# Paul and the Gentiles

# PAUL AND THE GENTILES

*Remapping the Apostle's Convictional World*

Terence L. Donaldson

Fortress Press / Minneapolis

*To Lois,*
*Meredith,*
*and Graeme*

PAUL AND THE GENTILES
Remapping the Apostle's Convictional World

First published by Fortress Press in 1997.

Library of Congress Cataloging-in-Publication Data

Donaldson, Terence L.
    Paul and the gentiles : remapping the Apostle's convictional world
/ Terence L. Donaldson.
       p.   cm.
    Includes bibliographical references and index.
    ISBN 0-8006-2993-0 (alk. paper)
       1. Paul, the Apostle, Saint.   2. Bible. N.T. Epistles of Paul—
Theology.   3. Gentiles in the New Testament.   I. Title.
BS2651.D66   1997
225.9′2—dc21                                              97-202
                                                          CIP

The paper used in this publication meets the minimum requirements of the American National Standard for Information Sciences—Permanence of Paper for Printed Library Materials, ANSI Z329.48-1948.                                         ∞

Manufactured in the U.S.A.                                  AF 1-2993

01    00    99    98    97    1    2    3    4    5    6    7    8    9

# CONTENTS

v

# PART II
# THE STRUCTURE OF PAUL'S CONVICTIONS
# ABOUT THE GENTILES

# PART III
## THE ORIGIN OF PAUL'S CONVICTIONS
## ABOUT THE GENTILES

# Preface

The question addressed in this study emerges at the intersection of two of my long-standing scholarly interests. One concerns the Gentilization of early Christianity. What I mean by this neologism is that process by which the church was transformed from a renewal movement located more or less entirely within a multifaceted Judaism, into a distinct and separate Gentile religion. This process, complex but inexorable, has had far-reaching implications, not only for Christian self-understanding, but also for the history of the church's relations with Judaism.

Sooner or later, of course, an interest in Gentilization must lead to that self-described apostle to the Gentiles, Paul himself. But here a second factor comes into play. In the past two decades—especially since the publication of E. P. Sanders's *Paul and Palestinian Judaism* (Philadelphia: Fortress, 1977)—the scholarly study of Paul has been undergoing a decisive shift in approach and understanding. Older approaches, especially those stemming from the Reformation, have been increasingly perceived as inadequate, their frameworks of interpretation having to be forced upon central elements of Paul's life and thought with greater and greater difficulty. At the same time the recognition that Paul's questions were not the same as those of the Reformers has produced new approaches, and the emergence of what might be described as a post-Reformation Paul.

One consequence of this shift has to do with Paul's concern for the Gentiles. What was taken as axiomatic in the older approaches now appears, I believe, as something in need of explanation. The purpose of this book is to carry out a fresh exploration of this aspect of Paul, and to offer such an explanation.

While this book was taking shape, when students, colleagues, or friends would ask me what it was about, I would occasionally reply, tongue somewhat in cheek: "How are we to understand Paul's Gentile mission, now that we know how Luther misunderstood Paul?" This may appear as an uncharitable—and even impolitic—way of putting it, given that a Lutheran publishing house has graciously agreed to publish it! But a glance at a Fortress Press catalog will be enough to dispel such impressions. For by publishing such seminal works as Sanders's *Paul and Palestinian Judaism* and Krister Stendahl's *Paul among Jews and Gentiles* (1976), Fortress Press has itself made a major contribution to this increasing recognition that lenses polished on the grinding wheel of the Reformation do not provide us with a clear picture of Paul. I am very grateful to Fortress for accepting my manuscript for publication as well and would like to express my appreciation to Marshall Johnson and his staff for all their work in bringing this project to completion.

Scholarship is a collegial enterprise; as scholars we are ever needful of the minds of others (to rephrase the old table grace), even—perhaps especially—those who see things differently. The notes in this volume provide some indication of the debt I owe to Pauline scholars past and present, whose labors and insights have greatly enriched my own. In particular, I would like to express my appreciation to a number of colleagues who have helped and encouraged me with this project. I am grateful to Alan Segal, Larry Hurtado, Paula Fredriksen, Lloyd Gaston, and Steve Wilson, who read the manuscript in its penultimate form. In addition, at earlier stages in the process, these same colleagues and others (especially William Campbell, Richard Hays, Robert Jewett, and Tom Wright) have helped to sharpen my thinking, as they have interacted in critical and constructive ways with various papers (both published and orally presented) in which I attempted to work out aspects of my thesis in preliminary forms.

Scholarship is also a costly enterprise; without the support of institutions of various kinds, scholarly work could not be produced. I am grateful for support received from several sources: from the College of Emmanuel & St. Chad, which has granted me six-month study leaves on two occasions, once in 1988 when I was in the initial stages of this research and again in 1995 when I was able to finish the writing; from the Anglican Church of Canada, which on both occasions provided me with a sabbatical grant from its Continuing Education Plan; and from the Social Sciences and Humanities Research Council of Canada, for a research grant (1992–95) that contributed in significant ways to the research project of which this book is a part.

Finally, scholarship is a human enterprise; scholarly work should contribute in some way to the well-being of the larger world, which requires in turn that scholars themselves be rooted in and nurtured by smaller-scale human communities. Any contribution that this book might make (I am under no grand illusions here!) will be due in no small measure to the influence of various communities that shape my life and provide it with meaning. I have been greatly enriched by the community of faculty, staff, and students at the College of Emmanuel & St. Chad, and the common life of study and worship in which we share. Further, I am grateful for the stimulating and collegial environment provided by the larger scholarly community in Saskatoon, especially the other schools of the Saskatoon Theological Union and the Department of Religious Studies at the University of Saskatchewan. But most of all I would like to acknowledge the love and support of my immediate family—of Meredith and Graeme, who have grown along with this book, and in decidedly delightful and gratifying ways; and especially of Lois, my wife and life partner, who has done much to humanize a husband who does too much of his living inside his head, but who nevertheless cherishes her deeply in his heart.

# Acknowledgments

Material from the following articles has been incorporated into the present work at several points:

"Zealot and Convert: The Origin of Paul's Christ-Torah Antithesis," *CBQ* 51 (1989) 655–82 (chapters 6, 11);

"'Riches for the Gentiles' (Rom 11:12): Israel's Rejection and Paul's Gentile Mission," *JBL* 112 (1993) 81–98 (chapter 8);

"Thomas Kuhn, Convictional Worlds, and Paul," in Bradley H. McLean, ed., *Origins and Method: Towards a New Understanding of Judaism and Christianity. Essays in Honour of John C. Hurd* (JSNTSup 86; Sheffield: Sheffield Academic Press, 1993) 190–98 (chapter 2).

This material is reproduced with the kind permission of the publishers (respectively, the Catholic Biblical Association, the Society of Biblical Literature, and Sheffield Academic Press).

# Abbreviations

1. *Greco-Roman, Hellenistic Jewish, pseudepigraphal, and early patristic literature*

| | |
|---|---|
| *Apoc. Abr.* | *Apocalypse of Abraham* |
| Aristides *Apol.* | *Apology* |
| *2 Bar.* | *Syriac Apocalypse of Baruch* |
| *4 Bar.* | *4 Baruch* |
| *1 Enoch* | *Ethiopic Enoch* |
| *Ep. Arist.* | *Epistle of Aristeas* |
| *Jos. Asen.* | *Joseph and Asenath* |
| Josephus | |
| *Ant.* | *Antiquities of the Jews* |
| *Ap.* | *Against Apion* |
| *War* | *Jewish War* |
| *Jub.* | *Jubilees* |
| Justin *Dial.* | *Dialogue with Trypho* |
| Philo | |
| *Abr.* | *De Abrahamo* |
| *Leg. all.* | *Legum allegoriae* |
| *Migr. Abr.* | *De migratione Abrahami* |
| *Omn. prob. lib.* | *Quod omnis probus liber sit* |
| *Praem. poen.* | *De praemiis et poenis* |
| *Q. Exod.* | *Quaestiones in Exodum* |
| *Q. Gen.* | *Quaestiones in Genesim* |
| *Spec. leg.* | *De specialibus legibus* |
| *Virt.* | *De virtutibus* |
| *Vit. Mos.* | *De vita Mosis* |
| *Ps.-Philo* | *Pseudo-Philo's Biblical Antiquities* |

| | |
|---|---|
| Ps.-Phoc. | Pseudo-Phocylides |
| Ps. Sol. | Psalms of Solomon |
| Sib. Or. | Sibylline Oracles |
| T. Mos. | Testament of Moses |
| T. Job | Testament of Job |
| T. 12 Patr. | Testaments of the Twelve Patriarchs |
| T. Ash. | Testament of Asher |
| T. Benj. | Testament of Benjamin |
| T. Dan | Testament of Dan |
| T. Jos. | Testament of Joseph |
| T. Jud. | Testament of Judah |
| T. Levi | Testament of Levi |
| T. Naph. | Testament of Naphtali |
| T. Sim. | Testament of Simeon |
| T. Zeb. | Testament of Zebulon |
| Tacitus Hist. | Histories |
| Tertullian Scorp. | Scorpiace |

2. *Qumran and related literature*

| | |
|---|---|
| CD | Cairo Genizah text of the *Damascus Document* |
| QTemple | *Temple Scroll* |
| 1QH | *Thanksgiving Hymns* (Qumran Cave 1) |
| 1QM | *War Scroll* (Qumran Cave 1) |
| 1QpHab | *Pesher on Habakkuk* (Qumran Cave 1) |
| 1QS | *Rule of the Community* (Qumran Cave 1) |
| 4QpNah | *Pesher on Nahum* (Qumran Cave 4) |

3. *Mishnaic and related literature*

| | |
|---|---|
| m. | Mishna |
| t. | Tosephta |
| b. | Babylonian Talmud |
| 'Abot | 'Abot |
| 'Abod. Zar. | 'Aboda Zara |
| B. Batra | Baba Batra |
| Bek. | Bekorot |
| Ber. | Berakot |
| B. Meṣ. | Baba Meṣia |
| B. Qam. | Baba Qamma |
| Demai | Demai |
| Giṭ. | Gittin |

| | |
|---|---|
| Ḥul. | Ḥullin |
| Ker. | Keritot |
| Meg. | Megilla |
| Ned. | Nedarim |
| Pesaḥ. | Pesaḥim |
| Sanh. | Sanhedrin |
| Šabb. | Šabbat |
| Soṭ. | Soṭa |
| Sukk. | Sukka |
| Yeb. | Yebamot |

4. *Other rabbinic and Targumic literature*

| | |
|---|---|
| Mek. | Mekilta |
| Mid. Gen. | Midrash on Genesis |
| Pesiq. R. | Pesiqta Rabbati |
| Pesiq. R. Kah. | Pesiqta de Rab. Kahana |
| Rab. | Rabbah (following abbreviation for biblical book) |
| Sipra | Sipra |
| Sipre | Sipre |
| Tg. Neof. | Targum Neofiti I |
| Tg. Onq. | Targum of Onqelos |
| Tg. Ps.-J. | Targum Pseudo-Jonathan |

5. *Abbreviations of commonly used periodicals, reference works, and serials*

| | |
|---|---|
| APOT | R. H. Charles, ed., *Apocrypha and Pseudepigrapha of the Old Testament* |
| ATR | *Anglican Theological Review* |
| BAGD | W. Bauer, W. F. Arndt, F. W. Gingrich, and F. W. Danker, *A Greek-English Lexicon of the New Testament* |
| BARev | *Biblical Archaeology Review* |
| Bib | *Biblica* |
| BJRL | *Bulletin of the John Rylands University Library of Manchester* |
| BR | *Biblical Research* |
| CBQ | *Catholic Biblical Quarterly* |
| CRINT | Compendia rerum iudaicarum ad Novum Testamentum |
| EThL | *Ephemerides theologicae lovanienses* |

| | |
|---|---|
| *ExpT* | *Expository Times* |
| HTR | *Harvard Theological Review* |
| ICC | International Critical Commentary |
| *Int* | *Interpretation* |
| *JBL* | *Journal of Biblical Literature* |
| *JSJ* | *Journal for the Study of Judaism in the Persian, Hellenistic, and Roman Period* |
| *JSNT* | *Journal for the Study of the New Testament* |
| JSNTSup | Journal for the Study of the New Testament Supplement Series |
| *JSOT* | *Journal for the Study of the Old Testament* |
| *JSP* | *Journal for the Study of the Pseudepigrapha* |
| *JTS* | *Journal of Theological Studies* |
| LSJ | Liddell-Scott-Jones, *Greek-English Lexicon* |
| NICNT | New International Commentary on the New Testament |
| NIV | New International Version |
| *NovT* | *Novum Testamentum* |
| NovTSup | Supplements to *Novum Testamentum* |
| NRSV | New Revised Standard Version |
| *NTS* | *New Testament Studies* |
| OTP | James H. Charlesworth, ed., *The Old Testament Pseudepigrapha* |
| *RHPhR* | *Revue d'histoire et de philosophie religieuses* |
| SBLDS | Society of Biblical Literature Dissertation Series |
| SBT | Studies in Biblical Theology |
| SNTSMS | Society for New Testament Studies Monograph Series |
| *SR* | *Studies in Religion/Sciences religieuses* |
| *StTh* | *Studia Theologica* |
| *TDNT* | G. Kittel and G. Friedrich, eds., *Theological Dictionary of the New Testament* |
| *ThBei* | *Theologische Beiträge* |
| *ThLZ* | *Theologische Literaturzeitung* |
| *ThZ* | *Theologische Zeitschrift* |
| *USQR* | *Union Seminary Quarterly Review* |
| WBC | Word Biblical Commentary |
| WMANT | Wissenschaftliche Monographien zum Alten und Neuen Testament |

# PART ONE

# The Problem of Paul's Convictions about the Gentiles

## CHAPTER ONE

# A New Paradigm and a New Problem

Recent developments in Pauline scholarship have led a growing number of observers to conclude that a "paradigm shift" is underway.[1] As in the world of science for which the term was originally coined,[2] this paradigm shift has been preceded and accompanied by a growing conviction that the old framework of understanding is no longer able to account satisfactorily for the range of relevant observations. As in the scientific parallel, this shift has resulted in the emergence of new questions and problems, as a new framework of understanding forces the reconstrual of old problems and places formerly innocuous observations in new and perplexing light.

There are several dimensions to the shift in question, but broadly speaking it has to do with Paul's attitudes toward Israel and the nature of his criticism of Judaism. It has been occasioned by dissatisfaction with traditional explanations in three areas: (1) the nature and function of Paul's language of "justification by faith"; (2) the nature of Paul's conversion experience; and (3) the place of Romans 11, with its insistence on the eventual salvation of "all Israel," in the argument of the epistle as a whole. The resultant shift has led to new and more satisfying accounts of what Paul has to say about the law, works, faith, righteousness, and other topics that figure centrally in scholarly discussion of Paul (although not always in Paul's letters themselves, a distinction instructive in itself). But, in ways not yet fully recognized, it has also rendered problematic Paul's fundamental concern for the Gentiles. For if, as is now being argued, Paul's language about justification by faith represents not a foundational insight into generic human existence but a tactical argument developed to defend a Torah-free mission to the Gentiles, if Romans 9–11 is to be seen not as a puzzling excursus but the climax of the letter, if, to condense a range of scholarly argumentation into a single point, Israel is a much more central category and concern for Paul than heretofore supposed—

then the fact that Paul came to see a mission to the Gentiles as a person-ally urgent corollary to the kerygma is a matter requiring some expla-nation.

To put this into perspective, it will be helpful to look at the place of the Gentile mission in older approaches to Paul. I think it can be fairly said that in traditional approaches to Paul his concern for the Gentiles was considered not as a "topic" or a "problem"—an aspect of his life and thought requiring reflection and explanation—but as axiomatic—a basic assumption about his life and thought that formed part of the framework for reflection on and explanation of the rest.[3] In particular, it was within this universalistic framework that his arguments against the Jewish and Judaizing Christian understanding of the Torah were interpre-ted. Recent chronicles of the interpretive shift have emphasized the Refor-mation, especially Lutheran, roots of the old paradigm.[4] Certainly the Reformation has had an important impact on Pauline scholarship, and more recent approaches have been worked out in conscious debate with Reformation emphases. But the new appreciation of the place of Israel in Paul's thought replaces a framework of understanding—a universalistic paradigm, we might call it—the main contours of which were much more widely shared and more deeply rooted in Christian tradition.

For present purposes it is not necessary to spell out this universalistic paradigm in systematic detail. A sufficiently clear picture of it will emerge as I examine in more detail the three main areas of perceptual shift men-tioned above. In each area of discussion I will pay particular attention to the way in which the Gentile mission was accounted for in the older framework of understanding, so that we can then clearly see how the interpretive shift has rendered the Gentile mission problematical.

### Faith and Works: Traditional Approaches

Since the Reformation it has been common to see Paul's juridical lan-guage—guilt and condemnation on the one hand, righteousness and jus-tification on the other—as constituting the central theological category around which everything else finds its proper place. In this reading it is assumed that where Paul uses this language (especially in Galatians and Romans), his central theological problem is that of universal human sin-fulness, so that his argumentation is driven by the question, How can sinful humanity find acceptance before a righteous God? Paul's answer to this fundamental problem, it is asserted, is faith: God counts as righteous (that is, God justifies) those who in faith accept the offer of forgiveness made possible by the atoning work of Christ. What gives Paul's concept of "justification by faith" its particular character in this approach is that it is defined in terms of a fundamental contrast with "justification by works," the latter being interpreted as the attempt to claim acceptance with God on the basis of one's own meritorious moral achievement. Judaism enters into Paul's argumentation because it represents a conspicuous and pertinent example of the wrong way to seek justification. What makes it wrong is not only that the pervasiveness of sin makes it impossible to achieve justification this way but also—and especially—that, even if it were possible, this way would result in prideful self-confidence instead of humble dependence on God's grace. Paul's concern with Judaism, then, operates at a secondary level; his primary concern is with the faith-works duality, a category that includes Torah religion as a particular case.

This way of construing Paul's thought and its place in scholarly interpretation from Luther through Bultmann to the present is well known. But so that we will be able to see clearly how the recent shift in approach has rendered problematic Paul's concern for the Gentiles, we need to look more closely at the way in which the Gentile mission is accounted for in this traditional approach. In fact, this way of stating it is misleading, for it suggests that the Gentile mission was consciously perceived as something that needed to be accounted for. But, in the Reformation view of things, Paul's interest in the Gentiles required no explanation at all. For Luther ("Paul's Gospel [is the message] of *man's* free justification by faith in Christ Jesus"),[5] Bultmann ("Paul's theology can best be treated as his doctrine of *man*"),[6] and all in between, it is assumed that Paul's starting point is the plight and salvation of the offspring of Adam and Eve, generically considered. Any distinction Paul might make between Jew and Gentile is secondary to his primary interest in the terms on which individual sinful "man" can be accounted righteous before a holy God. In this understanding of Paul, his interest as a Jew in the salvation of the Gentiles does not arouse the slightest curiosity because the reigning paradigm, which creates the rules for admissible problems and legitimate solutions,[7] assumes that for him distinctions between Jew and Gentile were not—or, to anticipate the discussion of Paul's conversion below, were no longer— of fundamental significance.

This assumption about the universal framework and starting point of Paul's juridical language was not restricted to the Reformers and the Augustinian tradition to which they laid claim.[8] It was no less axiomatic for the framers of the Tridentine response to Luther, who defined justification as "a translation, from that state wherein man is born a child of Adam, to the state of grace . . . through the second Adam, Jesus Christ, our Savior."[9] Indeed, the Reformation debate occurred within a framework of understanding regnant since the second century, when the church-synagogue separation was complete and the church came to see itself as a Gentile (that is, universal) religion. Nor did the arrival of historical-critical approaches call this framework into question. Both Baur's reconstruction of Paul as the defender of "a higher and freer state of religious consciousness" against Jewish Christian opposition[10] and attempts by the History of Religions school to interpret Paul as the Hellenizer of primitive Christianity[11] operate within a similar universalistic framework. Despite their differences, these various readings of Paul approach him within the same interpretive framework, one in which humankind as such—individually or collectively, but always generically and without further ethnic differentiation—is taken to be his fundamental soteriological category.

### Conversion and Call: Traditional Approaches

The second dimension of the interpretive shift has to do with the nature of Paul's Damascus experience. Until recently, it was taken for granted that this experience could be described simply as a conversion experience, with the assumption that this experience represented for Paul a transition from one religion, centered on Torah and thus based on a fundamental distinction between Jew and Gentile, to another, in which this distinction was transcended and rendered secondary and obsolete.

This view of Paul's conversion appears in the Lutheran tradition, most notably in the work of Bultmann, who interprets Paul's conversion experience as a recognition of "God's condemnation of his Jewish striving after righteousness by fulfilling the works of the Law."[12] But again it is by no means restricted to this tradition, originating rather as part of the basic framework within which Paul has been read and understood since the emergence of the church as a Gentile institution. John Chrysostom's paraphrase of Paul's account of his conversion experience may be taken as typical: "As soon as I passed over to the doctrines of the Church I shook off my Jewish prejudices."[13] And again, while the emergence of historical-critical study produced a great deal of interest in Paul's conversion experience[14] (to which I will need to return), the basic paradigm continued intact. One line of interpretation, drawing on psychological insights, attempted to account for Paul's conversion by seeing it as the result of a long period of struggle with the law and of dissatisfaction with Judaism.[15] Another, interested in accounting for Paul's later pattern of thought, attempted to explain it with reference to his preconversion reasons for persecution: the conversion experience produced an inversion of previously held opinions about the incompatability of Christ and Judaism.[16] But in either case it was assumed that Paul's experience was in essence a conversion away from Jewish particularism to a universalistic pattern of salvation. As a later example of the first approach, Stewart describes how Paul's "growing sense of the failure of Judaism" gave way to the sudden conviction "that he had found the truth for which all men everywhere were seeking";[17] typifying the second, Baur argued that Paul's conversion transformed his earlier fear that Christianity would "undermine" Judaism because of its "refusal to regard religion as a thing bound down to special ordinances and localities" into the belief that Christ represented an inner, spiritual religion available to all.[18]

Again, in this reading of Paul's conversion, his commitment to a Gentile mission is not so much something that needs to be explained as it is an implicit feature of the interpretive structure itself.

### Israel and the Church: Traditional Approaches

The third dimension of the shift in interpretation has to do with the significance of "Israel" for Paul, especially in view of Romans 11, with its often seen as surprising attempt to preserve a place in salvation for "all Israel" (v. 26). Until recently it was generally assumed that insofar as "Israel" continued to be a significant theological category for Paul it was as an appellation that had now been carried over to the church without remainder. Indeed, since Justin Martyr[19] the church has seen itself as "the true spiritual Israel" (*Dial.* 11), the sole inheritor of the promises, scripture, and name of the Old Testament people of God, and the people in whom the line of salvation history beginning with Abraham found its unique continuation.

This assumption, of course, is a necessary corollary of the assumptions discussed already. For if Paul's basic concern is how humanity, generically considered, can find justification with God, and if his conversion was essentially a conversion away from an ethnic and particularist religion centered on the Torah to a Christ who is the universal savior of all, then it follows that "Israel" can be retained as a positive category only if it is redefined in a nonethnic manner.

Romans 11, with its patently tortuous struggle—against both the canons of logic and the facts of Paul's own experience—to argue for the eventual salvation of "all Israel," presented traditional interpreters with something of an anomaly. In a bold tour de force, Calvin maintained consistency (at the price of rendering Paul's argument stunningly anticlimactic!)[20] by interpreting "Israel" in Rom 11:26 as the church comprised of the elect of both Jews and Gentiles (appealing to Gal 6:16).[21] More often the chapter is seen as a digression, deviating from the main current of Paul's thought and inconsistent with it, in which Paul has allowed his understandable concern for his kinsfolk to draw him away from

"his own fundamental position that all men are in the same position before God."[22]

In the older paradigm, then, Romans 11 was seen as an anomaly, an
"irritant" to be explained away[23] in one manner or another. This passage
aside, Paul's language about Christ, salvation, and the church was understood within a framework in which the elimination of any fundamental
Jew-Gentile distinction was taken to be axiomatic. Insofar as Paul was
interested in the term "Israel" at all, it was as a nonethnic term taken over
and redefined to denote the church composed of Jews and Gentiles.

On the basis of such observations, it is quite appropriate to speak of a
"universalistic paradigm" that held sway over Pauline interpretation from
the emergence of Gentile orthodoxy in the second century until comparatively recently and that continues to be influential into the present. In this
century, however, and increasingly in recent decades, the foundational assumptions of this paradigm have been widely called into question within
Pauline scholarship. Such questioning has resulted, in part, from the more
accurate and detailed understanding of first-century Judaism made possible by recent discoveries and studies. But it has also been stimulated by
changes in the climate of investigation effected by broader social factors,
including the development of the Jewish-Christian dialogue and especially the sobering impact of the Holocaust.

This is not the place to trace this shift and its precipitating factors in
any detail. Our interest lies in the way the collapse of the old paradigm
has exposed the problematic nature of Paul's Gentile mission. Our purposes here will be served by returning to the three areas of Pauline studies
mentioned above, looking briefly at the seminal works that have caused
the old paradigm to totter and collapse.

### *Faith and Works: Toward a New Paradigm*

In the old paradigm it was assumed that Paul's central concern had to do
with the terms on which an individual human being could be acceptable
to God (that is, justified), given the pervasiveness of sin; and that his answer (by faith) was worked out in terms of a contrast with a justification
based on meritorious self-achievement (by works). The most sustained
argument against this line of interpretation has been developed by E. P.
Sanders in his books on Paul,[24] although to a certain extent his work
builds on and brings to more widespread attention significant studies on
Paul done earlier in the century.

Sanders's first contribution has to do with Paul's supposed depiction
of Judaism as a legalistic religion of works-righteousness. Much earlier in

this century, Jewish scholars such as Claude Montefiore and S. Schechter, together with Christian scholars sympathetic to Judaism such as James Parkes and George Foot Moore, had complained that the popular Christian depiction of Judaism, based largely on Paul, was simply wrong.[25] Those who knew the sources best, they declared, recognized that the Torah, far from being the categorical opposite of grace, was God's gracious gift to Israel, to be received with joy. Jews kept the Torah, not to become acceptable according to the stringent standards of a scrupulous God, but to respond with gratitude to a God who in grace had chosen Israel to be a special divine people. Nor did sin represent any fundamental impediment to the effective functioning of a religious system based on the law. For the Torah itself, with its provisions for repentance, atonement, and forgiveness—provisions studiously ignored by Paul—recognized the reality of sin and afforded the means by which it could be dealt with within the covenant. Taking the popular understanding of Paul as an accurate account of his thought, these scholars concluded that Paul must have misunderstood Judaism, probably because he knew only an inferior Hellenized version of it.

Building on this earlier work,[26] Sanders argued, at length and convincingly, that the "pattern of religion" reflected in all the Palestinian literary material at our disposal[27] is one not of legalism, but of what he termed "covenantal nomism." In this religious system, the law is understood as functioning within a covenantal relationship between God and Israel, a relationship established and maintained by God's grace; the law provides the means by which, on the human side, this relationship can be affirmed and maintained; all members of the covenant people, except those who, by willful disregard of the law's provisions for repentance, atonement, and forgiveness, repudiate their membership, belong to the company who in the end will experience divine salvation. In covenantal nomism, then, "election and ultimately salvation are considered to be by God's mercy rather than human achievement."[28]

None of this, however, affects our understanding of Paul, except, perhaps, to lower our estimate either of his perspicacity or of the cogency of his argumentation. But Sanders goes on to ask whether there is not an alternative to the conclusion that Paul must have misunderstood Judaism, namely, that popular interpretation has misunderstood Paul. Here again he builds in part on the work of significant predecessors, in this case Schweitzer and (consequently) Wrede.[29]

Pauline interpretation has long recognized two distinct spheres of discourse in Paul's discussion of salvation. On the one hand there is the juridical language, in which salvation is described in terms of a change of sta-

tus from one situation ("condemnation") to another ("justification"). On
the other there is what, at least since Schweitzer, has been called the mystical, in which salvation is conceived more in terms of the believer's sharing
with Christ in the process of death and resurrection. In the Reformation
tradition, these two spheres of discourse were synthesized into two successive stages (justification and sanctification, respectively) in a single process of salvation. In this way justification was preserved as the center and
starting point of Paul's soteriology. When it was subjected to more critical
examination in the nineteenth century, however, this neat sequential solution began to break down, although without any more satisfactory explanation emerging to take its place. The best the History of Religions school
could offer was the suggestion that Paul "bore two souls within his
breast";[30] that is, two distinct conceptions of salvation—one (the mystical) drawn from Hellenism and the other (the juridical) from Judaism—
dual conceptions that Paul had not been able to homogenize into a
single coherent theory.[31]

The first significant step forward was taken by William Wrede. For
Wrede, previous Pauline scholarship had badly misunderstood Paul, precisely because it had failed to recognize the great gulf fixed between his
world of understanding and our own. Interpretation at least since the
Reformation had approached Paul with the assumption that he, too,
viewed salvation as the deliverance of the individual from the consequences of sin, with sin conceived of in terms of individual moral failing,
and the consequences of sin as guilt before God. With such a starting
point it was no wonder that Paul's juridical language loomed larger than
it should have. For Paul, however, the human problem was of a different
nature: the enslavement of humankind as a whole under the cosmic powers of the flesh, sin, and death. Christ in his death accomplishes redemption, not in the form of atonement for guilt and forgiveness for sins, but
in the form of a victory over these enslaving powers and the opening up
of a new sphere of existence beyond their reach. What, then, of Paul's
juridical language? Noting that this appears only where Paul is engaged
in "strife against Judaism,"[32] he argued that this is to be seen as his "polemical doctrine," brought into play only in defense of his more basic assumptions, which are: "(1) the mission [i.e., to the Gentiles] must be free
from the burden of Jewish national custom; (2) the superiority of the
Christian faith in redemption over Judaism as a whole must be assured."
He concludes that *the doctrine of justification is nothing more than the
weapon with which these purposes were to be won.*[33]

Wrede's influence on current discussion of Paul and the law, while
extensive, has not been fully recognized, largely because this influence

has been mediated through the more widely known work of Albert Schweitzer.[34] In *The Mysticism of Paul the Apostle*, Schweitzer takes up these insights of Wrede and sets them in the framework of a dazzling, though idiosyncratic, presentation of the way Paul's thought unfolded from its eschatological and christological underpinnings. His work represents an advance on that of Wrede in its demonstration both that Jewish eschatology provides the framework for Paul's doctrine of redemption and that Paul's "mysticism"—his language of "being in Christ," and related concepts—is to be understood within this framework. But on the place and function of Paul's juridical language, Schweitzer essentially reiterates what Wrede had already said: Paul's doctrine of justification by faith "is only a fragment from the more comprehensive mystical-redemption doctrine, which Paul has broken off and polished to give him the particular refraction he requires"[35]—requires, that is, to defend his law-free mission to the Gentiles. His contribution is to provide further grounding for Wrede's conclusion by demonstrating (1) that some aspects of Paul's thought, especially his ethics, cannot be derived from justification by faith, and (2) that there are places where the underlying derivation of the juridical from the mystical breaks through to the surface.

Standing on the shoulders of these giants, Sanders confidently lays out for his readers a clear course through the bewildering terrain of Paul's theological argumentation. Those who try to find a point of entry in Paul's juridical language, he says in effect, are doomed to become lost, since they are coming at things backwards. With verve and vigor he argues persuasively that in passage after passage Paul's cycle of argumentation concerning justification and the law, faith and works, depends on and functions in the service of a more fundamental assumption, namely, that "in [Christ] God has provided for the salvation of all who believe"[36] (with salvation being understood, in a manner similar to that of Schweitzer, as "participationist eschatology"). Since salvation is through Christ, and since it is to include Gentiles ("of all"), the law cannot be imposed as an entrance requirement.

But Sanders takes a decisive step beyond his predecessors—both with respect to Palestinian Judaism and with respect to Paul—in the conclusion he draws concerning Paul's criticism of Judaism in general and his language of "boasting" and "works" in particular. Paul uses these terms to refer, not to meritorious human achievement with its consequent self-confidence, but to the Jewish assumption that keeping the law guarantees a special privileged status not available to those outside the circle of the law. In other words, Paul does not misunderstand Judaism at all. He understands the structure and claim of covenantal nomism very well, but rejects it because he has come to believe that the community of salvation is to be found in Christ.[37]

All this could be developed at greater length,[38] and many aspects will come up for more detailed scrutiny below. But for our present purposes the important point is the observation, common to Wrede, Schweitzer, and Sanders, that Paul's juridical language is not to be located at the center of his thought, laying bare his fundamental concern for the plight of the individual human being, generically considered. Instead, it is peripheral and derivative, arising out of and fashioned to defend a set of independent and already-held convictions, among which was the conviction that the Gentiles were included in the salvation accomplished in Christ.

Where then did this more fundamental conviction about the Gentiles come from? How was it that Paul came to believe that the death and resurrection of the one whom the earliest Jewish church identified as the Messiah had accomplished salvation for *all*, Jew and Gentile alike? Each of the three authors surveyed here answers this question in different, and not fully consistent, ways. For Wrede, Paul's concern for the Gentiles arose out of his belief in the universal significance of Christ, an understanding of the Messiah that was already part of his Jewish beliefs prior to Damascus. And yet he can also argue, paradoxically, that this concern was not present from the time of Paul's conversion, but was something that developed only after an unsuccessful period of mission within Judaism and as a result of his experience in the Antioch church.[39] Why his prior conception of the universal scope of the Messiah's work took so long to manifest itself in his Christian thinking, he does not explain.

Schweitzer's approach to Paul's Gentile mission is too complex to be described briefly. In general terms, however, he sees it as a combination of the widely held Jewish expectation that the Gentiles would have a share in eschatological salvation, together with Paul's own unique conceptions of the interim state (only those who are "in Christ" in the present period between the resurrection and the parousia will share in the life of the Age to Come) and the maintenance of the status quo (believers are to remain in the condition in which they had been at the time of their entrance "into Christ").[40]

For Sanders, there is certainty about Paul's fundamental convictions (1) that the Gentiles are included in the salvation made available through Christ, and (2) that he himself was called to be the apostle to the Gentiles.[41] But he is much less certain about the origin of such convictions. He recognizes that these convictions are not the self-evident corollaries of belief in the resurrected Jesus; others in Paul's situation came to different conclusions. But beyond this he will only speculate. His speculations move along two lines. First, he suggests that perhaps prior to his Damascus experience, Paul experienced "secret dissatisfaction" about the exclusion, or at least secondary status, that was the Gentiles' lot in Jewish understanding. Second, he argues that Paul came to understand his mission as a fulfillment of the expected eschatological ingathering of the Gentiles, which suggests that the origin of his convictions is to be found in Jewish eschatological expectation.[42] But neither of these speculations is pursued in any detail. Paul believed that he was called to be the apostle of the Gentiles; but how he came to this belief is left as an open question.

Thus, despite their significant area of agreement, there is a striking spectrum of opinion among these three scholars with regard to both the nature and the origin of Paul's convictions about the Gentiles and their place in salvation. As I begin to cast the net more widely, this spectrum will increase in both breadth and definition. In due course I will carry out a systematic analysis of this range of opinion. For the present, I make two observations. First, to the extent that the criticism of the old paradigm is accurate, Paul's concern for the Gentiles emerges as a problem requiring explanation. As long as his juridical language is seen as central to the structure of his convictions and thought, his concern for the Gentiles—to which it is always linked—falls naturally and smoothly into place. But when the juridical is displaced from the central position to which it has traditionally been assigned, the Gentile concern thrusts out awkwardly as an element of his thought and action. Second, the fact that the scholars discussed above by no means agree on the nature and origin of Paul's concern for the Gentiles indicates that the restructuring of our understanding of Paul required by this displacement will not be an easy matter. It is not a simple case of replacing one thing by another at the center with everything else remaining intact. A recognition of the derivative nature of the juridical language forces a reassessment of the relationship among a whole range of Pauline conceptions—Israel, the law, sin, Christ, the cross, and so on.

Before turning to such a reassessment, we need to look at other areas where the old paradigm is being called into question.

### Conversion and Call: Toward a New Paradigm
In the old paradigm Paul's Damascus experience was understood to be a conversion out of Judaism, with its particularistic way of viewing the world, and into a different universalistic religion, in which particularistic distinctions between Jew and Gentile were no longer relevant. But, as we will see, such universalistic construals of Paul's Damascus experience have been significantly undermined by a number of influential studies.

Universalistic interpretations of Paul's conversion have appeared in two main forms. The first of these emerges from the attempt to account for the conversion in terms of psychological preconditioning. In this approach, Paul's conversion is seen as the result and resolution of a long struggle with respect to his Jewish convictions and identity. Some would see this struggle as precipitated by a latent attraction to Hellenism,[43] and others by the cumulative impact of Christian apologetics and steadfastness under persecution.[44] These were usually linked, however, with another and more widely proposed factor, namely, an experience of frustration with respect to the law, in which Paul despaired of ever achieving the righteousness it demanded.[45] The appeal of this approach was not only that it provided a naturalistic explanation of what was on any reading a startling event and not only that it dovetailed neatly with traditional righteousness-by-faith readings of Paul (though it was not necessary for[46] nor did it necessarily lead to[47] such readings). This approach was compelling because it seemed to find firm support in Romans 7, where Paul, speaking in the first person singular, describes just such an experience of frustration over the impossible demands of the law.

Such interpretations of Paul's Damascus experience, however, have now been largely abandoned. Again, the main lines of the argument were first laid down by Wrede;[48] and again, his accomplishment has been overshadowed by the later work of another scholar, in this case that of W. G. Kümmel.[49] In his discussion of the origin of Paul's Christian ideas, Wrede acknowledges the popularity of the view that, prior to Damascus, Paul "was continually and vainly wrestling for righteousness before God" (p. 143), with its corollary that the doctrine of justification by faith was the immediate and necessary result of the Damascus experience itself. But, he asserts, this portrait is modeled more on "the soul-strivings of Luther" (p. 146) than on Paul himself.

Wrede buttresses this assertion with an argument that, at least in part, parallels his argument that justification by faith is to be seen as a derived doctrine. He points out that the main support for such a portrait of Paul—Rom 7:7-25—is found in a passage where the discussion is narrowly focused on the inadequacy of the law in comparison with Christ. Whenever Paul has occasion to speak directly of his own pre-Christian past, however, he does so with a sense of pride and accomplishment. Wrede points specifically to Paul's assertion in Phil 3:6 "that as a Pharisee he had lived irreproachably in the law" (p. 145). What then of the "I" of Romans 7? The statement in v. 9—"I was once alive apart from the law"—cannot be taken as a description of the experience of one whose life was governed by the law from the beginning (cf. Phil 3:5, "circum-

cised the eighth day"). The first person discourse is to be taken as a literary device to depict more forcefully the plight of unredeemed humanity
from the standpoint of redemption.

All this was sketched out very rapidly—four short paragraphs and several brief footnotes—and Wrede himself was aware of the need for more
rigorous and detailed argumentation.[50] This was supplied by Kümmel,
whose widely influential study, *Römer 7 und die Bekehrung des Paulus*,
generally developing the lines of argument laid down already by Wrede,[51]
has largely carried the day.[52] What needs to be noted here is that, to the
extent that Wrede and Kümmel are right, a common way of understanding Paul's conversion in universalistic terms has been closed off. If in his
conversion encounter with Christ Paul found what he had searched for in
vain in Judaism, then it could easily be assumed that Jewish particularism
was one of the things left behind when he left the one (Judaism) for the
other (Christ). But if his conversion experience was precipitated not by
an already-present dissatisfaction with Judaism but by an unanticipated
reestimation of the significance of Jesus (that is, as one raised by God),
there is no immediately apparent reason to assume that his experience
would have had these results. If, in the terms of Sanders's well-known
slogan, Paul's "solution" preceded any perception of a "problem" with
Judaism or the law, then it can no longer be simply assumed that Damascus represented the point of transition from a particularistic Jewish way
of viewing the people of salvation to a new Christian one in which the
Jew-Gentile distinction was no longer relevant. Certainly Damascus represented a profound shift in Paul's framework of understanding, entailing
a new estimation of the constituent elements of his old Jewish world. And
it is possible that one of the elements thrust up for reappraisal was his
inherited attitudes toward the Gentiles and their place in God's purposes.
But the implication of the "solution before problem" way of understanding Paul's conversion is that it can no longer be assumed that the experience was in essence and at bottom a conversion from particularism to
universalism. The experience was in essence and at bottom a new estimation of the significance of Christ. Any immediate change in his attitudes
toward the Gentiles would have been the more contingent result of the
way in which Paul perceived the significance of Christ with respect to his
inherited world of understanding.

This, however, leads to a second way in which Paul's Damascus experience has been interpreted as essentially a conversion to a universalistic
way of viewing salvation. It is not necessary to posit a prior dissatisfaction with Judaism to perceive the Damascus experience as a conversion
away from Judaism to something else. However it came about, this experi-

ence produced a new perspective not only on Christ but also on the Torah. Indeed, Paul's persecution itself could suggest that he came to the Damascus experience already convinced that in some way Christ religion and Torah religion were incompatible. The result of that experience could then be seen as not so much a new conviction concerning the incompatability of Christ and Torah, as a new perspective on that incompatability as he had already perceived it. But, in any case,[53] after Damascus Paul abandoned the conviction that Torah observance was necessary for membership in the community of salvation, and this abandonment has often been construed as an abandonment of Judaism, and even of Israel itself. If salvation is not through Torah, then (it is argued) the Torah-based distinction between Jew and Gentile is irrelevant, and Israel's status is reduced to that of one nation among many. Lucien Cerfaux's construal of the relationship between conversion, law, and Gentiles is typical:

> The principle by which Israel had lived is done away with. *The abolition of the law and the call to the pagans are correlated*, since in the divine plan revealed to Paul the heathens do not enter the Church through the intermediary of Judaism, but through the wide-open door of mercy. . . . The whole of Judaism is obsolete, the works of the flesh are useless. The death of Christ suppresses the law in its entirety.[54]

In other words, the Gentile mission is the natural outcome of Paul's Damascus experience, since that experience was in essence a conversion from Torah to Christ, and thus (it is assumed) a conversion from Judaism to a universal religion in which ethnic distinctions between Jew and Gentile have been eradicated. Discussion concerning this approach to Paul's Gentile mission belongs more properly to the next section, where I consider new approaches to Paul's convictions concerning Israel and the church. Here, however, I want to consider the concept of "conversion" itself.

Until comparatively recently, it was taken to be perfectly natural and obvious to describe Paul's Damascus experience as a conversion. Such a perception was not limited to biblical scholars. Indeed, from popular references to "conversion on the road to Damascus" to the paradigmatic role of Paul's experience in the seminal social scientific studies of conversion,[55] it is clear that Paul has come to be viewed as the convert par excellence, the one whose experience creates the type. For the past twenty years, however, the word "conversion" has either disappeared from scholarly discussion of Paul entirely, its place being taken by the word "call," or it is used only after a labored defense of its continuing appropriateness.

This shift in vocabulary is due almost entirely to the impact of Krister Stendahl's celebrated essay, "Paul among Jews and Gentiles."[56] Stendahl begins by observing that while we have assumed without question that Paul's experience can be described as a conversion, Paul himself describes it differently. Echoing language from Isaiah and Jeremiah, Paul's most explicit narrative of his "before" and "after" (Gal 1:13-16) depicts the intervening experience as a call, similar to that of the prophets, in which the same God whom he had been serving since birth has now given him a new task: through the risen Messiah, God "asks him as a Jew to bring God's message to the Gentiles" (p. 7). While Stendahl does not deny the fact that Damascus represented for Paul a striking shift in perspective, he argues that the word "conversion" conveys to the modern reader something that was foreign to Paul's own self-perception, namely, "the idea that Paul 'changed his religion': the Jew became a Christian" (p. 11). Both before and after the Damascus experience, Paul identified himself as a Jew, serving the one God of Jews and Gentiles, who had established an inviolable covenant relationship with Israel. It is in full consciousness of his identity as a Jew and of his membership in Israel that Paul carries out his calling as apostle to the Gentiles.

While Stendahl's "call rather than conversion" formulation may have overstated the case somewhat (the tendency of recent scholarship leans toward the view that "conversion" properly understood can be appropriately applied to Paul),[57] his emphasis on the Jewish self-consciousness of Paul the apostle has contributed significantly to the the paradigm shift under discussion. To a certain extent his essay leads us into the third area, the relative place of Israel and the church in Paul's set of convictions. Stendahl acknowledges his own indebtedness to Johannes Munck, whose work will figure prominently in the next section of discussion. Before moving on, however, we need to ponder for a moment Stendahl's description of Paul's experience as a call to go to the Gentiles.

Insofar as there has been a shift in our basic framework for understanding Paul, therefore, the fact of Paul's urgent concern for the Gentiles emerges as a problem requiring explanation. On the surface, Stendahl appears both to recognize the problem (Paul a Jewish apostle who nevertheless goes to the Gentiles) and to provide a solution (Paul's Damascus experience as essentially a call to take God's message to the Gentiles). But on further reflection, it can be asked whether this really explains much. For this "call" came to one who was in the process of persecuting the church because he perceived its message about Christ to be objectionable in some significant way. Before it was anything else, then, his Damascus experience represented a shift in his convictions about Jesus: the crucified

Jesus had indeed been raised by God (Paul felt himself compelled to believe); therefore his previous assessment of Jesus was clearly wrong.[58] Certainly Paul came to perceive his Gentile mission as the divinely purposed consequence of this new conviction: God "was pleased to reveal his Son in me in order that I might preach him among the Gentiles" (Gal 1:15). But any attempt to reduce this experience to that of a simple call to a Gentile mission without showing how this conviction related to other fundamental convictions (about Christ, Israel, the law, and so on) and without placing it intelligibly within a larger process of transformation by which his convictions were transformed from those of a zealous persecutor to those of an apostle of Christ does not really explain anything. Nor does Stendahl provide any real explanatory advance with his reflections about a two-covenant reading of Paul, that is, one in which Christ functions as God's provision for the Gentiles only, while the Torah covenant continues to be both valid and sufficient for Israel.[59] To account for Paul's Gentile mission simply by saying that his Damascus experience was really a call to be an apostle to the Gentiles is ultimately tautologous.[60] The problem remains.

### Israel and the Church: Toward a New Paradigm

In the older paradigm it was assumed that for Paul, the Christian, an ethnic definition of the people of God (Israel) had given way to one in which any differentiation between Jew and Gentile was categorically done away with (the church). Such statements as Rom 10:12, "for there is no distinction between Jew and Greek," were taken to mean that for Paul "Jew" and "Israel" as he had traditionally understood the terms now had no continuing theological significance. Only as redefined and used figuratively of the church did "Israel" have any categorical validity at all.

The tenacity of this paradigm for understanding Paul is quite understandable, given the dominance since the middle of the second century of various "new" or "true" Israel models for Christian self-definition and for its construal of the relationship between the testaments. Just as understandably, critical reexamination of these models and their development—spurred on in recent decades by increasing recognition of the legacy of Christian anti-Semitism—has helped to create the climate in which the older Pauline paradigm itself has lost its hold. As it became apparent that the seeds that bore such bitter fruit in the Holocaust were first sown in the "New Israel" displacement ecclesiology of the second century apologists,[61] it became increasingly difficult to hold with equanimity the opinion that this was Paul's own view.[62] And as it became apparent that the

"New Israel" patterns of thought were shaped by a configuration of factors quite distinct from those that obtained in the first century,[63] it was increasingly obvious that Paul's Israel-church discourse needed to be approached afresh and on its own terms.[64]

Important steps in this direction were taken by several scholars—notably Albert Schweitzer, W. D. Davies, and H.-J. Schoeps[65]—who demonstrated the possibility of explaining Paul's thought as that of a Jew who had come to believe that in Jesus of Nazareth the Messiah had appeared. The works of these scholars are significant for the general atmosphere they helped create, in which Paul's self-understanding as Christ's apostle to the Gentiles and as a member of the church is not seen as necessarily set over against his identity as a Jew and as a member of Israel.

But of more immediate significance is Johannes Munck's *Paul and the Salvation of Mankind*.[66] For in this book, he almost single-handedly rescued Romans 9–11 from the backwaters of Pauline interpretation and showed how Paul's mission to the Gentiles could be seen as the work of one still deeply committed to the centrality of Israel κατὰ σάρκα (according to the flesh).

As has already been noted, for the older universalistic paradigm Romans 9–11 represented an anomaly—a regrettable digression, a speculative fantasy, a lapse back into a set of theological categories that were really no longer operative for Paul. But Munck demonstrated that the lines connecting Romans 9–11 with central elements in Paul's self-understanding were too taut and numerous to allow the passage to be placed in the margins and left out of consideration. What strikes Munck about these chapters is the central role Paul assigns himself in his discussion of Israel: he has been "appointed by God to fill the key position in the last great drama of salvation" (p. 43). Paul begins by expressing his willingness, like Moses, "to sacrifice himself for Israel's benefit"(9:1-5),[67] and he ends by declaring that it is by means of the mission to the Gentiles—a mission in which he as apostle to the Gentiles (11:13) takes the leading role—that all Israel will be saved. What Paul is wrestling with in these chapters, then, is not simply the fate of Israel, but the goal and meaning of his own activity as apostle and missionary. This being so, it becomes much more difficult to disconnect Romans 9–11 from the central concerns of the apostle.

Munck argues that such an exalted view of Paul's apostolic role is not restricted to Romans 9–11, but shows up as well in 2 Thess 2:6-7; Rom 15:14-33; 2 Cor 3:7-18; and Gal 2:1-10. Moreover, the hope that Israel would be spurred by jealousy to repent seems to provide the key for understanding the collection project: Paul goes up to Jerusalem, "with a representative company of believing Gentiles" because "it is his intention to save the Jews by making them jealous of the Gentiles" (p. 303). Far from being idle speculation, then, the link posited in Romans 9–11 between Paul's labors among the Gentiles and the salvation of "all Israel" undergirds a project that occupied several years of his efforts and represented the culmination of his work in the east (cf. Rom 15:23).

Munck makes these observations about Paul's apostolic self-understanding in the context of a larger project of reinterpretation. Against those on the one hand who would approach Paul primarily as a theologian, and those who would read his letters instead as spontaneous and unreflective expressions of the emotional and religious life of an individual, Munck argues that Paul needs to be approached as a missionary: "It is the *apostle* Paul with whom research has to do" (p. 66). For Munck, Paul's call to be God's apostle to the Gentiles provides both the key and the starting point for understanding him and his letters. His theology is mission theology; it "arises from his work as apostle and directly serves that work" (p. 67). The significance of this emphasis for Stendahl's reexamination of Paul's "conversion" experience has already been noted. These two aspects of the paradigm shift are thus intimately connected.

Munck's work as a whole, however, needs scrutiny at some points. His reinterpretation is distorted considerably by an overreaction to Tübingen, and marred by an ungenerous treatment of Judaism and its attitude toward the Gentiles.[68] And, as we shall see in a moment, it provides no plausible explanation of how Paul came to his view concerning the Gentiles. Nevertheless, by establishing the centrality of Romans 9–11 for both the epistle and its apostle, he has closed off the entrance to one common approach to Paul's Gentile mission: no longer is it possible to assume that Paul went to the Gentiles because he believed that in Christ "Jew" and "Israel" had been emptied of their ethnic denotation. It is as a Jew, and for the sake of Israel, that Paul engages in his activity as apostle to the Gentiles.

How then did Paul come to his convictions about the Gentile mission? In part, Munck's answer is, like Stendahl's after him, that Paul's Damascus experience was in essence a call to apostleship among the Gentiles.[69] But, unlike Stendahl,[70] he also attempts to place Paul's call within a wider framework of perceptions and convictions.

This framework is built first of all on the idea of the eschatological salvation of the Gentiles.[71] Following J. Jeremias and others, he argues that both Jesus and early Jewish Christianity expected that the conversion of Israel to the gospel would result in salvation also for the Gentiles. Paul, too, operated within this framework; the collection visit to Jerusalem, for example, was understood against this background (p. 303). But Paul differed with the Jewish church before him in the conviction that a mission to the Gentiles was to take place prior to the parousia. Indeed, Paul's uniqueness consists in his inversion of the usual eschatological scenario: the salvation of the Gentiles would precede and make possible that of Israel rather than vice versa.

How did Paul arrive at this inverted program of salvation? Here is where Munck's reconstruction runs into problems.[72] On the one hand, he sees Paul's approach as arising from his experience of Jewish rejection of the gospel: "Paul realizes that the Gospel in the preaching of Jesus, and later of the apostles (including himself) had been rejected by the Jews, and that therefore the great thing was to take it to the Gentiles" (p. 276). But, on the other, he wants to see Paul's self-understanding as apostle to the Gentiles as an essential part of his Damascus experience,[73] which therefore was there from the beginning. It might be possible to argue that Paul began to turn to the Gentiles in reaction to a lack of response among the Jews, so that he gradually came to believe that "because of the Jews' unbelief and hardness of heart God has decided to have the Gospel preached [first] to the Gentiles"[74] (although this runs into problems of its own, as we shall see). But to argue that this framework of understanding was there from Damascus, as Munck clearly wants to do, is highly unlikely. For if his career as a persecutor tells us anything, we can be assured that Paul's experience to that point had been of the success of the gospel within Judaism, not its failure; one does not attempt to suppress a message that has been "rejected." If Paul shared with the church before him the basic eschatological understanding of the salvation of the Gentiles, one would have expected him after Damascus to embark with enthusiasm on a mission to increase the success of the gospel within Judaism. Munck's very success in convincing us of the importance of Paul's apostolic call undercuts his explanation of the structure of Paul's convictions about the Gentile mission.

I shall offer my own explanation of these convictions in due course. For the present, several conclusions emerge from the preceding discussion: (1) *The old universalistic paradigm has ceased to function as an explanatory model of Paul's thought.* At each of the key points—Paul's juridical language, his conversion experience and its significance, the relationship between Israel and church as he perceives it—it is no longer possible to account for the evidence within a univeralistic framework, that is, one in which it is assumed that Paul's basic concern is with humankind, generically considered. For Paul the apostle, "Jew" and "Gentile" continue to function as fundamental categories.

One result of this paradigm collapse is that (2) *Paul's apostolic interest in the Gentiles, formerly seen as axiomatic, now emerges as a problem in need of solution.* And since any solution must be able to account within a single framework for the diverse areas of Paul's thought and experience surveyed above, a range of diversity artificially masked in the old paradigm, the search for such a solution will not necessarily be simple and straightforward.

Finally, (3) *no full and satisfactory solution has yet been given of the resultant problem of Paul's apostolic concern for the Gentiles.* Munck's *Paul and the Salvation of Mankind* is the closest thing to a direct, full-scale study of Paul's Gentile mission. But it is flawed in many respects, predates the work of E. P. Sanders, and operates on an inadequate understanding of Second Temple Judaism. Where this problem has been recognized in more recent work, it is nevertheless usually treated as an adjunct to some other topic, for example, Paul's apostolic call (Stendahl), his attitude toward the Torah (Sanders) or toward contemporary Judaism (Gaston). The assumption seems to be that, once these topics have been addressed, all aspects of the Gentile question will have been taken up without remainder. While it may be appropriate to speak of the emergence of a new paradigm, there is by no means a consensus concerning the origin and nature of Paul's convictions about the Gentiles and their salvation.

The time seems to be ripe, then, for a thorough reexamination of the whole question of Paul and the Gentiles such as I propose to carry out in the pages to follow. To set the stage for such a reexamination, I want to expand on several aspects of the summarizing observations made above.

I begin with the range of scholarly opinion on the question. As has already become clear, there are two dimensions to the question: *chronological*, the identification of the stage (or stages) in Paul's biographial trajectory that was (were) determinative of his eventual apostolic concern for the Gentiles; and *convictional*, the nature of his concern for the Gentiles, and the way this concern relates to and perhaps results from his other fundamental convictions. Scholarly opinion then can be plotted along two axes, resulting in two distinct yet interconnected ways of surveying the terrain. We will begin with the chronological, surveying the alternatives in reverse order.

*Later Development*

While most scholars view Paul's consciousness of an apostolic mission to the Gentiles as a basic conviction—a basic element, or a direct corollary, of the Damascus experience, present more or less from the beginning—a few have argued that it was a later development. Generally speaking, this approach takes Romans 11, with its argument that the mission to the Gentiles was made possible by the obduracy of Israel, as a theological distillation of Paul's own experience. Paul began his career as a missionary to Jews (it is argued), but turned to the Gentiles out of frustration at the lack of Jewish response to the gospel, developing his more radical approach to the Torah in the context of the Gentile mission.[75]

*Conversion and Call*

Most scholars see Paul's concern for the Gentiles as a more basic conviction, part of his Christian faith from the beginning. Some see the Damascus experience itself, in one way or other, as the direct source of Paul's conviction about the Gentiles. Several in this group would account for it on the basis of an explicit verbal commissioning.[76] More importantly, as noted above, the recent "paradigm shift" in Pauline studies has involved the idea that Paul understood the Damascus experience as essentially a call to be apostle to the Gentiles.[77]

Others see Paul's concern for the Gentiles as present more or less from the beginning, but as a derivative conviction, the result of a more fundamental aspect of his Damascus experience. As noted already, older scholarship tended to see Paul's conviction about the Gentile mission as a direct corollary of his new attitude toward the Torah. In his conversion experience he abandoned his former conviction that Torah observance was necessary for salvation; salvation was to be attained through Christ, not through the Torah. While the logical link from "Christ" to "not Torah" is construed in a variety of ways,[78] the link from "not Torah" to "Gentiles" follows a single path: if salvation is not through Torah, then the Torah-based distinction between Jew and Gentile is irrelevant, and salvation is available to all humanity on equal terms.[79]

In a similar fashion, a smaller group of scholars would derive Paul's Gentile mission from his christology. In his Damascus experience Paul came to recognize Jesus not only as raised by God, but also as exalted to a position of universal lordship. The scope of Christ's saving significance, then, is cosmic and universal, embracing both Jews and Gentiles.[80]

Finally, some scholars believe that a mission to the Gentiles was part of the community into which Paul converted, and that an openness to

Gentiles was something that he accepted simply as part of the package. H. Räisänen is an example. Along with a number of other scholars, he believes that the church Paul persecuted had already begun a mission to the Gentiles and that Paul simply accepted this mission. Most of these scholars also believe that in his conversion Paul worked out the theological implications of such a mission for himself,[81] and thus belong more properly in one of the previous categories. But Räisänen, building on the work of G. Strecker, argues that this theological work took place only later.[82] The Hellenists were already admitting Gentiles without circumcision, but (he believes) they had not really thought through the theological implications of such a policy. The Gentile mission was a spontaneous development, arising naturally in the environment of eschatological enthusiasm within the church, and apparently confirmed by God in the bestowing of charismatic gifts upon uncircumcised Gentiles. When Paul converted, he simply adopted the unreflective liberalism of the Hellenists, treating the law as an adiaphoron. In this environment, he gradually internalized Gentile attitudes, with the result that he became alienated from the Torah, especially its ritual aspects. It was only later, in the Judaizing crisis, that these internal attitudes were transformed into an explicit theological position.

At first glance, Alan Segal's *Paul the Convert* seems to represent a second example. Drawing on sociological studies of conversion, and emphasizing the socializing role of the community into which one converts, he argues that Paul was converted into a Gentile Christian community and that his attitudes toward the Gentiles were shaped by this new environment. At the same time, however, he believes that for a time Paul continued to observe the Torah and to preach to Jews. I will consider this in more detail below, but it is probable that two successive stages are in view here, so that Segal's approach does not really conform to that of Räisänen.[83]

### Pre-Christian Attitudes

Several scholars see Paul's concern for the Gentiles as a basic conviction, but locate the roots of this conviction in his Jewish upbringing. In each case, the Damascus experience is an important factor; but its importance arises from its impact on already-developed convictions and concerns. As noted above, the traditional approach to Paul understood his conversion as the resolution of a period of frustration within Judaism, and with the demands of the law in particular. This idea of a preconversion dissatisfaction, for which the conversion experience provides a resolution, shows up

within the newer Pauline scholarship as well. Here, however, the dissatisfaction has to do not with the law's demands, but with its exclusion of
the Gentiles. In Davies's words, there was a conflict between his "creed,"
which condemned all those outside the Torah to perdition, and his "human sympathies" for the Gentiles so condemned.[84] In his conversion experience, Paul found a way that the Gentiles could be included in salvation. The roots of his Gentile mission, then, are to be found in the "uneasy
conscience" (Davies)[85] or the "secret dissatisfaction" (Sanders)[86] or the
"personal quandary" (Gaston)[87] that he experienced in his Jewish upbringing.

Finally, there are several approaches—more positive with respect to
Judaism in that they do not depend on any fundamental tension between
Paul's pre- and post-Damascus patterns of thought—that account for
Paul's Gentile concern on the basis of already existing Jewish "patterns
of universalism." For it is increasingly clear that Judaism was in its own
way universalistic (just as Paul, with his insistence on belief in Christ, was
in his own way particularistic). Within the Judaism of the Second Temple
period, there were several developing but distinct patterns of thought
which in differing ways created space for Gentiles within the scope of
God's saving purposes, without compromising in any way Israel's own
covenantal self-understanding.[88] A growing tendency in recent Pauline
scholarship has been to understand Paul's concern for the Gentiles as a
revision, in light of his Christ experience, of one or another of these patterns of universalism.

One common approach takes as its point of departure the Jewish tradition of the "pilgrimage of the nations," the expectation that at the time
of the eschatological deliverance of Israel Gentiles would come to share
in the blessings. Paul shared this common expectation (it is held) and,
when he came to believe that the Messiah had indeed appeared, he came
naturally to the conclusion that the time to invite the Gentiles to share
in the blessings of salvation had arrived.[89] Another approach works in
analogous ways with the belief, clearly emerging in the first century, that
there were "righteous Gentiles" who would have a share in the age to
come. That is, while the Torah was essential for membership in Israel, it
was not necessary for salvation; it was possible for Gentiles to be accounted righteous on other grounds. Several scholars have suggested that
Paul's insistence on "righteousness for Gentiles apart from works of the
law" is to be seen against this background. Gaston's two-covenant reading
of Paul—righteousness by faith through Torah for the Jews and through
Christ for the Gentiles—is one particularly striking example.[90] In more

mainstream (christocentric) readings of Paul's gospel, Paula Fredriksen and Alan Segal have, in differently nuanced ways, appealed to the phenomenon of "godfearers" to explain his attitude to the Gentiles.[91]

It is apparent that the various ways of accounting for Paul's Gentile concern are linked with a variety of ways of construing his basic convictions. The various positions can be arranged along this axis in two main groups: those that explain Paul in terms of a fundamental *rejection of Jewish particularism*, and those whose explanation is based instead on a *revision of Jewish universalism*.

### Rejection of Jewish Particularism

This approach is characteristic of the older paradigm discussed above. In turning to the Gentiles Paul was at the same time turning away from, or perhaps transcending, a view of the world in which humankind was divided into two basic categories—Jew and Gentile—by virtue of God's election of Israel. His Gentile mission is the natural result of a fundamental realization that "there is no distinction between Jew and Greek" (cf. Rom 10:12), for the one God is God of all (cf. Rom 3:29-30). What was it that caused Paul to abandon Jewish particularism? As noted above, at least four possibilities have been put forward: Paul's call to be apostle to the Gentiles; the rejection of Israel in favor of the Gentiles (based on Romans 11); the universal lordship of Christ; and, most frequently, the end of the Torah.

### Revision of Jewish Universalism

By contrast, a feature of the emerging paradigm is the tendency to see his mission as a revision, in light of his new convictions about Christ, of one of the ways in which Judaism itself had already conceived of Gentile salvation, namely, the eschatological pilgrimage tradition, or the notion of righteous Gentiles. Paul's call to be apostle to the Gentiles can be incorporated into these reconstructions as well.

There is thus wide diversity of opinion concerning both the nature and the origin of Paul's concern for the Gentiles. As to its nature, was it a core conviction, part of his basic framework of meaning either as a Christian or as an adherent of Judaism? Or was it derivative, a corollary perhaps of his new perspective on Christ or the Torah? And where are the origins of this concern to be found: in his early formation in Judaism, in his conversion experience, or later in his apostolic ministry?

More specifically, taking into account the general profile of the new perspective on Paul described above, the problem can be described as one of accounting for the following data: (1) Paul's "earlier life in Judaism" was characterized not by frustration nor misperception but by the stable framework of meaning described by Sanders as "covenantal nomism." (2) Within this world of meaning, Paul somehow perceived the Christian movement as a threat, and so "was violently persecuting the church of God and was trying to destroy it." (3) Paul's conversion experience resulted in a new estimation about Jesus ("God was pleased to reveal his Son to [in] me"), and thus undoubtedly a revision, but by no means necessarily an abandonment, of his earlier Israel-centered frame of reference. (4) At some point subsequent to this, Paul began to be engaged in a Torah-free mission to the Gentiles, perceiving it at least by the time of the writing of Galatians as the divinely intended outcome of his Damascus experience ("so that I might proclaim him among the Gentiles").[92]

Any full study of the issue, then, will need to be carried out in two dimensions: (1) *synchronically,* an examination of the structure of Paul's core convictions concerning God, Israel, the Torah, Christ, and so on as they pertain to the Gentile mission; and (2) *diachronically,* a reconstruction of the process by which Paul shifted from one set of convictions (centered on the Torah) to another (centered on Christ and a mission to the Gentiles).[93] Given the nature of the evidence, each line of investigation is fraught with problems and will require careful deliberation before proceeding. We will begin with the first of these dimensions, the examination of his mature convictions about the Gentiles as they can be ascertained from the letters. Such a starting point is suggested by the facts that the primary evidence for the process of Paul's conversion comes from letters that were all written after his Gentile mission was fully underway, and that any consideration of the developmental origin of his missionary concerns will very quickly require decisions concerning the nature of those concerns themselves.

## CHAPTER TWO

# A Conviction-Centered Approach

Because our knowledge of Paul is limited primarily to a handful of occasional letters, any attempt to investigate his convictions about the Gentiles, or anything else for that matter, needs to proceed with care and deliberation. One preliminary consideration—the list of letters to be included in the investigation—can be quickly disposed of. The seven letters commonly considered to be authentic provide us with more than enough material to work on and will comprise the main object of study. In addition, I hold 2 Thessalonians and Colossians to be authentic; they will be drawn into the discussion where appropriate. For the remainder, while Ephesians and 2 Timothy have the strongest claim to some direct connection with Paul,[1] the nature of that connection is so uncertain as to render them too problematical to be included here; they will be referred to only tangentially and by way of comparison. The issue of authenticity, however, is a preliminary matter. However one delimits the Pauline corpus, the problem of coherence remains, and it requires more detailed consideration.

At least some of the responsibility for the diversity of approaches surveyed in the previous chapter rests with Paul himself. For in the course of his letters the apostle makes statements that seem to ground the Gentile mission in a variety of *theologoumena*. We can observe at the surface of Paul's epistolary rhetoric statements suggesting a wide variety of theological rationales for the salvation of the Gentiles. These can be differentiated according to the significance assigned to the people of Israel and are presented here more or less in order of increasing positive significance.

1. *The Gentiles replace Israel in God's purposes, Israel having been rejected because of unbelief.* This position, which became the dominant view of the Gentile church from the second century onwards, finds prima facie support in specific statements made in Romans 11. Salvation has come to the world through Israel's trespass (vv. 11-12), failure (v. 12), and

rejection (v. 15). Gentiles have been grafted into the olive tree "in place of" (so the RSV and NRSV) the Jewish branches that have been lopped off (vv. 17-20).

2. *The abolition of the law removed the barrier that once stood between Jews and Gentiles.* Such a statement appears most explicitly in Ephesians (2:14-15), an epistle whose relationship to Paul is problematical. But the certainly authentic letters contain statements that can also be read in this way. Christ is the termination (one possible rendering of τέλος) of the law, making justification available to all—Jew and Gentile—who believe (Rom 10:4). Now that Christ has brought to an end the custodial role of the law, there is no longer any distinction between Jew and Greek, and Gentiles can become sons of God through faith (Gal 3:23-28).

3. *Because righteousness before God comes through faith rather than works of law, there is no distinction between Jew and Gentile; all humanity is acceptable to God on the same terms.* Recent reappraisals of Paul's faith-works language notwithstanding, statements remain which on the surface level at least suggest that the salvation of the Gentiles is predicated on the irrelevance of any Jew-Gentile distinction, which in turn is predicated on the fact that God desires to justify through faith rather than works. In Gal 2:14-16, for example, Paul criticizes Peter's behavior on the grounds that, since "a person is justified not by the works of the law but through faith in Jesus Christ," Gentiles need not "live like Jews" in order to be justified. Similarly in Rom 3:27-30: since people are "justified by faith apart from works prescribed by the law," the God of Jews and Gentiles "will justify the circumcised on the ground of faith and the uncircumcised through that same faith."

4. *Because God is one, there is no distinction between Jew and Gentile; all humanity is acceptable to God on the same terms.* This is stated explicitly in Rom 3:29-30: "Or is God the God of Jews only? Is he not the God of Gentiles also? Yes, of Gentiles also, since God is one; and he will justify the circumcised on the ground of their faith and the uncircumcised through their faith." Consequently Paul can say that there is no distinction between Jew and Gentile (Rom 3:22; 10:12), though the second of these texts fits more appropriately in category 6, below.

5. *The salvation of the Gentiles was God's plan from the beginning, a plan now being implemented.* In Col 1:25-27 Paul describes the glory of Christ's presence among the Gentiles as a "mystery that has been hidden throughout the ages and generations but has now been revealed to [God's] saints," a theme echoed in Eph 3:1-6 and in slightly different terms in Rom 11:25 (cf. Rom 16:25-27). Paul himself was appointed by God to

make this mystery known to the Gentiles (Col 1:25), having been set apart at birth and called for this very purpose (Gal 1:15-16). Somewhat at odds with the idea of a mystery just now being revealed is the set of statements proclaiming the salvation of the Gentiles as the fulfillment of scripture. The gospel of the justification of the Gentiles by faith was proclaimed beforehand to Abraham, says Paul in Gal 3:8 (citing Gen 12:3), and in Rom 15:9-12 he constructs a catena of texts to show that the scriptures anticipated a time when the Gentiles would glorify God for his mercy (also Rom 4:16-18; 9:25-26). Against the charge that it was unfair of God to allow the Gentiles to succeed where Israel failed (Rom 9:30-33), Paul replies that God is as free to make plans with humankind as the potter is with clay (Rom 9:19-26).

6. *Christ is lord of all, Gentiles as well as Jews.* The significance of the lordship of Christ for the Gentiles is at least implicit in the hymn of Phil 2:5-11: "at the name of Jesus every knee should bend, in heaven and on earth and under the earth, and every tongue should confess that Jesus Christ is Lord." This implication is made explicit by Paul in Rom 10:9-13, a passage which serves as a christological counterpart to the theological statements in 4 above: "For there is no distinction between Jew and Greek; the same Lord[2] is Lord of all and bestows his riches upon all who call upon him" (v. 12). Perhaps the statements to the effect that "in Christ" there is no distinction between Jew and Gentile (Gal 3:28; Col 3:11) can be placed in this category as well.

7. *"Israel" is not to be defined in purely ethnic terms; in Christ, Israel has been redefined, so as to include both Jews and Gentiles irrespective of Torah observance.* Such redefinition takes several forms. In Gal 3:6-9 and Romans 4, those who have faith, whether circumcised or not, are the true descendants and heirs of Abraham. Later in Galatians 3, Christ alone is identified as Abraham's true "seed" and heir, those "in Christ" being linked to Abraham only by extension. Elsewhere Paul can describe the church as the "[true] circumcision" (Phil 3:3; cf. Col 2:11; Rom 2:26-29), and perhaps as the "Israel of God" (Gal 6:16).

8. *Gentiles are beneficiaries of the fulfillment of God's dealings with Israel; Gentile salvation is a consequence of the salvation or blessing of (the remnant of) Israel in Christ.* In Rom 15:8-9 Paul sums up his argument with the striking declaration that Jesus' significance for the Gentiles is somehow dependent on the success of his ministry to Israel: "For I tell you that Christ has become a servant of the circumcised on behalf of the truth of God, in order that he might confirm the promises given to the patriarchs, and in order that the Gentiles might glorify God for his mercy." The verse is difficult in several respects, and will come up for

detailed discussion later.[3] But it seems to assign a more positive role to Israel in the extension of God's salvation to the Gentiles than any text canvased so far. In light of this conclusion to the argument of the epistle, the statement with which Paul begins—"to the Jew first and also to the Greek" (1:16)—may suggest a priority for Israel going beyond merely the right of first refusal. That this positive role for Israel is not taken over by Christ without remainder is suggested by various statements apparently assigning significance to the Jewish Christian remnant. The collection project is a means for the Gentile Christians to acknowledge the debt incurred when the Jewish Christians shared with them their spiritual blessings in Christ (Rom 15:26-27). Gentile Christians have been grafted in "among" (so JB) the Jewish Christian branches to share in the life of the vine of Israel (11:17).[4] The theme developed in Eph 2:11-22, then, that in Christ Gentile Christians have been incorporated into "the commonwealth of Israel" to share with the natural born members the goodness of the household of God, is not absent in the certainly authentic epistles of Paul.

This catalog of texts slides over a number of critical and exegetical issues that will have to be addressed. For the present this survey is sufficient to make the point: Paul can provide diverse and even conflicting theological justifications for his Gentile mission. Are Israel and its election, for example, irrelevant for the theology of the Gentile mission (categories 3, 4, 5, and 6 above)? Are they a negative factor (1, 2), or perhaps a positive (7, 8)? Is the salvation of the Gentiles a new and unforeseen divine initiative (that is, a mystery), or is it simply the culmination of a pattern whose shape and direction could have been anticipated from scripture? Is the distinction between Jew and Gentile totally abolished in Christ or do these remain as significant theological categories even within the church? Is the salvation of the Gentiles based on a particular kind of religious attitude toward God (such as faith), or is it based on the confirming of the promises made by God to the patriarchs of Israel through Jesus the Christ? The problem of what to do with conflicting and even apparently contradictory statements is by no means confined to this aspect of Paul's thought, and is generally recognized in Pauline scholarship.

The problem of conflicting statements in Paul's letters has been nicely described by Schweitzer in his typically vivid fashion:

> In the effort to understand Paul some started out from his anthropology, others from his psychology, others from his manner of thought in his pre-Christian period (as though we knew anything about that!), others from his personal idiosyncrasy, others from his attitude to the Law, and others

from the experience on the way to Damascus. In thus taking hold of any thread which came to hand they tangled the skein to start with, and condemned themselves to accept an inexplicable chaos of thought as Pauline teaching.[5]

The problem is so fundamental to any critical investigation of Paul that a full description of the various approaches to the tangle would require a complete history of Pauline scholarship.[6] One approach has been the attempt to identify the center or core around which the remaining elements can be suitably arranged. Schweitzer himself took this approach, as he relegated another putative center—justification by faith—to the status of a subsidiary crater existing within the main crater, Paul's mystical doctrine of "being in Christ."[7] Another approach has been to search in Hellenism or Judaism for the religious background to his thought, finding here either a coherent framework presupposed in the foreground[8] or the poles of an unresolved tension or duality in his thought.[9] As already noted, others have argued that Paul's conversion (or call), often taken together with his preconversion opposition to the Christian movement, provides the necessary interpretive starting point. Still others have posited theories of development, seeking a dynamic rather than static pattern of coherence.[10] And a few have denied that Paul was a systematic thinker at all, arguing that the attempt to reconstruct a system of "Paulinism" is misconceived, either because it is in his religious life and pastoral concern that his true significance is to be found,[11] or because his argumentation is so riddled with contradiction and systemic inconsistency as to render it fundamentally incoherent.[12]

Drawing on the results of more recent study, however, it is possible to speak in terms of a significant methodological advance. In part, this advance is due to new angles of approach opened up by the application of social-scientific insights to New Testament study. Just as important, however, has been the appearance of a number of detailed and perceptive studies of Paul himself. I will begin with the latter, singling out the significant and comprehensive treatments by J. C. Beker, D. Patte, and E. P. Sanders,[13] and attempting to develop some methodological clarity in dialogue with them.

The differences among these authors, both in detail and in approach, are not to be minimized. Nevertheless, each in his own way suggests that a distinction needs to be made between the surface elements of the text and an underlying set of basic commitments or convictions. At the surface level, Paul's letters represent various attempts through rhetorical device and theological argumentation to deal with practical problems that have emerged in his congregations. But underlying these contingent and conceptual levels in the text is a set of basic convictions (about Christ, Israel, the Torah, the Gentiles, and so on) that seldom emerge explicitly but nevertheless provide the tacit "semantic universe" in which the text in all its aspects has its being. The relationship between this underlying structure and the text itself is construed differently by each author, and conflicts and contradictions at the surface level are seen in different terms. But the idea that we need to interpret the text in terms of different structural levels, and especially that we should begin by identifying the basic convictional structure, represents a real step forward.

Beker identifies with those who are concerned to locate a "coherent center" to Paul's thought, but he is quite critical of most previous attempts to do so. In part this is just because he disagrees with the identifications others have made.[14] More significantly, however, he feels that much scholarship has gone astray by trying to identify one symbol or element (for example, justification, righteousness, reconciliation, freedom, being-with-Christ) out of the whole kaleidoscopic array of Pauline terms and concepts as the center around which the rest are forced to revolve. He argues instead that we need to recognize two levels in the structure of Paul's thought. There is indeed a coherent core, which he identifies as the coming apocalyptic triumph of God, already announced and inaugurated in Christ. But Paul is a pastor and a hermeneut, concerned to translate the core of his gospel into terms appropriate to the situations addressed in his letters. One needs to reckon, then, with a second level in his thought, that of contingent interpretation. The array of theological symbols and concepts, so fascinating and perplexing to scholars, needs to be recognized as the hermeneutical means by which Paul "translates the apocalyptic theme of the gospel into the contingent particularities of the human situation" (p. ix). A symbol such as the "righteousness of God," then, belongs to the surface or contingent level of the structure, and is to be understood only in the context of its relationship to the "deep structure":

> Therefore the primary language of the symbolic structure or its "deep structure" signifies the Christ-event in its meaning for the apocalyptic consummation of history, whereas the secondary language of the symbolic structure, or its "surface structure," signifies the contingent interpretation of Paul's Christian apocalyptic into a particular situation. (p. 16)

The strength of Beker's proposal is that it does not require us to choose between Paul the thinker and Paul the pastor. It gives full value to the contingent and occasional nature of the letters, without forcing us to sacrifice coherence of thought. It opens up middle ground between a Paul who simply imposes an already formulated dogmatic system on his readers without consideration of their particular situations, and a Paul who uses arbitrary and purely utilitarian arguments to gain a following or to have his way.

But Beker's approach requires caution. My concern here is not so much with the content of the "coherent center" as he conceives it; his insistence on the centrality of apocalyptic and his stubborn refusal to transmute it into something else are commendable. My concern, rather, has to do with the way in which the two-level structure has been construed. One needs to ask whether these levels have not been too sharply differentiated and whether their relationship to the text has not been construed in such a manner that important aspects of the "coherent core" have gone unrecognized.

Different facets of what turns out to be a single problem come into view in the two sections—"The Contingency of the Gospel" and "The Coherence of the Gospel"—into which Beker's study is divided. I begin with his treatment of contingency, and in particular with his discussion of the midrash on Abraham and the Torah in Gal 3:6—4:11 (pp. 47–56), a discussion that illustrates the problem nicely. Beker is certainly correct in his insistence that in Galatians Paul addresses a different situation than in Romans, so that his treatment of the Abraham story differs in logical development and in function in each case. In Galatians Paul is countering Judaizers who have neatly and smoothly synthesized Abraham, Torah, Christ, and the Gentiles, and thus is forced to emphasize discontinuity in salvation history; in Romans he defends himself against Jewish charges that he has denied God's faithfulness to Israel, and so emphasizes continuity. But the resulting exegesis of Gal 3:6—4:11 both overestimates the degree of logical inconsistency at the surface level and underestimates its significance for the deeper level.

In Beker's understanding of this passage, Paul constructs the link between Abraham and the Gentiles, promised in Gen 12:3, in three distinct ways, with three completely different estimations of the role of Christ. In vv. 6-9 those who have faith, Gentiles included, belong to Abraham's seed; faith, rather than Christ, establishes the connection. In vv. 10-14 Christ is the one who enables the blessing of Abraham to flow to the Gentiles, by removing the curse of the law. But in vv. 16-29 Christ is the sole recipient of the promise to Abraham; only as they are "in Christ," the "true seed of Abraham," do Gentiles share in Abraham's inheritance.

Because of its relevance for the Gentile question, I will return to Beker's reading of this passage later. What needs to be noted here is that Beker's "contingent hermeneutic" approach to Paul's argumentation renders him seemingly unconcerned about such logical discontinuities and abrupt shifts in argument.[15] Paul's contingent purpose, Beker believes, is to reduce Abraham's significance from that of a model proselyte (faith plus circumcision) to the symbol of a promise of a "faith" that became possible only with Christ. His argument shifts from one soteriological pattern to another until he reaches the conclusion that suits his purpose (vv. 26-29). This passage is admittedly one of the most obscure and impenetrable in the whole New Testament. In Beker's approach any attempt to find coherent logical structure in the passage—even peculiar logic unique to Paul—is ruled out at the outset in the name of contingency. He construes contingency in such a way that there seems to be no place in between "coherent core" and "contingent interpretation" for a body of theological explication, in which the theological implications of Paul's core convictions for significant topics (the place of Abraham, the role of faith, the inclusion of the Gentiles, and so on) were developed for their own sake rather than for their usefulness in a particular situation. This is not to underestimate the role of specific pastoral situations in spurring the development of Paul's theological thinking, but it is to suggest that Beker posits too much of a disjunction between the contingencies of the situation and the development of a coherent pattern of theological thought.

Beker insists with equal stress that there is such an underlying theological pattern, "a paradigmatic structure of Paul's thought that forms its basic coherence and must be derived from the contingent variety of his arguments in his letters" (p. 41). Coherence is by no means to be swallowed up in contingency. Because of the sharp distinction he makes between core and contextual argumentation, however, he is able to restrict tensions and logical difficulties to the surface level without having to reckon with the possibility that they say something about the nature of the core. In other words, he overestimates not only the contingency of the surface but also the coherence of the core. Returning to his treatment of Galatians 3, he recognizes that in Gal 3:19-26 Paul struggles, against what could be seen as the logical flow of his argument, to retain nevertheless a role for the law. But the locus of the tension, in his view, is restricted to the situational level, where to counter his opponents Paul has had to construe Christ and Torah in antithetical terms. Beneath the surface, however, at the core level, Paul's thinking about the law is characterized by a coherence undisturbed by the storms raging above.[16] But it needs to be asked whether Paul's struggle in Galatians 3 stems, at least in part, from the fact that he is committed to two potentially conflicting convictions: (1) salvation is through Christ, and therefore not through law; (2) the law was given by God.[17]

This emphasis on coherence runs throughout the second main section of Beker's book, where he reconstructs Paul's thought on a variety of topics (for example, sin and death, the law, life in Christ, Israel) within the framework of Paul's christological apocalyptic. In his reconstruction, Paul was able to combine quite smoothly and without tension belief in the salvatory significance of the cross and resurrection with traditional apocalyptic expectation. But Paul himself gives us sufficient ground to wonder whether the marriage of convictions old and new was made so easily.

Beker's attempt to preserve a place in Pauline interpretation for both contingency and coherence is on the right track. But he has perhaps made too sharp a differentiation between the two levels,[18] overemphasizing the contingency of the surface and the coherence of the core in the process. It seems to me that these difficulties arise, at least in part, because he fails to recognize the existence of two levels in what he calls the "consistent core," with the result that in his structure three levels have been unnaturally compressed into two.

A statement made in the course of his discussion of the law provides us with a point of entry. His purpose in this chapter, he says, is to show that Paul's various and conflicting arguments concerning the law "cohere in an intelligible pattern consistent with the organizing center of his thought" (p. 235). Despite his attempt to include Paul's developed thinking about the law within the category of the "coherent core," Beker seems here to recognize a distinction between Paul's basic convictions ("the organizing center") and his developed (and developing) thought about the implications of those convictions for the law ("an intelligible pattern consistent with the . . . center"). The core itself has a structure: at the center there is a set of basic convictions—traditional Jewish apocalyptic expectation, modified by the belief that the expected triumph of God has been inaugurated in the cross and resurrection of Jesus[19]—providing the framework within which the theological implications of these convictions are explored and a body of theological explication developed. While he does not recognize it explicitly, then, Beker's approach to Paul really assumes a threefold structure: convictional core, theological explication, and contingent hermeneutic. It is my contention that many of the difficulties of his approach can be overcome by recognizing that, between the fixity of the convictional core and the fluidities of the contextual hermeneutic, is to be found a developing and unfinished body of theological explication. To explore this further, the structuralist approach of Daniel Patte will be of considerable assistance.

While Beker notes in passing that his approach could be described in structuralist categories (p. 16), Patte sets the development of a structural introduction to Paul's letters as his main aim. To be sure, some might wonder whether this approach can be of any assistance in understanding the thought of a historical person such as Paul. As Patte concedes in his introduction, structuralism is usually associated with a studied indifference toward the historical particularities of a text and its author.[20] But structuralism is not fundamentally ahistorical. Certainly, in contrast to traditional approaches in which an author is seen as simply a creator of signification, with complete autonomy over a text and its meaning, structuralism has insisted that authors also have signification imposed on them, that meaning in a text is the result not only of an author's intentions but also of the deeper structures of language itself.[21] But in its broadest conception, the "structures" with which it is concerned are not necessarily ahistorical. Structuralism assumes that the surface elements of a text—words strung together to form syntactical units—become meaningful with reference to an underlying structure that provides an organizing principle linking the syntactical units in some significant way. These underlying structures can be of a variety of types: so-called deep structures, buried in the unconscious and part of every event of human communication; cultural codes; narrative grammars; and—important for our purposes—structures pertaining to the convictions of an author and to the author's intentions with respect to the situation being addressed. In the case, then, of Paul's letters—occasional writings that allow only brief and partial glimpses into the system of convictions on which they are based—structuralism provides us with an appropriate and useful conceptual framework.

To this point, the term "conviction" has been used in a loose and intuitive way. Patte uses it as a key concept, however, defining it more precisely by means of a contrast with the term "idea." An idea is a proposition, assent to which is dependent on a demonstration of its truth or validity. A conviction, by contrast, is a self-evident truth. Ideas can arise out of convictions, but they have to do with different dimensions of human existence: "Conviction is closely associated with faith and believing, while idea is associated with knowledge and thinking" (p. 11). Ideas and convictions can overlap in substance; for example, both could involve assent to the proposition "God exists." But the relationship in each case between the human subject and the proposition is quite different. In the former case, assent would be withdrawn if the human "thinker" lost confidence in the arguments on which the truth of the proposition rested. In the latter case, the assent of the human "believer" is independent of logical demonstration; the proposition is of the order of an axiom. Further, while we have control over ideas and can manipulate them for our own ends, convictions have control over us, motivating our actions and configuring our existence.

Convictions are not isolated entities, however, but are generally linked together within a convictional pattern or system. By establishing what is real and what is desirable, such a system of convictions constitutes a "semantic universe," relating the various elements of human experience together in an orderly way and providing a framework of meaning for human existence. Such a system of convictions Patte labels a "faith."

As the title of his book suggests, Patte's concern is to discover the nature of Paul's faith, so defined. His study differs in essential ways, then, from traditional attempts to outline Paul's thought. For Patte, thought is to faith as idea is to conviction. His goal is to abstract from the text of the letters the structure not of Paul's thought (a system of ideas) but of his faith (a system of convictions). To do this he proposes a structural analysis of the letters, in which the structure being pursued is that of the convictional system undergirding them. Paul's letters consist of a string of ideas hierarchically organized in order to perform a rhetorical function appropriate to the epistolary occasion. But the principle of organization—the framework within which the rhetoric becomes effective—is provided by the semantic universe of Paul's faith. This is what Patte sets out to discover.

Patte's analysis provides us with a significant step forward. As was argued above, Beker's coherence/contingency model, while valuable in several ways, is nevertheless too simple to be effective as a tool of structural analysis. His concept of the "coherent core" is too broad in that it includes two distinct and discernible levels, that of Paul's basic convictions, and that of the pattern of thought built up on the basis of those convictions. But by defining conviction and faith as he does, Patte provides us with a way of conceiving these two levels. In fact, in Patte's categories, what Beker treats as a single block (coherent core) consists of two quite distinct entities (convictions and ideas). But Patte seems also to compress two levels into one. For what he calls Paul's "ideas" really includes both theological explication ("theological discourse" by means of which Paul "makes sense of [his] faith" both for himself and for others)[22] and contextual application ("arguments" designed to alter the readers' thought and action).[23] If with his concept of a "system of convictions" he helps us to make an appropriate distinction within Beker's category of the "coherent core," Beker's concept of "contingent hermeneutic" allows us to make an appropriate distinction within Patte's category of Paul's "ideas." But in order to develop further the category lying in between—that of theological explication, differentiated from convictions on the one side and contextual argumentation on the other—it will be useful to look briefly at aspects of Sanders's treatment of Paul.

In his two significant books on Paul, Sanders provides us with both a penetrating analysis of the problems facing anyone who desires to discover a coherent pattern in Paul's theological statements—especially his statements about the law—and stimulating proposals for a solution. Simply stated, his suggestion is that clarity can be achieved if one recognizes an essential distinction between Paul's basic convictions and other levels of his thought and argumentation. Paul is to be seen, he asserts, as "a 'coherent,' though not a 'systematic' thinker."[24] "His complicated and often obscure reflections"[25] on the implications of the gospel are governed by a set of basic and unchanging convictions about the saving significance of Christ. This set of convictions, as Sanders perceives it, is not to be confused with his well-known concept of a "pattern of religion," which in Paul's case he identifies as "participatory eschatology." As he insists in his later book,[26] this concept is only an analytical tool employed for the specific purpose of comparing Paul and Judaism. Instead, Paul's basic convictions are identified as follows: (1) God has provided for salvation in Christ; (2) this salvation is for all—Jew and Gentile—on the same terms; (3) God has appointed Paul as apostle to the Gentiles.[27] Because of the place of the Gentiles in this description of Paul's convictional core, we shall have to return to it later. For now, our concern is more with form than with substance.

What is the nature of the relationship between these basic convictions and the content of the letters? How are we to understand both Paul's coherence and his lack of system? To a certain extent, Sanders's views coincide with those of Beker, in that he sees the divergencies and conflicts in Paul's theological arguments as due in part to contextual factors. "Different questions" about the function and significance of the law require "different answers."[28] The *arguments* Paul uses to defend a position are not always good indicators of his *reasons* for holding the position in the first place.[29] But the unsystematic appearance of Paul's theological statements is not fully accounted for on the basis of the constraints of the dialogic situation alone. Sanders also makes room for an unfinished body of thought, related to and yet distinct from both the convictional core on the one hand and contextual argumentation on the other. Paul is not only a preacher, convinced of certain truths that he wants to share; and not only a pastor, concerned to address "words on target"[30] to a particular situation. In addition he is a thinker, occupied—albeit in an unsystematic way—with working out the implications of his convictions and resolving the logical conflicts that they present.[31] Several aspects of his approach to Paul's convictions, his thought, and the relationship between them will be useful for our purposes here.

First, although Sanders does not put it in these terms, it can be said on the basis of his analysis that there is a *structure* to be perceived within Paul's set of basic convictions. In Patte's phrase, we have to do with a *system* of convictions. My point here has to do with Sanders's (convincing) argument that Paul's belief that the law cannot provide salvation is *derived* from his basic conviction that salvation is to be found in Christ: "If salvation is by Christ . . . it is not by the Jewish law."[32] Sanders does not classify the belief that "the Torah is not an entrance requirement [for salvation]" among Paul's set of basic convictions. But it is clear that in Patte's definition of the term—a self-evident truth, undergirding argument and constraining action—this belief can indeed be described as a conviction. If this is so, then not all convictions stand on the same level; convictions can give rise to other convictions. It will be necessary, therefore, to inquire into the relationships among convictions. In particular, is Paul's conviction about the Gentiles—that they are to be included in the salvation provided for in Christ—a fundamental conviction, or is it subordinated to and even derived from something more basic? When Sanders identifies the basic conviction underlying Paul's argumentation as "God had sent Jesus Christ to provide for the salvation *of all*,"[33] is he presenting as a single conviction something that in reality is structurally more complex?

The second aspect of Sanders's analysis that will be helpful for our own is the observation that conflict can exist between basic convictions. While it is not inappropriate to talk about a structured system of convictions, we need to allow for the presence of tension within the structure. Two examples of conflicting convictions are addressed by Sanders, and in each case the conflict arises between a native conviction stemming from Paul's Jewish upbringing, and a conversion conviction stemming from his new Christian faith. The first of these, of course, has to do with the law. While Paul became convinced that salvation was not to be found through the law, he nevertheless continued to believe that the law had been given by God, and therefore must have had some divinely ordained role to play. The attempt to hold these two convictions together, Sanders argues, gives rise "to some of the most difficult and tortured passages in the surviving correspondence."[34] Despite several attempts, Paul never fully resolved the conflict to his own satisfaction, and continued to struggle with it, in Sanders's understanding of his letters, to the end.

The other conflict has to do with Israel and the Gentiles, and thus concerns us here even more directly. On the one hand, Paul was convinced that salvation was to be found in Christ for all, Jew and Gentile, on equal terms; much of Paul's argumentation is aimed at demonstrating the equal status of Jew and Gentile in both plight and salvation. But, on the other hand, Paul continued to believe that God's election of Israel was "irrevocable" (cf. Rom 11:29). Romans 9–11 represents Paul's anguished attempt to seek "a formula which would keep God's promises to Israel intact, while insisting on faith in Jesus Christ."[35] While the substance of this attempt will occupy our attention later, for now the point is that Paul's system of convictions does not necessarily mesh smoothly into a harmonious whole. In particular, in the case of Paul we are dealing with a convert, one whose new Christian convictions did not totally displace the old and therefore needed to be correlated with another, partially disjunctive and potentially conflicting set of convictions.

The final observation to be made from Sanders's treatment of Paul has to do with the connection between Paul's convictions and his thought. As has just been mentioned, internal conflicts and tensions within Paul's basic convictions give rise to various attempts to think through the implications of the gospel and to find a satisfactory resolution of the problems raised by Paul the apostle for Paul the Jew (and vice versa). His "ideas" are not generated entirely by the exigencies of his pastoral ministry, though these may have provided him with the immediate occasion and stimulus. He has to be seen, at least in part, as a thinker, someone concerned to work out the implications of his basic convictions for their own sake and not simply for their effectiveness in a specific context. This is not to posit a false distinction between Paul's "thought" and his apostolic calling; it is precisely in order to defend and enhance his apostolic ministry that he struggles with the explication of his basic convictions. But the fact remains that his theological discourse and argumentation has to be understood within a three-level framework: At one end there is a system of basic convictions, derived both from his native Jewish upbringing and from his conversion experience. At the other end, there is the rhetorical situation of the letters themselves, as Paul represents and responds to particular sets of circumstances in his ministry with local congregations. In between, mediating the two and driven in different but interconnected ways by each, is a process of theological reflection and development. What we are accustomed to call Paul's theology, then, is to be seen as a dynamic process taking place in the space between his structured set of convictions on the one hand, and his contextual ministry on the other.[36]

With the exception of Patte, the scholars discussed above have proceeded in an apparently instinctive exegetical fashion; explicit theoretical reflection on their interpretive procedure is rare. Patte's structuralist approach is more self-consciously theoretical. For my purposes, however, his structuralism is not as useful as is his concept of a structured set of convictions that provides a "semantic universe" within which people order their lives and make them meaningful. This concept could be elaborated in connection with work being done in the social sciences, especially the sociology of knowledge,[37] linguistics,[38] and cultural anthropology.[39] Sociology of knowledge, in particular, offers a way of seeing Paul's letters in their full social dimension (and not simply as collections of "ideas"), while retaining a place for what has more traditionally been investigated under the category of Paul's "thought": Paul's letters can be seen as attempts to present, defend, and preserve a particular "social world" (or construction of reality), with inner symbolic structures and outer social forms.[40]

But for utilitarian purposes, I would like to develop an approach to Paul's convictions with the aid of Thomas Kuhn's book *The Structure of Scientific Revolutions*.[41] His analysis of cognitive structures is strikingly congruent with sociology of knowledge approaches[42] and thus provides just as useful a theoretical framework for the three-level approach to Paul described above. It has two added advantages. Because of its origin with reference to the world of science and scientific innovation, where individual perception plays an important role,[43] it is more adaptable to the case of a semantic universe as perceived by an individual. And, more importantly, since his central concern has to do with shifts of convictional framework (in his case, those accompanying scientific revolutions), his approach provides conceptual tools that will aid in incorporating the phenomenon of conversion into our analysis.[44]

Kuhn's intention in the book is to refute a view of science and scientific progress that he labels "development-by-accumulation"—the idea that scientific discoveries and innovations are added one by one to an "ever growing stockpile that constitutes scientific technique and knowledge" (p. 2). Instead, as his title suggests, he sees scientific progress as consisting of revolutions, in which one way of ordering the world as it pertains to a particular scientific field is thrown over and replaced by another. The major and truly significant scientific discoveries represent qualitative as well as quantitative changes, in that they involve shifts from one "worldview"—one "network of commitments . . . that tell [the scientist] what both the world and his science are like" (p. 42)—to another. Kuhn sets himself against an empiricist view of science, then, arguing for the primacy not of detached observation but of a set of basic convictions which define the world within which the scientist operates and without which no science is possible.

Kuhn's best known and most characteristic category is that of the "paradigm," and this is as good a place as any to begin a more detailed description of his analysis. Actually he uses the term in two distinct (though organically connected) ways. In its most basic sense, a paradigm is a specific scientific achievement—including "law, theory, application and instrumentation together" (p. 10)—successful enough in resolving a set of hitherto intractable problems that it sets a pattern and a framework for scientific work to follow. Copernicus's theory of a rotating earth revolving with other planets around a stationary sun is a good example. Providing a simpler and more satisfying account of astronomical observations than the earth-centered system of Ptolemy, it set the framework for astronomical investigation from that time onward. Kuhn also uses "paradigm" in an extended sense to refer more broadly to the set of basic assumptions and convictions described in the previous paragraph. But it is clear from his discussion that the two are closely linked. Not only does the paradigm in the narrow sense provide the foundation out of which the set of guiding convictions develops. But since the convictions are implicit in the paradigm, the paradigm itself, rather than an explicitly formulated set of assumptions, rules, and procedures, often provides the more immediate point of reference for scientific work.[45]

Paradigms, of course, do not solve all of the problems in a given scientific field; they represent the beginning, not the end, of what Kuhn calls "normal science." Normal science involves extending the accomplishment of the paradigm to the whole field of knowledge. Such "paradigm articulation," as he calls it, includes the attempt to replicate the achievement of the paradigm in the case of other recognized problems, and the exploration of new problems suggested by the paradigm itself. The paradigm thus sets the framework for normal science, providing the criteria for appropriate problems, the rules for tackling the problems, and the standards for admissible solutions.

Kuhn's main concern has to do with the process by which one convictional framework—and the normal science to which it gives rise—is replaced by another, a process he describes as a "paradigm shift." An important element in the process is the recognition of an anomaly—a counterinstance unforeseen by, or not consistent with, the predictions of the theory. By themselves anomalies do not cause the rejection of a paradigm; at most they create a sense of crisis, a feeling that the tools a paradigm supplies are no longer capable of solving the problems that emerge. A paradigm is never simply abandoned; it is always exchanged for another more suitable:

> The decision to reject one paradigm is always simultaneously the decision to accept another, and the judgment leading to that decision involves the comparison of both paradigms with nature and with each other. (p.77)

It is in this discussion of paradigm shifts that the congruency between his concept of paradigm, especially in its extended sense, and Patte's categories of "conviction" and "faith" becomes most apparent. Once a paradigm has been accepted, Kuhn asserts, it takes on an axiomatic quality. What within the former paradigm were seen as anomalies—irritants to be explained away—now "seem very much like tautologies, statements of situations that could not conceivably have been otherwise" (p. 78). A paradigm in its extended sense, then, corresponds closely to Patte's definition of "faith" as a system of convictions that relate various elements of human experience together in an orderly way, providing a framework of meaning for human action and existence. Indeed, Kuhn can describe a paradigm as a "set of received beliefs" (p. 5). Further, because a paradigm shift represents a shift of allegiance from one system of convictions to another, he describes the process as a "conversion" (p. 150). A paradigm cannot simply be accepted as the result of a logical proof, since it is the paradigm itself that provides the rules governing the standards for such proofs. A paradigm shift is not a step-by-step process of logical reasoning, but a transfer of allegiance from one set of convictions to another.

Kuhn's analysis provides a suggestive model for looking at the structure of Paul's thought. In what follows, I will be arguing that Paul can be seen as one who underwent a paradigm shift, a transfer of allegiance from one set of world-structuring convictions to another. Paul began with a semantic universe defined by the Torah and the "traditions of [his] fathers" (Gal 1:14). His commitment to this way of ordering the world was anything but casual: he describes himself as a "zealot" who "advanced in Judaism beyond many of [his] contemporaries" (Gal 1:14). Because of this commitment, when he encountered the early Christian movement, he perceived—perhaps more clearly than the Jewish Christians themselves—the incompatibility of the message of a crucified and risen Messiah with his Torah-centered way of looking at the world. I will have to leave until later any attempt to specify with precision the nature of the conflict between Christ and Torah as Paul perceived it. Nevertheless, it is clear from Gal 1:13-14 and especially Phil 3:6 that he attempted to suppress the Christian message precisely because he perceived it as posing in some way a threat to the Torah.

The message of a crucified and risen Messiah presented itself to Paul, then, as an anomaly, or at least as something that would have been an anomaly if he believed it were true. In this connection, it is worth noting Kuhn's observation that commitment to an established paradigm is a prerequisite for recognizing the presence of an anomaly: "Novelty ordinarily emerges only for the man who, knowing with precision what he should expect, is able to recognize that something has gone wrong" (p. 65). With his experience outside Damascus, the anomaly ceased being merely hypothetical, and Paul came to believe that something had indeed "gone wrong" with his inherited world of meaning. Contrary to his expectation, God had raised Jesus from the dead. Though it threatened to shatter his semantic universe, Paul became convinced that the crucified Jesus was, after all, God's anointed Messiah.

How Paul was able to make sense of this new conviction and to resolve the conflicts it presented for his old system of convictions are questions that will need to be examined in due course. Resolve these conflicts, however, he did. In Kuhn's categories, this initial resolution of the conflict between Christ and Torah can be see as a basic paradigm, in the more restricted sense of the term—a new discovery that set the pattern for what was to follow. This basic paradigm provided the framework for a more general reconsideration of the convictions that made up Paul's former semantic universe or system of convictions. The result of this reconsideration was a new constellation of convictions, a new way of ordering the world in a meaningful way—a new paradigm, in the more extended sense of the term. Within the framework provided by this new Christ-centered paradigm, Paul began to work out its implications and deal with its residual tensions (the apostolic equivalent of what Kuhn calls normal science), and to respond, on the basis of his "basic paradigm," to a series of contingent situations that demanded his apostolic attention (the analogue, perhaps, of applied science).

The validity of this particular reading of Paul in Kuhnian terms will need to emerge from the detailed argumentation to follow. To summarize the approach, however, I am suggesting that behind or beneath the surface of Paul's letters we can find three structural levels that constrain the discourse and govern its meaning: (1) *contextual or circumstantial*, the complex of factors having to do with the situation of the readers being addressed, Paul's intentions with respect to that situation, and the nature of the relationship between Paul and his readers; (2) *theological*, the pattern of Paul's thought as it has developed to this point; (3) *convictional*, the basic set of convictions, or the semantic universe, that structures Paul's apostolic ministry and undergirds his thought. Kuhn's analysis provides us with both a helpful analogue to this three-level structural approach, and workable categories that will enable us to extend this approach to include the phenomenon of conversion. I propose, then, to investigate Paul's statements about the Gentiles in order to determine the nature of his conviction about their salvation, the place of this conviction within his basic system of convictions, and the origin of this conviction in the trajectory of his life experience from Pharisee to apostle.

I begin with an investigation of the structure of Paul's set of basic convictions (about Christ, the cross and resurrection, sin, Torah, Israel, the Gentiles) as they can be ascertained from his letters, with particular attention to the place of the Gentiles within that structure (Part II). Given the definition of "conviction" developed above, it seems reasonable to assume that Paul's convictions undergo no significant change or development in the period represented by the letters. While his letters may provide evidence for development in his *thought*, since they all stem from a relatively brief period characterized by his fixed self-perception as apostle to the Gentiles, we can proceed on the assumption that they are grounded on a mature and stable system of *convictions*. The goal of Part II, then, can be said to be *synchronic* in nature. Building on the results of this synchronic investigation, Part III will be *diachronic*, attempting to trace Paul's transition and development from zealot and persecutor to apostle of the Gentiles, with a view to determining the origin of his conviction about the Gentiles and their place in the salvation accomplished by Christ. At the appropriate point in Part III I will need to engage in supplementary methodological considerations, particularly with respect to contemporary thinking about conversion and to the elements of continuity and discontinuity in a paradigm shift.[46] To lead into Part II, however, I need to ask how one goes about identifying Paul's system of convictions.

Patte's structuralist approach represents the most detailed attempt to develop the requisite methodology.[47] As he describes it, a didactic discourse (the category to which he assigns Paul's letters) can be seen in terms of two levels: the *dialogic* level, containing the description of the effect on the readers' knowledge, action, or belief toward which the discourse is directed; and the *warranting* level, aimed at motivating the readers to recognize the validity and the value of the main argument.[48] It is primarily in the warranting statements that Patte expects to find a manifestation of an author's fundamental convictions.

Such warranting statements, however, might not be the best indicators of basic convictions, especially in the case of someone who openly pursues a policy of "sanctified inconsistency" in order to win people to his point of view (cf. 1 Cor 9:19-22). As has already been mentioned, Paul can defend a position with arguments that do not really correspond with his reasons for holding the position himself. Warranting statements have more to do with an author's assumptions about what the readers will find effective than with the author's own basic convictions. Paul's convictions govern and constrain his argumentation, to be sure. But the link between argument and conviction varies from case to case. Sometimes convictions are most clearly apparent in the premise, sometimes in the conclusion, sometimes in the assumptions at work in the argumentative logic. If we use the term "predication" to refer to the full range of statements that are asserted, assumed, or agreed to in the course of an argument (in the premises, the warranting statements, the logical inferences, or the conclusions), we can say that a conviction might be reflected in any of the predications of an argument. Paul's convictions cannot simply be read off in any mechanical way from an analysis of his argumentative rhetoric.[49]

But, at the same time, Paul's convictions will not be discovered apart from a careful analysis of his rhetoric, guided by discussions of rhetoric both ancient and modern.[50] In such an analysis, we need to be particularly alert for "disjunctions" of various kinds—"claims" that Paul wants to establish over against his opponents, non sequitur jumps in his argumentative logic, arguments against the plain sense of scriptural texts, apparent inconsistencies, and so on. On this point, Patte's advice is right on target:

> Since they are not ideas which fit neatly into a logical argument, the convictions are to be sought "in the cracks," in what is odd in the argument, in what does not contribute to the unfolding of the argument or even hinder it [sic].[51]

One way of proceeding would be to take the letters one by one, building up a picture of Paul's convictional world as we go. While this would have the advantage of respecting the uniqueness of the rhetorical situations represented in each of the letters, it would make for much repetition. If it is valid to assume that Paul's convictions remain essentially unchanged throughout his letters—that is, if there is any validity to the threefold interpretive framework developed above—then a topical or categorical approach will be both more appropriate and more economical. And so, I will proceed according to the basic categories of Paul's convictional system (God, humankind, the Torah, Christ, Israel, Paul's own call and apostolic mission), in each case examining the material in his letters bearing on the salvation of the Gentiles, with a view to ascertaining the structural relationship of his underlying convictions. In the case of the Torah, for example: Is Paul's conviction about the Gentiles (that they can receive salvation in Christ without adhering to the Torah) a consequence of a more fundamental conviction that the (Jewish) Torah is nonsalvific ("not Torah" leads to the obliteration of the Jew-Gentile distinction)? Conversely, does his opposition to the Torah stem from a more fundamental conviction concerning the salvation of the Gentiles? Or are his convictions about the Torah and the Gentiles related in some other way?

There is one more preliminary point to be made. As described in chapter 1, this book has been precipitated by a perceived paradigm shift in the study of Paul, one in which scholars have come to believe (in part) that Paul did not misunderstand Judaism in any fundamental way and that his conversion represented a reconfiguration rather than a repudiation of his essential Jewishness. This suggests that "covenantal nomism" can function appropriately as a kind of "boundary condition" or "criterion of satisfaction" here. Any proposed reconstruction of Paul's convictional world needs to be one that could be plausibly inhabited by a covenantal nomist who had come to believe that God had raised Jesus from death.

This suggests a second dimension to the proposed investigation of Paul's convictions in Part II, in addition to the attempt to ascertain the convictional logic at work in his various statements about the Gentiles. In the case of each of the convictional categories referred to above, I will compare the structure of Paul's convictions with the structured semantic universe of covenantal nomism, noting where convictions are shared, where they are similar in form but different in substance, and where they are divergent. When this has been carried out, we should be well positioned to ascertain the nature of the paradigm shift occasioned by Paul's Damascus experience (Part III). In order to carry out such a comparative study, we need to know something about the place of the Gentiles within the world of covenantal nomism, a topic to which I now turn.

## CHAPTER THREE

# Covenantal Nomism and the Gentiles

The purpose of this chapter is to survey Jewish attitudes toward the Gentiles that were contemporary with Paul, paying particular attention to what I have called the "patterns of universalism," those ways in which Judaism had already created space for the Gentiles within their hopes of salvation. I am adopting, at least for heuristic purposes, the hypothesis that Paul is to be understood as a covenantal nomist who came to believe that God had raised Jesus from the dead. Such a hypothesis does not imply that Paul's Gentile mission represents a revision of some pattern of Jewish universalism; his new belief about Christ may well have caused him to reject covenantal particularism entirely. The procedure to be followed in Part II—a sequential examination of Paul's major convictions and their interrelation with his conviction concerning the Gentiles—is designed to allow for unbiased evaluation of all proposed interpretations of the Gentile mission. Thus the hypothesis makes an assumption about the beginning of the process but not about its outcome.

The main purpose of this chapter, then, is to survey the range of attitudes toward the Gentiles that were present in the Jewish world of meaning in which Paul was socialized and in which his Damascus experience took place. Although there is still perhaps a need for a full-scale study, the relevant evidence has been largely identified and various aspects of the issue extensively explored.[1] What follows is a kind of typology of the range of Jewish attitudes toward the Gentiles, constructed with a view to its usefulness for the investigation of Paul's convictional world. This typology is built on a kind of "criterion of multiple attestation": if an approach to the Gentiles is documented in more than one sociological strand of Judaism, and in time periods both before and after that of Paul, I have taken it to be one of the live options in Paul's own situation.[2] Further, while some strands of Judaism thought of Gentiles simply as enemies of Israel and sinners destined for destruction, the emphasis here will fall on the various patterns of universalism, ways in which Judaism could conceive of the "salvation" of (the) Gentiles that were consistent with its own covenantal self-understanding. These patterns will simply be identified and documented here; specific aspects will be explored in more detail later as the need arises.

"Attitudes" do not exist as disembodied entities. They are held by human beings in the context of structured social worlds. In any such world, inner symbolic structures are mirrored by and grounded in outer social forms and realities. The inner attitudes of interest in this chapter are integrally connected with corresponding outer realities of Jew-Gentile relationships in the Mediterranean world. One cannot divorce conceptual "patterns of universalism" from such social realia as the various levels of attachment to Judaism,[3] the intended function of Jewish apologetic literature and the degree to which Judaism engaged in "mission,"[4] the participation of Gentiles in worship at the Jerusalem temple, and so on. While our interest here is primarily in the former, it cannot be pursued in isolation from the latter.

The material to be considered falls into two broad areas—the present and the eschatological future. We shall begin with the present.

## 3.1 Aliens, Strangers, without Hope

Perhaps the most consistent way that Israel's covenantal self-understanding could be extrapolated to the situation of the Gentiles[5] was to see the covenant as a kind of Noah's ark outside of which there was no salvation. In one form of this type of thinking, Gentiles could avail themselves of the possibility of climbing into the ark by means of proselytism; we will look at this option in the next section. Here we are interested in a harsher pattern of thought in which proselytism is not entertained as an option at all, where Gentiles are seen as "aliens from the commonwealth of Israel, strangers to the covenants of promise, having no hope and without God in the world," to use the language of Eph 2:12.

Without a doubt, the most unrelentingly negative characterization of the status of the Gentiles is to be found in *Jubilees*. *Fourth Ezra* may be more pessimistic about the number of those to be saved and the ability of humankind to keep the Torah, but at least Ezra is distressed about the fact![6] For *Jubilees* the matter is simple: those who are born outside the covenant are thereby excluded from the circle of the saved:

> And anyone who is born whose own flesh is not circumcised on the eighth
> day is not from the sons of the covenant which the Lord made for Abraham

since (he is) from the children of destruction. And there is therefore no sign upon him so that he might belong to the Lord because (he is destined) to be destroyed and annihilated from the earth and to be uprooted from the earth because he has destroyed the covenant of the Lord our God. (*Jub.* 15.26)

The text perhaps should not be read as a categorical rejection of proselytism: the language concerning the "eighth day" is modeled on Gen 17:9-14, and the author is aware that Abraham himself was circumcised as an adult. Nevertheless, the possibility of proselytism is nowhere countenanced[7] and, furthermore, is even deliberately avoided: in the story of the rape of Dinah, *Jubilees* approvingly repeats Levi and Simeon's statement that it would be a reproach for a daughter of Israel to be given to an uncircumcised man (*Jub.* 30.12; cf. Gen 34:14), while pointedly ignoring that part of the Genesis account where Levi and Simeon offer circumcision as an option to the men of Shechem (Gen 34:15-24).[8]

While no other text is as categorical in restricting salvation to Israel, *Jubilees* is not alone in its pessimism about the Gentiles. As is well known, the Qumran community, whose outlook overlapped with that of *Jubilees* to a considerable extent, viewed all outside their own sect as "men of the lot of Satan," destined for destruction (e.g., 1QS 2.4–9). While a few texts retain גרים ("resident alien, proselyte") as a category within the community of Israel (e.g. CD 14.4–5, perhaps a reference to non-Israelite slaves;[9] cf. CD 12.11), rarely is there even a glimmer of interest in incorporating Gentiles into the community.[10] Indeed, 1QS 6.13–14 appears to restrict membership to native-born Israelites.[11] Similarly, in the *Testament of Moses*, Moses declares that God "created the world on behalf of his people, but he did not make this purpose of creation known from the beginning of the world, so that the nations might be found guilty" (*T. Mos.* 1.12–13), and looks forward to the day when God will "work vengeance on the nations" (10.7). Still other texts agree with *Jubilees* in prohibiting intermarriage, with no apparent option of proselytism.[12]

*Fourth Ezra* is typical of a number of other texts in which there is an attempt to justify the rejection and ultimate destruction of the Gentiles on the basis of their disregard for the law. For example, speaking of "Adam and all who have come from him," the angel says to Ezra:

For this reason, therefore, those who dwell on earth shall be tormented, because . . . though they received the commandments they did not keep them, and though they obtained the law they dealt unfaithfully with what they received. (7.72)

This theme of the culpability of the Gentiles because of their refusal to obey the law permeates the book (see esp. 3.28–36; 7.19–24, 37–38, 79–82; 8.55–58; 9.10–12). Sanders has characterized 4 *Ezra* as anomalous in its pessimism about those within the covenant,[13] but its treatment of those outside the covenant is paralleled elsewhere. *Pseudo-Philo*, for example, has God declare to Moses:

> [F]or I have given an everlasting Law into your hands and by this I will judge the whole world. For this will be a testimony. For even if men say, "We have not known you, and so we have not served you," therefore I will make a claim upon them because they have not learned my Law." (11.1–2)

A similar "ignorance of the law is no excuse" argument appears in 2 *Bar.* 48.40–47 (see also 82.6; cf. *t. Soṭ* 8.6).

In formal terms, such texts seem to hold open the option of repentance and proselytism; if Gentiles are condemned for disregarding the law, the possibility must have been there for them to be redeemed by keeping it. And so 4 *Ezra* can speak of the present age as a time when "an opportunity of repentance was still open to them" (9.12) (also *Apoc. Abr.* 31.6). But since these writings show little interest in encouraging proselytism and little optimism concerning the Gentiles' ability to respond,[14] this formal openness to proselytism is to be seen rather as a type of theodicy: the nations therefore have no grounds for complaint.[15] The rabbinic tradition that God offered the law to all nations but only Israel accepted it[16] is a later variation on the theme.

But for another strand within Second Temple Judaism, proselytism was more than merely a hypothetical reality. To this we now turn.

## 3.2 Proselytes

In the "didactic romance" that we know as the Book of Judith, just as Judith herself (as her name implies) represents the ideal Jew, so several other characters play the role of typical Gentiles. Nebuchadnezzar and his second-in-command, Holofernes, in their arrogance, cruelty, and impiety gather up all the features of Israel's persecutors from the Assyrians to the Seleucids.[17] The attitude of the author toward such Gentiles is as pessimistic as any of the writings surveyed in the previous section. But there is another Gentile character in the story, Achior, the "leader of all the Ammonites" (5:5). He appears first as a perceptive outsider, who in response to Holofernes' queries displays a better understanding of the Deuteronomic reading of Israel's history than many of the Jews in the story (5:5–21; cf. 7:23–28). In retribution for his forthright recognition of the power of the God of Israel, Holofernes stations Achior in the Jewish city of Bethulia, so that he might perish along with all those who doubt the power of Nebuchadnezzar, the "lord of the whole earth" (6:4). Achior's role, then, as determined by Holofernes, is that of a witness to the contest between the god Nebuchadnezzar (6:2) and the God of Israel. Holofernes' words to Achior (6:2–9), of course, are highly ironic: after Judith displays the severed head of Holofernes, Achior, seeing "all that the God of Israel had done, . . . believed firmly in God . . . was circumcised, and joined the house of Israel" (14:10).

In the context of the narrative, Achior's conversion functions primarily as a means of vindicating the view of Israel's self-understanding advocated by the author. But the story goes beyond similar scenes of vindication[18] in its description of the vindicating witness as a *conversion*; Achior plays the ideal proselyte to Judith's ideal Jew. Consequently, the story exemplifies a second widespread attitude toward the Gentiles and their place in salvation, one in which the possibility of becoming a proselyte is not simply a stratagem of theodicy, but a real and desirable option.

The concept of proselytism in Second Temple Judaism is rooted in the preexilic category of the גר, or "resident alien" (differentiated from the נכרי, "foreigner"). To call these people converts would be anachronistic; Israel was an ethnic entity to be entered only by birth.[19] Nevertheless, the tendency in the Torah was in the direction of the incorporation of such resident aliens into the covenant community (e.g., Exod 12:19; 20:10; Deut 26:1-11) and of equality before the law (e.g., Num 9:14; 15:16; Lev 24:22). Only rarely are they differentiated from the native born (Exod 24:28-29; Deut 14:21), and even in these cases there are parallel texts in which they are included (Num 9:14; Lev 17:8-16).

With the experiences of the exile and the diaspora, the older understanding of Israel as an ethnic entity living on its ancestral land gradually gave way to that of a religious community defined by the Torah.[20] Along with this shift came the possibility of the full assimilation of Gentiles into the community, that is, proselytism. But the link with the older notion is clear; except where גר clearly indicates the resident alien, the LXX generally renders it by προσήλυτος ("proselyte"; πάροικος is the preferred term for the exceptions). Similarly, in rabbinic usage גר (sometimes with the addition of צדק ["righteous"]) refers to the proselyte proper; to designate the resident alien, the modified term גר תושב was adopted.[21]

Real worlds are seldom as tidy as narrative worlds. While the author of Judith can present Achior's incorporation into the house of Israel as full and complete, in the real world inhabited by Jews and Gentiles the boundary between the two was not as sharply defined. As Cohen has

observed, there was a whole range of degrees of attachment to Judaism—
from simple admiration of some aspect of Judaism, to full conversion[22]—
and differences of opinion as to the point at which it could be said that
the boundary had been crossed. Mirroring this ragged boundary in the
real world, Israel's symbolic map was in the process of being redrawn in
such a way as to allow for the inclusion of Gentiles in salvation without
their full incorporation into the community of Israel. In our period of
interest, however, this process had not yet reached the point where new
and clearly defined categories had emerged; Philo is only a particularly
prominent example of a much wider tendency to use proselytism language to refer to a quite different way of conceiving the status of righteous
Gentiles.[23] To put it somewhat differently, the evidence that leads McEleney to posit the existence of uncircumcised proselytes[24] is in my opinion
more properly to be taken as an indication of a not-yet-resolved situation
of category confusion; more on this in subsequent sections. Partially overlapping with this is the further matter of terminological diversity. While
גר/προσήλυτος is the most widely used terminology, full conversions could
be recounted without its use, as the story of Achior itself demonstrates.
Writing for more Hellenistic audiences, Philo and Josephus tended to
avoid this Septuagintal term, preferring either better known terms like
ἔπηλυς or ἐπήλυτος ("incomer"; Philo) or nonstandardized circumlocu-
tions (Josephus).[25]

But while giving full recognition to the degree of ambiguity and blurri-
ness around the edges, the point remains that, at its ideal center, proselytism represents a clearly defined and widely recognized pattern of universalism. One can make the point economically simply by setting alongside
the text from Judith this statement of Tacitus:

> Those who are converted to their ways follow the same practice [i.e., cir-
> cumcision], and the earliest lesson they receive is to despise the gods, to
> disown their country, and to regard their parents, children and brothers as
> of little account. (*Hist.* 5.5.2)

When one makes allowances for the jaundiced perspective with which
Tacitus views the phenomenon, the path to proselytism is the same for
the Roman historian as for the Palestinian novelist: to believe firmly in
God, to be circumcised, and to join the house of Israel (cf. Jdt 14:10).

References to the making of proselytes are widely distributed within
the literature of the period: Palestinian pseudepigrapha (Jdt 14:10; Tob
1:8; 2 *Bar.* 41.4); Josephus, referring to Fulvia in Rome (*Ant.* 18.82),
Helena and Izates in Adiabene (*Ant.* 20.34–53), and others in between;[26]

Philo (*Virt.* 102; *Spec. leg.* 1.51–52; 4.178); Tannaitic sources (e.g., *m. Bik.* 1.4; *b. Pesaḥ.* 87b; *m.* 'Abot 1.12; *b. Šabb.* 31a; *Sipre Num* §108; *Mek.* on Exod 20:10; *b. Sanh.* 97b; petition 13 in the *Shemoneh 'Esreh*; etc.); Christian literature (Matt 23:15; Acts 2:11; 6:5; 13:43; Justin *Dial.* 122); Greek and Roman authors (Dio Cassius 37.17.1; 57.18.5; 67.14.1–3; Juvenal *Satire* 14.96; Horace *Satires* 1.4.142–3); and Jewish inscriptions.[27]

In these texts the profile of proselytism that arises from the two passages discussed above is repeated and confirmed. Proselytism involves:

1. *Exclusive devotion to the God of Israel* (Achior "believed firmly in God"). The abandonment of idolatry and acknowledgment of the one true God, revealed in the Torah and worshiped in the temple, was non-negotiable, even for those strands of Judaism that wanted to present a softer edge to the Gentile world. It was Abraham's abandonment of idolatry that led to his designation as the first and prototype proselyte (e.g., *Mek.* on Exod 22:20; *Gen. Rab.* 38.13; *b. Sukk.* 49b; Philo *Virt.* 212–19; *Apoc. Abr.* 1–8). To go over "into Jewish ways" is, from the Greco-Roman perspective, to become atheist (Dio Cassius 67.14.1–3), that is, to abandon the traditional worship of the gods. Josephus presents King Izates of Adiabene as an example of those who "fix their eyes on [God] and trust in him alone" (*Ant.* 20.48). And while diaspora literature needs to be treated in a separate section, on this point at least it is aligned firmly with the proselyte material: for Philo, converts are those who have abandoned the "ignobility . . . of monstrous customs which assigned divine honors to stocks and stones and soulless things in general" (*Virt.* 219); Aseneth can be renamed the "City of Refuge" for those nations who "take refuge with the Lord God" (*Jos. Asen.* 14.7) only after she has renounced her idols and turned to the God of the Hebrews (11.7–11).

2. *Incorporation into the people of Israel* (Achior "joined the house of Israel"). As recent studies have demonstrated, conversion is as much the incorporation into a new social group as it is the acceptance of a new set of beliefs.[28] In 2 *Baruch*, accepting "the yoke of [God's] Law" (41.3), "[fleeing] under God's wings" (41.4) and "mingl[ing] with the seed of the people who have separated themselves" (42.4) are equivalent descriptions of proselytes. As this passage illustrates, to say that proselytism involves the acceptance of the Torah (e.g., *Ant.* 20.44–45; *t. Demai* 2.5; *m.* 'Abot 1.12; *b. Šabb.* 31a) is to say that it involves entrance into the Jewish community. Hence the ideal, espoused from such different points on the spectrum as those occupied by Philo and by the Rabbis, that proselytes deserved the same social status as native-born Jews.[29]

The emphasis in the literature on the proselytes' experience as one of separation or estrangement from their communities of origin is therefore not surprising. This, for example, is the source of Izates' hesitation with respect to circumcision (*Ant.* 20.39-42). What is surprising, at least in the initial encounter, is to find this emphasis even in those diaspora writings that downplay circumcision in the apparent interest of lowering the barriers to proselytism (to be discussed more fully in the next section). In *Joseph and Asenath*, for example, when Asenath renounces her former gods, she becomes an "orphan," disowned by her family and hated by all (*Jos. Asen.* 11.4-5; 12.5-15). Philo similarly describes converts as those who have "abandon[ed] their kinsfolk by blood, their country, their customs and the temples and images of their gods, and the tributes and honors paid to them" (*Virt.* 102; also *Spec. leg.* 1.51-52), and in the process have seen their kinsfolk turned into "mortal enemies" (*Spec. leg.* 4.178). As Collins has perceptively pointed out, however, functional monotheism, even without circumcision, would effectively exclude a person from participation in Gentile society, given the degree to which cultic worship was intertwined with civic and social affairs.[30]

3. *For male converts, undergoing circumcision was an entry ritual* (Achior "was circumcised"). As would be expected, crossing the boundary that set the Jewish people apart from the wider Gentile world was accomplished only by means of a recognized ritual of initiation. In the rabbinic material, it is taken for granted from the earliest levels of the tradition that the admission of a proselyte required circumcision, ritual immersion, and the offering of a sacrifice at the temple (e.g., *Sipre* on Num 15:14 [§108]; *m. Ker.* 2.1; *b. Ker.* 9a). Both the early date and the lack of controversy[31] suggest strongly that the tradition was in place at least among the Sages in the first century.

But elsewhere there is clear evidence only for circumcision. The only possible allusions to ritual immersion—neither of compelling clarity— are in *Sib. Or.* 4.165 and Epictetus (*Diss.* 2.9.20). Proselytes like Helena are depicted as offering sacrifices at the temple (*Ant.* 20.49); but then again, so are many others who are clearly not proselytes (e.g., *Ant.* 11.87). Nothing in the account of Izates and Helena suggests that sacrifice was necessary as a condition of membership.[32]

The evidence for circumcision, by contrast, is generally clear and unambiguous. To be sure, Ananias's advice to Izates that he "could worship God even without being circumcised" (*Ant.* 20.41), together with Philo's oft-discussed description of a proselyte as one "circumcised not in foreskin but in pleasures, desires, and other passions of the soul" (*Q. Exod.* 2.2), has given rise to the dubious notion that some strands of Judaism could countenance the possibility of uncircumcised proselytes.[33] As I will show, these texts open an important window on other aspects of Jewish universalism. But in neither do we find the crucial combination of uncircumcision plus full membership that would be necessary before there could be any talk of proselytism. These passages aside, the requirements were clear: any males[34] wanting to be accepted as full proselytes to Judaism needed to be circumcised. This was certainly Izates' understanding of the matter prior to Ananias's intervention (*Ant.* 20.38); and even then Ananias was not able to dissuade him for long. Circumcision was perceived by the Herodians as a nonnegotiable requirement in the case of Gentiles marrying into the royal family (*Ant.* 16.225; 20.145–46). Similar recognition is to be found both by Gentile observers with no interest in conversion whatsoever (Juvenal; Petronius)[35] and by those offering to convert out of fear for their lives.[36] Cohen concludes: "as far as is known no (non-Christian) Jewish community in antiquity accepted male proselytes who were not circumcised."[37]

Despite widespread agreement within Second Temple Judaism on what was needed for full proselyte status, there was at the same time broad diversity with respect to both the eagerness with which proselytism was encouraged and to the religious status of those who did not become proselytes. On the first point, the issue has sometimes been raised—most recently by McKnight and Goodman[38]—concerning the extent to which Judaism was a "missionary religion." Both convincingly argue that a distinction needs to be made between a willingness to receive proselytes and a more active desire to search them out, especially when this active desire is assumed to be universal and worldwide in scope. Still, one wonders whether the basic question has not been wrongly put. In the first place, the idea of a "missionary religion" (institutionally organized, with traveling evangelists) seems to have been constructed too much on the basis of Christian models. What is needed is not simply a denial that Judaism was a missionary religion in this definition of the term but a more positive recognition of the distinctive ways in which some Jews, at least, did attempt to draw Gentiles under the wings of the Shekinah. For example, as Moore pointed out long ago, Judaism did not need to send out missionaries; given the reality of the diaspora, they were already there.[39]

In addition, and more to the present point, the evidence suggests a considerable range in the degree to which proselytes were sought and proselytism encouraged. At one end, the authors of *4 Ezra* and *Pseudo-Philo* used the hypothetical possibility of proselytism simply as a justification for the condemnation of the wicked, displaying no interest at all in moving beyond the hypothetical (e.g., *4 Ezra* 7.72; *Pseudo-Philo* 11.1–2).

*Second Baruch* also uses proselytism in the interests of theodicy, but at least is aware of the existence of actual proselytes (41.4). Close in attitude to 2 *Baruch* would be Shammai (e.g., *b. Šabb.* 31a) and other rabbis suspicious of the motives of proselytes (*b. Yeb.* 24b) and skeptical of their value (*b. Yeb.* 47a–b; *Mek.* on Exod 22:20-21; *Lev. Rab.* 27.8). At the other end, evidence as disparate as Matt 23:15[40] and Horace (*Satires* 1.4.143) suggests that Ananias was not the only one to take deliberate initiative in seeking out potential converts (*Ant.* 20.34-35; also 18.81-82). Falling somewhere in between, the conversion of Achior in Jdt 14:10 is probably reflective of the most prevalent Jewish attitude. Achior "joined the house of Israel" not because of any attempt to seek him out, but because he was attracted by "all that the God of Israel had done."[41] Probably sharing this attitude are those texts that refer to Israel (or the Torah) as a light to the nations, as a priest among nations, and so on.[42]

A second aspect of diversity in Judaism's understanding of proselytism has to do with those Gentiles who do not become proselytes. Again, the texts from 4 *Ezra*, *Pseudo-Philo*, and 2 *Baruch* discussed above represent one end of the spectrum, in which the only hope Gentiles have of sharing in the life of the age to come lies in becoming a full proselyte to Judaism in this age.[43] But Ananias was not alone in his opinion that, while proselytism was preferable, uncircumcised Gentiles could still enjoy a positive relationship with the God of Israel. Proselytism was not the only model of universalism on offer.

### 3.3 Natural Law "Proselytes"

I have alluded to texts that used proselyte language, but with reference to Gentiles who had apparently not undergone circumcision. There are two such texts in which the lack of circumcision is explicit. One is *Ant.* 20.41, where Ananias informs Izates that he could "worship God even without being circumcised if indeed he had fully decided to be a devoted adherent of Judaism, for it was this that counted more than circumcision." The other is a comment of Philo on Exod 22:21:

> [Scripture] demonstrates most clearly that he is a proselyte who is circumcised not in foreskin but in pleasures, desires, and other passions of the soul. For in Egypt, the Hebrew race was not circumcised. . . . Because of this it adds, "For you know how a proselyte feels." But what is the way of thinking [διάνοια] of a proselyte? Abandonment of the belief that there are many gods, and appropriation of the worship of the one God who is Father of all.[44]

Taken at face value, these texts seem to suggest that Ananias and Philo were prepared to count as proselytes people who, while adhering to some set of reduced requirements, were not circumcised. Understandably, these texts have precipitated considerable debate. Some scholars are of the opinion that face value is just the way in which the texts should be taken.[45] Others argue that the texts provide no solid evidence for uncircumcised proselytes in the full sense of the word[46] or that they represent some category distinct from proselytism.[47]

These texts are part of a larger apologetic pattern found in the literature of Hellenistic Judaism. This pattern has been traced in detail by John J. Collins in his highly stimulating and persuasive book *Between Athens and Jerusalem*, whose insights inform much of the discussion in this section. Collins uses Festinger's concept of "cognitive dissonance,"[48] seeing this literature as motivated by a desire to reduce the dissonance felt by diaspora Jews in their minority situation. On the one hand, members of diaspora communities were identified by a tradition that encouraged separation and thus fostered Gentile suspicion; on the other, they found much to admire in Hellenism and so desired to participate in the wider Gentile world.

In response to this situation, Jewish writers developed an apologetic, addressed as much to a Jewish audience as to a Gentile,[49] that operated on two broad fronts. One of these, represented, for example, by Josephus's *Against Apion*, was concerned to refute what were considered to be mistaken and sometimes slanderous Gentile views of Judaism. The other consisted of an attempt to present Judaism in terms that would be congenial and appealing to those Gentiles whose respect and approval was most coveted. In this presentation, those aspects of Judaism that most set Jews apart and rendered them peculiar in Gentile eyes (esp. circumcision, food laws) were downplayed in favor of a few core elements that were both nonnegotiable and most likely to win the approval of enlightened Gentiles (monotheism and its negative counterpart, the rejection of idolatry; the Jerusalem temple as the shrine of the one true God; heightened morality, especially sexual morality). In addition, the attempt was made to align this "reduced essence" of Judaism with the loftier ideals of Hellenism, presenting the Torah as simply the purest manifestation of a natural law recognized by Hellenistic culture at its best and accessible to all. This apologetic receives its most sustained and self-consciously philosophical treatment, of course, in the writings of Philo. But it comes to expression in a wide body of literature.[50]

For our present purposes what is of interest is the way in which conversion or proselyte language is often used to describe those Gentiles who merely abandon idolatry and turn to worship the God of Israel. Formally speaking, such Gentiles seem to be described as proselytes to Judaism; but substantially, given the way in which "Judaism" is presented in this literature, one needs to ask whether they are really something else. In the third *Sibylline Oracle*, for example, the "law" is universal, binding on the nations as well as Israel. The nations are condemned for "transgressing the holy law of immortal God" (600; also 69–70, 686–87), and are enjoined to repent (545–50, 624–34, 762–66). When at last[51] the nations do repent, their conversion takes the form of temple worship and law observance:

> Come, let us all fall on the ground and entreat the immortal king, the great eternal God. Let us send to the Temple, since he alone is sovereign and let us all ponder the Law of the Most High God, who is most righteous of all throughout the earth. (716–20)

By "law," the Sibyl clearly means the law given through Moses at Sinai (254–58) and practiced by the Jews (573–600). But in describing the law—for example, in two hymns in praise of the Jews (218–64, 573–600)—the author slides over those aspects of the Torah that separate Israel from the nations (circumcision, dietary regulations, and so on).[52] Rather, one fulfills "the word of the great God, the hymn of the law," by abstaining from astrology and sorcery (221–33), not loving money (235) or committing robbery (238–39), maintaining just measurements (237), caring for the poor (241–45), etc. Or one shares in "the righteousness of the law of the Most High" (580) by worshiping the one true God at the Jerusalem sanctuary (575–79) and engaging neither in idolatry (586–90) nor in sexual immorality (594–600).

One the one hand, then, the opinion of the Sibyl is that Gentiles need to abandon their sinful ways and adhere to the law of God. On the other, the essence of the law is to be found in the avoidance of idolatry, worship of the God of Israel as the one true God, and adherence to a basic code of morality. While an element of particularism remains in that Gentiles were expected to worship God at the temple in Jerusalem, this by no means implied full proselytism in the Second Temple period; as we will see in more detail later, offerings from Gentiles as Gentiles were readily accepted at the temple. In formal terms, then, the Sibyl wants Gentiles to become converts to the law, that is, proselytes (though the word itself does not appear); but in substance such conversion seems to fall short of the strict requirements of full proselytism.

A similar picture emerges from the narrative in *Joseph and Asenath*. Asenath's experience is definitely presented as a conversion. A sharp barrier is present between Jews and Gentiles, so that Joseph will neither eat with her family (7.1) nor kiss her in greeting (8.4–5). When she repents of her "lawlessness" (11.10, 17; 12.3–4) and abandons idolatry she is cut off from her own people as an orphan (11.4–6). In turning to God, however, she is numbered among God's chosen people (8.9), her name being written "in the book of the living in heaven" (15.4). Indeed, in an angelic visitation she is declared to be virtually the prototypical proselyte:

> Your name shall no longer be called Asenath, but your name shall be City of Refuge, because in you many nations will take refuge with the Lord God, the Most High, and under your wings many people trusting in the Lord God will be sheltered, and behind your walls will be guarded those who attach themselves to the Most High God in the name of Repentance. (15.7)

But the substance of her conversion is centered almost entirely on idolatry. Joseph's separatism is based not on any cultic dietary regulations but on the need to remain separate from idolatry. The process of Asenath's conversion begins with the destruction of her idols (10.12–13). Idolatry is the central theme of her soliloquies (11.3–14, 16–18) and prayer of repentance (12.1–13.14). While the transition to her new state is marked with a symbolic ritual involving bread, wine, and a honeycomb (16.1–16), the ritual bears no resemblance to anything connected with proselytism. Even when full allowance is given to the fact that, as a woman, Asenath would not be subject to circumcision, and that Joseph predates Moses and the giving of the law, Asenath's conversion cannot be said to conform to the pattern of proselytism outlined in the previous section.

The attempt to align Jewish tradition with the best of Hellenistic philosophy by means of a concept of natural law reaches its high-water mark in the massive apologetic enterprise of Philo. This is not the place to discuss Philo's enterprise in any detail. But for our present purposes, before we look at the "uncircumcised proselyte" of *Q. Exod.* 2.2, we need to observe that Philo's appeal to the wider Gentile world is characterized by the same contrast between form and substance noted above.

On the one hand, for Philo the law is to be observed by the whole of humankind. In *Vit. Mos.* 2.36, for example, the translators of the law into Greek speak for Philo when they pray "that the greater part, or even the whole, of the human race might be profited and led to a better life by continuing to observe such wise and truly admirable ordinances." Or, Philo longs for the day when "each nation would abandon its peculiar ways, and, throwing overboard their ancestral customs, turn to honoring our laws alone" (*Vit. Mos.* 2.44). Philo makes frequent reference to con-verts (προσήλυτοι, or, more characteristically, ἐπήλυτοι) who "have left their homes and taken refuge with God" (*Som.* 2.273).

But, on the other hand, this universal law in its written form is but a "copy" of an "unwritten law" that stands "in conformity with nature" (*Abr.* 3–6). The purpose of the patriarchal narratives, for example, is to demonstrate that the life of virtue prescribed in the written law was exem-plified already by the patriarchs who lived in accordance with nature; indeed, the written law is to be seen as something of a concession for those not able to ascertain the path of virtue directly from nature (*Abr.* 60–61). Further, when he discusses proselytes, he never mentions circum-cision or other specific Torah requirements, defining conversion primarily in terms of the abandonment of idolatry and the acceptance of monothe-ism and virtue (*Virt.* 102, 181–82, 212–19; *Spec. leg.* 1.51, 4.178). In addition, among those put forward as models of virtue and righteousness are Gentiles who certainly were not Torah observers (*Spec. leg.* 2.42–48; *Omn. prob. lib.* 72–74).

What then of the moral or spiritual "circumcision" of *Q. Exod.* 2.2? Would Philo have been prepared to accept as a full member of his syna-gogue community a male "convert" who had not been circumcised? The texts already cited might lead one to expect an answer in the affirmative. But one further text, *Migr. Abr.* 89–90, suggests a more cautious assess-ment. Here Philo denounces those radical allegorizers in his community who, while agreeing with him that specific prescriptions of the law are "symbols of matters belonging to the intellect," take the next step of treat-ing the literal observance "with easygoing neglect." One would expect, then, that he would equally object to those who believed that since cir-cumcision was ultimately a matter of excising the "pleasures, passions and other desires of the soul," the physical symbol could be dispensed with. The fact remains, however, that he avoids any explicit reference to the circumcision of converts, while at the same time using conversion lan-guage of Gentiles who were clearly not converts in the formal sense.

What are we to make of this aspect of Hellenistic Jewish literature? Does it provide evidence that some strands of diaspora Judaism were pre-pared to accept pious but uncircumcised Gentiles as proselytes in some real sense of the term? Probably not. To be sure, the degree to which monotheism itself would lead to a dissociation from much of non-Jewish society is not to be discounted. And there were individuals, like the allego-rizers rebuked by Philo, whose extreme universalism would probably lead to the elimination of any boundary distinctions. But King Izates' percep-tions are certainly accurate: to become a full member of the Jewish com-munity, circumcision was necessary.

At the same time, however, the distinguishing feature of diaspora literature as traced above is to be given full weight. There is no reason to
believe, for example, that this approach to the Gentiles was merely part
of a self-conscious tactical strategy—one in which the more rigorous requirements for proselytism were deliberately underemphasized, but only
until Gentiles had made too much of a commitment to turn back. It might
have worked this way in practice, as is demonstrated perhaps by Juvenal's
satirical description of the sabbath-observing father with the circumcised
son (*Satire* 14.96). But the literature seems to reflect a sincere struggle to
find a way, consistent with the Jewish frame of reference, of including
within the circle of the righteous those Gentiles who met some minimum
standards of piety but who were not full proselytes.

The nature of the struggle, I suggest, is that Philo, the Sibyl, and others
were implicitly making a distinction—between full proselytes and what
could be called "natural law proselytes"—for which they did not yet have
the categories or the vocabulary. They wanted to affirm that those Gentiles who rejected idolatry, worshiped the God of Israel, revered the
temple, and followed a basic moral code, were thereby acceptable to God
(though not thereby full members of Israel); and they adapted the only
category and vocabulary at their disposal—that of proselytism—to do so.
There is evidence, however, that the desired category was in the process of
development elsewhere within Second Temple Judaism.

## 3.4 Righteous Gentiles

There is a well-known discussion between R. Eliezer and R. Joshua—
Tannaim active around the turn of the second century C.E.—concerning
the fate of the Gentiles. The passage begins with the anonymous statement, "The children of the wicked among the heathen will not live [i.e.,
in the world to come] nor be judged." It continues:

> R. Eliezer says: None of the Gentiles has a portion in the world to come, as
> it says: "The wicked shall return to Sheol, all the Gentiles who forget God"
> [Ps 9:17]. "The wicked shall return to Sheol" are the wicked Israelites. R.
> Joshua said to him: If it had been written, "The wicked shall return to
> Sheol, all the Gentiles," and then said nothing further, I should have main-
> tained as you do. But in fact it is written, "All the Gentiles who forget God,"
> thus indicating that there are also righteous people among the nations of
> the world, who do have a portion in the world to come. (*t. Sanh.* 13.2)

It is clear from the context that the Gentiles under discussion—even those
designated "righteous" by R. Joshua—were not proselytes. R. Joshua is
well aware of the phenomenon of proselytism, and even debated aspects

of it with R. Eliezer.[53] From his perspective, then, there is a category of "righteous Gentiles" existing alongside that of the proselytes. What differentiates the two is a distinction between salvation and conversion: Gentiles may have a share in salvation without becoming full converts to Judaism.[54] Gentile converts will be saved as well, but Gentiles do not need to become converts to be saved.

R. Joshua's opinion is by no means an isolated one. First, as Sanders has pointed out, the anonymous (and hence generally accepted) statement with which the passage begins, presupposes that some Gentiles (at least the children of those who are not "wicked," perhaps all but the wicked) will have a share in the age to come; otherwise, there would be no point in singling out the children of the wicked.[55] In addition, one can point to other equally generous statements appearing in the Tannaitic period, such as that of R. Johanan: "Just as the sin-offering makes atonement for Israel, so charity makes atonement for the heathen" (b. B. Batra 10b).[56] Indeed, according to one tradition, so unacceptable were Eliezer's intransigent opinions concerning proselytism that he was expelled (b. B. Meṣ 59b). Eventually, when linked with the related concepts of the Noachian decrees[57] and the ger toshab legislation,[58] the "righteous Gentiles" concept becomes the normative Jewish position on the matter.[59]

Our concern, however, is not with the development of rabbinic attitudes, but with the first century. Is there evidence of a "righteous Gentile" concept in this earlier period? Certainly, the conditions were right for such a concept to flourish. Judaism had attracted to itself many Gentile sympathizers—the so-called "God-fearers"—who identified to some extent with the Jewish community and its ways without becoming full proselytes. To be sure, A. T. Kraabel has attempted to minimize the phenomenon, seeing the "God-fearers" as in large measure a Lukan invention.[60] He is quite right in his assertions that the language often associated with such Gentiles (σεβόμενοι/φοβούμενοι τὸν θεὸν, θεοσεβεῖς) is also used of Jews and full proselytes, and thus is not to be seen as technical terminology; and that Gentile friendliness toward, or association with, Jews does not necessarily imply the kind of recognized religious status traditionally associated with the term "God-fearer." But, as most scholars have recognized,[61] the phenomenon itself does not thereby disappear; the existence of Jewish sympathizers is amply attested in Jewish,[62] Greco-Roman,[63] and inscriptional[64] evidence. Indeed, the evidence from the Aphrodisias inscription seems to confirm the fact that "God-fearer" could be used to refer to a class of people differentiated from both native-born Jews and proselytes.[65]

But the mere existence of Jewish sympathizers does not by itself demonstrate the existence of a "righteous Gentile" category. For one thing, sympathizers came in various shapes and sizes, including those who merely admired Judaism, or were friendly toward Jews, or included the God of Israel within a polytheistic pattern of worship;[66] one would hardly expect many Jews to consider such Gentiles "righteous." And even in the case of Gentiles who had embraced monotheism and identified with the Jewish community, the mere presence of such persons at the synagogue does not in itself tell us how they were viewed by Jews. In Josephus's account of the conversion of Izates, for example, Eliezer clearly sees Izates' "God-fearing" stage (the phrase is used in *Ant.* 20.34) as just a way station on the way to full proselytism, with no legitimacy of its own.[67] Further, many of the relevant texts are clearly apologetic in intent; the accounts of "God-fearing" Gentiles often are intended to function as a vindication of the claims of Judaism, for the benefit of Gentile, or, occasionally, Jewish (e.g., 2 Macc 3:33-40) readers, rather than as an indication of how such Gentiles would have been viewed and received by the Jewish community itself.

Nevertheless, there is enough evidence not simply of the existence of Gentile adherents but of Jewish attitudes toward them to suggest that it is appropriate to speak of a "righteous Gentile" concept in the first century. We can begin with the discussion between R. Eliezer and R. Joshua in *t. Sanh.* 13.2. As was observed above, the anonymous statement with which the discussion begins also assumes the existence of righteous Gentiles who have a share in the age to come (else why single out wicked ones?). Since "anonymous statements are generally earlier than the comments on them,"[68] and since the two rabbis in question flourished toward the end of the first century, it is quite likely that at least some rabbis in the pre-70 period were prepared to recognize the existence of righteous Gentiles.

Next there is the phenomenon of the Noachian decrees. As articulated in the Tannaitic period, these were the injunctions that God had laid on Adam (six) and Noah (a seventh added after God gave permission for the consumption of meat), and that consequently were binding on all of humankind.[69] While an explicit connection with the concept of "righteous Gentiles" does not appear until much later, the implicit assumption in these texts is that those Gentiles who fulfill these requirements have done all that God requires of them, and are therefore acceptable to God (i.e., righteous).[70] Two pieces of evidence can be appealed to in support of the contention that a similar pattern of thought was present in the earlier period.[71] The first of these is *Jub.* 7.20:

> And in the twenty-eighth jubilee Noah began to command his grandsons
> with ordinances and commandments and all of the judgments which he

knew. And he bore witness to his sons so that they might do justice and
cover the shame of their flesh and bless the one who created them and
honor father and mother, and each one love his neighbor and preserve
themselves from fornication and pollution and from all injustice.

It might be thought that *Jubilees* would be the last place to look for evidence in support of a doctrine of tolerance and universalism; the writing,
after all, denies salvation to all who are born outside the covenant (*Jub.*
15.26). But the function of the passage is to provide grounds for God's
judgment on the Gentiles; Torah obedience aside, they did not measure
up even to this minimum set of commandments. Because these commandments bear at least a family resemblance to the Noachian decrees, the
passage probably provides evidence, in its own negative way, for the belief
that through Noah God had imposed a minimal standard of righteousness on the whole of humankind.[72] A more positive indication is the
apostolic decree of Acts 15:28-29, which in a very similar manner serves
to set a minimum list of requirements for Gentiles who (despite urgings
from some quarters to the contrary) are included within the sphere of
salvation without the requirement of circumcision.[73] Even if Finkelstein
is correct in his assertion that the Noachian decrees originated in the Hasmonaean era as a practical solution to the question of the degree to which
the Torah was binding on Gentiles under Jewish rule,[74] these two texts
are much more general in their reference, and suggest that the concept
was more widely applied.

Third, one can cite the stance taken by Ananias in the process leading
to the conversion of King Izates of Adiabene, as recounted by Josephus
in *Ant.* 20.34-48. What is of interest here is the argument put forward by
Ananias in an attempt to dissuade Izates from undergoing circumcision:
"The king could, he said, worship God even without being circumcised
if indeed he had fully decided to be a devoted adherent of Judaism, for
it was this that counted more than circumcision" (*Ant.* 20.41). What is
Ananias saying about Izates' status with respect to Judaism? Some have
argued that by describing the king as one who, lack of circumcision notwithstanding, had resolved to be "a devoted adherent of Judaism"
(ζηλοῦν τὰ πάτρια τῶν Ἰουδαίων), Ananias was recognizing him as a full
proselyte.[75] The omission of circumcision, in this reading, is to be seen as
an allowable concession in view of the potentially dangerous consequences, somewhat akin to the omission of circumcision in the case of a
hemophiliac.[76] While not impossible, such a reading is unlikely. The potential danger to Izates comes, not from circumcision per se, but from
what circumcision would signify, namely, full conversion to Judaism: his

subjects "would not tolerate the rule of a Jew over them" (20.39). One would expect that a king who was a proselyte in every respect but circumcision would be equally as intolerable. It is better to conclude that Ananias is counseling Izates to remain in the state he was prior to his awareness of his mother's conversion, namely, as one who worshiped God (τὸν θεὸν σέβειν [20.34]; cf. τὸ θεῖον σέβειν [20.41]) but had not yet become a "confirmed Jew" (βεβαίως Ἰουδαῖος) through full conversion (μεταθέσθαι [20.38]).[77]

Other pieces of evidence could be adduced in support: the acceptance of sacrifices by and for Gentiles at the temple;[78] the recognition of the legitimacy of Gentile altars to God apart from the temple;[79] the reference to the salvation of the "righteous from among the nations" in T. Naph. 8.3;[80] texts describing Israel as a priest among the nations[81] (priests occupying a distinct status and bound by more stringent legislation than the remainder of the people). But what has been presented is sufficient, I believe, to establish the point: in the first century there were segments of Judaism that saw the Torah as God's special gift to Israel; the Gentiles, bound by a lesser set of requirements, could attain righteousness without having to become full converts to Judaism.

## 3.5 Eschatological Pilgrims

As is true of most aspects of Second Temple Judaism, a survey of Jewish attitudes toward Gentiles is not complete without a consideration of the eschatological future. Indeed, in what has come to be known as the "eschatological pilgrimage of the nations,"[82] we encounter one of the most distinctive of the Jewish patterns of universalism.

The various attitudes toward Gentiles in the present, as surveyed above, generally carry with them implications for the eschatological future. If Gentiles are forever outside the covenant and fit only for destruction (Jub. 15.26), for instance, then destruction is what awaits them at the eschaton. Alternatively, in the case of proselytism, while there is no clear statement to the effect, it seems reasonable to believe that for at least some within Judaism, proselytism is an option limited to this age: those who fail to become proselytes in this age will have no share in the age to come.[83] Others, as we have seen, believe that there are "righteous Gentiles" who will have a share in the age to come; the wicked, correspondingly, will not.

But this does not exhaust the material. The Gentiles are frequently included in Jewish expectations of future salvation, and in ways that are not simply extrapolations of the patterns already examined. In particular, the so-called "eschatological pilgrimage" tradition anticipates a Gentile share in salvation based not on any action or disposition in the present (conversion, "righteousness") but on their response to God's saving vindication of Israel in the eschatological future.

While there is considerable variation in Jewish expectations for the future, for our present purposes it is sufficient to observe that most of these expectations conform to the general pattern of what might be termed "Zion eschatology," or, in Sanders's phrase, "Jewish restoration eschatology."[84] Central to this pattern, rooted in the Hebrew scriptures themselves, is the hope that "on that day" the lamentable conditions of Israel's present existence—dispersion among the Gentiles, oppression by foreign nations, unfaithfulness to the covenant within Israel—will be reversed: Israel's enemies will be routed,[85] Jerusalem/Zion will be glorified,[86] the scattered exiles will stream back to Zion,[87] where they will enjoy a life of peace and prosperity,[88] and the universal rule of God and/or God's Anointed One will be inaugurated.[89]

The place of the Gentiles in this eschatological restoration varies from passage to passage. Sometimes their complete annihilation is envisaged.[90] More often they appear in a subservient role—bringing the exiles back to Jerusalem, rendering tribute to Zion, and serving Israel.[91] But in another strand of the tradition, the Gentiles are presented as full participants in eschatological salvation, worshiping the God of Israel and sharing in the blessings of the new age. This expectation, rooted in the Hebrew scriptures themselves,[92] was a widespread and continuing feature of Second Temple Judaism, appearing throughout the period[93] in both Hellenistic and Palestinian texts. Although a pilgrimage to Zion is often in view, it is not always present, and the heart of the pattern lies elsewhere—in the salvation of the Gentiles as a kind of by-product of the end-time restoration of Israel.

We begin our survey of the main passages of interest[94] with the book of Tobit. Here we find two examples of restoration eschatology, with Gentiles mentioned in each. Chapter 13 consists of a hymn in praise of restored Jerusalem, and includes the declaration, "Many nations will come from afar to the name of the Lord God, bearing gifts in their hands, gifts for the king of heaven" (v. 11). Tobit's deathbed testament in chapter 14 includes a second restoration passage (vv. 5-7), which, while shorter, features the Gentiles more prominently:

> Then [i.e., after the restoration of Jerusalem] all the Gentiles will turn to
> fear the Lord God in truth, and will bury their idols. All the Gentiles will
> praise the Lord, and his people will give thanks to God, and the Lord will

exalt his people. And all who love the Lord God in truth and righteousness will rejoice, showing mercy to our brethren. (vv. 6-7)

A similar generous attitude toward the Gentiles in the age to come is found in *1 Enoch*. In a passing reference, *1 Enoch* 10.21 anticipates the time "when all nations shall worship and bless [God], and they will all prostrate themselves to [God]." A more substantial reference is to be found in 90.27-33, a passage appearing in the context of Enoch's second "Dream Vision" (chaps. 85–90). The vision is a symbolic recital of the history of Israel from the creation to the era of eschatological fulfillment, fulfillment which the author, evidently living in the Maccabean period, expected to see shortly. In this vision Israel is symbolized by sheep, and the Gentile nations by various beasts and birds. The events of the end include the defeat and destruction of the Gentile oppressors (90.18-19), the judgment of the angelic "shepherds" (vv. 20-27), and the erection of a new "house" (Jerusalem or the temple,[95] vv. 28-29). Then in vv. 30 and 33 the "animals" and "birds"—presumably those Gentiles who had no part in the oppression of Israel, since these have already been destroyed (vv. 18-19)—come into the picture again. Verse 30 depicts merely the subjugation of these Gentiles (and other Israelites) to those "sheep" who had been faithful through the time of crisis:

> Then I saw all the sheep that had survived as well as all the animals upon the earth and the birds of heaven, falling down and worshiping those sheep, making petitions to them and obeying them in every respect.

But in v. 33 the Gentiles appear in a more positive light. Here they join with the resurrected Jewish martyrs ("destroyed") and the diaspora Jews ("dispersed"), worshiping God in the temple and experiencing the favor of the Lord.

> All those [sheep] which have been destroyed and dispersed, and all the beasts of the field and the birds of the sky were gathered together in that house; and the Lord of the sheep rejoiced with great joy because they had all become gentle and returned to his house.

In this passage, then, full participation of the surviving Gentiles in the final state of affairs is envisaged.

An equally bright future for at least some of the Gentiles is found in *2 Bar.* 72–73. Such a glimmer of light is unexpected in *2 Baruch*, which elsewhere portrays the Gentiles in darker terms: all except proselytes (41.1-6) are destined for eternal punishment or destruction (30:4-5;

44:15; 51:6; 82:3-9). The most probable explanation is that the "Cloud and Waters Apocalypse" of chapters 53–74 was a pre-70 C.E. unit taken over and incorporated into 2 *Baruch*.[96]

In any case, after the sequence of "black waters" has run its course and the enemies of Zion are vanquished, God's Anointed One will summon the nations (72.2). Those who have afflicted Israel will be delivered up to the sword, but those who have "not trodden down the seed of Jacob will live" (72.4). The life to which they are granted access, apparently, is that of the age to come, for the description of the kingdom in chapter 73 is strikingly universal in tone: the Messiah rules over "everything which is in the world" (v. 1); a time of health and peace will appear "among men" (v. 2); "joy will encompass the earth" (v. 2); "nobody will again die untimely" (v. 3); all that has made "the life of men" miserable will disappear (v. 5); wild beasts will serve "men" (v. 6). The Gentiles who are spared, it would appear, are full participants in this time of peace and joy.[97]

The eschatological sections of the *Testaments of the Twelve Patriarchs* contain frequent references to the future salvation of the Gentiles. Some of these are probably Christian interpolations,[98] but the theme is unmistakably there in the Jewish core material. In *T. Levi* 18, the eschatological priest "shall be extolled by the whole inhabited world" (v. 3); under his rule "the nations shall be multiplied in knowledge on the earth, and they shall be illumined by the grace of the Lord" (v. 9). *T. Naph.* speaks of the gathering of the "righteous from among the nations" (8.3-4). In *T. Jud.* the nations who "call upon the Lord" will be "judged" and "saved" (24.6; cf. 25.5). *T. Zeb.* 9.8 declares that all nations, freed from Beliar, will be "zealous" for God. In *T. Benj.* 10.9, the nations, like Israel, will be judged and appointed for either honor or dishonor.

The eschatological pilgrimage tradition is found in the literature of Hellenistic Judaism as well. *Sibylline Oracles* 3.657–808 contains a fairly typical presentation of restoration eschatology. After the final defeat of Israel's enemies, Israel will live in peace around a restored Zion:

> But the sons of the great God will all live peacefully around the Temple, rejoicing in these things which the Creator, just judge and sole ruler, will give. (702–4)

And then "all islands and cities," abandoning their idols and recognizing the God of Israel, say:

> Come, let us all fall on the ground and entreat the immortal king, the great eternal God. Let us send to the Temple, since he alone is sovereign and let

us all ponder the Law of the Most High God, who is most righteous of all throughout the earth. (716–20; also 767–775)

The final text to be mentioned here is found, somewhat surprisingly, in Philo. One would not expect to find material relevant to the present investigation in an author closer to Platonic philosophy than to apocalyptic speculation. Nevertheless, a plausible argument can be mounted in favor of seeing the following text as a reworking of traditional Zion eschatology:

> Thus the laws are shown to be desirable and precious in the eyes of all . . . though our nation has not prospered for many a year. It is but natural that when people are not flourishing their belongings to some degree are under a cloud. But, if a fresh start should be made to brighter prospects, how great a change for the better might we expect to see! I believe that each nation would abandon its peculiar ways, and, throwing overboard their ancestral customs, turn to honoring our laws alone. (*Vit. Mos.* 2.43-44)

Granted, "a fresh start . . . made to brighter prospects" is a far cry from the pungent apocalyptic style of *1 Enoch* or *2 Baruch*. But the underlying pattern is the same: the restoration of Israel triggering a turn to God among the Gentiles. The decisive factor, however, is another Philonic text (*Praem. poen.* 164–72), in which restoration eschatology is clearly to be seen: the redemption of Israel (164); the deliverance from Gentile oppressors (164; cf. 168); the pilgrimage of exiles to Zion (165); prosperity in the land (168); and so on. While the latter passage contains no expectation of Gentile salvation, its similarity to the text cited above suggests strongly that the expectations about the Gentiles in the former text are to be seen as a Philonic reworking of traditional restorationist themes.[99]

To sum up, then: the texts surveyed here demonstrate the existence of a distinct pattern of universalism. In contrast to the patterns discussed earlier, where the inclusion of the Gentiles in the life of the age to come was dependent on their attitudes and actions in the present, in the eschatological pilgrimage pattern it is dependent on what God will do in the future. When God acts to fulfill the divine promises and to restore Israel, the Gentiles will abandon their idols, turn to worship God, and share with Israel in the blessings of the eschatological era.

But on what terms? The tendency in scholarly discussion has been to speak of the end-time "conversion" of the Gentiles, implying (though usually without addressing the issue directly) that these Gentiles are to become proselytes.[100] But with the increasing awareness of the "righteous

Gentile" strand of Jewish thought, there has been some recognition that the status of eschatological pilgrimage Gentiles with respect to Israel and to the Torah requires more careful consideration.[101] I have dealt with the question at length elsewhere,[102] and will simply summarize my conclusions here.

Given the explicit reference to the Torah in the seminal text of Isa 2:2-4—"for Torah will go forth out of Zion"—one would not be surprised to see the tradition develop in the direction of full conversion. But this is not what is found. Only in diaspora literature do we find explicit references to Gentile conformity to the law in the age to come (*Sib. Or.*3.719, 757–58; Philo *Vit. Mos.* 2.44). But as we have already had occasion to observe, this literature tends to redefine "law" in terms of a natural law, closer in its substance to the Noachian decrees than to the detailed law of Moses. Elsewhere, the language is more vague. While there is no clear indication that the Gentiles are to remain outside the Torah as a separate community of salvation, neither is there any indication that these Gentiles will undergo circumcision or accept any of the other observances that serve to mark out the boundary between Jew and Gentile. What gives added weight to the latter observation is that references to these boundary markers are absent in literature that elsewhere stresses law observance for Jews (esp. Tobit; *2 Bar.* 53–74).

The tendency of the tradition, it seems to me, is to view these Gentiles *as Gentiles*, rather than as converts to Judaism. But at the same time, the ambiguity of the texts at this point suggests that the distinction was not as significant for the original authors as it is for contemporary scholars. Indeed, the central concern of the former lay elsewhere—in the vindication of Israel and of Israel's view of its place in the world. "On that day," the dissonance between its self-understanding as the covenant people of the one true God and its present humble status among the nations of the world would be removed: the preeminence of the God of Israel, of the Jerusalem temple, and of Israel itself would be universally established and acknowledged. Wherever the Gentiles appear in this tradition, their treatment, positive or negative, is subservient to this central theme.

## 3.6 Implications for Pauline Interpretation

My purpose in this survey is not to predetermine the end of the process, the nature of Paul's postconversion convictions about the Gentiles, but instead to enable a clearer grasp of the presumed start of the process, the pre-Damascus Paul as a covenantal nomist. Some concluding reflections are in order.

When we raise the question of what a covenantal nomist, such as we are assuming Paul to have been, would have thought about the Gentiles, we are quickly confronted by a paradox. On the one hand, Gentiles figure prominently in the core convictions of covenantal nomism. At every point, Israel's covenantal self-understanding is defined over against the nations: Israel's God is no mere local deity, but the one true God, sovereign over all things, including all the nations; Israel has been chosen from all other nations to be God's special possession; in the present time, faithfulness to the covenant involves (among other things) remaining distinct from the nations, who, nevertheless, can become God's agents of punishment when Israel is unfaithful; in the eschatological future, Israel's covenantal status will be vindicated for all the nations to see. Implicit in every facet of Israel's self-identifying narrative, then, is a counterassertion of one kind or another about the Gentile nations. Jews could not define themselves without at the same time considering their relationship with non-Jews.

On the other hand, the literature of Second Temple Judaism displays no single clear and agreed-on position regarding the Gentiles themselves—their status vis-à-vis God in the present or their destiny in the eschatological future. Not that there were no opinions on the matter; as we have seen, the literary and other remains of the period bear witness to a lively interest in the issue, and a rich range of approaches. But most of these are consistent with covenantal nomism, and none of them can be taken as normative.

In part, this is due to the fact that the function of the nations in covenantal formulations is more that of a foil for Israel than an item of interest in its own right.[103] In part it is due to a tension inherent in the covenant idea itself: in that Israel's God is the creator and sovereign of all, the Gentiles cannot be excluded from God's purposes; but in that Israel has been chosen in distinction from the other nations, the Gentiles cannot simply be included without the potential of a threat to Israel's special status. Israel's self-identifying story provides no clear indication of how this tension is to be resolved. It is also due in part to the changing variety of sociopolitical contexts in which Jewish communities encountered Gentiles throughout the Second Temple period.

We cannot make a simple move, then, from the supposition that Paul was a covenantal nomist to a fixed reading of his pre-Damascus attitudes toward the Gentiles. But while "Judaism" may have had no clear and fixed opinion of the Gentiles, individual Jews certainly did. What about the possibility, then, of making such a move on the basis of a biographical profile, an argument that a person such as Paul (first century C.E., dias-

pora upbringing, zealous Pharisee, and so on) would have thought thus
and so about the Gentiles? Again we confront diversity, and of a kind that
cannot simply be plotted along chronological, geographical, or sociological lines. To be sure, some broad tendencies can be discerned. Chronologically, the term ger (גר), for example, undergoes quite a transformation
from the preexilic "resident alien" to the detailed rabbinic discussions
concerning proselytes. Geographically, one is much more likely to find a
Philo or a *Letter of Aristeas* in the diaspora, and a *Jubilees* or *War Scroll*
in Palestine. And sociologically, if Paul had been a member of the Qumran
community, one could predict his attitudes toward the Gentiles with a fair
degree of confidence. But Second Temple Judaism is too diverse in many
respects, attitudes toward the Gentiles included, to allow us to plot these
with any precision.[104] If we can encounter both Eleazar and Ananias in
Adiabene, both the Teacher of Righteousness and Josephus in Judea, both
Philo and the allegorists in Alexandria, and both R. Eliezer and R. Joshua
among the Tannaitic rabbis, who is to say what a Tarsus-born Pharisee
must have been like?

I am assuming that Paul can be viewed as a covenantal nomist who
came to believe that God raised Jesus from the dead, and I am asking how
he also came to see a law-free mission to the Gentiles as an urgent personal corollary of this belief. If we could know for certain what Paul
thought of the Gentiles prior to his Damascus experience, our task would
be easier. But we do not have the benefit of such a fixed point of reference.
Jewish attitudes toward the Gentiles and their salvation were too diverse—even within sociologically identifiable groups—to allow us to ascertain, simply on the basis of what we know of Paul, the shape of his
preconversion attitudes toward the Gentiles. A covenantal nomist such as
Paul might be supposed to have been could, in principle, have held any of
the attitudes surveyed above.

The process of our investigation, then, is more complicated, and cannot be short-circuited. The shift in Paul's convictional world can be traced
through several stages, each of which has some fixed points and some
unknowns: (1) *Upbringing in Judaism*: We "know"—that is, we are assuming as a plausible working hypothesis—that Paul's native convictions
were those of a covenantal nomist. We do not know what he thought of
the Gentiles and their possibilities of salvation. (2) *Persecutor of the
church*: We also know—on the basis of his self-description as a zealous
persecutor—that his initial perception of the Christian gospel was that it
was incompatible with his Jewish convictional world. We do not know
precisely why this was so, or how the Gentiles might have figured into his
perceptions at this point. (3) *Conversion*: We "know"—again as a plausi-

ble hypothesis—that his conversion experience represented a dramatic shift in perception concerning the person and status of Jesus, necessitating a reconfiguration of his native convictional world, rather than an abandonment of that world altogether. While we also know that he later linked his Gentile mission to this experience, we cannot be certain that a concern for the Gentiles was immediately present as an explicit part of the experience. Nor do we know how his previous attitudes toward the Gentiles were affected by this convictional shift. (4) *Apostle to the Gentiles*: Finally, on the basis of the most tangible evidence at hand—the letters themselves—we know that Paul was urgently concerned to carry out a law-free mission to the Gentiles. In the letters, as he explains and defends this mission and deals with a whole range of emergent circumstances, he forges (or assumes) links between the Gentiles and various elements in his convictional universe, some from his native social world (for example, God, the law, Israel), others from his Christian (for example, faith, sin, Christ, the cross).

Our task in what follows will be to explore these links in order to ascertain the structure of Paul's convictional universe. We must begin with our point of most immediate access, the letters themselves. In each case we will probe beneath the surface of Paul's rhetorical logic, with the aim of discerning the shape of the convictional logic lying underneath. In each case as well we will compare the linkages in Paul's argumentation (between Gentile salvation and these various other convictional elements) with similar linkages in Judaism, asking what convictions need to be added or altered to move from the Jewish pattern to the Pauline. Differently put, I am attempting a kind of process of triangulation, in which we use two or more of our "knowns" to arrive at the most plausible identification of the "unknowns." At the end of the analysis I hope to be able to propose a way of plotting the points in the four stages identified above that both satisfies the boundary conditions represented by our fixed points of knowledge, and provides a plausible accounting of Paul's convictions concerning the Gentiles and their place in salvation.

When I began researching the topic, I was among those who felt that Paul could be explained within an eschatological pilgrimage framework.[105] But while working on Romans 11, I became increasingly dissatisfied—for reasons that will be presented in due course (see §7.1 and §8.1 below)—with the ability of this hypothesis to explain significant aspects of Paul's convictions. At the same time, I became increasingly convinced that a more satisfactory account could be given by seeing him within the framework of Jewish proselytism. My thesis can be sketched out briefly by referring to the four stages in Paul's reconfiguration mentioned above. (1) *Upbringing in Judaism*: I will argue that prior to his Damascus experience Paul—like Eleazar in Adiabene—was interested in attracting proselytes to Judaism; "preaching circumcision" was how he put it in his letter to the Galatians (5:11). (2) *Persecutor of the church*: Paul's zealous persecution of the church was rooted most fundamentally in his perception that Christ was being presented as a rival boundary marker for the people of Israel, the community of the righteous who were promised salvation in the future. (3) *Conversion*: As a result of his new conviction that the crucified Jesus had been raised from death by God, Paul accepted what he had previously resisted, namely, that the boundary marker of Israel is constituted by Christ, not by the Torah. Paul did not reject his Israel frame of reference; rather, he redefined it in light of his Christ experience. (4) *Apostle to the Gentiles*: Though it is altered in substance, the *form* of Paul's convictions about the Gentiles remained the same through his conversion experience. Both before and after, he believed that God had chosen Israel to be a channel of salvation for the Gentiles, and that the Gentiles' share in salvation was dependent on their becoming full members of Israel ("the true circumcision"; cf. Phil 3:3) on equal terms with the Jews ("there is no distinction"; Rom 10:12). But the *substance* of his conviction was reconfigured: the equal terms are to be found not in the Torah, but in Christ.

The plausibility of this thesis will need to emerge from the detailed exegesis itself.

# PART TWO

# The Structure of Paul's Convictions about the Gentiles

## CHAPTER FOUR

# God

At various points in his letters, but especially in Romans, Paul links his concern for the Gentiles with basic statements about the character and purposes of God. There are four categories of such statements to be examined. (1) The oneness of God, linked explicitly with the justification of the Gentiles in Rom 3:29-30. (2) The impartiality of God, defined in terms of the evenhanded meting out of divine justice to "the Jew first and also to the Greek" (Rom 2:11). (3) The righteousness of God, now revealed for all who believe without distinction (Rom 3:21-22). (4) Scripture, through which God promised the gospel (Rom 1:2), a gospel which Paul understands as inclusive of the Gentiles almost by definition (Rom 1:5, 16).

When Paul is viewed in the broadest perspective, this grounding of the Gentile mission in basic beliefs about God is of fundamental significance; Paul's literary and missionary activity in the service of the gospel can scarcely be understood apart from a basic belief that the gospel is the work of the one God who created all things.[1] But within the narrower perspective arising from the specific concerns of this study, Paul's *theolog*ical statements will not by themselves shed much light on his Gentile convictions. For his beliefs about God are not in any significant way distinguishable from those of his Jewish compatriots or, for that matter, other Jewish Christians. But the inferences he draws from these basic beliefs are so distinctive that one cannot understand them without taking into account the intervening links represented by his convictions about Christ, Israel, the law, and so on. A discussion of Paul's *theo*logical defense of his gospel for the Gentiles, then, will not take us very far. Nevertheless, it provides us an opportunity for an initial survey of the field, a convenient way of raising the questions to be explored more fully in subsequent chapters.

## 4.1 God's Oneness

The clearest use of monotheism as an argument for the salvation of the
Gentiles is found in Rom 3:29-30, which can be rendered (somewhat
woodenly) as follows:

> Or is God the God of Jews only? Is he not the God of Gentiles as well? Yes,
> of Gentiles as well, since (εἴπερ) God is one, [the God] who (ὅς) will justify
> the circumcised from faith and the uncircumcised through faith.

The argument here can be structured in two different ways. First, taken
on their own, vv. 29b-30 contain a more or less complete argument for
the justification of the uncircumcised, developed from the starting point
of the oneness of God. The chain of inference for this line of argument is
established by εἴπερ ("since"), used here as elsewhere to indicate the
grounds for a preceding statement,[2] and by the relative ὅς ("who"), which
introduces its corollary.[3] The explicit sequence of the argument, then, is
this: (1) God is one; therefore (2) God is God of both Jews and Gentiles;
consequently (3) God will justify circumcised Jews and uncircumcised
Gentiles on the same[4] basis of faith.

At the same time, however, this argument links in with another line of
argument signaled by v. 29. This verse is tied to what precedes by means
of the connective ἤ ["or"]. Verse 29a, then, introduces a new line of argumentation in service of the claim that "a person is justified by faith apart
from works of law" (v. 28). The premise implied by v. 29a is: (1) If justification is by works of law, God is the God of Jews only. Then the argument
continues: but (2) God is God of Jews and Gentiles (since God is one);
therefore (3) circumcised and uncircumcised alike will be justified on the
basis of faith, and not works of law.

While we need to keep this larger argument in view, our primary concern here is with the other argument nested within it, one that begins
with God's oneness and ends with the justification of circumcised and
uncircumcised alike. Paul's Jewish (or Jewish Christian) interlocutor
would be able to follow him part way along this chain of inference. With
the first step in the argument there would be full agreement: the declaration "God is one" goes back, directly or indirectly, to the Shema (Deut
6:4), the basic statement of Jewish monotheism. Likewise, there would
be general agreement on the second: since the one God is the creator of
the universe, he is the Lord of all, Gentiles as well as Jews.

This point deserves to be underlined, especially in view of attempts
by some commentators to set Pauline universalism over against Jewish

particularism. Nils Dahl quite rightly criticizes Ernst Käsemann on this score,[5] and his criticisms can justly be extended to C. E. B. Cranfield as well. Only in a one-sided and tendentious reading can the rabbinic text cited by Käsemann and Cranfield[6]—a rather typical declaration of Israel's election—be seen as closed to universalistic concerns. Jewish particularism is in its own way universalistic, just as Paul's universalism, requiring as it does belief in Christ, is undeniably particularistic. This observation, that Judaism could combine covenant and election with various patterns of universalism, has been explored already, and can be taken as established. But the oneness of God is central to Jewish self-understanding vis-à-vis the nations (e.g., Sir 36:5; 2 Macc 7:37) and indeed is explicitly referred to in each of the categories of texts discussed in the preceding chapter.

(1) *Proselytism:* The story of Judith, for example, turns on the question of whether Nebuchadnezzar (3:8; 6:2; 11:1) or the God of Israel (8:20; 9:12; 13:18) is to be recognized as "lord of the whole earth" (6:4). Judith's victory demonstrates to Achior that there is "no other god" (8:20) than the God of Israel, which leads directly to his conversion (14:10). (2) *"Natural Law" proselytism:* Philo emphasizes the oneness of God: proselytes are those who have come to worship "the one and truly existing God" (*Virt.* 102; also 179, 214; *Spec. leg.* 1.52); further, "since God is one, there should also be only one temple" (*Spec. leg.* 1.67). Likewise, in *Joseph and Aseneth,* Joseph can have no relationship with Aseneth (8.5-7) until she renounces her idols and turns to the "Lord God of the ages, who created all things and gave them life" (12.1). (3) *Righteous Gentiles:* As described by R. Joshua, righteous Gentiles are those who do not "forget God" (*t. Sanh.* 13.2). The renouncing of idolatry is a constant element in the related Noachian precepts (e.g., *t. 'Abod. Zar.* 8.4); indeed, this is so essential that the one "who denies it [i.e., idolatry], it is as if he accepts the whole Torah" (*b. Ḥul.* 5a; cf. *b. Meg.* 13a). (4) *Eschatological Pilgrims:* In *Sib. Or.* 3, the nations come to recognize "the immortal king, the great eternal God," and worship God at the temple, "since he alone is sovereign" (717–18). In Tob 14, the Gentiles who turn to God in the end times "will abandon their idols . . . and . . . praise the eternal God" (vv. 6-7).

To tie these observations in with the main line of discussion: Paul's Jewish interlocutor would agree with him not only that God is one, but also—as these texts make clear—that in consequence God is the God of Jew and Gentile alike. This means that unless Paul's debating partner shared the minority view found, for example, in *Jubilees* (where the oneness of God is used to deny salvation to all outside Israel; see 15.25-32), there would be agreement as well that Gentiles are not to be excluded from the sphere of righteousness and salvation, although the terms on which these Gentiles would relate to the one God would vary, in accordance with the various patterns of universalism that we have delineated.[7]

But for most Jews or Jewish Christians following his argument to this point, Paul's next step would have appeared as a reckless leap into the absurd:[8] because God is one, God will justify circumcised and uncircumcised alike on the sole ground of faith. John A. Ziesler observes that the logic of Paul's argument here requires "an unexpressed minor premise";[9] in fact, there are at least two. For Ziesler, what is required to make the argument work is the assumption that Gentiles cannot be asked to keep the whole Torah. Certainly some assumption having to do with the Gentiles and the Torah is required. For the group of Paul's interlocutors would include advocates of proselytism, who would have no problem agreeing with his argument to this point—(1) God is one, and therefore (2) is God of both Jews and Gentiles—but who could then in all plausibility continue: (3) the one God has given the law to be the one means of righteousness for Jew and Gentile alike. Paul's rejection of #3 indicates that he rejects the idea that the law is the means of righteousness for Gentiles.

But this cannot be the whole story. Ziesler's "unexpressed premise"—that Gentiles cannot be asked to keep the whole Torah—needs to be seen as shorthand for something longer. Construed in this way, the submerged premise seems to pertain only to the Gentiles, considered separately. But this fails to take into account another important element taken for granted in the argument here, the equality of Jew and Gentile. This assumption has already bobbed to the surface in v. 22 ("for there is no distinction"); and it is equally present in v. 30, where faith is designated as the grounds of justification for circumcised and uncircumcised alike.

This can be put in another, and more pointed, way by comparing Paul's argument here with "righteous Gentile" patterns of thought. As we have seen, there were those who believed that full Torah observance, while required for Jews, was not necessary for Gentiles. Some segments within Judaism, then, would have been prepared to grant Ziesler's minor premise as it pertains to Gentiles, while holding to full Torah observance for Jews. As Ziesler has construed it, Paul's argument would have been similar to a "righteous Gentile" approach:[10] Gentiles can be righteous without adhering to the full requirements of the Torah. Basic to this approach, however, is the idea of differentiation: the Torah is God's special gift to Israel alone; Gentiles can be righteous apart from the Torah, but they remain distinct from the covenant people. But this not only runs counter to explicit statements of equality in the larger context of the argument ("there is no distinction," v. 22); it is unlikely that Paul would attempt to derive such a pattern of Gentile inclusion so directly from the oneness of God, monotheism lending itself much more easily to ideas of uniformity (cf. Philo *Spec. leg.* 1.67).

The first part of the premise left unexpressed in the enthymeme[11] of v. 30, then, is the belief that Jew and Gentile stand on the same ground before God; God treats them equally as far as "justifying" is concerned. The second part, having to do with the Torah, will require at least a chapter of its own before it can be stated with any precision. But to begin to get some purchase on it, we can recall that the monotheism argument of vv. 29-30 serves as another way of establishing the conclusion of v. 28, namely, that justification is by "faith" and not by "works of law." As we have noted, some of Paul's interlocutors, agreeing with him that Jews and Gentiles are to be justified on the same grounds, would hold to the position that the Torah itself provides this common ground of justification. They could argue that such a position is logically consistent with the set of assumptions they share with Paul; they could even concede that "faith" was an important part of the equation. That Paul reaches the conclusion he does requires the intervening assumption that Torah, on the one hand, and justification and faith, on the other, are somehow mutually exclusive. To say more will require a detailed examination of how Torah, faith, and justification figure in Paul's arguments for the Gentile mission. But for now we can say this: the unexpressed premise in v. 30 is not simply that Torah is not to be imposed on Gentiles; rather, there is one way for circumcised and uncircumcised alike to relate to God, and this way is not the Torah.

Before leaving the passage, there is one final observation to be made. As was noted above, vv. 29-30 stands in rhetorical parallelism with the argument of v. 28. Indeed, the use of ἤ (or) with an interrogative (as in v. 29) is a favorite Pauline device for introducing an additional argument for some claim, standing in parallel with a preceding argument or arguments.[12] But v. 28, together with the preceding verse to which it is tightly connected, stands in a highly significant position in the argument that has been developed to this point. After describing the situation of all humankind under the wrath of God (1:18–3:20), and subsequently the disclosure for all who believe of the righteousness of God (3:21-26; cf. 1:17), the discourse moves with v. 27 into the rhetorical payoff: "Where then (οὖν) is boasting . . . ?" If this payoff consisted only of vv. 27 and 28, there might be grounds for the Reformation view that justification by faith rather than by meritorious works was the "main proposition"[13] of Paul's argument. But he goes on in vv. 29-30 to provide an alternative statement of his conclusion,[14] one in which any reference to "works" and "boasting" has fallen away, and justification by/through faith is instead set over against any attempt to restrict the righteousness of God to the Jews. I will explore in a subsequent chapter the way in which the statements concerning "works of law" and "boasting" are linked to the salvation of the Gentiles. But in any case we can say that the inclusion of the Gentiles is an important part of the goal toward which Rom 1:16—3:26 has been moving.[15]

The oneness of God is introduced as an argument in another passage whose main theme concerns the inclusion of the Gentiles, Gal 3:19-20: "[The law] was ordained through angels in the hand of a mediator. But the mediator is not of one, but God is one." In the usual reading of this passage, v. 20 is taken as a generalized argument, one in which the process of mediation is set over against the oneness of God, in order to establish the inferiority of the law (given through the mediation of Moses) in comparison with the promise (given directly by God to Abraham). While opinions differ as to the precise way in which mediation is to be contrasted with monotheism (about which more in due course), the argument as a whole, as customarily interpreted, bears on the matter of the inclusion of the Gentiles only indirectly, by way of the law.

Paul's letter to the Galatians has been prompted by the willingness of some of the Gentile Christians in Galatia to consider circumcision (5:2). In response, Paul denounces any attempt to impose the law on Gentile converts. While the argument in Gal 3:6-29 is as dense and complex as any in the Pauline corpus, the thread that concerns us here is spun out as follows: (1) The promise to Abraham included the promise of blessing for the Gentiles, which Paul interprets as the "gospel" that "God would justify the Gentiles by faith" (v. 8). (2) The promise cannot be subordinated to, or made conditional on, the law. Verses 10-24 consist of a series of arguments crafted to establish this proposition; the inferiority of mediation (vv. 19-20) stands alongside other arguments—for example, that the law brings a curse (vv. 10-14), that the law came in later (vv. 15-18), that the law had only a preparatory role (vv. 23-24)—in the service of the claim that (3) the promise is to be given to those who are in Christ by faith, Jews and Gentiles alike—not to those who rely on works of law. In this customary reading of the passage, the oneness of God is related primarily to the law, and thus only in an indirect fashion to the inclusion of the Gentiles.

But in a recent study of Gal 3:15-20, N. T. Wright has argued for a different interpretation of the passage, one that brings these two

themes into direct relationship.[16] The usual interpretation takes v. 20—
ὁ δὲ μεσίτης ἑνὸς οὐκ ἔστιν ("the mediator is not of one")—as a global
statement pertaining to mediators in general. Wright points out that it
would be more common in such a statement for the noun to be anarthrous, and argues instead that the mediator in question is the one just
mentioned in v. 19, Moses himself. "One" (ἑνὸς)[17] is similarly anaphoric,
in his view, referring back to the one "seed" of v. 16, that is, Christ, who
in due course is revealed as a corporate figure, one "in whom" is to be
found a new family of Jews and Gentiles (vv. 25-29). Verse 20a, then, is
not an argument but a statement, making the assertion that Moses is not
the one through whom the one family promised to Abraham will be
brought into being. The upshot of this is that the argument of v. 20b has
the same structure as that of Rom 3:29-30, albeit in compressed form:
"God is one; therefore he desires one people; therefore the law cannot be
the means of bringing his people into existence,"[18] for the law divides
people into separate groups of Jews and Gentiles.

Interesting as this suggestion may be, it renders the verse much too
elliptical to be convincing. If v. 20 is a simple assertion—that Moses is
not the agent of God's promised family—then the description of Moses as
*mediator* is wholly gratuitous. The oneness of God, in Wright's reading, is
introduced not by way of contrast with the duality of mediation but by
way of explanation of the one family presumably in view in the first part
of the verse. This leaves the designation of Moses as mediator in v.
20 with no significance whatsoever; the sense would remain the same
(indeed, would even be clearer) if the second μεσίτης ("mediator") were
simply omitted.[19] Further, the presence of the article with "mediator"
does not militate against a generic reading; a similar usage appears within
several paragraphs (ὁ κληρονόμος ["the heir"], in 4:1). The generic reading of v. 20, then, is much more likely.

The question remains as to the way in which mediation stands in contrast to the oneness of God. But, given the function of v. 20 in the argument of the chapter as a whole, we do not need to decide this question
here. For the present discussion, the only other place where Paul refers
directly to God's oneness is in 1 Cor 8:4-6, which is not connected to any
explicit reference to the salvation of the Gentiles. Nevertheless, the letter
is addressed to a Gentile Christian community, which means that the passage reflects the practical application of what Paul was arguing for in
Rom 3:29-30. That is, given the probability that the slogan "there is no
God but one" goes back to Paul's original preaching in Corinth,[20] the
passage provides evidence that monotheism was part not only of his de-

bating strategy with Jews, but also of his basic message to Gentiles. What this basic message might have had to say about the status of Gentile believers with respect to Jews is not immediately apparent.[21] But it is worth noting that the passage itself omits any intervening consideration of Jew and Gentile and moves directly from God's oneness to the undifferentiated group of believers[22] who acknowledge the one God and the one Lord. This is not to say that the Jew-Gentile distinction has necessarily lost all significance for Paul; this will come up for discussion in the next section, and more directly in the next chapter (§5.3). But it means that at least from one angle, God's oneness can be expressed in simple universalistic terms: God has created all things, and "we"—an undifferentiated group of believers (though mixed, since Paul includes himself)—exist for God.

## 4.2 God's Impartiality

In Rom 2:9-11 Paul picks up another common Jewish maxim concerning the nature of God and presses it into the service of his argument for Gentile salvation; this time it has to do not with God's oneness but with God's impartiality. While not as central to Jewish self-understanding as the monotheistic credo of the Shema, God's impartiality is nonetheless firmly rooted in the Hebrew scriptures and widespread in postbiblical Jewish literature.[23] Paul's statement is as follows:

> There will be anguish and distress for everyone who does evil, the Jew first and also the Greek, but glory and honor and peace for everyone who does good, the Jew first and also the Greek. For there is no partiality (προσωπολ- ημψία) with God.

Paul moves from the notion of divine impartiality to that of Gentile salvation along two different routes. The shorter route is contained in the verses quoted above: since God is impartial, God will punish those who do evil and reward those who do good, Jews and Gentiles alike. That it is not inappropriate to describe the "reward" in view here as "salvation" can be seen from the parallel assertions in vv. 6-8 and 13, where those who "do" the good, or the law, are promised eternal life (v. 7) or justification (v. 13).

This declaration of God's impartiality, however, is not limited in its relevance to these few verses in chapter 2. As Jouette Bassler has rightly observed, 2:11 sums up the theme of the whole of 1:18—3:20;[24] and given the presence of related themes in 3:22 (no distinction) and 3:29

(God the God of Jews and Gentiles alike), this observation could be extended to include 3:21-31 as well. This being so, one can discern a link between divine impartiality and Gentile salvation in this larger context too; but the route between the two is quite different, a fact which creates significant problems for the interpretation of chapter 2. In the shorter route described in 2:6-13, Paul appears to take for granted that there are those—Jews presumably, but especially Gentiles—who actually do the good, or the law, to a sufficient degree that they receive justification and eternal life. But the penultimate destination of the larger argument is the conclusion "that all, both Jews and Greeks, are under the power of sin" (3:9), "that there is no one who is righteous" (3:10), and that consequently "no human being will be justified in [God's] sight" on the basis of law observance (3:20). The longer route from divine impartiality to Gentile salvation, then, goes through the territory of universal sinfulness, and of the inability of the law to do anything more than reveal sin (3:20), before arriving at its final destination—the justification of all without distinction "through the redemption that is in Christ Jesus" (3:21-26).

The line of argument in 2:6-13 is so blatantly at odds with the overall drift of Paul's thought development in 1:18—3:20 that exegetical attempts to force the two into alignment have gone on from very early times.[25] In modern discussion, a variety of approaches to the problem have been taken,[26] of which the most significant are the following: (1) Paul is speaking only hypothetically, describing the state of affairs if one actually did keep the law, while ignoring for the sake of his larger argument the fact (as he understands things) that no one can do so. (2) The human activity Paul has in view is really the obedience of faith that leads to justification.[27] (3) Paul is really referring to Christians, who—as the argument of Romans eventually asserts—are able to do what the law requires because of the empowerment of the Spirit (cf. Rom 8:1-4). (4) The contradictions are real and unresolvable.[28]

For present purposes, it is not necessary to discuss Romans 2 in detail; the passage will come up again in subsequent discussions concerning the theme of universal sinfulness (see §5.2 below). For now, it will suffice to note that Bassler is probably close to the mark when she speaks of the anticipatory nature of the argument here. That is, while Paul is constrained by the nature of his argument at this early stage to speak in general and ideal terms, he writes in full knowledge that "the final stage of his argument" is that it is "only the Christian who can fulfill the demands of the Law."[29] The most forceful argument against the idea that Paul has Christian "doers" in mind here is the unlikeliness of Christians being described as keeping the law "by nature" (φύσει; v. 14) rather than by the Spirit (cf. 8:4).[30] But if allowance is made for the anticipatory nature of the argument, this can be seen as the result of Paul's not wanting to tip his hand at this early stage of the game (although the fact that he is playing an essentially Christian suit becomes apparent, a little ahead of time, in v. 16).

What, then, can we learn from the rhetorical use to which Paul puts the idea of divine impartiality? How does his argument compare with the function of the notion in traditional Jewish usage? The word translated "partiality" (προσωπολημψία) is a neologism, found for the first time in the New Testament. It is commonly agreed, however, that it is based on the Hebrew נשא פנים (lit. "to lift up the face"), used in the two Old Testament passages speaking of God's impartiality (Deut 10:17; 2 Chron 19:7).[31] As Bassler has demonstrated, the notion of divine impartiality is common in Judaism. It appears in two broad contexts, one pertaining to Israel alone, the other with the nations in view.

In the first of these, found in the Old Testament and elsewhere,[32] the fact that God "is not one who accepts persons, and he is not one to accept bribes" (*Jub.* 5.16) is used as a warning to Israelites. God is sure to punish those who "withdraw from the commandments of the Mighty One" (2 *Bar.* 44.4); therefore "you shall fear the Lord your God; him alone you shall worship" (Deut 10:20). Divine impartiality functions here within the context of the covenant, to exhort Israelites to remain faithful to it.

In the second set of texts, the implications of divine impartiality are extended to include the nations as well. These texts generally assume a situation where Israel has been suffering at the hand of the Gentiles, such suffering being understood as divine punishment. This punishment itself can be seen as the outworking of divine impartiality (*Ps. Sol.* 2.18). But the real cutting edge of these texts is to be found in the extension of the theme of impartiality to the Gentiles. These texts declare that the Gentiles are not to gloat over Israel, not to feel smug about their role as an instrument of divine punishment, for the impartiality of God's judgment means that in due time they will be punished for their sins as well. Such punishment may be experienced in the present (e.g., the death of Pompey, *Ps. Sol.* 2.22-35; also Wis 6:1-11), or in the eschatological future (2 *Bar.* 13.1-12, esp. v. 8; *1 Enoch* 63.1-12, esp. v. 8). But this extension of the notion of divine impartiality to include the Gentiles is carried out in such a way that there is no blurring of the covenantal line of distinction between Jew and Gentile. Baruch addresses the nations who have laid Zion to waste:

You who have drunk the clarified wine, you now drink its dregs, for the judgment of the Most High is impartial. Therefore he did not spare his own sons first, but he afflicted them as his enemies because they sinned. Therefore, they were once punished, that they might be forgiven. But now, you nations and tribes, you are guilty. (2 *Bar.* 13.8-11)

Divine impartiality leads to punishment for sin in the case of Jews and Gentiles alike. But the punishment of Israel leads to forgiveness; the punishment of the nations to destruction. In these texts, then, the theme of impartiality serves a paraenetic role—to comfort and encourage Israel in times of distress.

On the basis of her study of these texts, Bassler draws a sharp contrast between Paul and Judaism. In the case of Judaism, there is

no evidence . . . of the universal potential which the concept . . . could have acquired. God's impartiality certainly concerned the relationship between Jews and Gentiles, yet it was never seen as specifically blurring the distinction between the two groups.[33]

Paul, however, uses this axiom in a radically new way:

He dissolves in the name of divine impartiality every distinction between Jew and Gentile and thus approaches, using as a starting point the language and doctrines of Judaism, the highest ideals of universalism to be found in Greek philosophy.[34]

That Paul uses the concept differently than does Judaism is certainly not to be denied. But Bassler's description of the difference, depending as it appears to do on a questionable antithesis of Pauline universalism and Judaic particularism, is somewhat overstated. I have two corrective observations to make, one concerning Jewish particularism, centered on the shorter argument linking impartiality and Gentile salvation; the other concerning Pauline universalism, and centered on the longer argument.

First, Paul's Jewish dialogue partner would be able to give wholehearted assent to the statements linking impartiality and the Gentiles in 2:6-13, not only on the negative side (anguish and distress for everyone who does evil, Gentiles included), but also on the positive side (glory and honor and peace for everyone who does good, Gentiles included). For as we have seen, Jewish particularism is in its own way universalistic, and the concept of divine impartiality is at least implicit in these patterns of universalism, especially those that emphasize the law as equally binding on the Gentiles, namely, proselytism, and its diaspora reinterpretation (see §3.2 and §3.3 above).

This comes to explicit expression, at least in a negative way, in the Jewish material currently under discussion. In the preceding chapter I observed how the universality of the law and the possibility of proselytism were introduced in a number of Jewish texts as a kind of theodicy, to justify God's punishment of the Gentiles (see §3.1 above). While these texts did not evince much enthusiasm about proselytism, they at least held it open as an option, and were thus formally linked to those passages more positive about the option. Such a use of proselytism is found in two of the texts dealing with impartiality that were mentioned above. In 2 Bar. 13.8 the ultimate—and impartial—judgment of the nations is justified in these terms: "For I have always benefited you, and you have always denied the beneficence." The force of the argument depends on the—at least hypothetical—possibility of Gentile gratitude for divine beneficence. In 1 Enoch 63, we actually witness a change of heart on the part of the rulers of the Gentiles. They "worship before the Lord of the Spirits, and confess their sins before him," declaring, "Now we have come to know that we should glorify and bless the Lord of kings—him who rules over all kings" (vv. 2, 4). Unfortunately for them, however, their "conversion" comes too late. Their doom is sealed (for the Lord's "judgments have no respect of persons," v. 8), and all they can do is lament lost opportunities: "Would that someone had given us a chance so that we should glorify, praise and have faith before his glory" (v. 5). Again, their remorse that "now . . . we have no chance to become believers" (v. 8) implies that "formerly" there was at least the hypothetical possibility that they might have "had faith" and "glorified the Lord of Spirits and kings" (cf. v. 7).

These texts, while not enthusiastic about proselytism, nevertheless provide explicit evidence for the logical connection between divine impartiality and the proselyte option. Bassler's conclusions, then, need to be modified. Paul's argument, at least within the narrow confines of Rom 2:6-13, is not to be radically set over against Judaism. A Jewish interlocutor, open to proselytism, would be prepared to grant that since God is impartial, Gentiles who do the law will be justified. Paul's equal and evenhanded treatment both of Jews and Gentiles and of judgment and blessing might have aroused some suspicions about the ultimate destination of the argument. But this section of the argument, at least, is fully consistent with covenantal nomism.

It is in the longer argument, then, that Paul's appeal to the theme of impartiality parts company with Judaism and begins to blur the covenantal lines. For he goes on to declare that in actuality the group of those "doers of the law who will be justified" (cf. 2:13) is a null set: all have sinned, Jew and Gentile alike (3:9); the most the law can do is make this universal sinfulness apparent (3:19-20). God's impartiality is evident—negatively in that the whole world, without distinction, is held accountable for its sin (3:19); and positively in that the righteousness of God is available for all without distinction (3:22). It is at this point—not the move from impartiality to Gentile salvation per se, but the intermediate moves in which sin is used to nullify the traditional covenantal function of the law—that Paul can be said to be turning this Jewish axiom against the basic convictions of covenantal nomism.[35]

But is it correct to say that in the process he "dissolves . . . every distinction between Jew and Gentile"?[36] Is it really the case that Paul, under the banner of impartiality, abandons Jewish particularism entirely? Taken in isolation, his declarations of "no distinction" (Rom 3:22; 10:12; cf. Gal 3:28; 1 Cor 12:13; Col 3:11) could be read in this way.[37] But the most forceful statements against such a reading come from Paul himself: there is much advantage in being Jewish, much benefit in circumcision (Rom 3:1); God has not rejected his people (Rom 11:1); the gifts and the calling of God are irrevocable (Rom 11:29); and so on. Undoubtedly the presence of both sets of statements furnishes evidence of a certain degree of conceptual confusion, a phenomenon to be explored more fully in subsequent chapters. But at the same time it strikes a cautionary note: one should not be in haste to read the statements of "no distinction" in a global and categorical way; the distinction being denied may well pertain to a much more limited domain.

## 4.3 The Righteousness of God

In addition to the oneness of God and the impartiality of God, there is another divine "attribute" rhetorically linked with the salvation of the Gentiles, namely, the righteousness of God (δικαιοσύνη θεοῦ). While the appearance of the phrase is not limited to Romans (see 2 Cor 5:21; cf. Phil 3:9), the passages of interest are all found in this epistle. In 1:17, the gospel, just introduced as "the power of God for salvation for everyone who has faith, to the Jew first and also to the Greek" (v. 16), is described as the means by which the righteousness of God is revealed. In 3:21-22, Paul turns from the revelation of the wrath of God (1:18—3:20) to the manifestation of the righteousness of God, "the righteousness of God through the faith(fulness) of Jesus Christ for all (πάντας) who believe"—"all" in the context of the passage meaning "Gentiles as well as Jews." And in 10:3-4, Paul accuses Israel of not submitting to "the righteousness of God," contrasting the righteousness that Israel seeks to establish for itself with the righteousness coming through Christ "for all who believe."

Contemporary understanding of the phrase "the righteousness of God" has been profoundly affected by two widely accepted semantic insights, insights that have resulted in an interpretation differing from that of the Reformers and resolving several of the tensions inherent in Reformation theology and that need to form a part of any new Pauline paradigm. One has to do with the term "righteousness" itself. Since the work of H. Cremer,[38] it has increasingly been recognized that the word group (δικ—, צדק) in biblical usage has to do with conformity not to some absolute standard of ethical requirement but rather to the terms and requirements of a specific relationship. More particularly, in Paul's Jewish world of discourse, to be righteous is to act in a manner consistent with the covenant.

The other development has to do with the specific construction, "the righteousness of God." In Reformed interpretation, this has sometimes been viewed as the divine standard of righteousness (an objective genitive)—"that which is approved at his tribunal" (Calvin),[39] but more frequently as the righteous status that comes from God (genitive of origin), freely given to those who believe (Luther).[40] But in a well-known and widely influential article, Ernst Käsemann[41] has argued persuasively that while the sense "righteousness as gift" is not to be excluded, the term is used in at least some instances—including the passages of interest here—in a subjective way to refer to God's powerful saving activity. Such usage represents no fundamental innovation on Paul's part; while Käsemann may have overreached himself in arguing that the phrase (δικαιοσύνη θεοῦ) was already a fixed formulation in Paul's day, the general sense is fully present in Hebrew usage, where "righteousness" appears frequently in parallel with "salvation."[42] Putting this insight together with the previous one, then, Käsemann can say that to speak of God's righteousness is to speak of "God's covenant-faithfulness."[43]

Käsemann takes this line of development a step further, and in a manner that brings the Gentiles squarely into the picture. But before turning our attention to the place of the Gentiles in these Pauline texts, it is appropriate to ask what connections might have been present already within Judaism between the righteousness of God and the salvation of the Gentiles. The answer is of necessity speculative, since the two concepts are not explicitly connected in any text from Second Temple Judaism.[44] But in several passages from the Hebrew scriptures, the two are linked by means of the theme of vindication: the nations comprise the audience who witness the "righteousness" of God's deliverance of Israel (Ps 98:2;

Isa 62:2). This could have easily been linked further to the eschatological pilgrimage tradition: because they see the "righteousness of God" exhibited in God's deliverance of Israel, the nations abandon their idols and turn to worship the God of Israel.[45] This additional link, however, while fully consistent with the logic of covenantal nomism, appears nowhere in the literature of the period.

In the Pauline texts under discussion, however, the righteousness of God and the salvation of the Gentiles are spoken of in the same breath. How are they linked? There have been two distinct lines of scholarly interpretation in which the latter is seen as a direct result or manifestation of the former. One of these is Käsemann's analysis, where the two are intimately connected, but in a manner that sets Paul sharply over against a Jewish pattern of understanding. In his reading, the relationship to which God is shown to be faithful is not with Israel—"God's righteousness cannot now for Paul be primarily the divine covenant-faithfulness toward Israel"[46]—but with the whole creation. Paul conceives of Christ not as (for example) a second Moses, but as a second Adam; and the righteousness made manifest through Christ is not that of God as Israel's deliverer, but of God as the world's creator. Israel's role in the story is not the covenantal one of the divinely chosen means by which God's universal purposes are being worked out; Paul's "universalization" is more "unprecedented" and "radical" than that. Instead, Israel comes into the picture simply as a particular example, "the archetype of the religious man."[47]

In terms of the categories introduced in chapter 3, then, Käsemann falls into the camp of those who understand Paul's universalism as grounded in a rejection of Jewish particularism. Since one of my goals is to demonstrate that Paul's universalism is instead to be understood as a Christ-motivated reworking of Jewish universalism, it should come as no surprise that I feel that this aspect of Käsemann's position is a fundamental misreading of Paul—as are many others.[48] Given the brevity and paucity of the texts referring to the "righteousness of God," the point cannot be easily established on the basis of these texts themselves. Nevertheless, one observation can be made here.

In Rom 15:7-13—increasingly being recognized as a concluding summary of the body of the letter as a whole[49]—the work of Christ is summed up in terms that both include the Gentiles, while at the same time being explicitly and strikingly Israel-centered:

> Christ became a servant of the circumcised for the sake of the truthfulness (ἀλήθεια) of God, to confirm the promises given to the patriarchs, and in order that the Gentiles might glorify God for his mercy. (vv. 8-9)

The relevance of this statement for the "righteousness of God" theme emerges from a comparison with 3:3-7. In this earlier passage Paul uses the phrases "faithfulness (πίστις) of God," "righteousness (δικαιοσύνη) of God," and "truthfulness (ἀλήθεια) of God" in essentially parallel ways. To speak of God's "truthfulness," then, as he does in 15:8, is another way of speaking of God's righteousness.[50]

Käsemann himself recognizes this point,[51] but slips quickly to v. 9, which he reads as standing in contrast to v. 8 and thus as "surpassing" it: "covenant faithfulness . . . cosmically extended."[52] Certainly v. 9 needs to be included; we will draw it into the discussion in a moment. But before getting into the knotty syntactical problems it presents, it is worth pausing over the clearer statement of v. 8. Here the truthfulness (= righteousness) of God is linked tightly with Christ's ministry to Israel[53] and with the confirming of the promises to the Jewish patriarchs: Christ's ministry to Israel is carried out for the sake of God's truthfulness, and thus has as its goal the confirming of the patriarchal promises. However the Gentiles come into the picture, the truthfulness (= righteousness) of God remains indissolubly linked to Israel and its story. Pauline universalism is not the abandonment of the covenant for the sake of the cosmos.

Nevertheless, the Gentiles do come into the picture in v. 9, so that one can appropriately raise the question concerning the nature of the connection between the truthfulness (= righteousness) of God in v. 8, and inclusion of the Gentiles. To do so, however, lands us in a difficult syntactical tangle. The sentence in vv. 8-9 presents the interpreter with two areas of ambiguity. First, the infinitive δοξάσαι (to glorify, v. 9): is it (1) an expression of purpose, standing in parallel with εἰς τὸ βεβαιῶσαι (to confirm) and thus dependent on γεγενῆσαι (became), with the result: "Christ became a servant . . . so that he might confirm . . . and so that the Gentiles might glorify . . . "; or is it (2) dependent on λέγω (I say, v. 8) and parallel with γεγενῆσαι (became), with the result: "I say that Christ became . . . and/but that the Gentiles glorify . . ."? The second has to do with the phrase "for the sake of the purposes of God": is it (a) simply in apposition to "to confirm," and thus independent of v. 9 (". . . for the sake of the truthfulness of God, that is, to confirm the promises . . . ") or (b) an integral part of the clause on which both purposes constructions depend ("Christ became a servant of the circumcision for the sake of the truthfulness of God, in order that: [i] he might confirm . . . and [ii] the Gentiles might glorify . . . ")?

The passage is difficult, perhaps resistant to any fully satisfactory solution. To keep the discussion within manageable limits, I will not attempt anything like a full treatment of the options,[54] organizing my comments instead according to the range of possible links between the truthfulness (= righteousness) of God and the salvation of the Gentiles. In one way of construing the passage, the two are seen as quite distinct, even standing over each other in contrast. This construal takes the infinitive construction in v. 9 as dependent on λέγω (I say) in v. 8a, so that the statements concerning the Jews (v. 8b) and the Gentiles (v. 9) are separate and independent. It also sees a contrast between ὑπὲρ ἀληθείας (for truth, v. 8b), the goal of Christ's ministry with the Jews, and ὑπὲρ ἐλέους (for mercy, v. 9), the occasion of the glorying of the Gentiles. Käsemann is one who translates the passage this way (even though the translation is not supported by the comments in the commentary): "For I tell you that Christ became a servant of the circumcision for the sake of God's truth, namely, to confirm the promises to the fathers as valid. The Gentiles (may) nevertheless glorify God for his mercy, as it is written. . . ."[55]

But this rendering is less likely than one in which the infinitive in v. 9 is taken as a purpose construction standing in parallel with the similar construction in v. 8b, that is, where both βεβαιῶσαι (to confirm) and δο-ξάσαι (to glorify) are dependent on εἰς τὸ (in order that). Despite the awkward change in subject, this is still the closest and most natural structural indicator; λέγω (I say) stands too far back in the sentence to be plausibly linked with δοξάσαι (to glorify), especially in view of the intervening εἰς τὸ (in order that). Further, a construal with λέγω (I say) would have the unlikely result of severing the Gentiles from Christ: Christ came to confirm God's truthfulness for the Jews; but the Gentiles glorify God for his mercy. With most commentators, therefore, I take vv. 8b and 9 as two parallel statements concerning the purpose of Christ's becoming a servant of the Jews.

If this is the case, then Paul is able to link the salvation of the Gentiles with Christ's ministry to Israel: "Christ became a servant of the circumcised . . . (1) in order that he might confirm the promises given to the patriarchs and (2) in order that the Gentiles might glorify God for his mercy." The nature of this link, especially at the level of his underlying convictions, is something to be explored (see esp. §8.3 below). For the present, however, we turn our attention to another way of construing the verse, representing the other way in which the truthfulness (= righteousness) of God and the salvation of the Gentiles have been tightly linked together.

This construal assumes that v. 9 stands in parallel with v. 8b, but assumes further that the phrase "for the sake of the truthfulness of God" is an integral part of the clause on which the two purpose constructions depend, rather than standing in apposition to the first of them. That is, the truthfulness (= righteousness) of God issues both in the confirming of the promises made to the patriarchs (v. 8b) and in the salvation of the Gentiles (v. 9). In such a construal, the salvation of the Gentiles is one manifestation of the righteousness of God. How might this be understood? The most forceful argument along these lines is developed by Sam K. Williams, who argues both that the "truthfulness of God" in Rom 15:8-9 is equivalent to the "righteousness of God" and that God's righteousness (= truthfulness) is precisely God's faithfulness to the promise to Abraham of a blessing that would extend to all nations.[56]

The full assessment of this claim will need to wait for a discussion of Paul's argument concerning Abraham and the Gentiles (see §5.1). For the more narrowly focused purposes of this chapter, however, there are three considerations that tell against such a linkage. First, nowhere in Romans is the salvation of the Gentiles presented as a fulfillment of God's promises to Abraham. The one place where a connection is made between promise, Abraham, and Gentiles is Rom 4:16. But here the structure of the statement is not: the promise to Abraham was that the Gentiles would be blessed; rather, the promise was given to all Abraham's descendants, and believing Gentiles are to be included among these heirs of the promises. The point of the argument is that believing Gentiles are eligible to share in the promised inheritance, not that the promise was that Gentiles would be included among the heirs. Nowhere in the rhetoric of Romans, the epistle in which the righteousness of God is a prominent theme, is the salvation of the Gentiles seen as the product of God's faithfulness to a promise made to Abraham.

Second, in all of the passages where the righteousness of God and the salvation of the Gentiles are mentioned in the same context, they are present as parallel but not explicitly linked aspects of the gospel. In Rom 1:16-17, the gospel is both the power of God for salvation for all who believe, Gentiles included, and a revelation of the righteousness of God; but the salvation of the Gentiles is not said to be a manifestation of God's righteousness. In 3:21-22, the righteousness of God accomplished through the faithfulness of Christ[57] is for all who believe; but the inclusion of the Gentiles within the "all" is not an explicit part of that righteousness itself. This pattern is repeated in 10:3-4: the righteousness of God is for all, but this universality is not presented as a product of God's righteousness. Similarly, with respect to Rom 15:8-9, the fact that the two purpose clauses are separated (by δὲ ["and, but"]) and are in parallel suggests that they are distinct. That is, Christ's ministry to Israel has two goals or intended results: (1) the confirming of the patriarchal promises (v. 8b), and (2) the creation of a situation where Gentiles would glorify God (v. 9). In fact, this corresponds to what can be seen as the twin thrusts of Paul's argument in Romans. On the one hand, he wants to argue that righteousness and salvation are available in Christ to believing Gentiles simply on the basis of their faith; Gentiles do not have to conform to the Torah to be considered righteous. But on the other, he wants to insist that such a gospel of righteousness apart from the Torah represents a fulfillment, rather than a repudiation, of God's covenant promises to Israel. In the rhetorical context of Romans, the two elements stand in a certain degree of tension: acceptance of the one (the law-free mission to the Gentiles) does not entail (Paul is at pains to argue) the abandonment of the other (God's faithfulness to Israel). My argument, then, is that Rom 15:8-9 represents a recapitulation of this twofold argument. What Christ has made possible as a result of his ministry carried out in the context of Israel (v. 8a) is, on the one hand, the confirmation of God's covenantal promises, and on the other, the creation of a situation where the Gentiles, too, can give glory to God. But these twin results are not directly correlated; they represent the two sides of a bifurcated argument.

Third, there is the probable contrast between the "for the sake of God's truthfulness" (ὑπὲρ ἀληθείας) in v. 8 and "for the sake of [God's] mercy" (ὑπὲρ ἐλέους) in v. 9. True, given the tight connection in the Old Testament between the related Hebrew words (חסד ואמת),[58] "truthfulness" and "mercy" are not to be set over against each other in any absolute way. Nevertheless, within the context created by the argument in Romans, a contrast is probably to be inferred here. For in Romans, the term "mercy" has figured prominently in Paul's presentation of the sovereign freedom in which God has hardened (part of) Israel (for a time) and turned to the Gentiles (Rom 9:15, 16, 18, 23; 11:30-32), a divine initiative that he describes as a "mystery," (11:25; that is, something not previously known). The sense of vv. 8-9, then, is that Christ's ministry represents both a demonstration of God's truthfulness (faithfulness to promises already made to Israel) and God's mercy (unexpected inclusion of the Gentiles in Christ, on equal terms with the Jews).

To sum up this argument in grammatical terms, the phrase "for the sake of the truthfulness [= righteousness] of God" is to be seen as an anticipation of, or a phrase in apposition to, the first purpose construction, "to confirm the promises made to the fathers," rather than something on which both purpose constructions depend. That the Gentiles are glorifying God is a result of Christ's ministry to the circumcised, but it is not part of God's righteousness (that is, faithfulness to the patriarchal promises); these are parallel correlates of the one work of Christ.

## 4.4 Scripture

The preceding discussion concerning the righteousness of God leads naturally to the wider question of scripture. That is, while it is not the case (so I have argued) that Paul describes the salvation of the Gentiles explicitly as a manifestation of God's faithfulness to the covenantal promises made to Abraham (that is, God's righteousness), he nevertheless appeals explicitly to scriptural texts, Abrahamic and otherwise, in support of his gospel for the Gentiles. What can we learn about his convictions concerning the Gentiles from the way he cites and handles scripture?

As has been the case throughout this chapter,[59] our observations here will be preliminary and provisional. The highest concentration of scriptural citations is found in Romans and Galatians, where they function as support for the central themes of those epistles: namely, that righteousness is through faith, not works of the law; that such faith—exhibited by Jew or Gentile—provides one with membership in Abraham's family; and that the salvation of the Gentiles does not represent the failure of God's purposes with Israel. Consequently, Paul's use of scripture will figure prominently in the chapters to follow, where these themes will be addressed directly. For present purposes I will comment only on those passages where scripture is cited or referred to in direct and explicit connection with the Gentiles and their salvation. Further, my concern is to discern the shape of Paul's underlying convictions; other aspects of his use of scripture—textual basis, methodological parallels, rhetorical function, and so on[60]—will be drawn in only insofar as they serve this purpose.

The relevant passages fall into four categories. (1) On two occasions, Paul makes general statements about scripture and the Gentiles without citing any specific text. In Rom 1:2 he describes the gospel as a message that God "promised beforehand through his prophets in the holy scriptures," a message that—as he says later in the same sentence (v. 5)—he has been commissioned to bring to the Gentiles. Later in the epistle he refers to the "righteousness of God for all who believe" as something "attested by the law and the prophets." (2) References to ἔθνη ("nations, Gentiles") in the Genesis account of Abraham are cited on two occasions—Gen 17:5 ("I have made you the father of many nations/Gentiles") in Rom 4:17 and 18; and Gen 12:3 ("all the nations/Gentiles shall be blessed in you") in Gal 3:8, described as a declaration of the gospel to

Abraham "beforehand" (προευηγγελίσατο).[61] (3) In Rom 15:9-12 Paul strings together four texts—from the Psalms (18:49; 117:1), the law (Deut 32:43), and the prophets (Isa 11:10)—to establish the point that "Christ became a servant of the circumcised . . . in order that the Gentiles might glorify God for his mercy" (Rom 15:8-9).[62] (4) Finally, there are four occasions in Romans 9 and 10 where Paul argues for the legitimacy of the Gentile mission by citing texts which in their original context refer not to the nations but to Israel: Hos 2:23 and 1:10 in Rom 9:25-26; Isa 28:16 in Rom 10:11; Joel 2:32 in Rom 10:13; and Isa 65:1 in Rom 10:20.[63]

Without engaging in detailed exegesis, several observations can be made. The first concerns the priority of conviction over exegesis. In a discussion of Paul's attempts to justify the Gentile mission on scriptural grounds, Cerfaux wonders aloud "whether the texts led Paul to formulate his theory, or if the theory impelled him to search the Bible to find them there."[64] The latter is clearly the case. In most instances the texts establish what Paul wants them to establish only if one shares his convictions at the outset. This is patently clear with the fourth category in the previous paragraph, where the texts did not originally refer to the Gentiles at all. While the ground is firmer in the Abraham story, Paul nevertheless cites the texts in an attempt to make the scripture "say" (cf. Rom 4:3) something that the plain sense of the Genesis text clearly does not want to say, namely, that uncircumcised Gentiles can be part of Abraham's "seed," a state of affairs categorically excluded in Gen 17:9-14.[65] The catena of texts in Rom 15:9-12 is more in line with Paul's purposes, especially the messianic reference to the "root of Jesse" in Isa 11:10 (v. 12). But even here there is nothing that would of itself lead to the characteristic features of Paul's Gentile Gospel, namely, that Gentile believers did not have to observe the law but nevertheless shared equal status with Jewish believers. We encounter here a process that moves from conviction to exegesis. Paul begins with the conviction that Christ has accomplished salvation for all and reads scripture in that light, rather than reading scripture and coming to the conviction that it promises salvation for the Gentiles.

This observation is supported by two other considerations. One concerns the absence from the list of citations of some obvious texts. We would expect that in any attempt to canvas the scriptures directly for passages holding open the possibility of salvation for the Gentiles, two categories of texts (in addition to the Abraham story) would result. One is the eschatological pilgrimage expectation, found in such passages as Isa 2:2-4/Mic 4:1-4, Isa 25:6-10a, 56:6-8, and Zech 8:20-23. The other, having to do instead with the present age, concerns Israel's covenantal role as a "light to the nations" (Isa 42:6; 49:6), a light that finds its source of illumination in the Torah (Isa 42:4; cf. Wis 18:4; *T. Levi* 14.4).

With the exception of the citation of Isa 11:10 in Rom 15:12, the eschatological pilgrimage passages are completely absent from Paul's scriptural repertoire;[66] even here, Paul's interest in the text seems to be governed more by its messianic significance than by any eschatological pilgrimage associations. The "light to the nations" theme, while perhaps of some significance for Paul's own self-conception as a Gentile apostle,[67] appears explicitly only in the polemical context of Rom 2:17-24 (where the "light" evokes only Gentile blasphemy). These passages represent the clearest Old Testament reference to Gentile salvation, and thus, one would expect, would be of primary interest for a Christian missionary concerned to show that the promise of righteousness "for all," Gentiles included, was "attested by the law and the prophets" (Rom 3:21-22). Their absence therefore is striking, suggesting that other factors are at work in Paul's use of scripture, and that his thinking concerning the Gentiles is not simply a matter of "reading off" what the scriptures have to say on the topic.

A second consideration pointing in the same direction arises from Paul's use of the term "mystery" with reference to the Gentile mission— "mystery" as elsewhere in biblical usage designating something not known beforehand but now revealed.[68] The matter is complicated by the fact that three of the four instances[69] are texts whose authenticity is disputed or suspect. The clearest and most general statement is found in Ephesians: "[the mystery] that the Gentiles are fellow heirs, members of the same body, and sharers of the promise in Christ Jesus through the gospel" (3:6). Similar but less explicit notes are struck in the probably appended[70] doxological conclusion of Rom 16:25-27, where the mystery once hidden but now disclosed has to do with "the obedience of faith for all the Gentiles,"[71] and in Col 1:26-27, where the mystery is linked with the presence of Christ "among the Gentiles" (τοῦ μυστηρίου τούτου . . . , ὅ ἐστιν Χριστὸς ἐν ὑμῖν). In the one certainly authentic usage, the "mystery" has to do not with the inclusion of the Gentiles per se nor even with the equality of their status but with the narrower matter of the timing of God's purposes: first the "full number of the Gentiles," and then "all Israel" (Rom 11:25-26).

But on the assumption that Colossians is authentic, it is reasonable to conclude that the Ephesians passage accurately reflects Pauline usage, that is, that Paul can describe the inclusion of the Gentiles as a "mystery." The syntactical connection between μυστήριου ("mystery") and ἐυ τοῖς ἔθνεσιν ("among the Gentiles") in Col 1:27 is not entirely clear. It is unlikely that the latter phrase is to be taken as modifying the infinitive ("to make known among the Gentiles"; so NIV), for this creates a redundancy with the relative pronoun "to whom"[72] ("God desired to make known among the Gentiles to his saints"). The phrase is more probably adjectival, linked with "mystery" or, more likely, τὸ πλοῦτος ("the wealth"; so: "the wealth among the Gentiles of the glory of this mystery"). While this does not explicitly designate the inclusion of the Gentiles as the content of the mystery, it points in that direction. Further, since Paul goes out of his way to describe his readers as Gentiles ("you were dead in . . . the uncircumcision of your flesh" [2:13; cf. 1:21; 3:11]), his description of the substance of the mystery as "Christ in *you*" would seem to confirm it.

In any case, it is clear that Paul's conviction that salvation is for the Gentiles is not to be seen in any simple way as the product of his reading of the scriptures. To be sure, his convictions are at every point so intertwined with his reading of scripture that we are not to suppose that he would have been able to differentiate the two. Nevertheless, his use of scripture is governed by and in the service of his convictions, rather than the other way around. Indeed, this statement is already implied in the term "mystery." As it was used in Paul's environment, the term was essentially hermeneutical, denoting an approach to scripture in which its message was presumed to remain hidden until God should provide the necessary interpretive key.[73] While Paul never uses the term in connection with any specific instance of scriptural exegesis,[74] this approach corresponds closely nonetheless to the way in which such exegesis is actually carried out.

But given the priority of conviction over exegesis, are there any other observations to be made from the way in which Paul appeals to scripture? Two aspects are suggestive, though their full exploration will have to wait for later chapters. One is the absence of eschatological pilgrimage texts. Given the prominence of such texts among the collection of scriptural passages that refer positively to the Gentiles, it is surprising that Paul made no use of them. Why press into service in Romans 9 and 10 texts that do not refer to the Gentiles at all, when Mic 4:1-4 and Isa 25:6-10a lay ready to hand? The question is intriguing, especially in view of the widespread scholarly opinion that Paul's Gentile mission was undergirded by precisely this type of eschatological pilgrimage conception (see §7.1 below).

The other observation concerns Paul's appeal to the Abraham story, especially in Romans 4, where he attempts to swim upstream by arguing—against the plain sense of Gen 17:9-14—that the inclusion of uncircumcised Gentiles within Abraham's "seed" is according to scripture.

Why did he feel compelled to argue in this way? Possibly, the answer is to be found in the rhetorical situation; that is, perhaps he is just trying to do his best on argumentative turf staked out by his opponents. Nevertheless, it is curious and worthy of further exploration that in a Jewish context where there were other options for Gentile salvation than that of becoming full members of Abraham's family (proselytes), Paul felt compelled to argue—against the text—for just such a status for his Gentile converts (see §5.1 below).

## 4.5 Findings and Implications

We began with the recognition that while Paul's *theo*logical convictions were basic, they would not by themselves shed much light on his concern for the Gentiles. Indeed, as we examined the connections between his various premises concerning God and their corresponding conclusions concerning the Gentiles, we observed how other convictions came into play in the intervening warrants and logical inferences of the developed argument.

The move from "God is one" to the justification of the Gentiles, for example, involves intervening assumptions concerning the equality of Jew and Gentile and the impossibility of righteousness through the law, the latter also expressed in terms of the mutual exclusion of "faith" and "works." Likewise, the argumentative path beginning with divine impartiality leads through the terrain of universal sinfulness and the consequent inability of the law to produce righteousness. The link between the righteousness of God and the salvation of the Gentiles is less direct, since these seem to be parallel results or characteristics of Christ's ministry to the circumcised. Nevertheless, this link brings into view Paul's stated commitment to the idea that his gospel does not imply the end or failure of God's faithfulness to Israel. Finally, his appeal to the scriptural "oracles of God" (cf. Rom 3:2) is revealing both for his evident lack of interest in apparently relevant material (especially the eschatological pilgrimage tradition), and for factors that appear to govern his reading of those scriptures that do attract his interest, namely, the new revelation that provides the key to the "mystery" of scripture and the status of Gentile believers as full members of Abraham's family and "seed."

This survey of intervening assertions and assumptions obviously represents a list of many of the major topics in the scholarly discussion of Paul's thought. While I will look at these topics sequentially in the subsequent chapters, the procedure will not be the typical one of analyzing the various scholarly positions in an attempt to adjudicate the discussion. My specific concern, to identify the structured set of convictions underlying Paul's rhetoric and coming to expression in different ways in the various predications[75] of his argumentation, will result in a procedure distinct in two ways.

One distinction is the concern with the *structure* of the convictions, the pattern of relationships among them. Consider, for example, the assertions concerning (1) the equality of Jew and Gentile as far as righteousness is concerned and (2) the impossibility of righteousness through the law. How are these two statements related? Is the second foundational and the first derivative? That is, is Paul's fundamental conviction the inability of the law to produce righteousness, which then leads to the conclusion (a second-order, or derived, conviction) that the Torah-determined differentiation between Jew and Gentile was only apparent or no longer relevant, with the result that there was "no difference" between them? Or might it have been the other way around, a fundamental perception of Jew-Gentile equality leading to the conclusion that the law, with its inherent tendency toward differentiation, was to be rejected? In either case, what connection is there between these predications and that of the universal sinfulness of humankind?

These are questions to be pursued in due course. For the present it might be helpful to describe the procedure by means of an analogy from the study of semantics. Linguists agree that the basic unit of meaning is not the individual word, but the sentence. While a word may have multiple meanings, both denotive and connotive, the meaning in any given instance is determined by its context in a sentence, that is, by its syntagmatic relations with the other words in the structured unit of the sentence. In the analogy, Paul's various predications (expressive of, but not simply to be equated with, his convictions) can be compared to a collection of individual words. In the attempt to ascertain the structured set of Paul's convictions, what we are looking for is the "sentence" in which these "words" are linked together in syntagmatic relationship. It is this structured set of relationships that will determine the meaning of any one of its parts; such determination will allow us to speak not simply of a "predication" but specifically of a "conviction."

The second distinction has to do with the function of covenantal nomism as a "boundary condition." That is, we are assuming that Paul's writings are not to be explained in terms of a fundamental misunderstanding of Judaism; his conversion experience may have produced a significant reconfiguration of his native convictional world, but that world was one which conformed to the basic patterns of covenantal nomism. This boundary condition has come into play already in this preliminary chapter. With respect to the examples discussed just above, for instance, it is unlikely that Paul's criticism of the Torah can be seen simply as derivative of a more fundamental conviction concerning the equality of Jew and Gentile. For covenantal nomism provides in a very natural way for the combination "no difference" plus "righteousness through the Torah," which is to say that Gentiles have the opportunity (through proselytism) to stand on equal ground before God. Consequently, we need to look for other convictional influences at play.

The procedure in what follows, then, is to attempt to ascertain the structured set of convictions that we have called Paul's (Christian) convictional world, using his (assumed) native convictional world as a point of reference and boundary condition. We begin with those predications having to do with humankind in general or as a whole.

## CHAPTER FIVE

# Generic Humanity

In this chapter I turn to those passages where Gentile salvation is linked rhetorically with statements pertaining to generic humanity—humankind conceived of as an undifferentiated whole. Three such sets of statements are of interest here: those that contrast righteousness by works with righteousness by faith; those that assert the universal plight of humankind under sin; and those that declare there to be no difference between Jew and Gentile. These rhetorical linkages raise the possibility in one way or another that Paul's basic category is humanity in general; that all of his argument and activity is grounded in a view of the world in which the categories of "Jew" and "Gentile," of Israel and its covenantal identity, have in the end no fundamental significance (or are at most second-level categories); in other words, that his Gentile mission is the natural outcome of a generic universalism that shapes his convictional world from the outset.[1] This is no mere hypothetical possibility; the "old paradigm" of Pauline interpretation described in an earlier chapter read these statements in precisely these terms.

Given the nature of Paul's argumentation, it is inevitable that our examination of these passages will lead us into areas—especially concerning "the law" and "Christ"—that will occupy our direct attention in subsequent chapters. But what gives each chapter its distinctive thrust is the desire to determine the point at which the concern for the Gentiles first appears in Paul's convictional structure. In the chapter on the law, for example, I will explore the possibility that this point is to be located in his convictions about the law. In one way of construing the sequence: a conviction that righteousness does not come by the law leads to the perception that any distinctions between Jew and Gentile are invalid or obsolete, which leads to the Gentile mission. In the present chapter, however, I examine the possibility that it is grounded in a universal conception of human existence that is structurally prior to any conviction about Israel or even about Christ.

## 5.1 Righteousness, Faith, and Works

In Rom 3:28, as he delivers the rhetorical payload of the argument begun at 1:16, Paul makes this declaration: "For we hold that a person (ἄνθρω-πον) is justified by faith apart from works of the law." In keeping with the nature of his argument to this point, ἄνθρωπον ("man, person") is explicitly inclusive: righteousness is for all who believe, without distinction (v. 22); the God who justifies is God of both Jews and Gentiles (v. 29); justification is for circumcised and uncircumcised alike (v. 30). Here, as in similar passages (Rom 4:1-8; 9:30—10:4; Gal 2:15—3:29), argumentative links are forged between the works/faith contrast on one hand and the justification of the Gentiles on the other. In this section I explore the nature of these links.

The place to begin, of course, is with the Reformation reading of Paul, both because it is hard to avoid, having played such a powerful role in shaping the environment in which these texts are read and, more to the point, because it represents the prime example of an interpretation that grounds Paul's Gentile mission in faith/works categories generically understood. Calvin, for example, reads the verse cited above (Rom 3:28) as a statement of Paul's "main proposition," now demonstrated to be "incontrovertible" as a result of the argumentation to this point, with the next statement—that God is the God of Gentiles as well as Jews (v. 29)—as a "second proposition" subordinate to and following on from the first.[2]

For the purposes of our analysis, however, I refer to Bultmann's reconstruction, partly because he elevates these statements to an even more central place in Paul's thought than did the classical Reformers. For the Reformers continued to treat "sin" as an independent category, coordinated (as we shall see) somewhat uneasily and not always successfully with that of "works." They attempt to give full weight *both* to statements suggesting that the problem with the law is that sin makes it impossible to fulfill the law's requirements fully *and* to statements suggesting that, even if the law were completely kept, it is still the case that law is based on works and so cannot lead to a righteousness possible only through faith. The problems attendant on such a combination will come up for consideration later. But Bultmann neatly avoids these problems, defining sin at bottom and in its essence as a universal human desire for self-sufficiency and (divine) recognition on the basis of meritorious achievement, that is, as "works." Note the subtle way in which this redefinition clicks into play in the middle of each of the following two sentences:

> It is not merely evil deeds already committed that make a man reprehensible in God's sight, but man's intention of becoming righteous by keeping the Law and thereby having his "boast." "*Man's effort to achieve his salvation by keeping the Law* only leads him into sin, indeed this effort itself in the end *is already sin.*"[3]

The result is that all of Paul's statements critical of the law are gathered together under the heading of "works," defined as a false self-understanding centered in a misguided striving after security through achievement. This, in turn, is set over against the life of "faith," defined as an authentic self-understanding that accepts God's judgment against such strivings after self-sufficiency and recognizes one's creaturely dependence on God. And this antithesis is made the center and organizing principle for the whole of Paul's thought.

Bultmann's reconstruction is well known, and there is no need to burden the world with yet another description of it.[4] What requires a closer look, however, is the way the Gentiles enter the picture. Or perhaps this should be rephrased as the way the Jews are eased to the margins of the picture. For in Bultmann's reconstruction, Paul's faith/works categories are generic and universal right through to their core. This is apparent already in the use of the generic "man" in the quotations cited above. And it is resoundingly clear in his choice of an anthropological organizing schema: "Paul's theology can best be treated as his doctrine of man: first, of man prior to the revelation of faith, and second, of man under faith" (1:191). For Bultmann's Paul, Judaism functions simply as an example— the one closest to Paul's own experience, of course, but an example nonetheless—of the general human plight. Jewish boasting in law performance, for example, is but one manifestation of a "natural tendency of man in general . . . to have his 'boast'" (1:242), a tendency showing up among the Greeks as well in their boasts about wisdom (1 Cor 1:19-31). The function of the law within Judaism has its Gentile counterpart in the workings of human conscience (Rom 2:14-15), so that everything said about the Jews in Romans "holds true for the Gentiles too" (1:250; also 261).

The Gentiles enter the convictional structure of Bultmann's Paul, then, at precisely the same point as the faith/works polarity, which is to say, at the foundational level. This polarity is to be understood as the essence of his Damascus experience: to accept the crucified Jesus as the expected Messiah meant, for Paul, that he

> was willing to acknowledge in the cross of Christ God's judgment upon his self-understanding up to that time—i.e., God's condemnation of his Jewish striving after righteousness by fulfilling the works of the law.[5]

Bultmann evidently assumed that prior to Damascus Paul understood the law ("his self-understanding up to that time") as a religion of works ("his Jewish striving after righteousness by fulfilling the law").

On the basis of the preceding, we can sketch out the structure of Paul's convictions as Bultmann perceives them. Leaving the Gentiles aside for the moment, we have the following:[6]

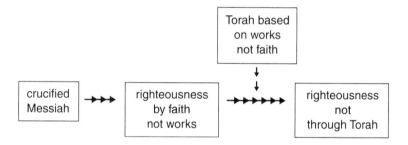

There are two distinct ways by which the Gentiles might enter this picture. One is as a logical consequence of this whole structure: if righteousness does not come through Torah, then the ground for the Jew-Gentile distinction has been removed, resulting in righteousness by faith for all.

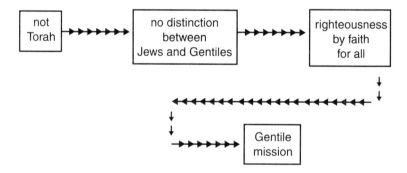

In this case, the Gentiles enter the picture as a result of a new conviction about the law; this convictional sequence is discussed in chapter 6.

The other possibility is that the foundational conviction, "righteousness by faith not works," is already universal in scope. That is, while Paul can conceive of two possible routes to righteousness—by works or by faith—he just takes it for granted that the routes apply equally to Jews and Gentiles in either case. Clearly this is Bultmann's understanding. For he reads Gal 5:11 ("if I am *still* preaching circumcision") as evidence for pre-Damascus "missionary activity among the heathen,"[7] thus implying that even when Paul believed that righteousness came by "works of the law," he saw this as the required route to righteousness for Gentiles as well. In such a reconstruction, then, Paul's universalism is a native conviction, carried over from his pre-Damascus world in a manner altered in substance but similar in form. He may have come to a new conviction about the terms on which righteousness is to be found; but in either case the terms apply to Jew and Gentile alike. Paul's convictional structure, then, as Bultmann understands it:

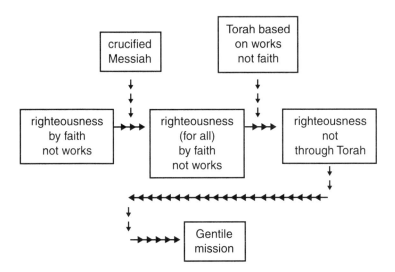

As was observed in chapter 1, this reconstruction of Paul's convictional structure has been effectively demolished by Wrede, Schweitzer, Sanders, and others, and there is no need to try to redo their work here. Rather, in what follows I will summarize and build on their analysis, paying special attention to the Gentiles. I begin with some general observations, then turn to a closer reading of the relevant texts.

First, as Sanders has exhaustively and conclusively demonstrated in *Paul and Palestinian Judaism,* if this is indeed how Paul conceived of To-

rah religion, then he has fundamentally misunderstood it.[8] For the literature of the period knows nothing of a law that functions as a means of
earning a status of righteousness before God. Far from being antithetical,
grace/faith and law/works are complementary: one obeys the Torah out
of a sense of gratitude for a covenantal relationship already and freely
established by God; the Torah was given as a means of responding to
God's grace, thus maintaining (never earning) one's place in the covenant
community.[9] If Paul's letters say what Bultmann hears them to be saying,
they represent a misperception of Judaism of monumental proportions.

Such a conclusion is not to be ruled out simply because it might be
unpalatable.[10] Nevertheless, there are general observations drawn from
the Pauline corpus as a whole that weigh in against it. First, it is striking
that the deadly danger posed by "works" seems to be present only in the
situation of Gentiles tempted to Judaize. Elsewhere (that is, outside of
Romans, Galatians, and Philippians 3), even where his subject matter
would have provided him plenty of opportunity to do so, Paul shows no
concern whatsoever to warn his Gentile converts about the dangers of
self-justification with respect to achievements relating to other moral systems. In virtually every letter, he himself issues commands, injunctions,
and exhortations of various kinds. Why, then, if Bultmann is right, does
Paul not balance these commands with a warning about the danger of
"works"? When he urges the Corinthians to contribute to the collection
project or to forgo marriage, why does he not add a cautionary statement
warning them not to suppose that by so doing they were earning a meritorious standing with God? Paul's silence here suggests strongly that his
works/faith contrast plays a much more limited role than Bultmann assumed.

Second, there is Schweitzer's astute observation that while ethics is an
obviously important concern for Paul, he makes no attempt to ground his
ethical concerns in juridical conceptions.[11] Even in Romans, when pressed
to demonstrate that his argument for justification by faith does not open
the door to immorality, he develops his response (chap. 6) on the basis of
the believer's participation in the death and resurrection of Christ, not on
that of faith and works. The result of both observations is that Paul develops his ethical teaching without reference, either negatively (in terms of
warnings of the dangers of works) or positively (in terms of a derivation
from justification by faith), to this supposedly foundational set of categories.

Third, where Gentile Judaizing is not in view, Paul can quite happily
use the vocabulary of "works" and "boasting"—his supposed bête
noire—in a positive sense, both of himself and of others. Christians are

to excel "in every good work";[12] Paul "boasts" not only of his missionary success generally,[13] but also of his material self-sufficiency (!) that allows him to be financially independent of his churches.[14] His statement in Gal 6:4—"But let each one test his own work (ἔργον), and then his reason to boast (καύχημα) will be in himself alone and not in his neighbor"—is enough all by itself to put skids under the notion that what drives his thought and mission is a fundamental rejection of meritorious achievement. That the statement appears in Galatians adds grease to the skids!

It is in this context that we are to read 1 Cor 1:29: "so that no one might boast in the presence of God." Bultmann uses the passage as grounds for his universalizing of the problem of works and boasting,[15] but the text is too slender to bear the weight. The antithetical pairing in the whole passage (vv. 18-31) is not between one subjective attitude (faith) and another (boasting), but between one objective ground of salvation (the cross of Christ) and anything else. As v. 31 indicates, as long as boasting is "in the Lord," Paul is all for it (also 2 Cor 10:17).[16]

The preceding considerations create the strong suspicion that the faith/works antithesis is a secondary formulation, a way of defending the law-free Gentile mission against Jewish or Jewish-Christian objections, rather than the convictional ground for that mission in the first place. If this suspicion is borne out by a closer consideration of the relevant passages (which indeed will be the conclusion of the discussion to follow), then we shall have to look for that convictional ground elsewhere.

### Gal 2:16—3:29

The passage begins on a promising note for a Bultmannian type of reading: "We know that a person is justified not by the works of the law but through faith in Jesus Christ" (2:16). The statement appears to take it for granted that righteousness is a generic human category—"a *person* (ἄνθρωπος) is justified"—and formulates the route to righteousness in terms of a contrast: not by works of law, but by faith in Christ. Similar contrasts—works/faith (3:2,5,10-12), law/faith (3:24-25), law/promise (of faith; 3:15-18,21-22)—reappear throughout the passage.

To be sure, a closer look at the statement in 2:16 raises the possibility that the contrast has been overstated in the NRSV rendering cited above; ἐὰν μή usually has exceptive rather than adversative force, which if taken in this sense would produce a less contrastive reading: "we believe that a person is not justified by works of law *except through* faith in Christ."[17] The NRSV itself now indicates in a footnote the possibility—increasingly accepted among scholars—that the faith in question is not that of the individual believer but that of Christ himself: "the faithfulness of Jesus

Christic."[18] Nevertheless, given that at least by the end of v. 16, works and faith do emerge as sharply contrasted alternatives,[19] and that the believer's faith in Jesus does come into view in the next clause in the verse, Bultmann's reading of the passage is not to be eliminated at the outset.

In such a reading, the genitives (of law/in Christ) recede into the background, the stress falling instead on the preceding nouns (works/faith). These terms are taken as indicative of the essential nature of the contrast under discussion in all that follows; that is, what is at issue is a contrast between two possible human attitudes, those of works and of its opposite, faith. The other contrast—law/Christ—is taken to be derivative, arising from the fact that the law is essentially a works system while Christ represents faith or somehow makes it possible.

Those who believe this to be the shape of Paul's underlying convictions see 3:11-12 as the point where it breaks through to the surface of the argument most clearly. Here Paul grounds the conclusion "no one is justified by the law"[20] on the propositions (1) that the righteous person is one who lives by faith and (2) that the law is based not on faith but on works, the latter apparently defined in terms of "doing" (ποιήσας). In keeping with the putative structure of Paul's convictions concerning the Gentile mission as analyzed above, the underlying logic of the argument here would be constructed as follows:

1. There is a single path to righteousness for all, Jew and Gentile alike (unstated premise).
2. That path rests on the attitude of faith rather than the doing of meritorious works (v. 11).
3. The law is based on works, not faith (v. 12).
4. Thus righteousness is available to Gentiles through faith, and not through doing what the law prescribes. Specifically, the Galatians should abandon all desire to come "under the law" (4:21) by submitting to circumcision (5:2).

But it is virtually impossible to account for the actual argument of 2:16—3:29 (or 2:16—5:12, for that matter) on the basis of such logic. Several observations lead to this conclusion; I will begin with the immediate context of 3:11-12. The first thing to note is that while the argument in these verses leads very quickly to a conclusion concerning the salvation of the Gentiles (v. 14), it gets there by an argumentative route quite different from that described above. If Paul's rhetoric were governed by this sort of logic, we would expect that he would have summed up the argument in vv. 6-12 (that "blessing" comes through "faith" while the "law" brings a "curse") with a statement to the effect that Christ came to reveal the efficacy of the one and the dead-end nature of the other. To put the words in his own mouth, "And so I say, to Jew and Gentile alike: faith brings blessing, works brings a curse; so choose faith." Instead, the conclusion in v. 14 depends on the premise that only when those who are subject to the curse are redeemed from it (by Christ in his death) will the promised blessing of the Spirit be able to pass to the Gentiles.[21] Since the curse seems to stem not from the "doing" of the law (works) but from the failure to "do" what the law requires (so v. 10), the path from the propositions in vv. 11-12 to Gentile salvation seems to lead through the territory of sin—sin not in Bultmann's terms as "man's intention of becoming righteous by keeping the Law and thereby having his boast" but as "evil deeds" that contravene the law's requirements.[22] We must defer any attempt to reconstruct the logic of vv. 10-14, noting here only that in doing so we will need to address the tension between the bracketing statements of vv. 10 and 13 on the one hand (where the problem with the law apparently stems from an inability to keep it) and the bracketed statements of vv. 11-12 on the other (where the problem seems to concern its principle of operation even where it is kept). But if the convictional links between Paul's faith/works language and the law-free mission to the Gentiles are as Bultmann understands them to be, Paul missed a golden opportunity at the end of v. 12 to make this clear.

This observation, valid as far as it goes, may not go all that far, given our basic assumption of a distinction between surface rhetoric and underlying convictions. For we need to leave open the possibility that vv. 11-12 are nonetheless to be seen as an outcrop of bedrock conviction, the rest of the argument consisting largely of loose soil and surface vegetation. But other considerations render this unlikely.

One of these leads on directly from vv. 10-14. Not only are the faith/works statements of vv. 11-12 sandwiched between other statements linking the law inevitably with a curse (vv. 10, 13). But the statements in vv. 10-14 themselves represent just two of a whole series of arguments in defense of the conclusion that the Galatian Gentiles should not come under the law by submitting to circumcision. In addition to the arguments in vv. 10-14—that the law brings a curse (vv. 10, 13) and that the law is based on works, not faith (vv. 11-12)—Paul argues that if justification were possible through the law, Christ's death would be pointless (2:21); that faith by itself had been demonstrably sufficient for the reception of the Spirit (3:1-5); that the law came later than the promise to Abraham (3:15-18); that the law was given through angels (3:19); and that the law was a temporary "pedagogical" measure (3:21-25). At the surface of the argument, then, the constrast between faith and works appears as just one of a dazzling kaleidoscope of arguments. To change the metaphor, the argument of vv. 11-12 may simply be one of an array of spokes used to support the rim (the goal of the argument, that the Gentile Galatians are not to submit to circumcision), rather than the hub of the wheel itself.

In response, it might be argued that the presence of works/faith language at the launching of the argument (2:16) is enough to identify 3:11-12 as the hub. But is it indeed the case that the contrast introduced in 2:16 is really one of two different human stances or dispositions (namely, meritorious doing versus humble believing)? If so, then in appealing to Abraham Paul paints himself into a tight rhetorical corner. For if the hub of his argument is that the key to salvation is the cultivation of a particular attitude, and if that attitude was possible in the case of an Abraham who lived long before Christ appeared on the scene, what need is there for a Christ to appear on the scene at all? Christ becomes just another spoke on the wheel, so that Paul's insistence on Christ (for example, 2:21; 5:2) is an arbitrary and unnecessary jump from one spoke to another.

It is possible that these apparent difficulties in logic reflect tensions in Paul's basic convictions themselves, that he holds firmly *both* to Christ *and* to faith (in the Bultmannian sense) as necessary and sufficient prerequuisites for righteousness, without ever working out the inherent tensions between them. The bumpy rhetorical ride in this case would be the result of a wheel trying to rotate around two hubs (if one can conceive of such a thing!). The possibility will need to be explored more fully in connection with Romans 4, where he appears to move even farther out from a faith/works hub before jumping to Christ (v. 24).

In the case of Galatians, however, there are good reasons—the appearances of 3:11-12 notwithstanding—to doubt that the faith/works contrast introduced in 2:16 has to do fundamentally with mutually exclusive *human* stances and dispositions. The contrast is between Christ and law, not faith and works; between the second of each of the noun pairings, not the first. To put it another way, 2:16 sets up a contrast between two objective means of righteousness—Christ or Torah—rather than between two subjective human attitudes.

This is certainly the case if, as is increasingly being argued and as I myself believe, Ἰησοῦ Χριστοῦ (of Jesus Christ) in 2:16 and 3:22 (along with τοῦ υἱοῦ τοῦ θεοῦ [of the Son of God] in 2:20) is a subjective genitive, denoting Christ's own faith or faithfulness. But even if the traditional reading of the phrase be accepted, there is nothing in the passage—apart from the example of Abraham, to which we will turn in a moment—to suggest that Paul conceived of faith in a nonchristocentric sense—faith in the abstract, or faith as a general stance toward God without reference to Christ. First, in 2:16-21, identified by Betz as the *propositio* of the argument,[23] wherever the vocabulary of "faith" or "righteousness" is used,[24] it is explicitly linked with Christ. And "Christ" appears in three of the remaining clauses or sentences. The christocentric nature of the argument for which this is the *propositio* could not have been more emphatically set out.

Further, there is the synonymous use of "faith" and "Christ" in 3:23-25: "before faith came / until Christ [came][25] / now that faith has come." The case of Abraham notwithstanding, Paul presents "faith" as an option that becomes possible only with the arrival of Christ and, indeed, is so tightly bound up with Christ that the arrival of one is the arrival of the other.

Finally, there is the curious construction οἱ ἐκ πίστεως (the ones of faith) that Paul uses as he brings Abraham into the argument: since Abraham was justified by faith, "the ones of faith" are "sons of Abraham" (3:7; also v. 9). As Hays has observed, if what Paul meant to say was that those who believed/had faith were Abraham's offspring, his construction is unnecessarily awkward;[26] it would have been more natural to describe them as οἱ πιστεύοντες (the believers). The construction that actually appears has the effect of identifying the group as characterized somehow by faith,[27] but without specifying this characteristic any further. The faith in question may be that of the group members. But the fact that "faith" is used in the wider context to refer not only to the activity of believers,[28] but also (perhaps) to Christ's own faithfulness and (certainly) to the new state of affairs ushered in by Christ (3:23-25), means that this cannot be its only or exclusive sense. Indeed, it is probable that the awkward phraseology was chosen precisely because of its vagueness. That is, as Hays has suggested, it provided Paul with a condensed but convenient way of designating the new group brought into being by means of a complex process, centered on Christ and characterized by faith at each stage, a process which Paul accordingly refers to as ἡ πίστις, "the faith."

But what of Abraham, to whose family "those of faith" are said to belong? Is it not the case that Abraham's faith was patently nonchristocentric, so that the appeal to his example in 3:6-9 firmly establishes faith—with God as its object and works as its defining negative counterpart—as the essential prerequisite for righteousness?

Certainly Abraham is introduced into the argument as one who exhibited faith in God, and whose faith was reckoned as righteousness (3:6).

But we need to pay careful attention to the way in which Paul uses the example of Abraham in the argument. First, the inference drawn in v. 7: "know, then,[29] that those of faith are sons of Abraham." Paul's point is not that faith is therefore the route to righteousness for all, Abraham functioning as a model of justifying belief; but instead that "those of faith" (οἱ ἐκ πίστεως) are "sons" of Abraham, Abraham functioning as the patriarch of an extended family. The question on which the example of Abraham is being brought to bear, then, is not in the first instance "How does one get to be accounted righteous?" but "How does one get to be part of Abraham's family?"

Second, the theme introduced in v. 7 reappears in v. 29, as Paul brings the argument to this point to a kind of preliminary conclusion: "If you are of Christ, you are Abraham's seed, heirs according to promise." This suggests strongly that we see vv. 6-7 not as a complete argument in itself, nor simply as the introduction to vv. 8-9, but instead as the thesis statement for the whole argument to follow.[30] This means that any interpretation of the Abraham argument needs to take fully into account the christocentric nature of the argument from 3:13 on, and in particular the absolutely central role of Christ in v. 29 as the means by which Gentile believers are part of Abraham's "seed."

Still, the fact remains that in vv. 6-9 Paul can declare that Gentiles are part of Abraham's family and share in his blessing, without mentioning Christ at all. How does Paul understand the faith of Abraham? J. Christiaan Beker's analysis of the argument in 3:6-29 provides a convenient anvil on which to hammer out an answer to this question. He makes the astute observation that the passage contains three different and apparently distinct rhetorical linkages between Abraham and the Gentiles, constituted, respectively, by (1) the faith exhibited by each (vv. 6-9); (2) the work of Christ as "enabler," in that he removes the curse and so allows the blessing to flow (vv. 13-14); and (3) Christ himself as the sole (but inclusive) "seed" of Abraham (vv. 16, 26-29).[31]

But in keeping with his "coherent center but contingent interpretation" framework for understanding Paul, he argues further that we have to do here with three disjunctive arguments, linked only by their common conclusion, but otherwise disconnected and not to be harmonized. We must understand Paul's arguments as determined by the contingencies of the situation, says Beker. Faced with the necessity of countering the position of the rival teachers in Galatia, Paul develops several utilitarian lines of argumentation that need to be understood with reference to their common rhetorical goal rather than to any coherent theological schema within which they each find their place. While this would mean on the one hand that the argument concerning Abraham's faith does not necessarily tell us much about Paul's convictions, it would mean on the other that in vv. 6-9 he does attempt to link Gentiles with Abraham on the sole basis of faith.

Since Romans 4 begins with an extended discussion of the structure of Abraham's faith, and thus represents at least a prima facie attempt to treat him as a model believer, Beker's analysis needs to be taken seriously. But one wonders whether he is reading Galatians 3 too much in the light of Romans 4.[32] Nowhere in these verses is faith itself thematized as the connecting link. Instead, we find loaded constructions that seem to point ahead to the more developed (and christological) arguments to follow. One of these is ἐν σοί (in you) in v. 8. The gospel proclaimed beforehand to Abraham is not that *like you* the Gentiles will be justified by faith, but that *in you* the Gentiles will be blessed. The relationship is not analogous, but corporate, a theme stated more fully in the "in Christ Jesus" statements of vv. 14, 26-29. The other is οἱ ἐκ πίστεως (those of faith) in vv. 7 and 9. As noted already, this phrase designating the group of Gentile believers seems to have been chosen to avoid an identification formulated simply on the basis of faith, thus pointing ahead to the whole complex story of the arrival of "faith" rehearsed in vv. 13-25. Although there are other themes to be explored before our interpretation of Galatians 3 is complete, I agree with Hays against Beker that 3:6-29 constitutes a single, story-based argument, an argument stated most fully and clearly in the "participationist soteriology" of vv. 16, 26-29.[33] In sum, while it is Abraham's own faith that sets this story in motion and elicits the divine promise of blessing for the Gentiles, it is only as this story of faith "comes" to its conclusion in Christ (vv. 23-25) that, by virtue of their own faith in Christ, Gentiles can become part of the community of blessing designated as "those of faith."

There is no foundation, then, for the position that Paul's purpose in the argument of Gal 2:16—3:29 is to argue for one human attitude toward God (faith) over against another (works). These terms are catchwords for more complex entities, entities that come more clearly into focus as the argument unfolds. But what can we learn from the way Paul constructs his argument about the nature of his underlying convictions? The question can be posed in terms of the connection between the way in which the argument begins and the way it ends. Paul begins (as we have already seen) with the proposition that a person is justified not from works of law but through faith in (of) Christ, and ends with the proposition that those who are in Christ belong to the seed of Abraham. The intervening argument, then, establishes a correspondence of some kind between two sets of terms:

| | |
|---|---|
| righteousness | membership in Abraham's family |
| by faith | by being in Christ |
| not by works | not by circumcision and law adherence |

The Reformation view of Paul saw the first set of terms as foundational, and the second as its corollary in a specific set of circumstances: Paul's basic belief is that people are justified by faith, so that, derivatively, believing Gentiles can be said to be part of Abraham's family. This position cannot be maintained. But a more adequate description of the relationship between these corresponding terms requires—and here Beker is right on target—that the specific set of circumstances be brought into the discussion. While various aspects of the situation prompting Galatians are open to scholarly debate, there is general agreement that Paul brings Abraham into his argument in response to an appeal to Abraham made already by the rival teachers in Galatia.[34] This is fully understandable. The fact that Genesis 17 declares circumcision to be the unconditional prerequisite for membership in Abraham's "seed" means that the story of Abraham provided much more evident support for the position of the rival teachers than for that of Paul. The latter's lengthy discussion of Abraham and his "seed" in 3:6-29 and 4:21-31 should be seen as his attempt to defend his own position on territory staked out by his rivals in Galatia.

This has three consequences for the question at hand. First, it suggests that we understand the terms in which Paul's opening statement is formulated ("A person is justified not by works of law but by faith in/of Christ") as tactical rather than fundamental, as the result of a strategic choice rather than as a window into his basic convictions. The terms on which he presents this statement are highly instructive; he introduces it not as his own unique position for which he will argue but as a proposition to which he expects any Jewish Christian to assent ("we Jews know . . .")[35] and from which he will develop the argument to follow. The terms righteousness and faith are chosen not necessarily because they reflect his fundamental conviction, but because they are present in the Genesis account and thus provide an opening for a christological rereading of the Abraham story that will blunt the impact of the argument of the rival teachers.[36] "Works" is to be seen not as a categorical term describing the negative of two antipodal stances toward God, but as a pejorative way of referring to circumcision and other "ethnic identity markers," as Dunn calls them,[37] when these are imposed on Gentiles as conditions for entry into the community of salvation. Paul's fundamental convictions appear much more clearly at the end of this section than at the beginning: salvation is to be found in Christ; therefore[38] Jewish ethnic identity markers are not to be imposed on Gentiles as a membership condition.

Second, following from this, it can be observed that covenantal nomism is the explicit framework within which the debate over "righteousness" is being carried out. Righteousness is understood—both by Paul and his interlocutors—in precisely the same covenantal way, as a membership term describing the status of those who belong to the community of God's people, a community living in the promise of God's eschatological salvation, a community described by all participants in the debate as the family of Abraham.[39] Far from misunderstanding covenantal nomism, Paul demonstrates through the rhetoric of the epistle that he understands it completely—understands it, but rejects it. Or, more precisely, Paul accepts its form (righteousness as a way of designating membership in the community of salvation) but rejects its substance (Christ, not the ethnic identity markers prescribed by the Torah, as the community entrance requirement).

But this leads, finally, to the use of Abraham as a designation for this community of salvation. Paul feels constrained to argue not only that believing Gentiles, like Abraham, are righteous, but further that they are thereby members of Abraham's family. Thus the premises shared by Paul and his opponents in the debate include not only the general definition of righteousness as community membership, but also the specific designation of that community as the family of Abraham, together with the specific assumption that Gentiles need to become part of that family to be able to participate in the promised salvation. What is to be made of this shared set of premises? Is it just a product of the high-stakes rhetorical situation, Paul not wanting to concede an inch of territory to his rivals? Or might it indicate something about his own basic assumptions about the Gentiles?

To be sure, the issue was raised in these terms by the rival teachers and Paul's argument needs to be seen as a response. But was this his only rhetorical option? As we have seen, within first century Judaism as a whole there were ways of conceiving of the salvation of the Gentiles that did not require them to become full members of Abraham's "seed" through proselytism. Paul appears to share with his interlocutors an assumption (about Abraham and the Gentiles) that gets him into difficult—but easily avoidable—argumentative territory. Similar factors are at work in Romans 4, where Paul's manner of argumentation puts this shared assumption into even clearer light. To move our analysis forward, we shall leave Galatians for now and turn our attention to this related passage.

### Romans 3:27—4:25

In Romans 4 Paul introduces Abraham as a case study for the conclusions to which he has arrived in 3:27-31. The sequence of the argument as it unfolds in chapter 4 parallels the sequence of the propositions in 3:27-30, a declaration (1) that justification is by faith apart from works of the law (3:27-28; 4:2-8) followed by a statement (2) that God will justify believing but uncircumcised Gentiles on the basis of their faith (3:29-30; 4:9-17a). The question being addressed in this chapter, then, is whether this *sequence* reflects an underlying logical *consequence*, especially at the level of Paul's convictions. Does Paul understand proposition (2) to be a corollary implied by a more basic conviction found in proposition (1)?

Bultmann's reading of Paul finds its most substantial support in this passage.[40] In vv. 4-8, works, presented as the defining opposite to faith, are themselves defined as accomplishments that provide grounds for boasting and, as it were, present God with an invoice for payment due. Faith, by contrast, is something exhibited by the ungodly, to whom God owes nothing. Further, while Galatians 3 contains only the bare mention of Abraham's faith, its nonchristocentric character remaining implicit and submerged, in Romans 4 we encounter a full description of the structure of his faith, as it is exhibited in his response to the divine promise of offspring (vv. 17b-22). While its nonchristocentric character is no more explicit here than in Galatians 3, it is much more readily apparent. Finally, even though Abraham functions here again as the patriarch of a family of believers and not simply as a model believer, parallels are drawn frequently enough between his faith and that of the members of his family (vv. 11-12, 16) to lead the reader toward the conclusion that what it takes to become a member of Abraham's family is faith itself, defined not with respect to its object (Christ)[41] but with respect to its opposite (works).

Thus while the goals to which the arguments of Galatians 3 and Romans 4 are directed can be formulated in similar terms (faith rather than circumcision and law as the prerequisite for Gentiles to be reckoned as righteous, or as members of Abraham's family), the routes which they take to that goal are strikingly distinct. In Galatians 3—at least by the end of the chapter—Christ functions as the essential link between the Gentile believer and Abraham. In Romans 4, the christological element is virtually absent; Christ is introduced awkwardly almost as an afterthought in vv. 24-25, and faith in God provides the sole and direct link between the two.[42] Does Romans 4 provide us then with evidence for the convictional structure described above, that is, justification by faith (not works) as Paul's fundamental conviction, with the justification of Gentiles by faith (not law) as a necessary corollary? A careful analysis of the argument in the chapter is revealing, not only because it demonstrates that the answer to this question is no, but also because it provides a clear indication of the operation of some fundamental convictions under the surface of the rhetoric.

We begin our analysis with another point of contrast between Romans 4 and Galatians 3, namely, the positive status assigned to a group of identifiably Jewish believers in vv. 11b-12 and 16. In each passage we have to do with two clans within Abraham's family of faith—uncircumcised Gentile believers ("all those who believe without being circumcised" [v. 11]; "the one who is of the faith of Abraham" [v. 16]) and circumcised Jewish believers ("the circumcised who follow the footsteps of Abraham's faith" [v. 12];[43] "the one who is of the law" [v. 16]).[44] Thus in apparent contrast with Galatians, circumcision and law have an ongoing significance as the identity marker for one segment of Abraham's "seed."

This has a major, negative impact on the cogency of Paul's argument here. In vv. 2-11a Paul develops two interrelated lines of argumentation in support of his position on the inclusion of the Gentiles, one based on faith and works (vv. 2-8), the other on the temporal priority of justification over circumcision in the case of Abraham (vv. 9-11a). But in each case, the legitimacy extended to the distinctively Jewish clan within Abraham's family of believers in vv. 11b-12, 16 renders the argument ineffectual unless one is prepared to assume what is to be proved.

First, in vv. 2-8 Paul argues that Abraham was declared righteous on the basis of faith, not works (presumably works of the law, at least by extension; cf. vv. 13-15). But from this one would be able to infer that believing Gentiles can be declared righteous apart from the law only if one went through an intervening step in which law and faith are in some real and universal way mutually exclusive. As soon as he allows the combination "faith plus law" for one segment of Abraham's family, he has no ground for denying it to the other, unless one assumes that it is inappropriate for Gentiles to come under the law, which, of course is the very thing he is trying to establish.

Similarly with the temporal priority of righteousness to circumcision in vv. 9-11a. Since circumcision can act as a legitimate seal of righteousness not only for Abraham but also for Jewish believers, the priority of righteousness over circumcision supports the inclusion of uncircumcised Gentile believers only if one assumes that circumcision, appropriate for Jews, is illegitimate for Gentiles—again, the very thing to be proved. As soon as he is prepared to allow some legitimacy to law and circumcision for one group of believers, he has left himself with no real answer to the argument that faith should be followed by circumcision—as it was for Abraham—for all who want to be part of Abraham's family.

Paul's readiness to make concessions in the direction of identifiably Jewish believers (if concessions they be) results in a short-circuiting of his Abraham argument. But before considering the implications of this, we need to recognize another, equally serious problem with the logic of the argument, this time with respect to the argument from scripture.

"What does the scripture say?" With this rhetorical question in Rom 4:3, Paul sets off on his breathtaking rereading of the Genesis story of Abraham. While the ensuing argument is confusing in many respects, one thing at least is clear: Paul wants to argue on the basis of Genesis 15 and 17 that uncircumcised but believing Gentiles can call Abraham "father" (vv. 11, 16-18), and thus are to be numbered among his "seed" (σπέρμα; vv. 13, 16, 18) and "heirs" (κληρονόμος; vv. 13, 14). But it is just as clear to anyone familiar with the Genesis story that such an argument finds no ready ally in the text itself. For what *does* the scripture say? Abraham and his "seed" (σπέρμα appears seven times in the LXX of Gen 17:7-19) are, according to God's command, to be identified by circumcision; any male not circumcised is thereby cut off from the family (עם [MT: people]; γένος [LXX: race]), and thus excluded from the inheritance (cf. v. 8).

Paul is a consummate tactician, and a pliant reader is easily swept along by the dazzling exegetical moves by which he subordinates the circumcision of Genesis 17 to the righteousness of Genesis 15, all under the overarching banner of the promise that Abraham would be the father of "many Gentiles" (ἐθνῶν; Gen 17:5, cited in vv. 17 and 18). But, as in Galatians 3, the impression of cogency is created only by keeping significant aspects of Genesis 17 out of the arena of discussion. If Paul's interlocutor were allowed to draw attention to the tight link between "seed" and "circumcision" in Gen 17:9-14, it would, as Ziesler has observed, "destroy his argument."[45]

Neither the logical difficulties confronting Paul's argument nor the audacity of his response have gone unnoticed by commentators. Typically, however, the contratextual nature of Paul's argument has been overlooked at its sharpest point, and attention is directed to less central matters. Often, for example, Paul is said to be arguing against a "Jewish theologoumenon"[46] or a "traditional Jewish argument"[47] having to do with proselytism, as if Jewish insistence on circumcision for proselytes had no exegetical foundation. Or, where scriptural objections to Paul's argument do enter the picture, it is often in the form of an inference from Abraham

("If circumcision could serve as a sign of Abraham's faith, why not of later believers?")[48] rather than the explicit scriptural injunction that Abraham's "seed" be circumcised as a condition of membership. Only occasionally does this explicit injunction in Gen 17:9-14 receive explicit attention.[49]

The question with which we began was whether Rom 3:27—4:25 provides evidence that the faith/works contrast was the fundamental conviction underlying Paul's concern for the Gentiles; that is, whether the logical structure is one of a basic conviction, "justification by faith, not by works," which has as its corollary "faith, not circumcision and law, as the prerequisite for justification for the Gentiles," with Abraham being brought in as a biblical example to prove the point. While several aspects of vv. 2-8 might point in this direction, the rhetorical surface of the argument shows such signs of strain as to suggest that the convictional forces at work underneath the surface are quite differently arranged. More specifically, the choices Paul makes as he develops his Abraham argument suggest strongly that his major concerns have to do with Abraham and Gentile Christians rather than with faith and works.

First, as was observed, Paul's concession to Jewish believers in vv. 11-12, 16—that is, his willingness to recognize a continuing role for law and circumcision in defining a specific subgroup within Abraham's family of believers—serves to cut his faith/works argument of vv. 2-8 off at the root. The goal of his argument is clear and must be seen as a firm conviction: Gentile believers are fully acceptable to God on the basis of their faith, so that law and circumcision are not to be imposed on them as prerequisites. But his willingness (even if inadvertent) to compromise the logic of the faith/works argument suggests that this argument is not foundational but tactical, a device used to defend the legitimacy of Gentile believers against certain lines of objection rather than the basis for openness to the Gentiles in the first place.

The fact that the example of Abraham as Paul develops it does not do what he wants it to do but simply begs the question suggests that here as in Galatians Abraham is introduced into the discussion not by Paul himself but by his opponents in debate. Attempting to establish his credentials in Rome over against Jewish or Jewish Christian criticism of his gospel for the Gentiles, Paul finds himself fighting on turf staked out by his opponents. They have appealed to the Abraham story, drawing on the already existing tradition of Abraham as "father of proselytes" and arguing from Genesis 17 that circumcision is the necessary entrance requirement for membership in Abraham's family.[50] Forced to engage on ground not of his own choosing, Paul makes the best of an unpromising situation, taking advantage of those few footholds available to him in the text, namely, the words faith, righteousness, and Gentiles.[51]

The broad rhetorical framework of Romans 4, then, is as follows: Paul's fundamental claim is that uncircumcised Gentile believers enjoy full and legitimate status before God (which he refers to as righteousness) on the basis of their faith. He has to defend this claim in a situation where others are defining legitimacy and righteousness in terms of Abraham's "seed" (Genesis 17), and thus are positing circumcision as a prerequisite for Gentiles. Because of the concurrence of faith, righteousness and Gentiles in the biblical story of Abraham, he develops the faith/works argument as a means of turning Abraham into a witness for the defense. To put it another way, the argument of Romans 4 is grounded on 3:29-30[52] rather than 3:27-28[53] (or, for that matter, 3:31);[54] as has already been observed, the statement about the Gentiles in 3:29-30 is presented not as a logical inference from the preceding one about faith and works (v. 28) but as a parallel formulation in different but analogous terms.[55]

If this is the lay of the rhetorical land, then the nonchristological nature of faith in Romans 4 is not to be taken with any great seriousness. Paul concludes the chapter with a statement that is as categorical in its restriction of justifying faith to *Christian* believers as it is awkward in its transition from what precedes (vv. 24-25). The very awkwardness of the transition[56] points to the convictional forces at work beneath the surface; while the constraints of the rhetorical situation compelled Paul to develop a line of argumentation threatening to pierce the hull of his christological vessel,[57] before the threat was too far advanced his christocentric convictions came into play to deflect the thrust. The faith of Paul's Gentile believers—and Jewish believers as well[58]—is thus clearly Christian in its nature and object.

Despite differences between Romans and Galatians, then, a similar set of convictions appears to underlie the arguments of each. But Romans 4 allows us to press a question merely noted in passing in the discussion of Galatians 3, having to do with the assertion that uncircumcised Gentile believers are members of Abraham's family. In both rhetorical situations, Paul appears to share with his interlocutors the assumption that membership in Abraham's family is necessary for the full legitimacy of Gentile believers. What do we make of this assumption? Is it rhetorically driven, simply a case of Paul not wanting to concede any argumentative ground, even ground staked out by his opponents in debate? Or does it tell us something more fundamental about Paul?

The answer to this question emerges from the recognition that Paul had other options open to him. The strategy he adopts is the result of argumentative choices, perhaps subconscious, but nevertheless reflective of some basic convictions that shape the argument. He could have avoided the tricky terrain of seed and paternity entirely, leaving that to his opponents. But he seems to have been constrained to choose otherwise.

As we have seen, the Judaism of Paul's day provided other options besides that of full proselytism for those interested in the Gentiles and their inclusion in "salvation." Were he so disposed, Paul could have argued on the basis of eschatological pilgrimage patterns, countering Genesis 17 with passages such as Isa 25:6-10a or Zech 8:20-23,[59] which envisage Gentile participation in salvation without any mention of Abraham. Alternatively, he could have followed the example of Ananias (in Adiabene) and others within contemporary Judaism who were prepared to differentiate between "salvation" and "conversion," and to entertain the possibility of pious Gentiles being acceptable to God—being "righteous"—without becoming full proselytes. In response to those who wanted his Gentile Christians to become proselytes to Judaism, he could have argued simply that in Christ God had provided a means for Gentiles to be righteous as *Gentiles,* without having to become part of Abraham's seed. Rather than challenging the premise of his interlocutor—that righteousness and salvation are possible for Gentiles only through membership in Abraham's family—Paul demonstrates by his refusal of this simpler option that he is equally committed to it.

But this choice of strategy can be put into even sharper relief. The "righteous Gentile" option is present not only in the religious culture generally, but also, at least potentially, in the specific text under discussion. While the story in Genesis 12–22 has as its focus Abraham and his "seed," the "nations" are also present in a positive way, especially in the LXX, the text read by Paul, which translates the hithpael (Gen 22:18; 26:4) or niphal (Gen 12:3; 18:18; 28:14) of ברך (to bless) with the passive; for example, Gen 18:18: "in [Abraham] shall all the nations of the earth be blessed." While the nature of the blessing remains unspecified in the text, it is clear that the nations are blessed *as nations.* Their blessing is not dependent on their being circumcised and becoming part of Abraham's "seed"; indeed, the idea of proselytism is foreign to the story.

The text under debate, then, would have readily lent itself to a "righteous Gentile" reading.[60] Had he so desired, Paul could have avoided the circumcision-seed issue entirely. He could simply have argued that in Christ the promised blessing of the nations has been realized,[61] a blessing coming to the believing Gentiles as ἔθνη (Gentiles) not as σπέρμα (seed). Alternatively, he could have used the ambiguous reference to Abraham as the "father of a multitude of nations" (Gen 17:5)[62]—the one "nations" text cited in Romans 4—in a framework in which this multitude of Gentiles was differentiated from Abraham's family of seed and heirs as defined by the covenantal sign of circumcision. Instead, he argues against the text, turning uncircumcised ἔθνη (Gentiles) into σπέρμα (seed) by sheer force of will. The very difficulty of the argument provides evidence of how firmly Paul is committed to the belief that Gentile Christians are members of Abraham's family. In other words, we are in touch here with a fundamental conviction.

As in the case of a sailboat tacking into the wind, the stubborn progression of Paul's argument against the drift of both logic and scripture provides evidence of other forces at work beneath the surface. It is the combined force of his underlying convictions that drives the rhetoric of Romans 4 in such difficult directions. On the basis of the preceding analysis, we can identify four such forces in particular: (1) faith in (what God has done through) Christ is the sole entrance requirement for the community of salvation; (2) circumcision (and any other Torah-based ethnic identity marker) is not to be imposed on the Gentiles as a condition of membership; (3) believing Gentiles are of necessity to be seen as full members of the family of Abraham's "seed" and "heirs"; and (4) an identifiably Jewish group, differentiated from Gentiles by traditional means (including circumcision), still occupies a legitimate place within the community of believers. The first three of these clearly are basic convictions, with "righteousness by faith not by works" to be seen as a contextually shaped argument mounted in their defense ("righteousness" "by faith" "not by works" functioning as particular articulations of [3], [1], and [2] respectively). The fourth, seemingly at odds with Paul's frequent assertions of "no difference" between Jews and Gentiles, will require further consideration below.[63]

### Romans 9:30—10:4

The final passage that might lend itself to a Bultmann-style explanation of Paul's concern for the Gentiles is Rom 9:30—10:4.[64] Once again we encounter faith and works as contrasting routes toward the goal of righteousness, in a context dealing with the righteousness of Gentiles. With its "What shall we say then?" v. 30 begins a section where Paul reflects on the state of affairs described in 9:6-29 that, as it has turned out, God's "people"(v. 25)[65] is made up of only a remnant of Israel together with those called from the Gentiles (v. 24).

The passage contains a number of well-known cruxes, one of which has been the subject of a full monograph.[66] For our present purposes the most economical point of entry is v. 32, especially as interpreted by

C. E. B. Cranfield.[67] The statement is notoriously elliptical; but, sounding a note not heard before,[68] it seems to suggest that Israel's striving for righteousness through the law[69] would have been successful if they had approached it from a standpoint of faith rather than from one of works. In Cranfield's words, "had they pursued it ἐκ πίστεως [from faith] instead of ὡς ἐξ ἔργων [as from works], they would have been doing what was required."[70] If faith and works are given their traditional Reformation sense, as Cranfield does, the text can be understood as saying that the law is not inherently a system of works, that all along it had been possible for Israel to have approached it in faith, and that if it had done so it would have achieved righteousness. Paul condemns Israel "not on account of the *fact that* it had pursued the law," but "for the *way in which* it had pursued the law."[71] "Had Israel pursued the law *in a different way*"—so Sanders summarizes this position—"not as external deeds to be done to establish self-righteousness, but in reliance on the gift of God, fulfilling the law would have produced righteousness—apart from Christ."[72]

Read in this way, the text seems to provide support for the view that Paul's basic concern is a generic human one—faith and works as two human stances equally possible for Jew and Gentile alike—so that Paul's concern for the Gentiles is to be seen as a logical outworking of a generically human category and conviction. But, on closer inspection, the way he develops his argument in these verses makes it impossible to construct the convictional linkage this way. The situation is analogous to that in chapter 4, except that what was a reality in the case of Abraham is only a hypothetical possibility in the case of Israel. In each case, one of the firmest elements of Paul's convictions about the Gentiles, that they are not to undergo circumcision or otherwise accept those parts of the law differentiating Jew from Gentile, remains unexplained. For if by "works" Paul means only a legalistic misunderstanding of the law,[73] so that it is possible to pursue the law ἐκ πίστεως (from faith), as Cranfield understands these terms, then Paul has no grounds to deny to the Gentiles such a faith-based adherence to the law. The fact that he does so, and with such vehemence, suggests that the origin and nature of his Gentile convictions are to be found elsewhere.

In any case it is quite unlikely that Paul's faith/works criticism of Israel in 9:30-32 is to be understood as a distinct line of argumentation independent of Christ.[74] Israel's failure, in the passage as a whole, is not that they pursued the law in the wrong way, but that they failed to accept Christ. Or better: to pursue the law of righteousness ἐκ πίστεως (from faith) *is,* by (Paul's) definition, to accept Christ as God's means of righteousness. What Paul sets over against "works" is not a human attitude available to Israel at each point in its history, but a "faith" centered on Christ leading to a righteousness made possible by Christ. In support of this conclusion are the following considerations.

To begin with, there is the stone testimonium in v. 33. While several scholars have argued that the stumbling stone is the Torah itself,[75] it is almost certain that Christ is in view. Even if we leave out of account the christocentric use of the same texts (Isa 8:14; 28:16) in 1 Pet 2:6-8, such a conclusion is virtually required by the context. If by "stone" Paul meant the Torah, then we would have the almost unthinkable (for him) concept of faith in the Torah: "whoever believes in it (ἐν αὐτῷ)," the Torah. The statement must be "whoever believes in him," and since God is speaking in the first person singular ("See, I am laying in Zion . . ."), the "him" in question must be Christ. Further, in 10:11 Paul repeats this part of the quotation; while αὐτῷ (in him) might possibly refer to God in this instance (though Christ is more likely), it certainly does not refer to the Torah.

Second, the Gentiles are said to have attained what Israel failed to attain (vv. 30-31). The goal of righteousness for which Israel was striving has been realized by the Gentiles. To discern the shape of this goal, then, we have only to look at the case of the Gentiles. Despite the difficulties involved in Paul's scriptural argument in 10:5-9,[76] the christocentric character of faith throughout the passage is unquestionable. Clearly, the righteousness-producing faith of the Gentiles is characterized by its object (God's work in Christ; 10:9-13), not by its contrast with an attitude of meritorious self-justification (works). This is the faith that Paul condemns Israel for not displaying.

Finally, despite all the exegetical difficulties posed by 10:4,[77] the verse clearly reveals the christocentric nature of the argument in 9:30—10:4. Paul brings the argument to a conclusion by saying not that the law should be approached by faith instead of works, but that Christ is the "end" (τέλος) of the law. Since this statement is given as grounds for the statement made in v. 3 (cf. γὰρ [for], v. 4), the contrast between the righteousness of God and "their own" righteousness (v. 3) is determined by the acceptance or rejection of Christ, not by the distinction between faith and works, as these terms have traditionally been understood. "Their own" is to be set over against not only "God" but also (and perhaps especially) the "all" (παντὶ) of v. 4 (their *own* righteousness/righteousness for *everyone* who believes). That is, their own righteousness is one that is exclusively the preserve of Jews, one that is not possible for Gentiles as long as they are Gentiles.[78]

We find ourselves on familiar ground. In the language of 9:32, we can conclude that to pursue the law "by faith" (ἐκ πίστεως) is to see that its goal is Christ;[79] to pursue it "by works" (ἐξ ἔργων) is to assume that possession of the requisite ethnic identity markers guarantees one a place in the community of salvation. "Works" is a kind of theological short-hand referring to the belief that the law places Jews in a privileged posi-tion vis-à-vis the Gentiles (namely, to covenantal nomism itself), just as "faith" is theological shorthand for the whole state of affairs brought into being through Christ. The Gentiles are present at the end of the race course not because of a generic entrance requirement (faith) open to all humankind, but because the salvation accomplished by Christ is available (for reasons yet to be fully understood) to all.

## 5.2 The Universality of Sin

Paul's statement in Romans 3:22b-24 reflects the shape of his argument in the first half of the epistle as a whole: he begins by identifying a univer-sal plight ("for there is no distinction, for all have sinned and fall short of the glory of God"; cf. 1:18—3:20) and then moves to the divinely provided solution in Christ ("[all] being justified by his grace as a gift, through the redemption that is in Christ Jesus"; cf. 3:21—8:39).[80] As E. P. Sanders has observed, the "from plight to solution" progression of the argument in Romans 1–8 has led to the belief, particularly in the Ref-ormation tradition of exegesis, that Paul's basic convictions are similarly structured.[81] That is, Paul's conviction that all of humankind is sinful and in need of salvation is structurally and logically prior to his conviction that God has provided the necessary salvation in Christ. For the purposes of our investigation, this aspect of Paul's argument raises a different ver-sion of the possibility explored in the previous section, that his interest in the Gentiles emerges from a universality built into his convictional start-ing point. As in the previous section, then, we need to reckon with the possibility that one of Paul's basic categories is humanity in general; the difference here is that the starting point is not a set of two possible human stances before God (faith/works) but the universal reality of sin.

This way of accounting for Paul's interest in the Gentiles arises not simply from his assertions of the universality of sin, but more specifically from the way he uses such assertions, particularly in Galatians and Ro-mans,[82] to argue for the ineffectiveness of the law and thus the "plight equality" of Jew and Gentile. The universal reality of sin makes it impos-sible to fulfill the law, with the result that possession of the law by the

Jews leaves them no better off than the Gentiles. A survey of the relevant passages will serve to put the material on the table for discussion.

Such a line of argumentation seems to be present, albeit elusively, in Gal 3:10. Here, in support (cf. γάρ [for]) of the assertion in vv. 6-9 that "those of faith" are descendants of Abraham and therefore blessed along with him, Paul cites Deut 27:26 as evidence that those "of law" are under a curse. The text itself, however, assigns the curse not simply to those "of law" but to those who do not "continue in all the things written in the book of the law to do them." For the text to say what Paul wants it to say, a further assumption appears to be necessary—that no one is able to do everything written in the law. Only in such a way can the two groups—those "of law" in Gal 3:10 and those cursed in Deut 27:26—be equated.[83] To be sure, if this is the thrust of v. 10, it stands in considerable tension with vv. 11-12, which identify as the problem with the law the fact that it is based on "doing," not on faith,[84] a point to which we will return. For now we simply observe the clear implication of the verse: because no one is able to perform the law fully, those within its sphere will inevitably be under a curse.[85]

The ineffectiveness of the law in a situation dominated by sin comes into view again later in the chapter. In vv. 21-22, the fact that "all things" are "under sin" means that the law is unable to produce righteousness and life. Why this is so is not stated explicitly. But it seems to be hinted at just previously in v. 19, the other place in the chapter where law and sin are linked. Here it is said that the law was added τῶν παραβάσεων (transgressions) χάριν. The force of this phrase depends on the sense of the preposition χάριν. One possible sense of χάριν with the genitive is that of cause (because of). If the noun were "sin," a causal sense might have been intended ("because of [in some not fully specified way] sin"). But, as we will presently have occasion to point out, Paul tends to differentiate between "sin" and "transgression" (and its synonym "trespass" [παράπτωμα]). The latter is a special kind of sin, the violation of a specific divine commandment (cf. Rom 4:15; 5:14); transgression, then is sin quantified by law. Thus it makes more sense to take χάριν in a purpose sense[86] (cf. Tit 1:5, 11): the law was added "for the purpose of transgressions," that is, to make it possible to identify specific instances of sinful wrongdoing. Its role is simply to clarify the situation of those "under sin"; it has no power (returning to vv. 21-22) to produce life. Compare 4:8-9, where Paul says that if the Galatians give in to the pressure to be circumcised, they will be returning to a situation of bondage under the "weak and beggarly elemental spirits" (see 1:4).

Moving to Romans, we discover that what is elusive and unstated in Galatians becomes explicit and repeated. In 1:18—3:20, as already observed, Paul moves toward his climax in 3:21-31 by arguing that both Gentiles (1:18-32) and Jews (2:1—3:8)[87] are "under sin" (3:9) and thus unable to find justification by "works of law" since all the law can do is bring an awareness of sin (3:19-20). At several points he appears to accept the possibility that justification can be achieved through doing what the law requires (2:6-16, esp. vv. 8, 10, 13). But by 3:20 this possibility is shown to be merely theoretical; the group of those justified by the law is a null set.

The universality of sin and the resultant ineffectuality of the law comes up again in the second main section of Romans, chapters 5–8. Questions concerning the relationship between this section and what precedes, as well as the point of division between the two,[88] are central to any discussion of the epistle as a whole. Since such questions bear directly on that of the basic structure of Paul's understanding of "salvation," they are of direct relevance to this whole investigation. For now, though, a few brief comments indicating my approach to the epistle will suffice.

The problem, as A. Schweitzer observed some time ago,[89] is that, instead of moving on to a new area of discussion in chapters 5–8, Paul picks up the same topics—the universality of sin, the role of the law, the death of Christ, the saving benefits made available by that death to the believer—albeit from an altered perspective. The difference in perspective is this: In Romans 1–4, these topics are treated from an "objective" or juridical point of view, the concern in each case to specify the *status* of persons in relationship to God. Here sin is conceived of primarily in terms of culpability, the law functions to establish this guilty status (e.g., 3:19-20), and Christ's death makes possible the new status of justification (3:21-26). In Romans 5–8, the topics are revisited from a "subjective" or participatory point of view, the concern now being to describe the actual human *experience* at each point. Here sin functions more as a power that holds humankind under its sway,[90] delivering all over to death; the law functions to make this situation of bondage painfully clear (7:7-25); Christ's death is not so much the basis of a transaction "for" believers as an event in which believers participate, thereby moving out of the reach of the powers of sin and death and into a new sphere of existence empowered by the Spirit (chapters 6 and 8).[91] Romans 5:1-11 serves as a transitional section, using the language of chapters 1–4 to raise questions not fully answerable until chapter 8.[92]

Moving into this section, the universality of sin comes up first in 5:12-21, in the context of a comparison of the two human solidarities brought into being by Adam and Christ. Here, while "status" language (condemnation, justification) is not absent, sin is described more as a quasi-personified "power" that has gained entry into the human situation through the disobedience of Adam (v. 12), bringing death in its train (v. 12), and both of them together having dominion (βασιλεύειν; vv. 14, 17, 21) over the human solidarity with Adam at its head (cf. 1 Cor 15:22).

What is particularly striking, especially in view of the questions with which we come to this passage, is the generic and universal nature of the categories with which Paul works here. The Jew-Gentile distinction, so dominant throughout chapters 1–4, seems to be in total eclipse. Christ is set over against Adam, the progenitor of the whole human race, whose act of disobedience has resulted in sin and death for *all* (vv. 12,18; cf. 15, 19), apparently without distinction. To be sure, the shadow of the Jew-Gentile distinction can be seen in the references to Moses (v. 14) and the law (v. 20). But if the arrival of the law creates a distinction among Adam's progeny, the line that is drawn still falls within the domain of sin, and is thus of much less significance than the line enclosing the domain as a whole. The law's role, again, is merely to quantify sin and make it fully visible: it makes it possible for sin to be "reckoned" (v. 13).[93] The sins committed by people between Adam and Moses could not, unlike those of Adam and of people after Moses, be called transgressions (v. 14), presumably because they were committed in the absence of an explicit, divine standard such as the law (or the Edenic injunction; Gen 2:17) provided; the law "came in, in order that trespass might be multiplied" (v. 20). In this latter statement a new note can be heard, to be sounded more clearly in chapter 7. The law not only reveals the presence of sin (making it possible for trespasses to be identified); it actually stirs sin up (trespasses are *multiplied*). But in any case, at least at the surface level of the argument, Paul moves from a universal plight "in Adam" to an equally universal remedy "in Christ"; generic humanity appears to be the fundamental category from the beginning.

The role of the law vis-à-vis sin comes in for further examination in chapter 7. Unlike the other passages in Romans mentioned to this point, here we find no explicit emphasis on the universality of sin. Paul addresses his comments not to people in general but "to those who know the law" (v. 1) in particular; the experience of life under sin as it is described in the chapter is predicated not of "all" but of "me"; most strikingly, he makes statements apparently suggesting that sin is an active reality only within the sphere of the law ("Apart from the law sin lies dead. I was once alive apart from the law"; vv. 8-9).

Nevertheless, there can be little doubt that the experience described here is to be generalized. Even if it were the case that the "I" is autobiographical, the personal story of life under sin appears in a context where the universality of sin has already been established, and is followed immediately by a general description of the salvation made available for all in Christ (8:1-4). But in reality, it is now generally agreed that Paul uses the first person singular here not to tell his own story but to describe the situation of life "in Adam" as it can now be perceived from the standpoint of life in Christ.[94] In particular, Adam is the one—indeed, was the only one[95]—who was once alive apart from the law; vv. 7-10 is undoubtedly Paul's retelling of the narrative in Genesis 1-3.[96] Chapter 7 as a whole picks up and amplifies the description of the Adam solidarity introduced in 5:12-21.[97] Consequently it covers the same ground as 1:18—3:20, but from the perspective of the actual subjective experience of human existence under sin and law, not the perspective of the objective status of sinful humanity before God.

Accordingly, we hear again that life through the law is possible at least as a hypothetical reality: the law "promised life" (v. 10; cf. justification to the doers of the law in 2:13). But in reality, because it is unable to enable, the law cannot deliver on its promise; all it can do is show sin to be sin (vv. 7, 13), functioning as a kind of divine litmus paper to reveal sin's presence, and in the process making those who know the law agonizingly aware of their bondage under sin's power (vv. 14-25). Further, in a move that threatens to make the law an instrument more of sin than of God, Paul describes the law as the means by which sin gained entry into the human solidarity, the catalyst (to continue the chemical analogy) that stirred up the deadly chemical reaction between flesh and sin (vv. 8-14). So, while the emphasis falls on the wretchedness of the experience under sin's power (v. 24) instead of the objective declaration of the sinner's guilty status before God (3:19-20), the rhetorical progression is the same: the thorough establishment of the universal human plight under sin, prior to any presentation of the solution made available by Christ. Further, in each case the universal plight is rhetorically and temporally prior to the appearance of the law and the resultant distinction between Israel and the Gentiles; indeed, the emergence of that distinction does nothing to qualify or diminish the solidarity in sin of humankind generically considered.

The ineffectiveness of the law in face of the universal reality of sin comes up once more (in 8:3), as part of a passage (8:1-4) that sums up the argument to this point and introduces the climactic presentation of life in the Spirit (8:5-39). Here the juridical is clearly subordinated to the participatory:[98] justification [= no condemnation] is made available to those who are "in Christ Jesus" not because Christ's death has effected atonement in any juridical sense but because through Christ sin has been defeated,[99] making possible the liberation of those who had been under its sway (vv. 1-2). But in any case, again we encounter (albeit in muted terms) the universality of sin: "flesh" (σάρξ; v. 3) is used here as elsewhere to refer to the whole of humankind (cf. Rom 3:20), especially humankind under the sway of sin (cf. Rom 7:14).[100] Again it is the universal reality of sin that renders the law ineffectual ("what the law, weakened by the flesh, could not do"; v. 3). And again, this universal plight is presented as the apparently necessary backdrop to the (again universal) solution accomplished by Christ.

I have skated quickly over a textual surface that is anything but smooth; a slower pace would require that we take more careful account of the many exegetical cracks and bumps. But for present purposes it will suffice. Our interest in this "from plight to solution" pattern of argumentation is its *universal* dimensions. Can we find the starting point of Paul's apostolic interest in the Gentiles in a fundamental conviction that "all have sinned"?

In the old Pauline paradigm described in chapter 1, and especially in the Reformation version of it, it was widely assumed that the progression of the argument in Romans reflected the basic structure of Paul's thought. That is, Paul begins with the fundamental belief that all have sinned; this leads him to the conclusion that the law is powerless to save (since God demands perfect performance); but he finally finds the solution to this dilemma in Christ. Paul's problem with the law in this reading of him, then, is that the universal presence of sin makes law religion unworkable. The inadequacy of the law is apparent apart from Christ and can be established apart from Christ.

On the surface of it, this criticism of the law is difficult to square with the objection that the law is based on or encourages an attitude of "works." How can law religion be faulted both on the basis that no one can fully perform the law, and on the basis that those who strive to perform it are ipso facto attempting to establish a relationship with God on the false grounds of meritorious achievement rather than on the divinely ordained grounds of grace and faith?[101] It seems to be a case of Paul wanting both to have his cake (sin⟶no righteousness for those who fail to perform the law) and to eat it (works⟶no righteousness for those who succeed). Indeed, the experience of reading Calvin's or Luther's commentaries on Romans 3–4 or Galatians 3:10-12 is one of being carried along by a train of thought that jumps back and forth between one set of tracks (works/faith) and another (sin/Christ), without any awareness on the part of the engineer of the way in which passengers and luggage are thrown about as a result! Still, to be fair, the issue does from time to time come somewhat into focus, allowing us to say that for the Reformers the attitude characterized as "works" arises from a *false* sense of achievement, false in that no one can ever fully perform what the law demands.[102]

This produces the following convictional structure:

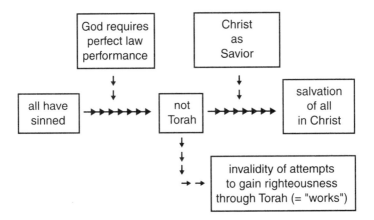

As with other similar diagrams in this study, the arrows are meant to indicate logical rather than chronological progression; diachronic questions will not be addressed directly until Part III. Nevertheless such a structure—where convictions about the universality of sin and resultant inadequacy of the law stand logically prior to any conviction about Christ—virtually requires as a correlative the view that prior to his conversion Paul had already despaired of the law's ability to deal with sin. If "from plight to solution" describes the structure of his convictions, it most probably describes the process of his conversion as well. In any case, the element of universality is important: if "all have sinned" is Paul's convictional starting point, scuttling his law religion and leading him to Christ, then his emergent concern for the Gentiles is just the outworking of a universal element ("*all* have sinned") fed into the structural system at the outset.

This convictional structure has come under intense scholarly criticism, both in its representation of Judaism and also as an accurate portrayal of Paul. First, as in the discussion of "works" in the previous section, if this represents Paul's convictions, then he has fundamentally misunderstood (or willfully distorted) Judaism. The point is actually much easier to make than in the case of "works," because of Paul's glaring omission of what

C. G. Montefiore calls "the very keynote of Judaism," namely, repentance, atonement, and forgiveness.[103] The existence of the temple itself testifies to the fact that perfect fulfillment of the law was never expected. What Paul (on this reading of him) takes as the vitiation of Torah religion, the existence of sin, is provided for already within the law itself. The law both anticipates sin and makes provision for it. That Paul fails to mention this at all affords ample evidence either of his lack of understanding of the religion he criticizes or of his lack of good faith.

Such criticisms of Paul have been made by both Jewish and Christian scholars alike since the early part of this century and have been amply chronicled by Sanders and others.[104] I turn to Sanders's own analysis, since, as is widely recognized, it represents a scholarly watershed and a new point of departure for any discussion of sin, law, and the Gentiles in Paul.

According to Sanders, it is not so much a case of Pauline misunderstanding of Judaism as it is of a scholarly misunderstanding of Paul. Sanders argues, quite convincingly, that the surface argument moving "from plight to solution" is in defense of a set of underlying convictions structured the other way round, moving from "solution" to "plight." Paul's critique of law religion is at bottom not anthropological (works, sin) but christological and soteriological. His fundamental conviction is that God has provided in Christ a means of salvation for all. His rejection of the law as a condition of salvation is derivative: "Since salvation is only in Christ, therefore all other ways toward salvation are wrong," the way of the law included.[105] Derivative also are the arguments based on universal sinfulness: if God has provided for universal salvation in Christ, it follows that all are enslaved to sin and in need of salvation.[106]

If Sanders's analysis is correct—and I believe it is, at least in its overall thrust—it leads to the collapse of the convictional structure sketched above; Paul's concern for the Gentiles cannot be accounted for on the basis of an axiomatic starting point of universal sinfulness, at least in this way. At the same time, Sanders posits another universal element as a primary conviction—the universal salvation made available in Christ. Before analyzing the resultant convictional structure, I consider the criticisms directed by Sanders and others[107] against the traditional "problem before solution" reading of Paul.

First, the evidence of the letters in no way supports the conclusion that prior to his Damascus experience Paul ever thought of the law as impossible to fulfill. Whenever he looks back on his experience, he does so with palpable satisfaction (Gal 1:13-14; Phil 3:4-6), even declaring that with respect to the law's demands he was "blameless" (Phil 3:6). No sign of

despair over an unattainable standard here! Once the nonautobiographi-
cal character of Romans 7 is recognized,[108] nothing remains to suggest
that apart from Christ Paul ever experienced the law as incapable of fulfillment or perceived sin as a categorical problem for law religion.

Next, there is the "double standard"[109] apparently operative in the way
he handles transgressions—a matter of grave seriousness when committed by those under the law, but of much less consequence when committed by those in Christ. If the presence of transgression is enough to render
law religion unworkable, why does it not do the same for Christ religion?
Why is it that the case of an incestuous Christian (a type of sin "not even
found among pagans"!) provokes only a reprimand of the individual (1
Cor 5:1-13), while the (undoubtedly rare) case of a Jewish temple robber
(Rom 2:22)—or, more to the point, that of a Jewish adulterer (v. 22)—is
evidence of the impossibility of righteousness through the law? Why hold
one group to a standard of perfection not applied to the other? Why is
one sin just an isolated disciplinary case while the other is a fundamental
systemic flaw? If the problem of sin was as central in Paul's thinking as
the structure described above portrays it, one would expect that the all-
too-evident reality of Christian transgression—reflected in all his letters—would have posed just as fundamental a problem for the system of
Christ religion as it did for that of the law. It is much more likely that
universal sinfulness is being used as an argument for a position arrived at
from a different starting point.

With respect to the argument of Romans 1–3 itself, one is struck first
by the exaggerated and artificial nature of the argument for universal sinfulness, especially for Jewish sinfulness. The treatment of Gentile sin in
1:18-32 is stock synagogue preaching, and would have carried weight
with Paul's audience here. But his attempt to establish Jewish sinfulness
consists of two lines of argument that even Paul himself must have found
unconvincing. First, he cites a short list of sins—stealing, adultery, temple
robbery (2:21-22)—that, while admittedly gross, were certainly far from
universal. Did he really think that all Jews were guilty of one or other of
these? As Räisänen observes, the move from "some commit gross sins"
to "all are under sin" is "a blatant non sequitur."[110] Second, Paul clinches
his argument by quoting a catena of scriptural texts in 3:10-18.[111] Taken
as they stand, the texts appear to make the point: they begin with a declaration of universal sinfulness (vv. 10-12), and move on to a vigorous denunciation of the wicked (vv. 13-18). But their probative value is only
apparent. Anyone of Paul's readers who looked at these texts in their
scriptural context would immediately see that in every case without exception a distinction is made between the righteous and the wicked, with

the former identified in terms of their faithfulness to the law and the covenant, and the latter the sole target of the denunciation. The texts sum up Paul's argument with an effective rhetorical flourish; but neither they nor the seemingly empirical arguments that precede would have been convincing to anyone not predisposed to the conclusion on other grounds.

Romans 1–3 is characterized not only by arguments that fail to convince, but also by internal inconsistencies. Most striking of these is the reference to Gentiles who fulfill the law (2:14-16, 26-27).[112] The rhetorical function of this reference is clear and its impact forceful. Paul contrasts Gentile law observers with Jewish lawbreakers in order to undercut claims of ethnic privilege: "Those who are physically uncircumcised but keep the law will condemn you that have the written code and circumcision but break the law" (v. 27). But such clarity and forcefulness come with a cost. By grabbing hold of law-keeping Gentiles as a battering ram to use against the walls of Jewish privilege, Paul inadvertently pulls the props out from under his siege ramp. For his argument to this point has been predicated on the assertion of universal sinfulness, of the Jew first (at least in rhetorical importance) but also of the Greek. These concessions in chapter 2 significantly undercut the foundation of the argument laid in chapter 1.

Various attempts have been made to soften the contrast and salvage the argument.[113] Paul speaks here in a hypothetical way, it is said (but how could one establish the point with a hypothetical example?), or he is really speaking of Christians (but do Christians really fulfill the law "by *nature*" [φύσει; v. 14]?). Even if he does have Gentile Christians in mind, anticipating in guarded fashion the results of an argument to be stated more clearly later (8:1-4),[114] a reader attempting to follow the flow of the argument would perceive these verses as damagingly inconsistent with the point already established. The ease with which Paul moves from "all Gentiles are given over to sin" to "some Gentiles keep the law," while arguing consistently toward a conclusion that righteousness comes through Christ not through law (3:19-31), demonstrates the degree to which any conviction about universal sinfulness is subordinate to more fundamental convictions concerning the inadequacy of the law (which in turn is subordinate to his christological starting point).

From the reference to Gentiles in Romans 2, we turn finally to the treatment in this chapter of the Jews. Here too we find the argument unfolding in surprising and telling ways. As Sanders has observed, the conclusion in chapter 3 is not what one would expect on the basis of 1:18—2:29.[115] Taken on its own, the argument of this section moves more in the direction of "Repent and become a better Jew" than of "Realize that it is impossible to fulfill the law and so to achieve righteousness." Paul argues that all will be judged in one way or another by the same standard of the Mosaic law (vv. 12-16); that those who do the law will be counted righteous (v. 13); that Jewish shortcomings are exposed by the instinctive law-keeping of some Gentiles (vv. 14-16); that true Jewishness is a matter not of external factors but of keeping the law from the heart (vv. 25-29); and that God has been patient in order to evoke repentance (v. 4). Surely the conclusion to which such an argument seems to lead is: "Repent, keep the law from your heart, and seek the righteousness that comes to those who truly do the law."

The actual conclusion in 3:9-31, of course, is something else. Looking back, one can see how the preceding material serves Paul's purposes, in that much of it has a leveling effect, putting Jew and Gentile on an equal footing. But what is of significance for our present discussion (in addition to the mention of repentance, with its implication that Paul was well aware of the structure of covenantal nomism),[116] is this: to prepare for his declaration of the righteousness of God in Christ (for all, and on equal terms), he uses arguments that, while placing Jews and Gentiles together on level ground, do so in a way that undercuts the argument for universal sinfulness. For the implication of the argument of chapter 2, as one moves through it, is that the fulfillment of the law is a real possibility. Paul's willingness to let down his guard at this point (universal sinfulness as the law's fatal flaw) in order to capture other argumentative territory (equal status for Jew and Gentile, salvation in Christ), suggests that his fundamental convictions are to be found more in the latter than in the former.

My intention here is heuristic rather than destructive. My purpose is not to demolish or deconstruct Romans 1–3. Full appreciation of it as a text needs to take into account its character as rhetoric, thus evaluating it with respect to the circumstances in which it was written and the effects on its intended readers toward which it was crafted. Paul was trying to win over a skeptical audience, not to construct a textbook example of logical argumentation. The assumption underlying my analysis is that by looking carefully at the way he argues we can discover something about his underlying convictions.

In Sanders's reading of Paul, then, both universal sinfulness and the ineffectiveness of the law are corollaries of the more fundamental conviction that Christ is the Savior of all on equal terms. For the purposes of the present investigation, this means, negatively, that the origins of Paul's concern for the Gentiles are not to be found in a primary conviction of universal sinfulness; but positively, that his primary conviction nevertheless contains the element of universality in a different way. The concern for the Gentiles arises from a universality embedded in his fundamental conviction—universality in this case not of sinfulness, but of divinely provided salvation. The convictional structure can be sketched as follows:

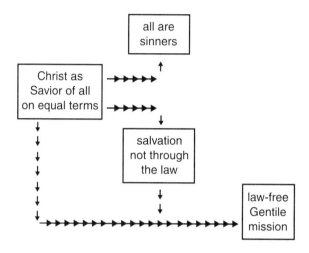

There is widespread agreement that Sanders is on the right track; anything Paul has to say about sin and the law is best understood within a framework provided by fundamental convictions concerning salvation in Christ. If we start here, we can find a more certain path through the difficult argumentative terrain of Romans and Galatians. Paul does not misunderstand the law; he just views it from a quite different perspective than that of covenantal nomism.

But at the same time, significant objections have been raised about the larger picture that results.[117] The problem is the almost complete disjunction between Paul's pattern of religion and that of covenantal nomism (and thus between Paul's former self and his apostolic self). Paul (as Sanders sees him) and Judaism end up as ships passing in the night, talking past each other from within completely disjunctive worlds of discourse. By so privileging Paul's new conversion convictions, Sanders trades a "Lutheran Paul" for an "idiosyncratic Paul," to use Dunn's delightfully apt phrase.[118] The trade renders some aspects of Paul's argumentation more understandable, but at the expense of making Paul himself inexplicable. In particular, his conversion, the process of transition from covenantal nomist to Gentile apostle, remains arbitrary and impenetrable.

Such criticisms raise large issues. For present purposes, I focus on the issue of arbitrariness as it pertains to the element of universalism in Paul's basic conviction. Granted, we can make better sense of Paul if we assume that he argues on the basis of the fundamental conviction that God has provided Christ as a means of salvation for all, on equal terms. But where does this conviction come from? No explanation is needed for the conviction of Christ as Savior; this was part of the kerygma inherited from the earliest church.[119] But given the complexity and uncertainty within early Jewish Christianity on the question of the Gentiles (no apparent conception among the earliest Christians of a Gentile mission at all, and sharp controversy over the conditions of entry when such a mission did emerge), the firmness of Paul's conviction that Christ was the Savior *of all* (which means that the Gentile mission was an urgent necessity) and on *equal terms* (which means that law observance is not to be added to faith in Christ as an entrance requirement) stands in real need of explanation. Simply to posit this as a basic conviction—as Sanders does[120]—begs a whole lot of questions. But if we can in some measure account for it, this will both render Paul less idiosyncratic (or at least explicably idiosyncratic) and provide a more satisfactory description of the convictional transformation centered on his conversion experience.

To give Sanders his due, he is not completely silent on the question. Toward the end of his *Paul, the Law, and the Jewish People,* he makes a connection between Paul's activity as a Gentile missionary and contemporary Jewish expectations concerning the eschatological pilgrimage of the Gentiles: "Paul's entire work . . . had its setting in the expected pilgrimage of the Gentiles to Mount Zion in the last days" (p. 171). This, as we have already had occasion to observe, is a common way of understanding Paul, one that I will investigate thoroughly in a subsequent chapter (§7.1). In Sanders's case, however, the notion is marginal, brought in without much discussion at various points where it is needed,[121] but not really integrated into the substance of his reconstruction. Indeed, at the one point where the idea comes up in *Paul and Palestinian Judaism* he appears to reject the connection.[122] If he is more favorable to the position in subsequent writings, he nevertheless makes little attempt to show how the individual elements in the traditional picture (restoration of Israel, glorification of Zion, gathering of the exiles, pilgrimage of the Gentiles, and so on) are reconfigured around their putative new center in Christ. He simply says that Paul "altered the traditional picture,"[123] and is content to leave it at that.[124]

Let us consider more closely the way Sanders sees the move from "Christ as savior of all on equal terms" to "all have sinned." Sanders can describe this in ways that suggest that universal sinfulness is entirely a derivative notion, which would mean that it would have nothing to tell us about Paul's convictions concerning the Gentiles. The basic conviction "Christ as savior"—so Sanders's argument runs—suggests the corollary that there must be a problem (sin) for which nothing else was able to provide a solution; the conviction "Christ as savior *of all*" leads to the derivative conclusion that *all* are subject to this problem of sin. Universal sinfulness is simply a corollary of universal salvation; any bearing that the latter might have on the Gentile question is just carried over in toto from the former.

But as Sanders himself recognizes, this is not where Gentile sinfulness first appears in Paul's convictional world. The language of Gal 2:15 is instructive: "We ourselves are Jews by nature and not sinners of the Gentiles [ἐξ ἐθνῶν ἁμαρτωλοί]." This language reflects typical Jewish attitudes,[125] suggesting that for Paul the sinfulness of the Gentiles was a native conviction, part of his view of the world from the outset. In Sanders's words, "before then [his conversion], he must have distinguished between Jews, who were righteous (despite occasional transgressions), and 'Gentile sinners' (Gal 2.15)."[126] What his new Christian conviction does, then, is not to create the idea of Gentile sinfulness (as part of a wider belief in universal sinfulness) but to erase the distinction between Jew and Gentile as far as sin is concerned. Since salvation is to be found in Christ, the law, which differentiates Jew from Gentile, can have no saving effect, which in turn eliminates any Jewish claim for exemption from the problem besetting the rest of humankind. Jews are in the same sinful boat as the Gentiles. The structure of this aspect of Paul's system of convictions, then, can be represented in part as follows:

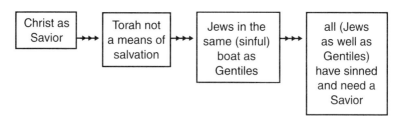

But while this accounts for the inclusion of the Jews within the "all" of universal sinfulness ("all have sinned"), it still leaves ambiguous the inclusion of the Gentiles within the "all" of universal salvation ("Christ provides salvation for all"). One possibility is that it too is a derivative conviction, another result of the new convictional starting point in Christ. More specifically, Paul might have concluded that the elimination of the Torah as a means of exempting Jews from the problem of sin serves to

eradicate the distinction between Jew and Gentile altogether. In this reading, Paul begins with a belief in Christ as Savior and ends with generic
humanity. If Jews are in the same sinful boat as Gentiles, then no distinction remains between them; the elimination of the Torah as a means or
condition of salvation is at the same time the elimination of any special
role or status for Jews. In this reading of the situation, it is the removal
of the Torah-imposed wall between Jew and Gentile that opens up the
wider Gentile world for Paul. In schematic terms:

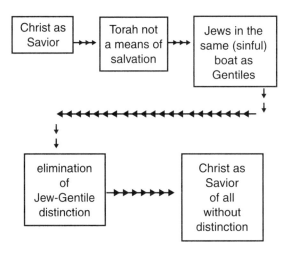

    This way of reading Paul is an example of what was described above
as an abandonment of Jewish particularism. Structurally it is similar to a
variety of approaches that, while taking different routes to arrive at the
position of "not Torah," follow a very similar path from here to the Gentile mission. Such explanations will be explored in more detail (and rejected) in the next chapter (§6.3). But the elimination of the Torah as a
condition of membership in the community of the to-be-saved does not
necessarily require the total eradication of the distinction between Jews
and Gentiles, especially when—conditions of entry aside—such distinctions appear to play a continuing part in Paul's thinking. Paul's "not Torah" conviction is by no means a global one; "not Torah" is not the convictional equivalent of "not Israel." I will return to this discussion in due
course.
    The other way of fitting Gentile salvation into the structure of Paul's
convictions is to see it as another carryover from his native universe of
meaning. That is, just as the belief that Gentiles are unrighteous sinners

was part of his convictional makeup prior to Damascus, so too was the expectation that they could change their status and gain a share in salvation. His conversion, centered in a new conviction that such salvation was to be experienced only in Christ, inevitably effected a new configuration of these native convictions; but the conception that Gentiles, too, might escape their sinful state and be included in salvation is (in this reading of things) part of the structured system of convictions from the outset. To refer again to the distinction defined earlier, this way of understanding Paul is to see his concern for the Gentiles as a christologically reinterpreted form of Jewish universalism.

As we have seen, there are several patterns of such universalism. The question, then, is to identify which of them, as a postulated point of departure for Paul, makes best sense of his later statements concerning sin, the law, and the Gentiles. The question is a complex one, partly because of the intervening event of his conversion and the concomitant reconfiguration of convictions, and partly because of the conflicting nature of the statements themselves. We will begin with the latter.

Scholars have frequently commented on the puzzling nature of what Paul has to say about the role of the law for Gentiles.[127] On the one hand, possession of the law is clearly presented as that which separates Jew from Gentile and differentiates the two. Gentiles are those who do not have the law (ἔθνη τὰ μὴ νόμον ἔχοντα; Rom 2:14), and who therefore sin (and perish) apart from the law (ἀνόμως; Rom 2:12). Paul behaves differently with Jews who are "under the law" (τοῖς ὑπὸ νόμον) than with Gentiles who are "outside the law" (τοῖς ἀνόμοις; 1 Cor 9:20-21).[128]

On the other hand, we encounter statements and lines of argumentation suggestive of a much wider view of the law, one in which the requirements of the law seem to be binding on all without distinction, and where the Gentiles as well appear to be subject to the law and its demands. The phenomenon appears already in Rom 2:12-15. Here, as part of his attempt to undercut notions of Jewish privilege, Paul brings forward the example of what can be described (without prejudging the issue) as "righteous Gentiles." These Gentiles are "doers of the law" and thus (by implication) are justified (v. 13); they "do instinctively what the law requires" (v. 14), thus demonstrating that "the work of the law is written in their hearts" (v. 15). A similar line of argumentation is found in 2:25-29: the Gentiles in question "keep the just requirements (δικαιώματα) of the law" (v. 26). To be sure, Paul's Jewish interlocutor might well have questioned his understanding of precisely what was involved in "doing the law," just as his later interpreters will try to ascertain how his understanding of "the just requirement of the law" has been altered by his new Christian conviction. But the point is the assumption that the law's significance (however it has been reinterpreted) is (at least potentially) the same for Jew and Gentile.

A similar conclusion emerges from the extended discussion concerning sin, law, and the human situation in Romans 5–8. While a Jewish frame of reference clearly pervades the whole, equally pervasive is the assumption that this Jewish experience can be generalized and applied to Gentiles as well. When in 7:5 Paul declares that "while we were living in the flesh, our sinful passions, aroused by the law, were at work in our members to bear fruit for death," he gives no reason to believe that he is addressing only the *Jewish* Christians in Rome.[129] A similar observation can be made with respect to the first person plurals in 6:15 ("we are not under law but under grace;" cf. v. 14) and 8:4 ("so that the just requirement of the law might be fulfilled in us"). Likewise, the first person singular in 7:7-25 seems to be used to describe the situation of Adamic humanity as a whole.[130] In Stephen Westerholm's words: "The Jewish situation is in mind, but Paul treats it as though it was universal."[131] Similar conclusions could be drawn about statements concerning the law in 1 Cor 9:8-9; 14:34; 15:56.[132]

What light might be shed on Paul's convictional starting point by this curious combination of particularism and universalism in his statements about the law? The reference made above to the "righteous Gentiles" of Rom 2:13-16 suggests one possibility. Indeed, when one looks at Paul's Gentile converts from the outside, they conform in significant ways to the Noachide or righteous Gentile model. On the one hand, they are counted righteous even though they are not circumcised, do not follow the food laws, and, in short, are not proselytes; on the other hand, they are enjoined to abstain from idolatry (for example, 1 Corinthians 8–10) and sexual immorality (1 Corinthians 5–6), to affirm monotheism (1 Cor 8:6), and so on. The case has been stated most strongly by Tomson, who adds a fresh dimension to the discussion of "Paul and the law" by focusing on passages dealing not with abstract theological statements but with practical halakic matters.[133] He concludes that Paul sees his Gentile converts as Noachides: that is, on the one hand, they are righteous as Gentiles and are not required to become full law observers; on the other hand, they are to observe those parts of the law that pertain to them as Gentiles.[134]

The position is not without merit, and will come up again for more complete discussion later (§8.2). But on the more limited basis of Paul's statements linking Gentiles with sin and law, it is readily apparent that when he is engaged in foundational and theological (rather than practical and halakic) argumentation, he does not make the kinds of distinctions that would be expected on the basis of Tomson's conclusions. When in Rom 2:13-16 and 25-29, for example, Paul puts forward the example of Gentile "doers of the law" in order to undercut Jewish notions of covenantal privilege, there is no hint that "the law" bears differently on Gentiles than on Jews; it is referred to throughout as a single, indivisible standard, making equal demands on Jew and Gentile alike.[135] Paul certainly creates headaches for later interpreters by saying *both* that those who have died with Christ are "not under law but under grace" (Rom 6:14) *and* that "the just requirement of the law" is fulfilled by those who walk according to the Spirit (Rom 8:3). The law seems both to be no longer operative for Christians and yet at the same time to have continuing relevance. But in neither case is there any hint of differentiation between Jews and Gentiles. To be sure, when one asks what this fulfilling of "the just requirement of the law" might look like in practice, the only relevant statements have to do with such universal moral demands as "Love your neighbor" (Rom 13:8-10; Gal 5:13-14). But nowhere is there any suggestion that these statements function in a context where the law is differentiated according to those parts that pertain to Gentiles (or to humankind in general) and those referring specifically to Jews. Indeed, in Romans 4, Gentiles who are righteous (by faith) are said to be part of the family of Abraham (not Noah!), a statement unparalleled in any Noachide or righteous Gentile material.[136] Tomson's approach is one of a series of unsuccessful attempts to account for the conflicting nature of Paul's statements concerning the law by positing a distinction in the use of the term νόμος ("law") itself.[137]

Nevertheless, Tomson's work serves to bring the problem clearly into light. On the one hand, Paul speaks of his Gentile converts as if they were proselytes; on the other, from the outside they look all the world like "righteous Gentiles." This way of stating the problem serves at the same time to suggest one possible solution. As we have seen, there is evidence within Hellenistic Judaism especially for an approach to the Gentiles—I called it "natural law proselytism"[138]—that is strikingly analogous to that of Paul. On the one hand, the law was put forward as an undifferentiated, universal entity, binding on Jew and Gentile alike; on the other, it was described in such a way as to downplay or eliminate those aspects that served to differentiate Jew from Gentile. From the inside, the vocabulary of proselytism was used to describe those Gentiles who conformed to such a "natural law" Torah; but from the outside, especially since attempts to take the next step and to abandon Jewish distinctive altogether were rare and subject to sharp disapproval,[139] such Gentiles looked more like righteous Noachides.

But it is unlikely that the parallel, however instructive, tells us anything about how the peculiar Pauline configuration of Gentiles, law, and sin *originated*. It is quite unthinkable that Paul, a self-proclaimed Pharisee (Phil 3:5) and "zealot for the traditions of [his] ancestors" (Gal 1:14), would, in his pre-Damascus days, have conceived of the non-Jewish world with anything like the synthesizing and accommodating program of a Philo of Alexandria.[140] The points of similarity are much more likely due to the impact of Paul's new Christ-conviction than to the shape of his pre-conversion convictional universe. In fact, one might speak of an analogical (as set over against a genealogical) parallel, in that both Paul and, for example, Philo find themselves in a situation of wanting to resolve the dissonance between a traditional conviction (the divinely given nature of the law) and a new conviction (Christ on the one hand, Hellenistic philosophy on the other).

Whatever similarities are present between Paul and the "natural law proselytism" of Hellenistic Judaism, I suggest, are due to the fact that prior to Damascus he held to proselytism as the only hope of salvation for "Gentile sinners." When due allowance is made for the reconfiguring effect of his new Christ-conviction—when Christ is removed from the equation, as it were—a very similar pattern emerges: the law functions to differentiate Jew from Gentile; nevertheless, the law is potentially binding on all, without distinction; those who fail to fulfill the law's requirements are sinners. As we have seen, such assumptions underlie Paul's argumentation, appearing frequently and at critical junctures. But they are also the basic assumptions adhered to by Eleazar of Adiabene, Rabbi Eliezer, and other strict advocates of proselytism. While Paul's new Christ-conviction leads to the displacement of the law as a vehicle for righteousness, he nevertheless continues to be committed to its divinely given nature, and thus has to find a place for it within his new universe of meaning. We can account most economically for the phenomena under discussion (statements linking Gentiles, sin, and law) if we assume that Paul carried over into his new symbolic world a pattern of thinking about the Gentiles that in the terms of his old world would conform to that of proselytism.

Such a construal of Paul's convictional transformation can be found in the important work of Ben Meyer, *The Early Christians: Their World Mission and Self-Discovery*.[141] His analysis of Paul's treatment of the law is just as christocentric as that of Sanders: Paul's critique of the Torah is grounded in his new conviction about the saving significance of the cross. But at the same time he maintains that Paul's depiction of the human plight under sin is not simply a utilitarian argument developed to support a universal mission.[142] Universal sinfulness is a native conviction, part of his convictional point of departure. The change effected by the conversion experience was the giving up of the former belief that the law was part of the solution:

> From the fact of the cross, then, it followed as the night the day that the Torah, which was supposed to succeed Chaos as the solution of man's benightedness and aberrancy, had really been futile. If this futility were not to have meant the failure of God's purposes, it must never have been God's intention that Torah should function as a solution. (p. 164)

While I take issue with several aspects of Meyer's analysis, the basic framework of his analysis corresponds with the findings in this section: Paul had understood the law to be the divinely provided solution for the human plight, and thus had thought of proselytism as the only path of salvation for Gentiles. But Paul's Damascus experience led him to see Christ as this solution, thus displacing the Torah in the structure of his convictions. In schematic terms:

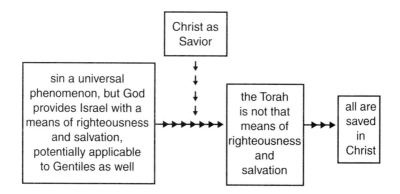

In this analysis of the convictional structure, then, Christ and Torah are paratagmatic elements, that is, they occupy analogous positions in systems of convictions that, to some extent at least, were parallel in their structure. The issue differentiating the two segments of Paul's life, yet at the same time binding them irrevocably together, is whether the universal means of righteousness and salvation, given to Israel by divine initiative, is the Torah or Christ.

I believe that the structure outlined above gives a consistent explanation of what Paul has to say about Gentiles, sin, the law, and Christ, but consistency is not enough to establish proof. In any case, statements about sin constitute too narrow a basis on which to rest a case. But the structure provides us with a promising way forward. In particular, it suggests two questions to be kept in mind. One concerns Israel: What happens to Israel in the reconfiguration of convictions? Does it lose its significance in the transition, or does it, as the immediate recipient of the divine gift, continue to have an important role to play in Paul's Christian world of meaning? The other has to do with Christ and Torah. Viewing Christ and Torah as paratagmatic elements is plausible, given the way he seems to perceive them as rival means of righteousness, and the way he can speak of their functions (purported on the one hand, actual on the other) in analogous terms (for example, in Christ, "God has done what the law could not do"; Rom 8:3). But what precisely is the point of conflict between them? Why does Paul perceive them as rival means of righteousness?

Before proceeding with such questions, there is one other aspect of Paul's discourse to be considered here.

## 5.3 Equality of Jew and Gentile

Paul asserts that there is no distinction (οὐ γάρ ἐστιν διαστολή) between Jew and Gentile. The primary texts to be considered here are Rom 3:22 and 10:12, where the explicit assertion appears. The statements in Gal 3:28 and Col 3:11 (in Christ "there is no Jew nor Greek"; cf. 1 Cor 12:13) strike a similar note. But these statements link the equality of Jew and Gentile with Christ, leaving open the possibility that the absence of distinction rests on a more fundamental christological conviction.[143] What is of interest in the texts from Romans is the absence of such a christological element (at least in the statements themselves). This suggests, again but in a different way, the possibility that Paul operates with a fundamental category of generic, undifferentiated humanity, a category more basic than any Jew-Gentile distinction, one that functions as an independent and underived entity in his convictional structure and provides the ultimate ground for his law-free Gentile mission.

This possibility can be brought into clearer focus by explaining more precisely what is meant by the description of this conviction as independent and underived. It is possible, of course, that Paul's belief in the equality of Jew and Gentile is derived from more basic Christian convictions. In the most common construal, his new commitment to Christ leads him to abandon the law. Since it is the law that differentiates Jew from Gentile, the abandonment of the law carries with it (in this way of reading him) the abandonment of the Jew-Gentile distinction. This possibility will be explored in the next chapter. But what is being explored here is the possibility that Jew-Gentile equality is independent of Christ in Paul's convictional scheme, and that this is the conviction lying behind both the abandonment of Torah and the concern for the Gentiles. This section of the convictional structure can be diagrammed as follows:

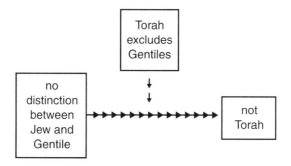

Several preliminary observations may be made. First, if a conviction is independent of Paul's belief in Christ, then for all intents and purposes it is to be seen as a native conviction, carried over from his pre-Damascus way of viewing the world. Second, the convictional structure diagrammed above appears to stand in sharp contrast with the basic framework of covenantal nomism. On the one hand, the belief in election, fundamental to covenantal nomism, carries with it an element of differentiation: out of all the nations of the world, God has chosen Israel for a distinct role and relationship. On the other hand, while the Torah differentiates Israel from the Gentiles, it in no way *excludes* them necessarily from a share in salvation, as the existence of the various patterns of universalism demonstrates. Putting these two observations together, we can conclude, then, that if the diagram provides an accurate reflection of Paul's convictional structure, he has seriously misunderstood or misrepresented the nature of Judaism. Such a conclusion runs counter to our working hypothesis, that Paul can be understood as a covenantal nomist who came to believe that God raised Jesus from death. Nevertheless, since no possible explanations are to be eliminated in an a priori way, we need to explore this structure further.

Given the universalistic framework of the previous paradigm of Pauline interpretation, it is not surprising to find this convictional structure in older work. In the History of Religions approach, for example, it was common to understand Paul as one who had been torn between Judaism with its particularism, and the universalism of Hellenism, with his conversion being understood as the resolution of this conflict of convictions.[144] But more surprisingly, this convictional structure shows up as well in the work of several contemporary scholars who accept much of the "new perspective on Paul" (to use the title of an article by one of them, James D. G. Dunn), but who at the same time identify as a fundamental Pauline conviction the belief that God's saving purposes have to do with the whole of humankind without distinction, and see this as the direct source of the convictions underlying Paul's Gentile mission.

The clearest example of this way of construing Paul's thought is the work of N. T. Wright. In *The Climax of the Covenant,* Wright presents us with glimpses of a comprehensive, and in many ways compelling, account of Paul's system of thought and conviction.[145] The most convenient point of entry into his reconstruction is his treatment of sin and the law. While in wholehearted agreement with Sanders on several of his main points (Judaism as a religion of covenantal nomism; Paul's criticism of Torah religion not to be understood in terms of legalistic works righteousness), at the same time he argues that Sanders has misunderstood and thereby significantly underestimated the place of sin in Paul's thinking about the law.[146] Wright grants Sanders the point that the law clearly makes provision for repentance, atonement, and forgiveness when an individual sins. But the point is "quite irrelevant" to Paul's line of argument (p. 146). In Gal 3:10-14, for example, the curse to which Paul refers is not something that pertains to individuals in isolation. Rather, as the reference to Deuteronomy 27 demonstrates, Paul is thinking corporately— of Israel as a whole, and of the curse about which Israel is warned if it as a whole people fails to live according to the Torah. What concerns him is

> not so much the question of what happens *when this or that individual sins,* but the question of what happens when *the nation as a whole fails* to keep *the Torah as a whole.* (emphasis in the original; p. 146)

What happens in the latter case is exile, a consequence foreseen by the Torah itself (Deuteronomy 27–30).

Wright argues further that in contemporary Jewish self-understanding (Paul's included), the exile by no means came to an end with the return under Cyrus. As long as Israel lived under the domination of foreign empires, and as long as Israel's own leaders were sinful and corrupt, the "curse of the law" first experienced in the exile to Babylon was a continuing reality. In this set of circumstances, Israel was unable to carry out the role that God had intended from the beginning.

This mention of Israel's intended role leads out into the wider dimensions of Wright's reconstruction. Far from seeing Paul as misunderstanding Judaism, Wright wants to align him closely with Jewish patterns of thought, especially the "plight and solution" patterns of thought characteristic of Jewish "restoration eschatology" (to use Sanders's term).[147] Included in this pattern is the anticipated salvation of the Gentiles, especially as it comes to expression in the eschatological pilgrimage tradition. Wright argues that the universal concern reflected in the eschatological pilgrimage tradition is an expression of a universal dimension inherent in the covenantal frame of reference from the beginning. In his reading, both Paul and significant segments of contemporary Judaism generally thought of Israel's election as having taken place not for Israel's sake alone but for the sake of the whole world. God chose Israel in order to bring to fruition intentions for humanity that were present from the beginning but were frustrated by human sin. Quoting *Midr. Gen.* 14.6, he puts it this way:

> "I will make Adam first," says Israel's god in the midrash on Genesis, "and if he goes astray I will send Abraham to sort it all out." The creator calls a people through whom, somehow, he will act decisively within his creation, to eliminate all evil from it and to restore order, justice and peace.[148]

Indeed, the call of Abraham contained within it the promise of a blessing to all nations. But, as the ongoing reality of the exile demonstrates, the persistence of human sin, now within the boundaries of the people Israel, continues to frustrate God's purposes. Enter Christ, who, as Messiah, functions as a representative Israelite and thus as a new Adam, and who, as representative Israelite and representative human being, draws the curse onto himself once and for all, "so that the blessing of covenant renewal might flow out the other side, as God always intended."[149]

Wright attempts to ground Paul's critique of the law in the reality of the exile and thus in the universality of sin. But closer examination reveals that for Wright its real ground is a conception of undifferentiated humanity.[150] He strives to present Paul's critique of the law not as something uniquely determined by Paul's particular circumstances and perspective but as a logical and natural outcome of the exile itself, apparent (at least in principle) to anyone:

> The Torah, however, held out over this people, the agents of promise, the curse which had in fact come true, and was still being proved true, in the events of the exile and its strange continuance right up to Paul's day and beyond. How could the promises, the blessings promised to Abraham, now

reach their intended destination? *The Torah looks as though it might render the promise to Abraham, and to his worldwide family, null and void.* (emphasis added; p. 142)

Thus there is nothing wrong with the law in itself; indeed, the Torah functioned exactly as it was intended to function. But in so doing, in rendering Israel liable to the curse of the exile, the Torah is part of the problem. All who embrace the Torah (for example, the Gentile Christians of Galatia) are consequently under the same curse (p. 147).

Wright thus attempts to ground Paul's critique of the law in covenantal nomism itself. But simply to describe the attempt is to refute it. Wright's Paul makes the inference that if (1) the exile was the manifestation in history of the curse threatened in the Torah, then (2) it is the Torah that stands in the way of God's intentions for the world. While many of Paul's contemporaries would grant the first inference, none would accept the second as valid. If the *problem* is nonobservance of the Torah, why should the solution involve its *elimination?* Jewish restoration eschatology may well have understood the present situation as a continuation of an exile resulting from Israel's corporate failure to keep the Torah (Wright is quite convincing here); but the restoration it anticipated was one in which the Torah would be fully observed.[151] No Jew would have taken the (thus understood) historical outworkings of the law's sanctions as a warrant for dispensing with (some of) its requirements, in the expectation of thereby receiving its promised blessings. If anything stands in the way of God's intentions for the world, it is not the Torah but sin.

It is apparent that Wright understands the real ground of Paul's Torah criticism to lie elsewhere. The problem with the law—the reason that it cannot be part of the Christian gospel of fulfillment—is not its connection with the exile and sin[152] but that it inevitably introduces into the human family a line of demarcation between one group and another. God's intention from the beginning was for a single, undifferentiated humanity; the law by its very nature differentiates between Jew and Gentile; therefore the law cannot be part of the consummation of God's purposes for humankind. This argument appears most clearly in Wright's treatment of the "single seed" of Gal 3:15-18:

> The argument of vv. 15-18 would then run: it is impossible to annul a covenant; the covenant with Abraham always envisaged a single family, not a plurality of families; therefore the Torah, *which creates a plurality by dividing Gentiles from Jews,* stands in the way of the fulfilment of the covenant with Abraham; and this cannot be allowed. (emphasis added; pp. 163–64)

For Wright, then, more fundamental than any of Paul's convictions about Israel and its election is a conviction asserted in Rom 10:12: "there is no distinction between Jew or Greek."[153] This assumption crops up over and over again at crucial points in Wright's argumentation. On Gal 3:10-14: the Torah "cannot be as it stands the boundary-marker of the covenant family promised to Abraham and spoken of by Habakkuk, i.e., the family that is a single worldwide family, the family that is created the other side of judgment, the family characterized by πίστις" (p. 150). On the same passage: "Paul argues that from the perspective of the Old Testament itself the Torah could not be thought of as accomplishing its apparent task of demarcating the covenant family. . . . God all along envisaged another demarcation line, namely faith" (p. 155). On Gal 3:15-20: "Monotheism demands as its corollary a single united family; the Torah, unable to produce this, cannot therefore be the final and permanent expression of the will of the One God" (p. 170). On Rom 9:30-33: "Israel is . . . guilty of a kind of meta-sin, the attempt to confine grace to one race" (p. 240). Again and again, then, the assumption of a single, undifferentiated humanity is brought in to clinch the argument and move it forward.[154]

This way of construing Paul's convictions as they pertain to the Gentile mission can be diagrammed as follows:

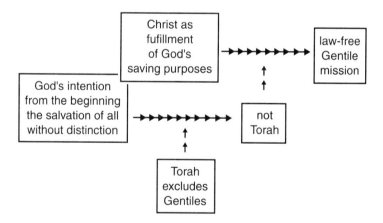

In this construal, Paul's fundamental conviction—the point of departure for the whole structure—is the belief that God's intention from the beginning was to work in history toward the salvation of all of humankind without distinction. Since this conviction is understood to be integral to Jewish self-understanding, and since there is no indication that this conviction was produced by Paul's Christ-experience in any way, it is probably to be assumed that this was a native conviction, something that shaped his convictional universe on both sides of the Damascus experience. The essence of his Damascus experience was the belief that in Christ God's saving intentions had reached their goal and "climax."[155] This new conviction is in a sense independent of the first; it neither produces it nor is produced by it in any strictly logical way. Yet it is intimately connected, in that the former provides the basic frame of reference for giving meaning to the latter. Hence in the diagram the two are depicted as overlapping.

For our purposes the most significant part of the structure is the way Paul's law-free Gentile mission is rooted in the fundamental conviction and thus is independent of his new Christian conviction. Both aspects of the mission—the inclusion of the Gentiles in salvation per se, and the exclusion of the law as a condition of their salvation—are presented as the necessary logical outcome of the universalistic conviction with which Paul begins (and not the christological conviction to which he comes).

When this structure was first introduced in general terms at the outset of this section, it was observed that it apparently stands in fundamental tension with the structure of covenantal nomism. Nothing in Wright's analysis requires us to alter this perception. Despite the brilliance of his thesis and the laudable passion with which he develops it, the fact remains that the convictional structure outlined above, far from being a necessary inference from covenantal axioms, is in essential conflict with covenantal nomism as it is known to us. Indeed, it is interesting to note the way in which Israel, as a Torah-delineated, ethnic group, gets squeezed out of the picture. For Wright, the role of Israel is taken over by Christ without remainder, so much so that any hope of the eschatological salvation of ethnic Israel is eliminated from Romans 11, "all Israel" being read to mean "all in Christ."[156] In order to preserve a Paul who stands in greater continuity with Israel's traditions, Wright is prepared to abandon ethnic Israel itself.[157]

The problem with this reconstruction is the role of the "no distinction" element in the structure. On the one hand, many within Judaism would have agreed that God's saving purposes for the world would ultimately include the Gentiles. But this did not necessarily mean that in the end there would be no distinction between Jew and Gentile. As we have seen, in several of the Jewish patterns of universalism there was the expectation that the Gentiles would be saved *as Gentiles,* the Torah continuing to differentiate between the covenantal elect at the center of God's saving purposes, and those from the other nations invited to gather around them to share the benefits of salvation. One cannot avoid the impression that at various parts of Wright's argument as surveyed above, the idea of "God's intention for a single united family" is brought in by a kind of exegetical sleight of hand. On the other hand, there were those within Judaism who would have agreed that in the end Gentiles would share in salvation with Jews on the same basis without differentiation; but this by no means required the elimination of Torah. For as we have seen, there were those within Judaism who saw proselytism as the sole avenue to salvation for Gentiles. The way into the age to come was the same for Jews and Gentiles without distinction; if Gentiles wanted a share in salvation, they needed to become equal members of the community of salvation marked out by covenant and Torah. Why should Torah be seen as any more of a hindrance to a "single united family"—as introducing any more fundamental a principle of differentiation—than was the case with Christ?

The problem with the position represented by Wright, then, is the assumption of a tight logical linkage among three elements: (1) that final salvation would include the Gentiles; (2) that there could be no distinction between Jews and Gentiles in salvation; and (3) that the Torah is not to function as a boundary marker for the community of salvation. While #1 is commonly found within covenantal nomism, it is not necessarily paired with #2. While #1 and #2 were held by some covenantal nomists, #3 would never have been seen as a necessary—or even as a possible—consequence. Either Wright is right, in which case the conclusion is unavoidable that Paul has misunderstood or misrepresented Judaism, or we need to find some other way of accounting for the presence of these three elements in Paul's set of convictions.

One possibility, of course, is that Paul's "no distinction" conviction is secondary, a corollary of a more fundamental abandonment of the Torah. For one reason or another, Paul comes to the belief that the Torah is not a means or a condition of salvation. Already within this chapter, for example, we have seen how several of Paul's arguments against the law (those based on works and on sin) make sense only on the basis of an underlying logic in which "salvation through Christ" leads to "therefore not through Torah." But since the law is the mechanism by which Jew is differentiated from Gentile, one might argue that for Paul "not Torah" brought with it as an unavoidable next step, "therefore no distinction between Jew and Gentile." Such a possibility will be explored in the next chapter (§6.3).

A closer examination of Paul's "no distinction" statements, however, leads to results that both raise questions about Wright's construal and lead in the direction of a different possibility. Paul's "no distinction" statements are by no means global assertions. He does not believe that the traditional, Torah-based distinctions between Jew and Gentile are completely irrelevant or have been totally obliterated, Jews simply being absorbed into a larger undifferentiated humanity with no ongoing significance. The statements in question are as specific and limited in their applicability as are the statements about works and faith. In the contexts of both Rom 3:22 and 10:12 the issue is that of entrance requirements into the community of salvation, and the point being argued is that Torah observance is not to be imposed on Gentiles as a condition of membership. But when this is not at issue, Paul's language betrays at many turns the fact that the Jew-Gentile distinction continues to play a fundamental role in his system of convictions.[158] The following observations are relevant here.

1. As the argument of Romans 9–11 indicates—in particular, the surprising argumentative turn at 11:11 toward the conclusion that "all Israel will be saved" (11:25)—empirical Israel, that differentiated segment of humanity identified by ancestry and Torah observance, has by no means disappeared from Paul's set of theological categories. Israel's story may be one strand of a wider human story, but that strand remains distinct and discernible to the end.

2. While Paul can assert that "in Christ there is no Jew nor Greek," this does not prevent him from assigning ongoing theological significance to the identifiably *Jewish* portion of the Christian community. It constitutes a remnant, of which Paul himself is a representative and prominent member (Rom 11:1-5), and which by its very existence demonstrates God's ongoing faithfulness to Israel as a whole (11:16). Further, it has functioned as the means by which Israel's spiritual blessings have been extended to the Gentiles (Rom 15:27).

3. Paul describes the sphere of his apostleship, the mission field in which he has been commissioned to proclaim the gospel, not as humankind in general but as the Gentile world in particular;[159] while he often uses city and province terminology to refer to local congregations, when he wants a term to refer to his churches as a whole, ἔθνη (Gentiles) is invariably his choice.[160] The term gives clear evidence of a frame of reference in which humanity is divided into two distinct groups by virtue of Israel's special election, and thus betrays a continuing Israel-centered viewpoint. Indeed, such casual usage is even more compelling than any direct and explicit statement about Israel itself. Paul sees himself as a Jewish apostle to the Gentiles, not simply as the bearer of a universal message to an undifferentiated humanity.

Statements that assert no distinction between Jew and Gentile, then, do not function in a global, categorical, and unqualified way. At the very least they coexist with patterns of speech that reflect a view of the world in which the Jew-Gentile distinction is a basic building block. But is it simply a case of coexistence? Do we have to do here with two uncoordinated and ultimately divergent strands of thought? Here a second observation becomes relevant. As we saw earlier with respect to Romans 4, Paul insists that Gentile believers, on the basis of their faith and despite their uncircumcision, are to be seen as members of Abraham's family ("seed"). Indeed, so insistent is he on getting to this destination that he runs through all the red lights in the texts under discussion (esp. Genesis 17), while ignoring other roads in the text that would have led him to the territory marked "Gentile blessing" without having to go through that marked "Abraham's seed." In other words, Paul's argument in Romans 4 is driven by a concern to place Jewish and Gentile believers on the same ground "without distinction." Far from calling the traditional covenantal differentiation into fundamental question, however, this concept of "no distinction" actually depends on it for its meaning: the gospel proclaimed by Paul offers Gentiles a place in Abraham's family on equal terms with Jews. As the epistle to the Ephesians puts it, those who once were "aliens from the commonwealth of Israel" (2:12) are now full and equal "members of the household of God (2:19).[161]

In formal terms, then, Paul's use of the idea of "no distinction" is similar to that found among Jewish advocates of proselytism, especially those who took the stricter line that only those Gentiles who became proselytes would have a share in salvation.[162] In both, Abraham's family stands at the center of the story of salvation; in both, membership in Abraham's family is a prerequisite for salvation; in both, Gentiles need to become equal members of Abraham's family in order to have a share in salvation; in both, then, there is "no distinction" between Jew and Gentile as to the prerequisites for salvation. The difference is that in Paul's reconfiguration, Christ plays the role elsewhere assigned to Torah.

The pattern of Paul's "no distinction" statements is therefore consistent with the thesis that he thinks of the Gentiles as proselytes to an "Israel" whose boundary marker is Christ rather than Torah. Since he also seems to attach ongoing theological significance to an Israel identified in traditional Torah terms, if this thesis were correct we would have to reckon with a certain element of category-confusion: the boundary of Abraham's family being marked here by Christ (e.g., Gal 3:29) and there by circumcision (e.g., Rom 11:25); Gentiles being equal members with

Jews of the former but categorically differentiated from Jews in the latter; and so on.[163] But no one ever said that Paul was not confusing!

## 5.4 Findings and Implications

In this chapter I have investigated Paul's use of three universalistic-sounding constructs (works, sin, equality of Jew and Gentile). My goal has been to test the possibility that in one way or other Paul begins with a fundamental conviction pertaining to humankind as a whole and without distinction and that his interest in the Gentiles and their salvation is grounded ultimately in this basic conviction.

The stakes have been high. If Paul's statements in key passages of Galatians and Romans can be taken as an accurate indication of how the underlying convictional logic is structured, then Paul has fundamentally misunderstood covenantal nomism. In each case, however, careful investigation has led to the conclusion that these universalistic constructs are to be seen instead as devices used to defend a more fundamental conviction that underlies the law-free mission to the Gentiles, namely, that in Christ salvation has been made available for all, Gentiles included, without the prerequisite of Torah observance (in particular, those aspects of the Torah serving to differentiate Jew from Gentile).

This is not an original conclusion, but an essential part of the emerging new paradigm. What is new is the attempt to keep the Gentiles in focus, with particular attention to the point at which they might enter into the convictional structure. My findings can be divided into two areas, one concerning the law-free aspect of Paul's Gentile mission, the other concerning the interest in the Gentiles itself. With respect to the first, we can state firm conclusions. In each of the cases under discussion, it is clear that the arguments (concerning works, sin, and equality) function as support for a more basic convictional structure that can be represented as follows:

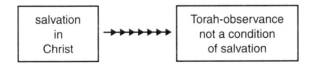

That is, Paul's rejection of Torah observance as a condition of membership in the community of salvation arises not from any basic conviction concerning humankind as an undifferentiated whole but from a conviction that the community of salvation is to be determined by the boundary marker of faith in Christ, and that as a result no other boundary marker—including that set of Torah-prescribed observances marking the boundary between Jew and Gentile—is to be imposed.

For this section of Paul's convictional structure to be fully established, however, two additional aspects need to be explored. First, while we have ruled out any general conception of "humankind as a whole" as the basis for his "not Torah" conviction, what about a more specific conviction that Christ has accomplished salvation for the Gentiles? The former would have been a fundamental conviction, independent of Christ and presumably part of Paul's native convictional framework, while the latter would have stemmed directly from his Christian experience. As we will see in later chapters, attempts have been made to derive Paul's concern for the Gentiles directly from his belief in Christ or from his commissioning as an apostle of Christ. Is it possible, then, that "not Torah" is the *result* of "salvation for Gentiles," so that another step needs to be added to the convictional sequence ("Christ"→→→→"Gentiles"→→→→"not Torah")?

The second question concerns the linkage between "Christ" and "not Torah." Why is it that for Paul (unlike some other Jewish Christians) the belief that salvation had been accomplished in Christ led to the belief that the Torah could not continue as before?

Both of these questions will be picked up in the next chapter. But while the resulting convictional structure will account for the *law-free* nature of Paul's Gentile mission, what about the interest in the Gentiles itself? As was mentioned above, some would derive this directly from Paul's encounter with Christ in one way or another; these possibilities will be addressed in chapters 7 and 9. But another common construal links it more directly with the Torah, seeing it as the *result* of the convictional sequence sketched above. Because what differentiates Jews from Gentiles is the Torah, the elimination of Torah as a prerequisite for salvation could bring with it the elimination of the Jew-Gentile distinction as a meaningful category. "Not Torah" leads to "no distinction," which leads in turn to "Gentiles too." This possibility will be picked up in the next chapter as well.

While such possibilities need to be explored, the material examined in this chapter suggests that the Gentile part of the equation was there from the beginning as a fundamental conviction. This conviction about the Gentiles is to be understood not in the Israel-denying sense which served as our point of departure (the possibility that undifferentiated humanity was Paul's basic category, eventually doing away with the Jew-Gentile distinction) but in an Israel-centered sense that arises from the universalistic dimensions of covenantal nomism itself. In other words, what has been suggested by the evidence is the possibility of a *revision of a Jewish pattern of universalism*. In particular, the pattern of argumentation in the passages under discussion is at least congruent with—and at one point is best explained by—the conceptual structures of Jewish proselytism, the one difference being that for Paul Christ plays the boundary-marking role traditionally associated with the Torah.

Paul's statements concerning sin exhibit formal parallels with the pattern of proselytism. In each case, while sin is a basic feature of human existence, God has provided Israel with a means of righteousness and salvation (Torah/Christ); and in each case, this means is also available to the Gentiles as well. Further, with respect to the law, even when Paul's Christ-centered revision of the law's role is given full weight, he still sees it (in a manner similar to that of proselytism) as a divine instrument that both differentiates Jew from Gentile, and is of at least potential applicability to Gentiles as well as Jews.

Further, despite surface appearances, Paul's statements about the equality of Jew and Gentile are also parallel to the pattern of proselytism. On the one hand, these "no distinction" statements are by no means global assertions; questions of membership requirements aside, Jew and Gentile continue to be distinct and meaningful categories for Paul. More importantly, on the other hand, the group to which Jewish and Gentile believers belong on the undifferentiated basis of their faith in Christ is none other than the family of Abraham. These statements function not to dissolve the special place of Abraham's family, but to establish Gentile believers as equal members within it. While differing in substance (Christ replacing Torah as the boundary marker of Abraham's family), the two structures are parallel in form.

But the significance of Abraham goes beyond mere formal parallelism. In our discussion of Paul's works/faith duality, we saw how Paul is so committed to the position that Gentile believers belong to Abraham's family that he develops an argument (in Romans 4) running directly counter to the plain sense of the scriptural text, even though the Genesis passage under discussion provided him with ample opportunity for a weaker "blessed but not family" position on the Gentiles. At issue between Paul and his interlocutor are two different ways of viewing Gentiles as proselytes (members of Abraham's family); alternative conceptions represented by the other "patterns of universalism" appear not to have entered into Paul's considerations.

I conclude, therefore, that Paul thought of Gentile believers as prose-lytes, except that for him Christ has replaced Torah as the boundary marker of the family of Abraham. At this point, the hypothesis is simply a possible explanation. Before concluding that it is a probable or even a necessary one, other convictional elements must be explored.

## CHAPTER SIX

# The Torah

The scope of this chapter is much more modest than its daunting title might suggest. My concern here is not to carry out a full discussion of Paul and the law—an impossible task in any case—but to explore the possible connections between Paul's convictions concerning the law (not to be imposed as a condition of salvation in Christ) and those concerning the Gentiles (to be included within the sphere of salvation made available in Christ). These issues were raised in the discussion of works, sin, and equality in the previous chapter. But three questions concerning Paul's "not Torah" conviction remain and need to be settled.

(1) The first is similar in structure to that arising from Paul's "no distinction" statements (see §5.3). Might it be the case that for Paul "not Torah" is the result of an already-present concern for the Gentiles, this time in the form not of a general commitment to the equality of all humanity but of a Christian belief that Christ has accomplished salvation for the Gentiles? That is, in one way or another, Paul's beliefs about Christ include or produce the belief that Christ has accomplished salvation for the Gentiles, and this in turn has led him to reject the law ("Christ" →+++→ "Gentiles" →+++→ "not Torah"). In chapter 5 I gave a negative answer to the earlier version of this question, concluding that "not Torah" was more likely the result of the belief that salvation was in Christ. As we will see, the evidence brought forward in §5.3 is sufficient to establish a similar conclusion here as well; "not Torah" is directly derived from "salvation in Christ," not from "salvation for Gentiles."

This conclusion will lead to two further questions. (2) One of these concerns the christological displacement of the law itself. If Paul's convictional logic moves from "Christ" to "therefore not Torah," why does he conceive of the two in such antithetical and mutually exclusive terms? What is there about Christ that displaces the law from the role it plays within covenantal nomism? (3) Given a negative answer to the first question posed above, might it be the case that the connection between the Torah and the Gentiles runs in the opposite direction, "not Torah" leading to the corollary "therefore, Gentiles too"? In other words, is the origin of Paul's concern for the Gentiles to be found in the displacement of the law ("not Torah"→→→→→"Gentiles")?

We will deal with these questions in turn.

## 6.1 From "Gentiles" to "Not Torah"?

There are several possible ways of deriving a concern for the Gentiles directly from the belief in Christ itself. One of these is rooted in eschatological pilgrimage ideas: if the Messiah has appeared, the time has arrived for the final inclusion of the Gentiles. Another is found in the emergence of elevated christological conceptions: if Christ is Lord (κύριος) of all, then the Gentiles are included within his lordship. For present purposes we need neither a full listing of these nor a complete description of their structure. They are of interest here because of the possible implication they have in common, namely, that however Paul might have moved from a basic belief in Christ to a derivative one that the Gentiles are to be saved, it was this resultant interest in the Gentiles that produced his distinctive position on the law.

This way of connecting Torah and Gentiles is not suggested as frequently as the inverse. One of the reasons for this, no doubt, is the absence of any Pauline statement explicitly linking Christ, Gentiles, and Torah in this sequence; if such a convictional linkage were operative in Paul, its workings would have to be discovered beneath the surface of the text. Nevertheless, such a reading of Paul is at least latent in those constructions in which his apostolic call to a Gentile mission is foundational, although, as we will see, the inner structure of his call tends to remain unexamined in these treatments.[1] It is found more explicitly, however, in several recent attempts to link it with eschatological pilgrimage ideas. One example is R. David Kaylor's study of Jews and Gentiles in Romans. While his understanding of the origin of Paul's concern for the Gentiles tends to vacillate,[2] in the most frequently encountered construal, eschatological pilgrimage ideas lead Paul to the Gentiles, and this in turn leads to the dethroning of the law:

> He came to believe that he was living in the new eschatological time in which God extended the covenant to include Gentile as well as Jew. The logic of that conviction led Paul to affirm that if the gospel is for Gentile as

well as for Jew, then there can be no distinction: the new covenant must be
offered to both on the same basis.[3]

Similar construals can be found in other studies as well.[4] Schematically:

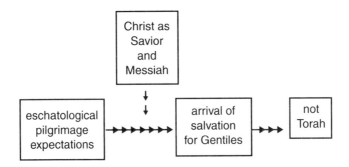

What is of interest here is not the eschatological pilgrimage starting
point, but the resultant sequence, "Gentiles"→→→→→"not Torah." This
way of putting Paul's convictions together is certainly more plausible than
the related one explored in §5.3; it is easier to think of him coming to see
the Gentiles as somehow included within Christ's saving work than it is
to think of the self-confessed "zealot for the traditions of [his] ancestors"
(Gal 1:14) as also holding firmly to the equality of all humanity without
distinction. Nevertheless, the considerations leading to the rejection of
the earlier possibility weigh just as heavily here. At the very least, if this
represents the flow of Paul's convictional structure, we would need to
abandon all thought of him beginning as a covenantal nomist.

To be sure, there have been one or two attempts to see Paul's "not
Torah" conviction as consistent with Judaism. An older approach, now
largely abandoned, was the attempt to argue that Judaism itself expected
the Torah to be abrogated in the age to come.[5] More plausible is the attempt to build on righteous Gentile concepts: Paul believes that Christ
has accomplished salvation for the Gentiles, but he combines this with a
native conviction that the Gentiles do not need to become converts to
Judaism in order to be considered righteous. Such an assumption lies
close to the heart of the "two covenant" approach of L. Gaston, J. Gager,
and others (see below, §8.2). While this approach is unlikely (if Paul believed that the Mosaic covenant continued to be in effect and sufficient
for Jews, he would have had plenty of occasion to say so), righteous Gentile patterns of thought can be more plausibly combined with eschatological pilgrimage expectations, as in the work of P. Fredriksen: in believing

that the law is not to be imposed on Gentiles, Paul is simply adhering to "the traditional Jewish apocalyptic view."[6]

But the convictional element that renders this particular reconstruction unlikely also makes it difficult in the more general case to square such a proposed sequence of convictions ("Christ"→→→→→"Gentiles"→→→→→ "not Torah") with the boundary condition of covenantal nomism as Paul's pre-Damascus convictional framework. I refer to his insistence that believing Gentiles are ipso facto full and equal members of Abraham's family. Such an assertion would have been totally incompatible with righteous Gentile conceptions, the essence of which was the assumption that Gentiles could be righteous without becoming full Torah adherents, and thus *without* becoming full and equal members of Abraham's family. The tenacity with which Paul holds to the contrary conviction—amply illustrated in our study of Romans 4—demonstrates the inadequacy of any attempt to account for his position in terms of righteous Gentile conceptions, whatever surface similarities there might have been in the practical outworking of things.

But at the same time, it makes it difficult both to hold to a "Christ" →→→→→"Gentiles"→→→→→"not Torah" explanation of his law-free Gentile mission, and to avoid the conclusion that he fundamentally misunderstood covenantal nomism. With respect to Kaylor's eschatological explanation of Paul's Gentile concern, I showed in chapter 3 that covenantal nomism would have provided two options for someone who believed both that Jesus had ushered in the age of messianic fulfillment and that this age of salvation included the Gentiles. One of these was a righteous Gentile pattern, in which Gentiles would be included *as Gentiles,* the Torah-based lines of demarcation between Jew and Gentile remaining intact. The other was a proselyte pattern, where Gentiles would be expected fully to embrace the Torah and become, like native-born Jews, members of Abraham's family. Jewish expectations about the status of Gentiles in the eschatological age do not appear to have been fixed (*pace* Fredriksen); the evidence suggests that both possibilities would have had adherents. What the evidence does not allow, however, is the combination—Gentiles who remained Gentiles but were nevertheless equal members of Abraham's family.

Paul cannot be explained, then, on such premises as Kaylor suggests. If Paul had (1) started within a framework of covenantal nomism, had then (2) come to the belief that the era of Gentile salvation, anticipated within that framework, had been opened up in Christ, but (3) understood Christ in a way that did not itself challenge his native understanding of the Torah, then his convictions about the Gentiles could not have developed the way they did. Unless we are prepared to give up covenantal nomism as a boundary condition, we need to see the conviction "not Torah" as a result of his new convictions about Christ, not simply of the inclusion of the Gentiles.

And what is true of this eschatologically based reconstruction would be equally true of *any* possible "Christ"→→→→"Gentiles" sequence. The belief that the Gentiles were to be saved by Christ would not, alone and by itself, produce the distinctive profile of Paul's Gentiles, that is, uncircumcised, but Abraham's seed nonetheless. Any attempt to explain him in this way would require us to assume what needs to be proved; only if there were additional factors (probably resulting from his perception of Christ), leading him to believe that the Torah was not to be imposed on Gentiles, would his convictions have emerged as they did. His new perception of Christ as Savior and his elimination of the Torah as a condition of membership must have been linked directly—the one somehow a direct corollary of the other—rather than indirectly through the intervening step of the inclusion of Gentiles in salvation. As Sanders has observed, the shape of Paul's thinking on the matter comes most clearly to expression in Gal 2:21: "If righteousness comes through the law, then Christ died for nothing."[7] The law is eliminated not because it excludes the Gentiles but because it has been replaced by Christ.

## 6.2 The Christ-Torah Antithesis

The conclusion reached in the previous paragraph is in agreement with Sanders's way of characterizing Paul's pattern of argumentation, summed up in his famous slogan, "the solution as preceding the problem": salvation is through Christ; therefore, it cannot be through Torah. But why this "therefore"? Why should law and Christ be antithetical in this way? What was there about Christ or the gospel as Paul perceived it that was categorically at odds with the Torah? What convictional logic is at work here?

A significant lacuna in Sanders's work is that, while he recognizes the question, he provides no real answer to it. He recognizes that many other Jewish Christians, while agreeing with the first half of the argument (salvation through Christ), would find the second half (therefore not through Torah) a total non sequitur. And so he asks the pertinent question, "Why did he [Paul] draw conclusions which others in his situation, or in similar situations, did not?"[8] But he offers no real answer.

A full answer to this question would need to include the diachronic component, the identification of the stage in Paul's experience (upbring-

ing in Judaism, activity as a persecutor, conversion, or later Christian experience) in which his Christ-Torah antithesis was rooted or in which it
emerged. If Paul is to be understood as a covenantal nomist who has come
to believe that salvation is through Christ, the most likely point at which
he first perceived a Christ-Torah antithesis would have been his initial
contact with the Christian message, namely, as a persecutor of the church.
Indeed, since it is precisely as a zealot for the Torah that Paul persecuted
the church (Gal 1:14; Phil 3:6), the most plausible and economical way
of accounting for his later view of the law is to see it as a Damascus-
produced inversion of an already-perceived Christ-Torah antithesis.[9]
Here, however, I concentrate on the synchronic aspect, and ask what convictional structure is reflected by the statements in the letters themselves.
What in his convictions about Christ and the Torah constrains Paul to say,
"If righteousness comes through the law, then Christ died for nothing"?

The most common answer to this question centers on the means by
which "Christ died," the cross itself. It is argued that from the perspective
of first-century Judaism, the idea of a suffering and dying Messiah was
not only a contradiction in terms, totally unanticipated in Jewish eschatological expectation; more than that, it was categorically ruled out by Deut
21:22-23. This verse of the Torah declares that those who are "hanged
on a tree" are "accursed of God." Evidence from Qumran indicates that
already by the first century this text was being read in connection with
crucifixion.[10] Accordingly, it is argued that the message of a crucified
Messiah would have been perceived by faithful Jews as an affront to the
Torah itself. By proclaiming as divinely favored one upon whom the Torah
had pronounced a curse, the Christians were proclaiming a message categorically at odds with Torah religion. In his conversion experience (so this
line of interpretation goes) Paul came to believe that Jesus had indeed
been raised by God. God had overturned the judgment of the Torah,
which carried with it the inevitable conclusion that God's truth was to be
found on the Christ side of the categorical divide. In this common way of
understanding him, then, it is the scandal of a crucified Messiah in general
(see 1 Cor 1:23), and the curse pronounced by the Torah on such a person
in particular (see Gal 3:13, which cites Deut 21:23), that accounts (at
least in part) for the sharp antithesis between Christ and Torah in Paul's
convictional structure.[11]

But I do not believe that such an explanation stands up to scrutiny.[12]
First, it is not readily apparent that a first-century Jew like Paul would
have seen a crucified person as necessarily and for that reason under a
curse. The text of the MT is difficult (קללת אלהים); while the LXX renders
it "cursed by God" (also Gal 3:13; 11QTemple 64.12), it could also be
read as "an affront to God" (Aquila; Theodotion) or even "one who

curses God" (Symmachus; *Tg. Onq.*; *m. Sanh.* 6.4).[13] In the latter cases, "hanging" or crucifixion would not in itself constitute a curse. Further, if this reasoning holds, then Saul and Jonathan (2 Sam 21:12), the eight hundred crucified by Jannaeus (*Ant.* 13.380), and the many put to death in a similar way by the Romans should have also been seen as dying under God's curse. Both common sense and the lack of any corroborating evidence[14] indicates the fallacy of such a line of reasoning. As P. Fredriksen has observed, "the spiritual status of the deceased cannot be inferred from the disposition of the body."[15] While one could understand how Deut 21:22-23 might have been useful as an anti-Christian polemical text,[16] it is difficult to imagine anyone coming to the conclusion, on the basis of this text alone, that the message of a crucified Messiah was in fundamental conflict with Torah religion.

To expand on this a little, a Jewish Christian, convinced both of the validity of the Torah and of the message of a crucified Messiah, could have resolved any tensions between the two, particularly the problem apparently posed by Deut 21:22-23, in a much simpler fashion. One could simply say that in this case the court made a mistake; Jesus was not guilty of "a crime punishable by death" (cf. Deut 21:22).[17] Alternatively, since Jesus had been put to death by the Romans, he could have been seen as a martyr for the cause of God. Or this text could have been countered by others, such as the suffering servant of Deutero-Isaiah or the righteous sufferer of the Psalms. Indeed, it could be argued that Gal 3:10-14 represents just this kind of attempt to resolve the problems raised (for Christian interpretation) by Deut 21:23.[18] In any case, the point is this: if a "zealot for the traditions of [his] ancestors" (such as Paul; cf. Gal 1:14) came to believe that God had raised Jesus from the dead, one would expect that he would have been inclined to search for a *resolution* of any perceived tension between Christ and the law, before concluding (in Meyer's words) that "if Torah had no room for Christ's crucifixion, so much the worse for Torah."[19] It is difficult to imagine anyone coming to the conclusion, simply on the basis of Deut 21:22-23, that there was no room for a crucified Messiah in Torah religion. Paul's Christ-Torah antithesis must be rooted somewhere else.

I have noted the way in which Paul's argument against the law centers on its role as a boundary marker, as a means of community identification. Righteousness, for example, is a membership term: to say that one is righteous is not, in the first instance, to say that the person conforms with some absolute standard of moral perfection, but that the person is a member in good standing of the covenant community.[20] The "works of the law" have to do with those aspects of the law by which Jews are differentiated from Gentiles, with the concomitant assumption that these define the boundary of the people of God and thus are required for righteousness.[21] The debate over Abraham in Galatians 3–4 and Romans 4 has to do with the issue of membership in his family: is it based on law and circumcision, or on faith in Christ? What has been emerging from much of the argumentation to this point, then, is that Paul's Christ-Torah antithesis is fundamentally sociological (or, if a more theological term is desired, ecclesiological) in nature. Paul perceives Christ and Torah as rival boundary markers, rival ways of determining the people of God, rival entrance requirements for the community of salvation.

Indeed, there are significant formal parallels between the function of the Torah in covenantal nomism and of Christ in Paul's pattern of religion. Both have to do with a community of salvation, formed by God in the present and awaiting full salvation in the future. The Torah in one, and Christ in the other, function as entrance requirements and marks of membership. Further, just as living in conformity with the Torah is the means of maintaining one's membership in the covenant community ("staying in," in Sanders's phrase), so continuing to "walk in Christ" (cf. Col 2:6-7) is the means of maintaining one's membership in the new community of salvation. And in each case, "righteousness" functions as a membership term, a way of indicating one's status as a member in good standing. It is surprising, then, that Sanders perceives the two patterns of religion (as he calls them) as being so distinct.[22] Differences there are, indeed; but they arise from Paul's convictions about Christ, who, differences in substance notwithstanding, plays a very similar role in the *formal* structure of his religion.[23]

My position, then, is that Paul's Christ-Torah antithesis is rooted in a perception that Christ and Torah represent mutually exclusive boundary markers, rival ways of determining the community of salvation. This perception emerged in conjunction with Paul's persecuting activity prior to his Damascus experience; this experience in turn, understood as signifying God's vindication of Christ, produced the conviction that the community of the righteous, awaiting salvation at the "end of the ages" (cf. 1 Cor 10:11), was marked and determined by Christ. My position is similar to that developed by U. Wilckens, except that I perceive the similarity between Christ and Torah not to be limited to apocalyptic material, but to pertain to covenantal nomism as a whole.[24]

The vigor with which Paul the apostle resisted any measure suggesting that Christ's role was being usurped by the law indicates that his perception of an antithesis was just as categorical after Damascus as before. Why was this so? Why was he not able to find some way of resolving the perceived tension between the Torah and the Christ?

Torah and messianism are not intrinsically opposed, of course. As long as they are related *sequentially,* with the Torah defining the community assured of salvation when the Messiah comes, Judaism could tolerate a range of opinions on the nature and status of the Torah in the messianic age.[25] Similarly, given the very fluid nature of Jewish messianism, there is no reason to believe that Jews would categorically reject any notion of a Messiah who endured suffering in the process of bringing salvation to the community defined by the Torah and of ushering its members into the age to come. The point at which the problem emerges is the peculiar already/not yet structure of early Christian messianism, which had the effect of replacing the sequential relationship of Messiah and Torah with a *parallel* or *overlapping,* and thus potentially rival one. In early Christian proclamation, the Messiah has appeared in advance of the final eschatological era of salvation, and participation in that era of salvation is made dependent on acceptance of this Messiah. In consequence of this, Christ becomes, at least implicitly, another—and hence rival—way of drawing the boundary in this age, of the community assured of salvation in the age to come. Instead of being smoothly continuous and congruent ways of describing the *same community* in *different eras* of salvation, Christ and Torah become, at least potentially, conflicting ways of determining the community of salvation in the pre-parousia period.[26] While the notion of a suffering and dying Messiah was indeed unprecedented, the cross appeared scandalous to Paul not so much in itself as in its temporal location, and thus in its community-defining role.

I suggest that from his pre-Damascus point of observation—outside the Christian movement and a zealot for the traditional Torah-defined way of life—Paul was able to see, probably more clearly than the Christians themselves,[27] that the kerygma implied a rival definition of the community of salvation, and thus that Christ and Torah were in fundamental conflict. His acceptance of the kerygma meant a radical shift in the perspective from which he viewed the conflict, but it did not lessen or remove it. If "Christ," then "not Torah."

## 6.3 From "Not Torah" to "Gentiles"?

This brings us to another possibility for the origin of Paul's turning to the Gentiles. Might it have been the case that this Christ-driven displacement of the law as a membership requirement meant the elimination of that which differentiated Jew from Gentile, and thus meant for Paul that the door of salvation now stood wide open to the Gentiles? While we have rejected the possibility that Paul's convictions ran from "Gentiles in" to "no Torah" (§6.1), might the movement have been in the reverse order? Many scholars would answer in the affirmative. One example is James Dunn, who suggests that the vindication of one who had been cursed by the law meant, for Paul, the end of the law "in its function of marking the boundary between the righteous and the sinner, the Jew and the Gentile. . . . The *immediate* corollary for Paul would be that God must therefore favour the cursed one, the sinner outside the covenant, the Gentile."[28] But to examine this position in more detail, I have chosen as a representative figure someone whose key work was done in the pre-Sanders period,[29] W. D. Davies and his seminal *Paul and Rabbinic Judaism*.

Davies's reconstruction is of intrinsic interest here because his work was instrumental in opening up the search for a new paradigm. Given his agenda—to understand Paul as a Pharisee who came to believe that in Jesus the Messiah had come—it might be expected that he would have understood Paul's Gentile mission as an outworking of eschatological pilgrimage expectations. His reading of Judaism would not have really allowed for this, however, since in his view such expectations had fallen away for the most part by the first century, being replaced by a "narrow nationalism" (p. 61) in which proselytism was the "only hope" for the salvation of the Gentiles (p. 63). And so instead, he finds the origins of Paul's later mission to the Gentiles in two aspects of his pre-Damascus frame of mind. One is what he describes as the "uneasy conscience" (pp. 63, 66) which Paul shared with many of his contemporaries as they contemplated the fate of the Gentiles according to the hard doctrines of their tradition. The other—coming to more explicit expression in several later works[30]—has to do with the perceptions of the early Christian movement that fueled his persecuting zeal. These perceptions, as Davies sees them, are twofold: christologically, the Christians were proclaiming as Messiah one who, by virtue of his crucifixion, was subject to the curse pronounced by the law (Deut. 21:22-23); ecclesiologically, the Christians were prepared to admit as full members many who fell far short of the law's demands. On both counts, then, the early Christian message represented a fundamental challenge to a Torah-centered way of life. Because this provided the framework in which Paul's Damascus experience took place, this experience meant not only that the formerly rejected message had been vindicated in the resurrection of Jesus, but at the same time that the Torah had been replaced by Christ as the identifying mark of the people of salvation.[31]

What is of concern is the way things develop from here. The unfolding logic of Paul's conversion experience leads him inexorably from Christ, to the displacement of Torah, and thus to the Gentiles. The displacement of the law dissolved the nationalistic character of the people of the Messiah, which in turn opened the door to the Gentiles. Paul experienced

> the realization that it was no longer devotion to the Torah which was primary but faith in Christ; and because this faith in Christ or personal relationship to Christ was possible for anyone he could become the friend of sinners and publicans and those who were far off, the strangers and foreigners, the Gentiles, and they could become joint heirs with him in the blessings of God. The religion of the Torah was essentially a national religion. . . . Christ was, however, a revelation of God apart from the Law. *This meant that one could be a Christian without being a Jew, and so the doors were open to the Gentiles.* In Judaism all had to be Jews, there could be no Greek or Scythian. In Christ there could be both Jew and Greek and Scythian, *the national principle had been transcended.*[32]

Or again:

> All this made Paul's head swim. And he had to face an even more staggering fact. If God had, indeed, visited these "people of the land," would he not also visit the Gentiles? The answer could not be in doubt. All the conversion accounts connect Paul's vision with a call to the Gentile world. The God who had given his Messiah freely to the despised among the Jews, would also include all in his mercy. *The barriers between Jew and Gentile were down. The Gentile world had become the object of God's grace.*[33]

Of course, this experience would have resolved the uneasy conscience that Davies posits for the pre-Damascus Paul.[34] But the notion of an uneasy conscience—resting as it does on questionable assumptions about first-century Jewish thinking concerning the Gentiles[35]—is not an essential part of the convictional structure for which Davies is serving as a representative. The essential link, rather, is the assumption that for Paul the end of the law is equivalent to, or leads inevitably to, the end of the distinction between Jew and Gentile. This structure can be depicted as follows:

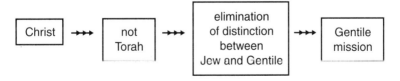

One text that might be appealed to in support of such a structure is Rom 10:4: "For Christ is the end of the law so that there may be righteousness for everyone who believes." One could also adduce those texts that have come up already in §5.3, Rom 3:22 and 10:12, where Paul asserts that there is no distinction between Jew and Gentile; and Gal 3:28 and Col 3:11, where we read that in Christ "there is no Jew nor Greek" (cf. 1 Cor 12:13).[36] But the popularity of this way of structuring Paul's convictions depends not so much on this or that specific text as on its ability to provide a plausible link among three convictions apparent throughout his discourse as a whole: Christ as Savior; Torah not a prerequisite for salvation; salvation includes the Gentiles on equal terms.

The problem with such a linkage, however, is that the Jew-Gentile distinction, supposedly dissolved and eliminated by the abolition of the Torah, stubbornly refuses to disappear. Paul persists in making statements suggesting that an ethnically identified Israel, differentiated from the Gentiles in traditional Torah-determined ways, continues to be a significant category even in the new sphere of reality determined by Christ. "Not Torah" does not seem to be equivalent to "not Israel"; "no distinction" does not seem to be a global and fundamental conviction. The bridge constructed between "not Torah" and "Gentiles" in the diagram above, then, seems to be without its necessary middle span.

Questions about this middle span emerge most strikingly with respect to the concern for the status of Israel in Romans 9–11 and, in particular, the argument for the eventual salvation of "all Israel" in 11:11-32. Given the flow of the argument in chapters 1–8, especially the attempts in the first three chapters to undercut any notion of Jewish privilege and to place Jew and Gentile on equal terms, the emergence of such a concern here has always been the occasion of surprise. Dodd speaks for many when he questions the logical consistency of Paul's argument here, suggesting that his conclusions stand in fundamental conflict with his premises.[37] While Dodd's commentary is representative of an older brand of scholarship, the collapse of the previous paradigm has by no means caused the perception of logical inconsistency to disappear.[38] Before reflecting on the significance of this phenomenon for our discussion, let us look at it a little more closely.[39]

The question raised in 9:1-6a—Has God's word to Israel failed?—is not itself entirely unexpected, having been raised in a provisional way in 3:1. As Paul responds to the question, however, it is really not until 11:11 that we encounter a substantially unanticipated turn in the argument, leading to the apparently inconsistent conclusion. Perhaps the most economical way of describing it is to say that while in 9:1—11:10 Paul seems to be arguing that the present situation is in no way inconsistent with God's promises to Israel,[40] after 11:11 the argument proceeds on the assumption that only if the present situation is reversed will God be proved faithful. Up to 11:10, Paul has defined Israel solely in terms of the faithful remnant (9:6b-9; 11:1-10), defended God's elective freedom to choose the children of promise from the Gentiles as well as the Jews (9:10-29), and demonstrated the culpability of the remainder of Israel for rejecting the gospel (9:30—10:21). The burden of the argument clearly seems to be that the *present situation*—a remnant of believing Jews, a growing body of faithful Gentiles, and a hardened majority of Abraham's natural off-spring—in no way indicates that "the word of God" to Israel has "failed" (cf. 9:6).

But from 11:11 on, the argument is clearly driven by the assumption that only if he can establish the eventual salvation of "all Israel"—a category just as Jewish as, but much larger than, the "remnant"—will he be able to affirm that "God has not rejected his people" (cf. 11:1).[41] Accompanying this argumentative shift are bewildering semantic shifts, not only with respect to the proportion of Israel that has to experience salvation in order for God's promise to be confirmed, but to other key terms as well. Prior to 11:11, the remnant is presented as the "true Israel" (cf. 9:6), the few who have been chosen, called, and prepared for salvation (9:11-12, 23-24, 27); after, they are the sanctifying core, the firstfruits whose holiness assures the eventual sanctification of the whole.[42] There is a corresponding shift with respect to the unbelieving remainder: from "vessels of wrath" (9:22) who are not really part of Israel (cf. 9:6b-7a), to a temporarily hardened but nevertheless continuing part of the whole body of Israel yet to be saved (11:25-26). Similarly with election: in the earlier section, God's elective mercy results in glory for the vessels of mercy and destruction for the vessels of wrath (9:22-23); in the latter, its modus operandi is the consignment of all to disobedience so that mercy can be shown to all (11:28-32). Likewise with the believing Gentiles: before 11:11, the emphasis is on their inclusion in the people of God on equal basis with the Jewish remnant (9:24-29; 10:9-13); after, the distinction between Israel and the Gentiles is to the fore, the "full number of the Gentiles" introduced as the factor precipitating the salvation of "all Israel" (11:25-26).

Davies is fully aware of these shifts, of course, and of the logical inconsistencies they produce and represent. But his tendency is to view Paul's continuing concern for Israel simply as an emotional leftover not really integrated into his Christian pattern of thought. In his reading of things, Paul's nationalism and his Christianity existed in a state of unresolved tension. The universalism inherent in the latter should have had as its logical consequence the abandonment of the former; but the "emotional intensity" exhibited in Romans 11 demonstrates his "refusal utterly to sacrifice his nation to logical consistency."[43]

Even if Davies were right about Romans 9–11, the evidence it provides of Paul's continuing attachment to his "kindred according to the flesh" and of the agonizing passions which arise when he considers the all-too-apparent possibility of their exclusion from God's grace, serves in itself to raise questions about the way Davies accounts for the Gentile mission. For if Paul retains an emotional attachment to Israel, so that he is not prepared to abandon Israel even if the logic of his convictions leads to that conclusion, why was this not operative when the basic convictional sequence concerning the Gentiles was unfolding? For "not Torah" (as Davies understands it) could easily have been combined with a continuing attachment to Israel; Paul could easily have undertaken a mission to Israel, preaching a message of salvation through a crucified and risen Messiah rather than through Torah observance. The conviction posited by Davies (quite rightly) as Paul's point of departure, that righteousness comes through Christ and thus not through Torah, would lead to a Gentile mission only if "not Torah" = "not Israel." This clearly is Davies's position. But if Romans 9–11 provides us with any real indication of Paul's feelings on the matter, it is hard to account for his passionate commitment to a Gentile mission on these terms. For it is precisely his passionate commitment to Israel that has to give way if his new convictions about Christ and Torah are to lead to universalism and Gentile mission. But even if this commitment is simply an emotional leftover, not logically consistent with his new convictions, why would Paul be any more prepared to abandon it here at the beginning of his apostolic career than he was toward its end when he wrote to the church in Rome? If Paul's lingering attachment to Israel is enough of a factor in Romans 9–11 to overthrow the logic of the preceding argument, it surely would have been enough, in the case of the logical sequence from Christ to Gentiles as Davies envisages it, to stop it dead in its tracks.

There are good reasons to believe that Romans 9–11 is driven not simply by a lingering emotional attachment, a residual unwillingness to allow head to rule fully over heart, but by a firm and continuing conviction. For it is not only in Romans 9–11 that we find evidence of a continuing categorical differentiation between Jew and Gentile. Assertions of "no distinction" notwithstanding, it is clear that, except when the issue concerns the imposition of the Torah as an entrance requirement, Jew and Gentile continue to function as significant categories for Paul. Two bodies of evidence are relevant here.

First, there is Paul's perception of a Jewish Christian remnant as constituting a distinct, foundational, and essential element in the church. Remnant language appears explicitly only in Rom 9:27 (where its smallness is stressed) and 11:5 (where it is put forward as evidence that God has not "rejected his people").[44] Even so, it is worth noting the way the remnant is described in the latter passage. Citing himself as an example, Paul presents his remnant credentials in traditional, ethnic-specific terms: he is an Israelite, of the seed (σπέρματος) of Abraham, of the tribe of Benjamin. Here where God's faithfulness to Israel is the issue, an ongoing "difference" between Jew and Gentile continues to function as a significant category for Paul.

But the concept of the remnant is much more widespread than the terminology. The concept (but not the term) reappears in Rom 11:17. Paul's grammar may be rough, but the thought is clear: the Gentiles who have been grafted onto the olive tree have come to join the natural branches already there (ἐν αὐτοῖς [among them]), the latter sharing (συγκοινωνός [copartners]) with the newcomers the goodness that was naturally theirs.[45] The NRSV unfortunately perpetuates the RSV's mistranslation of ἐν αὐτοῖς (rendering it "in their place"); the thrust of the verse is that Gentiles join the Jews who believe, not that they replace the Jews who do not.

Remnant concepts appear elsewhere in Romans as well. As we have already seen,[46] in Romans 4 Paul describes Abraham's family as consisting of distinct Jewish and Gentile "clans" (vv. 11-12, 16). Again these Jewish Christian believers[47] are differentiated from Gentiles in traditional ways: they are "of the circumcision" (ἐκ περιτομῆς; v. 12) or "of the law" (ἐκ νόμου; v. 16).[48] To be sure, in both verses they are "not only" (οὐ . . . μόνον) Jews, but believers as well; nevertheless faith does not obliterate the distinction.

The significance of a Jewish Christian remnant appears again but in a new way in Rom 15:25-27. What we encounter in these verses is not simply the remnant's existence (as in Romans 4 and 9), nor its role in guaranteeing the eventual salvation of the whole of Israel (as in Rom 11:16), but its significance for the Gentile mission. Here, as Paul describes the collection project and his upcoming journey to Jerusalem, he sets out the relationship between the Jewish and Gentile sections of the church in such a way that there is a clear sense of priority on the one hand and dependence on the other. The spiritual blessings enjoyed by the Gentiles belong by right and in the first instance to the Jewish Christians (τοῖς πνευματικοῖς αὐτῶν ["*their* spiritual blessings"]), the one having been invited in to share (ἐκοινώνησαν) the blessings of the other. While there may be no distinction between Jew and Gentile with respect to basis of membership (see Rom 3:22; 10:12), there certainly is with respect to the origin and progression of the gospel community of which they are both members: the Gentiles are in a position of indebtedness vis-à-vis the Jews (ὀφειλέται εἰσὶν αὐτῶν [they are in debt to them]), to whom the blessings first were given and who then shared them with the Gentiles. Indeed, in his role as both prototype member of the remnant of Israel (Rom 11:1-5) and apostle to the Gentiles (11:13; 15:16), Paul has been the primary means by which this sharing of spiritual blessings has taken place; in the collection for the saints in Jerusalem, he has brought into being a tangible means by which the resultant debt might be acknowledged (though certainly not repaid).

Less clear, but probably reflecting a similar viewpoint, is the statement earlier in the chapter about Christ's ministry to the circumcised (vv. 8-9). As we have seen,[49] this difficult construction is probably to be construed as two parallel purpose clauses: "Christ became a servant of the circumcised . . . in order that he might confirm the promises given to the patriarchs, and in order that the Gentiles might glorify God for his mercy." Here Christ's ministry with respect to the Jews has as one of its intended ends the conversion of the Gentiles. There is no explicit reference to a Jewish remnant in either of the first two clauses. Nevertheless, the statement is preceded by the injunction to "welcome one another" (v. 7), which puts vv. 8-9 squarely in the context of actual and distinct groups of Christians. Further, both the Jew-Gentile flavor of chapters 14 and 15, and the explicit mention of actual Gentiles in v. 9, serves to imply that Paul has Jewish Christians in mind when he speaks of "the circumcised" for whom Christ became a servant and for whom the patriarchal promises were confirmed. The Gentiles are able to glorify God, then, because of what Christ has accomplished for the remnant of Israel.

Outside of Romans, remnant ideas are more elusive.[50] I want to discuss one additional passage, however, where I believe that remnant conceptions play an important role. In Gal 3:13-14 Paul declares, "Christ redeemed us from the curse of the law . . . in order that in Christ Jesus the blessing of Abraham might come to the Gentiles." It is my contention that the "us" (ἡμᾶς) of the first clause refers not to believers in general but to Jewish believers in particular. If such a reading of the first person plural can be established, it would mean that different groups are in view in the two clauses and, specifically, that the extension of the blessing of Abraham to Gentiles is being predicated on the redemption of Jews.[51]

In support of this reading, one can point first to the contrast in 2:15 between "us Jews" and the Gentiles. The verse occupies a significant rhetorical juncture; in H. D. Betz's analysis, it begins the thesis statement (*propositio*; 2:15-21), for which 3:1—4:31 provides the demonstration (*probatio*). If the thesis is presented in such ethnic-specific terms, we should not be surprised to find other instances where the first person plural refers to Jews in contradistinction to Gentiles.[52] Second, the parallel placement of ἡμᾶς (us) and εἰς τὰ ἔθνη (to the Gentiles), both in an emphatic position before the main verb, suggests that they are to be seen as distinct and contrasting entities.[53] Finally, there is the fact that the "we" who are redeemed from the curse of the law are described as "those who rely on the works of the law" (ὅσοι ἐξ ἔργων νόμου; 3:10), presumably the same group referred to as those "under the law" (ὑπὸ νόμον) in 3:23 and 4:5. Since possession of the law is what differentiates Jew from Gentile (see 2:15-16), the prima facie sense of the terms suggests that those under the law and subject to its curse must be Jews.[54]

To be sure, this reading is not universally accepted. Of the arguments put forward against it, however, some simply beg the question, for example, that Christ's saving accomplishments are universal,[55] or that such a reading would mean that Paul was making the blessing of the Gentiles dependent on the redemption of the Jews, a pattern of thought (so it is claimed) difficult to comprehend.[56] Equally invalid is the argument that the "we" of v. 14b is undoubtedly inclusive.[57] The second purpose (ἵνα) clause can easily be taken as parallel to the first, but larger in scope: Christ redeemed us Jews from the curse of the law, so that the Gentiles might be blessed, and so that we all, Jews and Gentiles alike, might receive the promise of the Spirit through faith.

A somewhat weightier objection has been made on the basis of the universalized description of the human plight in 4:1-11. Verses 3-5 are parallel in construction to 3:13-14: "we" were "under the law" or "under the elements of the universe" (ὑπὸ τὰ στοιχεῖα τοῦ κόσμου); Christ was born under the law to redeem those under the law; so that we might receive adoption as sons.[58] What is striking here is that Gentile Christians who become circumcised, and thus presumably come "under the law," are said to be "turn[ing] back *again* (πάλιν)" to "the elements of the universe," to whom they had been enslaved in their pre-Christian past. On the basis of these features of v. 9, B. Reicke, in an oft-cited article, concludes that "under the law" and "under the elements of the universe" are equivalent terms, so that the human situation has been universalized in the passage:[59] in their natural state, all—Jew and Gentile alike—are "under the law" (= "under the elements of the universe"); Christ was born "under the law" (= born into the human situation); Christ redeems those "under the law" (= humankind as a whole).

In response to Reicke, however, it needs to be pointed out that nowhere in the passage (or elsewhere, for that matter) does Paul say that uncircumcised and non-Christian Gentiles are "under the law." Undoubtedly, "under the elements of the universe" is an inclusive phrase; for Paul, all humanity apart from Christ is in bondage to sin. Gentile Christians who abandon Christ by becoming circumcised (cf. 5:2-4) will be returning to that state of bondage. But this does not, in and of itself, imply that such Gentiles are returning to a situation "under the law." In our discussion of the universality of sin in chapter 5, we observed that while Paul views the law as having potential significance for Gentiles as well as Jews, only the latter are ever said to be "under the law."[60] All of humankind is under the power of sin; but only Jews are under the law. The law may have a preparatory part to play in the process leading up to the liberative activity of Christ (e.g., Gal 3:24; Rom 7:7-13). Nevertheless, to be under the law is just a special case of the more general human condition of bondage to the elemental spirits of the universe. While Gentile Christians who Judaize can be said to be entering the former situation, they can be said to *return* (cf. πάλιν ["again"]) only to the latter.

Thus in Gal 3:13-14 Paul asserts that the blessing of the Gentiles is dependent in some (yet to be determined) way on the deliverance, from the "curse of the law," of a body of Jewish believers. Assertions of "no distinction" notwithstanding, a Jewish remnant—differentiated by means of the ordinary, Torah-based identity markers—continues to function as an important category for Paul.

In addition to remnant ideas, a second indication that the traditional distinction between the two is of continuing significance for Paul is his use of the term "Gentile" (ἔθνη) itself. What needs to be observed at the outset—a point both obvious yet seldom recognized[61]—is that this represents a thoroughly Jewish way of perceiving the world. "Gentiles" do not think of themselves as such, any more than the majority of Canadians consider themselves as "mainlanders." The term betrays the standpoint of the one using it—Newfoundland, in the latter instance, Jewishness in the former. Indeed, Paul's hearers might well have been mildly offended by the designation; the term was current in Hellenistic usage with the sense of "outsiders" or "foreigners."[62] Paul conceives of himself as apostle not to an undifferentiated mass of humanity in general, but to the *Gentiles* in particular; such a self-conception betrays an underlying view of reality in which the distinction between Jew and non-Jew is fundamental.

Not surprisingly, given the issues under discussion, the term appears most frequently in Romans and Galatians. For our purposes what is of particular interest is the way Paul uses the term both to describe his own apostolic role as apostle to the Gentiles (Rom 1:5, 13; 11:13; 15:15, 18; Gal 1:16; 2:2, 8, 9) and to refer to his readers as belonging to the sphere of his apostolic activity so described. To the Galatians, Paul asserts that he rejected the demand that Titus be circumcised so that "the gospel that I proclaim among the Gentiles" (2:2) might be preserved for *"you"* (cf. 2:5). He begins his letter to the Romans by declaring that through Christ he has "received grace and apostleship to bring about the obedience of faith among all the Gentiles, . . . *including yourselves"* (1:5-6), and draws it to a close by saying that his boldness in writing *to them* is "because of the grace given me by God to be a minister of Christ Jesus *to the Gentiles* (15:15-16).

But while the term appears more frequently in Romans and Galatians, its usage elsewhere is perhaps more telling. Here, where Jew-Gentile issues are not nearly so pressing, we are surprised by the almost matter-of-fact way in which he uses the term to describe his converts and to refer to his sphere of apostolic activity. First Thessalonians provides an instructive example. Describing its readers as people who "turned to God from idols" (1:9), the letter is therefore addressed to a community of "Gentile" Christians (the fact that the term comes so readily to hand is an indication of how thoroughly we are under the sway of Paul's usage!). In the course of encouraging the Thessalonians to stand firm in the midst of persecution, Paul describes his mission as that of "speaking to the Gentiles so that they may be saved" (2:16); the context implies that the readers, who had heard and responded to his preaching (2:13), were part of that Gentile sphere of mission.[63] If he goes on to warn his readers not to behave "like the Gentiles who do not know God" (4:5), he is in effect reminding them that before they came to know God through his preaching (cf. 1:9), they too were such Gentiles. Such a note is sounded explicitly in 1 Cor 12:2: "You know that when you were Gentiles (ἔθνη), you were led astray to dumb idols" (see 5:1; 10:20). In Colossians as well, Paul speaks of the "wealth among the Gentiles" of the mystery of the gospel, making it abundantly clear at the same time that the Colossians are counted among the Gentiles.[64] Implicit in all these passages is something that becomes explicit in Rom 11:1: by describing his field of apostolic activity as the world of the *Gentiles*, Paul demonstrates that he continues to identify himself as a Jew. Set apart since his (Jewish) birth (Gal 1:15) and called by the God of Israel who has not rejected his people (Rom 11:1), Paul understands himself to be the *Jewish* apostle to the Gentiles.[65]

Of similar significance is the gratuitous way in which Jew/Gentile distinctions often appear without any apparent contextual motivation. Take 1 Cor 1:18-25, for example, where Paul develops the contrast between God's foolishness and human wisdom. While the contrast is first set up in generic and universal terms (for example, "the debater of this age," "the wisdom of the world"), unexpectedly in the middle of the passage we discover that human wisdom comes in two forms—that of Jews (for whom the cross is a stumbling block) and that of Gentiles/Greeks (for whom it is folly). Likewise in 1 Cor 9:20-23 (where "all people" are subdivided into Jews under the law, and those outside the law), 1 Cor 10:32 (where we find the tripartite division of Jews, Greeks, and the church of God), and 2 Cor 11:26 (where Paul has faced danger both from Gentiles and from "my own people").[66] One could include here even the statements of 1 Cor 12:13; Col 3:11; and Gal 3:28, which in their assertions of unity and lack of differentiation seem to push in the opposite direction, but which nevertheless do so in terms of the categories of Jew and non-Jew.

To be sure, Paul can speak of the gospel in universal terms, a message of salvation for "us" or for "all" without distinction (see §7.2). But his usage indicates clearly that for him "all" means "Gentiles as well as Jews," and that while his apostolic mission was directed toward the former, he himself belonged to the latter.

Contrary to Davies's reading of Romans 9–11, then, the evidence presented here suggests strongly that for Paul the end of the Torah did not carry with it the end of ethnic Israel as a significant category nor of the Jew/Gentile distinction that flows from it.[67] Paul's concern for "Israel according to the flesh" cannot be restricted to Romans 9–11 and then dismissed as an aberration. Paul continues to do his thinking and carry out his mission in a world subdivided into Jew and Gentile, Israel and the nations.

What this means for our question is that it is really not possible to understand Paul's concern for the Gentiles as a corollary of his new conviction about the Torah. "Not Torah" does not imply "not Israel, and therefore no distinction." There is no through road from "not Torah" to "Gentiles"; the bridge is out, and no construction permits can be granted. Paul's commitment to a law-free Gentile mission will need to be arrived at by some other route.

## 6.4 Findings and Implications

This chapter has produced two main findings, one positive and the other negative. Positively, we confirmed the position toward which we were

moving in chapter 5, namely, that Paul's rejection of the law is christologically based. It is his new convictions about Christ—rather than about the
contrast between faith and works, the universality of sin, the equality of
Jew and Gentile, or the inclusion of Gentiles in salvation—that lead him
to reject the law as a condition of membership. Further, we have presented
reasons to believe that his Christ-Torah antithesis was sociological or ecclesiological in nature, that both before and after Damascus he perceived
them as rival ways of determining membership in the community of salvation. Negatively, we have seen that Paul's continuing interest in Israel and
his tendency to assume the continuing validity of a traditional Jew-
Gentile distinction (at least where membership requirements are not at
issue) makes it very difficult to maintain that his interest in the Gentiles
was the result of the displacement of Torah.

But what are we to make of the perdurance in Paul's thought of an
ethnically determined distinction between Jew and Gentile? The attempt
to identify it as a residue of the past rather than a native conviction carried
over into the present is understandable, given the apparent conflict with
what seem to be clearly demonstrated convictions about existence in
Christ. Up to this point, I have identified basic convictions concerning
*membership requirements* (membership is granted through faith in
Christ, and therefore not through Torah observance), *status* (Jew and
Gentile are on equal terms in Christ; there is no distinction), and *identity*
(all those in Christ are members of Abraham's family). How can we add
to these the additional conviction that an ethnically identified Israel, differentiated from the Gentiles in traditional Torah-determined ways, continues to have significance within the new sphere of reality determined
by Christ?

With the benefit of hindsight, we can easily discern a certain instability
in such a set of convictions. They could not be held together in any consistent way for very long. *If* the community is defined solely on the basis of
faith in Christ; *if* Torah observance is not to be imposed on Gentile converts; *if* indeed the Torah-observant need to give way when such observance interferes with community life; *if* this community, precisely on the
basis of its Christ-identity, is the real family of Abraham; *if* there is no
distinction in terms of entrance requirements and membership privileges
between Jew and Gentile; then inevitably as time goes on and one generation succeeds another, any distinction between Jew and Gentile would
inevitably fall away, identifiably Jewish portions of the community would
inevitably become assimilated, and "Israel" would inevitably become (as
it did by the time of Justin Martyr)[68] a purely allegorical or nonliteral
designation for a decidedly non-Jewish entity.[69] But from the standpoint
of the first generation of the new movement, or, as would be a more accu-

rate representation of Paul's view of the matter, the *last* generation prior to the parousia, things looked quite different. However Paul (or any other Jewish Christian) had changed as a result of his new Christian identity, he was still ethnically Jewish. He had been circumcised, he had been shaped with a Jewish identity from his mother's womb, and he would carry that identity through to the end. And so it was quite possible for him, in the final generation before the end, to conceive of a community of Jews and Gentiles for which faith in Christ was the only membership requirement, but within which Jew and Gentile remained distinct and significant categories.

This means that we are not to see Paul's continuing interest in Israel as simply an emotional leftover, a failure to follow his conviction about Christ though to its logical conclusion. The broken rhetorical path of Romans 9–11 needs to be seen as evidence of convictional interplay at work beneath the surface. The defense of his Gentile mission (on the basis of the first three convictions listed in the penultimate paragraph) has led Paul into terrain that might be perceived as indicating the abandonment of Israel. But at this point a fourth conviction, concerning God's faithfulness to Israel, is triggered into action, producing the abrupt argumentative turns apparent at 9:1 and, especially, 11:11.

The nature of this conviction about Israel and its significance for the Gentile mission will be explored in chapter 8. Before turning to this, however, we need to look more directly at Christ, and in particular at several possible ways of deriving a concern for the Gentiles from convictions concerning Christ himself.

## CHAPTER SEVEN

# Christ

The evidence considered in chapters 5 and 6 suggests that Paul's rejection of the Torah is the direct result of his new convictions about Christ. God has provided a means of salvation in Christ; therefore Torah observance is not a prerequisite for salvation. But what of the *universality* of the salvation provided in Christ (Christ as Savior *of all*)? We have found it to be unlikely that this derived from his reestimation of the law. But might it be possible that the new Christ conviction was the origin not only of his rejection of Torah but of his universalism as well? Can we locate the driving force of Paul's convictions about the Gentiles in his christology itself?

In this chapter I will consider two broad categories of such an explanation. One of these builds on Paul's perception of Jesus as an eschatological figure (Messiah) and especially on eschatological pilgrimage conceptions. The other takes as its point of departure the universal and cosmic elements in Paul's christology—Christ as Lord and Savior of all.

## 7.1 Eschatological Pilgrimage Expectations

While "not Torah" reconstructions represent the dominant way of accounting for Paul's Gentile mission, eschatological pilgrimage explanations certainly run a close second. Indeed, within the newer paradigm, where the concern for the Gentiles tends to be explained as a revision of Jewish universalism rather than as a rejection of Jewish particularism, this is the most frequently encountered approach. This approach places Paul's Gentile mission within the general framework of Jewish eschatological expectation. Jesus is Israel's Messiah (Rom 9:5),[1] the promised root of Jesse (Rom 15:12). Through his death and resurrection, the eschatological age of salvation has begun to dawn (see 1 Cor 10:11); consequently, the time for the long-awaited ingathering of the nations has arrived. To quote Sanders once again: "Paul's entire work . . . had its setting in the expected pilgrimage of the Gentiles to Mount Zion in the last days."[2]

This idea, however, is frequently put forward imprecisely and with lack of rigor. E. P. Sanders, for example, does not integrate this explanation of the Gentile mission with Paul's central convictions as he understands them, but simply assumes that the eschatological dimension alone is sufficient to connect Paul with this pattern of Jewish thought.[3] Equally unconvincing is the argument that the sequence of Rom 11:25-27 (where the "fullness of the Gentiles" triggers the salvation of "all Israel") is to be seen as a simple reversal of the traditional end-time scenario (where the pilgrimage of the nations *follows* the eschatological deliverance of Israel) and thus is to be taken as proof that Paul's Gentile mission was rooted in the traditional expectation. Moxnes's interpretation is typical:

> In Paul's view the prophecy of the pilgrimage of all nations to Jerusalem at the end of time was fulfilled when the uncircumcised entered the church. But this was offensive to many Christian Jews—because it meant that the "nations" had arrived at Zion *before* the Jews.[4]

Such an inversion would be not so much offensive as incomprehensible. For in the eschatological pilgrimage tradition, the salvation of the Gentiles follows the restoration of Israel as a matter not simply of *sequence* but of *consequence:* it is *because* they see the redemption of Israel and the glorification of Zion that the Gentiles abandon their idols and turn to worship the God of Israel. The inversion of the sequence represents not a simple modification of the tradition, but its evisceration. Without the restoration of Israel in some form, the hypothesis is deprived of its explanatory power.[5]

A similar judgment is to be made concerning Schoeps's argument, in which he appeals to eschatological pilgrimage expectations in support of the position that Paul understood his Gentile mission as a means of hastening the arrival of the messianic age:

> He shared the faith of many of his Pharisaic contemporaries that by missionary work the coming of the Messianic time might be hastened, *since the prophets had prophesied that its dawning would coincide with the conversion of the nations.* Since the Messiah had now appeared, the missionary task was all the more incumbent on him.[6]

The urgency with which Paul approached his mission and the belief that its completion would hasten the coming of the end need explanation. But they are not to be explained in this way. The prophets had prophesied the "conversion" of the nations as a by-product of the messianic restoration of Israel, not as a means to bring it about. To use an "already" pattern of prophetic thought as a way of accounting for a "not yet" aspect of Pauline thought, by means of the vague language of coincidence ("coincide"), amounts to little more than exegetical sleight of hand.

These observations do not by themselves invalidate an eschatological pilgrimage approach to Paul's Gentile mission. Certainly he can think of Christ as Israel's Messiah, and link the salvation of the Gentiles with Christ's messianic role (Rom 15:12, citing LXX Isa 11:10). Further, one might find evidence for such a reading in the collection project which, as a number of scholars have observed,[7] can be brought into relation with the expectation that Gentiles would bring gifts to Jerusalem in the end times.[8] Nevertheless, for an eschatological pilgrimage interpretation of Paul's Gentile mission to be convincing, it would need to demonstrate in one way or another that Paul perceived Christ as having accomplished the restoration of Israel (appropriately redefined), thus precipitating or making possible the overflow of eschatological blessings to the Gentiles. There are two ways in which this redefined "restoration of Israel" might be conceived: (1) by seeing Christ himself as Israel personified; (2) by identifying it with the existence of a Jewish-Christian remnant. We will deal with each of these in turn.

The most forceful and cogent example of the first of these approaches is to be found in the work of N. T. Wright.[9] Wright's reading of Paul can be described briefly as follows. Paul shares with his Jewish contemporaries the belief that God has called Israel to be the means by which the problems introduced into the human situation by Adam's sin are to be reversed. But Israel has run aground on the same problem; Israel's own sin has resulted—just as the law said it would (Deut 28, esp. vv. 64-68)—in the curse of the exile, a situation that, despite the return to the land, still continues.

It is against this background (and here Paul's Christian convictions begin to distinguish him from the general Jewish view of things) that Christ is to be understood. As Messiah (Wright insists that Χριστός never loses its titular sense for Paul), Christ is a corporate figure, who sums up Israel in himself, accomplishing in his death and resurrection what Israel was called to do. The "curse of the law" experienced by Christ on the cross (Gal 3:13) is precisely the curse of the exile pronounced against sinful Israel by Deuteronomy 28. In his role as Israel's representative, Jesus "took the brunt of the exile on himself" in his death, so that "the blessing of covenant renewal might flow out the other side, as God always intended."[10] Paul's Adam christology (Romans 5; 1 Corinthians 15) is thus an Israel christology, linked in a process of successive narrowing. Abraham's family was called into being to reverse the problem of Adam; to this family God gave the Torah "to be the means of concentrating the sin of humankind in one place . . . in order that it might then be concentrated yet further, drawn together on to Israel's representative, the Messiah—in order that it might there be dealt with once and for all."[11]

Wright's Paul thus operates within the framework of traditional restoration eschatology, with the whole experience of exile and restoration understood as being summed up and brought to a climax in the death and resurrection of Jesus, Israel's Messiah and representative. Not surprisingly, then, Wright sees Paul's Gentile mission as a revised, christocentric version of the eschatological pilgrimage expectation, an expectation often found within such restoration eschatology. In Christ, "the true restoration was beginning, a restoration in which Gentiles were, quite properly, being invited to share. As the great prophets believed, when Israel is restored, then the Gentiles will share in the blessing." Paul's Gentile mission is nothing other than the eschatological ingathering of the nations anticipated in Isa 2:2-4, Tobit 14:6, and other similar texts.[12]

In order to represent this schematically, there is no need to include Wright's understanding of the "not Torah" element in Paul's convictional structure.[13] The two constructions are separable, and the eschatological pilgrimage construal of his conviction about the Gentiles could be combined with other views of the law (such as the belief that with the coming of the Messiah the age of the Torah is at an end).[14] With the Torah left out of account, this aspect of the structure is quite simple:

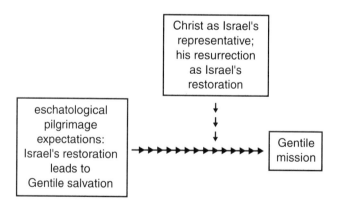

Wright's reconstruction draws support from the evidently corporate nature of Paul's "in Christ" patterns of thought, and in particular the "seed" argument of Gal 3:16, according to which Christ (and by extension the community of all those who are in him; v. 29) is said to be the promised "seed" of Abraham. In addition, such an Israel-centered reading makes plausible sense of what Paul has to say about Adam, the role of the law, and the representative function of Christ (see also §8.3 below).

But one important element of Paul's thought left out in such a reconstruction is the Jewish Christian remnant and its role with respect to Gentile salvation. Indeed, Wright redefines "Israel" so thoroughly in terms of Christ and those "in Christ" that, as we have seen,[15] he is forced to deny the clear ethnic sense of the term in Rom 11:26, seeing this as a reference to the mixed church of Jews and Gentiles in the present. Christ gathers up Israel's story so completely that he and those "in him" constitute Israel without remainder. But we have seen (chapter 6) that Jew and Gentile continue to have significance for Paul, even within the "in Christ" domain. Jewish Christians constitute a remnant that continues as an identifiable group within Abraham's family (Rom 4:11-12, 16). More than that, in several places the existence of the remnant is somehow the prerequisite of the salvation of the Gentiles—the Gentiles being grafted in to share the richness of the olive tree with the natural branches already there (Rom 11:17); the Gentiles' glorification of God as the intended result of Christ's ministry to the circumcised (15:8-9); the collection as a means by which the Gentiles can acknowledge their indebtedness to the Jewish Christians who shared their spiritual blessings with them (15:25-27).

This leads to a second way of understanding Paul's Gentile mission as a reconfiguration of traditional eschatological pilgrimage expectations. In this reconstruction, the restoration of Israel, on which the ingathering of the Gentiles depends, is to be seen not simply in Jesus' resurrection, but in the emergence of a Jewish Christian remnant, for whom "the promises given to the patriarchs" have been "confirmed" (cf. Rom 15:8). This remnant provides the necessary link between Christ and the Gentiles; representing the eschatological restoration of Israel, it provides by its very existence the grounds and impetus for the long-awaited salvation of the Gentiles.

I am aware of only one example of this way of construing Paul's convictions about the Gentiles—my own essay on Gal 3:13-14.[16] I have changed my mind since then and therefore am in the curious situation of citing myself as the only exemplar of a position I no longer hold.

The focus of my earlier essay was centered on the purpose construction in Gal 3:13-14: "Christ redeemed us from the curse of the law ... *in order that* (ἵνα) in Christ Jesus the blessing of Abraham might come to the Gentiles." The first step was to demonstrate that the first person plural in the first clause ("us") referred not to believers in general but to Jewish

Christians exclusively. Thus the passage asserts that the blessing of the Gentiles was somehow dependent on the redemption of the Jews, that is, on the existence or creation of a Jewish Christian remnant.[17] The second step was to argue that the passage is best understood "as a radical reinterpretation, in light of the cross event, of a Jewish pattern of thought in which the inclusion of the Gentiles is seen as a consequence of the eschatological redemption of Israel."[18] This conclusion was based primarily on the parallelism between the two patterns of thought and the absence of any other compelling explanation of this aspect of Paul. I will return to this conclusion in a moment, after the following schematic representation:

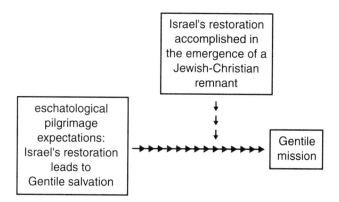

Both of these eschatological pilgrimage reconstructions (Wright's and my earlier position) identify important aspects of Paul's thought that need to be taken into account in any investigation of his convictions. For Paul, Israel is to be seen as a kind of representative sample of humanity, the law functioning within Israel to lay bare the plight of bondage to sin that Israel shares with the rest of the nations; Christ in turn functions as a representative of Israel, and thus by extension a new Adam; and the existence of a Jewish Christian remnant is a presupposition of the Gentile mission. But I no longer believe that these aspects of Paul's argument reflect an underlying eschatological pilgrimage pattern of thought.

The process by which I came to change my mind conforms closely to the structure of a paradigm shift as analyzed by Thomas Kuhn. Since I have already put this forward as a model for understanding Paul's own shift,[19] it is not out of place to speak autobiographically here for a moment. Paradigm shifts generally begin with the perception of an anomaly, something that simply cannot be accounted for within the ruling interpretive structure.[20] In my case the anomaly was Paul's readiness in Romans 11 to ground the Gentile mission on the stumbling (παράπτωμα; vv. 11-12), the defeat[21] (ἥττημα; v. 12) or the rejection (ἀποβολή; v. 15) of Israel. If at a fundamental convictional level Paul understood his Gentile mission to be grounded in and made possible by the eschatological *restoration* of Israel, how could he possibly, even for contingent rhetorical purposes, describe it as grounded on and made possible by Israel's *rejection*? To be sure, the idea of Israel's rejection appears only as part of an argument culminating in the eventual salvation of all Israel (vv. 25-26). But this simply underscores the anomaly, since it reveals the degree to which Paul perceives the restoration of Israel as having not yet happened. Christ and the Jewish Christian remnant notwithstanding, Paul's agony over Israel's present failure to respond, and his confidence, despite all appearances to the contrary, of Israel's eventual full salvation, make it very difficult to believe that what propelled him into a passionate and all-consuming mission to the Gentiles was the conviction that Israel had somehow already been restored. Underscoring the anomaly even further is the fact that the Gentile mission occupies a fixed period of time *prior to* the full manifestation of the eschatological state of affairs. It is the "fullness of the Gentiles"—the completion of the Gentile mission—that brings the period of Israel's rejection to an end, and triggers the final salvation of "all Israel" (vv. 25-26), the resurrection of the dead (v. 15), and so on. Israel's full restoration, far from setting the stage for an eschatological pilgrimage of the nations, actually brings the period of Gentile salvation to an end. The Gentile mission is linked more to the "not yet" of Paul's eschatological duality than to its "already."

Anomalies do not by themselves destroy paradigms, as Kuhn points out. In the absence of a new and more adequate paradigm, they simply remain as anomalies—to be finessed, explained away, or put on the shelf for future reference. The shift in paradigms occurs when a new and rival way of perceiving the field presents itself, one that not only accounts satisfactorily for the once-shelved anomaly but also reconfigures the whole field so thoroughly that what once was perceived as anomalous now is taken virtually as axiomatic. In my case, this aspect of Romans 11 continued for quite a while to be simply an annoying loose thread that I tried to ignore while working on other aspects of the investigation. But when I finally turned to Romans 11, it suddenly occurred to me during a period of intense consideration of the passage that this aspect of the argument could be accounted for very simply with reference to a pattern of Jewish thinking about proselytism, in particular a strict version of this pattern in which it was considered necessary for Gentiles to become proselytes to Judaism in this age if they wanted to have a share in salvation in the age to come.[22] This insight not only turned an anomaly into a self-evident datum; it illumined the whole terrain of Paul's Gentile rhetoric, revealing a more orderly and satisfying pattern of convictions than had been hitherto perceived. In short, it emerged as a new paradigm, in the service of which the present study is being carried out.

If I were really writing autobiography, I would go on to describe details of how the terrain was illumined and the convictional pattern perceived. But, in keeping with Kuhn's observation that there is usually a difference between the way scientific discoveries are arrived at and the way they are written up and presented to the scholarly community, I will leave further discussion of this new paradigm for chapter 8, and turn back to the pattern of systematic argumentation.

The personal experience just described represents one set of considerations weighing in against an eschatological pilgrimage reading of Paul: Despite some surface similarities and possible points of contact, Paul's statements about the Gentile mission stubbornly resist any attempt to force them into the Procrustean bed of eschatological pilgrimage patterns of thought.

A second consideration (see §4.4 above) is the virtual absence of eschatological pilgrimage texts. Such texts were plenteous and close at hand.[23] Given Paul's desire to ground the Gentile mission in scripture,[24] there would have been plenty of opportunity for him to cite such texts if he had so desired. To be sure, the citation of LXX Isa 11:10 in Rom 15:12 might be put forward as a counterexample.[25] In its Isaiah context the verse is part of a description of end-time peace and righteousness established by the messianic descendant of Jesse (11:1-16). The wicked are judged (v. 4), the poor vindicated (v. 4), the remnant of Israel gathered (v. 12), and the earth "will be full of the knowledge of the Lord as the waters cover the sea" (v. 9). Especially in the LXX version, where the Gentiles are said to hope (ἐλπιοῦσιν) in the root of Jesse rather than simply to inquire (ידרשׁו) of him, the text can be included among the collection of eschatological pilgrimage texts.

If one were convinced on other grounds that Paul carried out his Gentile mission within an eschatological pilgrimage framework, there would be justification for reading Rom 15:12 in similar terms. But it is doubtful that the citation can support such an interpretation on its own. The citation is the fourth and final item in a catena of texts that Paul brings forward in the grand finale of his argument (15:9-13). None of the other three (Ps 18:49; Deut 32:43; Ps 117:1) is eschatological in nature; what binds them together is simply the term "Gentiles" (ἔθνη), used in a context asserting, calling for, or implying the inclusion of the Gentiles in the praise and worship of God. As has often been noted, Paul is here employing a "keyword" pattern of argumentation, paralleled in rabbinic exegesis, in which texts from the Torah, the prophets, and the writings are chained together in support of a point.[26] What we learn from Rom 15:9-12 as a whole is that Paul believes his convictions about the Gentiles to be supported by scripture; what we learn from v. 12 in particular is that he believes that the salvation of the Gentiles is linked in some way with the ministry of the Messiah of Israel (cf. vv. 8-9); but we will have to look elsewhere to find solid evidence concerning the nature and structure of his Gentile convictions.

Third, Paul's firm conviction of the equality of Jew and Gentile in both plight and salvation, and his concern to establish full membership in Abraham's family for his Gentile converts is not easily explained on eschatological pilgrimage terms. While it was not impossible within Jewish tradition for such Gentiles to be perceived as proselytes, this was certainly not to the fore in the literature surveyed in §3.5 above.[27] The emphasis falls instead on the ongoing distinction between Jews and Gentiles; those who make the eschatological pilgrimage to Zion are undeniably *Gentiles*, clearly differentiated from Jews. Galatians 3:13-14 can serve as an example of the contrast: Here the pattern is not that the Gentiles witness the salvation of Israel and turn to worship Israel's God but that they are blessed by becoming members of Abraham's family.

Finally, parallels between Paul's Israel-centered view of the Gentile mission and Jewish patterns of universalism are by no means restricted to eschatological pilgrimage expectations. The belief that God would use Israel to bring salvation to the Gentiles—or, echoing the language of Rom 15:27, that God had showered spiritual blessings on Israel that were to be shared with the Gentiles—is found just as frequently with respect to Israel's role in the present, especially with respect to proselytism (although not exclusively so). Philo, for example, speaks repeatedly of Israel's priestly role vis-à-vis the other nations, Israel being consecrated "to offer prayers for ever on behalf of the human race that it may be delivered from evil and participate in what is good."[28] Such language will be of special interest when we turn to the cultic dimensions of Paul's Gentile mission; here we note only Israel's present role as an instrument of blessing for the world. Not surprisingly, this role often is defined in terms of the Torah:

Israel is the agency "through whom the imperishable light of the law was to be given to the world" (Wisd 18:4); "the light of the law . . . was granted to you for the enlightenment of every man" (*T. Levi* 14.4).

The belief that Israel has been entrusted with the Torah as a means of enlightenment and salvation for all the nations is especially interesting in view of Paul's Christ-Torah antithesis, as we have examined it in previous chapters. The parallelism here is every bit as striking as that proposed with eschatological pilgrimage patterns of thought. In each we have to do with a divinely bestowed means of righteousness (Christ/Torah) which Israel (or a remnant of Israel) has been commissioned to share with the Gentiles. Even the belief that Israel's commission has devolved upon a remnant is not without parallel in Judaism, given the development of the remnant motif in Israel's scripture and the continuing party rivalry characteristic of the post-Maccabean period, with the concomitant tendency to see the line of demarcation between the sinners and the righteous within Israel as constituted by adherence to the Torah.[29]

Likewise, the collection project, in which Gentiles journey with gifts to Jerusalem, has just as many parallels with "this age" phenomena within Judaism as with eschatological pilgrimage expectations. Indeed, given the prima facie absurdity in the suggestion that the tiny band of Gentile Christians is somehow to be equated with the vast procession of the nations envisaged in the tradition,[30] other parallels are much more appropriate. Gentile offerings were accepted at the temple, and the relevant literature is replete with references to Gentiles journeying to Jerusalem to offer gifts to the God of Israel and to honor God's temple.[31] Further, while the evidence is not conclusive, it is probable that making an offering at the temple was one of the required steps in the process of becoming a proselyte in our period.[32]

Those aspects of Paul's Gentile mission that have been put forward as evidence for an eschatological pilgrimage interpretation, therefore, can be accounted for just as easily on other terms. While parallels can be drawn between the Pauline material and eschatological pilgrimage traditions, the parallelism is not an exclusive one; there are equally striking similarities between Paul and other Jewish patterns of universalism. We will explore these similarities further in the next chapter. For present purposes, they simply reinforce the conclusion that an eschatological pilgrimage explanation of Paul's Gentile mission is unlikely.

This is not to deny the significance of the eschatological dimension in Paul's set of convictions. First, Paul can conceive of Jesus as the Messiah of Israel (Rom 9:5), whose role as "servant of the circumcised" results in Gentile salvation (Rom 15:8-9). This does not imply eschatological pilgrimage, but it represents an aspect of thought that needs to be addressed in our discussion of Israel in the next chapter.

Second, the "already" needs to be taken just as fully into account as the "not yet." If, as I have suggested, the evidence is best explained from the starting point of proselyte conceptions, it is not to be thought that we are to perceive Paul's post-Damascus set of convictions simply as a structurally identical analogue of the previous set, with the single substitution of Christ for Torah. No, Christ is an eschatological figure; his resurrection represents the firstfruits of the general resurrection (1 Cor 15:20), so that Christians are those for whom the age to come has begun to dawn (Rom 8:23; 1 Cor 10:11; 2 Cor 5:17). Eschatological considerations will need to be taken into account in any assessment of Paul's convictional structure. Nevertheless, eschatology—at least in the particular form of eschatological pilgrimage expectations—does not provide us with the key to his pressing concern for a mission to the Gentiles.

## 7.2 Lord and Savior of All

In section §5.3 above, regarding the "equality of Jew and Gentile," I postponed consideration of one category of texts, those where assertions of equality do not stand alone but instead are rooted in christology. I now consider a second way in which Paul's concern for the Gentiles might arise directly from his new convictions about Christ, this time not from Christ's eschatological significance (cf. §7.1), but from his role as universal Lord and Savior. While christology narrowly considered is not easily disentangled from soteriology in Paul's case, to facilitate the discussion I will make an artificial distinction between the two and begin with a consideration of Jesus' lordship.

In keeping with the kerygma Paul shared with the rest of early Christianity, he understood the resurrection of Jesus to be not simply a rescue from death but an elevation to a position of sovereignty "at the right hand of God" (Rom 8:34; Col 3:1; cf. Rom 1:3-4; Phil 2:9; etc.). Further, he stood close to the headwaters of that stream of christological development in which Christ's sovereign position was extended into the past, as he was declared to be the agent through whom "all things have been created" (Col 1:16; 1 Cor 8:6).

Two things are of interest here. One is the universal scope of Christ's sphere of significance. This comes to clearest expression in the hymn of Phil 2:5-11: ". . . so that at the name of Jesus every (πᾶν) knee should bend, in heaven and on earth and under the earth, and every (πᾶσα) tongue should confess that Jesus Christ is Lord." Elsewhere it is at least implicit in the use of the neuter plural πάντα ("all things") with reference to the scope of Christ's sovereignty at the end of human history (1 Cor 15:27-28; cf. Eph 1:10) and to his creative activity at the beginning (Col 1:16; 1 Cor 8:6).

The second is the absence of any reference to Israel, or to the distinction between Jew and Gentile. In its depiction of Jesus' earthly existence, the hymn of Philippians 2, for example, makes much of his humanity (ἄνθρωπος [human being] appears twice; v. 7) but nothing of his Jewishness. Even if Paul has taken over a preexisting hymn here, he apparently felt free to adapt it; Lohmeyer's suggestion that v. 8b is a Pauline gloss has been widely accepted.[33] If this is so, it means that he felt it more important to specify the form of Christ's death ("even death on a cross") than the (Jewish) form of his humanity. But whatever the tradition history of the Philippian hymn, Paul's christology is such that in presenting Jesus as Lord—in Philippians 2 or elsewhere—he appears to be under no compulsion either to make explicit the Jewishness of the Lord or to specify the ethnic makeup of the company of those who acknowledge him as such. Romans 10:12 is the one exception[34] that proves the rule: "For there is no distinction between Jew and Greek; the same Lord [i.e., Jesus; cf. v. 9] is Lord of all and is generous to all who call upon him."

These texts raise the possibility, then, that Paul's concern for the Gentiles enters into his convictional structure at the point of his elevated christology. His perception of the cosmic significance of Christ—Jesus as Lord of all—leads to the transcending of his Jewish frame of reference and the elimination of the Jew/Gentile distinction as a fundamental category of his thought. Such a construal has been suggested from time to time, though infrequently and rarely in a coherent and thoroughgoing manner. Wilhelm Bousset's *Kyrios Christos*,[35] for example, was built on the assumption that the ascription of κύριος (Lord) to Jesus was a clear indication of a Hellenizing abandonment of the Jewish frame of reference in favor of a universal religion.[36] The methodological deficiencies of this History of Religions approach have been amply demonstrated in the intervening years, and need not be dwelt on here. In any case, for Bousset, elevated christology was more a sign than a cause of the expansion of Christianity beyond its Jewish matrix and was in no way determinative for Paul in that it was already a fait accompli among the Hellenistic communities into which he converted.[37]

A more significant reconstruction of Paul's universalism from the starting point of an elevated christology is to be found in W. Wrede's work on Paul. As we have seen, Wrede's analysis has anticipated contemporary discussion in significant ways, even if its influence has been more second-hand, through the work of Schweitzer and others.[38] For Wrede, the themes of justification and faith versus works were not fundamental for Paul but tactical arguments developed in defense of his law-free mission to the Gentiles. This law-free mission, in turn, was rooted in Paul's perception of Christ as a celestial being—not simply the Messiah of Israel, but Son of God and redeemer of the world. In contrast to Bousset, Wrede's Paul represents a sharp break from the church before him:

> Once for all the whole horizon is altered: it is no more the Jewish nation that forms the frame for all ideas, but the world, humanity. Christ is no more the Jewish Messiah, but the saviour of the world; faith in him is therefore no more a form of the Jewish faith, but a new faith. And secondly the Christology is new . . . chiefly because in Paul the origin and nature of Christ has become celestial.[39]

Also in contrast to Bousset, Wrede finds the origins of Paul's celestial christology in his pre-Damascus, Jewish frame of reference: Like others of his circle within Judaism, "Paul believed in such a celestial being, in a divine Christ, before he believed in Jesus." The chief outcome of his Damascus experience, "when Jesus appeared before him in the shining glory of his risen existence," was that he was led to identify the two, and to ascribe to the figure of Jesus "all those mighty predicates which has already been established."[40] One might well ask why such a conception of a celestial Christ should have broken open Paul's Jewish horizon after his Damascus experience but not before. If Paul the zealous Jew could have held to the notion of a celestial Messiah with equanimity and no apparent uneasiness about its implication for the Jewish world of understanding, why should the mere addition of one further belief—that this being had taken human shape in the person of Jesus—have been enough to shatter that world in such a decisive fashion? I will return to this point later. For now, we simply note Wrede's role as an example of a reconstruction in which Paul's universalism is grounded in his elevated christology.

In contrast to other aspects of his analysis, on this point Wrede has failed to anticipate or influence later Pauline scholarship. Rarely does one encounter the suggestion that elevated christology is the motivating factor in Paul's universal mission. One exception to this is F. Hahn's work on mission in early Christianity. He says of Paul: "From the concept of the exaltation he realized, as no one did before him,[41] the all-embracing reality of the Christian message." In this realization he came to see Christ as not simply the fulfillment of Israel's particularist *Heilsgeschichte,* but as the new Adam, whose saving activity is of benefit for the whole of humankind.[42]

Hahn's comments on Paul are brief and not fully developed. It is not clear, for example, how this way of accounting for the Gentile mission is to be linked with his statements about eschatological pilgrimage traditions.[43] A more thoroughly worked out example is Seyoon Kim's *The Origin of Paul's Gospel.* Kim's thesis is ambitious. The burden of his argument is that the major strands of Paul's christology and soteriology are derived directly from his Damascus experience, an experience described more precisely as a vision of "the exalted Christ appearing in the bright glory from heaven."[44] The argument is intricately structured and thoroughly documented but it thins out considerably just at our point of interest. In his concluding paragraph Kim identifies several topics in need of further exposition, including the correlation of Paul's gospel with his universal mission and the place of that mission in *Heilsgeschichte.* Still, the main lines of such an exposition can be seen in the study itself.

With many other scholars, Kim sees the Damascus theophany as the source of Paul's belief that Christ was the end of the law. Paul had perceived the Christian proclamation to be blasphemous, especially in view of the curse pronounced on a crucified figure by the law itself (Deut 21:22-23), and so he carried out his zealous persecution of the church. The Damascus experience led him to the conclusion that with Christ the law as a medium of revelation and salvation has been brought to an end. The distinctive feature of Kim's work, however, is not this negative consequence of Damascus but the more positive content of the christophany itself. Drawing on the throne-theophany visions of Daniel 7 and Ezekiel 1, and the streams of tradition developing from them (especially apocalyptic visions in the former case, and *merkabah* mysticism in the latter), he argues that Paul understood his bright vision as "analogous to those [visions] of the open court of heaven granted to prophets and apocalyptic seers."[45] His vision of Christ as the exalted figure at the center of this heavenly setting, accompanied by the radiance of the divine glory, led him to identify Christ as the "image of God" (εἰκὼν τοῦ θεοῦ; cf. 2 Cor 4:4), the visible manifestation of the invisible God.[46]

Flowing out of this fundamental perception, as Kim reconstructs things, are two main lines of development.[47] In the more strictly christological line, Christ as the image of God is identified with Wisdom (replacing Torah in traditional Jewish patterns of thought), and thus functions as the divine agent of creation, revelation, and salvation. But it is in the other line of development that the universal mission comes into the picture. Paul's perception of Christ as the divine "image" (εἰκών) led him naturally, says Kim, to the description of Adam as created in God's image (κατ᾽ εἰκόνα ἡμετέραν [according to our image]) in Gen 1:26-27. Seeing Christ accompanied by the radiance of the divine glory, which, according to some traditions, Adam had possessed before losing it in the Fall, Paul perceived Christ as the means by which everything that humanity had lost would be restored. And not only humanity; just as the created order was disfigured through Adam, it will be restored through Christ: "This renewal or new creation is not confined to mankind alone; it encompasses the entire creation."[48] The restoration of humanity is part of a larger, cosmic restoration effected by Christ. But in any case, it is this restoration of humanity in Christ, the new Adam, that leads to Paul's universal mission. And this Adam christology, in turn, arises from a Damascus christophany in which Paul perceives Christ as the glorified, heavenly image of God.

Differences in detail notwithstanding, a substantial similarity exists between Wrede and Kim on the origin and structural placement of Paul's universal mission. Both begin with the Damascus experience and the radiant Christ whom Paul perceives. Both understand this experience to have been interpreted with reference to already-existing Jewish conceptions of heavenly figures of divine mediation. And both see a universal mission as the natural and inevitable result of this cosmic, elevated status of Christ (Kim adding the intermediate step of Adam christology).

In Wrede's case, at least, the universalism deriving from this elevated christology occurs in conjunction with an abandonment of a particularistic Jewish frame of reference. Is this true also of Kim? Unfortunately, the unfinished state of this part of the study makes it difficult to say for sure. Nevertheless, the general impression left by the book leads one to believe this to be the case. Despite the appearance of a fresh examination of Paul from the starting point of the Damascus experience, in the end much of the old paradigm remains in place; the work is essentially an attempt to show how main elements of the old paradigm (justification by faith, substitutionary atonement) can be derived from this new starting point. For example, "Israel" is redefined in christological terms, with no apparent ethnic remainder,[49] the centrality of a universalized doctrine of justification by faith is defended, and the statement in Rom 10:4 about the "end (τέλος) of the law" is read as a univocal assertion of the law's termination.[50] Kim's reconstruction, therefore, is structurally congruent to

Wrede's at this point as well: elevated christology has led to an abandonment of Jewish particularism and thus to a universal mission.

As noted above, Kim differs from Wrede in that he posits Adam christology as an intermediate step between elevated christology and Gentile mission (Adam also identified as the image of God). But while fully recognizing the Adam overtones in Paul's image of God language (cf. Gen 1:26), the links Kim attempts to forge between Paul's bright vision itself, the divine glory, and the term "image of God" are tenuous indeed.[51] Further, Adam christology, rather than being an essential step in Kim's reconstruction, functions more as an alternative way of stating the universalism following from the elevated christology itself. Consequently, Adam can be set aside for the moment. Indeed, Wright's observation needs to be given full weight: Adam themes represent not an abandonment of Jewish particularism, but a very Israel-centered way of perceiving the world and Israel's place in it.[52] We will therefore return to Adam christology in chapter 8.

In any case, the convictional structure held in common by Wrede and Kim can be sketched as follows:

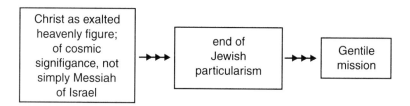

This reconstruction of Paul's convictional logic contains the seeds of its own destruction. For there is ample evidence that Jews could contemplate figures of universal lordship and cosmic elevation without any perceived challenge to covenantal self-understanding. This is patently the case with traditional messianism, where it was expected almost by definition that the coming Anointed One would both "destroy the unlawful nations with the word of his mouth" and "judge peoples and nations in the wisdom of his righteousness" (*Ps. Sol.* 17.24, 29; cf. Isa 11:10; Mic 5:4; Zech 9:10). This strand of tradition stands somewhat apart from the eschatological pilgrimage expectation; here the emphasis falls on the vindication of Israel and the subjugation of the nations rather than the participation of the nations in salvation. In any case, in messianic expectation, universal lordship in no way stands in tension with the particularism of covenantal nomism; indeed, it serves to reinforce it.

Of course, Paul's "Christ" is a more than simply "Messiah." Christ has been elevated to a position of sovereignty subject to God alone (1 Cor 15:27-28; Phil 2:9-11); he is identified as the agent through whom God created all things (1 Cor 8:6; Col 1:16-17); he is the image of God (2 Cor 4:4; Col 1:15) and in his face one can see the shining glory of God (2 Cor 4:6); in short, he is Christ the *Lord*. But, as Kim's work itself implicitly recognizes, such an elevated figure need not stand in any tension at all with a covenantal self-understanding.

As Kim perceives things, Paul understood his christophanic experience in very Jewish terms—by placing it against the background of apocalyptic and mystical visions of the heavenly court and identifying Christ with the visible manifestations of God's presence standing at the center of such visions (image, Wisdom, Son of Man, and so on). This reading of Paul's elevated christology (so distinct from Bousset's Hellenizing hypothesis) is certainly on the right track and is fully in keeping with contemporary scholarly trends. Larry W. Hurtado, in *One God, One Lord*,[53] convincingly argues that within first-century Judaism there was widespread interest in various heavenly figures of divine agency (personified divine attributes such as Wisdom, exalted patriarchs, chief angels) and that this explains how elevated views of Christ could have appeared within early Jewish (and therefore monotheistic) Christianity. With respect to Paul himself, one can mention Alan F. Segal's *Paul the Convert*.[54] His interpretation of Paul's conversion experience is similar in many respects to that of Kim. He too takes 2 Cor 4:6 as a reference to Paul's Damascus experience ("[God] has shone in our hearts to give the light of the knowledge of the glory of God in the face of Jesus Christ"). Likewise, he links this to Ezekiel's vision of the humanlike figure on the throne chariot which had "the appearance of the likeness of the glory of God" (Ezek 1:28) and thus to subsequent developments in apocalyptic and *merkabah* mysticism. For Segal, Paul is to be seen as a Jewish mystic—indeed, our primary first-century source for this type of Jewish mysticism—who had an experience in which he saw the divine Glory (*Kavod*) and equated it with the person of Jesus.

It is not necessary to analyze Paul's christology in precise terms here. Elevated christology, such as we find in Paul, is fully explicable in Jewish terms. It has counterparts in patterns of thought that emerge in a Jewish matrix and that nestle quite comfortably into texts that retain an Israel- and covenant-centered world of understanding (Ezek 1:26-28; *1 Enoch* 14.8-23; *Apoc. Abr.* 17–18). This being so, the convictional linkage in the diagram above becomes quite tenuous. It is highly questionable to derive

Paul's Gentile mission from elevated christology alone, at least if the essential intervening link is perceived as the shattering of a particularistic Jewish frame of reference. Cosmic divine agents and covenantal nomism coexist quite amicably; Paul's Gentile mission will have to be accounted for on the basis of some other point of departure.

Still, any reconstruction of Paul's pattern of thought and conviction will need to find a place for his belief in such an elevated, cosmic Christ. This is especially true if, as I contend, Paul's revised perception of the basic elements of covenantal nomism needs to be understood from the starting point of his new convictions about Christ. These new convictions differ in two crucial respects from the divine agents surveyed by Hurtado or the divine Glory in the apocalyptic and mystical material. (1) For Paul, Christ and covenantal nomism do not easily coexist; his new Christ-conviction necessitates a radical reconfiguration of his native Jewish frame of reference. (2) For Paul, as for some other strands of early Christianity, this elevated, heavenly figure is identified with the earthly human being, Jesus.

Undoubtedly these two distinctive features are linked. But how? The answer is not to be found simply in Paul's elevated christology. The shift away from a Torah frame of reference is not simply the result of his belief that the cosmic Lord has appeared in the person of the earthly Jesus. Rather, as was argued in §6.2, Paul's Christ-conviction precipitates a shift away from the Torah framework because he perceived Christ as a rival way of defining membership in the people of God, and this precisely because of the peculiar already/not yet structure of early Christian belief. Prior to his final manifestation as universal Lord, Christ has appeared as the dying and rising Savior. In the interim, membership in the community that will experience the full saving benefits of his lordship at the parousia is determined by identification with Christ. Since within covenantal nomism this membership-marking role in the period prior to the eschaton was played by the Torah, Christ and covenantal nomism stand in tension. Such tension is not produced by elevated christology—neither the elevation per se nor the identification of the elevated heavenly figure with a human being. The tension is not christological but sociological, or, to use more traditional language, soteriological and ecclesiological; Christ and Torah are two rival ways of defining and determining membership in the community of salvation.

This opens up another possible sequence of influence from elevated christology to Gentile mission, this time via the intermediate step of Torah displacement. Paul's vision of the glorified Christ results—for reasons just described—in the displacement of Torah, and this, in turn, is per-

ceived as eliminating the distinction between Jew and Gentile, resulting in
the Gentile mission. But this route has been explored—and abandoned—
already (§6.3); it runs into a dead end: the perdurance of the Jew-Gentile
distinction as an important convictional element in Paul's discourse.

Still, the observations with which we began this section remain: Paul's
perception of the gospel is such that he can formulate it in terms of
Christ's universal lordship and without any reference to Israel. If, as I
maintain, Israel continues to play a role in Paul's convictional framework,
it is one that can be compressed or left unstated when he speaks of Christ
as Lord of all. This element needs to be accounted for and will be considered later.

But, while elevated christology is not to be identified as the convictional starting point of Paul's Gentile mission, it is nevertheless important
for our investigation. First, in agreement with Sanders and others, I have
argued that "Christ→→→→not Torah" needs to be seen as the basic convictional logic governing what Paul has to say about the law and related
topics and thus as the key to any understanding of the reconfiguration of
convictions precipitated by his Damascus experience. But the term
"Christ" in this equation is not simply a cipher without content, a theological black box explaining everything else while remaining unquantified
itself. Part of any such "quantification" will involve Christ's role as a dying and rising Savior, an aspect to which we shall presently return. But an
important part of it also involves elevated christology, Christ as Lord of
all. For a covenantal nomist such as we are supposing Paul to have been,
the position indicated by "Christ→→→→not Torah" represents a dramatic
convictional shift, a personal reorientation of major proportions. The appearance of major shifts suggests the working of commensurate shifting
forces; one would expect that Torah could have been displaced from the
center of Paul's convictional world only by a Christ perceived in terms at
least as lofty. We will leave until later any consideration of the question
whether conversion autobiographies reflect the conversion experience itself or only the results of later socialization within the new community.[55]
But with respect to Paul's references to his encounter with the glorified
heavenly Lord, in either case—whether they reflect a powerful religious
experience or (less likely, to my way of thinking) only a stylized narrative
shaped by later patterns of thought—the result for present purposes remains the same. Only an elevated christology such as we find in Paul
would have been sufficient to account satisfactorily for the convictional
reconfiguration represented by "Christ→→→→not Torah."

Second, consider the connections leading back from Paul's elevated
christology to Wisdom conceptions and thus to Torah speculation. At

least since Windisch, it has been recognized that Paul clothes the figure
of Christ with material derived from the Wisdom tradition of Judaism.[56]
Not only does he call Christ "the wisdom of God" explicitly (1 Cor 1:24;
cf. v. 30); it is generally agreed that in various christological statements—
concerning Christ's origin ("firstborn of all creation" [Col 1:15]), his relationship to God ("the image of the invisible God" [Col 1:15]; "in him all
the fullness of God was pleased to dwell" [Col 1:19]; "being in the form
of God" [Phil 2:6]), his role in creation ("in him all things . . . were created" [Col 1:16]; "one lord, Jesus Christ, through whom are all things"
[1 Cor 8:6]) and his guiding presence in Israel's history (". . . and the rock
was Christ" [1 Cor 10:4])—Paul was using language and concepts derived from the traditions of personified Wisdom.[57]

Taking this one step further, W. D. Davies drew attention to the way
in which Wisdom had come to be equated with Torah in Jewish tradition.[58] The figure of Wisdom in Job and Proverbs has what Davies describes as "an international flavour," containing "nothing that is specifically Israelite."[59] Later developments in apocryphal and other postbiblical
material, however, serve to bring Wisdom within the covenantal framework by linking or equating it with Torah (Sir 24:8, 23; 1 Bar 3:37-4:1).
The identification continues in rabbinic material; Davies shows how familiar Wisdom themes (for example, that Wisdom was created before the
world and was the means by which the world was created) are attributed
to the Torah in Tannaitic literature. His purpose is to account for the
development of Paul's elevated christology, its Wisdom profile in particular:

> Once this step had been taken, however, that of substituting Jesus for the
> Torah of Judaism, Paul's mind would inevitably move forward to transfer
> to Jesus those attributes with which Judaism had honoured the Torah. We
> have seen, moreover, that the Torah had become identified in Judaism with
> the Wisdom of God and had been given the qualities of the latter, both pre-
> existence and participation in the creation of the universe as well as the
> moral discipline or redemption of mankind. The way was therefore open
> for Paul to identify Jesus with the same Wisdom of God and to ascribe to
> him pre-existence and creative activity.[60]

The parallels between the Wisdom-Torah linkage in Judaism and the
Wisdom-Christ linkage in Paul are sufficiently striking (a point also observed by Kim)[61] to justify the conclusion that Paul's christology was
shaped in significant ways at this point by his pre-Damascus perception
of the Torah.

This is significant in that it tends to confirm two conclusions reached previously. One concerns Paul's Christ-Torah antithesis. If these suggestions concerning Wisdom are correct, they provide additional confirmation that what was going on both prior to Damascus and after it was a perception that Christ was ascribed a role normally played by the Torah, and thus that Christ and Torah represented parallel and therefore rival ways of constructing the semantic universe. If Paul's christology per se is shaped by Wisdom conceptions along a line running parallel to Wisdom-Torah developments in Judaism, it is neither surprising to discover nor implausible to suggest that he perceives them as playing a parallel (and rival) soteriological role—that of marking the boundary of the people of God.

The other conclusion has to do with the Gentiles themselves. As Gaston has observed, once the Wisdom-Torah equation was made, the Torah becomes universalized, its significance no longer restricted to Israel alone: "As soon as the Torah is identified with *wisdom,* then all nations are under the Torah as they are under the laws of creation."[62] Gaston is correct in drawing out the negative consequences of this, that is, that the Torah becomes the universal standard by which the nations are judged and condemned (4 *Ezra* 7.72; *Ps.-Philo* 11.1-2; 2 *Bar.* 48.40-47). But there is a positive consequence as well, an almost inevitable tendency toward proselytism as the means by which the Gentiles too can find Wisdom and be assured of salvation.[63] This suggests another parallel between Paul's Torah conviction prior to Damascus and his Christ-conviction afterwards. The one or the other is the divinely provided manifestation of Wisdom and means of righteousness, given by God to Israel but available also to Gentiles on equal terms. As Wisdom, Christ stands in exactly the same relationship to the Gentiles as does the Torah in proselyte expectations. In other words, the shape of Paul's exaltation christology provides further confirmation that Paul thinks of the Gentiles as "proselytes" to an Israel defined not by Torah but by Christ. This position has the advantage of being able to account quite economically for an aspect of Paul's thought (exaltation christology) not easily incorporated into other explanations of his concern for the Gentiles (eschatological pilgrimage).

Christ is not only Lord for Paul; he is also Savior. Indeed, his descriptions of the message he proclaimed in Corinth (and presumably elsewhere) centers not on the exaltation of Christ but on the cross and its saving benefits (1 Cor 1:17-2:5; 15:1-8). We need then to give attention to Paul's soteriology, and to consider the possibility that his concern for the Gentiles emerges in some way from a perception of Christ as Savior of all.

When we look at Paul's language of salvation, we observe the same sort of universal scope as was noted with respect to his exaltation language. He understands Christ to be Savior of all, Jew and Gentile without distinction. Indeed, more often than not, any distinction between Jew and Gentile is kept out of view entirely, and the recipients of Christ's saving work are indicated by means of such inclusive terms as "all" (πᾶς, πάντες) or "human being" (ἄνθρωπος).

We can observe this first with respect to the "gospel" itself. Neither the summary of the gospel in 1 Cor 15:3-8 nor the argument based on it in the rest of the chapter contains any indication of the Jewish origins of the message. "Christ died for *our* sins," Paul proclaims (v. 3), the first person plural (ἡμῶν) embracing both the Jew Paul and his Gentile converts in an undifferentiated collectivity. What differentiation that does appear in the chapter has to do with those who die in Adam and those who are made alive in Christ (v. 22); in each case we encounter again the inclusive "all" (πάντες). Similarly in v. 49: "Just as *we* [note the inclusive first person plural] have borne the image of the man of dust, *we* will also bear the image of the man of heaven." Where the Jew/Gentile distinction does come into view in connection with the gospel (for example, Rom 1:16; 1 Cor 1:22-24), the point is that the gospel bears on each equally.

It is the same with the vocabulary of "salvation" itself, which appears in each of the passages mentioned in the previous paragraph. The gospel is "the power of God for salvation for *everyone* (παντί) who believes" (Rom 1:16). In 1 Cor 1:17-25, the significant line of division falls not between Jew and Gentile, but between "those who are perishing" and "*us* [Jew and Gentile alike] who are being saved" (cf. 1 Cor 15:2). Or again, in Rom 10:13, Paul quotes Joel (2:32) to the effect that "*everyone* (πᾶς) who calls on the name of the Lord shall be saved," the saving Lord already having been identified as Christ (v. 9).

What is true of the broad categories of "gospel" and "salvation" is true of more specific components of Paul's soteriology as well:

1. Statements of Christ's accomplishments for (ὑπέρ) the saved. "[God] gave him up for us *all*" (Rom 8:32); "[Christ] died for *all*" (2 Cor 5:15; also v. 14); "Christ died for *our* sins" (1 Cor 15:3).
2. Metaphors of changed status.[64] "*All* . . . are justified . . . through the redemption that is in Christ Jesus" (Rom 3:23-24); "Christ is the end of the law so that there may be righteousness for *everyone* who believes" (Rom 10:4); "*we* have been justified by his blood" (Rom 5:9); "*we*[65] know that a *person* (ἄνθρωπος) is justified not by the works of

the law but by the faith of Jesus Christ" (Gal 2:16); while *we* were
enemies, we were reconciled to God through the death of his Son"
(Rom 5:10); "in Christ God was reconciling the world to himself" (2
Cor 5:19; cf. Col 1:20).

3. Adam christology. "For as *all* die in Adam, so *all* will be made alive in
Christ" (1 Cor 15:22); "just as one man's trespass led to condemnation for all, so one man's act of righteousness leads to justification and
life for *all*" (Rom 5:18).

4. Participatory eschatology.[66] "If *we* have died with Christ, we believe
that *we* will also live with him (Rom 6:8); "one has died for all; therefore *all* have died" (2 Cor 5:14); "if *anyone* (τις) is in Christ, there is
a new creation" (2 Cor 5:17); "for *all* of you are one in Christ Jesus"
(Gal 3:28).

While this survey is far from exhaustive[67] and leaves open many questions about the shape and structure of Paul's understanding of salvation,[68]
it is sufficient to make the point. Paul's gospel finds its focus in the saving
significance of Christ's death and resurrection, a message of salvation that
includes all humanity. While categories of Jew and Gentile appear from
time to time (only to be set aside as of no significance as far as the nature
and terms of salvation are concerned), frequently and strikingly Christ's
saving work is presented as pertaining to humanity as a whole, directly
and without distinction. This leads us into the question of the structural
relationship between Paul's conviction concerning Christ as Savior and
his conviction concerning the salvation of the Gentiles. In particular, it
raises the possibility that it was Paul's perception of the nature and scope
of Christ's saving work that led to his Gentile mission. As we shall see,
however, any investigation of this possibility will lead us back very
quickly into terrain already traversed.

The question, then, concerns the possibility that the seeds of universalism were located somehow in the concept of a dying and rising Savior,
that somehow the gospel itself, as Paul perceived it, led him out into the
wider Gentile world. Such a possibility might find support in a statement
such as 1 Cor 1:23, where, with undoubtedly autobiographical overtones,
Paul describes the message of Christ crucified as "a stumbling block to
Jews." Might the cross (or perhaps the message of a crucified Messiah)
have been the thing to break down the particularistic structures of his
Jewish world of meaning and open him up to the Gentiles?

To my knowledge, no scholar has tried to construe Paul's convictions
in this way. Sanders has identified as Paul's fundamental conviction the

belief that Christ is the Savior of all on equal terms and has demonstrated that a highly satisfactory account of Pauline discourse can be thereby obtained. But this axiomatic starting point is itself left unaccounted for.[69] It contains too many discrete elements (Christ/salvation/universality/equality), with no indication of how they might be linked in an internal structure or of how they might have been precipitated by Paul's experience. In particular, Sanders's work contains no suggestion that the conviction concerning Christ as *Savior* was somehow the ground and origin of the concern for the Gentiles.

The only place to look for such a convictional linkage would be in the cross itself and the scandalous (from Paul's covenantal nomistic perspective) notion of a crucified Messiah. But the only possible route from here to Gentile salvation would appear to lead through the intervening territory of the Torah. The necessity for the Messiah to die to accomplish salvation demonstrates (Paul could have thought) the inadequacy of the law to deal with sin (cf. Gal 2:21); the dethroning of the law, in turn, puts Jews in the same sinful boat as Gentiles, thus removing the boundary between them; this, in turn, opens the possibility of a mission to all without distinction ("cross"→→→→"not Torah"→→→→"end of Jew/Gentile distinction"→→→→"Gentile mission"). This route has already been explored (§5.2, §6.3) and found wanting. For Paul, "not Torah" is not equivalent to "not Israel"; the Gentile mission is precisely that—a mission to those identified by their contradistinction from Jews, not to undifferentiated humanity as a whole. This is just another variation of the "rejection of Jewish particularism" approach characteristic of the old paradigm.

How, then, are we to construe the relationship between Paul's convictions concerning Christ as Savior and those concerning Gentile salvation? The basis of an answer to this question has been developed already in §5.2. The cross is to be seen as reconfiguring a pattern of convictions in which the Gentiles already appeared. The cross is not the point at which Gentile salvation enters the structure of Paul's Christian convictions. Instead, Christ replaces Torah in a convictional structure already universalistic in its own way. Paul had understood the Torah as the means by which Israel was covenantally differentiated from the sinful remainder of humanity and set apart for salvation. Further, Paul belonged to a segment of Judaism that believed that the Torah was available to Gentiles as well, as the sole means by which they might be delivered from sin and made righteous (proselytism). The result of the Damascus experience was to replace the Torah with Christ as the divinely appointed means of righ-

teousness and salvation. This convictional structure is represented in the
following diagram:[70]

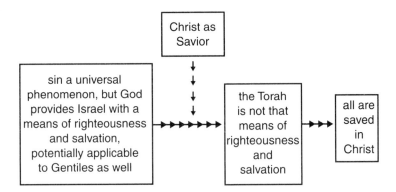

We have seen how well this construal accounts for Paul's statements
about sin and the Gentiles. I will need to show that it does the same for
material dealing with the Gentiles and salvation. What needs to be explained is this: On the one hand, Jew and Gentile appear to continue as
fundamental categories for Paul. The coming of Christ entails neither the
elimination of the Jew/Gentile distinction nor the end of Israel as a significant element in the divinely provided means of salvation. Yet, on the
other hand, Paul can discuss this salvation in terms that not only place
Jew and Gentile on equal footing but that even disregard the Jew/Gentile
distinction entirely, speaking of Christ as the Savior of all, of the whole
undifferentiated mass of humanity "in Adam." Only when we have shown
how these two facets fit together will we be able fully to understand Paul's
Gentile mission; only when I have shown how such a fit can be accomplished on the basis of the convictional structure diagrammed above will
I have confirmed my hypothesis.

The key elements of such a demonstration have already been identified
in the discussion of the eschatological pilgrimage model in §7.1. There I
noted several important aspects of the place of Israel in Paul's scenario
of salvation:

- the whole of humankind equally under the power of sin
- Israel as a kind of representative sample of humanity, differentiated
  from the rest by the law, whose function is to lay bare the plight of
  bondage to sin that Israel shares with the rest of the nations

- Christ in turn as a representative of Israel, and thus by extension a new Adam
- the Jewish Christian remnant as the primary beneficiaries of Christ's victory over sin, a victory also applicable, by the very nature of the sequence of representation, to the wider Gentile world

The place to spell this out in more detail, however, is in the context of a discussion of Israel itself, a discussion which we are now in a position to take up.

## 7.3 Findings and Implications

In this chapter I have examined and discarded several possible ways in which a concern for the Gentiles might have entered Paul's convictional structure by means of his new conviction about Christ. One of these is the eschatological pilgrimage interpretation, the idea that Paul perceives Christ as having accomplished that restoration of Israel which in traditional expectation was to trigger the end-time salvation of the Gentiles. While this falls into the category of a "reinterpretation of Jewish universalism," the others tend more to involve the "rejection of Jewish particularism." The first of these has to do with Christ's elevated status: Paul's perception of Christ as having been raised to God's right hand as universal Lord constituted a transcending of his particularistic Jewish categories and a widening of his horizon, resulting in the inclusion of the Gentiles. The other has to do with Christ as Savior, the means of Christ's saving work somehow having universal implications.

The result was uniformly negative. Despite the undeniable centrality and significance of Paul's new convictions about Christ, convincing arguments prevent us from identifying any of them as the primary point where the salvation of the Gentiles enters into Paul's convictional structure.[71]

At the same time, several observations and questions need to be carried forward. One observation concerns elevated christology and Paul's Christ-Torah antithesis. I have argued that Paul was a covenantal nomist who came to believe in Jesus as Christ, Savior and Lord, and that this, and not any independent grounds of dissatisfaction with the law, was what dislodged Torah from its position at the center of his universe of convictions. This approach assigns a high energy value to the role of Christ in the equation describing his convictional transformation. "Not Torah" results not from already-present concerns about the inadequacy of the law vis-à-vis the power of sin or the contrast between works and faith, and so on, but solely and simply from the conviction that membership in the community of salvation is to be determined by Christ. A transformation of such deeply rooted convictions requires a proportional transforming force. No one, perhaps, could have predicted the shape of Paul's christology from these factors alone. But for these factors to have produced the observable results, Paul's new Christ convictions must have had the kind of explosive energy that certainly is consonant with the elevated view that we actually do find. Paul's elevated christology supplies something needed for the basic hypothesis to work.

Another observation concerning elevated christology bears more directly on the matter of the Gentiles. We found reason to believe (1) that Paul's christology has been shaped in significant ways by Wisdom traditions, (2) that it is thus formally parallel to the Wisdom-Torah connection already present in Jewish tradition, and (3) that prior to Damascus Paul probably thought of the Torah in these Wisdom terms himself. This, in turn, brings the Gentiles into the picture, and in a manner tending toward proselyte patterns of thought. The equation of Wisdom with Torah universalizes the latter, makes Torah the means of instruction for the whole of humankind, Gentile and Jew alike, and thus provides a cosmic rationale for proselytism. This Wisdom connection means that both the Torah on the one hand and Christ on the other stand in an analogous relationship vis-à-vis the Gentile world. Thus is added another dimension to the parallel roles played by Christ for Paul, and by the Torah for the proselyte strand of covenantal universalism to which he (it is being argued) once belonged: not only as a membership marker (entrance into Abraham's family, on equal terms), but also as the earthly manifestation of Wisdom (universal revelation of God and God's will).

Two other observations raise questions about the place and importance of Israel with respect to the salvation of the Gentiles. On the one hand, the investigation of the eschatological pilgrimage option turned up considerable evidence suggesting an important role for Israel and the Jewish Christian remnant in the ongoing story of salvation. While this did not add up to the eschatological pilgrimage option, it nevertheless indicates that Paul can tell that story in a form in which Israel plays an important intermediary role between Christ and the Gentiles. Yet, on the other hand, there is plenty of evidence for a version of the story that moves directly from Christ to the Gentiles (or to all of humankind), skipping the intermediary Israel link entirely (or dissolving Israel into an undifferentiated mass of humanity). Any adequate explanation of Paul's convictional world will need to account for both observations; an Israel-centered explanation, such as is being attempted here, will need to show how a putatively important element of the story can be omitted. The lineaments of such a demonstration have begun to be visible in the discussion to this point. To fill in the picture, I turn to a discussion of Israel itself.

## CHAPTER EIGHT

# Israel

Our attempts to traverse the territory toward Gentile salvation have, in one way or another, invariably led us to Israel and, in particular, to the question of Paul's post-Damascus perception of Israel and its role in Gentile salvation. More specifically, we have repeatedly observed how the various paths leading to Paul's Gentile concerns are mapped most economically and convincingly with reference to a particular pattern of Pauline conviction, one where Gentiles are perceived as proselytes to a redefined Israel, in which Christ has replaced Torah as the mark of community membership. The time has come, then, to explore the territory from the starting point of Israel itself.

Three aspects of Paul's discourse need to be examined here: (1) statements in Romans 11 in which Gentile salvation is predicated on Israel's rejection; (2) sections of Romans that envisage righteousness and salvation for Israel but with no reference to Christ, opening up possibilities of a two-covenant or righteous Gentile model; and (3) a set of passages, most of which have been encountered already, in which Gentile salvation is mediated through Israel, or is somehow made possible by God's dealings with Israel. I shall examine these in turn.

## 8.1 The Rejection of Israel[1]

At four points in Romans 11, Paul makes statements linking the salvation of the Gentiles with the lack of response in Israel: "Through their misstep[2] salvation has come to the Gentiles" (v. 11); "if their misstep means riches for the world" (v. 12); "if their defeat[3] means riches for the Gentiles" (v. 12); "if their rejection[4] means the reconciliation of the world" (v. 15). The identical construction of the latter three statements indicates that no real significance should be attached to the variation in vocabulary describing Israel's failure; the statements function in the same way—to ground Gentile salvation in Israel's failure "to obtain what it was seeking"

(v. 7). But how? What cause-and-effect logic are we to supply[5] to link the misstep/defeat/rejection of Israel and the riches/reconciliation of the Gentiles?

The most common reconstruction of this logic interprets these statements with respect to (a particular reading of) the olive tree analogy of vv. 17-24. In this analogy, unbelieving Jews are likened to natural branches broken off, and believing Gentiles to wild olive shoots grafted in (v. 17). Not only do we once again find Jewish failure and Gentile salvation in close juxtaposition but, at least in the NRSV and RSV, the two are linked in a particular way: "If some of the branches were broken off, and you, a wild olive shoot were grafted *in their place* to share the rich root of the olive tree. . . ."

As the phrase "in their place" indicates, this rendering assumes that what is at work in the verse is a kind of "displacement logic." Such a reading of the verse has had a long history in the church. John Chrysostom, for example, paraphrased Paul's address to the Gentiles in these terms: "For it is into their place that you have been set, and their goods that you enjoy" (*Homilies on Romans* 19 [on Rom 11:18]). Paul Achtemeier sounds a similar note in our own day: "Israel's stumbling was the occasion for redemption to be opened to gentiles. There is almost a spatial analogy here. Only if some Israelites have been cleared out will there be room for gentiles."[6] As these quotations illustrate, the logic of displacement operates on the basis of place, or space. The Gentiles occupy the place—in the people of God, in God's sphere of attention, in the ongoing course of salvation history—that had been the exclusive preserve of the Jews. It is the removal of the great majority of the Jews that makes possible a place for the Gentiles.

Such a reading of v. 17 is very easily extended to the statements in vv. 11-12 and 15, with which we began. Indeed, Achtemeier's comment, cited above, was made with reference to v. 11, not to v. 17.[7] Taken together, they provide the basis for this additional way of accounting for Paul's interest in the Gentiles. Israel's loss is the Gentiles' gain; because Israel has rejected the gospel, God offers it instead to the Gentiles. At least one other statement could be drawn in to such a reading, namely, the sharply polemical statement about God's wrath against "the Jews" in 1 Thess 2:14-16. The resultant construal of Paul's convictional logic can be represented schematically as follows:

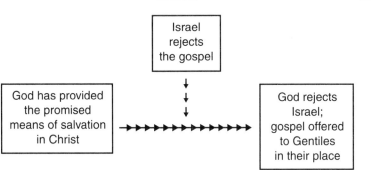

As was mentioned already, such a reading of Romans 11 has been common in Christian tradition, especially given the prevalence since at least the time of Justin Martyr of various displacement theories concerning the relationship between Israel and the church (the church as "new" or "true" Israel).[8] Paul's questions are different from those of Justin; the issue for Paul has to do with the inclusion of the Gentiles within the sphere of the gospel and thus with the relationship of the Gentiles (rather than of the church as a whole) to Israel and the Jews (including Jewish members of the church). In any case, I am interested in those instances where such a reading of Romans 11 is seen to be indicative of Paul's basic convictions about Gentile salvation.

The most common such approach takes Romans 11 to be a theological distillation of Paul's own experience: it was the frustrating experience of a period of unsuccessful missionizing among the Jews that convinced him to turn to the Gentiles.[9] In a few instances, the (temporary) displacement of Israel is taken to be a basic part of the framework within which Paul conducted the mission to the Gentiles, without any indication of the process of experience or reasoning by which he arrived at this point.[10] Less common (and less plausible) is the view that displacement notions were there from the outset.[11] Such a reconstruction is hard to reconcile with Paul's persecuting activity. His zealous persecution of the church suggests that up to the time of his Damascus experience, he felt that the mission to Israel was being *too* "successful"! It is hard to imagine that shortly afterwards he undertook a mission to the Gentiles on the grounds that the Jewish mission was a failure.

In any case, there are weighty objections to be raised against this way of linking the "failure" of Israel and the "riches" of the Gentiles. First, since apparently in the end there will be plenty of room not only for the "fullness of the Gentiles" but also for "all Israel" (vv. 25-26), it hardly seems necessary for some to be cleared out in order to make way for others; there is no shortage of space on God's olive tree! This observation may seem pedantic; analogies can be pressed only so far. Nevertheless it does draw attention to an aspect of Romans 9–11 that should act as a caution against any simple account of Paul's logic here, namely, his insistence, against the evidence of his senses and the flow of the argument from 9:1—11:10, on the ultimate salvation of "all Israel." To this we shall return below.

Second, and more significantly, there is no justification for the displacement reading of v. 17 ("in their place"). If this is what Paul intended to say, he would have said ἀντὶ αὐτῶν; ἐν αὐτοῖς can only mean "among them." Paul's focus here is on the branches that remain, rather than on those ("some") broken off; his point is that the wild shoot has been grafted in *among* the Jewish believers, not *in place of* the Jewish unbelievers. This conclusion is supported further by the next statement made about the ingrafted Gentiles. They are συγκοινωνός (copartners)[12]; the term is morphologically redundant, thus doubly confirming that the statement has to do with Gentile Christians joining with the Jewish believers already there, rather than replacing those who have been removed. Admittedly, the nearest antecedent for αὐτοῖς (them) is τῶν κλάδων (the branches; v. 17). But in view of the evidence from v. 17 as a whole, scholarly opinion is virtually unanimous that a shift in antecedent is much more probable than the alternative.[13] For the true antecedent one does not have to look far; it is found in the "holy branches" of v. 16. It is regrettable that the NRSV has perpetuated the unfortunate RSV rendering.

But these observations, though compelling, are not decisive. What clinches the argument against a displacement reading of the passages in question is that the one time such an interpretation of the Gentiles' status comes up for discussion, Paul rejects it emphatically. I refer to vv. 19-24. The displacement idea, placed in the mouth of Gentile Christians, appears in v. 19: "You will say, 'Branches were broken off so that I might be grafted in,'" the displacement logic coming to expression in the balanced contrast of the ἐκ- (ἐξεκλάσθησαν; broken *off*) and ἐν- (ἐγκεντρισθῶ; grafted *in*) prefixes, linked by ἵνα (so that). Paul's reply gives the initial impression that he agrees with the proposition: καλῶς (well; v. 20). But as he continues, he makes it clear that he does not accept any direct cause-and-effect displacement link at all. It is faith, or the lack of it, that determines one's place on the tree.[14] Any smug Gentile assumption that they are in because the others are out is sharply condemned.

What then of καλῶς? Clearly it does not indicate wholehearted agreement; once again the RSV and NRSV rendering (that is true) is unnecessarily anti-Judaic. Used as a reply, καλῶς can have a range of meanings, from full approval ("well said") through ironic concession to polite refusal ("no, thank you").[15] Since Paul sees some connection between the "failure" of the Jews and the "riches" of the Gentiles, καλῶς should probably not be taken in the latter sense of refusal. Manson is probably closer to the truth when he says: "The adverb καλῶς is probably ironical and should be translated 'Well, well!' rather than, 'That is true.'"[16] In any case, while the ingrafted branches may have benefited somehow from the lack of faith of the others, it was not by the direct means of simple displacement.

Other attempts have been made, however, to account for the logic at work in Paul's linkage of Jewish stumbling and Gentile riches. Two of these can be mentioned here.[17] The first is based on a different understanding of the nature of Israel's misstep/defeat/rejection. The usual assumption, and certainly the assumption at work in displacement readings, is that Israel's failure consisted in its rejection of the (post-Easter) gospel.[18] But Karl Barth, followed with some qualification by C. E. B. Cranfield, has suggested that Israel's misstep was the crucifixion itself.[19] Cranfield finds justification for such a reading in the parallel statement in v. 15, where Israel's failure is said to have accomplished the reconciliation (καταλλαγή) of the world, since the only other occurrence of reconciliation language in Romans (5:10-11) is with reference to Christ's death. In such a reading, the logical link would be found in the universal saving significance of Christ's death: Israel stumbled, by "[delivering] up their rejected Messiah to the Gentiles for crucifixion,"[20] but God used this to bring salvation to all.

This reading is intriguing but, in the end, unconvincing. First, even if παράπτωμα (misstep, transgression) were not a continuation of the foot-race metaphor (9:30-33; 11:11),[21] Israel's failure has clearly been defined in 10:5-24 in terms of a rejection of the gospel of Christ dead and risen. Further, in the passage as a whole, "misstep" stands in contrast both with the action of the believing remnant (vv. 5-7)—where surely the point is not that these were not involved in Christ's crucifixion but that they have believed his death to be salvific—and with the future "full inclusion" (v. 12; cf. vv. 25-26), which will involve not an un-crucifying of Jesus, but (presumably)[22] an acceptance of the crucified Messiah. The presence of καταλλαγή (reconciliation) is not significant enough to outweigh these considerations.

Another line of interpretation takes Israel's failure in its usual sense but sees the argument simply as second-order theological reflection, with no real connection to Paul's fundamental convictions about Gentile salvation. As he writes—so this line of interpretation goes[23]—Paul is aware that his own preaching among the Gentiles has met with much greater success than that of other apostles among the Jews. Believing that what has happened must be part of God's plan, and that God's plan must include the eventual salvation of Israel itself, Paul links together in a sequence the failure of the Jewish mission, the success of the mission to the Gentiles, and the eventual salvation of "all Israel" (perhaps as a reworking of traditional Gentile pilgrimage expectations). Because the sequence is divinely intended, Paul can assume that the stumbling of the Jews and the salvation of the Gentiles are causally linked somehow, and so can write as he does in vv. 11-12 and 15.

In this approach, then, the nature of the causal link is not to be identified precisely. At most, Paul has in mind the fact that Jewish rejection of the Gospel has forced the apostles to turn to the Gentiles and to expend more energy on the Gentile mission. But the logic is essentially circumstantial, a reflection on experience, a belief that what has happened must have been the result of divine purpose. In Dahl's words:

> We should not overstress the correlation of cause and effect. We do not
> need to consider Jewish rejection of the gospel a necessary condition for its
> acceptance by the Gentiles. Paul interprets what actually happened.[24]

What is significant for our purposes about this approach is the assumption that the passage sheds no real light on Paul's convictions. The questionable nature of the logic suggests that the argument is purely circumstantial, the circumstances in question having developed long after Paul had begun his work among the Gentiles.

I certainly believe that we must see the argument of Romans 11 as experience-driven, as a reflection on his experience as a Gentile missionary and thus not something that he could have written at the outset of his apostolic career. Further, as has already been mentioned, I agree that the argument, especially from v. 11 on, is characterized by a startling lack of logical consistency.[25] But this does not mean that the argument is irrelevant for our purposes. On the contrary, it is precisely the cracks in the argument that open a window into the set of underlying convictions. Romans 11 is a parade example of what has been maintained throughout this study—the necessity of differentiating between argumentative logic, operative at the rhetorical surface of Paul's letters, and convictional logic, the deeper interplay of his fundamental convictions. At the surface level, Paul's letters represent various attempts through rhetorical device and theological argumentation to deal with practical problems that have emerged in his congregations. But underlying these contingent and conceptual levels in the text is a set of basic convictions (about Christ, Israel, the Torah, the Gentiles, and so on) that seldom emerge explicitly but nevertheless provide the tacit "semantic universe" in which the text in all its aspects has its being. We need, then, to look at the argument more closely.

As already observed, the unexpected shift in the argument at v. 11 signals the depth of Paul's conviction that God would not ultimately abandon ethnic Israel. Paul's basic conviction that God had provided Christ as a means of salvation for all on equal terms, the logic of his argument up to 11:10, the undeniable failure of the Jewish mission—all these seem to suggest that if "Israel" had any ongoing significance between the resurrection and the parousia it was in the form of the remnant without remainder. Paul's determination to swim against this current indicates the presence of another conviction, that God's elective calling of Israel is irrevocable (Rom 11:28-29). As E. P. Sanders puts it in his discussion of these chapters, the failure of the Jewish mission presents Paul with a "dilemma": "How could God have willed the election and ultimately the redemption of Israel *and* have appointed Jesus Christ, whom most Jews were rejecting, for the salvation of all without distinction?"[26] The anguished argument of chapters 9–11 represents Paul's struggle to hold these convictions together in a situation where history was bringing them into open contradiction and conflict.

But what about that part of the argument linking the rejection of Israel and the riches of the Gentiles? The first thing to observe is that it does not stand alone but appears as part of the larger argument moving toward the salvation of all Israel. Indeed, three of the four statements in question form the protases of first-class conditional sentences, the apodoses of which speak of Israel's "full inclusion" (v. 12) and "acceptance" (v. 15). Again we encounter curious logic.[27] In its formal structure, the argument in these verses corresponds to a *qal waḥomer* pattern of reasoning, arguing from the lesser to the greater.[28] But even though the ultimate "full inclusion" of Israel is precisely the question under discussion (cf. v. 11a), Paul simply assumes it; if Israel's defeat brings positive results, Israel's inclusion will bring results that are even more positive. But "inclusion" itself is the argument's premise, rather than its outcome. Further, the correlation between the two halves of the argument is puzzling. While the effects move from lesser (riches for the Gentiles/reconciliation of the world) to greater ("how much more"/life from the dead), the causes do not; here we have to do with a reversal (from "rejection" to "acceptance"). Why a *reversal* of cause should lead to an *intensification* of effect is not immediately apparent and nowhere explained.

Logical curiosities in vv. 12 and 15 serve only to underline what is apparent from the chapter as a whole: Paul is convinced, so much so that he assumes it rather than argues for it, that the present situation of Israel's rejection is temporary and that it will be reversed at some time in the future. Actually, Paul is more explicit than this about the termination point. What brings this temporary situation to an end,[29] what coincides with the reversal of Israel's condition from "rejection" to "acceptance" (v. 15) and from "hardened" to "saved" (cf. vv. 25-26), is the completion of the Gentile mission ("until the fullness of the Gentiles comes in") and the parousia of Christ[30] ("the deliverer") (vv. 25-26). The Gentile mission, then, occupies a distinct period of time, coinciding with the period in which partial hardening has come upon Israel, and terminating in the parousia of Christ and the consummation of salvation.

While this observation is a commonplace, its implications—both for our understanding of the logic at work in vv. 11-12 and 15 and for the larger question of Paul's Gentile concern—have not yet been fully explored.[31] There are two implicit assumptions in Paul's statements about the period that ends at the parousia. First, Paul apparently believed that the opportunity of salvation for the Gentiles would come to an end with the parousia. This is clearly implied by the use of τὸ πλήρωμα (fullness) in v. 25; the salvation of Israel would take place once the Gentile mission has been brought to fulfillment, that is, *completed*. This belief is frequently encountered elsewhere in Paul's letters: It is (only) those who are Christ's who will be raised at the parousia (1 Cor 15:23); the time for Gentiles to respond to Paul's message of reconciliation in Christ is *now* ("now [νῦν] is the day of salvation;" 2 Cor 6:2); those who are not in Christ are without hope at the parousia (1 Thess 4:13-17) and will find no escape from the sudden destruction that will come upon them (1 Thess 5:2-10).[32]

Second, Paul apparently believed the reversal of Israel's present situation of stumbling/defeat/rejection to be the event that would precipitate the eschatological age itself. In v. 12 Paul leaves undefined (πόσῳ μᾶλλον [how much more]) the blessings that will accompany Israel's πλήρωμα (fullness). In v. 15, however, the consequences are made explicit: Israel's acceptance (presumably of Christ,[33] spurred on by their "jealousy" of the Gentiles [v. 11]) will trigger the resurrection (ζωὴ ἐκ νεκρῶν [life from the dead])[34] and thus will coincide with the parousia itself.

If Israel's acceptance of Christ will accompany—indeed, precipitate—the parousia, and if the parousia represents the termination of the Gentiles' opportunity for salvation, then Israel's immediate acceptance of the gospel would have meant the closing of the door to the Gentiles. If Israel had accepted the gospel, there would have been no opportunity for the Gentiles to participate in salvation. To adapt Paul's language here, Israel's "success" would have meant the "impoverishment" of the Gentiles. Salvation would not have been nearer to Paul's Gentile readers than when they first believed (cf. 13:11); it would have passed them by entirely. It is only because Israel "stumbled," a stumbling brought about by God's act of "hardening," that the Gentiles had the opportunity of getting into the "race for righteousness" (see 9:30-32) at all.

My suggestion, then, is that the logic at work in Paul's statements here is not the spatial logic of displacement but the temporal logic of delay. Israel's failure to respond to the gospel makes possible the "riches for the Gentiles" by opening up, not some space, but some time.[35] If Israel had responded to the gospel immediately (so Paul's argument assumes), if God had not been prepared to harden all but the remnant, then the Gentiles would have remained branches of a wild olive tree and vessels fit for destruction. God has set aside some of the natural branches, not to replace them with those drawn from the Gentiles, but to provide an opportunity for the Gentiles to be grafted into the tree so that they might share the goodness of the root with the natural branches—only some of them now, but all of them in the end.

Richard Hays has drawn attention to Paul's use of the phrase "God did not spare" (οὐκ ἐφείσατο) with respect both to Christ (8:32) and to Israel (11:21). He suggests that the repetition is deliberate:

> What Paul has done, in a word, is to interpret the fate of Israel christologically. . . . Israel undergoes rejection for the sake of the world, bearing suffering vicariously.[36]

This statement is an apt summary of the logic I suggest is at work in Paul's statements in Rom 11:11-12, 15.

But this by itself does not shed any light on Paul's convictions. The shift from space to time does not alter the conclusion reached above, that, unless it was only later that he developed an interest in the Gentiles, Paul's Gentile mission could not have been based on the notion of Israel's rejection. Underlying convictions begin to become visible, however, when we look at Jewish parallels to the two assumptions discussed above—that Israel's "obedience" to the righteousness of God will trigger the parousia and that the Gentiles' opportunity for salvation will come to an end with the parousia.

The first of these parallels has been firmly established in a perceptive article by Dale C. Allison.[37] Marshaling texts drawn from apocalyptic and rabbinic sources,[38] Allison demonstrates a widespread expectation in Second Temple Judaism that the arrival of the end "is contingent upon the repentance of Israel";[39] that is, Israel's sinfulness is what is delaying the end, and Israel's repentance is what will usher in the promised day of the Lord. Except for the typical absence in Paul of the notion of repentance—its place being taken by such things as faith (vv. 20, 23) and obedience (vv. 30-32)—the pattern is the same: "The conversion of a hardhearted Israel will be the last act of salvation-history, the event that will usher in the end."[40]

The second assumption is of greater significance here. For this assumption—that the eschatological salvation of Israel will terminate the period in which salvation is open to the Gentiles—is identical (apart from the revisions entailed by his new belief in Christ) with assumptions present within one strand of Jewish proselyte tradition. As observed in chapter 3,[41] there were those within Second Temple Judaism who believed that the only hope a Gentile had of experiencing salvation in the age to come was by becoming a proselyte to Judaism in this age.

One line of evidence for such a view comes from documents which admittedly show little interest in encouraging proselytism but which nevertheless hold open the formal possibility of becoming a proselyte in the present, even if simply to justify the punishment of Gentiles in the future. In 2 *Baruch*, for example, all Gentiles will face eternal punishment or destruction (30.4-5; 44.15; 51.6; 82.3-9), except for those who take upon themselves the yoke of the Law (41.1-6).[42] Similarly in *4 Ezra*, it is because the nations chose not to keep the Law (7.37-38) that they will be tormented (7.72) and perish (8.56-58) in the final judgment. On that day those who "manifestly kept [God's] commandments" will rejoice at the downfall of the idolaters, for, as the "Eternal, Mighty One" says, "I waited so that they might come to me, and they did not deign to" (*Apoc. Abr.* 31.1-8). Here might also be mentioned R. Eliezer, R. Joshua's interlocutor in the oft-discussed "righteous Gentiles" text of *t. Sanh.* 13.2. While Eliezer had an even more jaundiced view of proselytes than the house of Shammai as a whole, he did not reject them categorically.[43] But when the discussion concerned Gentiles as Gentiles (not proselytes), he was categorical: "None of the Gentiles has a portion in the world to come."

As for pre-70 C.E. material, a similar expectation is present at Qumran. In the period between the death of the Teacher of Righteousness and the arrival of the end, the community was prepared to receive "converts," both from Israel (1QS 6.13-15) and, if גר (sojourner, proselyte) has its usual meaning, from among the Gentiles as well (CD 14.4-5). But when the end arrives, the door to converts will be closed:

> And until the age is completed, according to the number of those years, all
> who enter after them shall do according to that interpretation of the Law

in which the first were instructed. . . . But when the age is completed, according to the number of those years, there shall be no more joining the house of Judah. (CD 4.7-12)

The material discussed to this point is generally hostile toward Gentiles. But a similar framework seems to be at work in Eleazar's successful attempt to encourage Izates to become circumcised. If the king does not take this step, warns Eleazar, he will be "guilty of the greatest offense against the law and thereby against God." [44] While not an explicit statement that this is the only hope a Gentile has of sharing in future salvation, it certainly points in that direction. Further, in Tannaitic literature we find the combination of an eschatological terminus ad quem for proselytism together with a more receptive attitude toward proselytes this side of the eschaton. In striking contrast to the eschatological pilgrimage expectation, for example, an early Tannaitic tradition declares that such twelfth-hour converts will be turned away:

In time to come, idol worshipers will come and offer themselves as proselytes. But will such be accepted? Has it not been taught that in the days of the Messiah proselytes will not be received? [45]

Indeed, in a text dating from the same period, [46] it is anticipated that the existence of those who have become proselytes in this age will be used to justify the condemnation of those who spurned the opportunity to do likewise. Commenting on Zech 2:11, R. Hanina b. Papa declares:

This refers to the day when God will judge all the nations in the time to come. Then he will bring forward all the proselytes in this age and judge the nations in their presence and say to them, "Why have you left me to serve idols in which there is no reality?" The nations will reply, "Sovereign of the universe, had we come to thy door, thou wouldst not have received us." God will say to them, "Let the proselytes from you come and testify against you." At once will God bring forward all the proselytes who will judge the nations and say to them, "Why did you abandon God and serve idols that are unreal? Was not Jethro a priest of idols, and when he came to God's door, did not God receive him? And were we not idolaters, and when we came to God's door, did not God receive us?" At once all the wicked will be abashed at the answer of the proselytes. (*Pesiq. R.* 161a)

In view of the fact that Zech 2:11 is an eschatological pilgrimage text, R. Hanina b. Papa's exclusion of the Gentiles from the age to come is highly ironic.

Admittedly, most of the texts cited are post-70 c.e., and not all of them are positive toward proselytism. Nevertheless, on the basis of this evidence and of the full discussion in chapter 3 above, we can make the following observations with confidence: (1) many within Judaism expected the exclusion and judgment of the Gentiles in the future; (2) most of Judaism was prepared to receive proselytes in the present; (3) these two opinions can be easily combined within the framework of covenantal nomism, as the Tannaitic evidence demonstrates; and (4) the likelihood of such a combination is in no way dependent on the events of 70 c.e. There is every reason, then, to suppose that for one strand of Judaism, at least, the Gentiles' hope of salvation in the age to come depended on their becoming proselytes in the present age.

If this is so, we have a clear parallel to the assumptions at work in Romans 11 and thus a framework for understanding the logic by which Paul connects the "stumbling of Israel" and the "riches of the Gentiles." What makes Paul's logic work here is an assumption—and thus an underlying conviction—identical to a conviction held by the more rigorous advocates of proselytism. In both instances it is believed that Gentiles can gain a share in the age of salvation to come by being grafted into the people of Israel in the present—except that for Paul Christ has replaced Torah as the means of entry into this community of salvation. This suggests that prior to his Damascus experience Paul viewed Gentiles in just this way, that is, that "there was no hope for the gentiles except for those who had been brought under the wings of the Divine Presence, that is, as proselytes."[47] His post-Damascus view of the Gentiles is formally similar, except that Israel has been redefined in terms of Christ.

Once again, the distinction between conviction and argument needs to be stressed. I am not suggesting that the *argument* in Romans 11 necessarily predated Romans;[48] even if it did, it would be unlikely that it corresponds to the theological framework within which Paul embarked on the Gentile mission at the outset. But the *conviction* underlying the argument, that Gentiles are to be seen as proselytes to an Israel reconstituted around Christ, is another matter. Not only does it account for the argument in Romans 11, with all its jumps and curiosities; but since we have discovered a similar conviction underlying other aspects of Paul's Gentile discourse, it provides us with a way of explaining, simply and elegantly, a whole array of seemingly disparate data. In the particular case of Romans 11, the tortuous line of argumentation constructed by Paul as a means of holding his two, apparently conflicting convictions together, can be traced most clearly if we see it as built on and constrained by the underlying conviction that Gentile salvation is dependent on their becoming proselytes to an Israel redefined by Christ.

Two other related passages deserve mention. First, 1 Thess 2:14-16, with its embarrassingly vehement polemic against the Jews, could be cited in support of an explanation of Paul's Gentile mission in terms of the rejection of Israel. On the one hand, we have Paul's passionate concern to "[speak] to the Gentiles so that they may be saved"; on the other, we have the grim declaration that "God's wrath has overtaken [the Jews] at last."[49] It would seem but a small step to link the two in a causal sequence: the offer of salvation is extended to the Gentiles because it has been spurned by the Jews.

The passage raises a host of questions.[50] But I note the absence of any connection, either explicit or implicit, between God's wrath on the Jews and the preaching to the Gentiles.[51] Indeed, no theological foundation is provided for the Gentile mission at all; it is simply taken for granted. Paul's mission may be hindered by Jewish opposition, but it is not occasioned by Jewish unbelief. The Jewish activity so displeasing to Paul (and, he believes, to God as well) emerges as a *response* to, rather than a *cause* of, the mission to the Gentiles. The grounds for the mission itself are left unstated.

We observe also the surprising connection Paul makes between the Gentile Christians of Thessalonica and the Jewish Christians of Judea. Why does Paul hold up the Judean Christians as a model? Surely there were other models of Christian suffering closer to hand.[52] Even if the Thessalonian troubles were instigated in part by Jews, as in the account in Acts (17:1-9), it is a long way, both geographically and rhetorically, from Thessalonica to Judea. Paul goes out of his way, then, to stress solidarity between the Jewish and Gentile wings of the church. And not only solidarity. Paul describes the Thessalonians as "imitators" (μιμηταί) of the Jewish Christians, using language usually reserved, in 1 Thessalonians and elsewhere, for the type of foundational modeling provided by Paul (and other missionaries) and by Christ himself.[53] The passage does not go as far as Romans 15:27 in making Gentile Christians spiritually dependent on the Judean church, but it certainly moves in this direction.[54]

But the identification goes even deeper. In vv. 15-16a, Paul extends the connections to include the persecuted prophets,[55] making use of a traditional Jewish motif, probably as reworked in Jewish Christian and then Gentile Christian circles.[56] He thus establishes a line of continuity from the prophets to Christ to the Judean churches to Jewish Christian missionaries and, finally, to the Gentile Christians of Thessalonica. Later, when the separation of church and synagogue was complete and the church was almost exclusively Gentile, the "persecution of the prophets" theme was used to buttress a decidedly displacement and supercessionist type of theology.[57] But at this early point in Christian history, when the center of the Christian movement was still very much Jewish, Paul's use of the tradition serves quite different ends, namely (borrowing appropriate language from elsewhere), to identify the Thessalonians as part of a Gentile Christian shoot grafted into the tree of Israel, taking their place alongside the Jewish Christian branches already present. I do not mean to suggest by this allusion to Romans 11 that the two passages are identical. On the basis of 1 Thess 2:14-16 one would not have been able to predict the kind of agonizing over the situation of the unbelieving Jews that we find in Romans 9–11, let alone the elaborate scenario of their ultimate salvation.[58] Still, we find here something we have found to be at work elsewhere—a basic assumption that the Gentile mission rests on, and is linked with, the already existing Jewish Christian remnant.

The other passage of interest here also comes from the Thessalonian correspondence. In 2 Thess 2:1-7, Paul speaks in highly enigmatic fashion about "the restrainer" (ὁ κατέχων; v. 7) whose "restraining influence" (τὸ κατέχον; v. 6) is holding back the "man of lawlessness" (v. 3), a figure of supreme evil who will appear in conjunction with "the rebellion" (v. 3) that precedes the final day of the Lord and parousia of Christ (vv. 1-2). Paul can assume that because of prior instruction his intended readers will readily identify the various characters in this apocalyptic scenario (v. 5). Later readers, not privy to this information, might well wish it had been otherwise. For, while the general apocalyptic shape of the passage is manifestly clear, what Paul had in mind with the references to the restrainer and his restraining influence is anything but.

Interpreters ancient and modern have made a variety of suggestions: Caesar and the Roman empire; God, or some mythological divine agent; figures hostile to God (who "hold sway" rather than "restrain"); Paul and the Gentile mission.[59] The latter possibility was first suggested by Oscar Cullmann and then taken up by Munck and incorporated into his larger reconstruction of Paul's missionary theology.[60] The main planks of Cullmann's argument are as follows: (1) the belief elsewhere in early Christianity that the Gentile mission was the task to be completed before the coming of the end (for example, Mark 13:10); (2) evidence from Rom 11:25-26 that Paul perceived the Gentile mission in a similar manner; (3) Paul's elevated apostolic self-consciousness; (4) the parallel expectation in Judaism that the arrival of the age to come was dependent on the repentance of Israel. The points of contact with my own reading of Romans 11 should be apparent.

While this reading has not received wide acceptance among commentators, there are several things to be said in its favor. First, both this passage and Romans 11 deal with the question of the factors determining the timing of the end-time events, and thus clearly are connected and should not be interpreted in complete independence of each other. Further, since Rom 11:25-26 is the clearer of the two (at least on the point in question), it is quite appropriate to appeal to it for guidance on the interpretation of the more obscure but obviously related passage.

At the same time, there are major difficulties.[61] First, even if one grants Cullmann's arguments, if my reading of Romans 11 is correct, what is restraining the parousia in this passage is not so much the Gentile mission per se, but the hardening of Israel (cf. vv. 7, 25)—the eventuality that made the Gentile mission possible in the first place. Further, in view both of the lapse of time between the writing of 2 Thessalonians and Romans and of the differences in context, it is not self-evidently the case that the two passages need to correspond in any detailed way. Developments in thought and variations in rhetorical strategy need to be given due allowance. The biggest problem with Cullmann's position, however, is posed by what is said about the restrainer in v. 7: ". . . until the restrainer is *removed*."[62] Both Cullmann and Munck take this to be a reference to Paul's death. But Paul's statement in 1 Thess 4:17 indicates clearly that at this stage of his ministry he expected to live to see the parousia.[63] Only by studiously avoiding this text can Cullmann and Munck maintain their thesis.

But while exaggerated attempts to press 2 Thessalonians 2 into the mold of Romans 11 are to be avoided, the former passage is nevertheless significant for our study. Whatever Paul meant by his enigmatic references, he is clearly working within an underlying framework characterized by these elements: (1) an interim period between the cross and the parousia as the temporal setting for his mission to the Gentiles; (2) the parousia as bringing an end to the opportunity of salvation proclaimed by Paul in his gospel (1:8-10; cf. 2:9-12); (3) this interim period as a "mystery" (2 Thess 2:7), that is, something just recently revealed. While 2 Thessalonians 2 and Romans 11 may not correspond fully in their details, they nevertheless represent separate outworkings of a common underlying temporal structure, the elements of which, moreover, are discernible throughout Paul's writings.

The significance of this observation can be drawn out by means of a brief comparison with A. Schweitzer. Schweitzer accounts for Paul's Gentile mission on the basis of the interaction of three factors: (1) traditional eschatological expectations, including that of the eschatological pilgrimage of the nations; (2) the belief that Jesus is the Messiah; and, complicating matters and preventing us from seeing Paul simply as an eschatologically oriented Jew who believed that the Messiah had come,

(3) "Being-in-Christ" as an unforeseen form of existence for the elect in the interim period between cross and parousia.[64] Schweitzer's reconstruction of the dynamics of this interim period is idiosyncratic, overly complex, and ultimately unpersuasive.[65] But the identification of the interim period itself as an important aspect of any proper understanding of Paul deserves to be rescued from obscurity and rehabilitated. The role of an interim period in Paul's thought can be accounted for more economically on the basis of two factors: (1) a conviction that Gentiles must become proselytes to Israel in this age if they are to share in the age of salvation to come (which accounts both for the eschatological urgency of Paul's mission and for his emphasis on equality of status); and (2) a belief that the Messiah has already appeared, in the form of Jesus crucified and raised (which results in Christ displacing Torah as the identifying boundary of Israel).

## 8.2 Righteous Gentiles

I have noted that, from some perspectives at least, Paul's converts look for all the world like "righteous Gentiles." They are to be considered righteous, even though, unlike proselytes, they neither undergo circumcision nor adhere fully to the Torah. And yet they are expected to conform to a pattern of behavior not unlike that prescribed by the Noachian decrees— avoidance of idolatry (1 Cor 8, 10) and sexual immorality (1 Cor 5-6), strict adherence to monotheism (1 Cor 8:6), and so on.[66] In addition, they exist alongside an identifiably Jewish group, righteous as well but continuing to be identified by circumcision (Rom 4:12), law-adherence (Rom 4:16), the covenants, the patriarchs (Rom 9:4-5), and all of Israel's irrevocable gifts and calling (Rom 11:29).[67] Not surprisingly, such similarities cause some to suggest that in Paul's view (to use Segal's words) "the gentiles are to be added to the community of the faithful through the model of the Noachide commandments."[68]

Each time these parallels have come into view in this book, I have rejected the possibility that they represent anything more than surface similarities. Standing in the way of any underlying structural connection is Paul's insistence that Gentile believers are full and equal members of the family of Abraham.[69] Nevertheless, it is necessary take a direct look at righteous Gentile readings of Paul.

The readings to be discussed here fall into two categories, one "harder" than the other. The harder version is associated most widely with the name of Lloyd Gaston, although earlier comments by Krister Stendahl provided important stimulus, and subsequent endorsement by

John Gager has given his work wider visibility.[70] Gaston's views were first advanced in his contribution to a series of essays in response to Rosemary Ruether's *Faith and Fratricide;*[71] this and subsequent essays appeared in a later collection, also entitled *Paul and the Torah.*[72]

Gaston's reconstruction is audacious and revolutionary. For Gaston's Paul, the Torah and the covenant of which it is a part continue to be valid and efficacious *for Jews;* he differs from other covenantal nomists only in his belief that God has provided Christ as a means of righteousness *for Gentiles.* What is being propounded then is a two-covenant reading: two parallel paths to salvation, two distinct forms of justifying faith, two different covenant communities. In his words:

> Had all Israel followed Paul's example, we could have had an Israel loyal to the righteousness of God expressed in the Torah alongside a gentile church loyal to the righteousness of God expressed in Jesus Christ and his fulfillment of the promises to Abraham.[73]

Likewise Gager:

> The principle of faith applies not just to Gentiles, whose justification is through Christ, but to Jews, whose justification is through the Torah.[74]

To maintain such a position, against the current both of Pauline scholarship and of the prima facie sense of Paul's letters themselves, requires considerable ingenuity and resolve. Gaston demonstrates both. He finds a firm anchor for his position, as one would expect, in Romans 11, that "stunning" passage where Paul can speak of the final salvation of all Israel "without using the name of Jesus Christ"[75] (see also Romans 4). For the rest, he simply deflects the current. Paul's letters are all written to *Gentile* Christians, dealing with *Gentile* issues. His statements about the law do not address Judaism itself but only the situation of Gentiles and the inappropriate attempt to impose the Jewish law on them. Paul "said nothing against the Torah and Israel, but simply bypassed them as irrelevant to his gospel."[76] Where he criticizes Israel for their attitude to Christ or the gospel, it is because they have refused, not to become Christians, but to recognize Christ as God's means of righteousness for the Gentiles.

Gaston's Paul conforms in significant measure, then, to the "righteous Gentiles" pattern of universalism sketched out in §3.4 above. The Torah is the divinely provided means of righteousness for Jews. Gentiles are not required to become proselytes to Judaism and full members of the covenant community; righteousness is possible for them as Gentiles. Such a

Paul would differ from Izates' adviser Ananias only in his firm conviction that God had provided Christ as this alternative means of righteousness.

As it is developed in detail, however, Gaston's position is more complex than this. He recognizes the righteous Gentiles material within Second Temple Judaism, but sees it as a more ambiguous, less optimistic phenomenon. On the one hand, in his view, the terms on which a Gentile might be assured of righteousness were unclear;[77] on the other, the equation of Torah with Wisdom tended to universalize the Torah's power to condemn while continuing to exclude Gentiles from covenant relationship with God. These two factors combined to encourage Gentile Judaizing, the observance of some or many Jewish practices in order to establish righteousness. Paul's specialized terminology must be seen (says Gaston) against this background. By "under law," Paul refers to the situation of the *Gentiles* where they "must keep all the laws given to Israel without being part of the covenant God gave to Israel";[78] by "works of law," those observances adopted by *Gentiles* in order to establish righteousness.

In a certain sense, then, Gaston rules out the "righteous Gentiles" concept as a live option for the first century. He at least does not see it as an already fully formed viewpoint ready and waiting for Paul to adopt. If I understand him correctly, his Paul is more of an innovative figure, the first one really to have developed the positive conception of Gentile righteousness outside and apart from the covenant with Israel. Thus he was misunderstood by Jews and Jewish Christians alike, a situation leading to various degrees of opposition. His innovation was the result of his Damascus experience. Prior to this, he shared the Shammaitic outlook that there was no hope for Gentiles apart from proselytism. What he found in Christ was an answer to "his quandary concerning gentiles and the law,"[79] a quandary also pervading any contemporary Jewish discussions about righteous Gentiles.

I interpret the material dealing with righteous Gentiles in a more positive way than Gaston. He combines material from two distinct patterns of thought—the more pessimistic forms of proselytism, on one hand, and righteous Gentiles, on the other—and produces a "quandary" that is quite artificial. But for the purposes of our analysis here, and of the model for which Gaston is an example, we can leave this particular aspect of his reconstruction to one side. One could just as easily argue (as does P. Lapide,[80] for example) that God-fearing or Gentile righteousness was a well-established Jewish concept and that Paul differs from his compatriots only in his identification of Christ as the means. But whether it was already fully present within Judaism, or the result of his Damascus experience, the resulting convictional structure is the same:

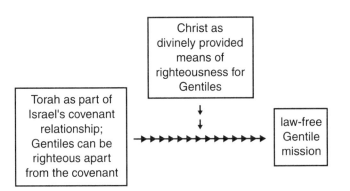

Several aspects of Gaston's approach have been criticized in the subsequent scholarly discussion.[81] Certainly Romans 11, with its evident concern for the ongoing validity of election and the ultimate certainty of Israel's salvation, needs to be given full weight. But the chapter does not exist in a vacuum. Prior to this point, Paul has argued that Jews as well as Gentiles are under sin and guilty before God (1:18-3:18; 5:12-21); declared that the law does not exempt Jews from this universal plight (3:19-20; 5:20); stated that the righteousness of God, testified to by law and prophets, has been manifested in Christ (3:21-22); declared that all, without distinction, can attain the righteousness not available through the law by being ἐκ πίστεως Ἰησοῦ (of the faithfulness of Jesus; 3:22-26); argued that only those who walk according to the Spirit of Christ (8:9-11) can fulfill the just requirement of the law (8:1-4); and lamented over Israel, because they have not recognized that righteousness is to be found in Christ (9:30-10:4) and have not believed the message of salvation in Christ (10:9, 14-21). By the time one arrives at chapter 11, then, Paul has established a christocentric semantic range for the key vocabulary of this seemingly nonchristological discourse, for example, "saved" (vv. 14, 26; cf. 10:9-13); "unbelief" (v. 20; cf. 10:17); "foreknew" (v. 2; see 8:29). If Paul's position were as Gaston describes it, so that most of his troubles with Jewish and Jewish Christian opponents were based on a misunderstanding, he would have had plenty of opportunity in the argument to make himself clear.

An additional weakness of Gaston's position has to do with Paul's insistence on the equality of Jew and Gentile and, in particular, their equal status within the family of Abraham.[82] Even if one were prepared to grant an "equal but distinct" type of argument (both are justified equally by faith, even if the grounds, object, or vehicle of their faith is different), the incontrovertible fact remains that membership in Abraham's family ("seed"; Gal 3:29; Rom 4:16) requires circumcision, and thus, for Gentiles, proselytism (see Gen 17:7-19). In addition, if Paul really held to a two-covenant, righteous Gentiles position, there would have been no need for such a dangerous exegetical venture as we find in Romans 4; as noted above, Genesis 17 contains softer statements about the Gentiles that would have suited his purposes admirably. Paul's unshakable determination to defend not only the Gentiles' righteousness but also their membership in Abraham's "seed" is a serious difficulty for Gaston's thesis.[83] In addition, Gaston's interpretation of Israel's "misstep" as Israel's failure to recognize that God has provided Christ as a separate and distinct route to salvation for the Gentiles can scarcely be the thing that makes the success of the Gentile mission possible. If anything, it makes it more difficult (cf. 1 Thess 2:14-16). While Gaston's conclusions might be appealing, they are not supported by the texts themselves.

A softer version of the righteous Gentiles approach to the question could be constructed, however, one where Christ is the means of salvation for all, but where the "law-free"[84] nature of Paul's message is explained in terms of a righteous Gentiles pattern of thought already present within Second Temple Judaism. There does not appear to be any pure example of such an approach, one in which righteous Gentiles material is appealed to as the sole and fundamental explanation of Paul's urgent concern for the Gentiles. Nevertheless, it is brought into play in several recent studies.

The most pertinent example is provided by Paula Fredriksen.[85] She argues that such conceptions were widespread in first-century Judaism. Indeed, neither in the quotidian nor in the eschatological situation was it considered necessary for Gentiles to convert in order to be considered righteous and to share in salvation. In her reconstruction, the Christian movement shared this attitude toward Gentiles right from the beginning. Precisely because it was Jewish, the Jewish Christian church accepted Gentiles into their communities without insisting on circumcision and conversion. Paul was by no means unique, in her view; his Gentile mission conformed to a pattern already present in the church and widespread within Judaism itself. The innovators were the Judaizers, who were responding to the specific set of circumstances produced by the delay of the parousia.

Fredriksen appears to have overestimated the place of this attitude toward the Gentiles. Far from being an aberration or innovation, the stance of the Judaizers was a particular Christian manifestation of another Jewish attitude that can be just as widely documented. Even if we limit our attention to Paul, however, righteous Gentiles ideas are at best a secondary factor in her reconstruction. In her reading, Paul's approach to the

Gentiles was fundamentally driven by eschatological pilgrimage expectations.[86]

Righteous Gentiles conceptions also appear in Alan Segal's work on Paul, but again in a secondary way. He argues that "Paul has adopted God-fearing as the model of righteous behavior" for his Gentile converts.[87] At the same time, however, he denies that this provides any real insight into his turning to the Gentiles, because it leaves out of account his conversion experience. He notes in particular that in Paul's insistence that Jewish and Gentile believers constitute one community in Christ and that uncircumcised Gentile Christians have the status of members of Abraham's family, Paul goes far beyond anything found in the God-fearer tradition.[88] God-fearing is simply a model Paul adopts for a Gentile mission conceived of and undertaken on other grounds. Those grounds are provided by the conversion experience itself. Segal brings contemporary sociological studies of conversion to bear on the interpretation of Paul, placing particular stress on the idea that conversion is as much a shift in community membership as in intellectual commitment. In his view Paul converted into a Gentile Christian community, and this experience, shaped by the new community itself, provided Paul with his impetus and model for Gentile conversion.

Segal's interpretation of Paul's conversion will be examined in chapter 10. For the present, we note simply that his reconstruction is not a real example of the position under examination here. In his reading of Paul, God-fearing or righteous Gentiles patterns of thought are only of secondary importance. They are to be seen as a model—or even an analogy[89]—that Paul chooses, a surface similarity that does little to reveal the true underlying reality. Nevertheless, he draws attention to a crucial feature of Paul's rhetoric, one that serves to rule out the righteous Gentile model entirely. I refer to the insistence that Gentile believers are full and equal members of Abraham's family. As Segal says, "Paul must have known that the one thing that did not follow from these traditions [concerning righteous Gentiles] is that the gentiles were part of the Mosaic covenant."[90] While he does not consider the logical next step—that Paul thinks of his converts within a reconfigured model of proselytism—he certainly puts his finger on that which makes the righteous Gentile model highly unlikely.

Thus in both its harder and softer versions, righteous Gentile approaches to Paul fail to convince. Yet Gaston's harder version especially is important for our study in that it calls attention to Paul's stubborn refusal to abandon ethnic Israel as a theologically significant category.[91] As we have seen in §6.3 above, whatever else "not Torah" might mean for Paul, it does not mean "not Israel." This leads to the final section of this chapter.

## 8.3 Proselytes to a Reconfigured Israel

I have argued that the shape of Paul's rhetoric concerning Gentile salvation can be best accounted for in terms of an underlying pattern of convictions in which Gentiles are thought of as proselytes to an Israel reconfigured around Christ. Paul's statements concerning his own role as apostle to the Gentiles need to be examined, but we are nevertheless at the point where we can draw the various arguments together and provide a sketch of the thesis as a whole.

Simply stated, my argument is that Paul's new conviction about Christ precipitated the restructuring of a system of convictions in which the Gentiles already figured. Prior to his Damascus experience, Paul adhered to that particular version of covenantal nomism in which it was believed that the only hope Gentiles had of participating in the coming age of salvation was to become proselytes to Israel in the present age. The result of his Damascus experience was that Christ came to occupy the position in his convictional structure previously occupied by the Torah. Consequently the reconfigured convictional world is structurally similar in many ways to the native world, except that Christ has replaced Torah at the center. The most important similarity has to do with the Gentiles: Paul continues to believe that the only hope of salvation for Gentiles lies in their becoming proselytes to Israel prior to the eschaton, but his Damascus experience has led him to redefine Israel (and thus proselytism) in terms of Christ. This outline of the thesis will be filled in as we proceed with a summary of the arguments supporting it.

In part, my argument has been a negative one. I have examined a variety of ways in which a concern for the Gentiles might have emerged from Paul's basic convictions and have found significant obstacles in the way of accepting any of them. This includes the two most commonly encountered construals—those in which Paul's Gentile mission is understood within the framework of eschatological pilgrimage expectations and those in which it is a primary result of the abandonment of Torah.

It is necessary now to set out the positive argument. The starting point is *Paul's repeated and insistent tendency to treat his Gentile converts as members of a christologically redefined Israel.* This emerges from a compelling body of data, much of which has been examined already. First, there is the argument in Romans 4 and Galatians 3 that Gentile believers are full and equal members of the family of Abraham. The most striking thing emerging from our examination of this argument was its "contra-textual" nature.[92] Paul insists on his hard-line position that believing Gentiles belong to Abraham's "seed," despite the explicit restriction of such membership to the circumcised (Genesis 17), and despite the presence in the very passage (Genesis 17) of statements open to a softer, "righteous Gentile" type of interpretation.

Similar assumptions underlie Paul's insistence in Phil 3:3 that it is Christians—"we" who "worship in the Spirit of God and boast in Christ Jesus"—who are "the circumcision" (ἡ περιτομή). While it is not impossible that Paul is referring here to *Jewish* Christians like himself (cf. vv. 4-11), it is nevertheless unlikely. In contrast to the situation in Galatians, Philippians contains no explicit Jew-Gentile differentiation such as would indicate that the first person plural should be read in an exclusively Jewish Christian way.[93] Further, in Col 2:11-13, where Paul is clearly speaking to Gentiles (cf. v. 13: "the uncircumcision of your flesh"), he can say that in baptism they have experienced a kind of circumcision. While the terms used here—"a circumcision not made with hands"—might suggest simply a metaphorical or symbolic turn of phrase,[94] one should not overlook the very concrete language of v. 13: as a result of this "circumcision," Gentile Christians can no longer be described as "dead in trespass *and in the uncircumcision of your flesh*." Indeed, once Paul's converts have learned to say "Jesus is Lord," they cease to be Gentiles (1 Cor 12:2-3), and are no longer to live as the Gentiles do (1 Cor 5:1; 10:20; 1 Thess 4:5). As observed already, the term "Gentiles" presupposes a bifurcated, Jewish-centered way of viewing the world; thus to cease to be Gentile necessarily means in some fashion to become a member of Israel.

To this we can add the reference to "our ancestors" (οἱ πατέρες ἡμῶν) in 1 Cor 10:1. Again Paul is clearly addressing Gentiles (cf. 12:2), and again he includes them in the family of Israel. Trying to impress on the Corinthian Christians the need to avoid idolatry, he recites the experience of "our ancestors" during the wilderness sojourn. The first person plural is clearly inclusive (cf. vv. 6, 9, 11), indicating that Paul sees these Gentile believers as now part of the family[95] descended from the Exodus community.

The olive tree analogy of Rom 11:17-24 points in a similar direction. The olive tree clearly represents Israel as a whole (cf. v. 16b), comprising the root (the patriarchs),[96] the natural branches that remain (the Jewish Christian remnant), and the natural branches broken off (the unbelieving

Jews). The Gentiles are saved, not as a separate tree in the divine orchard, but by being grafted in to the tree of Israel.

The controverted and much discussed statement in Gal 6:16, where Paul bestows a benediction on "the Israel of God," is probably also to be included here. To be sure, E. Burton and, subsequently, P. Richardson have argued that Paul has two groups in view:[97] those who follow the rule articulated in v. 15, upon whom he bestows peace; and the Israel of God, upon whom he bestows mercy. The former are Christians, especially those who see things Paul's way; the latter are those Jews who will eventually come to the truth. The position is not without merit. It offers an explanation of the awkward placement of "and mercy" after "peace be upon them." (Why, if Paul wanted to say what he is usually taken to have said, did he not say simply "peace and mercy be upon them"?) And it has in its favor the fact that Paul nowhere else uses "Israel" of the church. But undermining the first point is the additional καί (καὶ ἔλεος καὶ ἐπὶ τὸν Ἰσραὴλ τοῦ θεοῦ), which is much more easily construed with the ascensive sense "even" (". . . and mercy, *even* upon the Israel of God"). Against the second is the whole argument of 3:6-29, culminating in the declaration that all who are in Christ, Gentiles included, are part of Abraham's "seed." As Rom 9:6-7 makes abundantly clear, Paul is well aware that the proper name of Abraham's "seed" (σπέρμα appears in v. 7; cf. 2 Cor 11:22) is Israel. The benediction, then, should probably read: "And all those who follow this rule—peace be upon them and mercy, even upon the Israel of God."[98] If so, Paul uses the unusual expression "the Israel of God" to refer to the community of the new creation (cf. v. 15) made up of Jews *and* Gentiles.

Finally, there are statements that assert divine impartiality (Rom 2:11) and the absence of any differentiation (Rom 3:22; 10:12) between Jew and Gentile.[99] While at first glance these might suggest the abandonment of Jewish particularism in favor of an undifferentiated humanity, when they are examined in context, it is clear that they function within the kind of Israel-centered framework represented by the material just surveyed. That is, divine impartiality consists in the fact that God accepts, as full and equal members of the family of Abraham, all those who believe, Jew and Gentile without distinction.

These observations are not new; this aspect of Paul's language has been used as justification for various "new Israel" or "true Israel" views of the church as early as Justin Martyr in the second century.[100] Such displacement approaches are characterized by the belief that the identity and privileges of an obsolete, ethnically determined Israel have been transferred to the church, a new and distinct community in which Jew and Gentile no longer function as significant categories. My approach is not to be confused with this older view. For it is able to account for some Pauline material that older displacement views usually have to treat as anomalous, given their general assumption that ethnic Jewishness has become obsolete and irrelevant for Paul, at least in principle. Two categories of material come into play here.

First, there is a set of statements that presupposes, in various ways, the *continuing significance of ethnic Israel*. The most striking of these is the insistence on the ultimate salvation of "all Israel" (Rom 11:11-32). The tortured logic of the argument leading up to this conclusion simply underlines the depth of Paul's conviction here.[101] In addition, there is Paul's use of the term "Gentile" itself as the most basic way of identifying his converts and his sphere of apostolic mission. By its very nature, the term presupposes a Jewish-centered way of viewing the world, a bipolar division of humanity depending for its very meaning on the existence of a distinct and identifiable Jewish entity.[102] Further, the significance of this division is not restricted to the world outside the church. More than simply an empirical datum—one of the facts of life in the present age[103]—the division is significant within the church as well. For it is clear that in Paul's perspective the existence of a Jewish Christian remnant is of fundamental significance. We have seen how he introduces the concept into the discussion of Abraham's family in Romans 4, even though it significantly undermines the logic of his argument.[104] Further, the remnant features prominently in Romans 9–11, and statements about it increase in significance as the argument develops. When first mentioned, Paul simply asserts its existence, with emphasis on its smallness (9:24, 27-29); next it is brought forward as evidence in itself that God has not "rejected his people" (11:1-10); finally, it points beyond itself as a sign and guarantee of the ultimate salvation of all Israel (11:11-27, especially v. 16).[105]

This does not exhaust what Paul has to say about the Jewish Christian remnant. The other relevant statements, however, fall into a second category, where he speaks of ethnic Israel not only as an entity with continuing theological significance, but also as the *means or vehicle of Gentile salvation*. Perhaps the clearest example is Rom 15:25-27, where Paul justifies his collection project in terms of Gentile Christian indebtedness to Jewish Christianity.[106] Jewish Christians have shared their spiritual blessings with the Gentiles, and so the Gentile Christians *ought*[107] to share their material blessings with the Jews in return. In v. 27 Paul sets these needy "saints in Jerusalem" (cf. v. 26) paratagmatically over against "the Gentiles" (τὰ ἔθνη), indicating that in some sense they represent or embody the community of Jewish believers, the remnant of Israel to whom the blessings of the gospel most properly belong. This remnant, then, constitutes an important intermediate link between Christ and the Gentiles, the primary beneficiaries of saving benefits that are only subsequently extended to the Gentiles.

Such a relationship between Jews and Gentiles is found elsewhere in Romans as well. Earlier in chapter 15 we have this statement: "Christ has become a servant of the circumcised on behalf of the truth of God, in order that he might confirm the promises given to the patriarchs, and in order that the Gentiles might glorify God for his mercy"( vv. 8-9).[108] The statement in itself is cryptic, but it serves to sum up the whole argument of 1:16—15:7, and its sense is clear: the salvation of the Gentiles has been made possible by the ministry Christ has carried out for the benefit of "the circumcised." Moving back to Rom 11:17, the Gentile believers are depicted as wild olive shoots grafted in among the (remaining) Jewish branches (*pace* the NRSV) to share with them the richness of the root.[109] Again, the Jewish Christian remnant has both temporal priority and first claim on the blessings, the Gentiles coming in to share what has, in the first instance, been provided for them. Moving back still further, this sense of temporal and (what might be called) mediational priority is signaled at the outset of the epistle, when Paul speaks of the gospel as "the power of God for salvation, *to the Jew first,* and also to the Greek" (1:16).

Outside Romans, the primary passage of interest is Gal 3:13-14, where Paul states that "Christ redeemed *us* from the curse of the law . . . in order that in Christ Jesus the blessing of Abraham might come to *the Gentiles.*" As I have observed,[110] the argument within which the statement is found begins with an emphatic differentiation between "us Jews" and the Gentiles (2:15). This, together with several other indications, suggests strongly that the us/Gentiles pairing in 3:13-14 represents a continuation of this programmatic differentiation. The salvation of the Gentiles has been made possible by the redemption of the Jews. To redeem those who were under the law (4:4-5), Christ became not only human ("born of a woman") but also Jewish ("born under the law"). This redemption of a Jewish remnant by a Jewish savior is what makes possible the fulfillment of God's gospel promise to Abraham about the Gentiles (cf. 3:8).

This, in turn, opens out into Paul's whole discussion of the law and its place in the divine program of salvation, which we will need to revisit in due course. For the present, what emerges from the preceding survey of material is that ethnic Israel continues to represent a significant category in Paul's system of convictions. As was observed earlier, "not Torah" does not mean "not Israel."[111] While Paul resists any attempt to impose Torah-based, Jewish identity markers on Gentiles as a condition of membership, he continues to find a place in his thinking for a continuing Jewish entity identified by precisely these Torah-based identity markers.

But this observation stands in considerable tension with the one made previously, concerning the redefined family of Abraham. How can Paul define Abraham's family in terms of Christ and faith, so that uncircumcised gentile believers are full and equal members, while at the same time affirming the ongoing legitimacy of a form of Abraham's family defined in terms of traditional, Torah-based, ethnic identity markers? While this phenomenon serves to refute any simple "new Israel" approach to Paul's ecclesiology, it remains at the same time something that any alternative approach must account for.

One popular approach has been to see Paul's Gentile mission as an outworking of eschatological pilgrimage ideas. Such an approach has definite appeal, especially since it can draw support from just these Israel-centered aspects of Paul's language. Indeed, I believe that if he had been so inclined at the outset, Paul could developed his thinking along such pilgrimage lines, arriving at a very similar mission to the Gentiles with only minor modifications in his theological discourse. But several aspects of Paul's discourse, especially his willingness to contemplate the "rejection" of Israel (Rom 11:11, 12, 15), render this interpretation unlikely (see §7.1, above).

But while this argument concerning Israel's rejection serves to close one door (an eschatological pilgrimage reading), it opens another which proves to be much more promising. As was argued above (§8.1), this argument lends no support to traditional displacement readings of Paul, in which Gentiles are brought in to fill up the space left vacant by Jewish unbelief. Rather, the decisive assumptions at work in the argument—that Israel's "acceptance" will coincide with the parousia and the arrival of the age of resurrection; that the Gentile mission will terminate with the parousia—suggest that Israel's "rejection" of the gospel (or, from a different perspective, the divine "hardening" of the major portion of Israel) functions to open up not an element of space but a segment of time—an interim period, during which a mission to the Gentiles can take place. Further, it was argued that in its essential elements—full membership in Abraham's family; an opportunity open only until the eschaton—Paul's approach to the Gentiles is structurally similar to that version of Jewish proselytism which held that Gentiles needed to become proselytes to Israel in this age if they wanted to share in the salvation of the age to come.

At several earlier points I have had occasion to peer through this door and to suspect that Paul considered his Gentile converts as proselytes to an Israel reconstituted around Christ—indeed, that his conversion experience represented (in part) a shift from a Torah-centered view of proselytism to a Christ-centered one. But the simple yet thoroughgoing way in which this thesis accounts for the otherwise difficult argument of Romans 11 serves to throw the door wide open and to beckon us to walk through with confidence. It is my contention that this thesis, together with the related notion of the (short) interim period between cross and parousia, provides an economical and satisfying account of all the relevant data, and thus is to be preferred. Let us look again at the relevant material.

1. The most straightforward and unambiguous supporting body of evidence is the material surveyed at the outset of this section, in which Paul treats his Gentile converts as members of the family of Abraham. Parallels with Jewish proselyte traditions are readily apparent.[112]

2. The Torah in covenantal nomism (especially the more exclusive proselyte version of it under consideration here) and Christ in Paul's new pattern of thought have parallel roles. In both cases we have to do with a divinely provided instrument of deliverance from an otherwise universal problem of sin;[113] both instruments function as boundary markers, defining and preserving the community called by God in the present and awaiting salvation in the future;[114] in both cases, "righteousness" is a membership term, a way of designating one as a member in good standing of such a community of salvation.[115] Further, both in Paul's revised view of things and in covenantal nomism, the Torah is applicable in principle to the Gentiles as well, though only Jews (and proselytes) are what Paul would describe as "under the law."[116] And finally, both Christ and Torah are linked with elevated Wisdom conceptions, and thus are both linked particularly with Israel but are also of universal significance.[117] At each point, the relationship between Christ and the Gentiles is parallel to the analogous relationship assumed in such proselyte patterns of thought. This degree of parallelism is fully consistent with the supposition that Paul was a covenantal nomist who in his conversion came to transfer over to Christ the central role formerly assigned to the law, including its character as a sine qua non for Gentile salvation.

3. A third supporting observation concerns the temporal terminus ad quem of the Gentile mission as Paul perceives it, and the resultant placement of the mission in the divine chronology of salvation. As we have seen, the mission occupies that period stretching from the cross to the parousia—and no further. For Paul the offer of salvation to the Gentiles is an opportunity available only until the parousia. The most important significance of this is the parallel it represents with the more hard-line version of Jewish proselytism, where the only hope Gentiles have of sharing in the age to come is to become proselytes in this age. This parallel

provides considerable support for the thesis being argued for here, support that is further strengthened by the fact that it is able to make good sense of the difficult argument in Rom 11:11-27.

But an interim period thus understood is able to account for two other observations we have made. The second of these will come up in the fifth point below; the first, to be dealt with here, concerns Paul's Christ-Torah antithesis. Why did Paul perceive Christ and Torah in such mutually exclusive terms? This question was explored in detail above (§6.2), and an answer based on the peculiar nature of the interim period was suggested. In traditional Jewish messianism, where Messiah and Torah are related sequentially, there is no tension or rivalry between them: the Torah functions in this age to mark out the community of the righteous that will be saved through the Messiah's agency in the age to come. Torah and Messiah play distinct and complementary roles. But in the gospel to which Paul shifted his allegiance, the Messiah has appeared *in advance of* the age to come. Since acceptance of Christ is a prerequisite for participation in that age of salvation, the kerygma assigns to Christ a role traditionally played by the Torah. Christ functions not only to deliver the righteous when he comes at the end of the age, but also to determine the community of the righteous in the period prior to the end. Because of the unexpected already/not yet structure of early Christian belief, then, Christ and Torah are put into competing and rival roles.

My suggestion is that Paul perceived this Christ-Torah rivalry even prior to Damascus, so that his persecution was fueled at least in part by a perception of a fundamental antithesis between Christ and Torah. After his conversion, he continued to see them as mutually exclusive, at least with respect to membership requirements, boundary markers, righteousness, and so on. But his new conviction was not simply the inverse of the old. He was in no way prepared to abandon his belief that God had given the Torah. If the Torah was from God, Paul had to find a new place and function for it. Paul's solution was to assign it a preparatory role. If the problem was the result of an unexpected overlap of Christ and Torah, the solution was to make them sequential again.

But the new sequence was construed quite differently than the old. Paul did not simply revert to the old schema, and say that since the Messiah had come they were now living fully in the age of salvation. The present period is a "mystery," something not anticipated in the traditional scheme of things, and consequently is still very much a "not yet" time for Paul. For all his idiosyncrasy, Albert Schweitzer was quite shrewd in his insistence on the significance of this interim period, a point with which eschatological pilgrimage readings do not fully reckon. While Paul has a

*Heilsgeschichte,* it represents a significant reconfiguration of traditional expectations, not the smooth continuation of them such as is defended, for example, by N. T. Wright. The coming of Christ, then, brings the era of the Torah to an end, by inaugurating not the final age of salvation, but an unanticipated interim period. In such a revised pattern of saving history, the role of the Torah cannot remain as it was understood before. Instead, Paul assigns it a preparatory function in a period lasting only until Christ, in which it serves to lay bare the human plight under sin.

Paul's restriction of Gentile salvation to the period between the cross and the parousia is parallel in essential respects to that version of proselytism in which Gentiles are required to embrace the Torah in this age if they are to share in salvation in the next. Not only does this provide direct support for my thesis, it offers indirect confirmation as well in that it leads us to recognize that Paul understood the period between Christ and the parousia as an *interim* period. This in turn accounts for his Christ-Torah antithesis, in that he perceived them as rival means of identifying the community (of Jews and Gentile "proselytes") destined for salvation in the age to come.

4. Moving back from the interim period to the period of the Torah, Paul's revised view of the purpose of the law accounts for what we have observed concerning the role of Jewish Christian remnant in salvation. As was argued at several points above,[118] Paul views Israel as a kind of representative sample of the whole of humankind. Sin entered the human story through Adam, and death through sin. The law was given, not to overturn the power of sin and undo Adam's work, but simply to provide a mechanism by which sin could be identified, so that it could be dealt with in Christ. Christ, in other words, was the "goal" toward which the law was intended (Rom 10:4). Prior to Christ, Jew and Gentile were equally under the power of sin, even if possession of the law meant that Israel was under sin in a distinct way. Nevertheless, the giving of the law and the emergence of Israel as a distinct people represented a significant preliminary step in the direction of redemption, in that within Israel's experience the reality of the human situation—in bondage to sin and to the powers of this age—was thrown into sharp relief.

But just as Israel was the special subgroup of the family of Adam in which the problem of sin was identified and clarified, so it was the arena where the divinely provided solution appears: Christ was "born under the law" (Gal 4:5); "from [the Israelites], according to the flesh, comes the Messiah" (Rom 9:5); he "became a servant of the circumcision" (Rom 15:8). Fully identifying with Israel's (and thus the human) situation—being "made sin" (2 Cor 5:21); "taking the form of a slave" (Phil 2:7);

"becoming a curse" (Gal 3:13)—Christ therefore serves to concentrate the human plight even further. He stands at the focal center of a two-stage process of representation, functioning as a representative of Israel (Abraham's true "seed" [Gal 3:16]; becoming "a curse *for us*" [Gal 3:13]), just as Israel functioned as a representative of the whole of humankind.[119] On this point, I agree wholeheartedly with Wright:

> God has deliberately given the Torah to be the means of concentrating the sin of humankind in one place, namely, in his people Israel—in order that it might then be concentrated yet further, drawn together on to Israel's representative, the Messiah—in order that it might there be dealt with once and for all.[120]

Several consequences flow out of this analysis. The most immediate one concerns Israel. Since Christ identifies first with Israel, the saving benefits made possible in his death and resurrection pertain in the first instance to Israel. Thus it is quite to be expected that we should find the Jewish Christian remnant perceived as the primary beneficiary of Christ's ministry, and the means by which those benefits are extended to the Gentiles. Further, since Israel functions as a representative sample of Adam's family as a whole, it is also to be expected that what Christ accomplishes for "the circumcision" is applicable in principle and available on the same terms to everyone, Jew and Gentile alike. This further explains why it was possible for Paul to formulate his soteriology in ways that move directly from Christ to "all," with no explicit mention of the Jewish middle term.[121] As the representative individual of the representative family, Christ is the representative of all (see 2 Cor 5:14). Because of the particular role assigned to Israel, Christ's redemption of Israel is at the same time and on the same terms the redemption of the whole human family. When it suits his purposes, Paul can pass over the intervening step in silence.

Having reached this point it would be possible to go on to show how such a christologically reconfigured understanding of Israel's role vis-à-vis the nations leads into Paul's presentation of salvation as "participatory eschatology,"[122] that is, Christ's death and resurrection as the defeat of the powers of sin and death (Rom 8:3-4, 31-39; 1 Cor 15:24-28; Col 2:15); Christ as the first to die to this age and rise to the age to come (Rom 6:4-11; 1 Cor 15:20); Christ as a representative figure, who thereby makes it possible for others to be liberated from the power of sin and to participate in the transition from this age to the age to come (Rom 8:1-4; 2 Cor 5:14-15); existence "in Christ" as the prerequisite, locus, and means of salvation (Gal 2:19-21; Rom 8:1-2); and so on. But for present purposes the main point of interest is the place of the Gentiles in all this, and in particular the fact that Paul's whole soteriology can be explained on the basis developed here, namely, (1) a proselyte form of covenantal nomism; (2) the interim period, putting Christ and Torah in a position of rivalry; (3) Jesus as the Christ, the anticipated agent of eschatological redemption; (4) the resultant reconfiguration of (1) on the basis of (2) and (3), in which the Torah is repositioned, becoming the means of clarifying the universal problem so that a solution might be accomplished for all in Christ, the offer of participation in which, however, is open to the Gentiles only until the end of the age.

5. This mention of the end of the age leads into the final aspect of the material under examination, the continuing significance of ethnic Israel. We have observed how this introduces a puzzling "category confusion"[123] into Paul's discourse. How is it that he can remain so committed to an Israel defined in traditional, Torah-based terms, while at the same time insisting on a redefinition of Abraham's family (Israel) based instead on Christ—a redefinition which, if followed through consistently, would sooner or later surely mean the disappearance of an ethnically identifiable Israel?

As argued earlier,[124] an answer suggests itself in the phrase "sooner or later." For Paul, there *was* no "later"! From the time of the Thessalonian correspondence, when he expects to be alive until the parousia (1 Thess 4:15), through to the writing of Romans, when he can still declare that the day of salvation is at hand (Rom 13:12),[125] he continues to expect the parousia to take place in the near future. The interim period is a brief one; Paul's generation was the final one of this age. In such a situation, those who had been born Jewish and whose identities had been shaped by the law would remain identifiably so to the end, even if—like Paul—they had come to understand the role of the law and the nature of Abraham's family in different terms. The brevity of the interim period allows us to understand how Paul can hold both to a definition of Abraham's family in which faith in Christ is the only membership requirement for Jew and Gentile alike, and to the continuing significance, both within and apart from the church, of the Jew/Gentile distinction and of ethnic Israel. Needless to say, it is a formulation that could not be carried intact into a church in which the parousia is indefinitely delayed; the very attempt to do so distorts it considerably. But our concern here is to understand Paul's thought in his own context, not to construct a theology for our own day.[126]

My argument, in sum, is that the structure of Paul's convictions can be represented as follows:

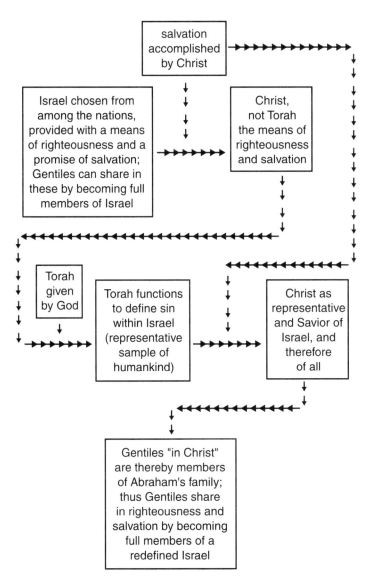

## 8.4 Findings and Implications

In the previous section (§8.3), I pulled together the various conclusions arrived at earlier, and summarized the resultant case for my thesis. The thesis is that Paul views the Gentiles in a manner analogous to that found in the more stringent forms of Jewish proselytism. In both cases it is held that only by becoming proselytes to Judaism in this age will Gentiles be able to share in the salvation of the age to come; the difference is that for Paul Christ has replaced Torah as the boundary marker of Israel, and thus as the prerequisite for proselytism. All that is necessary here is a comment on the first two sections of this chapter.

In the first section, I examined those statements in Romans 11 where Paul links the salvation of the Gentiles with the rejection of Israel. The logic at work here has usually been understood as a logic of space—the Gentiles come in to fill up the space given up by unbelieving Israel—and has thus provided the rationale for various displacement ecclesiologies. A more careful examination of the passage, however, led me to the conclusion that Paul's logic is based not on space but on time: Israel's rejection has opened up a period of time during which the offer of salvation is extended to the Gentiles. Since this offer apparently expires with the parousia, Paul's approach to the Gentiles conforms in a significant way to the stringent view of proselytism described in the previous paragraph. This similarity provides a strong indication that Paul's convictional framework can be understood as a Christ-centered reconfiguration of precisely this proselyte viewpoint, a conclusion further confirmed by the fact that it is able to include the heretofore difficult argument of Romans 11 within a consistent and economical framework.

In the second part of the chapter I examined those statements suggesting that a Torah-identified, ethnic Israel continues to function as a significant category for Paul. While I found unconvincing the position that Paul operated on a two-covenant basis—through Christ for the Gentiles, through Torah for the Jews—I noted that any explanation of Paul's Gentile mission needs to take this material into serious account. The position set out in §8.3, I believe, does precisely that.

We come finally, then, to Paul himself. Our study of his convictions about the Gentiles will not be complete until we examine the convictions at work in the statements he makes about his own role as apostle to the Gentiles.

## CHAPTER NINE

# Paul's Apostolic Call

## 9.1 The Call

In recent years, and particularly since the work of Krister Stendahl, one further element of Paul's universe of meaning has been put forward as the convictional starting point for his Gentile mission, namely, his sense of "call." As Stendahl puts it, Paul's Damascus experience is to be understood not as a conversion but as a call, an experience in which "God's Messiah asks him as a Jew to bring God's message to the Gentiles."[1] In one or two examples of this type of approach, we find a defense of an explicit, verbal commissioning such as is narrated in Acts.[2] More typically, however, the experience is described in vaguer terms, the call to carry out an apostolic mission to the Gentiles being understood as Paul's own perception of the import of the experience.[3]

There are two ways in which Stendahl's statement, and others like it, can be understood. One is to see it as a way of summing up a complex experience, the concern for a Gentile mission understood as emerging from the experience itself (and thus present from the beginning of Paul's existence as a Christian, rather than a later development), but at the same time as the result of a more complex shift of convictions (and thus not the convictional starting point in itself).[4] My argument, to a certain extent, is a case in point. Such cases, where the universality of the call itself is dependent on more fundamental convictions, are for that reason not of interest in this chapter.

But occasionally Paul's sense of call is presented as a much more fundamental datum, the essence of the experience itself and the fixed point from which everything else develops. E. P. Sanders provides us with a prime example. "We come to the following train of experience and thought," he says as he draws his discussion of Paul and the law to a conclusion:

> God revealed his son to Paul and called him to be apostle to the Gentiles.
> Christ is not only the Jewish Messiah, he is savior and Lord of the universe.
> If salvation is by Christ and is intended for Gentile as well as Jew, it is not
> by the Jewish law.[5]

Sanders goes on to describe in more detail how Paul's views about the law
unfold from here, but this is enough to illustrate the point: the call to
reveal God's Son to the Gentiles is the point of departure for everything
else.

This way of accounting for Paul's Gentile mission, however, can be
disposed of rather quickly. As we have observed,[6] it either begs the question or renders Paul's convictional shift arbitrary and inexplicable—or
both. Prior to the Damascus experience, Paul was, in his own terms, a
zealot for the law and a persecutor of the church (Gal 1:13-14; Phil 3:5-
6). Before his experience could have been understood, then, as a call "to
proclaim God's Son among the Gentiles" (Gal 1:15-16)—or, in Stendahl's
terms, as a call in which "God's Messiah asks him as a Jew to bring God's
message to the Gentiles"—it must have been an experience in which he
became convinced that the crucified Jesus was even so and after all the
"Messiah" and "Son of God." Further, since his persecution of those who
proclaimed the message of the crucified Messiah was linked to his zeal
for Israel's law and ancestral tradition, any revision of his estimation of
Jesus would necessarily entail a reassessment of these other fundamental
convictions as well. Moreover, since each of these convictions (about Israel, the Torah, messianic salvation, and so on) carried with it implications for the situation and status of the Gentiles, Paul could not have
arrived at the conviction that he was to proclaim a Christ-centered message of salvation to the Gentiles without the situation and status of the
Gentiles becoming part of this convictional reassessment. Kim's assumption of an explicitly verbal call ("Paul, I want you as a Jew to bring the
message of Christ to the Gentiles"!) would have made no sense to him at
all, unless it fit into a framework where Jew, Gentile, and God's message
about Christ made coherent sense. In other words, a perceived call to a
Gentile mission could not have been Paul's starting point. There must
have been a first stage in which a Christ-centered mission to the Gentiles
made sense before a there could be a second-stage perception that he himself was called to play a central role in such a mission.

Thus it is not possible to account for the convictions undergirding
Paul's Gentile mission simply from the starting point of a perception on
his part that he had been called to carry out a mission to the Gentiles.
The Damascus experience can be described as a call to such a mission

only in the larger sense in which the perception of a call is the outcome—
the focal result—of a shift in convictions centered on an altered assessment of Jesus.

As has become clear in the preceding chapters, my proposal is that
Paul's Gentile mission is to be accounted for in just this way, in conjunction with two other factors that stemmed from days as a Pharisee and a
persecutor: (1) His new assessment of Jesus and his salvific function was
shaped in decisive ways by his pre-Damascus perception of the kerygma,
in particular that Christ and Torah represented mutually exclusive ways
of defining the boundary of the elect people of God. (2) As a Pharisee, he
had held to the stringent view that only those Gentiles who in this age
became proselytes—full members of the community of the elect—would
have a share in the age to come. Such a reading takes just as seriously the
significant religious experience represented by the Damascus event as do
the approaches discussed above. Only a powerful experience could have
altered Paul's perception of Jesus and produced such a seismic shift in his
convictional world. But the experience in its initial impact and import, I
maintain, concerns Jesus and the belief that God had raised him, not Paul
and the belief that God had called him.

I believe that my proposal provides a consistent and economical accounting of the data represented by Pauline discourse, though before my
case can be said to be complete it will be necessary to show that the assumptions made about Paul's pre-Damascus convictions and perceptions
are plausible. Before turning to this final stage of the investigation, however, two aspects of Paul's apostolic self-consciousness require further discussion. The first has to do with the Gentiles and their place in salvation,
the second with Paul's own role.

1. In the material reflecting Paul's perception of his role as apostle to
the Gentiles, can we discern anything about his underlying convictions
about the Gentiles and their place in God's saving purposes? In particular,
is there anything with a bearing on the proposal that he perceives them
as proselytes to a redefined Israel? While a survey of the relevant material
reveals nothing to confirm the specific proposal (the proselyte parallel), it
nevertheless uncovers a rich body of evidence supporting the more general
contention that Paul perceived his apostolic mission to the Gentiles in a
very Israel-centered way.

The most explicit indication of an Israel-centered conception of the
mission is found in Rom 11:11-32, where Paul argues that the "fullness
of the Gentiles" will be the thing to trigger the final salvation of all Israel,
the latter's jealousy of the Gentiles' experience of salvation functioning in
some way to bring this about. While it would be going too far to conclude

that Paul saw himself as bringing in this "fullness" single-handedly, nevertheless he certainly assigns himself a central role in the mission from which it will result.[7]

I am by no means prepared to argue that this scenario, found only in Romans, represents in any essential way the framework within which Paul initiated and carried out his apostolic labors.[8] While the occasion of the letter to Rome was perhaps not the first time he tried to work his way through the argument,[9] the problem it addresses—the failure of Israel— was one that became apparent for Paul only subsequent to the start of his apostolic career.[10] Still, there are enough connections between this argument and the pattern of missionary activity reflected more widely in his letters to suggest that it was more than just a passing conceit. The collection project, for example, which occupied a considerable portion of his time and energy, is in all probability to be seen as one of the ways in which Paul sought "to magnify [his] ministry in order to make [his] own people jealous" (see Rom 11:13). Further, his evident concern to establish representative churches in a string of Roman provinces,[11] together with the belief that with the delivery of the collection project the eastern portion of the Gentile mission had been "fulfilled" (πεπληρωκέναι; Rom 15:19), provides a strong indication that he saw himself as working toward the kind of "fullness (πλήρωμα) of the Gentiles" anticipated in Rom 11:25.

But evidence of an Israel-centered conception of the Gentile mission is by no means restricted to the unique argument of Romans 11. In the first place, we can mention Paul's basic self-understanding as an apostle to the *Gentiles*.[12] As we have seen, Paul's use of the term "Gentile" (ἔθνη) betrays the essential Jewishness of his way of viewing the world.[13] While there is room for discussion as to the degree to which he saw himself as *the* apostle to the Gentiles in some unique sense,[14] as well as the extent to which ἔθνη retained its basic sense of "nations,"[15] the fact remains that ἔθνη means *non-Jews*. For Paul to define his apostolic role as having to do with *Gentiles* is to signal not his abandonment of a Jewish perspective, but the degree to which his mission depends on such a perspective for its rationale.

This is confirmed by a related point. When Paul identifies his mission field as that of the Gentiles in particular (in contrast to the world in general), he is thereby also identifying himself in his apostolic role as a *Jewish* missionary to the Gentiles. This is not only implied by the term itself; it is an explicit feature of his self-presentation as an apostle.[16] The most spectacular examples are found in those boasting passages where he feels compelled to establish his Jewish credentials over against the claims of rival Jewish missionaries (2 Cor 11:21-29; Phil 3:4-6)—a circumstance that tends to devalue the evidence to a certain degree. But this is not the extent of the evidence. For one thing, his Jewish origins and pre-Damascus persecution of the church seem to have been part of his initial preaching. In Gal 1:13-14, for example, he refers to this personal story as something about which the Galatians have already heard, presumably during his initial visit.[17] In addition, his recitation of the gospel as he first preached it to the Corinthians concludes with his own apostolic commissioning in the midst of his persecuting activity (1 Cor 15:3-11). The fact that this detail does nothing to advance the argument[18] suggests that it was part of the gospel message as he usually proclaimed it. To this we can add Paul's references to his own persecution at the hands of Jewish agencies (1 Thess 2:14-16; 2 Cor 11:24, 26; Gal 5:11), statements indicating both that he was perceived as Jewish by the synagogue and that this fact was recognized by his Gentile congregations.[19]

It is in Romans 11, however, that such self-identification receives its most weighty theological signification. Here Paul points to himself as an example—in actuality, the only example cited—of the remnant of Israel: "Has God rejected his people? By no means! I myself am an Israelite" (11:1). It is instructive to note how centrally Paul places himself in his answer to the question "Has God rejected Israel?" There are two parts to his answer: (1) Any rejection is only *partial*; there is a remnant (11:1-10). (2) Such rejection is only *temporary*; eventually all Israel will be saved (11:11-32). With respect to #1, Paul puts himself forward as an exemplary member of the remnant; with respect to #2, it is the Gentile mission, in which he is playing the primary role, that will bring about the eventual salvation of Israel. One even wonders whether Paul views his whole experience as paradigmatic of Israel as a whole, his own initial rejection of Christ being overturned in a christophany that not only made him part of the remnant but also prefigured the eventual reversal of the situation of Israel as a whole.[20] But at the very least, Romans 11 reveals the extent to which Paul perceives himself as a *Jewish* apostle, an apostle to the Gentiles on behalf of, and for the sake of, God's elect people Israel. While the rhetorical situation of Romans is no doubt a factor in his self-presentation in Romans, this presentation is nevertheless fully in keeping with information emerging from his other letters.

The Israel-centered character of Paul's apostolic consciousness is reflected in two other collections of textual material. First, as has been widely recognized, in Gal 1:15 Paul describes his "conversion" experience as a "call," using language rooted in prophetic call narratives.[21] The texts most frequently mentioned in this regard are Jer 1:4-5 and Isa 49:1-6; both passages describe a commissioning that begins in the womb and has to do with the Gentiles. The most significant verbal similarities, however, are to be found with respect to LXX Isa 49:1-6.[22] If intentional, the allusion is surprising: the passage from Isaiah concerns the call not simply of a prophet, but of the "Servant of the Lord." Elsewhere in the New Testament the "Suffering Servant" passages of Isaiah were read christologically, as referring to Christ. But the allusion is by no means isolated; while Paul does not cite these texts with reference to the suffering and death of Christ,[23] on at least three other occasions he draws them in explicitly with reference to his own apostolic mission.[24]

In 2 Cor 6:2 we find a direct quotation of Isa 49:8. In the larger context, Paul is discussing his own "ministry of reconciliation" (5:18) as an "ambassador of Christ" (5:20). The text in question is quoted with reference to the offer of salvation being made to the Gentiles now in the present era (6:1-2). Moving to Romans, in 15:20-21 Paul cites another Servant passage (Isa 52:15), in connection with his apostolic practice of working only where Christ has not yet been preached. The role assigned to the Servant in the Isaiah passage is assumed here by Paul himself. And earlier in the epistle, he cites Isa 52:7 and 53:1 with reference to the preaching of the gospel to Jews and Gentiles (Rom 10:15, 16). Admittedly, the reference in this case is to Christian preaching generally, especially to the Jews. But there is no indication in the passage that his own preaching was excluded from view.[25]

At the very least, these references confirm the Jewish framework within which Paul conceives his apostolic ministry. The casualness with which the texts are cited, especially in 2 Cor 6:2 and Rom 15:21, is striking. Almost instinctively, Paul reaches for parallel texts and figures from Jewish tradition to characterize and explain his ministry to the Gentiles. But the parallels with the Servant of Isaiah are too striking to be incidental; the Servant is somehow identified with Israel (49:3), is given the task to be a light to the nations (v. 6), and at the same time will "bring Jacob/Israel back to" the Lord (v. 5). Indeed, the parallels are much closer in the case of the Servant than in that of prophets in general; despite Jer 1:5, prophets were oriented toward Israel much more than to the nations.[26] While I would not go so far as to say that Paul thought of himself as *the* Servant, full stop, it is certainly not outreaching the evidence to say that he found in the Servant-missionary of Isaiah a model for the mission to the Gentiles within which he had been given a primary role.

One final point: While I am not prepared to place very much weight on it, it is at least worthy of comment that Paul can say that he was set apart *from his mother's womb* for the task to which God has now called him (Gal 1:15-16).[27] That the language is stylized is not to be denied.

Still, it suggests that Paul perceives his concern for the Gentiles not as a radical *novum* first coming into existence in the Damascus experience but instead as somehow part of God's dealings with him from the beginning. This is at least consistent with the suggestion that the roots of his Gentile concern are to be found in a pre-Damascus orientation toward the Gentiles.

We turn finally to a second set of texts reflecting an Israel-centered view of mission, where we find Paul in the role not of a prophet but of a priest. Actually, there is a hint of cultic language already in Gal 1:15; ἀφορίζειν (to set apart; found also in Rom 1:1) is frequently used in the LXX with reference to the setting apart of persons and things for holy use.[28] In any case, frequently in Paul's letters we encounter cultic and temple language being used with reference not only to Christian existence in general (for example, 1 Cor 3:16-17; 6:19), but also to the Gentile mission in particular, and to Paul's own role within it.[29]

The richest concentration of cultic language is found in Paul's description of his apostolic mission in Rom 15:15-16: "the grace given to me by God, so that I might be a *cultic minister* (λειτουργὸν) of Christ Jesus to the Gentiles, *doing priestly service* (ἱερουργοῦντα) with respect to the gospel of God, so that the *offering* (προσφορὰ) of the Gentiles might be *acceptable* (εὐπρόσδεκτος), *sanctified* (ἡγιασμένη) by the Holy Spirit." As an apostle, Paul serves God as a priest, striving to bring the "offering of the Gentiles" to an acceptable conclusion. But such usage is by no means limited to this verse.[30] Several chapters earlier, Paul urges his (Gentile) readers to present their bodies "as a living sacrifice (θυσίαν), holy and pleasing to God" (12:1). That he considers this exhortation to follow from the discussion just completed, concerning the mystery of Israel and the Gentiles in God's purposes, is indicated by the connective "therefore" (οὖν). Further, on several occasions he describes the initial converts in a geographical area as "firstfruits" (ἀπαρχή), implying that the whole church in the area would eventually comprise the full offering.[31] In his letter to the church at Philippi, he speaks of his death as a "libation being poured out"[32] over the "sacrificial service[33] of your faith" (2:17), and of their partnership in his apostolic ministry as "a fragrant offering, a sacrifice acceptable and pleasing to God" (4:18). In 1 Cor 9:13-14, arguing that apostles deserve to be supported in their work, he compares the work of an apostle with that of a priest in the temple.[34] Finally, while words of the λειτουργ- group (serve) do not always have cultic connotations,[35] his use of such terms with reference to the collection project (Rom 15:27; 2 Cor 9:12)—specifically to describe the service being rendered to the Jewish Christians in Jerusalem by the Gentile churches—probably is to be included here, especially as he expresses the wish that the collection prove to be "acceptable" (Rom 15:31).[36]

While cultic imagery is put to a variety of uses in these passages, it seems to cohere in the image of the Gentile believers as themselves being the offering. This is certainly the case in Rom 12:1 and in the "firstfruits" references. The faith of the Philippians, described in sacrificial terms in Phil 2:17, is not to be differentiated in any essential way from the believers themselves; such a description merely puts the focus on that which has effected their transition from "unsanctified" to "holy." Thus when in Rom 15:16 Paul speaks of "the offering of the Gentiles," the genitive should probably be interpreted as epexegetic: the offering consists of the Gentile believers themselves, though the offering is at the same time one made by the same Gentile believers (Rom 12:1). The remaining financial references—the Philippians' support of Paul; the contributions from the Gentile churches to the collection project—can be seen as particular manifestations of the greater offering represented by the Gentile mission as a whole.

What bearing does this material have on our question? On the one hand, and negatively, the usage is to a significant extent simply metaphorical. That is, Paul does not seem to be attempting to establish any "spiritualized" correspondence between his Gentile mission and some *specific* tradition or practice concerning Gentile involvement at the temple in Jerusalem. For example, while it would help my argument, I am not prepared to suggest that he sees this Gentile offering as the Christian replacement or fulfillment of the offering probably made by proselytes as part of the process of conversion.[37] Nor, by the same token, does the evidence suggest a specific background in either eschatological pilgrimage offerings[38] or sacrifices made by "God-fearers" of one kind or another.[39]

But, on the other hand, the usage is not so metaphorical that the terms now refer simply to Christian ministry in general, with any Jew/Gentile distinction having fallen away entirely. The acceptable offering that Paul is striving to bring to completion is specifically the offering of the *Gentiles* (Rom 11:16); the "firstfruits" are the first converts in *Asia* (Rom 16:5) or *Achaia* (1 Cor 16:15), that is, the initial offering of a mission that has Jerusalem as a point of departure and has now worked its way through a string of Roman provinces reaching right to Illyricum and heading for Spain (Rom 15:19).[40] Not only is it a *Gentile* offering; the mention of a Jerusalem point of departure indicates that the offering retains in some way a Jerusalem focus. And so it is to the example of *Israel's* temple that Paul appeals for support of his apostolic rights (1 Cor 9:13-14). While the "offering of the Gentiles" of Rom 15:16 cannot be simply equated with the collection from the Gentile congregations, there are nevertheless several indications—Paul's description of the collection as a sacrificial service (λειτουργῆσαι) rendered by the Gentiles (v. 27); his expressed desire that it, like the offering itself, be considered "acceptable" (εὐπρόσδε-κτος; vv. 16, 31); the fact that the delivery of the collection brings to completion (even sets the "seal" on; cf. v. 30) this phase of the mission—that the one is at least a sign and preliminary manifestation of the other. And Paul is prepared to undertake an elaborate and dangerous journey, with a representative number of Gentile Christians, so that this sacrificial sign and manifestation might be offered *in Jerusalem*.

The cultic elements in Paul's language of mission, then, join with the prophetic and Isaianic Servant elements to reinforce the Israel-centered nature of his understanding of his apostolic role. While not drawn from any particular "pattern of universalism," this language is very much in keeping with the more general cultic and temple focus found throughout the material surveyed in chapter 3. When all due allowances are given for the place of Christ in Paul's world of meaning, his perception is not unlike that of Philo, who understands Israel's role as that of a priest among the nations: Israel is "the nation dearest of all to God, which . . . has received the gift of priesthood and prophecy on behalf of all humankind"; "the Jewish nation is to the whole inhabited world what the priest is to the state."[41] In Paul's view, he has been called by the God of Israel to carry out Israel's prophetic and priestly task among the nations.

This examination of Paul's perception of his apostolic role confirms the general thrust of my thesis that he carried out his mission to the Gentiles within an Israel-centered framework and is at least consistent with its more specific contention that he considers his converts to be proselytes to a redefined Israel. But there is one final question to be addressed in this discussion of his call.

2. How do we explain Paul's conviction, not only that a mission to the Gentiles (on the distinctive terms that have come to be associated with him) is to be carried out, but also that he himself has been called to play a primary role in such a mission, a task that presses upon him with a considerable degree of urgency? The question, then, concerns both the personal role and the sense of urgency.

The sense of urgency is not difficult to account for, at least within the framework of the thesis being put forward here. If Paul believed both that Gentiles needed to respond to Christ (and thereby become part of Abraham's family) prior to the end of the age and also that Christ's parousia (which would usher in the end of the age) would take place in the near future, then the window of opportunity for Gentile salvation would be open for only a short time longer.[42] As for Paul's personal role, it is not difficult to understand why he would think of himself as an apostle. The concept of apostleship—a status grounded in an encounter with the risen Lord, a role centered on the proclamation of the kerygma—was a fully established part of the movement into which he converted (1 Cor 15:7; Gal 1:17). It is not surprising that he would have perceived his own experience of the risen Christ as grounds for an apostolic role on equal terms with those who were apostles before him. But while he insists on equality of status, he insists just as firmly on uniqueness of role: he is apostle to the *Gentiles*. How is this to be accounted for?

It is not enough simply to account for the *terms* on which Paul undertook the Gentile mission—the rejection of any requirement to adopt Jewish identity markers, the insistence at the same time that "in Christ" Gentiles were members of Abraham's family, and so on. We have provided a consistent, coherent, and, I believe, compelling account of how Paul arrived at this conception of Gentile salvation, by suggesting that prior to Damascus he held a particular view of the Gentiles and their place in an Israel-centered scheme of things. But while this might account for his post-Damascus perception of the Gentiles, it does not account for his compelling conviction of a personal role. While the author of 2 *Baruch* may have believed similarly that the end was near and that only those Gentiles "who have fled under the wings" of Israel's God would be saved,[43] this combination of beliefs, apparently, did not propel him to any concerted effort to encourage such flight.

But what if prior to Damascus Paul not only held such beliefs about the Gentiles but was also personally involved in some way in the process of receiving and instructing proselytes? What if his sense of having been called from his mother's womb (Gal 1:15) came to initial (but, from his later perspective, misguided; see Rom 10:2) expression in a time of "preaching circumcision" (Gal 5:11) to "God-fearers" and other interested Gentiles, a phase of his life that he now looks back upon as an abnormal birth (1 Cor 15:8), God's purposes in calling him having initially miscarried?[44]

Of course, it would be necessary to demonstrate that such a suggestion is plausible, with respect both to Paul's own orientation and activity prior to his Damascus experience, as far as this can be determined, and to the phenomenon of proselytism within Judaism more generally. For the present, the point is that it is fully consistent with the structure of Paul's Christian convictions as we have discerned it, and that it moreover supplies the piece missing from an otherwise convincing explanation of how such a convictional reconfiguration came to be.

This explanation can be summarized as follows: (1) At the outset Paul can be characterized as a covenantal nomist, and in particular as one who not only held to the more stringent view concerning Gentile participation in salvation (that is, limited to proselytes) but also had a personal involvement in the process of making proselytes. (The nature of that involvement does not have to be specified at this point.) (2) After encountering the Christian movement, he opposed it vehemently. The specific reasons for his opposition will require further discussion (§11.2), but at bottom he perceived the message of Christ as representing a rival and opposing way of defining the boundary of God's covenant people. (3) His experience of the risen Jesus not only convinced him that Jesus is Christ and Lord, requiring a radical shift in his way of understanding God's purposes with Israel and the Gentiles, but it also galvanized his own personal involvement with the Gentile world, infusing the already-existing structures of his concern for Gentile salvation with a new sense of apostolic mission and urgency.

My thesis does not assume the existence of a full-scale Jewish mission to the Gentiles, so that the only difference in the before and after picture of Paul's activity is the substitution of Christ for law in his missionary message.[45] The experience of the risen Jesus introduced powerful new factors into the situation, for example, a sense of eschatological urgency and of an apostolic call, and produced a new and different phenomenon. The early Christian mission, Paul's included, cannot be accounted for in its entirety by already-present Jewish patterns. But, at the same time, early Christianity being in no way hermetically sealed off from its Jewish environment, it is completely to be expected that Jewish patterns would contribute to the shape of the new movement, the new energy of the Christ-experience flowing at least initially along channels already present within Judaism. Paul's new world of meaning is the product of an interaction between a powerful religious experience and a framework of native convictions, with emphasis on both parts of the equation.

## 9.2 Findings and Implications

In this chapter we examined a final set of statements bearing on the Gentile mission, that is, those having to do with Paul's conviction that he was called as an apostle to preach the gospel among the Gentiles. We quickly concluded that the Gentile mission cannot be accounted for simply on the basis of a call. To attempt this is simply to beg the question, to pass a tautology off as an answer. The experience could not have been perceived as such a call without at the same time involving more basic convictions concerning Israel, the law, the Gentiles, and Christ.

An examination of the material reflecting Paul's apostolic self-consciousness reveals nothing to confirm the specific thesis set out in §8.3, that he views his Gentile converts as proselytes to an Israel redrawn around Christ. Nevertheless, it provides significant confirmation of a more general feature of the thesis, namely, the Israel-centered nature of Paul's missionary conceptions. The term "apostle of the Gentiles" (Rom 11:13), in and of itself, betrays a decidedly Jewish vantage point on the world. Moreover, to characterize his role Paul draws heavily on the model of the prophets of Israel, the Servant of Isaiah, and the priests of the temple. He goes to the Gentiles, then, not simply as an individual Jew but as a representative of Israel, sharing Israel's spiritual blessings with the nations.

At the same time, however, this material raises a question that will lead us into the final section of my study. The thesis sketched out in §8.3 will account for the shape of Paul's thinking about Gentile salvation. But what about his sense of personal urgency? Why did he feel that he himself was called to take the lead in this enterprise? My suggestion follows on directly from the one made already: If we can account for the structure of his convictions about the Gentiles on the assumption that prior to Damascus he believed that only proselytes would share in Israel's salvation, we can account for the urgency of his apostolic self-consciousness by assuming that in addition he had already been personally involved in the process by which Gentiles became proselytes. Conviction and activity were linked in each case.

This leads us into the final, diachronic section of my study. To this point our investigation has been synchronic. I have been examining the structure of convictions assumed to underlie the rhetorical surface of the epistolary discourse. While the discourse varies with the situation, and while the theology coming to expression in successive letters may have undergone a process of development, I have assumed that Paul operated on the basis of a set of core convictions that remained relatively fixed over the period represented by his letters. My attempt to describe and account for this structure, however, led me to posit a process unfolding in a temporal sequence: an initial convictional world (resulting in some specific activity vis-à-vis the Gentiles); an initial perception of the Christian message as a rival to Torah religion (resulting in persecution); a powerful experience understood to be an encounter with the risen Christ (resulting in an apostolic mission to the Gentiles). To complete the case, then, I need to confirm the plausibility of this temporal sequence, the suggestions about Paul's pre-Damascus convictions and activity in particular.

# PART THREE

# The Origin of Paul's Convictions about the Gentiles

## CHAPTER TEN

# Other Theories of Origin

In the preceding chapters I have developed the argument that Paul's Gentile convictions are best explained as the reconfiguration, under the impact of his Damascus experience, of convictions formed during his "earlier life in Judaism" (cf. Gal 1:13). My explanation, then, moves from the examination of a convictional structure, perceptible beneath the rhetorical surface of a set of letters, to a hypothesis about a transformational process that takes place in the temporal unfolding of a life experience. In this final part, I intend to demonstrate that such a hypothesis is plausible. It will not be possible to engage in thorough discussions of all the historical issues touched on in this chapter and the next; this would require a book-length study of its own, especially if one were to bring relevant material from Acts into the discussion. Here my intention is more modest— simply to demonstrate that the diachronic elements of the hypothesis are plausible.

As a first step in this direction, it is necessary to consider a few additional explanations of Paul's Gentile convictions. At the end of chapter 1, I presented a survey of the various approaches to the question, arranged chronologically, that is, arranged according to the point in Paul's experience at which the foundation of his concern for the Gentiles is to be located.[1] Most of these explanations have been dealt with in the course of the discussions in the previous chapters. A few, however, remain to be examined.

The full range of explanations is summarized in the list to follow. The survey is highly condensed; readers are directed to the previous discussion for full detail. One preliminary comment should be made, however, about the classification scheme. In the case of the approaches listed in the first and third categories, the Damascus experience is not irrelevant. In the first instance, Paul's apostolic concern for the Gentiles is seen to result from the impact of his Christ-experience on his previous frame of mind;

in the third, it is assumed that he drew on his new convictions about Christ to make sense of the later experience. The differentiating element in each case is the essential role played by factors in addition to the Damascus experience itself. By the same token, approaches listed in the second category do not necessarily assume that a concern for the Gentiles was instantaneous; it may have developed more gradually. But the characteristic feature here is the assumption that, whenever it did appear, it was the direct and immediate result of the Damascus experience.

1. Pre-Damascus Convictions

• dissatisfaction with Judaism as a solution to the universal human plight
* dissatisfaction with Judaism's exclusion of Gentiles from salvation
• commitment to one of Judaism's already-developed "patterns of universalism" (i.e., ways in which Gentiles might participate in Israel's salvation); in particular, eschatological pilgrimage expectations and righteous Gentiles conceptions

2. Damascus Experience

• an openness to the wider Gentile world as the result of the abandonment of Torah (this, in turn, the result either of an earlier dissatisfaction with Judaism, or of a new conviction about Christ)
• an openness to the wider Gentile world as the result of a new belief in Christ as universal lord and savior
• the experience as containing, or consisting of, an explicit call to a Gentile mission
* conversion to a form of early Christianity already engaged in a Gentile mission

3. Later Development

* a turning to the Gentiles after a period of unsuccessful mission among the Jews

Most of these possibilities have been dealt with in the course of our discussion to this point. Three remain to be examined, however, before we can bring this aspect of our discussion to a conclusion. They are indicated by asterisks in the preceding list.

1. Several scholars—W. D. Davies, E. P. Sanders, and L. Gaston included—have suggested that during his life within Judaism Paul had experienced both a sympathy for the Gentiles and a dissatisfaction with the

fact of their exclusion from God's saving mercies. His encounter with Christ, it is suggested, provided him with a resolution of his "uneasy conscience" or "secret dissatisfaction" or "personal quandary" with respect to the Gentiles.[2] Sanders's presence among this group gives rise to a certain irony, given his vigorous defense of a "solution before problem" approach to Paul. For he seems to be prepared to accept in the case of the Gentile mission what he emphatically rejects in the case of the Torah, namely, that the development of Paul's thought moved to a Christian solution from a prior Jewish problem.

In any case, the assumption here—quite correct, in my estimation—is that Paul had belonged to a form of Judaism that would consign all outside the covenant to perdition.[3] But even assuming that he had found this position troubling, the reality of the situation, as we have seen, was that Judaism itself provided the means to quiet such an unsettled conscience. One did not need to convert to Christianity to find a more comforting doctrine; one could join with those Jews who looked for the salvation of the Gentiles as Gentiles, in the eschatological future, or who were ready to consider the possibility of righteousness (without conversion) for Gentiles in the present. If Paul had indeed been troubled by an uneasy conscience about the Gentiles, less drastic solutions were close at hand.

But further, it can reasonably be asked whether someone who took such pride in his Jewish heritage (Phil 3:4-6) and who was filled with such zeal for the traditions of his fathers (Gal 1:14)—someone who in Krister Stendahl's words was characterized by a "robust conscience"[4] as far as his Jewish upbringing was concerned—would have felt any secret dissatisfaction about the Gentiles at all. For such a person, any concern about the fate of the Gentiles could easily have found expression in proselytizing activity. What cause was there to feel troubled or uneasy when the door was wide open for Gentiles to come in under the wings of God's mercy (see 2 Bar 41.4)? Moreover, it is not as if Paul's "solution" left him any better off. In his Christian soteriology he still had to countenance a mass of humanity outside of Christ "doomed to destruction."[5] The only difference in this regard from his former position had to do with the nature of the boundary line between saved and lost. Indeed (though this would not have become apparent until later), his new soteriology had the makings of an even more troubled conscience, in that it appeared to assign most of his own "kinsmen by race" (see Rom 9:3) to the company of the doomed. It is more probable, then, that if Paul the Pharisee had held a strict proselyte position with respect to the Gentiles, he did so with the same equanimity that characterized the Jewish proselytizing movement as a whole.

2. Working in chronological order, we come next to the suggestion that Paul was converted to a form of Christianity already engaged in a mission to the Gentiles, and that he accepted such a mission as part of the package.[6] As noted already in the survey at the end of chapter 1, most of the scholars who account for Paul's Gentile mission in this way also believe that part of the process of conversion was the working out of a system of convictions in which such a mission made theological sense. These approaches belong more properly elsewhere. But several other scholars— especially H. Räisänen, and (less clearly) A. Segal—assign a much more fundamental role to the assumed stance of the community into which Paul was received.

In Räisänen's reconstruction,[7] the Hellenistic Jewish Christian practice of admitting uncircumcised Gentile converts into their community emerged not as the result of any clearly articulated theology, but, more spontaneously, a product of the charismatic enthusiasm of the new movement. If any theological justification were needed, it was to be found in the fact that God had obviously poured out the Spirit on these believers as well. When he ceased persecuting this movement and instead became part of it, Paul simply adopted the unreflective liberalism of the Hellenists, accepting Gentile salvation as a given component of the new world to which he had given his allegiance. It was only later, when this approach came under fire from Judaizing Christians, that he was forced to develop a theological defense of the Gentile mission that would take into account the constituent elements of the old world he had left behind.

In his attempt to argue his case, Räisänen makes many astute observations about the logical difficulties present in Paul's argumentation. But he provides no solid grounds for believing that these lead necessarily to the position he expounds. The only other argument of substance concerns the fact that until the Antioch incident, Paul was able to function without difficulty in Antioch and alongside Barnabas. Since Barnabas's position on the law was less radical than that eventually defended by Paul (Gal 2:13)—so his argument goes—Paul could not have believed from the outset that "Christ is the end of the Torah." Now, it is not to be doubted that there were differences between Paul and Barnabas on the issue of the law and that these were exacerbated by the Judaizing crisis. Nevertheless, the fact that up to this point Barnabas had been prepared, as Paul can say, to "live like a Gentile" (cf. Gal 2:13-14) means that his association with Paul cannot be used as evidence against an early date for Paul's Christ-Torah antithesis.

But the major difficulty with Räisänen's thesis is that it ignores the fact of Paul's persecuting zeal. The idea that someone with zealous commitment to the Torah would after his conversion casually abandon it as an *adiaphoron,*[8] without having come to the conviction that this was a necessary corollary of his new faith in Christ, is incredible.[9] It is possible to imagine Paul the zealot becoming a Christian of the Judaizing type and then later coming to the conclusion that Christ meant the end of the Torah as a requirement for salvation. But to suggest that he would abandon what had been the central fact of his existence without pausing to think about it strains belief. Räisänen can argue his position only by ignoring entirely the implications of Paul's persecuting zeal.[10]

Alan Segal's reconstruction is more difficult to bring clearly into focus. He states that discovering how Paul's Gentile mission came about is a "crucial" element of his book.[11] But he seems to account for it in two different ways. On the one hand, he holds that Paul was received into and nurtured by a Gentile Christian community. Summing up a discussion of Paul's early experience in Damascus, Arabia, and Antioch, he states, "Paul lived in a gentile community during his formative years as a convert."[12] This is not simply an incidental observation but a basic element of his thesis. For he interprets Paul's conversion with the aid of models drawn from sociological theory, arguing in particular (and quite plausibly) that conversion needs to be seen as a shift as much from one social group to another as from one set of beliefs to another.

Yet, on the other hand, Segal leans decidedly in the direction that Paul came to perceive a call to a Gentile mission only later, after a largely unsuccessful period of missionary activity among Jews: "Paul's description of himself as the apostle to the gentiles could easily have been the result of his experience of success among gentiles and his rejection among Jews. Evidently there was a period of time when Paul tried less successfully to convince his Jewish brothers."[13] Paul's declaration in 1 Cor 9:21—that "to those outside the law I became as one outside the law . . . so that I might win those outside the law"—Segal takes not as a statement of ongoing practice, but as a reference to a specific shift in practice and belief, when Paul abandoned Torah observance in order to preach to the Gentiles.[14]

It is not clear to me how to fit these two elements together. It is difficult to take both as descriptive of Paul's situation immediately subsequent to his Damascus experience. Then we would have the the odd and implausible picture of a Torah-observant missionary to Jews living as a member of a Gentile Christian community. Probably we are to think of sequential phases—a brief initial phase in which he attempted, unsuccessfully, to evangelize Jews, resulting in a decisive turn toward the Gentiles (almost a second conversion) and incorporation into a Gentile Christian community. If this is the correct reading of Segal's position, then he belongs more properly in the next section.

Let us consider the idea, however, that Paul moved directly after his conversion into a Gentile Christian community. One obstacle immediately presents itself, an obstacle also standing in the way of Segal's position as described above—the unlikelihood that such a form of Christianity even existed at this point. There is no certain evidence even for Räisänen's position of a Hellenistic Jewish Christian mission to the Gentiles at the early date of Paul's conversion. This is certainly within the realm of possibility,[15] but, in the absence of solid evidence, it provides only a very precarious foundation for an attempt to account for the origin of Paul's Gentile concern. (Accordingly, while such a position would be consistent with my own argument—and even strengthen it—I am not prepared to place very much weight on it.) But Segal goes one step farther, resting his case on the assumed existence of *Gentile* Christianity at this very early date. At the very least, the term requires definition. Does it mean a community consisting primarily of Gentiles? If so, where is the evidence? Or does it mean a mixed community of Jews and Gentiles, such as is found later at Antioch? But even Antioch seems to have found Paul's position too radical (cf. Gal 2:11-14). Such an assumption provides a precarious foundation indeed.[16]

But let us suppose, for the sake of argument, that Paul the convert was nurtured in such a community. Far from explaining Paul's concern for a Gentile mission, such an approach would simply beg the question. For the crucial question to be answered in this case would be why Paul joined such a community in the first place. Early Christianity contained a variety of communities, with a spectrum of opinion on the terms of admission for Gentiles. Why did Paul—a Pharisee and zealous defender of Torah religion prior to his conversion—not join the community of those who advocated a more Torah-centered position vis-à-vis the Gentiles? Surely the original choice was not purely incidental, the Gentile church being the only one in the neighborhood! But if not, the question of the origin of Paul's particular attitudes toward the Gentiles would need to be pushed back a stage.

One cannot explain Paul's Gentile mission, then, simply on the basis of the community into which he converted. Even if it were the case that he joined a form of Hellenistic Jewish Christianity already including Gentiles (a possible but by no means certain proposition), he must—as part of the process of conversion itself—have come to a reassessment of his former convictions concerning the law. Otherwise membership in such a mixed community would not have been possible, and he would have aligned himself with some other form of Jewish Christianity.

3. What then of the second element of Segal's reconstruction, the idea that Paul abandoned the Torah as a condition of membership and turned to the Gentiles only after an unsuccessful period of missionizing among Jews? This has been argued by a number of scholars, most recently by F. Watson, who is not necessarily typical of the approach, but whose work contains the most complete treatment of the Pauline material.[17]

Watson argues that Paul and others in the Antioch church turned to the Gentiles because of the lack of response from Jews, abandoning the requirement of Torah observance when they discovered that Gentiles responded more readily without it. In his version of the thesis, then, the law-free mission to Gentiles developed for pragmatic reasons, theological justification emerging only later in response to opposition. This element of unreflective pragmatism (not dissimilar to that of Räisänen), however, is not a necessary part of the thesis. One could just as easily argue that the failure of the Jewish mission precipitated a more fundamental crisis of conviction, almost a second conversion.

In any case, the arguments put forward by Watson pertain to both versions of the thesis. For our purposes, there are two main lines of argument to be discussed. First, he cites evidence which, in his view, suggests a period when Paul preached only to Jews. Included here are 1 Cor 9:20-21 and 2 Cor 11:24, both of which refer to missionary activity among Jews. To these texts he adds the reference to "preaching circumcision" in Gal 5:11. Against the argument that Gal 1:15-16 makes the call to a Gentile mission coincident with the Damascus experience itself, he replies that "Paul is reflecting on his conversion as he now understands it, about seventeen years after the event" (p. 30), and, furthermore, in a highly polemical context. In such a situation, he asserts, one cannot easily eliminate the possibility that he is telescoping years of experience into the single event from which it eventually unfolded.[18] The second argument has to do with the turning to the Gentiles. This argument is constructed on "the remarkable series of statements in Romans 11 to the effect that Israel's unbelief has led to the salvation of the Gentiles." He believes that "it is hard to imagine how Paul could have come to such a view except through reflection on what had actually happened." Indeed, he rests his case here: "Here at last we are on solid ground in our investigation of the origins of the Gentile mission: it began in response to Jewish failure to believe the gospel" (p. 32).

On closer examination, however, Watson's "solid ground" disappears rather quickly. In 1 Cor 9:19-23, the parallel way in which Paul speaks of the various groups (Jews, those under the law, those outside the law, the weak) suggests clearly that he is treating them as equal categories, and thus is speaking of current practice, rather than a decisive shift in the past[19] (even though the practicalities of that practice might be hard to contemplate!). Likewise with 2 Cor 11:24; only if one assumes what is to be proven can one place the events of v. 24 at a different time than those of the surrounding verses. The statement of Gal 5:11, apparently implying that there was a time when Paul "preached circumcision" ("if I am still preaching circumcision"), while tantalizing, provides no support for Watson's position. For in the context of Galatians, "preaching circumcision" *means* insisting that Gentiles be circumcised if they want to be members of Abraham's family. The term necessarily has to do with preaching to Gentiles, not Jews.[20] It cannot be used as evidence of a period during which Paul restricted his preaching to Jews.

Still, the statement is interesting. When *did* Paul engage in preaching circumcision to Gentiles, if this is indeed the implication of the statement? In the next chapter we will look at this text in more detail, and consider the possibility that it reflects his pre-Christian involvement with the Gentiles. Here, though, we need to consider another possibility, a slight variant of Watson's position. Might the text provide evidence that for a time after his conversion Paul preached a more Torah-centered gospel among the Gentiles—one in which Torah observance was required along with belief in Christ—abandoning this only later?

Given our limited knowledge of Paul's activity for the first decade or so after his conversion, such a thesis cannot be rejected out of hand. But it runs up against not only the complete absence of any other clear evidence of such a phase in Paul's life, but also the argument of Galatians 1. Granted, one needs to admit the possibility that Paul's biographical account telescopes all the consequences of his conversion into the event itself. Further, as Paula Fredriksen has pointed out, conversion accounts often reveal more about the state of mind of the convert at the time of writing than at the time of conversion, and are shaped in significant ways by the values and self-understandings of the new social group into which the convert has been incorporated.[21] The significance of Galatians 1, however, lies not in Paul's statement itself but in the rhetorical context in which it is uttered. Paul is trying to defend the "gospel that [he] proclaims among the Gentiles" (cf. Gal 2:2) against the arguments of Judaizing rival teachers, and in this context he claims that he received this gospel independently at the time of his conversion and call. Not only does he dissociate his circumcision-free gospel from the "other gospel" of Christ-plus-circumcision in the strongest possible terms—declaring the latter to be no gospel at all and its advocates to be anathema (1:8-9)—but he asserts that his understanding of the gospel was there in its essentials from his conversion (1:12, 16). This argument, that the message now under dispute was his gospel from the beginning, would have been in serious jeopardy if his rivals could have trotted out the embarrassing fact that for a period of time after his conversion he had proclaimed the "other gospel" now being denounced in such vehement terms. In such a situation, his argument would have been open to ridicule. Paul may have been opportunistic, but he was no fool. The fact that Paul can make the statement without fear of contradiction and when he has raised the stakes so high weighs heavily against this position.

And so we are left with Romans 9–11. There is no need to repeat the discussion of this passage carried out in §8.1 above. Certainly Paul in these chapters is reflecting on "what had actually happened";[22] Gentiles "have attained righteousness through faith," while Israel (except for the remnant) has not (9:30-31; 11:7). But there is nothing in the passage to suggest that this experience was what had turned Paul to the Gentiles in the first place. Indeed, if this had been the case, the *absence* of such a line of thought from his earlier letters—letters written to the Gentile beneficiaries of such a shift—would be striking indeed. Romans 9–11 represents Paul's attempt near the end of his active ministry to make sense of the progress of the gospel among Jews and Gentiles. But it tells us nothing about the process by which he came to his own special understanding of the gospel in the first place; at least, it does not tell us what Watson and others think it does. A clearer indication of Paul's postconversion mentality is probably provided by the reference to his sojourn in Arabia (Gal 1:17) and the opposition it provoked from Aretas the Nabatean king (2 Cor 11:31-32). One does not rouse the anger of a ruler by engaging in a "period of silence and seclusion," as the Arabian sojourn has sometimes been romantically portrayed.[23] Instead, these references probably indicate that Paul was engaged in Gentile evangelization from the outset.[24]

In all likelihood, then, Paul's convictions about the Gentile mission were the direct result of the Damascus experience; there is no solid reason to believe that they were preceded by a preliminary phase in which he either preached only to Jews or preached a "Torah plus Christ" gospel to Gentiles. This is not to argue that the fully articulated conception of the Gentile mission such as is found explicitly (for example, Romans 15) or implicitly in the letters was there from the beginning. The fact that Paul spent at least the first decade after his conversion in the relatively circumscribed area of "Syria and Cilicia" (Gal 1:21), for example, suggests that the geographical ambitions reflected in a statement such as Rom 15:19

developed only gradually. Still, the convictional framework on which such ambitions were built were present in their essentials from the beginning.

Such are the other suggestions that have been put forward to account for the emergence of Paul's Gentile mission and the convictions within which it was carried out. I have attempted not only to point out their weaknesses and failures but also to demonstrate that my own suggestion provides a more economical, satisfying, and thoroughgoing explanation of the relevant material in Paul's letters. To complete this demonstration, however, it is necessary to look more closely at Paul's preconversion period and to examine the plausibility of my thesis as it bears on this phase of his life.

## CHAPTER ELEVEN

# Preacher of Circumcision, Zealot, and Persecutor

In Part II of this study, after examining the structure of convictions under-lying Paul's statements and arguments concerning the Gentiles, I suggested that the observed convictional structure could be most easily and satisfactorily explained if we made two assumptions about his pre-Damascus convictional world. (These were, in addition to a working assumption adopted at the outset, that Paul is to be understood not as one who misunderstood Judaism in some fundamental way but rather as one who prior to his Damascus experience shared the basic structure of convictions that has been described as "covenantal nomism.") One of these assumptions has to do with the Gentiles: Paul had held the opinion that only those Gentiles who became proselytes in this age would share in the age of salvation to come. Furthermore, it was suggested, he had had some active personal involvement in the making of proselytes. The other assumption pertains to the Christian movement: Linked with his persecution of the church was the perception that the Christ proclaimed in the "gospel" was functioning at least implicitly as a rival to the Torah in its role of defining membership in God's people. The purpose of this chapter is to demonstrate that both assumptions are plausible.

Two preliminary comments need to be made. First, it is not my intention to engage in a full-scale discussion of the "pre-Christian Paul."[1] Not only would this extend the present study unduly, but it is not really necessary. What my thesis requires is the demonstration that these assumptions are plausible. To accomplish this, it will be sufficient to sketch out the main lines of an argument.

The second comment has to do with the opinion expressed from time to time that our sources do not allow us to say much about Paul's pre-Damascus frame of mind. Recent studies of conversion by Beverly Gaventa and Paula Fredriksen in particular make the point that converts tend to construe both their former life and their conversion experience according to the norms and expectations of their new world, which means that autobiographical conversion accounts cannot be relied upon to provide accurate information about the past.[2] But while such cautionary comments need to be given due weight, warning us against any uncritical acceptance of texts at face value, they do not preclude the investigation being carried out here. Particularly because Paul's conversion was preceded by a period of opposition to the movement, some basic "facts" of his story were in the public domain, so to speak. In particular, these include his prior devotion to traditional Judaism, his persecuting activity, the conversion itself, and his later career as apostle to the Gentiles. For the same reason, various aspects of his self-description, such as those which refer to a widely familiar group such as the Pharisees (Phil 3:5), or to well-established religious tendencies such as zeal and zealotry (Phil 3:6; Gal 1:14), can also be taken as part of the public knowledge of his past. As A. E. Harvey has observed in another context, the range of interpretation of such "facts" is subject to constraints imposed by the known historical circumstances of the first-century world.[3] Despite the inevitable tendency of converts to reconstruct their past on the basis of their present new self-understanding, Paul's conversion accounts (and related material) do not present us simply with an impenetrable veil.

This is particularly true for the case (as in the present study) of an investigation of *convictions*. I am not attempting to re-create Paul's conscious frame of mind nor the psychology of his conversion experience nor the chronological sequence of events. As we have defined the term, "convictions" are not purely individual matters, but are socially constructed and socially maintained.[4] This means that they are operative at least partially at the subconscious level. While conscious perception is not to be ignored—especially when the case under examination includes a conversion, where the choice between competing convictional worlds impinges on an individual consciousness—the fact remains that convictional structures represent the way in which an individual is linked to a wider social world, without which any self-understanding or even self-consciousness is not really possible. While it has not been my purpose here to carry out a full-blown structuralist analysis, I draw on structuralism to the extent that I conceive of Paul's convictions at least in part as a deeper structure, not subject to the whims and contingencies of individual psychology, one that shapes and constrains his conscious expression and behavior.[5] I will return to this discussion in the final chapter. For present purposes enough has been said to support the claim that our knowledge of the social worlds of Judaism and early Christianity, together with the public knowledge of Paul's early activity and experience, provides us with sufficient material for the kind of plausible reconstruction being aimed at here.

## 11.1 Paul as "Preacher of Circumcision"

Before turning to evidence from Paul himself, it is appropriate to consider the Jewish environment to which he had belonged. As was demonstrated above,[6] one can identify a strand within Judaism holding to the rigorous position that only those Gentiles who became proselytes in this age would be granted a share in salvation in the age to come. The presence of this strand in Tannaitic material (*t. Sanh.* 13.2; *b. 'Abod. Zar.* 3b; *b. Yeb.* 24b; *Pesiq. R.* 161a) suggests the likelihood that it was present among the Pharisees as well. Unfortunately, we do not know enough about Pharisaism in the first century to locate the Pharisaic version of this strand with any certainty. To the extent that R. Hillel and R. Shammai represent first-century schools and tendencies, the traditional astringency of Shammai in general and the appearance of this strand in (the probably Shammaitic)[7] Eliezer in particular, suggest that this strand would more probably have been associated with the latter.[8] But in the final analysis, Paul himself might provide the most direct evidence for Pharisaic attitudes in the first century. In any case, the attitude we are supposing Paul to have held did exist, so that the supposition is not a priori implausible.

What about the additional supposition, that Paul had taken an active role in the making of proselytes? This inevitably raises the much-discussed question of whether Judaism was a "missionary religion." Recently several scholars, most notably Scot McKnight and Martin Goodman, have argued forcibly that it was not.[9] My argument here does not depend on showing that they are wrong. Indeed, as I have already indicated,[10] if by mission one has in mind the traditional Christian conception (universal scope, institutional organization, traveling missionaries), they are clearly right; this was not present in any wide scale way in Judaism.

Nor is it my argument that it was present in a more restricted strand of Judaism, so that Paul's activity might be accounted for on the basis of his prior involvement in such a more limited segment. For part of my proposal is that important aspects of Paul's missionary self-consciousness stem from the conversion experience itself, together with the already-existing conceptions of apostolic mission within early Christianity. I do not attempt to argue that the basic elements of his apostolic mission were already present and fully formed in his pre-Damascus days. The suggestion is a more modest one—that in this period Paul had formed decided opinions on the fate of Gentiles outside the covenant and on the terms of their inclusion, and had been involved (in a manner yet to be specified) in the process of incorporating proselytes into the covenant community. Such a suggestion is fully plausible in the context of first-century Judaism, and is not gainsaid by anything in recent discussion. Even if proselytism had been entirely a passive phenomenon—consisting solely of the reception of Gentiles attracted to Judaism who put themselves forward on their own initiative as potential proselytes—there would still have been a need for individuals to be involved in the process by which such persons were made full proselytes.

Ideally, one would like to know more about this process in the first century, and in particular the roles played by individual Jews within it. Unfortunately, "in regard to the instruction of proselytes before their reception, nothing is known."[11] Nevertheless, some things can be surmised and inferred. Two things are of particular relevance for the proposal to be made about Paul.

The first concerns the role of instruction. Given the importance of Torah instruction for Jews in general,[12] it is fully to be expected that instruction would be required for proselytes as well. Indeed, this is reflected in the comments of outsiders. Speaking of the circumcision of proselytes, for example, Tacitus says: "the earliest *lesson* they receive . . ." (*Hist.* 5.5.2). Likewise Juvenal: "and, *taught* the Roman ritual to deride, clings to the Jewish . . ." (*Satires* 14.101-2). Turning to Jewish sources, in Josephus's account of the conversion of Queen Helena and King Izates of Adiabene, one finds a similar emphasis on teaching: "Ananias . . . *taught* them to worship God after the manner of the Jewish tradition" (*Ant.* 20.34); "Helena had likewise *been instructed* . . ." (20.35); ". . . personally responsible because he had *instructed* the king" (20.41). The request of the would-be proselyte to Hillel and Shammai is similar: "*Teach* me the whole of the law while I stand on one foot" (*b. Shab.* 31a).

Presumably much of this instruction took place in the context of the synagogue. To be sure, there is no explicit mention of a synagogue in the most complete conversion account that we possess—the conversion of Izates (*Ant.* 20.34-48). Here we find only the activity of three Jewish teachers: the merchant Ananias, the unnamed Jew who had instructed Helena (20.35), and Eleazar. The picture is somewhat similar in Josephus's account of the unscrupulous Jew who, along with some others, took advantage of the proselyte Fulvia, by setting himself up as "an inter-preter of the Mosaic law and its wisdom" (*Ant.* 18.81). Of course, we are dealing here with swindlers, and not legitimate teachers. Still, the fraud could not have been carried out if Fulvia had not already known of legiti-mate Jewish teachers prepared to instruct interested Gentiles. Further, Jo-sephus assumes that the role of "an interpreter of the Mosaic law" was there to be played. Neither account can be taken as a typical proselyte story, of course; in both we are dealing with persons of the upper class, and in the latter case with a fraud. Further, one would expect the role of the synagogue to be more central than what is suggested here. Neverthe-less, the accounts serve to underline the role not only of instruction, but also of intentional instructors.

The second item of significance for our purposes also comes out of the Izates story, and concerns the activity of Eleazar. Eleazar appears not only as a teacher, but also as a forceful advocate: "He *urged* (προετρέψατο) him to carry out the rite" (*Ant.* 20.43). His stance is in sharp distinction to that of Ananias. Though Ananias thought proselytism was preferable in principle, he took the position that in Izates' case it was not necessary, "God-fearing" being an acceptable alternative.[13] By contrast, Eleazar, de-scribed as "extremely strict [πάνυ ἀκριβὴς] when it came to the ancestral laws" (20.43), rejects this position categorically, vehemently denouncing the idea ("guilty of the greatest offence" [20.44]; "what an impiety" [20.45]). Eleazar's role involves instruction; after all, the king was reading the law of Moses at the time. But it goes beyond mere instruction, to advocacy and strong encouragement. The account provides us with no clear indication of his motivation: was he concerned for the king, or only for the integrity of the Jewish community? One suspects that both con-cerns were in play. Nevertheless, in his view the line was clearly drawn, and he felt impelled (for whatever reason) to urge Izates to cross it.

Eleazar provides us with a model of the type of role I am proposing for Paul prior to his Damascus experience. I suggest that Paul is to be located in a Hellenistic Jewish community that was attracting Gentile ad-herents and proselytes. Like Eleazar, Paul held to a strict interpretation of the law; compared to many of his contemporaries, he was "much more a zealot for the traditions of his ancestors" (Gal 1:14). Like Eleazar (I sug-gest), Paul had a similar bifurcated attitude toward Gentiles. On the one hand, in his zeal to protect the integrity of the the covenant and the Jewish community, he was insistent that Gentiles needed to become full prose-lytes in order to enjoy God's favor; in his own language, he "preached *circumcision*" (Gal 5:11). Yet, on the other, he was not unconcerned about Gentiles who had not yet made that step, but took advantage of opportunities to encourage interested Gentiles to do just that; that is, he "*preached* circumcision."

Thus my position is to be differentiated from that of J. Jeremias, who argues that Paul's apostolic concern for the Gentiles (among other things) is to be accounted for on the basis of his prior identity as a (more open and liberal) Hillelite.[14] If there is validity to the distinction, Paul was much more likely a Shammaite.[15] My suggestion is closer to that of M. Hengel, who locates the pre-Christian Paul in a Greek-speaking synagogue in Jerusalem, where he both studied the Torah as a Pharisee and taught it to the "large and constantly growing number of Jewish and 'godfearing' pilgrims from the Diaspora."[16] While I lean in the direction of a Jerusalem location,[17] it is not a necessary part of my position. In support of Jerusalem is Paul's own statement that his (admittedly later and apostolic) mission activity reached "from Jerusalem to Illyricum" (Rom 15:19), together with the absence of any evidence of Pharisaism outside Judea.[18] The situation is complicated by another statement in which Paul says that in the period immediately after his conversion he was "unknown by sight" by the Judean churches (Gal 1:21). But the issue does not need to be decided here.[19] Even if Paul's pre-Christian activity had been centered outside Judea in Damascus, my proposal would be no less plausible.[20]

As might be inferred from the allusion to Gal 5:11 in the paragraph before last, I consider this verse—where Paul vehemently denies that he is "still preaching circumcision" (περιτομὴν ἔτι κηρύσσω)—as a primary piece of evidence for my position. While many others read the verse in the same way,[21] the reading is not universal,[22] and so requires further discussion.

As we have already observed, whatever other uncertainties there are it is clear that by "preaching circumcision" Paul is referring to proselytizing activity directed at Gentiles.[23] Watson's position, that Paul's statement refers instead to an earlier phase of his Christian activity when he confined his preaching to Jews, is untenable. Not only does the context in Galatians concern the circumcision of Gentiles, but it is quite unthinkable that a mission to circumcised Jews proclaiming "Jesus as the Jewish Messiah who came to save the Jewish community" would be described as "preaching circumcision."[24] For similar reasons, it is highly unlikely that Paul would have used this particular phrase simply to describe his former commitment to Torah religion. In the context of Galatians, "preaching circumcision" means encouraging *Gentiles* to submit to circumcision. But this raises the question: in denying that he is "still [ἔτι][25] preaching circumcision," is he conceding that at some time in the past he did attempt to make circumcised proselytes from among the Gentiles? What contrast to his present activity is implied by "still"?

The abruptness with which Paul takes up—and drops—the matter alluded to in v. 11 has led commentators to despair of ever knowing what prompted his retort.[26] It is tempting to bypass the issue altogether: whatever he was responding to, he appears to admit that at one time he did preach circumcision (to Gentiles); if there are good reasons to doubt that this was possible after his conversion, it must have taken place before; therefore before his conversion he had been active in proselytizing activity; Q.E.D. In a sense, this is what my argument will boil down to. But against this shortcut a legitimate objection can be raised. Paul is apparently responding to some statement about his teaching or practice, made by the rival teachers in Galatia in support of their circumcision campaign among the Gentile Christians there (5:2; 6:12). How, then (assuming such a reading of 5:11), did the matter of his preconversion activity come into the dispute? Was it introduced by his Galatian opponents? If so, what possible support could they derive for their campaign from Paul's attitudes and activity predating his conversion to Christ? Or was it introduced by Paul himself? If so, to what end? The prima facie irrelevance for the Galatian dispute of Paul's preconversion activity means that we cannot use his statement in v. 11 as evidence for this activity without considering the question of what prompted it.

As a point of entry, we need to consider the import of the word "still" (ἔτι). For our purposes, what is significant is Paul's understanding of the term as he uses it in this context. But to get a reading on this, it will be helpful to know something about both the range of possible meanings of the term and its point of introduction into the Galatian dispute (was it Paul's own term, or was he picking up a term that had already been used by his opponents?).

The primary sense of the adverb ἔτι[27] is temporal, denoting that a given set of circumstances continues to exist, for example, "you are still of the flesh" (1 Cor 3:3). By extension, it is used in nontemporal ways to denote quantitative or numerical addition (for instance, "that your love may abound still more and more" [Phil 1:9]) or logical contrast (as, "if through my falsehood God's truthfulness abounds to his glory, why am I still condemned as a sinner?" [Rom 3:7]). With this range of meanings in mind, let us turn to an exploration of the dialogical situation of which Gal 5:11 is a part.

No matter who first introduced ἔτι (still) into the discussion (the rival teachers, or Paul himself), it is clear from Paul's statement[28] that he is responding to an assertion about his present attitudes or activity. Even if his opponents have made reference to something in his past, they have done so not in isolation, but in support of and in conjunction with an assertion about the present. In some way they have said, or implied, that Paul "preaches circumcision." How might this statement have come about?

Some reconstructions of the dialogue need not be seriously entertained, for example, G. Howard's proposal that the Judaizers honestly thought that Paul agreed with their policy on Gentile converts, since he had only recently informed the Jerusalem church of his position;[29] or the "two front" interpretation of Lütgert and Ropes, which sees Gal 5:11 as a response not to Judaizers but to a radical Gentile party, precursors of a Gnostic or Marcionite attempt to sever the links with Judaism completely, who accused Paul of not being radical enough where Judaism was concerned.[30] The remaining reconstructions fall into two general categories.

First, many scholars take "preaching circumcision" as a face-value and literal indication of what the rival teachers were saying about Paul, understanding it as having been part of a charge of inconsistency. In the context of the Judaizing campaign in Galatia (so this line of interpretation goes), it was being said that Paul was not fundamentally opposed to circumcision, that he allowed it elsewhere, and that the reason he did not insist on it in Galatia was simply that he wanted to make it easier for Gentiles to accept his message (cf. Gal 1:10). Grounds for this assertion might have been found in Paul's own policy of pragmatic inconsistency (cf. 1 Cor 9:19-23), in his readiness to treat circumcision as an *adiaphoron* when it was not being imposed on Gentiles as a condition of salvation (1 Cor 7:18-19; Gal 5:6; 6:15),[31] or in his readiness to have Timothy circumcised (Acts 16:3).[32]

What about the place of ἔτι (still) in this reconstruction of the situation? One possibility is that it was used in Galatia in the sense of a logical contrast. That is, his opponents might have said: "Despite what he may have said to you about his gospel for the Gentiles, he still advocates circumcision when it suits his purpose." Here the sense would not be temporal, but adversative: "nevertheless." But even if the word was introduced into the dialogue in this way, it is quite unlikely that Paul used it in this sense in v. 11. The natural sense of the word is the temporal one. The adversative sense requires some clear indication in the context. If Paul did not have in mind a past period in his life when he did "preach circumcision," it is quite unlikely that he would just echo an adversative ἔτι without making its sense clear in the context. He would more likely have said simply, "If I preach circumcision," or "If I am preaching circumcision to please people" (cf. Gal 1:10). If Paul has picked up a term used adversatively by his opponents, it must have been because he wanted to give it a temporal twist of his own: "If I am *still* preaching the message that I once preached. . . ."

Alternatively, the term might have been used in Galatia in a temporal sense: "He used to advocate circumcision [either before his conversion[33] or in an earlier Christian phase][34] and, when it is expedient, he still does." In the former case the statement would have been purely opportunistic; in the latter, it could have had argumentative force ("If he saw no problem combining Christ and circumcision then, why should he now?"). In either case, Paul's use of the term would simply reflect its sense in the original statement. Finally, it is quite possible that the term was not used in Galatia at all, but that Paul introduced it himself. Again it would have had a temporal sense: "I did preach circumcision once, but I do so no longer."

Second, another group of scholars takes "preaching circumcision" less literally, seeing the assertion to which 5:11 is a response as part of a more nuanced position. The rival teachers (so it is argued) were presenting circumcision as the logical and natural completion of the gospel proclaimed by Paul and accepted by the Galatians.[35] They presented themselves not as Paul's opponents but as his coworkers, come to finish the work that he had begun (cf. Gal 3:3). Paul (they said) may have omitted some of the harder aspects of the gospel out of deference to Gentile sensibilities (cf. Gal 1:10), but these were implicit in his preaching. For in proclaiming Jesus as the Christ, he was proclaiming him as the fulfillment of God's promises to the seed of Abraham (see Gal 3:16, 29). To share fully in these promises, it was necessary, like Abraham, to become circumcised.

This approach, like the one above, appeals for support to those texts where Paul can treat circumcision as an *adiaphoron*. The essential distinction between the two is the absence of any assertion that Paul actually advocated circumcision in some circumstances. Circumcision as the natural complement to Paul's preaching rather than as an occasional part of his practice is the defining feature in this reconstruction.

What about the place and significance of ἔτι (still) in this approach? Its advocates tend to assume that the term originated with the Judaizers, though usually without attempting to determine its specific sense. It is possible that it was first used adversatively (in the grammatical sense of the term) to indicate a logical contrast: "Despite the fact that Paul did not mention it when he was here, circumcision is *still* the the goal to which his preaching was leading." Again, however, such a logical contrast could not have been carried over into Gal 5:11 simply by the repetition

of ἔτι. If Paul echoes his opponents' vocabulary here, it is because he
wanted to give it his own temporal twist: "I preached that way once, but
not anymore!"

That the term originated with the Judaizers in a temporal sense, while
not impossible, is less likely than in the previous approach. Here the Judaizers are not asserting that, in some circumstances at least, Paul actually
advocates circumcision. If they were, a link between past and present
would be persuasive: "He did once, and, when it suits him, he still does
now." Instead, in this second approach, the link that the Judaizers want
to establish is not between past and present but between implicit and
explicit, between premise and inference: "Whether Paul made it clear or
not, circumcision is really implied in the gospel you received." A temporal
ἔτι (still) would not really suit the argument.

The more likely possibility within this second approach is that the term
originated with Paul himself. In response to the assertion that he *really*
preached circumcision (in that circumcision was consistent with and implied by his preaching of the gospel), he declared that while he once
preached in this way he did so no longer; his (οὐκ) ἔτι ([not] still) responds to their ὄντως (really).

It is not necessary here to resolve the issue and to decide on one of
these reconstructions of the charge or assertion lying behind Gal 5:11. In
my opinion the interpretation outlined in the previous paragraph is the
most attractive; certainly the common assumption that the term originated with the Judaizers needs to be reexamined. But for the issue currently under discussion, we have gone far enough. Whatever the origin of
the term, it is most probable that it was used by Paul in a temporal sense.
Even if it was first used by the Judaizers in an adversative way, the absence
of any logical "over against" in the context suggests strongly that Paul
intended it to be taken in its natural temporal sense.[36] And so we are
justified in asking when it was that Paul "preached circumcision" to Gentiles.

One possibility is that he did so as a Christian missionary. Did he, at
some earlier point in his Christian experience, adhere to the strict Jewish
Christian position on Gentile circumcision? This position has already
been examined and rejected.[37]

The remaining possibility, then, is the one being advocated here, that in
Gal 5:11 Paul refers to preconversion involvement in Jewish proselytizing
activity. This provides a very plausible reading of Gal 5:11 in the context
of the epistle as a whole: "In my former life in Judaism I admit that I
preached circumcision to the Gentiles; but then God called me to preach

Christ crucified, and I preach circumcision no longer." In the absence of other plausible readings of the verse, it is undoubtedly to be preferred.

While Gal 5:11 provides the most solid confirmation of the position being defended here, one other bit of evidence—less explicit, yet still significant—can be cited in support. This appears in the context of Paul's skewering of Jewish self-confidence in Romans 2. I have already had occasion to note the curious nature of this chapter, and its awkward fit with the larger argument of Romans 1–3.[38] After having established Gentile sinfulness (1:18-32), Paul turns in chapter 2 to the situation of the Jews, wanting to demonstrate that they too are subject to sin, so that he can finally conclude that "all, both Jews and Greeks, are under sin," and that as a result "no one will be justified in [God's] sight by works of the law" (3:9, 20). But in order to demonstrate Jewish sinfulness, Paul seems to assume that the law is capable of fulfillment, that doing the law is the way to justification, and even that there are Gentiles who perform what the law requires (2:6-16). If chapter 2 were read in isolation, one would have expected that its conclusion would have been: "Repent, keep the law, and seek the righteousness that comes to those who truly do the law." More to the point, if Romans 2 were read in isolation, it would seem to be much closer to a synagogue sermon than to a Christian treatise. Indeed, E. P. Sanders is not alone in seeing it as just that.[39]

Present purposes do not necessitate a detailed discussion of the tradition history of Romans 2 or of its place in the larger argument. The only observation to be made here is that the chapter demonstrates Paul's familiarity with patterns of discourse associated with a Hellenistic synagogue.[40] It is in this context that vv. 17-20 become significant. For in these verses we find a clear—though biting—description of the kind of Jewish self-understanding typically associated with the attraction of Gentiles to the synagogue. The language resonates strongly with certain strands of Second Temple era literature: because it possesses the law, Israel is a "guide to the blind" (see 1 Enoch 105.1; Sib. Or. 3.194-95), and "a light to those who are in darkness" (see Isa 42:6; 49:6; Wisd 18:4; T. Levi 14.4; 18.9). Taken in the context of the chapter as a whole, these verses demonstrate Paul's thorough and intimate familiarity with the type of religious self-consciousness which made the attraction of God-fearers and the reception of proselytes possible.

This does not necessarily imply either that Paul once shared those attitudes or that he had played an active role in proselyte instruction and reception. But taken in conjunction with Gal 5:11, a text pointing strongly in this direction, it plays a significant corroborative role. For it confirms that Paul was well aware of precisely the attitudes and activities that, on the basis of Gal 5:11, can be predicated of him in his earlier life.[41]

Thus a plausible case can be made for the position that prior to his Damascus experience Paul was characterized by attitudes and activities similar to those of Izates' adviser Eleazar. Again, this is not to say that Paul was a "missionary," in any manner akin to the later Christian conception. Indeed, as the references to his earlier zeal (Gal 1:14; Phil 3:6) suggest, his activity was probably motivated as much by a desire to protect the integrity of the Jewish community as to "win the lost" for God and the law. It is even possible that the sharp criticism of Jewish Torah-laxity displayed in Romans 2 is not simply a function of his present Christian argument, but reflects an earlier stance; that is, he was just as aggressive—or, to use his language, zealous—in encouraging strict Torah observance among Jews as among interested Gentiles. Paul's self-attributed zeal requires further investigation, but this is more appropriately to be carried out with reference to his persecuting activity, a topic to which we must now turn our attention.

## 11.2 Paul as Zealot and Persecutor

The second supposition emerging from the investigation of Paul's convictional world in Part II had to do with his reasons for "persecuting" the early Christian movement. I concluded that his new convictions about Christ and the Torah could be most satisfactorily explained if we supposed that his persecution of the church was based (at least in part) on a perception that the Christ of the kerygma represented a rival to the Torah, the one functioning (at least implicitly) as a replacement for the other as the boundary marker of the people of God. Can a case be made for the plausibility of this supposition as well?

It is not necessary at this point to reenter the whole discussion of Paul's Christ-Torah antithesis. In previous sections of this study I have established several things that need only be recalled here. First, with respect to the nature of the antithesis, I have come to the firm conclusion that Paul's rejection of the law as a condition of membership "in Christ" is the direct result of his new convictions about Christ, rather than of factors pertaining to the law directly (for example, its basis in "works," its powerlessness with respect to sin).[42] Further, there are solid reasons to believe that the antithesis between Christ and Torah is based not on christology per se (such as Deut 21:22-23 and the proclamation of a crucified Messiah), but instead on "ecclesiology"; that is, that Paul rejected the Torah because he understood Christ and Torah to represent mutually exclusive ways of defining membership in the people of God—Christ and Torah as rival boundary markers for the community of the righteous (§6.2). Second, with respect to chronology, I have judged to be highly unlikely the suggestion that Paul's distinctive views concerning the law developed only later, at a point significantly removed in time from the Damascus event.[43]

These conclusions, taken together, constitute a strong a priori case for my suggestion. *If* the nature of the Christ-Torah antithesis found in the letters was as I have described it; *if* Paul's perception of this antithesis goes back to the conversion itself; *if* his conversion was preceded (as it certainly was) by opposition to the Christian movement—then the simplest way to account for the Christ-Torah antithesis in Paul's set of Christian convictions is to see it as an inversion of his preconversion perceptions of the Christian message.

It is at this point that Paul's characterization of his persecution as an act of *zeal* becomes important.[44] This characterization appears at two points. The most explicit reference is found in the "boasting list" of Phil 3:5-6, where he cites his persecution of the church as evidence of his zeal (ζῆλος; v. 6). In Gal 1:13-14, it is true that Paul's activity as "a zealot [ζηλωτής] for the traditions of [his] ancestors" is linked more directly with the superiority of his achievements over those of his contemporaries (v. 14), than with his persecution of the church (v. 13). Still, since the two statements—concerning his persecution and his zeal—are presented together as a summary of his "former life in Judaism," it is not inappropriate to take the former as one of the manifestations of the latter.

In order to see the significance of these references to zeal, we need to say something about the "zealot" ideal as it had developed in Second Temple Judaism. Since this has been thoroughly investigated,[45] here it is necessary only to sketch the most salient features. By the first century, zeal was a widely held Jewish ideal with a long and celebrated tradition. It seems to have come to special prominence in the Maccabean period, under the influence of Mattathias and his followers, who, "zealous for the law" and the covenant,[46] took up arms to defend Jewish tradition against the Syrian threat. But the ideal of zeal was neither the creation nor the exclusive preserve of the Maccabees. The ideal was deeply rooted in earlier scriptural tradition (Num 25:11,13; 1 Kgs 19:10,14; Sir 45:23; 48:2); it appeared across a broad spectrum of Judaism (e.g., 1QS 9.23; *m. Sanh.* 9.6; Philo *Spec. leg.* 2.253); and it was by no means exclusively linked with opposition to foreign oppression (for example, 2 *Bar.* 66.1-8). In this latter connection it might be mentioned that not until the war with Rome was "Zealot" taken over as a self-designation for a party advocating armed rebellion against Rome.[47] Prior to that time, and, in particular, when Paul described himself as a "zealot" (Gal 1:14), the term, contrary to popular belief, did not necessarily designate one as a member of an identifiable party.

The basic pattern of zeal was derived from the popular Old Testament prototypes—Phinehas (Num 25), Elijah (1 Kgs 18–19), and Simeon and Levi (Gen 34).[48] Zeal was more than just a fervent commitment to the Torah; it denoted a willingness to use violence against any—Jews,[49] Gentiles,[50] or the wicked in general[51]—who were contravening, opposing, or subverting the Torah. Further, zealots were willing to suffer and die for the sake of the Torah,[52] even to die at their own hand.[53]

The theological framework within which such zealous activity was carried out was also derived from the Old Testament material. As in the case of Phinehas, it was believed that God would honor and reward those who defended God's law.[54] As in the case of Elijah, it was expected that God would come to the aid of those who took up the cause of the covenant.[55] But perhaps the most significant theological motivation for zealous activity was the belief that, as in the case of Phinehas, zeal had atoning value: violent punishment of the wrongdoer would "turn back [God's] wrath from the people of Israel" (Num 25:11).[56]

By characterizing his persecuting activity as a demonstration of zeal, then, Paul was placing this activity within a very specific framework. He was signaling that his opposition to the movement was motivated not by unspecified antipathy or general dislike, but by very specific concerns: he perceived the Christian movement as posing a threat to the Torah, and to the community defined by its Torah allegiance.[57] While this does not in and of itself mean that he perceived this threat in the way being proposed here, it is nevertheless instructive to observe the covenant and community emphases in the zeal tradition. The concept of zeal is bound up with the twin covenant ideals of righteousness and community; zealous activity was undertaken to preserve the righteousness of the community, by disciplining the wrongdoer and upholding the Torah, and to restore the righteous status of the community, by atoning for its sins. Paul's alignment of his persecuting activity with Israel's tradition of zeal, then, at least renders plausible the suggestion being made here, that he understood the message about Christ to represent a different, and therefore rival, way of determining the constitution of the people of salvation.

At this point, however, a major difficulty needs to be addressed. In the persecution accounts in Acts 6–8, a distinction is made between the Hellenists, who were the prime targets of persecution, and a more conservative group which was largely untouched and able to carry on quietly in Jerusalem. While this account raises many more questions than can be discussed here,[58] there is general consensus that the persecution of early Jewish Christianity was not a universal and categorical phenomenon but was focused more selectively on specific segments and individual cases.[59] This raises the possibility that Jewish persecution of Christians (Paul's included) must have been motivated not by the kerygmatic message of a dying and rising Messiah per se (in which case no distinctions would have been made at all), but by some more specific feature of Hellenistic Jewish Christianity, for example, its criticism of the temple,[60] its Torah-laxity or even rejection of the law,[61] and/or its inclusion of uncircumcised Gentiles.[62] But if this was the case, it might seem to rule out the kind of suggestion being made here, where Paul's persecuting zeal is linked to more fundamental perceptions arising from the gospel itself.[63]

Certainly there is no need to doubt the evidence that persecution primarily affected only specific segments within early Jewish Christianity. A distinction needs to be made, however, between the factors leading to persecution in the first place and the perceptions about the deviant group that might be formed by an individual persecutor in the process. On the one hand, a case of "persecution" such as is under discussion here needs to be understood in the first instance as a sociological, and not merely an ideational or theological, phenomenon. Judaism did not engage thought police to ferret out those individuals or groups holding opinions differing from the norm. Indeed, Second Temple Judaism was characterized by a considerable degree of tolerance toward parties, sects, and other movements with diverse viewpoints. It is only when the activities and presence of such groups disrupted the social equilibrium, and were perceived as posing threats to the established community and its boundaries, that action was taken to preserve social boundaries and to protect group solidarity. The nature of such action was differently understood—as persecution by those on the receiving end, but as group discipline by those responsible for the well-being of the parent community.[64]

In any case, whether persecution or discipline, such pressure to conform was brought to bear not simply because the early Christians held to this or that belief about Jesus, or even because they drew this or that conclusion about his significance for the institutions of Judaism, but because they (or some of them) acted on these beliefs or conclusions in ways that seemed to threaten the established social cohesion of the larger Jewish community. The situation described in Acts is precisely what one should have expected: a group that was forceful and outspoken in its denunciation of the current Jewish leadership, that was prepared to criticize at least the temple on the basis of its new Christian beliefs,[65] and that showed itself disinclined to live within the established structures of Judaism, was the one targeted for persecution/discipline; while a group that held its beliefs more quietly, avoided confrontation with established authorities, and demonstrated a willingness to live within accepted structures and norms, enjoyed a greater degree of tolerance. In short, I take it as quite probable that Paul persecuted a type of (Hellenistic) Jewish Christianity such as was described in the previous sentence[66] (though I find much more doubtful the suggestion that the persecuted communities had already developed a full-blown critique of the law or had begun at this early date to admit Gentiles),[67] and that his persecuting zeal was aroused more by their distinctive stance and attitudes than by any beliefs shared by early Christianity as a whole.

But, on the other hand, it is quite another thing, and a logical non sequitur, to say that for this reason Paul could not have arrived at conclusions concerning the persecuted group or developed justifications for his persecuting activity that would have pertained to the Christian movement as a whole. To take but one example: It is quite probable that Deut 21:22-23 was first propelled into the Christian orbit by Jewish opponents of the new movement;[68] indeed, it is likely that Paul himself first used this text in connnection with Christ, not in his letter to the Galatians (see 3:13), but in his pre-Damascus persecution of the church. That this was his primary motivation is ruled out by the selective nature of the persecution, as discussed above,[69] but this does not mean that he could not have appealed to it to explain or justify his activity. (Whether it was the heart of his Christ-Torah antithesis, however, is quite another matter.)[70] The selective nature of the persecution, then, cannot be used to eliminate the proposal being put forward here. It is quite plausible to believe that even though persecution was undertaken on grounds pertaining to a specific segment, it was understood and justified—if not by everyone, then at least by perceptive individuals—in terms that would apply in principle to the movement as a whole.

There is no intrinsic implausibility, then, to the argument that in the context of his persecuting activity Paul had developed negative opinions of the Christian movement based not simply on peripheral or at least secondary factors but on its fundamental message of a dying and rising Messiah and savior and, in particular, on a perception that Christ and Torah represented mutually exclusive ways of marking the boundary of the people of God. Admittedly, the absence of intrinsic implausibility is not an argument for plausibility. We need to face squarely the fact that we have no direct and independent access to Paul's pre-Damascus opinions and perceptions. This is particularly true if we want to argue for a distinction between the broad, sociological reasons for persecution and the particular perceptions of an individual persecutor. Indeed, the strongest argument in favor of this understanding of Paul's pre-Christian perceptions is that it is congruent with and thus accounts for the shape of his Christian perceptions of Christ and Torah.

This means that we are running the risk of arguing in a circle. We have (1) arrived at certain conclusions concerning the structure of Paul's Christ-Torah antithesis; then we have (2) suggested that this structure is best explained on the basis of a supposition concerning the nature of his pre-Christian perceptions; but then we have (3) recognized that the best argument for the plausibility of the supposition is the way it accounts for the conclusions with which we began! The circle is not a closed one, however. Two independent factors can be drawn into it, which serve to anchor the argument in external reality. One is the fact that, as was demonstrated above,[71] Paul's law-free gospel—his Christ-Torah antithesis—goes back in all its essential elements to the experience of his conversion. The other is the fact of his persecuting *zeal;* he persecuted not simply because he disliked Christians and did not want his sister to marry one, but because he perceived this movement to represent a threat to the Torah-centered community. The combined effect of these two factors is this: on both sides of the Damascus experience one can identify a Christ-Torah antithesis as part of his convictional makeup. The simplest conclusion is that the two are congruent and thus linked. That is, his Christian conviction that "if righteousness comes through the law, then Christ died for nothing" (Gal 2:21) is simply a reconfiguration of the perceptions motivating his persecuting zeal.

The formal structure of this argument is independent of the particular nature of the Christ-Torah antithesis being argued for here. Indeed, my thesis is formally similar to a variety of suggestions going back as far as F. C. Baur,[72] which all share the following structure: (1) As a Pharisee Paul came to believe (for one reason or another) that the Christian message of salvation was incompatible with Torah faith, and so took steps to suppress it. (2) In his Damascus experience he became convinced that God had raised Jesus from the dead and thus that salvation was to be found in Christ. (3) This new conviction about Christ gave him a new perspective on the Christ-Torah antithesis of his earlier days: if salvation is through Christ, it cannot be through Torah. Paul's conversion experience, then, resulted not so much in a new perception of the relationship between Christ and Torah, as in a new perspective on that relationship as he already perceived it. The incompatibility of Christ and Torah was the constant element in a syllogism that, on one side of the conversion experience, led to persecution of the church and, on the other, resulted in fierce resistance to the Judaizers. This argument is characterized by the assumption that a tight convictional or cognitive connection can be found to link together Paul's persecution of the church, his conversion, and his later pattern of thought.

Shifting from form to substance, the nature of this connecting thread has been variously perceived, a function of the various scholarly understandings of the nature of Paul's Christian convictions about Christ and Torah. For Baur, it had to do with the rejection of the Jewish idea that true religion was a matter of "outward ceremonials":[73] first as a persecutor and then as an apostle, Paul understood the gospel as a "refusal to regard religion as a thing bound down to special ordinances and localities."[74] This idealistic approach to Paul characterized other nineteenth-century scholars as well.[75] In this century, Bultmann used a similar structure in his reformulation of the Reformation view. For him, the issue at stake in the persecution was faith versus works. Paul heard the gospel of Hellenistic Jewish Christianity as a message of "God's condemnation of his Jewish striving after righteousness by fulfilling the works of the Law" and so became a persecutor of the church. In his conversion "he submitted to this judgment of God," and so became a foe of all forms of human self-righteousness and boasting.[76] Others have seen christology as the connecting link: Paul the persecutor found the concept of a crucified Messiah objectionable—either in itself[77] or in light of Deut 21:22-23[78]—but had to revise his thinking in the light of his conversion.

In each case (my own included), the reasons proposed for Paul's persecuting activity[79] are grounded in the particular understanding of Paul's Christian convictions rather than any independent information pertaining to the persecution itself. Accordingly, it is not necessary to deal with these suggestions here, since they have been adequately discussed at various points in Part II. One point deserves repetition, however, a point made in the context of the discussion of Deut 21:22-23 in chapter 6 above.[80] If Paul as a zealous Jew had come to the conclusion that the Christian message represented a threat to Torah religion and then had come to believe that Jesus was indeed the Christ, one would have expected that he would have tried diligently to *reconcile* his formerly perceived antithesis between them and to find a way of combining Torah observance with Christian faith. The combination was not impossible, as the example of a large segment of the Jerusalem church demonstrates (Acts 21:20). The fact that Paul continued to see Christ and Torah as mutually exclusive means of righteousness (Gal 2:21), indicates that he was not able to resolve the antithesis—that it was of such a fundamental nature that it could not be resolved. One of the merits of my suggestion,

I believe, is that it accounts for this fully, and on the basis of convictions (rather than, for example, idiosyncratic aspects of individual psychology).

My position corresponds in part to suggestions that have appeared already in scholarly discussion. M. Dibelius, followed by several others,[81] located the problem not so much in the Christian claim about Jesus as in their claim about themselves. What was offensive, he suggests, was not the proclamation that the Messiah had appeared, but the claim that he had appeared *to them,* to a group of the *'am ha'aretz* and others on the margins of Judaism, rather than to those righteous according to the standard of the Torah. The problem, as Dibelius sees it, then, is more ecclesiological (or sociological) than christological—the claim that the people of the Messiah, the remnant of Israel, was to be found in this marginal movement rather than among the Torah and Temple mainstream.

This, in my opinion, pinpoints part of Paul's problem with the Christian movement: the Christian community included in its fellowship those whom the Torah would delare to be unrighteous; therefore the Torah was *not necessary.* But there is another aspect: Christian preaching declared that to be part of the community destined for salvation, everyone—even those whom the Torah would declare to be "righteous"; even (to bring matters closer to home) one zealous for the law like Paul himself—needed to believe in Jesus; therefore the Torah was *not sufficient.* The significance of this aspect has been clearly seen by Wilckens.[82] For Wilckens, the problem has to do not so much with christology as with soteriology. According to his interpretation, Paul perceived that in the Christian message Christ had displaced the Torah at the center of the process of salvation. In Paul's theological milieu (apocalyptic, not Pharisaic), the Torah served to identify and preserve the community of the righteous who were destined to receive salvation in the coming age. Even though the early church may not have been aware of the radical implications of its message, Paul recognized that the kerygma assigned this central role to Christ rather than to the Torah, and so took steps to defend Judaism from this danger.

I want to differentiate my position from that of Wilckens at several points. The distinction he makes between apocalyptic and Pharisaic views of the Torah is unwarranted. In all probability, the Pharisees understood the role of the Torah in similar covenantal nomistic terms. And I feel that "ecclesiological" describes this approach to Paul better than "soteriological." For in Paul's thought, soteriology always had the community in mind. The soteriological question for him was not "How can a sinful individual find salvation?" but "How does one belong to the true community of salvation?" But the basic insight—that Paul perceived the proclamation of the crucified Jesus as God's Christ to pose a threat to the role of the Torah in defining and maintaining the community of salvation—is, I believe, sound.

As was developed in more detail in §6.2 above, my suggestion is that the perceived threat—and thus the Christ-Torah antithesis—is rooted in the unique already/not yet nature of the early Christian message. There would have been no tension between Torah and Christ—even a crucified and risen Christ—if the age to come had been fully ushered in on Easter Sunday. Then the Torah would have completed its task of defining and regulating membership in the this-age community destined for salvation in the age to come. The function of the Torah and of the Messiah would have been sequential and complementary. But the kerygma proclaimed a Christ who had appeared in advance of the full manifestation of the reign of God, and thus it proclaimed a salvation dependent on one's acceptance of Christ and membership in the community that called him lord, Christ and savior. In the period leading up to the parousia, then, the Christ proclaimed in the gospel played a role that stood in direct competition to that of the Torah. Both functioned to define the boundary of the community to whom salvation had been promised, to determine membership in the people of God (righteousness).

When Paul experienced what he did near Damascus and came to believe that Jesus was indeed God's Christ, none of these perceptions were altered in the slightest. While he now had an entirely new perspective on Christ and Torah, nothing had happened to alter the mutually exclusive nature of their relationship. If the crucified and risen Jesus was God's Messiah, then membership in God's people—righteousness—could not come through the Torah. The convictional inversion was not total; since God had given the Torah, he could not reject it as categorically as he had done earlier in the case of Christ. And so it was necessary to come to a new perception of its function.[83] But the basic antithesis remained; since Christ did not die for nothing, righteousness could not come through the law (cf. Gal 2:21).

A plausible and compelling case can be made, then, for both elements of the hypothesis emerging from our study of Paul's convictional structure in Part II. Good grounds exist for supposing (1) that Paul had been involved in the reception and instruction of proselytes, believing that only by becoming proselytes could Gentiles share in the age of salvation to come, and (2) that his persecuting zeal was fueled by a perception that the Christ proclaimed in the gospel represented a rival boundary marker for the people of God. The most appealing feature of these suppositions is the thorough and economical way they account for Paul's Christian patterns of thought and action. Nevertheless, they are plausible on their own terms.

## CHAPTER TWELVE

# The Reconfiguration of Paul's Convictions

## 12.1 The Damascus Reconfiguration

Somewhere in the vicinity of Damascus, Paul had a powerful personal experience that decisively altered his world of understanding and framework of meaning. While he speaks of the event itself infrequently and tangentially (Gal 1:15-16; 1 Cor 15:8-10; and probably 1 Cor 9:1), the transition it effected, by which he became an apostle of Christ, is present in all his letters both as a fundamental assumption and as a recurring theme.[1] Any examination of this experience in all its dimensions lies well beyond the scope of this study (not to mention the abilities of its author). As a religious person, I am prepared to accept the reality of religious experiences and to approach Paul's own testimony sympathetically.[2] As a Christian, I am predisposed to understand it as an experience of the same divine mystery powerfully at work in Jesus' resurrection. As a scholar, I am intrigued by the various questions raised by Paul's own references to it and by the accounts in Acts and am ready to employ various linguistic, literary, rhetorical, and sociological tools to pursue them.

For present purposes, however, I am interested in one particular element of this experience and want to assess its significance from one specific angle. The element in question is the cognitive dimension of the experience. Its significance arises from the function of the experience in effecting a shift in the basic convictions with which Paul made sense of the world and his place in it. In the next section I will attempt to shed further light on this shift by placing it within an interpretive theoretical framework. But first I need to describe it.

In the previous chapter, the attempt was made to demonstrate the plausibility of a certain understanding of Paul's pre-Christian outlook and situation. This was done not for its own sake but for the purpose of bringing

Paul's "former life in Judaism" (Gal 1:13) into fruitful conjunction with the conversion experience itself, in order to arrive at a clearer understanding of the Paul revealed in the letters. The goal in investigating Paul's pre-Christian situation was not—as in many, especially psychologically oriented studies of the past[3]—to *account* for the conversion experience, to "explain" how and why this dramatic reorientation of his life took place. Rather, viewing that experience as a reality in its own right, one that introduced a new factor into the equation, the goal was to account for the shape of Paul's new convictional framework by seeing it as the result of the dynamic interplay between past dispositions and new experience. Paul's past dispositions comprise both his native Jewish convictions and the initial perceptions of the Christian message as these developed in conjunction with his persecuting activity. At the center of his new experience was the belief that Jesus had indeed been raised by God, and was thus (at least) Messiah and Savior. This new belief, once zealously rejected, now became his most fundamental point of personal adherence, precipitating a thoroughgoing reconfiguration of his former constellation of convictions.

Of course, these three biographical points—Jewish persecutor of the church, Damascus convert, Christian missionary to the Gentiles—define the persona of Paul in popular conception; and it is no surprise that scholarly attempts to align them go back at least as far as F. C. Baur.[4] Indeed, in this book I have observed a wide variety of such reconstructions, differing in the nature of the line proposed to link the three, but formally similar in their structure.[5] This diversity is occasioned by two related factors. First, it would not be difficult to draw a precise line if we were really dealing with biographical *points*. Instead, what we are trying to line up are more complex entities—at each end, convictional structures; and in between a profound personal experience. Perhaps it would be better to refer to them more generally as stages or moments. Second, we do not have direct and independent access to at least two of these moments. For both his pre-Damascus disposition and his conversion experience, we are dependent on his own retrospective accounts written much later. Further, even if we can convince ourselves of our ability to extract reliable information from them, we are left with an irreducible range of possible implications. For example, Paul may have persecuted out of zeal for the Torah, but what precisely was it about the Christian message or movement that aroused his zeal? He came to believe that Jesus had been raised by God, but what immediate implications did this have for him as to the significance of Israel, the role of the Torah, or the status of the Gentiles? And while the third moment—Paul's set of Christian convictions—is more accessible and directly discernible, at least in principle, the wide variety of scholarly construals makes for a considerable lack of resolution here as well.

Thus while there is an inherent plausibility to the approach—it is difficult to imagine these three moments *not* being linked—in each of them there is an irreducible range of points through which the connecting line can be drawn. The persuasiveness of any reconstruction, then, will be determined by its overall coherence and explanatory power. While information about the earlier moments (for example, zeal, preaching circumcision) is not insignificant and should be pressed for all it can yield, the plausibility of any suggested alignment of the three moments is to be judged by the degree to which all the elements of the emergent convictional structure can be accounted for.

The argument, then, is that Paul's concern for the salvation of the Gentiles is to be understood with respect to a convictional reconfiguration resulting from the dynamic sequence of three moments or stages: an initial (native) set of convictions and perceptions; a new, unanticipated and disjunctive experience, one which resists assimilation into the inherited world of understanding, and thus precipitates its disintegration; a reconfigured set of convictions and perceptions, one in which selected elements of the old world are retained, but organized now with reference to a new center and pattern.

### *Stage I*

1. The broad framework of Paul's initial convictional world was provided by covenantal nomism, a constellation of convictions which can be described as follows: God has chosen Israel from among the nations of the world, initiated a special relationship with them, and promised them blessing and salvation; God has provided the Torah as a means of identifying Israel as a special people and of maintaining the covenant relationship; Jews who are so identified and who avail themselves of the Torah-prescribed means of maintaining their membership in the covenant community (who are "righteous") are assured of divine blessing, especially that of salvation in the age to come. This was the working assumption with which we began our study, and it was borne out by our investigation of the relevant Pauline themes (works, faith, righteousness, law).

2. Within the broad framework of covenantal nomism, Paul is to be located specifically within the more stringent and zealous forms of Pharisaism and, in particular, among those who felt that the only hope Gentiles had of sharing in the salvation of the age to come was by becoming full

proselytes to Judaism in this age. One of the considerations leading to the latter supposition is his insistence, even as a Christian missionary, that Gentile converts are to be seen as Abraham's seed.

3. In addition, in his pre-Christian life Paul played an active role in the making of proselytes. The supposition here is not that he was engaged in a Gentile mission along the lines of his later apostolic mission, the two differing only in the content of the message. Rather, the activity being proposed conforms to patterns characteristic of Second Temple Judaism, with King Izates' adviser Eleazar serving as a prototype. The Gentiles in question were primarily those who had been attracted to the Jewish community, and the activity was motivated as much by a concern to preserve the community from an undesired blurring of the boundaries as it was by a concern for Gentiles and a desire to welcome them under the wings of the God of Israel (see 2 *Bar* 41.4). In support of this point and the previous one is Paul's statement in Gal 5:11, where he refers to a time when he once "preached circumcision."

4. Finally, in his initial encounter with the Christian movement and message, he perceived it as objectionable and so became involved in attempts to suppress it. In the terms of his later Christian vocabulary, he became a persecutor. His characterization of this persecuting activity as a manifestation of zeal indicates that it resulted not simply from some general and indeterminate antipathy, but more precisely because he perceived the Christian movement as posing a threat to the Torah and thus to the community shaped by its Torah adherence. A range of possible reasons has been suggested for Paul's persecuting zeal. But the shape of the Christ-Torah antithesis in his Christian discourse suggests that his objection to the Christian message had to do not simply with the Torah-laxity of some of its adherents, nor with the message of a crucified Messiah itself. Instead, the problem was more sociological or "ecclesiological"; he perceived the Christ of the kerygma as representing a rival to the Torah with respect to its role of determining membership in God's covenant people. The basis of this rivalry—the reason why he perceived Christ and Torah as mutually exclusive boundary markers—is to be found in the already/ not yet structure of the Christian message. The message that the Messiah had appeared in advance of the age to come, and that salvation was dependent on recognizing Jesus as this Messiah, implied an alternative way of determining the community of the "righteous," namely, by adherence to Christ, rather than to the Torah. While the rivalry between the two

remained implicit in the early days of the movement—many of the early Christians happily combining the two or at least unaware of any essential tension between them—Paul from his vantage point was able to perceive things more clearly. To the extent to which the early Christian movement was prepared to include as members those who were lax about Torah observance, simply on the basis of their adherence to Christ, they were implying that Torah was not necessary. Since it was necessary even for a conscientious Torah observer such as himself to believe in Jesus in order to be eligible for salvation, Paul perceived the message as implying that the Torah was not enough. The result, whether the Christians were aware of it or not, was that Christ was functioning as a de facto replacement for the Torah as a membership requirement. The fact that the Messiah in question had been ignominiously put to death on a cross only added to the scandal of the phenomenon.

### Stage II

5. Whatever else it may have been, Paul's conversion experience produced in him the solid conviction that God had raised Jesus from the dead, and thus that Jesus was—as the targets of his persecuting activity had been proclaiming all along—Messiah and Savior. To this extent, Paul's fundamental conviction did not differ from that of his predecessors in the faith (see 1 Cor 15:11). But because of his unique starting point as a persecutor, this new conviction brought with it an already-construed set of cognitive forces and inferences—a convictional dynamic primed to operate in such a way as to ensure a much more disjunctive and radical outcome. For this new conviction presented itself to one who was already convinced that Christ and Torah were antithetical, that they represented rival ways of marking the boundary around the community of the righteous. He could not come to the conviction that God had raised Christ without at the same time shifting to the other side of the Christ-Torah *Gestalt*,[6] thus setting in motion a set of cognitive forces that would reconfigure his whole constellation of native convictions.

### Stage III

The word "reconfigure" is important. Paul did not so much abandon his native convictional world as reconstruct it around a new center. True, in choosing Christ as both the center of his world and circumference of God's people he was forced to let go of Torah in that role. But quite a few of his native convictions—God, the election of Israel, Israel's role as a light to the Gentiles, the consummation of God's reign in the age to come, and others—were not directly implicated in the Christ-Torah either-or and thus continued as important elements in his convictional framework. And even the Torah was not left behind in totality; Paul continued to believe that it had been given by God, and that it therefore had a significant role to play. While there can be no doubt that important things were left behind, and at substantial personal cost (see Phil 3:7-8), his shift from Torah to Christ has to be understood not as the total abandonment of one set of convictions in favor of another, different and distinct, but as the reconfiguration of one set of convictions around a new and powerful center. In the process, some individual native convictions were abandoned, others radically altered, still others carried over more or less intact, and additional Christian ones introduced.

At the end of chapter 8, I attempted to describe the way in which this convictional dynamic played out, and to outline the resultant structure of Paul's Christian convictions.[7] I will not repeat this here but simply draw attention to those aspects that concern the Gentile mission.

6. As observed already, Paul shared with his fellow Jews the conviction that Israel had been chosen by God from among the nations, and had been provided with a means of righteousness and a promise of salvation. In addition, he shared with some of his Jewish kinsfolk the belief that righteousness and salvation were available to Gentiles as well, but only on the condition that they become full members of the people of Israel. In his conversion, Paul came to a different understanding of the means of righteousness: Christ, not Torah, served as the entrance requirement and boundary marker of the community. But while this made for an alteration in substance, the basic convictions just described were carried over into the new framework in essentially similar form: Gentiles could share in Israel's means of righteousness and hope of salvation, but only by being "in Christ" and thus becoming full members of a redefined Israel.

7. Paul's Gentile mission then needs to be understood as the combination of two factors. First, guided by models of apostleship operative within the Christian movement from the beginning, as these were supplemented by prophetic models drawn from scripture, he understood his conversion experience as constituting a call to be an apostle, that is, one authorized by the risen Christ to preach the gospel. Second, the energy experienced in this call was directed along channels already present from his past—a belief that Gentiles had to become part of Israel to be saved, and a personal involvement in the business of making proselytes. His former convictions reoriented around a new center, and his former activity energized

by a new experience, Paul understood himself to be called by Christ to a mission among the Gentiles.

8. One other important conviction is Paul's belief that the parousia was near—that his own generation was probably the last. While this might have been a native conviction, it would even in that case have still been strongly reinforced by his encounter with the risen Christ; more probably it originated with the conversion itself. The reason for giving it explicit mention here is that it accounts for the perplexing ambiguity in Paul's attitudes toward traditional distinctions between Jews and Gentiles, Israel and the nations. On the one hand, he can make statements suggesting that these old distinctions are obsolete: all who are "in Christ" are members of Abraham's family, with no ongoing distinction between Jew and Gentile. On the other, ethnic Israel continues to be a significant entity for Paul, with "all Israel" eventually to be saved. Such ambiguity is understandable in the context of what was perceived to be the last generation. While the boundary of Israel may have been radically redefined by Christ, nothing could alter the fact that Paul was ethnically as Jewish as his converts were (for the most part) Gentile. Only as his generation was succeeded by other ones would an ambiguous both/and be transmuted into a disjunctive either/or—either an Israel defined in ethnic and Torah terms, or a Gentile church defined (first by Justin Martyr) as "true Israel." Expecting Christ's soon return, Paul could (though not without difficulty) continue to hold on to both.

## 12.2 Conversion and the Reconfiguration of a Convictional World

It is necessary now to draw out the connections between the transformation described in the previous section and the theoretical discussions carried out in chapter 2. Of primary interest here is the notion that Paul's conversion experience can be understood as a reconfiguration of his convictional world.

For the most part, my discussion in the preceding chapters of Paul's "convictions" can be clearly understood on the basis of the common, intuitive sense of the word. Convictions are those things of which a person is convinced—foundational cognitions, basic beliefs about the nature of reality, things that can be taken for granted. As such, they serve as the framework within which new perceptions are understood and as axioms for further knowledge. My use of the term is fully in keeping with this generally understood sense. But in my analysis of Paul's letters, the term functions as a significant category within a more deliberate interpretive framework.

In keeping with emerging trends in Pauline interpretation, I attempt to understand what is commonly referred to as his "thought" or "theology" with reference to a three-level analytical structure. The bottom level, extending far beneath the surface of the texts, consists of an ordered set of convictions, providing the basic framework of meaning within which Paul makes sense of reality. What is in view here is not a single conviction, or even a collection of discrete, individual convictions, but a convictional structure—a more or less coherent arrangement of convictions which provides a more or less successful framework for making life meaningful. I say more or less, because of the possibility of conflicting convictions— for example, when latent tensions are magnified into what are perceived as explicit conflicts by the force of new experiences. In such a situation, the perceived conflict (or dissonance) has to be negotiated and sorted out at a second level of conscious reflection. Such a possibility is of particular relevance in the case of a convert such as Paul, whose convictional world comprises convictions both native and new.

The topmost level is that of the rhetorical surface of the letters themselves. This is the level of contingency, of situation, of active involvement with the everyday reality of the world. Here we find Paul attempting to shape the perceptions and actions of his readers in accordance with the norms and structures of his basic world of meaning. Inevitably, this involves second-order articulation of the nature of this world, and of the individual convictions of which it is composed.

In between the deep structure of Paul's convictions and the surface structure of his situationally conditioned rhetoric lies the intermediate structure of his theology. Driven on the one hand by the need to work out perceived conflicts, tensions, and unresolved questions arising from his basic convictions, especially as these are exposed by the developing circumstances of his life, and on the other by the need to respond in a reasoned way to the immediate needs of his congregations, Paul engages in second-order reflection on his basic set of convictions, thereby building up a developing structure of theological articulation.

As was indicated in chapter 2, this three-level approach to Paul's thought is not only in keeping with recent developments in Pauline studies but also is rooted in rich theoretical soil, nurtured by conceptions drawn from structuralism, cultural anthropology, and, especially, the sociology of knowledge. For a primary theoretical model, however, I looked not to Claude Lévi-Strauss, Mary Douglas, or Peter Berger, but to Thomas

Kuhn, and to his analysis of the role of "paradigms" within the world of scientific knowledge.[8] The model was developed in detail in chapter 2.

Kuhn uses the term paradigm in at least two senses—to refer both to the basic set of assumptions governing the scientific understanding of a particular field of observation and inquiry and to the specific scientific achievement by which the validity of this set of assumptions was demonstrated and within which it was at least implicit. Once established, a paradigm (in the broader sense of the term) provides the cognitive framework within which "normal science" can be carried out. By "normal science" he means the second-order process of paradigm articulation that makes up most quotidian scientific work: extending the paradigm to other areas of the field, identifying new problems to be investigated, predicting results that can then be tested in further confirmation of the paradigm, and so on. In my appropriation of the model, these two aspects of a scientific paradigm correspond to the bottom two levels of my analytical structure—the ordered set of convictions making up a convictional world and the developing structure of second-order theological reflection. The correlate of my third level—the rhetorical situation of the letters themselves—is not as clearly apparent in Kuhn's model. Appropriate correlations might be made with applied science, or perhaps the experimental side of normal science. In any case, for present purposes it is the lower two levels of the model that are more pertinent.

Two aspects of Kuhn's model make it particularly congenial for my work and thus determined its choice. One is that, while not neglecting the social dimension of the construction of knowledge, it places greater emphasis on individual cognitions. The other is that, as a theory developed primarily to describe and account for scientific revolutions—major shifts in the reigning paradigms—it is admirably suited to the analysis of the cognitive shift represented by Paul's conversion. There is no need to repeat what was said in chapter 2 about Kuhn's analysis of a paradigm shift. But further reflection is in order concerning these two aspects. We will begin with the phenomenon of conversion.

Until recently, there has been a kind of moratorium in effect among Pauline scholars in the use of the term "conversion" as a description of Paul's Damascus experience. This state of affairs was due primarily to the work of Krister Stendahl.[9] Understanding the term as referring to a radical break with the past and a decisive shift from one religion (or from no religion) to another, he felt that it did not do justice to the degree of continuity in Paul's self-understanding before and after Damascus, and so he rejected it in favor of Paul's own term, "call" (Gal 1:15). Stendahl's distaste for the word is understandable, given the influence of psychological studies of conversion earlier in this century, where the tendency was to see it as a manifestation of personality disorders and mental instability. Ironically, in these studies the case of Paul was often taken as the proto-type for such a conception of conversion.[10]

Stendahl's instincts were right. There was much more continuity in Paul's biography, and much more robustness in his personality, than the older models of "conversion" were prepared to recognize. Still, it cannot be denied that Paul's experience resulted in decisive shifts of values, orientation, and commitment of a kind not usually associated with a "call." No Isaiah was ever called to a change of direction as dramatic as that of the persecutor turned apostle (Gal 1:13-16). No Jeremiah ever transvalued his past the way Paul does in Phil 3:4-8. Further, in more recent times there have been significant developments in the social-scientific study of conversion, with the emergence of broader, more nuanced, more sympathetic, and less pathological models. For example, in a seminal study of conversion, Lewis Rambo applies the term to a broad array of personal reorientations and changes in religious affiliation, including: apostasy, intensification (of commitment to a religion with which one was already associated), affiliation (from no commitment to full participation in a religious group or tradition), institutional transition (from one branch of a religious tradition to another), and tradition transition (from one religion to another).[11] Accordingly, there has been a renewed willingness recently to view Paul as a convert, and to construct, with aid from the social sciences, a more satisfactory model of conversion within which his experience can be described.[12]

One clear result of the recent study of conversion, especially as the range of approaches has broadened to include not only psychology, but also sociology and cultural anthropology, is that conversion needs to be seen as a complex phenomenon, involving social and cultural as well as personal and religious dimensions.[13] This means that conversion cannot be reduced simply to the cognitive dimension. While the cognitive dimension is important and is not to be squeezed out in any reductionistic way,[14] we are not to suppose that by tracing the shift in Paul's convictional world we have provided a full account of his conversion. A full account would need to take note of personal dimensions in addition to the purely cognitive, and would need to place the resultant, already-complex personal experience within the further complexity of Paul's social and cultural environment.

In any such analysis, models drawn from the social sciences will have important contributions to make. But these need to be chosen and applied

with care so as to avoid hasty generalizations where one aspect of conversion analysis is seized on and applied to Paul's situation without due regard to the whole context. Models need to be applicable to the case under
discussion, and in Paul's case there are several distinctive elements not
found in a "typical" conversion. (1) Paul is converted into a new movement, one that has been in existence for only a few years at most. Models
drawn from conversions to more well established traditions—for example, as when Paul is compared to Augustine[15]—are thus not fully applicable. (2) This new movement is at the same time a renewal movement
within the larger religious tradition of Judaism. In Rambo's typology, for
example, it is not clear whether Paul's conversion should be seen as an
example of "institution transition" or of "tradition transition." The ambiguity is not to be finessed away; it is part of the dynamic under investigation. (3) Until the time of his conversion, Paul had been not only a devoted
adherent of the "parent" tradition, but also engaged in active opposition
to the new movement. While many conversions are preceded by a period
of hesitation and resistance which undoubtedly shape the convert's later
perception of things, Paul's active opposition intensifies this element considerably. (4) Partly as a result of the preceding factors, and partly because
of his own personality, Paul was a pioneering figure rather than a rank-
and-file convert.[16] While he was undoubtedly shaped by the community
into which he converted, he was by no means pressed into a mold, but
emerged the other side of his conversion as a leader of a segment of the
movement which he was able to shape in accordance with his own perception of things.

For all these reasons, Paul was not a typical convert. Any attempt to
construct an explanatory model would need to recognize these distinctive
features and seek to develop the model on the basis of comparable cases.
Now it is not my intention here to attempt any full-scale explanatory
model (although—irony of ironies, given the point of departure for this
study—the first comparable figure to come to mind is none other than
Martin Luther!). Rather, I make this point simply in defense of my focus
on the individual and cognitive aspects of Paul's conversion. While such
a focus would be legitimate and defensible in many cases of conversion,
I submit that it is particularly so in a case such as Paul's. His principled
opposition to the movement, his radical shift in orientation, his role as
a pioneering figure—all suggest that the cognitive element was a more
dominant component of his conversion experience than is typically
the case.

Because of its emphasis on the cognitive aspects of a scientific revolution, especially as they are experienced by scientific pioneers,[17] Kuhn's

model of a paradigm shift is particularly appropriate for the case of Paul.[18] Indeed, Kuhn describes the personal experience of a shift in paradigms as a kind of conversion.[19] My suggestion, then, is that Paul can be seen as one who experienced a paradigm shift. His Damascus experience represented a transfer of allegiance from one convictional world to another, a personal and cognitive shift in which he gave up one set of world-structuring convictions and embraced another. His native world was shaped by the paradigm provided by the Torah, a set of convictions which had successfully determined and accounted for his experience to this point. In his early encounters with the Christian movement, he came to realize the extent to which this set of beliefs functioned as a rival and incompatible way of structuring the world. To protect his paradigm, and the semantic universe to which it gave rise, he attempted to suppress the movement. His new conviction that Jesus had indeed been raised both shattered the framework of the old paradigm and, at the same time, provided the organizing center for a new one. What had been perceived as an anomaly now became an axiom, the hinge for the flip from one paradigm to another. Inverting his previous perception of the Christian message, he now became convinced that Christ, not Torah, is to be seen as the divinely given means of determining membership in the community destined for salvation. This new conviction became the center of a reconfiguration of his convictions, producing a new paradigm which was to shape his thought and activity from this point on.

Kuhn's model provides us with an illuminating way of balancing continuity and discontinuity. On the one hand, paradigms are sharply disjunctive and discontinuous. A scientific revolution involves the "rejection of one time-honored theory in favor of another incompatible with it."[20] Yet, at the same time, there is continuity; Ptolemy and Copernicus may represent rival and incommensurate ways of organizing the world of astronomy, but on both sides of the shift from one to the other one finds planets, stars, and the sun. In a paradigm shift, the old field of knowledge is reconfigured, not abandoned.[21] Many old observations, cognitions, and even convictions are carried over, but organized and understood with respect to a new structure.

In Paul's case, I submit, this is true especially of his conception of the Gentiles and their place in the world. Both before and after his conversion he was convinced that their one hope of salvation was to become part of the people of Israel. His conversion can be understood as a shift from a paradigm in which membership in Israel was determined by Torah, to one in which it was determined by Christ. His convictions about the Gentiles and their place in salvation did not originate with his conversion; rather, the conversion experience reconfigured a set of convictions in which the Gentiles were already firmly located.

## 12.3 Concluding Reflections: Paul and the Gentiles in Retrospect

There is an ambiguity, even an irreducible tension, within Paul's convictions about "Jews, Gentiles, and the church of God" (see 1 Cor 10:32). He seems to want to hold on to two conflicting definitions of "Israel." On the one hand, the family of Abraham—Israel—had been redefined in terms of Christ, so that "in Christ" the old, Torah-based differentiations between Jew and Gentile have been obliterated. And yet on the other, these differentiations continue to have a real validity. Paul understands himself to be a Jew called to proclaim the gospel to Gentiles. Further, he looks for the future salvation of an Israel defined in precisely these traditional terms, for "the gifts and the calling of God are irrevocable" (Rom 11:29).

Helmut Koester has described this desire "to establish a new Israel on a foundation that could include both Jews and Gentiles" as an attempt "to accomplish the impossible."[22] The impossibility of the enterprise is clearer in retrospect—and probably was clearer in the perception of Paul's opponents, both inside and outside the church—than it was to Paul himself. At several points in this study, I have attempted to argue that one can understand, at least to some extent, why Paul would make such apparently conflicting statements about the nature of "Israel" when one sees the situation from his perspective. In his perspective, there was not much of a possibility of retrospect at all—at least, not this side of the parousia. In his first-generation situation, expecting the return of Christ and the consummation of salvation to occur soon, he could insist, as his basic conviction impelled him to do, that membership in Israel was determined by Christ, not Torah, while at the same time continuing to take for granted—in accordance with another of his core convictions—the traditional, Torah-based distinctions between Jew and Gentile.

But there was at least a latent tension between these core convictions which Paul, even with the full panoply of his rhetorical powers deployed in the task, could not fully overcome. By the time of writing of his epistle to the Romans, events had unfolded in such a way as to bring this tension into the view even of Paul himself. The stunning expansion of Gentile Christianity through the Mediterranean world, coupled with the relative failure of the Jewish mission (see Rom 11:7-12), made it more difficult to contain the tension within his convictional structure. Romans 9–11 represents Paul's heroic attempt to hold on to divergent convictions in a situation where events were apparently bringing them into sharp conflict. But Paul did not see the situation as impossible. Inscrutable and unsearchable, perhaps; but not impossible, since his faith was unshakably in the God from whom and through whom and to whom are all things (11:33-36).

But history carried on; Paul's generation was replaced by another, and another, and yet another. By the time of Justin Martyr, Paul's both/and was clearly an either/or—either Christian or Jew; either Justin's "true, spiritual Israel" or Trypho's ethnic, empirical Israel. The church in its emerging normative form took a portion of Paul and left the other to one side. Indeed, his construction of a true family of Abraham, made up of Jews and Gentiles as equal members on the basis of their faith in Christ, seemed to be tailor-made for the emerging view of Christianity as a third race.[23] It is not surprising that Paul's stubborn commitment to natural Israel—Israel κατὰ σάρκα (according to the flesh)—was treated more and more as an anomaly—recognized, but not incorporated. The result was a more consistent theology, but a consistency purchased at the price of increasingly lamentable consequences.

There is a sense, then, in which Paul can be seen as a tragic figure. On the one hand, he was prepared to endure hardship, calumny, and eventually even death, because of his concern that the gospel continue to be seen as good news for Israel. The acceptance of synagogue discipline (2 Cor 11:24); the mental anguish testified to in Rom 9:2 and apparent through the subsequent three chapters; the difficulties of the collection project, faced willingly because of the prospect of confirming the solidarity of Jewish and Gentile Christianity—all bear witness to Paul's ongoing commitment to his kinsfolk according to the flesh. Yet at the same time, his prodigious labors, both as a missionary and as a thinker, helped to create conditions conducive to just the type of Gentile triumphalism foreseen and warned about in Rom 11:17-24. The success of his Gentile mission helped to ensure the eventual "Gentilization" of the church, while his passionate defense of the position that believing Gentiles were, on the basis of their faith in Christ, full members of Abraham's family, provided the conceptual framework for the spiritualization of "Israel" and the emergence of the displacement theology of the *adversus Judaeos* tradition.

Paul's efforts to accomplish his apostolic task, then, produced results that eventually ran counter to his conscious intentions. This is obviously not the place to explore the historical outworking of his missionary and theological enterprise. Nevertheless, it would be neither appropriate, nor true to Paul, to let tragedy have the last word. For in his Damascus experience Paul felt himself to be in the hands of a God able to turn tragedy to triumph, crucifixion to glory, weakness to strength. In obedience to this God, the God of Israel, the God who had set him apart from his mother's womb, he undertook the task of preparing an "offering of the Gentiles" that was "acceptable and holy" (Rom 15:16), holding firmly to his convictions even when they threatened to tear him apart, confident that the tensions would ultimately be resolved in God's final glorious demonstration of mercy to all (Rom 11:32).

# Notes

## Chapter 1

1. The term itself is used by Robert Jewett, "The Law and the Coexistence of Jews and Gentiles in Romans," *Int* 39 (1985) 341; John G. Gager, *The Origins of Anti-Semitism* (New York/Oxford: Oxford University Press, 1983) 198–199; Robert Morgan, as cited by Peter Sedgwick, "'Justification by Faith': One Doctrine, Many Debates?" *Theology* 93 (1990) 11; Daniel Boyarin, *A Radical Jew* (Berkeley/Los Angeles/New York: University of California Press, 1994) 47. Others make the same observation without the term, e.g., James D. G. Dunn, "The New Perspective on Paul," *BJRL* 65 (1983) 97, 100; Mary Ann Getty, "Paul and the Salvation of Israel: A Perspective on Romans 9–11," *CBQ* 50 (1988) 456.

2. The term originated with Thomas S. Kuhn, *The Structure of Scientific Revolutions* (2d ed.; Chicago: University of Chicago Press, 1970). For reasons that will be developed in due course, I will be making use of his theoretical framework in the present investigation of the structures of Paul's thought. Accordingly, a more complete description of Kuhn's categories can be found below; see pp. 43–45.

3. On the axiomatic nature of paradigms, see Kuhn, *Scientific Revolutions*, 122–28.

4. See, e.g., Stephen Westerholm, *Israel's Law and the Church's Faith* (Grand Rapids: Eerdmans, 1988) 3–12; Francis Watson, *Paul, Judaism and the Gentiles* (Cambridge: Cambridge University Press, 1986) 1–18.

5. From Luther's comment on Gal 1:1; *A Commentary on St. Paul's Epistle to the Galatians* (Grand Rapids: Zondervan, n.d.) 9.

6. Rudolf Bultmann, *Theology of the New Testament* (2 vols.; London: SCM, 1952) 1:191.

7. See Kuhn, *Scientific Revolutions*, 6.

8. For Augustine's discussion of justification, see esp. *The Spirit and the Letter*, ET in *Augustine: Later Works* (Library of Christian Classics, vol. 8; Philadelphia: Westminster, 1955).

9. Philip Schaff, *The Creeds of Christendom* (London: Hodder & Stoughton, 1877) 2:91.

10. This phrase appears in F. C. Baur, *Paul: The Apostle of Jesus Christ* (2 vols.; London: Williams & Norgate, 1876) 1:253.

11. See, e.g., Bousset's presentation of Paul as the one who systematizes and develops the Kyrios religion of primitive Gentile Christianity, with "faith" the point at which "Pauline religion is concentrated and crystallized"; Wilhelm Bousset, *Kyrios Christos* (Nashville/New York: Abingdon, 1970) 200.

12. Bultmann, *Theology* 1:187–88.

13. Chrysostom, *Commentary on Galatians,* on 1:14.

14. For a thorough survey, see Beverly Roberts Gaventa, "Paul's Conversion: A Critical Sifting of the Epistolary Evidence" (Ph.D. diss., Duke University, 1978).

15. E.g., H. J. Holtzmann, *Lehrbuch der neutestamentlichen Theologie* (2 vols.; Freiburg: Mohr, 1897); Adolf Deissmann, *St. Paul: A Study in Social and Religious History* (London: Hodder & Stoughton, 1912) 93–98; C. H. Dodd, *The Epistle of Paul to the Romans* (London: Hodder & Stoughton, 1932) 104–16; James S. Stewart, *A Man in Christ* (London: Hodder & Stoughton, 1935) 83–122; Edgar J. Goodspeed, *Paul* (Nashville/New York: Abingdon, 1947) 8, 11–19.

16. See Gaventa's discussion of Baur, Holsten, Pfleiderer, and others; "Paul's Conversion," 10–24.

17. Stewart, *A Man in Christ,* 119, 141.

18. F. C. Baur, *The Church History of the First Three Centuries* (2 vols.; London: Williams & Norgate, 1878) 1:46–48.

19. Richardson has drawn attention to the fact that Justin is the first one to have unambiguously laid claim to this title for the church; Peter Richardson, *Israel in the Apostolic Church* (Cambridge: Cambridge University Press, 1969) 1, 9–14.

20. As recognized by the generally Calvinist interpreter John Murray, *The Epistle to the Romans* (Grand Rapids: Eerdmans, 1959) 2:97, n. 52.

21. Calvin, *The Epistles of Paul to the Romans and to the Thessalonians* (London: Oliver & Boyd, 1961) 255. Luther, apparently, also inclined to this view; see the editor's comment in *Commentary on the Epistle to the Romans* (Grand Rapids: Zondervan, 1954) 146. See also N. T. Wright, *The Climax of the Covenant* (Minneapolis: Fortress, 1991) 231–57.

22. F. W. Beare, *St. Paul and His Letters* (Nashville: Abingdon, 1962) 97. So also Adolf von Harnack, *The Date of the Acts and of the Synoptic Gospels* (London: Williams & Norgate, 1911) 45–50; Dodd ("Paul tries to have it both ways"), *Romans,* 183; Bultmann ("speculative fantasy"), *Theology,* 2:132. W. D. Davies speaks of "Paul's refusal utterly to sacrifice his nation to logical consistency"; *Paul and Rabbinic Judaism* (London: SPCK, 1948) 85; for a more nuanced discussion, see his "Paul and the People of Israel," *NTS* 24 (1977–78) 4–39, esp. 31–35.

23. See Kuhn, *Scientific Revolutions,* 78.

24. Sanders, *Paul and Palestinian Judaism* (Philadelphia: Fortress, 1977); *Paul, the Law, and the Jewish People* (Philadelphia: Fortress, 1983).

25. C. G. Montefiore, *Judaism and St. Paul* (London: Max Goschen, 1914); S. Schechter, *Aspects of Rabbinic Theology* (New York: Schocken, 1961 [1909]); James Parkes, *Jesus, Paul and the Jews* (London: SCM, 1936); George Foot Moore, *Judaism in the First Centuries of the Christian Era* (3 vols.; Cambridge: Harvard University Press, 1927–30).

26. For Sanders's discussion of these earlier authors, see *Paul and Palestinian Judaism*, 4–6. Aspects of Sanders's analysis, including the use of "nomism" itself, were anticipated in significant ways by Richard N. Longenecker, *Paul, Apostle of Liberty* (New York: Harper & Row, 1964).

27. *Fourth Ezra* represents the only exception.

28. Sanders, *Paul and Palestinian Judaism*, 422.

29. Albert Schweitzer, *The Mysticism of Paul the Apostle* (New York: Seabury, 1968 [1931]); William Wrede, *Paul* (London: Green, 1907 [1904]). For Wrede's influence on Schweitzer, see his *Paul and His Interpreters* (London: A. & C. Black, 1950 [1912]) 166–71, and *Mysticism*, 36.

30. Schweitzer, *Paul and His Interpreters*, 72.

31. For a detailed survey, see Schweitzer, ibid., 63–99.

32. Wrede, *Paul*, 122.

33. Ibid., 127 (emphasis his).

34. Sanders's *Paul and Palestinian Judaism* is illustrative; while Schweitzer figures prominently in the discussion, Wrede rates only two brief and passing references.

35. Schweitzer, *Mysticism*, 220.

36. Sanders, *Paul and Palestinian Judaism*, 441; a second fundamental assumption, viz., that Paul himself was called to be the apostle to the Gentiles, will be taken up below.

37. See esp. Sanders, *Paul, the Law, and the Jewish People*, 46.

38. For a penetrating and invaluable study, see Westerholm, *Israel's Law*.

39. Wrede, *Paul*, 151–68; cf. 42–43.

40. Schweitzer's discussion of Paul and the Gentiles is to be found in his chapter "Mysticism and the Law," *Mysticism*, 177–204.

41. E.g., Sanders, *Paul and Palestinian Judaism*, 442.

42. See Sanders, *Paul, the Law, and the Jewish People*, 152–54, 171–72.

43. E.g., J. Klausner, *From Jesus to Paul* (New York: Macmillan, 1943) 312. This approach to Paul has been revived by Boyarin (*A Radical Jew*), who locates Paul's struggle precisely in the tension arising from a Torah that both proclaims a universal God and excludes most of humanity from the people of God (e.g., pp. 39–44). For further discussion of Boyarin, see §5.3 and chap. 10 below.

44. See, e.g., O. Pfleiderer, *Paulinism* (2 vols.; London: Williams & Norgate, 1891) 1:3–13; Klausner, *From Jesus to Paul*, 312–29; Goodspeed, *Paul*, 14–18.

45. For bibliography on this position, see above, chap. 1, n. 15.

46. Bultmann, for example, denies that Paul's conversion is to be viewed as the resolution of a long struggle of despair over the law's demands; Phil 3:6, rather than Rom 7, describes Paul's pre-Damascus experience with the law. See Rudolf Bultmann, "Paul," in *Existence and Faith* (Cleveland/New York: Meridian, 1960) 114–15.

47. Stewart eloquently defends the autobiographical nature of Rom 7 (see *A Man in Christ*, 99–103), but argues just as vehemently that union with Christ, rather than justification by faith, is to be seen as "the heart of Paul's religion" (147).

48. Wrede, *Paul*, 142–47.

49. Kümmel, *Römer 7 und die Bekehrung des Paulus* (Leipzig: Hinrichs, 1929).

50. In addition to his comments in the preface in defense of the popular manner of presentation, see his reference to "other grounds [that] might be adduced" in the note on p. 145.

51. Cf. Westerholm, *Israel's Law,* 53; Westerholm provides a clear and concise summary of Kümmel (pp. 53–65).

52. Admittedly, several recent studies have entertained the possibility that frustration with the law was a factor in Paul's conversion; see J. Christiaan Beker, *Paul the Apostle* (Philadelphia: Fortress, 1980) 240–43; H. Räisänen, *Paul and the Law* (Philadelphia: Fortress, 1986) 231–36. Nevertheless, in neither case does it play a central role, nor—more specifically—is it used to account for Paul's concern for the Gentiles.

53. Attempts to explain Paul in this way by positing a tight logical connection between his pre- and post-Damascus patterns of thought have both a long history (See Gaventa, "Paul's Conversion," esp. 74) and an innate probability; indeed, I will be developing one form of this argument in what follows.

54. Lucien Cerfaux, *The Christian in the Theology of St. Paul* (New York: Herder & Herder, 1967) 69 (emphasis added). For similar construals, see n. 79 below.

55. For a very helpful discussion, see Alan F. Segal, *Paul the Convert* (New Haven/London: Yale University Press, 1990) 285–300.

56. One of several essays included in Stendahl's book *Paul among Jews and Gentiles* (Philadelphia: Fortress, 1976).

57. See Beverly Roberts Gaventa, *From Darkness to Light: Aspects of Conversion in the New Testament* (Philadelphia: Fortress, 1986); Segal, *Paul the Convert.*

58. On the absence of Christ from Stendahl's account of Paul's call, see, e.g., William S. Campbell, *Paul's Gospel in an Intercultural Context* (Frankfurt: Peter Lang, 1992) 73.

59. The attempts by Gaston, Gager, and others to carry through such a reading of Paul in a detailed and rigorous way will be examined below; see §8.2 below.

60. Nor is the situation improved by arguing for an explicitly verbal divine commissioning. For to be intelligible at all, something perceived to be a message from God would need to be brought into coherence with the perceiver's semantic universe or system of basic convictions.

61. See esp. James Parkes, *The Conflict of the Church and the Synagogue* (New York: Atheneum, 1985 [1936]), written before the Holocaust, but widely influential after World War II.

62. See, e.g., Parkes, *Jesus, Paul and the Jews.*

63. See Marcel Simon, *Verus Israel: A Study of the Relations between Christians and Jews in the Roman Empire (135–425)* (Oxford: Oxford University Press, 1986 [1948]).

64. See, e.g., Richardson, *Israel in the Apostolic Church.*

65. Schweitzer, *Mysticism;* Davies, *Paul and Rabbinic Judaism;* Hans Joachim Schoeps, *Paul: The Theology of the Apostle in the Light of Jewish Religious History* (Philadelphia: Westminster, 1961).

66. First published 1954; ET (London: SCM, 1959). Part of the preparatory work for this book was published two years later (1956) in the form of a commentary on Romans 9–11 (ET: *Christ and Israel: An Interpretation of Romans 9–11* [Philadelphia: Fortress, 1967]).

67. Ibid.

68. E.g., "Jewish propaganda . . . was mainly trying to make proselytes, and was not a real mission for the kingdom of God"; ibid., 270.

69. This is the thrust of the first two chapters.

70. See above, p. 17–18.

71. For what follows, see §7.1 below.

72. The eschatological explanation of Paul's Gentile mission itself is problematical, as I will attempt to demonstrate below. Here I allude only to the more obvious weaknesses of Munck's explanation.

73. "It cannot be sufficiently stressed that with Paul it is not a matter of a call to apostleship in general, but of a clearly defined apostleship in relation to the Gentiles" (40–41).

74. Ibid., 276.

75. For a recent and thoroughgoing example, see Watson, *Paul, Judaism and the Gentiles,* 28–38. Segal contemplates the possibility of an early period where Paul observed the Torah and preached to Jews; see *Paul the Convert,* 8, 120, 142–43. See also Martin Goodman, *Mission and Conversion* (Oxford: Clarendon Press, 1994) 166, and Campbell (*Paul's Gospel,* 89–90), who sees the failure of the Jewish mission as a catalyst. Earlier examples of a similar approach can be found in Wrede, *Paul,* 10–11, 42–43; Morton Scott Enslin, *Reapproaching Paul* (Philadelphia: Westminster, 1972), 63–80; Edward P. Blair, "Paul's Call to the Gentile Mission," *BR* 10 (1965) 19–33; Klausner, *From Jesus to Paul,* 331–46.

76. E.g., Seyoon Kim, *The Origin of Paul's Gospel* (Grand Rapids: Eerdmans, 1982) 57; F. F. Bruce, *Paul: Apostle of the Heart Set Free* (Grand Rapids: Eerdmans, 1977) 75.

77. See above, pp. 16–18. Other scholars who approach Paul in these terms include: Beker, *Paul the Apostle,* 3–10, and Philip A. Cunningham, *Jewish Apostle to the Gentiles: Paul as He Saw Himself* (Mystic, Conn.: Twenty-Third Publications, 1986).

78. See §6.2 below.

79. This construal goes back as far as O. Pfleiderer; see *Paulinism,* 1:3, and *Primitive Christianity* (4 vols.; London: Williams & Norgate, 1906) 1:95–98. For other examples prior to Sanders, see: Cerfaux, *The Christian in the Theology of St. Paul,* 69; W. Grundmann, "Paulus, aus dem Volke Israel, Apostel der Völker," *NovT* 4 (1960), 274, 277; Wolfhart Pannenberg, *Jesus — God and Man* (Philadelphia: Westminster, 1968) 71–72; George Eldon Ladd, *A Theology of the New Testament* (Grand Rapids: Eerdmans, 1974) 368; J. Dupont, "The Conversion of Paul, and Its Influence on His Understanding of Salvation by Faith," in W. W. Gasque and R. P. Martin, eds., *Apostolic History and the Gospel* (Grand Rapids: Eerdmans, 1970), 192–93; W. D. Davies, *Paul and Rabbinic Judaism,* 67; idem, *Invitation to the New Testament* (Garden City, N.Y.: Doubleday, 1965) 263; idem, "The Apostolic Age and the Life of Paul," in *Peake's Commentary on the Bible,* ed. M. Black and H. H. Rowley (London/New York: Thomas Nelson, 1962) 873–74; Ulrich Wilckens, "Die Bekehrung des Paulus als religionsgeschichtliches Problem," in *Rechtfertigung als Freiheit: Paulusstudien* (Neukirchen-Vluyn: Neukirchener, 1974) 25; M. Dibelius, *Paul* (London: Longmans, Green, and Co., 1953) 52–53; F. J. Leenhardt, "Abraham et la conversion de Saul de Tarse," *RHPhR* 53 (1973) 350; B. Rigaux, *The Letters of Paul* (Chicago: Franciscan Herald Press, 1968) 61; Blair, "Paul's Call," 28. For more recent forms of this construal, see §6.3 below.

80. See esp. Ferdinand Hahn, *Mission in the New Testament* (SBT 47; Naperville: Allenson, 1965) 76–77, 100; Barnabas Lindars, "The Old Testament and Universalism in Paul," *BJRL* 69 (1987) 512–13; Dupont, "Conversion of Paul," 192–93. Cf. Pannenberg, who ascribes this view to the pre-Pauline originators of the Gentile mission, but not to Paul; *Jesus — God and Man*, 71–72. While Sanders characteristically identifies "Jesus as universal saviour" as a fundamental conviction, occasionally he links this with Jesus' lordship; see *Paul and Palestinian Judaism*, 441–42; *Paul, the Law, and the Jewish People*, 152.

81. E.g., Bultmann, *Theology*, 1:187–88; Beker, *Paul the Apostle*, 144, 185; Walther Schmithals, *Paul and James* (London: SCM, 1965) 28–37; William R. Farmer, *Maccabees, Zealots and Josephus* (New York: Columbia University Press, 1956) 178–79, n. 6; E. Barnikol, *Die vorchristliche und frühchristliche Zeit des Paulus* (Kiel: Walter G. Mühlau Verlag, 1929), 23–24. James D. G. Dunn, *The Partings of the Ways* (London: SCM/Philadelphia: TPI, 1991) 121–22.

82. Räisänen, *Paul and the Law* 251–63; idem, "Paul's Conversion and the Development of His View of the Law," *NTS* 33 (1987) 404–19; Georg Strecker, *Eschaton und Historie* (Göttingen: Vandenhoeck & Ruprecht, 1979); idem, "Befreiung und Rechtfertigung: Zur Stellung der Rechtfertigungslehre in der Theologie des Paulus," in J. Friedrich et al, ed., *Rechtfertigung* (Tübingen: Mohr [Siebeck] / Göttingen: Vandenhoeck & Ruprecht, 1976) 479–508.

83. On conversion into a Gentile community, see *Paul the Convert*, 6–11, 205, and esp. 26; on the possibility of an initial Jewish mission, see pp. 8, 120, 142. See also below, pp. 267–68.

84. Davies, *Paul and Rabbinic Judaism;* the terms quoted here are found on p. 67. See also Sanders, *Paul, the Law, and the Jewish People*, 152–53; Lloyd Gaston, "Paul and the Torah," in A. T. Davies, ed., *Antisemitism and the Foundations of Christianity* (Toronto/New York: Paulist, 1979) 61–62. E. F. Synge combines the notion of a preconversion frustration about Judaism's attitude to the Gentiles with the older idea that Paul was also frustrated over an inability to keep the Torah; see "St. Paul's Boyhood and Conversion and his Attitude to Race," *ExpT* 94 (1982–83) 260–63.

85. Davies, *Paul and Rabbinic Judaism*, 63.

86. Sanders, *Paul, the Law, and the Jewish People*, 152.

87. Gaston, "Paul and the Torah," 62.

88. These will be surveyed in detail in chap. 3.

89. This was an important element in the reconstructions of both Schweitzer (*Mysticism*, 177–87) and Munck (*Paul*, 255–78); in each case, however, the eschatological element is intertwined with other, equally significant, factors—an idiosyncratic view of the interim period (Schweitzer) or the temporary rejection of Israel (Munck). Both will be discussed further below. For others holding to an eschatological pilgrimage interpretation, see: Sanders, *Paul, the Law, and the Jewish People*, 171; Schoeps, *Paul*, 219; Hahn, *Mission*, 108–9; Markus Barth, *The People of God* (Sheffield: JSOT Press, 1983) 43; R. Bring, "The Message to the Gentiles: A Study to [*sic*] the Theology of Paul the Apostle," *StTh* 19 (1965) 32; Pinchas Lapide, "The Rabbi From Tarsus," in Pinchas Lapide and Peter Stuhlmacher, *Paul: Rabbi and Apostle* (Minneapolis: Augsburg, 1984) 48; R. David Kaylor, *Paul's Covenant Community* (Atlanta: John Knox, 1988) 7, 37; Cunningham, *Jewish Apostle to the Gentiles*, 41; Richard B. Hays, *Echoes of Scripture in the Letters of Paul* (New Haven/London: Yale University Press, 1989) 36–37, 71,

162; Wright, *Climax*, 150–51, 245; Bruce W. Longenecker, *Eschatology and the Covenant: A Comparison of 4 Ezra and Romans 1–11* (JSNTSup 57; Sheffield: Sheffield Academic Press, 1991), 264; Peter Stuhlmacher, "Zur Interpretation von Römer 11:25–32," in *Probleme biblischer Theologie*, H. W. Wolff, ed. (Munich: Kaiser, 1971), 555–70; idem, *Paul's Letter to the Romans* (Louisville: Westminster/John Knox, 1994) 170–71; Rainer Riesner, *Die Frühzeit des Apostels Paulus* (Tübingen: Mohr [Siebeck], 1994) 213–27; Karl-Wilhelm Niebuhr, *Heidenapostel aus Israel* (Tübingen: Mohr [Siebeck], 1992) 76, 110–11; Halvor Moxnes, *Theology in Conflict* (Leiden: Brill, 1980) 95; James M. Scott, "Paul's Use of Deuteronomic Tradition," *JBL* 112 (1993) 645; Paula Fredriksen, "Paul and Augustine: Conversion Narratives, Orthodox Traditions, and the Retrospective Self," *JTS* 37 (1986) 29–30; idem, "Judaism, the Circumcision of Gentiles, and Apocalyptic Hope: Another Look at Galatians 1 and 2," *JTS* 42 (1991) 33; Charles H. H. Scobie, "Jesus or Paul? The Origin of the Universal Mission of the Christian Church," in P. Richardson and J. C. Hurd, eds., *From Jesus to Paul* (Waterloo, Ont: Wilfrid Laurier University Press, 1984) 51–52.

90. Lloyd Gaston, *Paul and the Torah* (Vancouver: University of British Columbia Press, 1987).

91. Fredriksen, "Judaism, the Circumcision of Gentiles, and Apocalyptic Hope," 532–64; Segal, *Paul the Convert*, e.g., 121, 204.

92. These quotations from Galatians 1 are used solely for stylistic convenience. I am well aware of the problems involved in using a convert's later conversion narratives as evidence for the nature of the conversion process itself; see Fredriksen, "Paul and Augustine," 3–34; and below, pp. 273–275.

93. The problem to be explained is not the mere existence of the mission itself. Paul was by no means the only Jewish Christian engaging in a mission to the Gentiles. Such a mission, undertaken on one basis or another, appears to have been a widespread phenomenon in the early Christian movement; cf. Raymond E. Brown, "Not Jewish Christianity and Gentile Christianity, but Types of Jewish/Gentile Christianity," *CBQ* 45 (1983) 74–79. The problem has to do with the basis for such a mission as Paul perceived it. That is, how does Paul's conviction about the salvation of the Gentiles fit in with, or arise out of, his other convictions about God, Christ, Israel, etc., as we now understand them?

## Chapter 2

1. For a thoughtful departure from the conventional wisdom on these writings, see Luke T. Johnson, *The Writings of the New Testament* (Philadelphia: Fortress, 1986) 367–72, 381–89.

2. In view of the confession in v. 9, κύριος (Lord) in v. 12 undoubtedly refers to Christ.

3. See §4.3 below.

4. The question of the interpretation of ἐν αὐτοῖς (in them) in v. 17 will come up for discussion below, pp. 217–219.

5. Albert Schweitzer, *The Mysticism of Paul the Apostle* (New York: Seabury, 1968 [1931]) 40.

6. See the standard surveys, and the bibliography cited therein: Albert Schweitzer, *Paul and His Interpreters* (London: A. & C. Black, 1950); E. Earle Ellis, *Paul and His Recent Interpreters* (Grand Rapids: Eerdmans, 1961); B. Ri-

gaux, *The Letters of St. Paul* (Chicago: Franciscan Herald Press, 1968). See also J. Christiaan Beker, *Paul the Apostle* (Philadelphia: Fortress, 1980) 13–15.

7. Schweitzer, *Mysticism*, 205–26.

8. Schweitzer's own explanation of Paul's mysticism in terms of Jewish eschatology is a good case in point. See also W. D. Davies, *Paul and Rabbinic Judaism* (London: SPCK, 1948).

9. See the discussion in Schweitzer, *Paul and His Interpreters*, 28–32.

10. See, e. g., C. H. Dodd, "The Mind of Paul," *BJRL* 17 (1933) 91–105, and 18 (1934) 69–110; Lucien Cerfaux, *The Christian in the Theology of St. Paul* (New York: Herder & Herder, 1967); Hans Hübner, *Law in Paul's Thought* (Edinburgh: T. & T. Clark, 1984).

11. Adolf Deissmann, *St. Paul: A Study in Social and Religious History* (London: Hodder & Stoughton, 1912); James S. Stewart, *A Man in Christ* (London: Hodder & Stoughton, 1935).

12. So Heikki Räisänen, *Paul and the Law* (Philadelphia: Fortress, 1986).

13. Beker, *Paul the Apostle;* E. P. Sanders, *Paul and Palestinian Judaism* (Philadelphia: Fortress, 1977), and *Paul, the Law, and the Jewish People* (Philadelphia: Fortress, 1983); Daniel Patte, *Paul's Faith and the Power of the Gospel* (Philadelphia: Fortress, 1983). In addition, my thinking has been stimulated by work being done in the SBL Pauline Theology Group, the firstfruits of which are now available in Jouette M. Bassler, ed., *Pauline Theology, Volume I* (Minneapolis: Fortress, 1991), David M. Hay, ed., *Pauline Theology, Volume II* (Minneapolis: Fortress, 1993), and David M. Hay and E. Elizabeth Johnson, eds., *Pauline Theology, Volume III* (Minneapolis: Fortress, 1995). See also R. David Kaylor, *Paul's Covenant Community: Jew and Gentile in Romans* (Atlanta: John Knox, 1988), who makes a similar distinction between convictions and theology (e.g., pp. iii, 1–8).

14. Schweitzer's treatment of Paul, for example, is much closer to that of Beker's, at least in formal terms, than the latter is prepared to acknowledge. That is, Schweitzer, too, can be described as seeking to identify a coherent core or "deep structure" (Christ mysticism, or being-in-Christ, eschatologically understood), which provides an interpretative framework for an array of surface symbols and concepts (e.g., in Christ, dying and rising with Christ, suffering, baptism, righteousness, etc.), and which in turn translates aspects of that deep structure for particular situations (justification by faith as a "fragment" of the underlying pattern used to defend the mission to the Gentiles).

15. This is observed by Richard B. Hays, *The Faith of Jesus Christ* (Chico, Calif.: Scholars Press, 1983) 194–95.

16. Cf. Beker, *Paul the Apostle*, 243.

17. Cf. Sanders, *Paul, the Law, and the Jewish People*, 151.

18. Despite assertions to the contrary; see Beker, *Paul the Apostle, 33–35,* 352–55.

19. Ibid., esp. 143–53.

20. Patte, *Paul's Faith*, xiii.

21. See Daniel Patte, *What is Structural Exegesis?* (Philadelphia: Fortress, 1976), esp. 21–25.

22. Patte, *Paul's Faith*, 199–200.

23. Ibid., 11–12.

24. Sanders, *Paul, the Law, and the Jewish People*, 147–48.

25. Sanders, *Paul and Palestinian Judaism*, 442.

26. Sanders, *Paul, the Law, and the Jewish People*, 5–6.

27. Several such lists appear, with slight variations in detail; see Sanders, *Paul and Palestinian Judaism*, 441–42; *Paul, the Law, and the Jewish People*, 5, 47.

28. Sanders, *Paul, the Law, and the Jewish People*, 10, 143.

29. Ibid., 4. The same observation has been made much earlier by O. Pfleiderer, who notes that Paul often gives "somewhat far-fetched and not always very forcible arguments" for convictions which "he has other and internal grounds for believing"; *Paulinism* (2 vols.; London: Williams & Norgate, 1891) 1:6.

30. The phrase is Beker's; e.g., *Paul the Apostle*, 352.

31. E.g., Paul's various treatments of the topic of the law are to be seen as "varying attempts to solve the same problem"; Sanders, *Paul, the Law, and the Jewish People*, 145.

32. Ibid., 152; see also 47, and Sanders, *Paul and Palestinian Judaism*, 475.

33. Sanders, *Paul, the Law, and the Jewish People*, 5 (emphasis mine).

34. Ibid., 143; cf. Heikki Räisänen, "Paul's Conversion and the Development of His View of the Law," *NTS* 33 (1987) 410; idem, *Paul and the Law*, 11–12.

35. Sanders, *Paul, the Law, and the Jewish People*, 199.

36. On Paul's theology as an *activity*, see Jouette M. Bassler, "Paul's Theology: Whence and Whither?" in *Pauline Theology*, 2:3–17, esp. 9–13.

37. The seminal work in this area has been done by Peter L. Berger; see *The Sacred Canopy* (Garden City, N.Y.: Doubleday, 1967), and, with Thomas Luckman, *The Social Construction of Reality* (Garden City, N.Y.: Doubleday, 1966).

38. See Richard B. Hays's use of Chomsky in "Crucified with Christ: A Synthesis of the Theology of 1 and 2 Thessalonians, Philemon, Philippians and Galatians," in *Pauline Theology*, 1:227–46. Hays's argument that Paul operates on the basis of a foundational narrative (*The Faith of Jesus Christ*) is also pertinent here.

39. For an application of Mary Douglas's theory to Paul, see Jerome H. Neyrey, *Paul, in Other Words* (Louisville: Westminster/John Knox, 1990).

40. The basic category of "social world" as Berger defines it is congruent in essential respects to Patte's "faith." For a stimulating introduction to the whole New Testament from a sociology of knowledge perspective, see Johnson, *The Writings of the New Testment*.

41. Thomas Kuhn, *The Structure of Scientific Revolutions* (2d ed.; Chicago: University of Chicago Press, 1970).

42. The social basis of scientific paradigms is even more to the fore in the postscript to the second edition (1970).

43. I recognize and endorse fully Kuhn's emphasis on the social basis of scientific knowledge—indeed, of all knowledge. Nevertheless, the perceptions, discoveries, and theoretical proposals of individuals have had a decisive role in scientific revolutions, as Kuhn himself makes clear.

44. For the application of Kuhn's insights to the study of (Paul's) conversion, see Beverly Roberts Gaventa, *From Darkness to Light: Aspects of Conversion in the New Testament* (Philadelphia: Fortress, 1986) 1–13; Carl Raschke, "Revelation and Conversion: A Semantic Appraisal," *ATR* 60 (1978), 420–36. See further §12.2 below.

45. To use Polanyi's terminology, the "paradigm" in the extended sense of the term is just an articulation of what was *tacitly* apprehended in the basic paradigm; see Michael Polanyi, *Personal Knowledge* (New York: Harper & Row, 1964).

46. See §12.2 below.

47. See Daniel Patte, *What Is Structural Exegesis?;* "Method for a Structural Exegesis of Didactic Discourses. Analysis of 1 Thessalonians," *Semeia* 26 (1983) 85–136; *Structural Exegesis for New Testament Critics* (Minneapolis: Fortress, 1990).

48. See Patte, "Method for a Structural Exegesis," 87–97. A similar approach is taken by Kraftchick, drawing on Stephen Toulmin's analysis of argumentative rhetoric; see Steven J. Kraftchick, "Seeking a More Fluid Model: A Response to Jouette M. Bassler," in *Pauline Theology,* 2:18–34. In Toulmin's analysis, "warrants" and "backings" pertain to those parts of an argument justifying the rhetorical move from agreed on facts (the "data") to a conclusion (the "claim"); see Toulmin, *The Uses of Argument* (Cambridge: Cambridge University Press, 1958).

49. Patte's summary of Paul's convictions is scarcely revolutionary. He concludes that Paul's "faith" consists of three components: (1) *charismatic* (Christians' awareness that they are in a right relationship with God stems from their immediate experience rather than through the mediation of tradition or institution); (2) *eschatological* ("the only absolute and permanent convictions are the ones which will be established for the believers at the end of time"; all others are partial, relative, incomplete, and subject to change); (3) *typological* (Christ's own experience provides the model or type for explaining the experience of Christians); see *Paul's Faith,* 232–41. While valuable insights can no doubt be derived from this reconstruction, it is a less satisfying description of Paul's basic convictions than those identified, for example, by Sanders, who uses more conventional exegetical methods.

50. See esp. Chaim Perelman and L. Olbrechts-Tyteca, *The New Rhetoric: A Treatise on Argumentation* (Notre Dame: University of Notre Dame Press, 1969); for the New Testament, see Burton L. Mack, *Rhetoric and the New Testament* (Minneapolis: Fortress, 1990).

51. Patte, *Paul's Faith,* 39–40.

## Chapter 3

1. See esp.: B. J. Bamberger, *Proselytism in the Talmudic Period* (New York: Ktav, 1968); John J. Collins, *Between Athens and Jerusalem* (New York: Crossroad, 1983); Shaye J. D. Cohen, "Crossing the Boundary and Becoming a Jew," *HTR* 82 (1989) 13–33, and *From the Maccabees to the Mishnah* (Philadelphia: Westminster, 1987) 41–59; Paula Fredriksen, "Judaism, the Circumcision of Gentiles, and Apocalyptic Hope: Another Look at Galatians 1 and 2," *JTS* 42 (1991) 532–64 (esp. 533–48); K. G. Kuhn, "προσήλυτος," *TDNT,* 6:727–44; Scot McKnight, *A Light among the Gentiles: Jewish Missionary Activity in the Second Temple Period* (Minneapolis: Fortress, 1991); David Novak, *The Image of the Non-Jew in Judaism: An Historical and Constructive Study of the Noahide Laws* (New York/Toronto: Edwin Mellen, 1983); Gary Porton, *Goyim: Gentiles and Israelites in Mishnah-Tosefta* (Atlanta: Scholars, 1988); E. P. Sanders, *Jesus and Judaism* (Philadelphia: Fortress, 1985) 213–18; Emil Schürer, *The History of the Jewish People in the Age of Jesus Christ* (3 vols.; Edinburgh: T. & T. Clark, 1973–87) III.1:150–76; Alan F. Segal, *Paul the Convert* (New Haven/London: Yale University Press, 1990) 79–114; Martin Goodman, *Mission and Conversion* (Oxford: Clarendon, 1994). Other studies will be indicated in the notes.

2. For a similar statement of procedure, see Fredriksen, "Judaism, the Circumcision of Gentiles, and Apocalyptic Hope," 534.

3. See, e.g., Cohen, "Crossing the Boundary."

4. See, e.g., McKnight, *A Light among the Gentiles;* Goodman, *Mission and Conversion;* and the discussion in Collins, *Between Athens and Jerusalem,* 8–10.

5. Note Cohen's comment to the effect that only the extreme Hellenists and the extreme nationalists had what might be called a consistent policy vis-à-vis the Gentiles; *From the Maccabees to the Mishnah,* 58.

6. Even more so than God, as Bruce Metzger notes in his introduction to 4 *Ezra;* see *OTP,* 1:521.

7. The only glimmers of hope are found in the statements about the blessing of the nations in 27.23 and 31.20, statements modeled on Genesis (e.g., 28:14); more typical is the statement that for all except those chosen by God "there is no hope in the land of the living" (22.22).

8. Curiously, the narrator can nevertheless blithely recount Joseph's marriage to an Egyptian—the "daughter of the priest of Heliopolis," no less—without a murmur of disapproval (40.10).

9. So Geza Vermes, *The Dead Sea Scrolls in English* (4th ed.; London: Penguin, 1995) 14.

10. 11QT 63.10–15 envisages the possibility of a Gentile woman captured in battle and taken as a wife; the passage prescribes a seven-year period during which she was restricted from handling pure things.

11. Given other differences in detail among the scrolls, there is no point in trying to harmonize CD 14.4–5 and 1QS 6.13–14; note, however, Burrows's suggestion that גרים ("resident alien, proselyte") in the former text refers to (Jewish) novices who had not yet completed their period of probation; Millar Burrows, *The Dead Sea Scrolls* (New York: Viking, 1955) 263.

12. *Ps.-Philo* 9.5; 18.13–14; 21.1; 30.1; 44.7; 4 *Bar* 8.1–12; cf. Ezra and Nehemiah.

13. E. P. Sanders, *Paul and Palestinian Judaism* (Philadelphia: Fortress, 1977) 409–28.

14. Of the writings mentioned here, only 2 *Bar.* contains any note of optimism; see discussions of 41.1–6 and 72.1–6 below (sections §3.2 and §3.5 respectively).

15. While Wisdom of Solomon belongs more properly with the Hellenistic Jewish literature treated below (§3.3), its mention of the grace period granted the Canaanites (12:10), despite the fact that "they were an accursed race from the beginning," represents a similar theodical concern.

16. E.g., *'Abod. Zar.* 2b; *Lam. Rab.* 111.1§1.

17. For the probability of a Hasmonaean dating for the book, see Carey A. Moore, *Judith* (Anchor Bible; Garden City, N.Y.: Doubleday, 1985) 67–70.

18. Occasionally in narrative texts, significant Gentiles are moved by events to recognize and praise the God of Israel, without any further attempt in the narrative to specify or develop the consequences of the change of heart. Second Maccabees has several such scenes: Heliodorus (3:35); Nicanor (8:36); Antiochus himself, whose deathbed prayers are not accepted (9:11-18); and Lysius (11:13). Cyrus plays a similar role in Bel and the Dragon (28, 41); see also the general references to the Gentiles in Bar 2:15, Sir 36:22 and 1 Macc 4:11. These scenes

function simply to vindicate Israel's self-understanding; there is no narrative interest in the characters or their status vis-à-vis Israel once this function has been carried out.

19. Cf. Cohen: "In pre-exilic times 'conversion' to Judaism did not yet exist because birth is immutable"; *From the Maccabees to the Mishnah,* 50.

20. See, e.g., Lawrence H. Schiffman, *Who Was a Jew?* (Hoboken, N.J.: Ktav, 1985) 15–16.

21. For the terminological development, see Kuhn, "προσήλυτος," 727–44. In the targums, *Onqelos* and *Pseudo-Jonathan* always follow the rabbinic halakah in its decisions as to whether גר in the MT refers to a proselyte or a resident alien, while *Neofiti* makes no differentiation; see M. Ohana, "Prosélytisme et Targum palestinienne: Données nouvelles pour la datation de Néofiti I," *Biblica* 55 (1974) 317–32.

22. Cohen, "Crossing the Boundary." See also McKnight, *A Light among the Gentiles,* 91–100.

23. See §3.3 below.

24. Neil J. McEleney, "Conversion, Circumcision and the Law," *NTS* 20 (1973–74) 319–41.

25. Josephus uses a wide array of descriptive phraseology; for details, see Kuhn, "προσήλυτος," 731–32.

26. See esp. *Ap.* 2.123, 210; *Ant.* 16.225; *War* 2.454, 463, 560; 7.45.

27. For a descriptive list of Jewish inscriptions referring to proselytes, see Pau Figueras, "Epigraphic Evidence for Proselytism in Ancient Judaism," *Immanuel* 24/25 (1990) 194–206. Of particular interest are the ossuaries found in Jerusalem, all of which are earlier than Bar Cochba, at the latest. See E. L. Sukenik, *Jüdische Gräber Jerusalems um Christi Geburt* (Jerusalem: 1931), esp. 13.

28. See esp. Segal, *Paul the Convert,* 74, 285–300, with the literature cited therein.

29. See *Virt.* 103, 108; *Spec. leg.* 1.52; *b. Yeb.* 47b; 62a; *b. Bek.* 47a; cf. *Ps.-Phoc.* 39. Neither rabbinic suspicion of the motives of would-be proselytes (see Kuhn, "προσήλυτος," 736) nor special halakic enactments concerning proselytes (see Schürer, *History,* 3:175–76) should be seen as undercutting the basic principle of equality.

30. John J. Collins, "A Symbol of Otherness: Circumcision and Salvation in the First Century," in J. Neusner and E. S. Frerichs, eds., *"To See Ourselves as Others See Us": Christians, Jews, "Others" in Late Antiquity* (Chico, Calif.: Scholars, 1985) 175.

31. The debate between R. Eliezer and R. Joshua over whether one who had been baptized but not circumcised (or vice versa) could be called a proselyte (*b. Yeb.* 46a) should be interpreted as having to do with the point in the process (i.e., a process necessarily involving both rituals) at which one can be said to be a proselyte, rather than as evidence for the position that one could become a full proselyte on the basis of one (or another) of these rituals alone.

32. Contra Schiffmann, *Who Was a Jew?* 31.

33. See McEleney, "Conversion, Circumcision and the Law"; Gary Gilbert, "The Making of a Jew: 'God-Fearer' or Convert in the Story of Izates," *USQR* 44 (1991) 299–313.

34. What the requirements were for women is not clear. In any case, the fact that women were more readily attracted as proselytes than men (e.g., *Ant.* 18.82;

20.34; *War* 2. 560) attests to the resoluteness with which Judaism insisted on circumcision for full membership.

35. Juvenal *Satire* 14.96; the Petronius fragment is cited by Menahem Stern, *Greek and Latin Authors on Jews and Judaism* (3 vols.; Jerusalem: Israel Academy of Sciences and Humanities, 1974–84) §3195.

36. Both Josephus (*Ant.* 11.285) and the LXX add the mention of circumcision to Esth 8:17.

37. Cohen, "Crossing the Boundary," 27.

38. McKnight, *A Light among the Gentiles*; Martin Goodman, "Jewish Proselytizing in the First Century," in Judith Lieu et al., eds., *The Jews among Pagans and Christians in the Roman Empire* (London/New York: Routledge, 1992) 53–78; idem, *Mission and Conversion*.

39. George Foot Moore, *Judaism in the First Centuries of the Christian Era* (3 vols.; Cambridge, Mass.: Harvard University Press, 1927–30) 1:324. On McKnight's approach, see the review by Steve Mason, *IOUDAIOS Review* 1.001 (July 1991).

40. Whether or not the verse reflects the attitude of Jesus, at least the author of the First Gospel could assume that this reference to aggressive proselytizing activity would make sense to his readers. Goodman's argument, that the text refers to attempts by Pharisees to make converts of other *Jews*, fails to convince; see *Mission and Conversion*, 69–74.

41. For similar patterns of attraction, see: Josephus *War* 7.45; *y. Ber.* 2.8; also the rabbinic tradition that the making of proselytes was the purpose of the diaspora (*b. Pesaḥ* 87b; cf. 2 *Bar.* 1.4).

42. See *Sib. Or.* 3.194–95, 580–85; Wis 18:4; *T. Levi* 14.4; 18.4; Philo *Abr.* 98; *Spec. leg.* 1.97; 2. 163–67; *Vit. Mos.* 1.149; Justin *Dial.* 121–22.

43. A similar perspective appears to be present in Acts 15:1 and Eph 2:11-12. This point will become important later; see §8.1.

44. *Q. Exod.* 2. 2. The translation is based on the Greek fragment. The full text is found only in Armenian.

45. See esp. McEleney, "Conversion, Circumcision and the Law"; Gilbert, "The Making of a Jew."

46. See John Nolland, "Uncircumcised Proselytes?" *JSJ* 12 (1981) 173–94; E. P. Sanders, "The Covenant as a Soteriological Category and the Nature of Salvation in Palestinian and Hellenistic Judaism," in R. Hamerton-Kelly and R. Scroggs, eds., *Jews, Greeks and Christians: Religious Cultures in Late Antiquity* (Leiden: Brill, 1976) 27–38; Cohen, "Crossing the Boundary," 21.

47. In the case of Philo, Harry A. Wolfson (*Philo* [2 vols.; Cambridge, Mass.: Harvard University Press, 1948] 2:369–74) and S. Belkin (*Philo and the Oral Law* [Cambridge, Mass.: Harvard University Press, 1940] 47) suggest a distinct category of "spiritual proselytes." In the case of Ananias, many interpret his statement as a reflection of a "righteous Gentile" or "God-fearing" approach; see the literature cited by Gilbert, "The Making of a Jew," 310 (n. 4).

48. Leon Festinger, *A Theory of Cognitive Dissonance* (Stanford, Calif.: Stanford University Press, 1957).

49. Since the publication of Victor Tcherikover's influential essay ("Jewish Apologetic Literature Reconsidered," *Eos* 48 [1956] 169–93), scholars have debated whether this literature was directed outwards, in the interests of changing Gentile attitudes, or inwards, with the aim of the self-preservation of a cultural

minority. The choice is probably an artificial one, especially from the perspective of cognitive dissonance theory, where proselytism is recognized as one of the means by which minority views are reinforced.

50. Esp. *Sibylline Oracles* 3, 5; *Epistle of Aristeas; Joseph and Aseneth; Pseudo-Phocylides; Testament of Abraham; Testaments of the Twelve Patriarchs.*

51. For the most part, the conversion of the nations in *Sib. Or.* 3 is envisioned as a future event; the material will thus come up again in a later section of this chapter (see §3.5).

52. Besides the temple sacrifices (575–79), the only hint of particularistic observance is found in the obscure reference to daybreak prayers and lustrations in 591–93.

53. *B. Yeb.* 46a. With most scholars, I understand the discussion in this passage as having to do with the point in the process (circumcision, immersion) at which one becomes a convert, rather than as evidence for proselytism without conversion. See, e.g., McKnight, *A Light among the Gentiles,* 81; but cf. McEleney, "Conversion, Circumcision and the Law," 331–32.

54. For this distinction, see Alan F. Segal, "Universalism in Judaism and Christianity," *Bulletin of the Canadian Society of Biblical Studies* 51 (1991–92) 20–35.

55. E. P. Sanders, "Defending the Indefensible," *JBL* 110 (1991) 467.

56. The term "righteous Gentile" appears in *Sifra* on Lev 18:5 (par. *b. Sanh.* 59a; *b. B. Qam.* 38a; *b. 'Abod. Zar.* 3a); see also *Midr. Prov.* 17.1.

57. See below, pp. 67–68.

58. As observed already (above, p. 55), as גר came more and more to refer to a full proselyte, rabbinic tradition began, as early as the Tannaitic period, to use גר תותב (*ger toshab*) of the sojourner or resident alien (e.g., *b. 'Abod. Zar.* 64b; *Sifra* Behar 110a; *b. Git.* 57b).

59. According to Gaston, the explicit use of the Noachian precepts as a standard for determining "righteousness" appears first in Maimonides (*Mishnah Torah, Melakhim* 8.11); see Lloyd Gaston, "Paul and the Torah," in Alan T. Davies, ed., *Antisemitism and the Foundations of Christianity* (New York/Toronto: Paulist, 1979) 56–57. Nevertheless, passages such as *b. 'Abod. Zar.* 64b suggest a link with the seven Noachian decrees even in the Tannaitic period.

60. See A. Thomas Kraabel, "The Disappearance of the 'God-Fearers,'" *Numen* 28 (1981) 113–26; and, with Robert S. MacLennan, "The God-Fearers—A Literary and Theological Invention," *BARev* 12, no. 5 (1986) 46–53.

61. See, e.g., Schürer, *History,* 3:150–76; Collins, *From Athens to Jerusalem,* 165–66; Segal, *Paul the Convert,* 93–96; McKnight, *A Light among the Gentiles,* 110–14; Louis H. Feldman, "The Omnipresence of the God-Fearers," *BARev* 12, no. 5 (1986) 58–63; Tessa Rajak, "The Jewish Community and Its Boundaries," in Judith Lieu et al., eds., *The Jews among Pagans and Christians in the Roman Empire* (London/New York: Routledge, 1992) 9–28.

62. Various actions of reverence and identification are attributed to Gentiles who at the same time are clearly not proselytes: adoption of Jewish customs (Josephus *Ap.* 1.166; 2.123, 279–82; *Ant.* 3.217, 318–19); worship at the Jerusalem temple (Josephus *War* 4.262, 324; 5.15–18; 2 *Bar.* 68.5–6; *Ep. Arist.* 37, 40; 2 Macc 3:35); "Judaizing" (*War* 2.463; 2 Macc 9:11–18; Bel 28); being partially incorporated into the Jewish community (*War* 7.45); revering God (*Ant.* 11.87; 14.110).

63. The most important reference here is Juvenal *Satires* 14.96, with its description of a father who reveres the sabbath, but whose son goes the whole route to become a proselyte. Other texts more generally describe Gentiles who observe Jewish customs (Dio Cassius 37.17.1; Seneca, quoted by Augustine, *City of God* §186); these may be proselytes, but are not explicitly identified as such.

64. Especially the Aphrodisias inscription, with its differentiation between Jews, proselytes, and "God-fearers" (θεοσεβής); see Robert F. Tannenbaum, "Jews and God-Fearers in the Holy City of Aphrodite," *BARev* 12, no. 5 (1986) 54–57; and, with Joyce M. Reynolds, *Jews and Godfearers at Aphrodisias* (Cambridge: Cambridge Philological Society, 1987).

65. Josephus also describes Gentiles who "fear God" (σέβειν τὸν θεὸν; *Ant.* 11.87; 14.110; 20.34). To be included here also is Josephus's rejection of the forcible circumcision of Gentiles who had taken refuge with Jews during the war with Rome, stating his belief "that every one should worship God (τὸν θεὸν εὐσεβεῖν) in accordance with the dictates of his own conscience" (*Life* 113).

66. See Cohen, "Crossing the Boundary."

67. See also *b. 'Abod. Zar.* 65a, where a *ger toshab* is expected to become circumcised within twelve months; if he does not, he is to be considered a "heretic among idolaters." For a similar contemporary understanding of the "righteous Gentiles" material, see J. R. Rosenbloom, *Conversion to Judaism: From the Biblical Period to the Present* (Cincinnati: Hebrew Union College Press, 1978) 51.

68. Sanders, "Defending the Indefensible," 467.

69. See esp. *t. 'Abod. Zar.* 8.4; also *b. 'Abod. Zar.* 64b; *b. Sanh.* 56a-b; *Midr. Gen.* 16.6; 24.5; 34.8; 98.9; *Pesiq. R. Kah.* 12.1. The most thorough study is that of Novak, *The Image of the Non-Jew.*

70. Gaston's contention—that prior to Maimonides the Noachian decrees had only to do with the (hypothetical) case of resident aliens ("Paul and the Torah," 56–57)—is surely incorrect. The only Tannaitic text to link the two is *b. 'Abod. Zar.* 64b; all other statements are very general in their reference.

71. On both of these, see Segal, "Universalism," 26–30.

72. See also J. P. Schulz, "Two Views of the Patriarchs: Noachides and Pre-Sinai Israelites," in M. A. Fishbane and P. R. Flohr, eds., *Texts and Responses* (Leiden: Brill, 1975) 43–59.

73. See John C. Hurd, *The Origin of 1 Corinthians* (London: SPCK, 1965) 250–53.

74. Louis Finkelstein, "Some Examples of Rabbinic Halaka," *JBL* 49 (1930) 20–42; cf. Novak, *The Image of the Non-Jew,* 3–35.

75. So McEleney, "Conversion, Circumcision and the Law," 323, 328; Gilbert, "The Making of a Jew."

76. Uncircumcised Israelites are referred to in, e.g., *m. Ned.* 3.11; *m. Yeb.* 8.1. Gemara commentary identifies these as people whose brothers died as a result of the operation; e.g. *b. Yeb.* 64b; *b. Hul.* 4a.

77. So Cohen, "Crossing the Boundary," 23; Lawrence H. Schiffman, "The Conversion of the Royal House of Adiabene in Josephus and Rabbinic Sources," in L. H. Feldman and G. Hata, eds., *Josephus, Judaism and Christianity* (Detroit: Wayne State University Press, 1987) 293–312.

78. See Schürer, *History,* 2:309–13.

79. See Elias J. Bickerman, "The Altars of the Gentiles," in *Studies in Jewish and Christian History. Part Two* (Leiden: Brill, 1980) 324–46; P. W. van der

Horst, "A New Altar of a Godfearer?" in *Hellenism — Judaism — Christianity: Essays on Their Interaction* (Kampen: Kok, 1994) 65–72.

80. While one needs to be on guard for Christian interpolations in *T. 12 Patr.*, there seems to be no reason to suspect this text.

81. Philo *Abr.* 98; *Spec. leg.* 2.163–67; *Vit. Mos.* 1.149; cf. *Jub.* 16.17–18.

82. This term goes back at least to Joachim Jeremias; see *Jesus' Promise to the Nations* (London: SCM, 1958) 55–62.

83. This point is discussed further below; see pp. 224–26.

84. See Sanders, *Jesus and Judaism*, 77–119.

85. Isa 24:23; 29:8; Joel 3:9-21; *Ps. Sol.* 17.24,32; *T. Mos.* 10.7; 4 *Ezra* 12.31-33; 13.37-38; 2 *Bar.* 39.7–40.2; etc.

86. Isa 2:2-4/Mic 4:1-3; Isa 60:1-22; Jer 31:23,38-40; Ezek 17:22-24; 40:1—48:35; Zech 8:1-23; 14:10-11,20-21; *1 Enoch* 90.28-29; *Jub.* 1.15–17; *1 Bar* 5:1–4; *2 Bar.* 4.2–4; etc. See also the fourteenth and seventeenth prayers of the *Shemoneh 'Esreh*.

87. Isa 35; Jer 31:1-25; Ezek 20:33-44; Zech 8:7-8,20-23; *1 Bar* 4:36–37; 5:5–9; *Ps. Sol.* 11.1–3; 17.50; *Jub.* 1.15–17; 4 *Ezra* 13.39-47; *Apoc. Abr.* 31.1; *Tg. Isa.* 4:3; 6:13; *Tg. Jer.* 31:23; etc. See also the tenth prayer of the *Shemoneh 'Esreh*.

88. Isa 25:6-10a; 30:23; 35:5-6; 61:6; Jer 31:12; Joel 2:26; Amos 9:13-15; *1 Enoch* 90.32-38; *Ps. Sol.* 17.28–31; *Sib. Or.* 3.702-9, 741-60; etc.

89. Isa 24:23; 52:7; Ezek 17:22-24; 20:33,40; 34:11-16,23-31; 43:7; Mic 4:6-7; 5:2-4; Zech 14:8-11; *Jub.* 1.28; *Ps. Sol.* 17.23–51; *2 Bar.* 40.3; 73.1; *T. Mos.* 10.1; etc.

90. *Jub.* 15.26; 4 *Ezra* 12.33; 13.38; *2 Bar.* 40.1; *Apoc. Abr.* 31.2; 1QM; *T. Mos.* 10.10; etc.

91. Isa 18:7; 60:1-22; 66:18-21; Hag 2:21-22; *Ps. Sol.* 17.30–31; *Jub.* 32.19; *Tg. Isa* 25:6-10; etc.

92. Isa 2:2-4/Mic 4:1-3; Isa 25:6-10a; 56:6-8; Zech 8:20-23.

93. There is no real justification for the opinion, expressed by Jeremias (*Jesus' Promise*, 61–62), W. D. Davies (*Paul and Rabbinic Judaism* [London: SPCK, 1948] 61–62), Johannes Munck (*Paul and the Salvation of Mankind* [London: SCM, 1959] 258–59), and others that this expectation had fallen away by the first century C.E. Sanders's criticism of Jeremias, while overzealous, is solidly grounded; see "Defending the Indefensible," esp. 464–68.

94. Other texts are sometimes included in this category: (1) Klausner has argued such a case for *Ps. Sol.* 17.22–34 (J. Klausner, *The Messianic Ideal in Israel* [London: George Allen & Unwin, 1956] 321), but a subjugationist reading is more likely. (2) R. H. Charles (*The Book of Enoch* [2d ed.; Oxford: Clarendon, 1912] 272) and Sanders (*Paul and Palestinian Judaism,* 359) see a reference to the salvation of the Gentiles in *1 Enoch* 108.11–12, but the reference is too vague to be included here. (3) The *Similitudes of Enoch* (chaps. 37–71) contain a passage (50.1–5) that describes the final redemption, where "the others," seeing the destruction of the sinners and the vindication of the righteous, "repent and forsake the deeds of their hands," finding salvation in the name of the Lord of Spirits. Since there is as yet no evidence confirming the pre-Christian existence of this work, it is probably not to be included here. (4) In view of the unrelentingly negative view of the Gentiles in *Jubilees*, *Jub.* 31.20 should be seen merely as a reflection of biblical phraseology (Gen 12:3). (5) *Sib. Or.* 5.493–500 is similar in some ways to the relevant passages in *Sib. Or.* 3, but the temple to which the Gentiles

come is in Egypt (Leontopolis?) and is destroyed before the final judgment. (6) If it were found in a different context, the statement in 4 *Ezra* 6.26 might be included. But in view of the absence of any sign of hope for the Gentiles in 4 *Ezra*, it is more likely that only Israelites are included among the "earth's inhabitants" who remain after the final judgment and whose hearts are changed. (7) A stronger case might be made for 4 *Ezra* 13.13, which is probably a preexisting apocalypse taken over by the author. The distinction between the "peaceable multitude" and the "many people," together with the fact that some of the latter "were bringing others as offerings" (cf. Isa 66:20), could be taken to suggest that, despite the absence of any explicit indication, Gentiles are nevertheless in view.

95. In 89:50 the "house" seems to be Jerusalem and the "tower" the temple; so Charles, *The Book of Enoch*, 198. In 89:36, however, the "house" is the tabernacle, the cultic center of worship.

96. See A. F. J. Klijn, "2 Baruch," *OTP*, 1:617–18; R. H. Charles, "2 Baruch," *APOT*, 2:474–76.

97. So, e.g., S. Mowinckel, *He That Cometh* (Oxford: Blackwell, 1956) 316; Sanders, "The Covenant as a Soteriological Category," 18.

98. *T. Jos.* 19.11 and *T. Benj.* 3.8, 11.2–3 are part of clearly identifiable Christian interpolations. In other texts the reference to the nations is brief and easily excised from the text (*T. Sim.* 6.5; 7.2; *T. Levi* 2.11; 4.4; 8.14; *T. Jud.* 22.2; *T. Dan* 6.7; *T. Ash.* 7.3; *T. Benj.* 9.2); here allowance has to be made for at least the possibility of Christian interpolation. I accept the position that except for such interpolations the *Testaments* reflect a Jewish viewpoint; for the argument that they are thoroughly Christian in their present form, see H. W. Hollander and M. de Jonge, *The Testaments of the Twelve Patriarchs* (Leiden: Brill, 1985).

99. So Wolfson, *Philo*, 2:415–417.

100. So, for example, P. Volz, *Die Eschatologie der jüdischen Gemeinde im neutestamentlichen Zeitalter* (Tübingen: Mohr [Siebeck], 1934) 356–59; Mowinckel, *He That Cometh*, 314; George W. E. Nickelsburg, *Jewish Literature between the Bible and the Mishnah* (Philadelphia: Fortress, 1981), 33. Lamentably, this tendency has been carried over into the NRSV, which renders Tob 14:6 as "the nations . . . will all be converted" (rendering ἐπιστρέψουσιν ["they will turn"]).

101. See E. P. Sanders, *Paul, the Law, and the Jewish People* (Philadelphia: Fortress, 1983) 18–19; idem, *Jesus and Judaism*, 221; Christopher Rowland, *Christian Origins* (Minneapolis: Augsburg, 1985) 218–19; Paula Fredriksen, *From Jesus to Christ* (New Haven: Yale University Press, 1988) 150; idem, "Judaism, the Circumcision of Gentiles and Apocalyptic Hope," 546–48.

102. "Proselytes or 'Righteous Gentiles'? The Status of Gentiles in Eschatological Pilgrimage Patterns of Thought," *JSP* 7 (1990) 3–27.

103. On this point, see Porton's discussion of the Gentiles in the Mishnah and Tosefta; *Goyim: Gentiles and Israelites in Mishnah-Tosefta.*

104. On this general point as it pertains to Paul, see Wayne A. Meeks, *The First Urban Christians* (New Haven/London: Yale University Press, 1983) 33.

105. See my "The 'Curse of the Law' and the Inclusion of the Gentiles: Galatians 3.13-14," *NTS* 32 (1986) 94–112.

## Chapter 4

1. Note the emphasis on monotheism in recent works on Paul; see E. P. Sanders, *Paul* (Past Masters; Oxford/New York: Oxford University Press, 1991) chap. 5; N. T. Wright, *The Climax of the Covenant* (Minneapolis: Fortress, 1991) 1.

2. See James D. G. Dunn, *Romans* (2 vols.; Waco, Tex.: Word, 1988) 1:189.

3. See C. E. B. Cranfield, *A Critical and Exegetical Commentary on the Epistle to the Romans* (2 vols.; ICC; Edinburgh: T. & T. Clark, 1975, 1979) 1:222.

4. With most commentators, I see the shift in prepositions in v. 30 (from ἐκ ["from"] to διὰ ["through"]) as a stylistic variation rather than a distinction in substance.

5. Nils A. Dahl, "The One God of Jews and Gentiles (Romans 3:29-30)," in *Studies in Paul* (Minneapolis: Augsburg, 1977) 178–91.

6. "I am God over all who enter the world, but my name have I associated only with you; I have not called myself the God of the nations of the world, but the God of Israel" (*Exod. Rab.* 29); see Cranfield, *Romans*, 1:222; Ernst Käsemann, *Commentary on Romans* (Grand Rapids: Eerdmans, 1980) 103. The text is cited for similar purposes by Charles H. Giblin, "Three Monotheistic Texts in Paul," *CBQ* 37 (1975) 544.

7. Howard argues that Paul considered the position of the Judaizers as tantamount to polytheism, in that it implied that God was not universal, but merely the local deity of an ethnic cult; George Howard, *Paul: Crisis in Galatia* (Cambridge: Cambridge University Press, 1979) 78. The argument is curious, with no solid support in either Jewish monotheistic self-understanding or in Paul himself.

8. Note Halvor Moxnes, *Theology in Conflict: Studies in Paul's Understanding of God in Romans* (Leiden: Brill, 1980) 40–41. Cf. Sanders, who notes that prior to his conversion Paul, as a monotheist, would have given full assent to vv. 29-30a, but would by no means have accepted v. 30b as a necessary corollary; while Paul can use God's oneness as an *argument* for the Gentiles, it by no means reflects his central *conviction* on the matter (E. P. Sanders, *Paul, the Law, and the Jewish People* [Philadelphia: Fortress, 1983] 5).

9. John A. Ziesler, *Paul's Letter to the Romans* (London: SCM/Philadelphia: TPI, 1989) 118.

10. I am not saying that Ziesler would view Paul in this way; the point is, rather, that a more precise understanding of the range of Jewish "patterns of universalism" available both requires and makes possible a more precise construal of the unexpressed links in the argument.

11. A syllogism with a minor premise omitted; see, e.g., G. Walter Hansen, *Abraham in Galatians* (Sheffield: Sheffield Academic Press, 1989) 88–89.

12. See Rom 2:4; 7:1; 1 Cor 1:13; 6:9, 19; 9:6, 7; 10:22; 14:36.

13. John Calvin, *The Epistles of Paul to the Romans and to the Thessalonians* (London: Oliver & Boyd, 1961), on v. 28. While coming at the text from a Roman Catholic perspective, Giblin nevertheless sees Paul's main purpose in vv. 27-31 in similar terms, viz., the elimination of boasting; see "Three Monotheistic Texts," 545.

14. Note that Luther in his commentary on Romans skips over vv. 29-30 without comment. Describing it as a "second proposition," Calvin treats it as subordinate to vv. 27-28.

15. On this point, see George Howard, "Romans 3:21-31 and the Inclusion of the Gentiles," *HTR* 63 (1970) 223–33; Sanders, *Paul, the Law, and the Jewish People*, 33.

16. Wright, *Climax*, 168–72. He has been followed in his reading by Daniel Boyarin, "Was Paul an 'Anti-Semite'? A Reading of Galatians 3–4," *USQR* 47 (1993) 55.

17. Without insisting on the point, Wright suggests that "mediator" is the complement of "is," ὁ δὲ being the subject, so that "one" is anarthrous, to conform to the anarthrous state of "mediator"; ibid., 170. The verse would then read: "Now he [the mediator referred to in the previous verse] is not [the] mediator of [the] single family."

18. Ibid., 171.

19. As Wright has observed (see n. 17 above), ὁ δὲ could function by itself as the subject of ἔστιν ("is"). For the demonstrative use of the article referring back to a noun in an oblique case, see A. T. Robertson, *A Grammar of the Greek New Testament* (New York: Hodder & Stoughton, 1914) 695.

20. Hurd has argued convincingly both that Paul is quoting from the Corinthians' letter and that this Corinthian slogan derives ultimately from the initial preaching of Paul himself; see John C. Hurd, *The Origin of 1 Corinthians* (London: SPCK, 1965) 67–69, 120–22, 278.

21. See my discussion of this issue in "'The Gospel that I Proclaim among the Gentiles' (Gal 2.2): Universalistic or Israel-Centred?" in L. Ann Jervis and Peter Richardson, eds., *Gospel in Paul* (Sheffield: Sheffield Academic Press, 1994) 166–93.

22. Since in v. 6 ἡμῖν ("for us") is linked with both "one God" and "one Lord Jesus Christ," ἡμεῖς ("we [exist]") refers to believers rather than to humankind in general.

23. Explicit statements can be found in Deut 10:17; 2 Chron 19:7; Sir 35:15–16; *Jub.* 5.16; 21.4; 30.16; 33.18; *Ps. Sol.* 2.18; *1 Enoch* 63.8; *Ps.-Philo* 20.4; *2 Bar.* 13.8; 44.4.

24. Jouette M. Bassler, *Divine Impartiality: Paul and a Theological Axiom* (Chico, Calif.: Scholars, 1982) 3.

25. For references to the history of interpretation, see Klyne R. Snodgrass, "Justification by Grace—to the Doers: An Analysis of the Place of Romans 2 in the Theology of Paul," *NTS* 32 (1986) 72–93.

26. For lists of these, with references, see Snodgrass, "Justification by Grace," 73; Cranfield, *Romans*, 1:151, who lists no fewer than ten; Sanders, *Paul, the Law, and the Jewish People*, 125–26; Heikki Räisänen, *Paul and the Law* (Philadelphia: Fortress, 1986) 103–6.

27. So Snodgrass, "Justification by Grace," who adds the qualification "on the basis of the amount of light received" (e.g., p. 82), thus including here those counted righteous before Christ.

28. So, e.g., Räisänen, *Paul and the Law*, 101–9; Sanders, *Paul, the Law, and the Jewish People*, 123–32, who discusses Rom 2 in an appendix, treating it as a collection of diaspora homiletical material, taken over by Paul but not fully assimilated; and J. C. O'Neill, *Paul's Letter to the Romans* (Harmondsworth: Penguin Books, 1975) 40–42, who argues that the whole of 1:18—2:29 is un-Pauline and inserted by a later editor.

29. *Divine Impartiality*, 145; see the whole discussion on 141–45.

30. See, e.g., Räisänen, *Paul the the Law*, 104.

31. See E. Lohse, "πρόσωπον," *TDNT*, 6·779–80.

32. Sir 35:15–16; *Jub.* 5.16; 21.4; 30.16; 33.18; *2 Bar.* 44.4; cf. *T. Job* 43.13.

33. Bassler, *Divine Impartiality*, 44.

34. Ibid., 186.

35. Cf. Bassler, *Divine Impartiality*, 143, 169.

36. Ibid., 186. Boyarin moves in the same direction in his reading of 2:28-29 as exhibiting "an allegory that dissolves those [Jewish] essences and meanings entirely"; see Daniel Boyarin, *A Radical Jew* (Berkeley/Los Angeles/London: University of California Press, 1994) 94–95. See also Dunn, *Romans*, 1:89, 93.

37. And often are; see, e.g., Dunn, *Romans*, 1:93. For rejections of such a reading see Richard B. Hays, *Echoes of Scripture in the Letters of Paul* (New Haven/London: Yale University Press, 1989), 44–47; R. David Kaylor, *Paul's Covenant Community* (Atanta: John Knox, 1988) 18, 26–27.

38. H. Cremer, *Die paulinische Rechtfertigungslehre im Zusammenhänge ihrer geschichtlichen Voraussetzungen* (2nd ed.; Gütersloh: Bertelsmann, 1900); see also John A. Ziesler, *The Meaning of Righteousness in Paul* (Cambridge: Cambridge University Press, 1972).

39. Calvin, *Romans*, on 1:17.

40. Ibid.

41. Ernst Käsemann, "'The Righteousness of God' in Paul," in *New Testament Questions of Today* (London: SCM, 1969) 168–82; for a survey of subsequent discussion, see Manfred T. Brauch, "Perspectives on 'God's Righteousness' in Recent German Discussion," in E. P. Sanders, *Paul and Palestinian Judaism* (Philadelphia: Fortress, 1977) 523–42.

42. E.g., Ps 40:10; 51:14 98:2; Isa 46:13; 62:1; see further, Arland J. Hultgren, *Paul's Gospel and Mission* (Philadelphia: Fortress, 1985) 12–39.

43. Käsemann, "Righteousness of God," 177.

44. Gentiles who turn to God in the end times are said to be righteous (e.g., Tob 14:7); and the messianic "shoot" is described as the one through whom "will arise the rod of righteousness for the nations, to judge and to save all that call on the Lord" (*T. Jud.* 24.6); but the two concepts approach no more closely than this.

45. Cf. *Sib. Or.* 3.710ff.: "And then all islands and cities will say, 'How much the Immortal loves those men! . . . Come, let us all fall on the ground and entreat the immortal king . . .'"

46. Käsemann, "Righteousness of God," 178.

47. Ibid., 179; this line of thought is developed further in "Paul and Israel," *New Testament Questions of Today*, 183–87.

48. For criticisms of Käsemann on this score, see Wright, *Climax*, esp. 18–40; Sam K. Williams, "The 'Righteousness of God' in Romans," *JBL* 99 (1980) 241–90.

49. Hays describes Rom 15:7-13 as a *peroratio*, "a summation of the letter's themes" (*Echoes of Scripture*, 70); see also Dunn, *Romans*, 2:844–45; Williams, "Righteousness of God," 285; Wright, *Climax*, 235; Lloyd Gaston, "For All the Believers: The Inclusion of the Gentiles as the Ultimate Goal of the Torah in Romans," in *Paul and the Torah* (Vancouver: University of British Columbia Press, 1987) 133.

50. See Williams, "Righteousness of God," 268, together with the references cited there.

51. "God's ἀλήθεια, i.e., his covenant faithfulness as in 3:4" (*Romans*, 385).

52. Ibid., 386.

53. As is generally agreed, the abstract noun περιτομή ("circumcision") refers collectively to the circumcised. Williams is surely incorrect in reading its genitive

form as a genitive of origin—a "servant from Israel" ("Righteousness of God," 286–87; followed by Gaston, "For All the Believers," 133–34). Everywhere else in Paul διάκονος ("servant"; δοῦλος ["slave"] too, for that matter) followed by the genitive has an objective sense. Further, in his reading, the reference to Christ as a "servant" is gratuitous and disconnected: Christ became a servant from Israel—a servant of whom? for what? If this was Paul's intent, he could have said simply that Christ came "from the circumcised." Clearly, Christ's role as a servant to the Jewish people is in view here.

54. For a thorough presentation of the possible ways of construing the passage, see Cranfield, *Romans*, 2:742–44.

55. Käsemann, *Romans*, 384. Bromiley's translation is an accurate reflection of the original; see *An die Römer* (3d ed.; Tübingen: Mohr [Siebeck], 1974) 371.

56. Williams, "Righteousness of God," esp. 285–89. A similar position is argued by Wright, *Climax*, though Rom 15:8-9 is mentioned only in passing (see esp. 234–35; also 35–36, 142–44, 150, 155, 163); see also Howard, "Romans 3:21-31," 230–31.

57. With a growing number of Pauline scholars, I understand πίστις Χριστοῦ ("faith of Christ") in Rom 3:22 and related texts as a subjective genitive—Christ's faithfulness, rather than the believer's faith in Christ. Nothing in the present discussion, though, hinges on this reading. For a thorough airing of both sides of the debate, see the articles by Richard B. Hays ("ΠΙΣΤΙΣ and Pauline Christology: What Is at Stake?") and James D. G. Dunn ("Once More, ΠΙΣΤΙΣ ΧΡΙΣΤΟΥ") in Eugene H. Lovering, ed., *SBL Seminar Papers* (Atlanta: Scholars Press, 1991) 714–29, 730–44.

58. See Dunn, *Romans*, 2:848.

59. Because Paul can describe scripture as "the oracles of God" (Rom 3:2), reference to his use of scripture is not out of place in a chapter on "God."

60. For a survey of recent study, see Hays, *Echoes of Scripture*, 5–14. Hays's work represents a major contribution in its own right, and will come into the discussion in significant ways in subsequent chapters.

61. Cf. the similar προ- ("before") compound (προεπηγγείλατο ["promised beforehand"]) in Rom 1:2.

62. On the syntax of vv. 8-9, see the discussion in §4.3 above.

63. In a closely related fifth passage (Rom 10:19), he cites a text (Deut 32:21) which, while it does refer to some (unspecified) nation, can hardly be seen in its original context as a promise of Gentile salvation.

64. Lucien Cerfaux, *The Christian in the Theology of St. Paul* (New York: Herder & Herder, 1967) 68, n. 1.

65. This will come up for full discussion below (§5.1).

66. As noted by Wolfhart Pannenberg, *Jesus—God and Man* (Philadelphia: Westminster, 1968) 71–72; and Ernest Best, "The Revelation to Evangelize the Gentiles," *JTS* 35 (1984) 20–21. Best sees the citation of Isa 11:10 in Rom 15:12 as an exception; but see the discussion below (§7.1). Wright sees Isa 2:3 reflected in the shift from ἕνεκεν Σιὼν ("for the sake of Zion") to ἐκ Σιὼν ("out of Zion") in the citation of Isa 59:20 in Rom 11:26 (*Climax*, 250). But Ps 14:7 and 53:6 are much more likely as sources for the expression; nothing in Rom 11:25-26 parallels Isa 2:2-3, where God's word goes out from Zion to the Gentiles.

67. In Gal 1:15 Paul echoes the language of Isa 49:1 in describing his call to proclaim Christ among the Gentiles; see the discussion in chap. 9 below.

68. On the apocalyptic background of μυστήριον ("mystery") in Daniel and elsewhere, see, e.g., G. Bornkamm, *TDNT*, 4:813–20.

69. Paul's usage of the term is not restricted to the inclusion of the Gentiles; it appears elsewhere with reference to the gospel in general or to other specific aspects of it (1 Cor 2:1, 7; 4:1; 13:2; 14:2; 15:51; 2 Thess 2:7).

70. See the full discussion in Cranfield, *Romans*, 1:1–11.

71. Taking εἰς πάντα τὰ ἔθνη ("for all the Gentiles") with the preceding phrase; so Dunn, *Romans*, 2:916; Cranfield, *Romans*, 2:812.

72. Bowers has made the interesting suggestion that οἷς ("to whom") in v. 27 has been attracted to the case of its antecedent ποῖς ἁγίοις ("to the saints"). It should really be read as an accusative, functioning as the subject of γνωρίσαι ("to make known"). Arguing in addition that τοῖς ἁγίοις ("to the saints") refers not to Christians in general but to the primitive Jewish community, he renders the verse: ". . . to his saints, whom God wished to make known among the Gentiles the wealth of the glory of this mystery" (see the discussion in Peter T. O'Brien, *Colossians, Philemon* [Waco, Tex.: Word, 1982] 85). Intriguing though it may be, this suggestion, while not impossible, is probably disconfirmed by the previous references to "saints" in 1:2, 4, where Gentiles are clearly in view.

73. On "pesher" interpretation, see, e.g., Dunn, *Romans*, 2:678; F. F. Bruce, *Biblical Exegesis in the Qumran Texts* (London: Tyndale, 1960).

74. He does cite scripture in Rom 11:26, but here his concern is with the final redemption of Israel, not the salvation of the Gentiles.

75. By "predication" I mean the various statements asserted, assumed, or agreed to in the course of an argument; see above, p. 48.

# Chapter 5

1. By "outset" I do not necessarily mean that such "generic universalism" was part of Paul's convictional world prior to Damascus. Our analysis in this part of the book has to do with the structure of Paul's *Christian* convictions. "Outset" then is used more with reference to a logical sequence than to a temporal one. The temporal question (to be the focus of the final part of the book) is a separable one: if Paul's Christian convictions rest on such a foundation of "generic universalism," this might be the result of his Damascus experience (so, e.g., Bultmann) rather than of an earlier way of construing the world.

2. John Calvin, *The Epistles of Paul to the Romans and to the Thessalonians* (London: Oliver & Boyd, 1961), on 3:28 and 29.

3. Rudolf Bultmann, *Theology of the New Testament* (2 vols.; London: SCM, 1952) 1:267, 264; emphasis in the original.

4. For a recent and penetrating analysis, see Stephen Westerholm, *Israel's Law and the Church's Faith* (Grand Rapids: Eerdmans, 1988) 70–75.

5. Bultmann, *Theology*, 1:187; see also "Paul," in *Existence and Faith* (Cleveland/New York: Meridian Books, 1960) 145.

6. In this diagram and all those to follow, the "convictional logic" moves from left to right. That is, the statement in the leftmost box represents a more fundamental conviction, from which those to the right have been derived. The conviction entering the sequence vertically from above is independent of those to the left of the point of entry, but interacting with them to produce the derivative convictions to the right.

7. Bultmann, "Paul," 113.

8. E. P. Sanders, *Paul and Palestinian Judaism* (Philadelphia: Fortress, 1977). Cranfield's position—that Paul accuses his Jewish opponents of misunderstanding the law, treating it as a legalistic system based on works rather than as something to be approached in faith—will be discussed below.

9. On this point, see also Lapide's comment on pp. 37–38 of Pinchas Lapide and Peter Stuhlmacher, *Paul: Rabbi and Apostle* (Minneapolis: Augsburg, 1984).

10. Schoeps, in his perceptive and generally sympathetic treatment of Paul, comes to the conclusion nevertheless that Paul did misrepresent Judaism at this point, a fact that he attributes to Paul's upbringing within (an inferior) Hellenistic Judaism; see Hans-Joachim Schoeps, *Paul* (Philadelphia: Westminster, 1961), esp. 173.

11. Albert Schweitzer, *The Mysticism of Paul the Apostle* (New York: Seabury, 1968 [1931]) 220–25, 294–95.

12. 2 Cor 9:8; also 1 Cor 3:11-15; 1 Thess 1:3; Col 1:10; cf. Eph 2:10.

13. Rom 5:3; 15:17; 2 Cor 9:3; 10:15-17; 11:16—12:10.

14. He "would rather die" than be deprived of this "ground for boasting" (1 Cor 9:15).

15. Bultmann, *Theology*, 1:242.

16. For another criticism of Bultmann's use of 1 Cor 1:29, see Heikki Räisänen, *Paul and the Law* (Philadelphia: Fortress, 1986) 172–74.

17. See James D. G. Dunn, "The New Perspective on Paul," *BJRL* 65 (1983) 112–13; BDF §376.

18. The most recent and thorough airing of the question can be found in the articles by Richard B. Hays ("ΠΙΣΤΙΣ and Pauline Theology: What Is at Stake?") and James D. G. Dunn ("Once More, ΠΙΣΤΙΣ ΧΡΙΣΤΟΥ"), both found in E. H. Lovering, ed., *1991 SBL Seminar Papers* (Atlanta: Scholars, 1991) 714–29, 730–44.

19. If ἐὰν μή is taken in its usual sense ("except"), v. 16 can be read in terms of a rhetorical strategy that begins with a statement acceptable to Jewish Christians ("we believe that a person is not justified by works of law except through faith in/of Christ"), but then shifts to a stronger antithesis. Cf. Dunn, who sees Paul as pushing "what began as a qualification on covenantal nomism into an outright antithesis" ("New Perspective," 113).

20. The second ὅτι is causal, i.e., "because."

21. I will leave until later the question of the identity of the group referred to by ἡμᾶς ("us") in v. 13: does it refer only to Jewish Christians, or does it include Gentiles as well? See §7.1 below.

22. Cf. Bultmann, *Theology*, 1:267.

23. Hans Dieter Betz, *Galatians* (Philadelphia: Fortress, 1979) 14–25, 113–27.

24. δικαιόω (to justify: vv. 16 [3x], 17); δικαιοσύνη (righteousness: v. 21); πίστις (faith: vv. 16 [2x], 20); πιστεύειν (to believe: v. 16).

25. Most commentators take εἰς Χριστόν (to Christ; v. 24) in a temporal sense; see, e.g., Heinrich Schlier, *Der Brief an die Galater* (Göttingen: Vandenhoeck & Ruprecht, 1965) 170; Betz, *Galatians,* 178; Richard N. Longenecker, *Galatians* (Waco, Tex.: Word, 1990) 148–49. Such a reading seems to be required by the temporal sense of εἰς ("to") in the preceding verse.

26. Richard B. Hays, *The Faith of Jesus Christ* (Chico, Calif.: Scholars, 1983) 200–206, 231.

27. The οἱ ἐκ (those of) construction appears elsewhere to designate members of a group, the group being identified by the object of the preposition; e.g., Israel (Rom 9:6); the household of Caesar (Phil 4:22); "the circumcision" (Gal 2:12).

28. E.g., 3:22, where the participial construction τοῖς πιστεύουσιν (those who believe) is used; see also 2:15.

29. Longenecker translates γινώσκετε ἄρα ὅτι as "you know, then, that," seeing it as a disclosure formula, serving "to remind readers of what is known" (*Galatians*, 114; also G. Walter Hansen, *Abraham in Galatians* [Sheffield: Sheffield Academic Press, 1989] 31, 44–47). But this is unlikely. Certainly γινώσκειν ὅτι can function this way (Rom 6:2; 2 Cor 8:9). But in addition to the fact that οἶδα (know) seems to be preferred (some three dozen occurrences, against only two for γινώσκειν), the presence of ἄρα (then), usually inferential and never found in a disclosure formula, suggests strongly that in v. 7 Paul is drawing out an inference from the passage quoted in v. 6 (with γινώσκετε as imperative), rather than reminding the Galatians of something they already knew (with γινώσκετε as indicative); so Betz, *Galatians*, 141.

30. "What the Galatians are asked to recognize is not obvious, but is the result of the following argument here anticipated"; Betz, *Galatians*, 141. See also Longenecker, *Galatians*, 108.

31. J. Christiaan Beker, *Paul the Apostle* (Philadelphia: Fortress, 1980) 49–52.

32. A common tendency; see Luther's comments on Gal 3:6 for another striking example.

33. *The Faith of Jesus Christ*, esp. 193–235. See also my earlier treatment of Gal 3 in "The 'Curse of the Law' and the Inclusion of the Gentiles: Galatians 3.13-14," *NTS* 32 (1986), esp. 100–102.

34. See esp. Hansen, *Abraham in Galatians;* also Schlier, *Galater*, 123–24; Robert Jewett, "The Agitators and the Galatian Congregation," *NTS* 17 (1970–71) 206–7. See also my discussion of the various approaches to the Galatian situation in "'The Gospel that I Proclaim among the Gentiles' (Gal. 2.2): Universalistic or Israel-Centred?" in L. Ann Jervis and Peter Richardson, *Gospel in Paul* (Sheffield: Sheffield Academic Press, 1994) 166–93.

35. On this point, see Dunn, "New Perspective," 104–5.

36. On Paul's choice of OT texts, see E. P. Sanders, *Paul, the Law and the Jewish People* (Philadelphia: Fortress, 1983) 21.

37. James D. G. Dunn, "Works of the Law and the Curse of the Law (Galatians 3:10-14)," *NTS* 31 (1985) 523–42. See also Räisänen, *Paul and the Law*, 171, 176–77; Alan F. Segal, *Paul the Convert* (New Haven/London: Yale University Press, 1990) 124; Daniel Boyarin, "Was Paul an 'Anti-Semite'? A Reading of Galatians 3–4," *USQR* 47 (1993) 47–48.

38. The logic implied by this "therefore" will of course have to be explored in detail. See §6.2 below.

39. For righteousness as a membership term, see §4.3 above.

40. As recognized by Räisänen, *Paul and the Law*, 171; also Westerholm, *Israel's Law*, 113–14.

41. This way of putting it is not meant to deny that such faith would have an object, i.e., God.

42. This contrast has frequently attracted comment; see esp. Beker, *Paul the Apostle*, 95–104; Hans Hübner, *Law in Paul's Thought* (Edinburgh: T. & T.

Clark, 1984); Hendrikus Boers, *Theology out of the Ghetto* (Leiden: Brill, 1971) 82–84; Jeffrey S. Siker, *Disinheriting the Jews* (Louisville, Ky.: Westminster/John Knox, 1991) 59.

43. The repetition of τοῖς (the) before στοιχοῦσιν (following ones) might be taken to imply two groups in v. 12; so J. Swetnam, "The Curious Crux at Romans 4,12," *Biblica* 61 (1980) 110–15. But the resulting construction is just as awkward; one would have expected οὐ τοῖς ἐκ περιτομῆς μόνον (not those of circumcision only). So with most commentators I take v. 12 to be referring to a single group of Jewish believers; see James D. G. Dunn, *Romans* (Waco, Tex.: Word, 1988) 1:210–11; C. E. B. Cranfield, *A Critical and Exegetical Commentary on the Epistle to the Romans* (2 vols.; ICC; Edinburgh: T. & T. Clark, 1975, 1979) 1:237.

44. The phrase τῷ ἐκ τοῦ νόμου (the one of the law) in v. 16 is difficult, since ἐκ νόμου (of law) is used in v. 14 of a group set over in contrast to one defined by faith. With most commentators, I take v. 16 to be parallel to vv. 11b–12, thus referring to two distinct groups of Jewish (τῷ ἐκ τοῦ νόμου [the one of the law]) and Gentile (τῷ ἐκ πίστεως Ἀβρααμ [the one of the faith of Abraham]) believers. Other possibilities: Cranfield entertains but rejects the notion that with "the one of the law" Paul has Christ in mind (*Romans*, 1:243); Günter Klein takes it as a reference to non-Christian Jews, in an anticipation of chapter 11 ("Heil und Geschichte nach Römer IV," *NTS* 13 [1966–67] 45–46).

45. John A. Ziesler, *Paul's Letter to the Romans* (London: SCM; Philadelphia: TPI, 1989) 129.

46. Ernst Käsemann, *Commentary on Romans* (Grand Rapids: Eerdmans, 1980) 116; see also idem, "The Faith of Abraham in Romans 4," in *Perspectives on Paul* (Philadelphia: Fortress, 1971), esp. 86.

47. Dunn, *Romans*, 1:217. Cf. Hays, who describes Rom 4 as Paul's contention that "his reading of Scripture—juxtaposed to an ethnic misreading—is in fact the right reading of what Israel's Scriptures have always proclaimed"; see Richard B. Hays, *Echoes of Scripture in the Letters of Paul* (New Haven/London: Yale University Press, 1989) 57.

48. Awareness of this counterargument is at least as early as Calvin and Luther. Calvin argues in reply that baptism has replaced circumcision as the confirming sign of righteousness (*Romans*, on 4:11); Luther argues for a spiritual circumcision of "perverse desires" (*Romans*, on 4:11). For contemporary references, see C. K. Barrett, *A Commentary on the Epistle to the Romans* (London: A. & C. Black, 1962) 91; Räisänen, *Paul and the Law*, 190.

49. As noted already, Ziesler, *Romans*, 129. Sanders recognizes the force of the Jewish counterargument, but in connection with Galatians rather than Romans; *Paul, the Law, and the Jewish People*, 18. See also Segal, *Paul the Convert*, 121.

50. So, many commentators; see Beker, *Paul the Apostle*, 74–104; Sanders, *Paul, the Law, and the Jewish People*, 18–19; Dunn, *Romans*, 1:210–11.

51. See Sanders, *Paul, the Law, and the Jewish People*, 21.

52. So Sanders, *Paul, the Law and the Jewish People*, 32–33; Richard B. Hays, "'Have we found Abraham to be our forefather according to the flesh?' A Reconsideration of Rom 4:1," *NovT* 27 (1985) 83–88; Lloyd Gaston, "Abraham and the Righteousness of God," *Horizons in Biblical Theology* 2 (1980) 39–68.

53. The traditional interpretation; see, e.g., Cranfield, *Romans*, 1:224.

54. So Barrett, *Romans*, 84–86; Siker, *Disinheriting the Jews*, 59; C. Thomas Rhyne, *Faith Establishes the Law* (Chico, Calif.: Scholars Press, 1981).

55. See §4.1 above.

56. In a highly stimulating article ("Abraham Our Forefather according to the Flesh?") Hays attempts to reduce the awkwardness by arguing that Abraham appears in Rom 4 as a foundational rather than a model figure. His faith not so much sets the pattern for later believers as it opens up the possibility of a family for which he is the patriarch. If his faith is analogous to any other, it is as a prefiguration of the "faith of Christ" which opens up the possibility of a new human solidarity. Hays bases his case on a new construal of v. 1: "What then shall we say? Have we found Abraham to be our forefather according to the flesh?" The rest of chap. 4, then, is the argument that membership in Abraham's family is based on faith not ethnic identity markers.

His reading is appealing, and I am prepared to think that Paul himself would endorse it! But I wonder whether it is not a case of Hays thinking Paul's thoughts more coherently than Paul did himself. σάρξ (flesh) does not figure in the argument of the chapter at all; κατὰ νόμον (according to law) would have been a better way of posing Hays's version of the question than κατὰ σάρκα (according to flesh). Further, where τί [οὖν] ἐροῦμεν (what shall we say [then]) appears elsewhere to introduce a negative inference, the inference is immediately rejected by μὴ γένοιτο (certainly not; e.g., Rom 3:5; 6:1; 7:7; 9:14). The awkwardness remains.

57. As A. Jülicher put it; see Boers, *Theology out of the Ghetto*, 100–101. For a similar observation concerning the argument in Romans 2, see Bruce W. Longenecker, *Eschatology and the Covenant: A Comparison of 4 Ezra and Romans 1–11* (JSNTSup 57; Sheffield: Sheffield Academic Press, 1991), 194.

58. The contrary interpretation of Gaston, Gager, and others will be taken up in §8.2 below.

59. Isa 2:2-4, with its mention of Torah, would have been less suitable.

60. To be sure, there is no evidence that these "blessing of the nations" texts were being read in that way in Paul's day. The passages are either echoed without comment (Sir 44:19–21; *Jub.* 18.15; 24:11; *Tg. Onq.*), qualified (those who bless Israel will be blessed, while those who curse Israel will be cursed; *Tg. Ps.-J.*; *Frg. Tg.*; *Tg. Neof.*), or given a narrow or trivial reading (*b. Yeb.* 63a; *Midr. Lev.* 11.7; *Midr. Gen.* 39.12). I see no evidence, however, to support Siker's assertion that Jewish tradition interpreted the blessing of the nations in terms of the opportunity to become proselytes (*Disinheriting the Jews*, 174); his statement that the blessing texts played "a less significant role" than other aspects of the Abraham story (p. 20) is closer to the mark.

61. This line of argument is developed in Gal 3 (esp. vv. 8, 14). But here as well, differences from Rom 4 notwithstanding, he wants to say in addition that believing Gentiles are part of Abraham's "seed" and "heirs."

62. It is not clear whether this is a hyperbolic description of the expected size of Israel or a reference to the Ishmaelites and other Arabic tribes (Gen 25:1-18; cf. Exod 2:15-22; 18:1); the commentators are divided.

63. See esp. §5.3, §8.3.

64. For Bultmann's own comments on the passage, see *Theology*, 1:280–81.

65. Since λαός (people; v. 25) is parallel with the "seed of Abraham" in v. 7, we can presume that Paul would have seen these Gentiles as members of Abraham's family; but this is not made explicit.

66. Robert Badenas, *Christ the End of the Law: Romans 10:4 in Pauline Perspective* (Sheffield: JSOT Press, 1986).

67. Cranfield, *Romans*, 2:508–10; see also "Some Notes on Romans 9:30-33," in E. Earle Ellis and Erich Grässer, eds., *Jesus und Paulus: Festschrift für Werner Georg Kümmel* (Göttingen: Vandenhoeck & Ruprecht, 1975) 35–43.

68. Cranfield and others have found an explicit anticipation of vv. 30-31 in the νόμου πίστεως (law of faith) of 3:27; see Cranfield, *Romans*, 1:219–20; G. Friedrich, "Das Gesetz des Glaubens: Röm. 3,27," *ThZ* 10 (1954) 401–17. For a convincing refutation, see Westerholm, *Israel's Law*, 123–26.

69. To be sure, what Israel strives for, according to the literal sense of v. 31, is not righteousness but νόμον δικαιοσύνης (law of righteousness); and what they fail to attain is not righteousness but νόμον (law). After the declaration in v. 30 that the Gentiles have attained δικαιοσύνη (righteousness) even though they were not pursuing it, the phrasing of v. 31 is surprising and has precipitated substantial scholarly comment; see esp. Cranfield, *Romans*, 2:507–8; Dunn, *Romans*, 2:581–82; Sanders, *Paul, the Law and the Jewish People*, 36–37. While not wanting to undervalue the importance of this discussion, I feel that one does no disservice to the text to speak of "Israel's striving for righteousness through the law." Dunn is probably close to the mark when he says that Paul chose νόμον δικαιοσύνης (law of righteousness) for its rhetorical shock value.

70. Cranfield, *Romans*, 2:508.

71. Ibid., 2:509; emphasis his.

72. Sanders, *Paul, the Law, and the Jewish People*, 37; emphasis his.

73. Cranfield is of the opinion that Paul could have made himself clearer if contemporary Greek vocabulary had contained a word corresponding to our "legalism"; then it would have been clear that his negative comments pertained not to the law itself but to a legalistic misunderstanding of it (*Romans* 2:853). C. K. Barrett approaches this position in "Romans 9:30—10:21: Fall and Responsibility of Israel," *Essays on Paul* (Philadelphia: Westminster, 1982) 132–53. See also Daniel P. Fuller, *Gospel and Law: Contrast or Continuum?* (Grand Rapids: Eerdmans, 1980).

74. See esp. Sanders, *Paul, the Law, and the Jewish People*, 36–43; Westerholm, *Israel's Law*, 122–35; Räisänen, *Paul and the Law*, 174–75.

75. So Barrett ("Fall and Responsibility," 144), apparently having changed his mind since he wrote his commentary (cf. *Romans*, 194); Paul W. Meyer, "Romans 10:4 and the End of the Law," in J. L. Crenshaw and S. Sandmel, eds., *The Divine Helmsman* (New York: Ktav, 1980) 64.

76. See esp. Hays, *Echoes of Scripture*, 1–5, 73–83.

77. At least three separate decisions need to be made, resulting in a whole array of possible construals: (1) whether τέλος means "goal," "termination," or (combining the two) "fulfillment"; (2) whether εἰς δικαιοσύνην (to righteousness) modifies "end of the law" ("end of the law as far as righteousness is concerned") or the whole main clause ("Christ is the end of the law, resulting in righteousness"); and (3) whether παντὶ τῷ πιστεύοντι (to everyone who believes) is connected with "righteousness" (righteousness for everyone who believes) or the sentence as a whole ("for everyone who believes, Christ . . .").

78. On this point, see Dunn, *Romans*, 2:595; also Sanders, *Paul, the Law, and the Jewish People*, 37-38; Howard, "Christ the End of the Law," 335.

79. Given the footrace metaphor that weaves its way in and out of this section (also 11:11; see Badenas, *Christ the End of the Law*, 101), τέλος at least includes the sense of "goal"; see also Hays, *Echoes of Scripture*, 76.

80. The syntax is notoriously curious, especially since the major advance in the argument represented by the soteriological assertion of vv. 24-26 is introduced by a participle (δικαιούμενοι [being justified]) dependent on the subject (πάντες [all]; v. 23) of a clause which is itself part of an explanatory statement (beginning at v. 22b) dependent in turn on the πάντας [all] of v. 22; see the discussion in Cranfield, *Romans*, 1:205. Nevertheless, the sense is clear. There is no difference: all are equal in sin (v. 23) and in salvation (v. 24).

81. Sanders, *Paul and Palestinian Judaism*, 442-43.

82. Outside Galatians and Romans there is no explicit statement to the effect that all have sinned; the assertion in 1 Cor 15:22 that "all die in Adam," with the subsequent linkage of death with sin (v. 56) comes closest (cf. Eph 2:1-3). At the same time, though, the sinful state of all those outside of Christ seems to be assumed (see 1 Cor 15:3, 17; 2 Cor 5:21; Col 1:13-14).

83. So, many interpreters, e.g., Longenecker, *Galatians*, 118; Schoeps, *Paul*, 176-77; Barnabas Lindars, *New Testament Apologetic* (London: SCM, 1961) 228. Contrariwise, Sanders argues that Paul cites the verse simply because it links "law" and "curse" (the only Old Testament text to do so), and that the unfulfillability of the law does not drive the argument of v. 10-12 as a whole. (For Schlier's attempt to subordinate v. 10 to vv. 11-12, see the next note.) But given Paul's willingness elsewhere to take such a position (i.e., the unfulfillability of the law) and to develop it at length (i.e., Rom 1-3), it is difficult to avoid the presence of such an assumption at least at the surface level of the argument in v. 10; on this point, see Räisänen, *Paul and the Law*, 94-95. Sanders's significant contribution concerning the connection between sin and law at the level of Paul's underlying convictions will be taken up below.

84. Schlier attempts to bring the two into alignment by placing the stress in v. 10 on "to do them" rather than on "all"; *Galater*, 132-34; for the rebuttal, see Hübner, *Law in Paul's Thought*, 38-41.

85. I am disregarding neither the logical problems attendant on this reading of v. 10, as these have been pointed out by Sanders, Räisänen, and others, nor the conclusion following on from this that Paul's *convictional* logic was quite different. Here I am interested only in the surface sense of the text itself.

86. For the range of uses of χάριν, see BAGD, *ad loc.*

87. While the identity of the person addressed in 2:1 is left vague, it becomes clear by v. 9 that a Jewish interlocutor is in view; on the structuring of these chapters, see Dunn, *Romans*, 1:78-79.

88. Commentators have variously identified as the point of division in the argument of Romans 1-8, the sections beginning at 5:1 (so Bultmann, Nygren, Cranfield, Dodd, Käsemann, Lietzmann, Klein, Lyonnet, Dahl), 5:12 (Zahn, Leenhardt), and 6:1 (Luther, Calvin, Sanday and Headlam, Schlatter, Lagrange, Schweitzer, Dunn). See the discussions in Cranfield, *Romans*, 1:252-54, and Dunn, *Romans*, 1:242-44.

89. Schweitzer, *Mysticism*, 225-26.

90. On sin as a power, see, e.g., Beker, *Paul the Apostle,* 213–21; John A. Ziesler, *Pauline Christianity* (rev. ed.; Oxford/New York: Oxford University Press, 1990) 75–77.

91. The terms "juridical" and "participatory" are those of Sanders (e.g., *Paul and Palestinian Judaism,* 485–92, 502–8). The terms parallel Schweitzer's distinction between "righteousness by faith" and "mysticism" (e.g., *Mysticism,* 225).

92. For the connections between 5:1-11 and the previous chapters, see Cranfield, *Romans,* 1:253; for those between 5:1-11 and chap. 8, see Nils A. Dahl, *Studies in Paul* (Minneapolis: Augsburg, 1977) 81–83, 88–90; John A. T. Robinson, *Wrestling with Romans* (Philadelphia: Westminster, 1979) 56–57.

93. The relationship among the three statements in vv. 13-14 has puzzled commentators, since the middle statement stands in such apparent contrast with the other two. I read these verses as another example of the diatribe style of Romans:

Paul:　　　　　Sin was in the world prior to Moses;
Interlocutor: But sin is not counted when there is no law;
Paul:　　　　　But the reality of death in this period demonstrates the presence of sin, even when there was no law to reveal it clearly.

While Paul rejects the inference drawn from the statement in v. 13b, he does not deny the truth of the statement itself; indeed, the interlocutor may be throwing Paul's own definition of the role of the law back at him.

94. See, e.g., Dunn, *Romans,* 1:381–83; also above, pp. 14–15.

95. At least in Paul's perspective. Contemporary readers tend to be less willing to allow Eve to be pushed into the shadows.

96. So, most commentators (for example, Dunn, Cranfield, Käsemann, Barrett).

97. Just as chap. 8 picks up and amplifies the situation of the solidarity of life in Christ.

98. Cf. Schweitzer, who sees the former as a "subsidiary crater" formed within the rim of the "main crater" represented by the latter (*Mysticism,* 225); Sanders, *Paul and Palestinian Judaism,* 502–4. I take chaps. 5–8 to lie closer to the heart of Paul's soteriology than 1–4, his starting point in the earlier chapters being determined by rhetorical factors rather than the structure of his developed understanding of the gospel.

99. κατέκρινεν (condemned; v. 3) cannot mean simply that sin was identified and declared to be contrary to God's will; for the law certainly did that. Since the condemnation effected by Christ was something that the law could not do, it must have been more than a simple pronouncement; as F. Büchsel has observed (*TDNT* 3.951–52), the term here includes both pronouncement and execution.

100. While Bultmann's anthropological starting point is open to question, his treatment of "flesh" in Pauline usage is of continuing value (*Theology,* 1:232–46); see also W. David Stacey, *The Pauline View of Man* (London: Macmillan, 1956) 154–73.

101. On this inconsistency, see Daniel Boyarin, *A Radical Jew* (Berkeley/Los Angeles/London: University of California Press, 1994) 271, n. 5.

102. See, e.g., Luther's comments on Rom 4:6-8: "The former [those seeking righteousness on the basis of works] finally regard themselves as no longer sinners; the latter [those with faith] always acknowledge themselves to be sinners."

103. C. G. Montefiore, *Judaism and St. Paul: Two Essays* (London: Max Goschen, 1914) 76. While it does not negate Montefiore's argument, Paul does make one reference to repentance in Rom 2:4; on this passage, see below, p. 141.

104. Sanders, *Paul and Palestinian Judaism*, 1–12; see also Frank Thielman, *From Plight to Solution* (Leiden: Brill, 1989) 1–12. Early Jewish scholars include S. Schechter and C. G. Montefiore; counterparts on the Christian side were G. F. Moore and J. Parkes.

105. Sanders, *Paul and Palestinian Judaism*, 482.

106. Ibid., 475. Stendahl's *Paul among Jews and Gentiles* contains a similar insight (p. 81).

107. E.g., Räisänen, whose *Paul and the Law*, despite some differences in emphasis and conclusion, makes many of the same points, often in more detail (see esp. 94–119). The following summary will draw on his work as well. For Sanders, see esp. *Paul and Palestinian Judaism*, 442–44, 474–500; *Paul, the Law, and the Jewish People*, 29–36, 123–35.

108. See above, pp. 14–15.

109. The term is Räisänen's; see *Paul and the Law*, 100; also 113–17. The point is also considered by Longenecker, *Eschatology and the Covenant*, 280–81.

110. Räisänen, *Paul and the Law*, 99.

111. Ps 14:1-3; 53:1-3; Eccl 7:20; Ps 5:9; 140:3; 10:7; Isa 59:7-8; Ps 36:1. Cf. also the quotation in 2:24 (Isa 52:5, with a probable allusion to Ezek 36:20).

112. Sanders also observes conflicts between Rom 1–3 and 10:1-4 (where the Jews' failure with respect to the law is that of unenlightened zeal rather than lack of fulfillment) and 5:13 (where sin is not counted in the absence of law); *Paul, the Law, and the Jewish People*, 35–36, 124.

113. For a full survey, see Klyne R. Snodgrass, "Justification by Grace—to the Doers: An Analysis of the Place of Romans 2 in the Theology of Paul," *NTS* 32 (1986), esp. 73–75. See in addition, Glenn N. Davies, *Faith and Obedience: A Study in Romans 1–4* (Sheffield: JSOT Press, 1990).

114. See above, pp. 89–90.

115. Sanders, *Paul, the Law, and the Jewish People*, 129.

116. To the mention of repentance in 2:4, we can add the recognition in 4:6-8 that forgiveness of sin was a real possibility in the period prior to Christ.

117. See, e.g., Dunn, "New Perspective," 95–122; Beker, *Paul the Apostle*, esp. 236–42; Thielman, *From Plight to Solution*, 20–27; Morna Hooker, "Paul and 'Covenantal Nomism,'" in Morna Hooker and Stephen G. Wilson, eds., *Paul and Paulinism* (London: SPCK, 1982) 47–56.

118. Dunn, "New Perspective," 101.

119. E.g., "Christ died for our sins" (1 Cor 15:3); also the possible reflection of traditional formulation in Rom 3:24-26, Gal 1:4, etc.

120. Essentially, though not completely; see the next paragraph.

121. See, as well, *Jesus and Judaism* (Philadelphia: Fortress, 1985) 217; *Paul* (Past Master Series; Oxford: Oxford University Press, 1991) 2–4.

122. Responding to W. D. Davies, he says (p. 497): "It would seem to push Jewish expectations about the Messiah too far to say that Paul's view is simply a radicalizing of the expectation that Gentiles would be brought in at the eschaton. That view has to do with obeisance to the Jewish law and the worship of the one true God on Mount Zion, not the universalizing of the way of access to salvation."

123. Sanders, *Paul, the Law and the Jewish People*, 200, n. 3.

124. See §7.1 below. This later section of our discussion will be the appropriate point to address the position developed by Wright, Thielman, and others. In response to Sanders, they argue that Judaism *is* aware of a plight caused by sin. While granting Sanders's point about repentance, atonement, and forgiveness, they argue that this is overly individualistic, not taking into account the issue of the sinfulness of the nation as a whole, and of the exile, the result in history of Israel's corporate failure to keep the Torah. They argue—convincingly, I think—that for many Jews the present state of affairs was a continuation of the situation of the exile, in that corporate sinfulness was still, and the promised restoration was by no means yet, a concrete reality. See N. T. Wright, *The Climax of the Covenant* (Minneapolis: Fortress, 1992), e.g., 140-47; Thielman, *From Plight to Solution*; James M. Scott, "Paul's Use of Deuteronomic Tradition," *JBL* 112 (1993) 645-65.

This line of interpretation will be discussed in more detail below. While it is instructive in many ways, it faces two substantial problems: (1) the absence of any explicit attempt in Paul to describe Israel's plight along the lines of Deuteronomic history, despite opportunities to do so (e.g., Rom 2:21-24, where Jewish sinfulness is established by means of purely individualistic examples; or 9:30—10:4, where Israel's "stumbling" is defined in purely christological terms); and (2) the failure of this approach to account for Paul's Christ-Torah antithesis (exile-restoration patterns of thought leading more naturally to the expectation of full and complete performance of the Torah).

125. For the phrase itself, see *Jub.* 23:23-24; for Gentile sinfulness, see §3.1 above; see also Betz, *Galatians*, 115; Longenecker, *Galatians*, 83; Schlier, *Galater*, 88-89.

126. Sanders, *Paul and Palestinian Judaism*, 499; also *Paul, the Law, and the Jewish People*, 24-25.

127. See, most recently, Räisänen, *Paul and the Law*, 18-23; Segal, *Paul the Convert*, 200; Westerholm, *Israel's Law*, 192-95.

128. Gaston's argument that those "under the law" are Gentiles is forced; see "Paul and the Torah," 63. Gaston's position will be examined in §8.2 below.

129. 7:1 ("for I am speaking to those who know the law") notwithstanding. The statement is much less restrictive than 11:13 ("now I am speaking to you Gentiles"); Gentiles, especially Gentile Christians, are equally capable of knowing the law. See Westerholm, *Israel's Law*, 193.

130. See esp. v. 9, and commentary on it; e.g. Dunn, *Romans*, 1:381.

131. Westerholm, *Israel's Law*, 194.

132. The situation in Gal 3 and 4 is more complex; see the discussion in §7.1 below.

133. Peter J. Tomson, *Paul and the Jewish Law: Halakha in the Letters of the Apostle to the Gentiles* (Assen: Van Gorcum/Minneapolis: Fortress, 1990).

134. For scholars taking a similar position, see chap. 1, nn. 90 and 91.

135. Sanders sees 2:13, 27 as incompatible with Noachian patterns of thought, in that these verses assume "that, to be righteous, Gentiles must fulfill the entire law"; *Paul, the Law, and the Jewish People*, 130.

136. See, esp., Segal, *Paul the Convert*, 121.

137. See the survey in Räisänen, *Paul and the Law*, 16-18.

138. See §3.3 above.

139. See Philo *Migr. Abr.* 89-90.

140. Against Neil J. McEleney, "Conversion, Circumcision and the Law," *NTS* 20 (1973–74) 61. Thielman, too, wants to align Paul with such strands within Judaism (*From Plight to Solution*, 50–59), an approach rightly rejected by Boyarin ("Was Paul an 'Anti-Semite'?" 67).

141. Ben F. Meyer, *The Early Christians: Their World Mission and Self-Discovery* (Wilmington, Del.: Michael Glazier, 1986).

142. Meyer sees his position as standing "in contrast to proposals that make Paul's appointment as Apostle of the gentiles the commanding principle of the development of his thought" (p. 168).

143. A similar situation exists with a whole array of texts in which the beneficiaries of Christ's saving work are described in terms of an undifferentiated humanity (Christ died for all). Such possibilities will be taken up below; see §7.2.

144. See the popularized expression of this view in J. Klausner, *From Jesus to Paul* (New York: Macmillan, 1943) 312. While his work appeared too late to be fully taken into account in this study, this position has been revived by Boyarin, *A Radical Jew.* Aligning himself in significant ways with F. C. Baur (p. 11), Boyarin argues that Paul rejected "the notion that one particular people could ever be the children of God to the exclusion of other people" (p. 23). Indeed, this is what lay at the core of his conversion: Paul's revelation of Christ provided "the resolution of that enormous tension that he experienced between the universalism of the Torah's content and the particular ethnicity of its form" (p. 29). On this latter point, several recent scholars (Sanders, Davies, Gaston) come close to Boyarin, at least in their willingness to see uneasiness about the exclusion of the Gentiles as an element in Paul's preconversion frame of mind. But none of them identifies this as the ground of his later convictions about the Gentiles and the law. See above, p. 25, and further below, pp. 264–65.

145. See esp. chaps. 7, 8, 10, 13. We look forward to the volume on Paul in his multivolume project, *Christian Origins and the Question of God.*

146. A similar approach can be found in Thielman, *From Plight to Solution*, and Scott, "Paul's Use of Deuteronomic Tradition"; see above, chap. 5, n. 124.

147. See, e.g., Sanders, *Jesus and Judaism*, 77–90. For Wright's understanding of Judaism, see chaps. 9 and 10 of *The New Testament and the People of God* (Minneapolis: Fortress, 1992).

148. Wright, *People of God*, 251–52.

149. Wright, *Climax*, 141.

150. See also §7.1 and §8.3, below.

151. At least within Israel; as was seen in §3.5 above, the status of eschatological pilgrimage Gentiles with respect to the Torah is not entirely clear.

152. This is the reason for not discussing Wright in the section on sin (§5.2 above; see chap 5., n. 124).

153. On Rom 10:12, see *Climax*, 230, 237.

154. Several other recent scholars have suggested that "no distinction" functions as the convictional basis of Paul's concern for the Gentiles. One example is Boyarin, *A Radical Jew,* discussed in n. 144 above. R. David Kaylor also identifies this as a "fundamental and unalterable" conviction, one that determines "almost all of Paul's other attitudes toward the Jewish heritage"; *Paul's Covenant Community: Jew and Gentile in Romans* (Atlanta: John Knox, 1988) 173. A closer examination, however, reveals that for Kaylor "no distinction" is a derived con-

viction, a corollary of the dethroning of the Torah. Also to be mentioned is James D. G. Dunn, who in an early essay ("The New Perspective on Paul") takes a position very similar to that of Wright. (In subsequent writings, he tends to view the element of "no distinction" more as a derived conviction, stemming from the idea of a crucified Christ; see below, p. 174). In this essay he argues that universality was the intention of the covenant all along: from the beginning "God's eschatological purpose in making the covenant had been the blessing of the nations. So, now that the time of fulfilment had come, the covenant should no longer be conceived in national or racial terms. No longer is it an exclusively Jewish *qua* Jewish privilege" (p. 114). The assumption underlying this statement is that no differentiation is allowed: since the promised blessing is universal, there is no place for a law that differentiates one human group from another. Indeed, it is because God's grace is to be "freely bestowed without respect to race or work" (ibid.) that Paul rejects any attempt to impose the law as a boundary marker. Against Sanders, the problem with Judaism is not that it is not Christianity, but (Dunn asserts) that it is "too narrowly and nationalistically Jewish" (p. 122). Dunn apparently wants this generic universalism to be understood as something that should have been apparent all along. This is signaled on the one hand by phrases such as "as God had originally intended" and "as it had been bestowed in the beginning" (p. 114). On the other hand it is indicated by the suggestion that the role of the law as a boundary marker was somehow a Jewish misapprehension: Paul is opposed not to the covenant itself, but only to a "too narrowly and nationalistic Jewish" understanding of it (p. 120), or only to "the covenant and the law as taken over by Israel" (p. 121).

155. Cf. the title of Wright's book. It is interesting to note Dunn's use of similar language: "the covenant purpose of God now reached its climax in Jesus Christ" ("The New Perspective on Paul," 121).

156. *Climax*, chap. 13, esp. pp. 249–50.

157. A similar abandonment of ethnic Israel is to be found in the early essay by Dunn, "The New Perspective on Paul," discussed above (n. 154). He begins by indicating his agreement with much of "the new perspective on Paul" as initiated by Stendahl and worked out by Sanders. In particular, he agrees with Sanders that Paul's works/faith language is not to be understood in terms of a contrast between meritorious works-righteousness and unmerited grace. Instead, by "works of the law" Paul is referring to those aspects of the Torah (circumcision, food laws, etc.) that serve as boundary markers, differentiating Jew from Gentile; thus what he is rejecting is the assumption that those who live within this boundary are "righteous," a community destined for salvation. But Dunn goes on to say that Sanders has formulated his "solution before problem" reading of Paul in terms that are so stark and disjunctive as to render him inexplicable. The points of contact between Paul's old convictions (those of covenantal nomism) and his new ones (Christ as savior of all) are so few and the similarities between the resulting patterns of religion so minimal that the effect is to exchange a Lutheran Paul for an idiosyncratic Paul. But Dunn's solution to this unpalatable set of alternatives is to argue that by using the Torah as an ethnic boundary marker the Jews were misapprehending the nature of the covenant. But surely the idea of a family of Abraham's descendants, marked by circumcision, food laws, and so on, is an essential part of the covenant itself. Thus the price Dunn pays to render Paul more explicable is ethnic Israel itself.

158. On this whole paragraph, see Hays, *Echoes*, 44; J. Christiaan Beker, "The Faithfulness of God and the Priority of Israel in Paul's Letter to the Romans," in G. W. E. Nicklesburg and G. W. MacRae, eds., *Christians among Jews and Gentiles* (Philadelphia: Fortress, 1986) 13; Friedrich-Wilhelm Marquardt, *Die Juden im Römerbrief* (Zurich: Theologischer Verlag, 1971) 16.

159. 1 Thess 2:16; Gal 1:16; 2:2; Rom 1:5, 13; 11:13; 15:15-16.

160. In addition to Romans and Galatians, where the term appears frequently, see 1 Cor 1:23; 5:1; 10:20; 2 Cor 11:26; Col 1:27; 1 Thess 4:5.

161. Similar assumptions are at work in 1 Cor 10:1 ("*our* ancestors") and Phil 3:3 ("we are the circumcision"); see further below (§83).

162. On the theme of "no distinction," while there is no close verbal parallel in Jewish literature to these Pauline statements (Strack-Billerbeck, for example, passes over these verses in silence), it is a basic assumption in those passages that speak of the law as having been given for "the *whole* world" (*Ps. Philo* 11.1–2), for "*each* of the inhabitants of the earth" (*2 Bar.* 48.40), "for the enlightenment of *every* man" (*T. Lev.* 14.4), or simply "for those who came into the world" (*4 Ezra* 7.21); cf. *Ep. Arist.* 16, 195–97. For the stricter line, see further below, pp. 224–26.

163. See further, §6.4 below.

## Chapter 6

1. Beker is a good example (J. Christiaan Beker, *Paul the Apostle* [Philadelphia: Fortress, 1980]). He takes Paul's call to be Christ's apostle to the Gentiles as the starting point for any proper interpretation. While he recognizes at one point that the law-free nature of Paul's mission does not necessarily follow directly from the kind of gospel summarized in 1 Cor 15:3-5 (p. 128), and thus is in need of some explanation, he makes little attempt to provide one, simply taking "the gospel for the Gentiles without the Torah" (ibid.) as the substance of the apostolic call. "Gentiles"→▸▸▸▸"not Torah" would be one way of filling in the gap. Similar comments could be made about the reconstructions of Munck and Stendahl. See further, chap. 9.

2. See above, chap. 5, n. 154.

3. R. David Kaylor, *Paul's Covenant Community: Jew and Gentile in Romans* (Atlanta: John Knox, 1988) 37; see also 7, 10.

4. For example, Karl-Wilhelm Niebuhr, *Heidenapostel aus Israel: Die jüdische Identität des Paulus nach ihrer Darstellung in seinen Briefen* (Tübingen: Mohr [Siebeck], 1992) 111, 181. While he mentions it only in passing, Hurtado also sees Paul's thinking about the law as the result of his commissioning as a Gentile missionary; see Larry W. Hurtado, "Convert, Apostate or Apostle to the Nations: The 'Conversion' of Paul in Recent Scholarship," *SR* 22 (1993–94) 277. In his contribution to the G. B. Caird volume ("'A Light to the Gentiles': The Significance of the Damascus Road Christophany for Paul," in L. D. Hurst and N. T. Wright, eds., *The Glory of Christ in the New Testament* [Oxford: Clarendon, 1987] 251–66), James D. G. Dunn claims to be taking a similar position, asserting that the sharp Jesus-law antithesis "was more the corollary of 'therefore to the Gentiles' than vice-versa" (p. 263). But closer analysis reveals that the "therefore to the Gentiles" is rooted already in a Christ-Torah antithesis,

the crucified Jesus being for that reason cursed by the law (Deut 21:22-23); see esp. pp. 264–65 of his article, and below, p. 174.

5. So Albert Schweitzer, *The Mysticism of Paul the Apostle* (New York: Seabury, 1968 [1931]) 68–69, 189–93; Hans-Joachim Schoeps, *Paul* (Philadelphia: Westminster, 1961) 171–73. For the refutation of such a view, see W. D. Davies, *Torah in the Messianic Age and/or Age to Come* (Philadelphia: SBL, 1952); E. P. Sanders, *Paul and Palestinian Judaism* (Philadelphia: Fortress, 1977) 479.

6. Paula Fredriksen, "Judaism, the Circumcision of Gentiles, and Apocalyptic Hope: Another Look at Galatians 1 and 2," *JTS* 42 (1991) 561. I am not as certain that the "traditional" view, by which she means the eschatological pilgrimage expectation, was as clear-cut on the status of the Gentiles vis-à-vis the Torah as she makes out; see the discussion in §3.5 above.

7. Sanders, *Paul and Palestinian Judaism*, 443, 482, 484; idem, *Paul, the Law, and the Jewish People* (Philadelphia: Fortress, 1983) 27. While the "solution" in Sanders's "solution before problem" reading of Paul is that Christ is Savior of all, it is clear that for him the logic of Paul's treatment of the law is governed more fundamentally by the first part of this formulation (i.e., Christ as Savior) than by the second (i.e., for all).

8. Sanders, *Paul, the Law, and the Jewish People*, 153.

9. The inversion is not total, of course. The rejection of the Torah after Damascus was by no means as complete and unequivocal as was the prior rejection of the crucified Christ; Paul continued to believe that God had given the Torah, and so had to maintain a place for it in his reconfigured world. The discussion of this issue in the next few pages is based on my article "Zealot and Convert: The Origin of Paul's Christ-Torah Antithesis," *CBQ* 51 (1989) 655–82.

10. In 4QpNah 1.7–8, תלא (hang) is used with reference to the crucifixions carried out by Jannaeus; in 11QTemple 64.12 a discussion of crucifixion makes clear reference to Deut 21:23.

11. So, e.g., Dunn, "A Light to the Gentiles," 264–65; Ben Meyer, *The Early Christians* (Wilmington, Del.: Glazier, 1986) 162–63; Beker, *Paul the Apostle*, 185–86, 261; W. D. Davies, *Invitation to the New Testament* (Garden City, N.Y.: Doubleday, 1969) 260–61; idem, "The Apostolic Age and the Life of Paul," in M. Black and H. H. Rowley, eds., *Peake's Commentary on the Bible* (London/New York: Thomas Nelson, 1962) 115; Morton Scott Enslin, *Reapproaching Paul* (Philadelphia: Westminster, 1972) 55–66; Seyoon Kim, *The Origin of Paul's Gospel* (Grand Rapids: Eerdmans, 1982) 44–48; Martin Hengel, *The Atonement* (Philadelphia: Fortress, 1981) 40–44; idem, *The Pre-Christian Paul* (London: SCM/Philadelphia: Trinity, 1991) 79–86; Morna D. Hooker, "Paul and 'Covenantal Nomism,'" in M. D. Hooker and S. G. Wilson, eds., *Paul and Paulinism* (London: SPCK, 1982) 55; F. F. Bruce, *Paul: Apostle of the Heart Set Free* (Grand Rapids: Eerdmans, 1977) 70–71; Christian Dietzfelbinger, *Die Berufung des Paulus als Ursprung seiner Theologie* (Neukirchen-Vluyn: Neukirchener Verlag, 1985) 29–42; O. Pfleiderer, *Primitive Christianity* (4 vols.; London: Williams & Norgate, 1906) 1:84–95.

12. So also Christopher M. Tuckett, "Deuteronomy 21,23 and Paul's Conversion," in A. Vanhoye, ed., *L'apôtre Paul: Personnalité, style et conception du ministère* (Leuven: Leuven University/Peeters, 1986) 345–50; Paula Fredriksen, "Paul and Augustine: Conversion Narratives, Orthodox Traditions and the Retrospec-

tive Self," *JTS* 37 (1986) 1–13; Heikki Räisänen, *Paul and the Law* (Philadelphia: Fortress, 1986) 249–51.

13. Lightfoot's discussion of Deut 21:23 is still helpful; see J. B. Lightfoot, *The Epistle of St. Paul to the Galatians* (London: Macmillan, 1874) 150–52.

14. Hengel's argument from silence—to the effect that there is no instance in Jewish tradition in which one who had been crucified was seen as a martyr—is unconvincing; see *The Atonement,* 43.

15. Fredriksen, "Paul and Augustine," 12.

16. Christian use of this text (cf. Acts 5:30; 10:39) is easier to understand as a response to such polemical use; it is more difficult to imagine Christians picking it up as a christological text on their own.

17. It is too simple to argue that for Paul the law condemned Jesus to death, therefore the law was wrong; for this view, see R. G. Hamerton-Kelly, "Sacred Violence and the Curse of the Law (Galatians 3:13): The Death of Christ as a Sacrificial Travesty," *NTS* 36 (1990) 98–99.

18. In typical rabbinic fashion, by drawing in another text (i.e., Deut 27:26; cf. Gal 3:10) to resolve the tension posed by the first.

19. Meyer, *The Early Christians,* 163.

20. See above, p. 94, 121.

21. See §5.1 above.

22. "Paul presents an *essentially different type of religiousness from any found in Palestinian Jewish literature*" (*Paul and Palestinian Judaism,* 543; emphasis his); see the whole discussion in pp. 543–56.

23. Sanders does recognize the similarity between Paul and Judaism on the matter of grace and works: "salvation is by grace but judgment is according to works; works are the condition of remaining 'in', but they do not earn salvation" (ibid., 543). I want to give this recognition a much more prominent place in any overall assessment of the two patterns of religion. For a similar point, see Hooker, "Paul and 'Covenantal Nomism,'" 47–56; and Philip A. Cunningham, *Jewish Apostle to the Gentiles* (Mystic, Conn.: Twenty-Third Publications, 1986) 46–48.

24. Wilckens makes an unwarranted distinction between the apocalyptic and the Pharisaic understanding of the role of the law. In addition, I believe that "ecclesiological" is a better way of describing the Christ-Torah antithesis than is "soteriological" (his term). On his approach, see further below, pp. 291–92. See Ulrich Wilckens, "Die Bekehrung des Paulus als religionsgeschichtliches Problem," *Rechtfertigung als Freiheit: Paulusstudien* (Neukirchen-Vluyn: Neukirchener, 1974) 11–32.

25. See Davies, *Torah in the Messianic Age.*

26. Thus, while I would develop the insight differently, I believe that Schoeps and Schweitzer were correct in their emphasis on the importance of the interim period for Paul; see Schweitzer, *Mysticism,* 75–100; Schoeps, *Paul,* 88.

27. For the suggestion that before his conversion Paul perceived the implications of the kerygma more clearly than most of the Christians, see O. Pfleiderer, *Paulinism* (2 vols.; 2d ed.; London: Williams & Norgate, 1891) 1:22; Beker, *Paul the Apostle,* 185; J. Dupont, "The Conversion of Paul, and Its Influence on His Understanding of Salvation by Faith," in W. W. Gasque and R. P. Martin, eds., *Apostolic History and the Gospel* (Grand Rapids: Eerdmans, 1970) 190–91; cf. Heikki Räisänen, "Galatians 2:16 and Paul's Break with Judaism," *NTS* 31 (1985) 550.

28. Dunn, "A Light to the Gentiles," 264–65 (emphasis his); see the discussion above (p. 341), as well as *The Partings of the Ways* (London: SCM/Philadelphia: TPI, 1991) 120–23. In the latter work, he differentiates his position from what he calls a "common line in current scholarship" and describes in terms very similar to the structure under discussion here (p. 120). The differences, however, have to do with his emphasis on the social, boundary-marking function of the law, and with the fact that the corollary concerning the Gentiles was immediate, bound up with the conversion experience itself, rather than a second and subsequent stage. While I agree with him on both counts, this does not alter the basic structure of Paul's convictions as he perceives it. It is still the nullifying of the law in its boundary-marking role that opens the door to the Gentiles. (His comments about Adam christology, though, suggest another, distinct possible line of development, to be discussed in the next chapter.) For other recent examples, see: Ulrich Wilckens, "Zur Entwicklung des paulinischen Gesetzesverständnis," *NTS* 28 (1982), esp. 156; Kaylor, *Paul's Covenant Community*, 7, 181; Dietzfelbinger, *Die Berufung des Paulus*, 137–47; Jürgen Becker, *Paul: Apostle to the Gentiles* (Louisville: Westminster/John Knox, 1993) 62–78.

29. For other examples of this approach in the earlier period, see chap. 1, n. 79.

30. See Davies, *Invitation*, 260–63; "The Apostolic Age," 873–74.

31. See §11.2.

32. W. D. Davies, *Paul and Rabbinic Judaism* (London: SPCK, 1948) 67; emphasis added.

33. Davies, *Invitation*, 263. Emphasis added.

34. "It was from this conflict that Paul was released when he became a Christian"; *Paul and Rabbinic Judaism*, 67.

35. See further below, chap. 10.

36. While it has no real parallel in the certainly authentic epistles of Paul, Eph 2:13-15 can also be mentioned here: "now in Christ Jesus you who once were far off have been brought near . . . [for] he has broken down the dividing wall; . . . he has abolished the law with its commandments and ordinances."

37. C. H. Dodd, *The Epistle of Paul to the Romans* (London: Hodder & Stoughton, 1932) 182–83.

38. See esp. Sanders, *Paul, the Law, and the Jewish People*, 192–98; Heikki Räisänen, "Paul, God and Israel: Romans 9–11 in Recent Research," in J. Neusner et al., eds., *The Social World of Formative Christianity* (Philadelphia: Fortress, 1988) 178–206; also Becker, who notes the surprising shift at 11:11 (*Paul*, 468); cf. Bruce W. Longenecker, "Different Answers to Different Questions: Israel, the Gentiles and Salvation History in Romans 9–11," *JSNT* 36 (1989) 95–123.

39. Some of the material in the next two paragraphs is drawn from my article, "'Riches for the Gentiles' (Rom 11:12): Israel's Rejection and Paul's Gentile Mission," *JBL* 112 (1993) 89.

40. This is not to overlook the logical tensions within this section; see Räisänen, "Paul, God and Israel," 181–87.

41. Breaking with the majority of modern scholarship, Wright argues that in these verses Paul does not envisage a future, large-scale salvation of ethnic Israel (N. T. Wright, *The Climax of the Covenant* [Minneapolis: Fortress, 1991] 246–51). Rather, the statement "and so all Israel will be saved" (v. 26) refers to the

process going on in the present, viz., a "steady flow of Jews" coming into the church, together with the gathering in of the "full number of the Gentiles" (v. 25), who apparently are also part of Israel (he appeals to Gal 6:16 and Phil 3:3). His understanding of "Israel" will come up for more complete discussion in §7.1, but I find his nonethnic redefinition of "Israel" in v. 26 to be quite unconvincing. Not only does it require a significant semantic shift in the space of two sentences (the ethnic referent is clear in v. 25), one neither signaled in any way in the text nor (as to the inclusion of the Gentiles in the term) anticipated in what precedes. But such a shift has the effect of rendering Paul's argument stunningly anticlimactic, turning his anguish for his "kindred according to the flesh" into the apostolic equivalent of crocodile tears. How can the present situation—where the number of Jewish converts is small enough that it is perceived as a problem—be *both* the stumbling/hardening/defeat/rejection that makes the Gentile mission possible, *and* the full inclusion/acceptance/salvation? How can the present situation be both firstfruits and whole batch of dough? Such an argument may preserve logical consistency, but at a cost too high for me.

42. While this is the most natural reading of v. 16a, it is not universally held. The problem is that the metaphor in the second half of the verse seems to ground the eventual salvation of the whole of Israel (i.e., the branches; cf. the whole lump of dough) not on the remnant (cf. the firstfruits) but on the patriarchs (the root). On the assumption that Paul would not have changed metaphorical horses in midstream, various unitary readings have been attempted, with both firstfruits and root referring: to the *patriarchs* (W. Sanday and A. C. Headlam, *A Critical and Exegetical Commentary on the Epistle to the Romans* [Edinburgh: T. & T. Clark, 1902] 326; Johannes Munck, *Christ and Israel: An Interpretation of Romans 9–11* [Philadelphia: Fortress, 1967] 127), to the *remnant* (Dan G. Johnson, "The Structure and Meaning of Romans 11," *CBQ* 46 [1984] 91–103), or to *Christ* himself (Karl Barth, *Church Dogmatics*, II/2 [Edinburgh: T. & T. Clark, 1957], 285). But the assumption is unnecessary; with C. E. B. Cranfield (*A Critical and Exegetical Commentary on the Epistle to the Romans* [2 vols.; Edinburgh: T. &. T. Clark, 1975, 1979] 2:564–65) and Dahl (Nils A. Dahl, "The Future of Israel," *Studies in Paul* [Minneapolis: Augsburg, 1977] 151). I take both metaphors at face value. In v. 16 Paul is prepared to find confirmation of his conviction of the eventual salvation of all Israel both in God's original covenantal promise to the patriarchs and in the existence of a Jewish-Christian remnant.

43. Davies, *Paul and Rabbinic Judaism*, 58, 85. Also F. W. Beare, *St. Paul and his Letters* (Nashville: Abingdon, 1962) 97.

44. The term in 11:5 is the relatively rare λεῖμμα; ὑπόλειμμα, more common in the LXX, appears in 9:27.

45. Campbell is not strictly correct in identifying the remnant as the *root* of the tree: "Paul expects Gentiles to recognize the inalienable position of the Jewish Christians as the root on to which they, as branches, are grafted"; see William S. Campbell, *Paul's Gospel in an Intercultural Context* (Frankfurt: Peter Lang, 1992) 52. But his insistence on the importance of the Jewish church moves in the right direction.

46. See above, pp. 123–24.

47. Granted, Christ is notoriously absent from Rom 4, and Gaston's "two covenant" reading of Paul needs to be given due consideration (see §8.2 below).

But Rom 4 follows Rom 3; it requires prodigious effort to eliminate Christ from the pattern of belief under discussion here.

48. For a discussion of some of the difficulties in interpreting these phrases, see above, chap. 5, notes 43 and 44.

49. See above, pp. 96–100.

50. While it is not explicit, the rationale for the collection found in 2 Cor 8:13-15 probably echoes the assumptions at work in Rom 15:27. At first glance, the argument appears to be one of simple reciprocity: the present situation, in which the abundant wealth of the Corinthians makes it possible and appropriate for them to contribute to the relief of Jerusalem, might be reversed at some time in the future. But the second half of the statement is awkward, with no counterpart to "your *present* abundance" (ἐν τῷ νῦν καιρῷ); and further, it is difficult to imagine Paul arguing that there would ever come a time when Jerusalem would come to the material aid of the Corinthians. It is plausible, then, that the "abundance" of the Jerusalemites is to be interpreted in the same spiritual (πνευματικά) manner as Rom 15:27; so Keith F. Nickle, *The Collection: A Study in Paul's Strategy* (SBT 48; Naperville, Ill: Allenson, 1966) 120–21; Hans Dieter Betz, *2 Corinthians 8 and 9* (Hermeneia; Philadelphia: Fortress, 1985) 68. For a rejection of this view, see Victor Paul Furnish, *II Corinthians* (Anchor; Garden City, N.Y.: Doubleday, 1984) 419–20.

51. For a more detailed discussion of this point, see my essay, "The 'Curse of the Law' and the Inclusion of the Gentiles: Galatians 3.13-14," *NTS* 32 (1986) 94–112.

52. So Hans Dieter Betz, *Galatians* (Hermeneia; Philadelphia: Fortress, 1979) 148, n. 101.

53. So M.-J. Lagrange, *Épître aux Galates* (5th ed.; Paris; Gabalda, 1942) 71; G. S. Duncan, *The Epistle of Paul to the Galatians* (Moffatt; New York: Harper & Bros., 1934) 99; T. Zahn, *Der Brief des Paulus an die Galater* (2d ed.; Leipzig: A. Deichert, 1907) 148.

54. For others reading 3:13 in a similar way, see note 3 in Donaldson, "The Curse of the Law."

55. Heinrich Schlier, *Der Brief an die Galater* (Göttingen: Vandenhoeck & Ruprecht, 1965) 137.

56. So Schlier, ibid.; Bo Reicke, "The Law and this World according to Paul: Some Thoughts concerning Gal 4:1-11," *JBL* 70 (1951) 274.

57. So Schlier, *Galater*, 137; F. F. Bruce, *The Epistle to the Galatians* (Grand Rapids: Eerdmans, 1982) 167.

58. Here the final "we" is inclusive of Jews and Gentiles; the parallelism does not extend to the separate statement concerning the Gentiles as in 3:14a. For an analysis of the parallel structure in 3:13-14, 3:23-29 and 4:3-7, see Donaldson, "The Curse of the Law," 95–98.

59. Reicke, "The Law and this World."

60. Above, pp. 146–47.

61. One exception is Dieter Zeller; see *Juden und Heiden in der Mission des Paulus* (2d ed.; Stuttgart: Verlag Katholisches Bibelwerk, 1976) 13.

62. There is evidence for this usage at least from the time of Aristotle (*Politics* 7.2.5 [1324b.10]) through to Dio Cassius (*Hist.* 36.41.1). See also the entry in LSJ and the references cited there.

63. The context and content of this sharply polemical, anti-Jewish passage (2:14-16) will come up for detailed discussion in §8.1 below.

64. This "mystery" has been entrusted to Paul by God *"for you"* (1:25), a group pointedly described a little later with the phrase "the uncircumcision of your flesh" (2:13). On the syntax of 1:27, see above, pp. 102-3. The usage in Ephesians is fully consistent with the picture described here, both with respect to the use of ἔθνη ("Gentiles") to designate the Gentile readers (e.g., 2:11; 3:1) and with respect to Paul's own role (3:1-3, 8).

65. Paul's apostolic self-conception will come up for more detailed consideration in chap 9.

66. Literally ἐκ γένους; see Victor Paul Furnish, *II Corinthians* (AB; Garden City, N.Y.: Doubleday, 1984) 517.

67. See the similar comment in J. Christiaan Beker, "The Faithfulness of God and the Priority of Israel in Paul's Letter to the Romans," in G. W. E. Nickelsburg and G. W. MacRae, eds., *Christians among Jews and Gentiles* (Philadelphia: Fortress, 1986) 13.

68. See Peter Richardson, *Israel in the Apostolic Church* (Cambridge: Cambridge University Press, 1969).

69. Boyarin argues that this is precisely what Paul does with the term "Israel"; Daniel Boyarin, *A Radical Jew* (Berkeley/Los Angeles/London: University of California Press, 1994).

## Chapter 7

1. While Χριστός (Christ) does not always retain its titular sense for Paul, Rom 9:5 provides evidence that he certainly can think of Christ in these terms; see Nils A. Dahl, "The Messiahship of Jesus in Paul," in Donald H. Juel, ed., *Jesus the Christ: The Historical Origins of Christological Doctrine* (Minneapolis: Fortress, 1991) 15–25.

2. E. P. Sanders, *Paul, the Law, and the Jewish People* (Philadelphia: Fortress, 1983) 171; for this aspect of Sanders's analysis, together with additional references, see the discussion above, p. 143. For others holding to this line of thought, see above, chap. 1, n. 89.

3. See above, p. 143.

4. Halvor Moxnes, *Theology in Conflict* (Leiden: Brill, 1980) 95. See also Schoeps, Stuhlmacher, Scott, Scobie (listed in chap. 1, n. 89 above), as well as Ferdinand Hahn, *Mission in the New Testament* (Naperville, Ill.: Allenson, 1965) 108–9; Richard B. Hays, *Echoes of Scripture in the Letters of Paul* (New Haven/London: Yale University Press, 1989) 73; and Gerd Theissen, "Judaism and Christianity in Paul: The Beginnings of a Schism and Its Social History," in *Social Reality and the Early Christians* (Minneapolis: Fortress, 1992) 210. Scott notes, with tentative approval, the suggestion by O. Hofius that in some Old Testament texts the pilgrimage of the nations precedes the salvation of Israel; see James M. Scott, "Paul's Use of Deuteronomic Tradition," *JBL* 112 (1993) 664. But an examination of the suggested texts (Isa 45:14-17, 20-25; 59:19; Mic 4:1-8) shows the suggestion to be without foundation.

5. See Seyoon Kim, *The Origin of Paul's Gospel* (Grand Rapids: Eerdmans, 1982) 87–90; and Dieter Zeller, *Juden und Heiden in der Mission des Paulus* (Stuttgart: Verlag Katholisches Bibelwerk, 1976) 272–75.

6. Hans-Joachim Schoeps, *Paul* (Philadelphia: Westminster, 1961) 229–30. Emphasis added.

7. See Keith F. Nickle, *The Collection* (Naperville, Ill: Allenson, 1966) 129–42, esp. 138–39; Johannes Munck, *Paul and the Salvation of Mankind* (London: SCM, 1959) 303–5; J. Christiaan Beker, *Paul the Apostle* (Philadelphia: Fortress, 1980) 72; Sanders, *Paul, the Law, and the Jewish People*, 171; Markus Barth, *The People of God* (Sheffield: JSOT, 1983) 43; Hahn, *Mission in the New Testament*, 109; James D. G. Dunn, *Romans* (2 vols.; Waco, Tex.: Word, 1988) 2:874; Peter Stuhlmacher, *Paul's Epistle to the Romans* (Louisville: Westminster/John Knox, 1994) 242.

8. See Isa 18:7; 60:1-22; Hag 2:7; Tob 13:11; *Sib. Or.* 3.772–95; *Gen. Rab.* 78.12, 97; *Ex. Rab.* 35.5; *Esth. Rab.* 1.4; *Midr. Ps.* 87.6; *Tg. Isa* 16:1.

9. See §5.3 above. The work under discussion is *The Climax of the Covenant* (Minneapolis: Fortress, 1991).

10. Ibid., 146, 141.

11. Ibid., 196.

12. Ibid., 150–51, 245. In my *Jesus on the Mountain* (Sheffield: JSOT Press, 1985), I have argued for a similar reading of Matthew.

13. For a demonstration that this is founded on a basic assumption that there is "no distinction" between Jew and Gentile, see §5.3 above.

14. So Schoeps, *Paul*, 171; and, with complications, Albert Schweitzer, *The Mysticism of Paul the Apostle* (New York: Seabury, 1968 [1931]) 189–92. It would be a little more difficult, though perhaps not impossible, to combine it with the interpretation of the Christ-Torah antithesis developed in the preceding chapter. For that interpretation stresses the "not yet" side of the eschatological duality (Christ and Torah functioning as rival ways of determining God's people in the period prior to the final consummation), while Wright's christocentric eschatological pilgrimage model lays stress instead on the "already."

15. Above, chap. 6, n. 41.

16. "The 'Curse of the Law' and the Inclusion of the Gentiles: Galatians 3.13–14," *NTS* 32 (1986) 94–112. The approach is similar in many respects, however, to Jervell's reading of Luke-Acts; see J. Jervell, *Luke and the People of God* (Minneapolis: Augsburg, 1972).

17. See above, pp. 180–82.

18. Donaldson, "The Curse of the Law," 100.

19. As well as for describing the current state of Pauline interpretation; see above, pp. 1, 8–22.

20. See chap. 6 in Thomas S. Kuhn's *The Structure of Scientific Revolutions* (2d ed.; Chicago: University of Chicago Press, 1970).

21. The point here is not at all affected by the variation in meaning proposed for ἥττημα (defeat, failure, fewness).

22. An initial attempt to develop this insight in a systematic way can be found in my article "'Riches for the Gentiles' (Rom 11:12): Israel's Rejection and Paul's Gentile Mission" (*JBL* 112 [1993] 81–98), parts of which are being incorporated into the present study.

23. Esp. Isa 2:2-4/Mic 4:1-4; Isa 25:6-10; 56:6-8; 66:18-23; Zech 8:20-23. Paul quotes from Isaiah frequently.

24. The largest concentration of Old Testament citations in the Pauline corpus is to be found in Rom 9–11; see also Rom 4, Gal 3–4.

25. So, e.g., Hays, *Echoes of Scripture*, 73; Dunn, *Romans*, 2:850. For the rejection of the suggestion that there is an allusion to Isa 2:3 in Rom 11:26, see above, chap. 4, n. 66.

26. See, e.g., E. Earle Ellis, *Paul's Use of the Old Testament* (Grand Rapids: Baker, 1981 [1957]) 45–51.

27. While Isa 2:2-4 could have provided a point of departure for such an understanding, this was apparently not picked up to any significant degree in the tradition; see above, p. 74.

28. *Mos.* 1.149; also *Abr.* 98; *Spec. leg.* 1.97; 2.163–67. See also *1 Enoch* 105.1; *Sib. Or.* 5.328–32; *2 Bar.* 1.4.

29. It would take us too far afield to attempt any full documentation here; the point, however, is uncontroversial. See, e.g., the *Psalms of Solomon*, where the differentiation between righteous and sinners within Israel is a recurring theme, with the law at the center (esp. 1, 3, 4, 8, 12, 13, 15, 17). See also *TDNT*, 4:194–214.

30. On this point, see Zeller, *Juden und Heiden*, 282–84.

31. See Emil Schürer, *The History of the Jewish People in the Age of Jesus Christ* (rev. ed.; Edinburgh: T. & T. Clark, 1973–1987) 2:309–13. Most of Schürer's references have to do with sacrifices by or on behalf of foreign kings and emperors, in which case we have to do with acts of public policy, or simple expressions of goodwill toward the Jews. But these are not the only examples. It is clear that many—like Queen Helena of Adiabene (*Ant.* 20.49), or the pilgrims from beyond the Euphrates (*Ant.* 3.318–19)—came out of sincere piety and devotion to Israel's God (also *2 Bar.* 68.5–6; *War* 2.412–13; 4.262; Tacitus *Hist.* 5.5). The existence of the court of the Gentiles itself, together with the need for a warning sign forbidding Gentiles from penetrating beyond it, reinforces the point.

32. See above, p. 58; also Scot McKnight, *A Light among the Gentiles* (Minneapolis: Fortress, 1991) 85–87.

33. See, e.g., Reginald H. Fuller, *The Foundations of New Testament Christology* (London: Lutterworth, 1965) 204–7; F. W. Beare, *A Commentary on the Epistle to the Philippians* (London: A. & C. Black, 1959) 73–77.

34. In Rom 9:5, ὁ ὢν ἐπὶ πάντων [the one who is over all] is more probably to be construed with θεὸς [God] than with Χριστὸς [Christ].

35. W. Bousset, *Kyrios Christos* (Nashville/New York: Abingdon, 1970 [1913]).

36. E.g., ibid., 128: "conceivable only on the soil of the Hellenistic communities."

37. "The full current of the new universal religious movement was already at flood level when Paul began his work, and even he was at first carried by this current;" ibid., 120. Bousset provides no explanation at all for the spread of the Christian movement into the Gentile world, simply taking it as a given. Further, his main evidence for the type of Hellenistic Christianity that shaped Paul so thoroughly is Paul himself.

38. See above, pp. 10–11.

39. William Wrede, *Paul* (London: Green, 1907) 167–68; see also 85–87.

40. Ibid., 151.

41. Despite this assertion of Pauline uniqueness, Hahn has already posited a belief in Christ's universal lordship as the ground and origin of a pre-Pauline, Hellenistic-Jewish Christian mission to the Gentiles; see *Mission*, 76–77. For simi-

lar views about Hellenistic-Jewish Christianity (though with different under-
standings of Paul himself), see: Ben Meyer, *The Early Christians* (Wilmington:
Glazier, 1986) 82–83; Wolfhart Pannenberg, *Jesus — God and Man* (Philadelphia:
Westminster, 1968) 71.

42. Ibid., pp. 99–100; the quoted material appears on p. 100. One observes
in passing the absence of any explicit reference to Wrede on this point. For similar
brief and undeveloped statements linking universal lordship and Gentile mission,
see J. Dupont, "The Conversion of Paul and Its Influence on His Understanding
of Salvation by Faith," in W. W. Gasque and R. P. Martin, eds., *Apostolic History
and the Gospel* (Grand Rapids: Eerdmans, 1970) 193.

43. Hahn, *Mission,* 108–9.

44. Kim, *Origin,* 223.

45. Ibid., 223.

46. Ibid., 219. Dietzfelbinger builds on 2 Cor 4:4 in a similar manner; see
Christian Dietzfelbinger, *Die Berufung des Paulus als Ursprung seiner Theologie*
(Neukerchen-Vluyn: Neukirchener Verlag, 1985) 49–51, 62–64, 73–75.

47. Conveniently summarized in diagram form on p. 268.

48. Ibid., 263.

49. See Kim, *Origin,* 256.

50. On the latter two points, see ibid., 269–300.

51. See esp. James D. G. Dunn, "'A Light to the Gentiles': The Significance of
the Damascus Road Christophany for Paul," in L. D. Hurst and N. T. Wright,
eds., *The Glory of Christ in the New Testament* (Oxford: Clarendon, 1987) 259–
62. Paul's christological use of "image of God" in 2 Cor 4:4 does not by itself
imply anything about his Damascus perceptions two decades or so earlier.

52. Wright, *Climax,* 18–40.

53. Larry W. Hurtado, *One God, One Lord* (Philadelphia: Fortress, 1988).

54. Alan F. Segal, *Paul the Convert* (New Haven/London: Yale University
Press, 1990).

55. See Paula Fredriksen, "Paul and Augustine: Conversion Narratives, Orthodox Traditions and the Retrospective Self," *JTS* 37 (1986) 3–34; and below,
pp. 273–75.

56. H. Windisch, "Die göttliche Weisheit der Juden und die paulinische
Christologie," in A. Deissmann and H. Windisch, eds., *Neutestamentliche Studien*
(Leipzig: Hinrichs, 1914) 220–34.

57. On personified Wisdom generally, see Job 28:23-27; Prov 1:20-33; 3:13-
18; 8:1-9:12; Wis 6:12—11:1; Sir 24:1-22. On the origin of Wisdom prior to
creation, see Prov 8:22-31; Wis 9:9; Sir 24:9. On Wisdom's role in making God
manifest, see Wis 7:25–26; 9:4. On Wisdom and creation, see Prov. 3:19; Wis 8:4;
9:2. On Wisdom and the rock in the wilderness, see Wis 11:4; Philo *Leg. all.* 2.86.

58. Davies, *Paul and Rabbinic Judaism,* 168–71.

59. Ibid., 168.

60. Ibid., 172.

61. Kim, *Origin,* 127-29, 258-60. For Kim, the line of development is opposite to that of Davies: Paul perceives the Christ of glory as the image of God, and
thus as the Wisdom of God, and hence as endowed with everything associated
with wisdom, including the role formerly played by the Torah.

62. Lloyd Gaston, "Paul and the Torah," in A. T. Davies, ed., *Antisemitism
and the Foundations of Christianity* (New York/Toronto: Paulist, 1979) 60.

63. See the discussion in §3.3 above.

64. I use this term to describe not only Paul's juridical (or, better, covenant lawsuit) language (righteousness, justification, etc.), but other metaphor clusters that function in a similar way to describe the new status of those who are "in Christ." These clusters can be identified as follows: temple (sacrifice, blood, sanctified, etc.); personal relationships (anger, enmity, reconciliation); marketplace (sold, redemption, price); slavery (bondage, "under," freedom, adoption).

65. Here the first person plural refers only to Jews; cf. v. 15.

66. The term is borrowed from Sanders to describe those well-known aspects of Paul's discourse where "salvation" is described in terms of the believer's participation with Christ in a process of death to this age and resurrection to the life of the age to come.

67. For a related survey of material, see my article "'The Gospel That I Proclaim among the Gentiles' (Gal 2:2): Universalistic or Israel-Centred?" in L. Ann Jervis and Peter Richardson, eds., *Gospel in Paul* (Sheffield: Sheffield Academic Press, 1994) 166–68, 173–75.

68. E.g., concerning the relationship between the participatory language and the metaphors of changed status.

69. Above, pp. 142–43.

70. Found earlier on p. 150.

71. Of course, in the eschatological pilgrimage option, as with others in the "reinterpretation of Jewish patterns of universalism" category, the Gentiles enter the structure not with Christ, but with Paul's native convictions. It was dealt with in this chapter because most versions of this interpretation fail to take Israel into account at all, fastening the interpretation solely on Christ as an eschatological figure.

## Chapter 8

1. Some of the discussion in this section has appeared in a preliminary form in my article, "'Riches for the Gentiles' (Rom 11:12): Israel's Rejection and Paul's Gentile Mission," *JBL* 112 (1993) 81–98.

2. παράπτωμα is more often translated "trespass." But the image of stumbling in v. 11 suggests a rendering more etymologically transparent.

3. On the rare word ἥττημα, see James D. G. Dunn, *Romans* (2 vols.; Waco, Tex.: Word, 1988) 2:654.

4. Given the parallelism with the two previous statements, the genitive must be subjective (Israel's rejection of the message) rather than objective (God's rejection of Israel). Israel's acceptance (v. 15) is likewise to be seen as subjective. The action of rejection and acceptance is Israel's, not God's; God has hardened (v. 7) but not rejected (v. 1) the "rest." On this point, see Lloyd Gaston, "Israel's Misstep in the Eyes of Paul," in *Paul and the Torah* (Vancouver: University of British Columbia Press, 1987) 146.

5. Indeed, there is no verb at all in these sentences, subject and predicate simply being linked by an understood copula; the NRSV translators supplied the verb "means" to indicate (correctly) that some cause-and-effect sequence is in view.

6. Paul J. Achtemeier, *Romans* (Interpretation; Atlanta: John Knox, 1985) 180.

7. Similar comments on v. 11 (p. 180) and v. 17 (p. 183)—about the apostles turning to the Gentiles because of the lack of response among the Jews—show how in Achtemeier's reading the two verses are being interpreted with reference to each other.

8. E.g., Justin Martyr, who identifies the church with Rachel, the beloved wife, who displaces Leah (i.e., Israel) and takes over both the name and the family possessions (*Dial.* 134–35). This aspect of early Christian self-identification has been well studied; see, e.g., Marcel Simon, *Verus Israel* (Oxford: Oxford University Press, 1986 [1968]); James Parkes, *The Conflict of the Church and the Synagogue* (New York: Atheneum, 1985 [1936]); Rosemary Ruether, *Faith and Fratricide* (Minneapolis: Seabury, 1974).

9. For references to scholars holding this view, see above, chap. 1, n. 75.

10. See: Johannes Munck, *Paul and the Salvation of Mankind* (London: SCM, 1959) 44, 264, 275; W. Grundmann, "Paulus, aus dem Volke Israel, Apostel der Völker," *NovT* 4 (1960) 290; Wolfhart Pannenberg, *Jesus — God and Man* (Philadelphia: Westminster, 1968) 72; and (surprisingly) Krister Stendahl, *Paul among Jews and Gentiles* (Philadelphia: Fortress, 1976) 28–29.

11. See, esp. Seyoon Kim, *The Origin of Paul's Gospel* (Grand Rapids: Eerdmans, 1982) 83–95, where it is argued that Paul understood his call against the background of Isa 6, which contains both a call (vv. 1-8) and a statement of Israel's obduracy (vv. 9-13).

12. The singular form (συγκοινωνός) is due to the fact that Paul refers to Gentile Christians collectively as a single shoot—a point not without significance: a single shoot joining a sizable number of branches already there (those broken off being only "some" [τινες]).

13. See, e.g., C. E. B. Cranfield, *A Critical and Exegetical Commentary on the Epistle to the Romans* (2 vols.; Edinburgh: T. & T. Clark, 1975, 1979) 2:567; Dunn, *Romans,* 2:661; Ernst Käsemann, *Commentary on Romans* (Grand Rapids: Eerdmans, 1980) 308; also most English translations (KJV, NEB, JB, NIV); see also William S. Campbell, *Paul's Gospel in an Intercultural Context* (Frankfurt: Peter Lang, 1992) 52, 87–88. Somewhat surprisingly, given his sensitivity to the place of Israel in NT theology, Markus Barth accepts the translation "in their place," though he argues that the apparent "succession" theology of this statement is undercut in the rest of the passage; see Markus Barth, *The People of God* (Sheffield: JSOT, 1983) 42; so also Anders Nygren, *Commentary on Romans* (Philadelphia: Fortress, 1949) 399. For the (unlikely) opinion that "among them" refers to the branches lopped off, see W. D. Davies, "Paul and the Gentiles: A Suggestion Concerning Romans 11:13-24," in *Jewish and Pauline Studies* (Philadelphia: Fortress, 1984) 155.

14. To his credit, Chrysostom gives due weight to this point: "For even if these had fallen a thousand times, the Gentiles would not have been saved unless they had shown faith. As the Jews likewise would not have perished unless they had been unbelieving and disputatious" (*Homilies on Romans* 19 [on 11.12]).

15. See the entry for καλός in LSJ. An example of polite refusal appears in Aristophanes' play *Ranae* (line 888), where Euripides replies to the urging of Dionysus ("Now put on incense, you") in these words: "Excuse me, no [the whole clause rendering the single word καλῶς]; my vows are paid to other gods than these" (Loeb translation).

16. T. W. Manson, "Romans," in Matthew Black and H. H. Rowley, eds., *Peake's Commentary on the Bible* (London: Thomas Nelson, 1962) 949. See also Leon Morris, *The Epistle to the Romans* (Grand Rapids: Eerdmans, 1988) 414.

17. Gaston's interpretation of Israel's "misstep" will be touched on in the following section (§8.2).

18. See, e.g., Johannes Munck, *Christ and Israel* (Philadelphia: Fortress, 1967) 120; Achtemeier, *Romans*, 180.

19. Karl Barth, *Church Dogmatics* II/2 (Edinburgh: T. & T. Clark, 1957) 278–79; Cranfield, *Romans*, 2:556. Cranfield combines this reading with the more usual one. See also Pannenberg, *Jesus — God and Man*, 72.

20. Barth, *Church Dogmatics*, II/2:279.

21. So Cranfield, *Romans*, 2:555–56.

22. See the discussion in §8.2 below.

23. This approach is taken, with variations in detail, by many; e.g., Franz Mussner, *Tractate on the Jews* (Philadelphia: Fortress, 1984) 211; Achtemeier, *Romans*, 180; Paula Fredriksen, "Judaism, the Circumcision of Gentiles, and Apocalyptic Hope: Another Look at Galatians 1 and 2," *JTS*, 42 (1991) 561–64; Barnabas Lindars, "The Old Testament and Universalism in Paul," *BJRL* 69 (1987) 513; Nils A. Dahl, "The Future of Israel," in *Studies in Paul* (Minneapolis: Augsburg, 1977) 150; C. H. Dodd, *The Epistle of Paul to the Romans* (London: Hodder & Stoughton, 1932) 176–77; Dunn, *Romans*, 2:667; John Ziesler, *Paul's Letter to the Romans* (London: SCM/Philadelphia: TPI, 1989) 273–74; Cranfield, *Romans*, 2:556; Nygren, *Romans*, 395; W. Sanday and A. C. Headlam, *A Critical and Exegetical Commentary on the The Epistle to the Romans* (Edinburgh: T. & T. Clark, 1902) 321.

24. Dahl, "The Future of Israel," 150. Meyer assesses Paul's statements in Acts in similar terms, differentiating between "a condition of possibility (that without which the world mission could not have taken place at all)" and "a condition of actuality (that without which it would not have taken place in the way it actually did)"; see Ben Meyer, *The Early Christians* (Wilmington, Del.: Glazier, 1986) 93–94. For a similar reluctance to press the causal connection or to see the rejection of Israel as essential, see the comments of Calvin and Luther in their commentaries on this passage.

25. See above, pp. 176–78.

26. E. P. Sanders, *Paul, the Law, and the Jewish People* (Philadelphia: Fortress, 1983) 197.

27. As noted by Dahl, *Studies in Paul*, 150–51.

28. For a discussion of this type of argumentation, see, e.g., Richard N. Longenecker, *Biblical Exegesis in the Apostolic Period* (Grand Rapids: Eerdmans, 1975) 34, 117. Examples, usually with πόσῳ μᾶλλον ("much more"), can be found elsewhere in Paul; e.g., Rom 5:9, 10; 11:24; 2 Cor 3:9, 11.

29. Wright denies that v. 26 has to do with a future salvation of Israel at the end of the age, arguing that οὕτως ("so") indicates means rather than time, and that "Israel" refers to the new covenant community of Jew and Gentile being brought into being in the present period; N. T. Wright, *The Climax of the Covenant* (Philadelphia: Fortress, 1991) 246–51. On the latter point, see the discussion of his reading of "Israel" above (chap. 6, note 41). On the former point, while he is correct about οὕτως ("so"), the temporal framework has already been established in the previous verse with ἄχρις οὖ ("until"). If the hardening of part of

Israel is to last *"until* the fullness of the Gentiles comes in," then the salvation of all Israel cannot take place until after this—unless of course there is a dizzying shift in the meaning of "Israel" in full argumentative flight. This means that "some temporal weight cannot be excluded" from v. 26 (Dunn, *Romans,* 2:681).

30. A reference to the parousia here is widely accepted; see, e.g., Dunn, *Romans,* 2:682; Käsemann, *Romans,* 314; Cranfield, *Romans,* 2:578. For the unlikely suggestion that Paul is referring to a future, final mission to Israel prior to the parousia, see Jürgen Becker, *Paul: Apostle to the Gentiles* (Louisville: Westminster/John Knox, 1993) 468–72; for a similar view, where the "Deliverer" is identified as Yahweh, see Christopher D. Stanley, "The Redeemer Will Come ἐκ Σιων: Romans 11.26-27 Revisited," in C. A. Evans and J. A. Sanders, eds., *Paul and the Scriptures of Israel* (Sheffield: Sheffield Academic Press, 1993) 118–42.

31. Indeed, it was the observations discussed in the following pages that caused me to turn away from an eschatological pilgrimage reading of Paul; see above, pp. 192–94.

32. See also Rom 2:5-11; 1 Cor 1:18; 2 Cor 2:15-16; 1 Thess 1:10; 2 Thess 1:8-10. For a discussion of these texts, in conjunction with those suggestive of universal salvation, see M. Eugene Boring, "The Language of Universal Salvation in Paul," *JBL* 105 (1986) 269–92.

33. On "their acceptance" as a subjective genitive, see above, chap. 8, n. 4. On the christocentric nature of Rom 11, see the discussion in the next section (§8.2).

34. Most modern commentators see this as a reference to the resurrection; e.g., Dunn, *Romans,* 2:658; Cranfield, *Romans,* 2:563; W. D. Davies, "Paul and the People of Israel," *NTS* 24 (1977) 16.

35. This idea has been noted occasionally, but never pursued; see, e.g., Kim, *Origin,* 96–97.

36. Richard B. Hays, *Echoes of Scripture in the Letters of Paul* (New Haven/London: Yale University Press, 1989) 61.

37. Dale C. Allison, "The Background of Romans 11:11-15 in Apocalyptic and Rabbinic Literature," *Studia Biblica et Theologica* 10 (1980) 229–34; for a later version of the paper, see "Romans 11:11-15: A Suggestion," *Perspectives in Religious Studies* 12 (1985) 23–30. See also E. Elizabeth Johnson, *The Function of Apocalyptic and Wisdom Traditions in Romans 9–11* (Atlanta: Scholars, 1989) 125–26.

38. *T. Dan* 6:4; *T. Sim.* 6:2–7; *T. Jud.* 23:5; *T. Mos.* 1:18; 2 *Bar.* 78:6–7; *Apoc. Abr.* 23:5; 4 *Ezra* 4:38–43; *b. Sanh.* 97b, 98a ; *b. Šabb.* 118b; *Sipre* 41 (79b).

39. Allison, "The Background of Romans 11:11-15," 229.

40. Ibid., 232

41. See above, p. 60.

42. 2 *Bar.* 72.1–6 treats Gentiles more positively, granting them a place in the eschatological future. With R. H. Charles ("2 Baruch," *APOT,* 2:474–76) and A. F. J. Klijn ("2 Baruch," *OTP,* 1:617–18), however, I view the "Cloud and Waters Apocalypse" of chaps. 53–74 as an already existing unit incorporated into 2 *Baruch.*

43. *B. Yeb.* 47b; *b. 'Abod. Zar.* 24a; *b. B. Mes.* 59b; see George Foot Moore, *Judaism in the First Centuries of the Christian Era* (3 vols.; Cambridge, Mass.: Harvard University Press, 1927–1930) 1:341.

44. *Ant.* 20.44.

45. B. *'Abod. Zar.* 3b; also *b. Yeb.* 24b. The tradition is associated with R. Jose, a second-generation Tanna.

46. On the dating, see W. D. Davies, *Paul and Rabbinic Judaism* (London: SPCK, 1948) 65.

47. Lloyd Gaston, "Paul and the Torah," in A. T. Davies, ed., *Antisemitism and the Foundations of Christianity* (New York/Toronto: Paulist, 1979) 61. While I agree with Gaston on this starting point, I part company with him on his interpretation of Paul's subsequent experience; see the discussion in the next section (§8.2).

48. See the discussion in Dunn, *Romans,* 2:520.

49. The precise sense of εἰς τέλος remains uncertain; see, e.g., the discussion in Carol J. Schlueter, *Filling Up the Measure* (Sheffield: Sheffield Academic Press, 1994) 18–38; Ernest Best, *A Commentary on the First and Second Epistles to the Thessalonians* (London: A. & C. Black, 1972) 121. In view of the temporal sense of the first part of the sentence ("constantly filling up the measure of their sins"), a temporal sense seems preferable here as well.

50. On the preliminary question of authenticity, there is no solid evidence to support Pearson's interpolation theory; see Birger A. Pearson, "1 Thessalonians 2:13-16: A Deutero-Pauline Interpolation," *HTR* 64 (1971) 79–94. For a thorough and up-to-date treatment of the passage as a whole, see Schlueter, *Filling Up the Measure.*

51. See Peter Richardson, *Israel in the Apostolic Church* (Cambridge: Cambridge University Press, 1969) 110–11.

52. Best suggests that this was triggered by something in Paul's own experience at the time of writing; see *Thessalonians,* 115. On this verse as an indication of the significance of the Jerusalem church for Paul, see B. Rigaux, *The Letters of St. Paul* (Chicago: Franciscan Herald Press, 1968) 61.

53. 1 Thess 1:6; 1 Cor 4:16; 11:1; Phil 3:17; 2 Thess 3:7, 9.

54. Ironically, given the usual concerns about the anti-Jewish tone of the passage, this strong identification with the Judean Christians is also counted as evidence for inauthenticity; see Robert Jewett, *The Thessalonian Correspondence* (Philadelphia: Fortress, 1986) 54.

55. Koenig's suggestion, that Christian prophets are in view here, is unlikely; see John Koenig, *Jews and Christians in Dialogue* (Philadelphia: Westminster, 1979) 47.

56. The fundamental work on this material has been done by O. Steck, *Israel und das gewaltsame Geschick der Propheten* (Neukirchen-Vluyn: Neukirchener Verlag, 1967). For an analysis of the Jewish and Gentile elements in the passage, see Becker, *Paul: Apostle to the Gentiles,* 461–62.

57. See, e.g., the references collected in n. 60 of my article, "Moses Typology and the Sectarian Nature of Early Christian Anti-Judaism: A Study in Acts 7," *JSNT* 12 (1981) 51–52, together with the comments on pp. 44–45.

58. Munck attempts to align v. 16 with Rom 11:25-26 by reading εἰς τέλος (to the end) as if it were ἕως τέλους (until the end); see Munck, *Christ and Israel,* 64. Further, while it is clear that Paul has only particular groups of Jews in view here, the force of τῶν Ἰουδαίων (the Jews; v. 14) is not to be softened by eliminating the following comma, thereby rendering the participle (ἀποκτεινάντων) with a restrictive clause (i.e., "[only] those Jews who killed both the Lord Jesus and the prophets . . ."). For this suggestion, see Koenig, *Jews and Christians in Dia-*

*logue,* 47–48. Schlueter insists, quite rightly, that the passage needs to be taken on its own terms and not harmonized with Rom 11; see *Filling Up the Measure,* esp. 54–64.

59. For a thorough (though no longer fully up-to-date) survey, see C. H. Giblin, *The Threat to Faith: An Exegetical and Theological Re-examination of 2 Thessalonians 2* (Rome: Pontifical Biblical Institute, 1967). Best provides a very helpful shorter survey of the issues and options; see *Thessalonians,* 290–302.

60. Oscar Cullmann, "Le caractère eschatologique du devoir missionaire et de la conscience apostolique de S. Paul: Étude sur le κατέχον (-ων) de 2 Thess. 2:6-7," *RHPhR* 16 (1936) 210–45; Munck, *Paul,* 36–42.

61. See, e.g., the comments by John Knox, with which I am in considerable agreement; "Romans 15:14-33 and Paul's Conception of His Apostolic Mission," *JBL* 83 (1964) 1–11.

62. For the grammatical difficulties here, see Best, *Thessalonians,* 294–95.

63. If 2 Thess is authentic, it dates from the same time period as 1 Thess. One can assume that the expectation evident in 1 Thess 4:17 was still the case for Paul.

64. Schweitzer, *Mysticism,* esp. 181–87.

65. In chap 5, for example, he attempts to explain it as the result of Paul's attempt to combine two quite distinct forms of Jewish eschatology, a Son of Man form rooted in Daniel and *1 Enoch,* and a Davidic Messiah form going back to the prophets. But such a distinction cannot be maintained.

66. On these points, see pp. 147–48 above.

67. On this point, see §6.3 above.

68. Alan F. Segal, "Conversion and Universalism: Opposites that Attract," in Bradley H. Mclean, ed., *Origins and Method: Towards a New Understanding of Judaism and Christianity* (Sheffield: Sheffield Academic Press, 1993) 188; see also *Paul the Convert,* 204.

69. See esp. the discussion of Rom 4 in §5.1 above.

70. Stendahl, *Paul among Jews and Gentiles,* esp. 4, 132; John G. Gager, *The Origins of Anti-Semitism* (Oxford: Oxford University Press, 1983). See also P. Lapide (with P. Stuhlmacher), *Paul: Rabbi and Apostle* (Minneapolis: Augsburg, 1984); Philip A. Cunningham, *Jewish Apostle to the Gentiles* (Mystic, Conn.: Twenty-Third Publications, 1986); Sidney G. Hall, *Christian Anti-Semitism and Paul's Theology* (Minneapolis: Fortress, 1993).

71. Gaston, "Paul and the Torah," in Davies, *Antisemitism and the Foundations of Christianity,* 48–71.

72. Lloyd Gaston, *Paul and the Torah* (Vancouver: University of British Columbia Press, 1987).

73. Gaston, "Paul and the Torah," 66.

74. Gager, *Origins,* 218.

75. The quoted words are from Stendahl, *Paul among Jews and Gentiles,* 4; for Gaston, see "Israel's Misstep," esp. 147–48. He does not rule out completely a reference to the parousia in Rom 11:26, but "if Christ is meant, then it is Christ in a different role, Christ as the agent of the 'Sonderweg' of Israel's salvation."

76. Gaston, "Paul and the Torah," 66.

77. He believes that the identification of the Noachian decrees as the standard of righteousness for Gentiles was not made until Maimonides; see ibid., 56–57.

78. Ibid., 60.

79. Ibid., 62.

80. Lapide, *Paul: Rabbi and Apostle*, 69.

81. See esp. Johnson, *Apocalyptic and Wisdom Traditions*, 176–205; also Heikki Räisänen, "Paul, God and Israel: Romans 9–11 in Recent Research," in J. Neusner et al., eds., *The Social World of Formative Christanity* (Philadelphia: Fortress, 1988) 189–91; Segal, *Paul the Convert*, 129–33; Davies, "Paul and the People of Israel"; Sanders, *Paul, the Law, and the Jewish People*, 193–95; Robert Jewett, "The Law and the Coexistence of Jews and Gentiles in Romans," *Int* 39 (1985) 348–49; Paula Fredriksen, *From Jesus to Christ* (New Haven: Yale University Press, 1988) 161–63.

82. This weakness has seldom been observed. For this component of Paul's convictions, see pp. 124–28 above.

83. Again, see the discussion of Rom 4 in §5.1 above.

84. As Segal points out, it is not proper to say that in righteous Gentiles conceptions, the law does not apply to Gentiles; rather, the Gentiles are bound by those part of the Torah that apply to them in particular; see *Paul the Convert*, 129.

85. Fredriksen, "Judaism, the Circumcision of Gentiles, and Apocalyptic Hope." This article amplifies the discussion in her earlier work, *From Jesus to Christ*, 165–76. The book by Mark D. Nanos, *The Mystery of Romans: The Jewish Context of Paul's Letter* (Minneapolis: Fortress, 1996), appeared too late to be included here.

86. "He knew that he lived in the very last days. And in those days, according to his tradition, God would redeem the nations from their idolatry graciously, without the works of the Law"; Fredriksen, "Judaism, the Circumcision of Gentiles, and Apocalyptic Hope," 564.

87. This statement is made at several points; see Segal, *Paul the Convert*, 139, 204; cf. "Conversion and Universalism," 188. Somewhat similar is Peter J. Tomson, *Paul and the Jewish Law* (Assen: Van Gorcum/Minneapolis: Fortress, 1990); see the discussion above, pp. 147–48.

88. See Segal, *Paul the Convert*, 121, 201–7.

89. Ibid., 204.

90. Ibid., 121.

91. Cf. Jewett, "Coexistence of Jews and Gentiles," 349.

92. For the discussion, see §5.1 above.

93. Note the inclusive first person plurals in Phil 3:15, 16, 20, 21. On the contrasting situation in Galatians, see pp. 180–82 above.

94. Thus the NRSV rendering: "a spiritual circumcision."

95. Cf. "brothers" (ἀδελφοί) in v. 1; one wonders to what extent Paul's fictive kinship language is shaped by the belief that Christians are now members of the family *of Abraham*.

96. For a discussion (and rejection) of the suggestions that "root" refers either to the Jewish Christian remnant or to Christ himself, see above, chap. 6, n. 42.

97. E. W. Burton, *A Critical and Exegetical Commentary on the Epistle to the Galatians* (Edinburgh: T. & T. Clark, 1921) 357–58; Peter Richardson, *Israel in the Apostolic Church* (Cambridge: Cambridge University Press, 1969) 74–84.

98. See the discussion in Hans Dieter Betz, *Galatians* (Philadelphia: Fortress, 1979) 320–23; Richard N. Longenecker, *Galatians* (Waco, Tex.: Word, 1990) 296–99.

99. Discussed above in §4.2 and §5.3, respectively.

100. Richardson (*Israel in the Apostolic Church*) has made the important observation that Justin was the first to apply the name Israel unambiguously to the church.

101. See the discussion above, pp. 176–78.

102. See the discussion above, pp. 182–84.

103. Perhaps one gets closer to an empirical classification in the tripartite division of humankind into Jews, Greeks, and the church of God in 1 Cor 10:32.

104. Above, pp. 123–24.

105. Above, pp. 179–80.

106. For the discussion of this passage, see above, pp. 179–80.

107. They are "debtors" (ὀφειλέται; v. 27).

108. For a discussion of this verse, including the translation difficulties, see above, pp. 95–98.

109. See above, p. 218.

110. For the discussion of Gal 3:13-14, see above, pp. 180–82.

111. See §6.3 above.

112. See §3.2 above.

113. See §5.2 above, esp. pp. 149–51, and §7.2, esp. pp. 210–12.

114. Above, §6.2, esp. pp. 171–73.

115. Ibid.

116. Above, pp. 146–47.

117. Above, pp. 205–7.

118. See pp. 189–91, and 211–12.

119. Thus Israel is more than simply an example or archetype of the universal situation; so Ernst Käsemann, "'The Righteousness of God' in Paul," 179; and "Paul and Israel," 184–87; both in *New Testament Questions of Today* (London: SCM, 1969). I agree with Barth: "In Rom 9–11, God's chosen people . . . serves not only as a *model* but also as an *instrument* of God's mercy upon all mankind"; *The People of God*, 32.

120. Wright, *Climax*, 196.

121. As noted on several occasions; see pp. 197–98, 208–9.

122. The term originates with Sanders. There is a sense in which Hooker is correct when she says that Paul's participatory language is his way of explaining the salvation of the Gentiles, though the origins of both are much more deeply rooted than she seems to suggest; see Morna D. Hooker, "Paul and 'Covenantal Nomism,'" in Morna D. Hooker and Stephen G. Wilson (eds.), *Paul and Paulinism* (London: SPCK, 1982) 53.

123. E.g., see above, pp. 160–61.

124. See above, pp. 185–86.

125. Of course by this time, he has had to face the possibility of his own death (2 Cor 1:8-9; 4:7—5:10).

126. Any attempt to do so on the basis of Paul should work more from his underlying convictions than from his surface arguments and developed theology. See further, §12.3 below.

# Chapter 9

1. Krister Stendahl, *Paul among Jews and Gentiles* (Philadelphia: Fortress, 1976) 7.

2. E.g., Seyoon Kim, *The Origin of Paul's Gospel* (Grand Rapids: Eerdmans, 1982) 57; F. F. Bruce, *Paul: Apostle of the Heart Set Free* (Grand Rapids: Eerdmans, 1977) 75.

3. Stendahl was influenced in significant ways by Munck, who begins his study of Paul with a chapter entitled "The Call"; see Johannes Munck, *Paul and the Salvation of Mankind* (London: SCM, 1959) 11–35. Others to be mentioned here include E. P. Sanders, *Paul, the Law, and the Jewish People* (Philadelphia: Fortress, 1983), esp. 152; J. Christiaan Beker, *Paul the Apostle* (Philadelphia: Fortress, 1980), e.g., 3–6; Ferdinand Hahn, *Mission in the New Testament* (Naperville, Ill.: Allenson, 1965) 97–98; Ulrich Wilckens, "Die Bekehrung des Paulus als religionsgeschichtliche Problem," *Rechtfertigung als Freiheit: Paulusstudien* (Neukirchen-Vluyn: Neukirchener Verlag, 1974) 12–13; Christian Dietzfelbinger, *Die Berufung des Paulus als Ursprung seiner Theologie* (Neukirchen-Vluyn: Neukirchener Verlag, 1985); Philip A. Cunningham, *Jewish Apostle to the Gentiles* (Mystic, Conn.: Twenty-Third Publications, 1986) 23; Larry W. Hurtado, "Convert, Apostate or Apostle to the Nations: The 'Conversion' of Paul in Recent Scholarship," *SR* 22 (1993–94) 277.

4. As previous discussions indicate, many of those cited in n. 3 above fall into this category.

5. Sanders, *Paul, the Law, and the Jewish People*, 152. Though the point is not developed, Larry Hurtado seems to move in a similar direction when he suggests that "some sort of prophet-like sense of being divinely commissioned to the gentiles came to him and that subsequently and as a consequence and corollary of that eschatological commission, Paul developed his emphasis on salvation through Christ without observance of Torah;" "Convert, Apostate or Apostle to the Nations," 277.

6. See above, pp. 17–18, 142–43.

7. Knox strikes the right balance here; see John Knox, "Romans 15:14-33 and Paul's Conception of His Apostolic Mission," *JBL* 83 (1964) 1–11, esp. pp. 5–8.

8. Cf. Kim, who holds that Paul had come to such a viewpoint (with the aid of Isa 6 and 49) in the immediate aftermath of the Damascus experience; *Origin*, 91–99.

9. See James D. G. Dunn, *Romans* (2 vols.; Waco, Tex.: Word, 1988) 2:520.

10. See above, p. 217.

11. See, e.g., Knox, "Romans 15:14-33"; Rainer Riesner, *Die Frühzeit des Apostels Paulus* (Tübingen: Mohr [Siebeck], 1994) 204–73.

12. He uses the term ἔθνη ("Gentiles, nations") in connection with his apostolic role in Rom 1:5,13; 11:13; 15:15–18; Gal 1:16; 2:2,8,9; Col 1:25-27; 1 Thess 2:16. Similar usage appears in Eph 3:1-13; 1 Tim 2:7; 2 Tim 4:17.

13. Above, pp. 182–84.

14. Contra Dunn (*Romans* 2:656), the absence of the article in Rom 11:13 does not preclude the translation "*the* apostle of the Gentiles" (found in NIV, JB); predicate nominatives are often anarthrous. Probably Paul was prepared to recognize as apostles other missionaries to the Gentiles, such as Barnabas (1 Cor 9:5-6). But in Gal 2:1-10, he leaves Barnabas to one side, claiming for himself the unique role on the Gentile side of things as to one to whom "the gospel for the uncircumcised" was entrusted, a role matched only by that of Peter with respect to the "gospel for the circumcised." While he is aware that the church of Rome

was founded by others, he still feels that because of his special apostolic role it is quite appropriate to write to them (Rom 15:15-16) and to preach the gospel among them (1:5-6,11-13).

15. Certainly the term often is used of individuals rather than nations: only individuals can observe the law from the heart (Rom 2:14-16); one does not eat with nations (Gal 2:12). Still, the basic sense of (non-Jewish) nation does not fall away entirely. In Rom 9–11, for example, in three of the four occurrences ἔθνη is set over against "Israel," i.e., another nation. Further, the statement that he has completed his apostolic mission to the "Gentiles" (Rom 15:15-19) in the east makes little sense if he conceived his mission simply as having to do with non-Jewish individuals; see Munck, *Paul,* 52.

16. This point has been made, *inter alia,* by W. Grundmann, "Paulus, aus dem Volke Israel, Apostel der Völker," *NovT* 4 (1960) 267–91; Friedrich-Wilhelm Marquardt, *Die Juden im Römerbrief* (Zurich: Theologischer Verlag, 1971) 9, 36; Karl-Wilhelm Niebuhr, *Heidenapostel aus Israel* (Tübingen: Mohr [Siebeck], 1992).

17. There is nothing in Paul's tone to suggest that the information was first communicated to the Galatians by the rival teachers; it must have come from Paul during his initial evangelization, the only opportunity for such a communication prior to the letter itself; so Heinrich Schlier, *Der Brief an der Galater* (Göttingen: Vandenhoeck & Ruprecht, 1971) 49; Martin Hengel, *The Pre-Christian Paul* (London: SCM/Philadelphia: Trinity, 1991) 66. There is nothing in the text to support the NRSV rendering "you have heard, *no doubt.*"

18. Cf. Fee's observation: "By concluding the considerable enumeration of resurrection witnesses with his own, which in turn led to a short digression about his apostleship, Paul's argument has gotten away from him a bit"; Gordon D. Fee, *The First Epistle of Paul to the Corinthians* (Grand Rapids: Eerdmans, 1987) 736.

19. Cf. Sanders's comment on 2 Cor 11:24; *Paul, the Law, and the Jewish People,* 192.

20. Cf. Grundmann, who describes Paul as one in whom Israel's destiny is recognizable; "Paulus," 267.

21. The most complete study is Karl Olav Sandnes, *Paul — One of the Prophets?* (Tübingen: Mohr [Siebeck], 1991). See also Munck, *Paul,* 24–35; Stendahl, *Paul among Jews and Gentiles,* 7–23; Lucien Cerfaux, *The Christian in the Theology of St. Paul* (New York: Herder & Herder, 1967) 79–88; Kim, *Origin,* 91–99; Niebuhr, *Heidenapostel aus Israel,* 76; A.-M. Denis, "L'Apôtre Paul, prophète 'messianique' des Gentils," *EThL* 33 (1957) 245–318. For the suggestion that Gal 1:15-16 reflects "sapiental autobiography" (cf. Sir 51:13–22; Wis 7:7–22) as well, see Dieter Georgi, *Theocracy in Paul's Praxis and Theology* (Minneapolis: Fortress, 1991) 18.

22. Cf. ὁ ἀφορίσας με ἐκ κοιλίας μητρός μου καὶ καλέσας διὰ τῆς χάριτος αὐτοῦ (the one who set me apart from my mother's womb and called [me] through his grace; Gal 1:15) and ἐκ κοιλίας μητρός μου ἐκάλεσε τὸ ὄνομά μου (from my mother's womb he called my name; LXX Isa 49:1).

23. Apart from the kerygmatic summary in 1 Cor 15:3-4, Paul's use of scripture reflects very little of the concern attributed to him by Luke to prove by the scriptures "that it was necessary for the Messiah to suffer and to rise from the dead" (Acts 17:2-3). Ellis's argument—that he assumed it, but wanted to advance to the next stage—relies too much on silence; see E. Earle Ellis, *Paul's Use of the*

*Old Testament* (Grand Rapids: Baker, 1981 [1957]) 115. Paul's Old Testament exegesis is more typically in the service of ecclesiology (especially with reference to the Gentiles) than of christology.

24. Other passages from Isaiah are occasionally put forward as sources for Paul's sense of vocation, esp. chap. 6 (Kim, *Origin*, 85–99) and 66:18–19 (R. D. Aus, "Paul's Travel Plans to Spain and the 'Full Number of the Gentiles' of Rom XI 25," *NovT* 21 [1979] 232–62; Riesner, *Frühzeit*, 216–25). The absence of any specific citation or allusion, however, renders such suggestions speculative.

25. See Dunn, *Romans*, 2:620–32.

26. While he rejects it, a good discussion of this point can be found in Sandnes, *Paul*, 6, 61–65.

27. On Paul's use of birth imagery with respect to his call, see George W. E. Nickelsburg, "An Ἔκτρωμα, though Appointed from the Womb: Paul's Apostolic Self-Description in 1 Corinthians 15 and Galatians 1," in G. W. E. Nickelsburg and G. W. MacRae, eds., *Christians among Jews and Gentiles* (Philadelphia: Fortress, 1986) 198–205.

28. See K. L. Schmidt, "ἀφορίζω," *TDNT*, 5:454–55.

29. For discussions of this point, see Munck, *Paul*, 50–51; Grundmann, "Paulus," 282–84; Cerfaux, *The Christian in the Theology of St. Paul*, 96–97; K. Weiss, "Paulus—Priester der christlichen Kultgemeinde," *ThLZ* 79 (1954) 355–64.

30. Contra Jürgen Becker, *Paul: Apostle to the Gentiles* (Louisville: Westminster/John Knox, 1993) 73.

31. Rom 16:5; 1 Cor 16:15. The term appears in some MSS at 2 Thess 2:13; if original, this would represent the only place where a congregation itself is described as the "firstfruits." While the MS evidence is about evenly balanced, the fact that elsewhere Paul specifies the entity of which the ἀπαρχή is the firstfruits, suggests that the reading "from the beginning" (ἀπ᾽ ἀρχῆς) is more likely; so Ernest Best, *A Commentary on the First and Second Epistles to the Thessalonians* (London: A. & C. Black, 1972) 312–13.

32. This renders the single word σπένδομαι; for the cultic reference of the word, see O. Michel, "σπένδομαι," *TDNT*, 7:528–36. Hawthorne's attempt to deny a reference to Paul's death here—seeing instead a more general reference to his sufferings as an apostle—is unpersuasive; see Gerald F. Hawthorne, *Philippians* (Waco, Tex.: Word, 1983) 105–6.

33. Literally, "sacrifice and service" (θυσία καὶ λειτουργία); but since the words are linked with a single article, the phrase is to be taken as a hendiadys (see Hawthorne, *Philippians*, 105).

34. While Paul's Corinthian readers might have heard the statement in terms of the temples of their own Greco-Roman world (where a similar practice was found), the fact that he goes on to talk of the Lord's similar command for apostles (οὕτως [so]; v. 14) indicates that he himself has the Jewish temple in view. See Alan F. Segal, *Paul the Convert* (New Haven/London: Yale University Press, 1990) 171; Fee, *First Corinthians*, 412.

35. The root can refer to other types of service; in Rom 13:6, for example, he describes the governing authorities as God's servants (λειτουργοί).

36. For the cultic associations of εὐπρόσδεκτος, see W. Grundmann, *TDNT* 2:58–59. Paul uses this term with cultic connotations in Rom 15:16, and related terms in Rom 12:1 and Phil 4:18.

37. For discussion of this proselyte sacrifice, see above, p. 58.

38. Several scholars suggest Isa 66:20 as the background; e.g., Aus, "Paul's Travel Plans"; Riesner, *Frühzeit*, 218–19; Dunn, *Romans*, 2:860. But not only is there a difference in vocabulary (δῶρον [gift] in LXX Isa 66:20, but προσφορά [offering] in Rom 15:16), in the Isaiah passage it is the Diaspora Jews themselves who are the offering; it is quite a jump to think that Paul grounded his ministry as a Jewish apostle bringing Gentiles as an offering, on a text which speaks of Gentiles bringing Jews. Further, while understanding the attractiveness of Isa 66:18–21 for Pauline interpreters—it is, after all, the only Old Testament text that seems to speak of an actual mission to the nations—the complete absence of any citation or allusion by Paul himself cautions us against any substantial reliance on it.

39. Above, pp. 62, 69.

40. Whether Paul sees his goal as Spain (so Aus, "Paul's Travel Plans;" Riesner, *Frühzeit*, 204–73), or as a complete circuit of the Mediterranean (cf. κύκλῳ ["in a circle"], Rom 15:19; so Knox, "Romans 15:14-33"), the Jerusalem anchor and starting point remains the same. Other hints of the geographical dimensions of his goal are found in the Corinthian correspondence (1 Cor 14:36; 2 Cor 10:13-16); cf. Jerome H. Neyrey, *Paul, in Other Words* (Louisville: Westminster/John Knox, 1990) 93–94.

41. *Abr.* 98, and *Spec. leg.* 2.163. See also *Spec. leg.* 1.97; 2.163–67; *Vit. Mos.* 1.149. In Philo's view, Israel offers to God on their behalf the type of worship that all nations should themselves be giving.

42. Paul would think of it rather as a door! See 1 Cor 16:9; 2 Cor 2:12; Col 4:3.

43. 2 *Bar* 41.1-6; see above, pp. 224–26.

44. Cf. Nickelsburg, "An Ἔκτρωμα."

45. On the question of a Jewish mission, see above, pp. 59–60, and further below, pp. 275–78.

# Chapter 10

1. See above, pp. 22–26.

2. Respectively, W. D. Davies, *Paul and Rabbinic Judaism* (London: SPCK, 1948) 63; E. P. Sanders, *Paul, the Law and the Jewish People* (Philadelphia: Fortress, 1983) 152; and Lloyd Gaston, "Paul and the Torah," in Alan T. Davies, ed., *Antisemitism and the Foundations of Christianity* (New York/Toronto: Paulist, 1979) 62. See also R. David Kaylor, *Paul's Covenant Community* (Atlanta: John Knox, 1988) 170; Daniel Boyarin, *A Radical Jew* (Berkeley/Los Angeles/London: University of California Press, 1994) 29, 39, 44.

3. Gaston sees him as a Shammaite; "Paul and the Torah," 61.

4. Krister Stendahl, *Paul among Jews and Gentiles* (Philadelphia: Fortress, 1976) 14–15.

5. Davies's phrase; see *Paul and Rabbinic Judaism*, 67.

6. Some of the discussion in this and the subsequent section can be found in an earlier form in my article, "Zealot and Convert: The Origin of Paul's Christ-Torah Antithesis," *CBQ* 51 (1989) 660–64.

7. See Heikki Räisänen, *Paul and the Law* (Philadelphia: Fortress, 1986)

251–63; idem, "Paul's Conversion and the Development of his View of the Law," *NTS* 33 (1987) 404–19. He builds in significant ways on the work of Georg Strecker; see *Eschaton und Historie* (Göttingen: Vandenhoeck & Ruprecht, 1979); idem, "Befreiung und Rechtfertigung: Zur Stellung der Rechtfertigungslehre in der Theologie des Paulus," in J. Friedrich et al., eds., *Rechtfertigung* (Tübingen: Mohr [Siebeck]/Göttingen: Vandenhoeck & Ruprecht, 1976) 479–508.

8. Räisänen's term; see *Paul and the Law,* 254.

9. Rightly observed by Seyoon Kim, *The Origin of Paul's Gospel* (Grand Rapids: Eerdmans, 1982) 270.

10. His reponse to Kim's criticism on this point evades the issue; *Paul and the Law,* 256, n. 145. And his article, "Paul's Conversion," written in response to criticism that his book does not adequately deal with Paul's accounts of his conversion, continues to ignore the implications of his references to persecuting zeal.

11. Alan F. Segal, *Paul the Convert* (New Haven/London: Yale University Press, 1990) 7.

12. Ibid., 26. See also xii, 11, 205.

13. Ibid., 8. See also 120, 142–43.

14. Ibid., 143.

15. So, e.g., J. Christiaan Beker, *Paul the Apostle* (Philadelphia: Fortress, 1980) 143–44; James D. G. Dunn, *The Partings of the Ways* (London: SCM/Philadelphia: TPI, 1991) 122; Kaylor, *Paul's Covenant Community,* 37, 72.

16. See the comments by Larry W. Hurtado, "Convert, Apostate or Apostle to the Nations: The 'Conversion' of Paul in Recent Scholarship," *SR* 22 (1993–94) 283.

17. Francis Watson, *Paul, Judaism and the Gentiles* (Cambridge: Cambridge University Press, 1986), esp. 28–38. For other scholars holding this view, see above, chap. 1, n. 75.

18. So also William Wrede, *Paul* (London: Green, 1907) 10–11; E. P. Blair, "Paul's Call to the Gentile Mission," *BR* 10 (1965) 23. Schweitzer, too, is open to this possibility, but rejects the idea that the Gentile mission was grounded on the failure of the Jewish; Albert Schweitzer, *The Mysticism of Paul the Apostle* (New York: Seabury, 1968 [1931]) 181–82.

19. Watson's reference to the aorist (presumably ἐγενόμην [became] in vv. 20 and 23) does not support his case, since in v. 21, where the decisive break is supposedly indicated, no verb appears at all, the verb used with respect to the Jews in v. 20 simply being understood. Of more significance for the temporal signification of the passage is the present ποιῶ ("I am doing") in v. 20.

20. It is by no means equivalent to "the gospel of the circumcision" (Gal 2:7), as Watson holds; *Paul, Judaism and the Gentiles,* 30. On this point, see further below, pp. 278–83.

21. Paula Fredriksen, "Paul and Augustine: Conversion Narratives, Orthodox Traditions and the Retrospective Self," *JTS* 37 (1986) 3–34.

22. Watson's words; *Paul, Judaism and the Gentiles,* 32.

23. Edgar J. Goodspeed, *Paul* (New York/Nashville: Abingdon, 1947) 21.

24. See, e.g., Jerome Murphy-O'Connor, "Paul in Arabia," *CBQ* 55 (1993) 732–37. Even Enslin admits that the Arabia references pose problems for his interpretation; Morton Scott Enslin, *Reapproaching Paul* (Philadelphia: Westminster, 1972) 73.

# Chapter 11

1. Cf. Martin Hengel's book by that name (London: SCM/Philadelphia: TPI, 1991).

2. Beverly Roberts Gaventa, *From Darkness to Light* (Philadelphia: Fortress, 1986), esp. 17–51; Paula Fredriksen, "Paul and Augustine: Conversion Narratives, Orthodox Traditions and the Retrospective Self," *JTS* 37 (1986) 3–34. For an earlier example, see Albert Schweitzer, *The Mysticism of Paul the Apostle* (New York: Seabury, 1968 [1931]) 40.

3. Cf. A. E. Harvey, *Jesus and the Constraints of History* (Philadelphia: Westminster, 1982).

4. See the discussion in chap. 2 above.

5. See the discussion of Patte above, p. 43.

6. Pp. 224–26.

7. See S. Safrai, ed., *The Literature of the Sages. Part One* (Assen: Van Gorcum/Philadelphia: Fortress, 1987) 186, 198–200.

8. Cf. also the famous account of Hillel's and Shammai's contrasting responses to the would-be proselyte; *b. Šabb.* 31a.

9. Scot McKnight, *A Light among the Gentiles* (Minneapolis: Fortress, 1991); Martin Goodman, *Mission and Conversion* (Oxford: Clarendon, 1994).

10. Above, pp. 59–60.

11. Emil Schürer, *The History of the Jewish People in the Age of Jesus Christ* (3 vols.; Edinburgh: T. & T. Clark, 1973–87) 3:172; see the full discussion on pp. 172–76.

12. Cf. Josephus *Ap.* 2.178: "But, should anyone of our nation be questioned about the laws, he would repeat them all more readily than his own name. The result, then, of our thorough grounding in the laws from the first dawn of intelligence is that we have them, as it were, engraven on our souls." See the whole discussion about education in Schürer, *History,* 2:417–22.

13. For a discussion of Ananias's position, see above, pp. 68–69.

14. Joachim Jeremias, "Paulus als Hillelit," in E. E. Ellis and M. Wilcox, eds., *Neotestamentica et Semitica* (Edinburgh: T. & T. Clark, 1969) 88–94.

15. So Klaus Haacker, "War Paulus Hillelit?" *Das Institutum Judaicum der Universität Tübingen* (1971–72) 106–20; Lloyd Gaston, "Paul and the Torah," in Alan T. Davies, ed., *Antisemitism and the Foundations of Christianity* (New York/Toronto: Paulist, 1979) 61; Karl-Wilhelm Niebuhr, *Heidenapostel aus Israel* (Tübingen: Mohr [Siebeck], 1992) 56–57; Seyoon Kim, *The Origin of Paul's Gospel* (Grand Rapids: Eerdmans, 1982) 41–44; Hans Hübner, *Law in Paul's Thought* (Edinburgh: T. & T. Clark, 1984) 44, n. 16.

16. Hengel, *The Pre-Christian Paul,* 54–62; the quoted phrase appears on pp. 58–59.

17. Perhaps the "synagogue of the Freedmen" of Acts 6:9, which contained (among others) people from Cilicia (where Tarsus is found). See Hengel, *The Pre-Christian Paul,* 69; Peter van Minnen, "Paul the Roman Citizen," *JSNT* 56 (1994) 43–52.

18. On the latter point, see Hengel, *The Pre-Christian Paul,* 29–34; Niebuhr, *Heidenapostel aus Israel,* 47.

19. For a still-useful discussion of the issue, see Arland J. Hultgren, "Paul's Pre-Christian Persecutions of the Church: Their Purpose, Locale, and Nature," *JBL* 95 (1976) 97–111.

20. For evidence of proselytes in Damascus, see Josephus *War* 2.56–61.

21. The proposal goes back as early as E. Barnikol (*Die vorchristliche und frühchristliche Zeit des Paulus* [Kiel: Walter G. Mühlau Verlag, 1929] 18–24), and has since found a number of supporters: Rudolf Bultmann, "Paul," in *Existence and Faith* (Cleveland/New York: Meridian, 1960) 113; Günther Bornkamm, *Paul* (London: Hodder & Stoughton, 1971) 12; (with hesitation) Hans-Joachim Schoeps, *Paul* (Philadelphia: Westminster, 1961) 64, 219; F. F. Bruce, *Commentary on Galatians* (Grand Rapids: Eerdmans, 1982) 236; Hübner, *Law in Paul's Thought*, 44, 108; Douglas R. A. Hare, *The Theme of Jewish Persecution of Christians in the Gospel according to St. Matthew* (Cambridge: Cambridge University Press, 1967) 12; Gaston, "Paul and the Torah," 61–62; Pinchas Lapide (with Peter Stuhlmacher), *Paul: Rabbi and Apostle* (Minneapolis: Augsburg, 1984) 68.

22. See, e.g., Peter Richardson, *Israel in the Apostolic Church* (Cambridge: Cambridge University Press, 1969) 89; Jürgen Becker, *Paul: Apostle to the Gentiles* (Louisville: Westminster/John Knox, 1993) 39–40; Kim, *Origin*, 41–44.

23. See above, p. 270.

24. See Francis Watson, *Paul, Judaism and the Gentiles* (Cambridge: Cambridge University Press, 1986) 30. While the phrase "to preach circumcision" (περιτομὴν κηρύσσειν) has no doubt been constructed by Paul after the pattern of "to preach Christ" (κηρύσσειν Χριστὸν) (see Heinrich Schlier, *Der Brief an die Galater* [Göttingen: Vandenhoeck & Ruprecht, 1965] 239), there is no foundation to the argument that "since κηρύσσειν is a technical term for Christian proclamation, 'preaching circumcision' is probably equivalent to preaching τὸ εὐαγγέλιον τῆς περιτομῆς (Gal. 2:7)—proclaiming Jesus as the Messiah who came to save the Jewish community" (Watson, ibid., 30).

25. ἔτι is absent from a few, mainly Western, manuscripts (D* F G 6 1739 1881 a b vgmss Ambst). Since there is no evident reason why it should have been added, and since the repetition of the word later in the sentence might have been deemed inelegant, virtually all commentators accept it as original; but cf. Barnikol, *Die vorchristliche und frühchristliche Zeit des Paulus*, 19–20.

26. See, e.g., Hans Dieter Betz, *Galatians* (Philadelphia: Fortress, 1979) 268.

27. See Ernest de Witt Burton, *A Critical and Exegetical Commentary on the Epistle to the Galatians* (Edinburgh: T. & T. Clark, 1921) 33.

28. While the form of the sentence is that of a real condition (see A. T. Robertson, *A Grammar of the Greek New Testament* [2d ed.; New York: Hodder & Stoughton, 1915] 1008), in substance it is a condition contrary to fact (see Burton, *Galatians,* 286). Presumably, if the apodosis had been assertive rather than interrogative, the sentence would have been cast into the "contrary to fact" form.

29. George Howard, *Paul: Crisis in Galatia* (Cambridge: Cambridge University Press, 1979) 10, 44. In this case, if ἔτι ("still") is not Paul's own term, the Judaizers would have used in in a temporal sense, denoting the continuation of an attitude on Paul's part which (they assumed) he had always held. But Howard's reading of the epistle is both implausible and impossible to maintain.

30. J. H. Ropes, *The Singular Problem of the Epistle to the Galatians* (Cambridge, Mass.: Harvard University Press, 1929), 15, 21, 39; W. Lütgert, *Gesetz*

*und Geist* (Gütersloh: Bertelsmann, 1919). In this case, if ἔτι (still) is not Paul's own term, it would have been used by his opponents with reference to his preconversion life. In effect they would have been saying that his conversion did not really alter his attitude to Judaism and its attendant ceremonials. This approach requires such frequent, unannounced switching between "fronts" in the epistle, however, that it has found few supporters.

31. So, e.g., Burton, *Galatians,* 286; Schlier, *Galater,* 239.

32. So J. B. Lightfoot, *The Epistle of Paul to the Galatians* (London: Macmillan, 1890) 206; G. S. Duncan, *The Epistle of Paul to the Galatians* (London: Hodder & Stoughton, 1934), 159–160; Bruce, *Galatians,* 26, 236.

33. So Bruce, *Galatians,* 236.

34. Entertained, but rejected, by Bruce (ibid.) and Schlier (*Galater,* 238).

35. See Peder Borgen, "Paul Preaches Circumcision and Pleases Men," in *Paul and Paulinisim,* ed. M. D. Hooker and S. G. Wilson (London: SPCK, 1982) 37–46; Robert Jewett, "The Agitators and the Galatian Congregation," *NTS* 17 (1970–71) 198–212; Schlier, *Galater,* 239; Betz, *Galatians,* 269. Borgen appeals to connections made in Judaism between outer and inner circumcision (e.g., Philo *Migr. Abr.* 92; *Spec. leg.* 1.9, 305; *Q. Gen.* 3.52; 1QpHab 11.13; 1QS 5.5–6) to argue that the Judaizers used Paul's preaching against the "works of the flesh" as support for circumcision. Jewett suggests that they were responding to pressure (cf. Gal 6:12) from Palestinian "Zealots" who objected to any close association between Jews and uncircumcised Gentiles.

36. The second ἔτι, however, is more probably adversative: i.e., ". . . why am I *nevertheless* being persecuted." Persecution and preaching circumcision are mutually exclusive in Paul's view; this is true both of the present and of the past. If there had been a time when he had been preaching circumcision, he would not at that time have been persecuted. If both instances of ἔτι are to be interpreted temporally, we would have to assume different *termini a quo* for the two situations: "if I am still preaching circumcision [an activity beginning at some earlier point in Paul's life], why am I still being persecuted [a situation that could not have existed at that earlier point but must have begun later]." While not impossible, it is easier to take the second ἔτι adversatively.

37. Above, pp. 270–71.

38. Above, pp. 88–90, 140.

39. E. P. Sanders, *Paul, the Law, and the Jewish People* (Philadelphia: Fortress, 1983) 123–35.

40. As is generally recognized; see Ernst Käsemann, *Commentary on Romans* (Grand Rapids: Eerdmans, 1980) 70; C. E. B. Cranfield, *A Critical and Exegetical Commentary on the Epistle to the Romans* (2 vols.; Edinburgh: T. & T. Clark, 1975, 1979) 1:164.

41. So, e.g., Bultmann, "Paul," 113.

42. See §5.1 and §5.2 above.

43. See above, pp. 269–72.

44. Some of the material in this section is drawn from my paper, "Zealot and Convert: The Origin of Paul's Christ-Torah Antithesis," *CBQ* 51 (1989) 655–82.

45. For a summary, with bibliography, see my article, "Zealot," *International Standard Bible Encyclopedia* (4 vols.; Grand Rapids: Eerdmans, 1979–88) 4:1175–79.

46. 1 Macc 2:27; the language of zeal is present also in 2:24, 26, 50.

47. The popular view, in which the "Zealots" existed as a party agitating for rebellion from the time of its founding by Judas of Galilee until it was finally successful in 66 C.E., has been substantially discredited; see esp. Morton Smith, "Zealots and Sicarii, Their Origins and Relation," *HTR* 64 (1971) 1–19; Marcus Borg, "The Currency of the Term 'Zealot,'" *JTS* 22 (1971) 504–12; David M. Rhoads, *Israel in Revolution: 6–74 C.E.* (Philadelphia: Fortress, 1976); Richard A. Horsley and John S. Hanson, *Bandits, Prophets and Messiahs: Popular Movements in the Time of Jesus* (Minneapolis/Chicago/New York: Winston-Seabury, 1985). The nature of the Zealot party and the precise time of its emergence, though, are still matters of some dispute; see my "Rural Bandits, City Mobs and the Zealots," *JSJ* 21 (1990) 19–40.

48. These Old Testament figures are often held up as models of zeal: Phinehas in Sir 45:23–24; 1 Macc 2:26,54; 4 Macc 18:12; *Ps.-Philo* 47.1; Elijah in Sir 48:1–2; 1 Macc 2:58; Simeon and Levi (despite the negative attitude taken toward them in Gen 34) in *Jub.* 30.18; *T. Levi* 6.3; Jdt 9:2–4.

49. Num 25; 1 Macc 2:24; 2 *Bar.* 66.1–8; *m. Sanh.* 9.6; cf. Josephus *Ant.* 18.23.

50. Gen 34; Jdt 9:2–4; 1 Macc 2:25.

51. *T. Ash.* 4.2–5; 1QS 9.23; 1QH 14.4; Philo *Spec. leg.* 2.253.

52. 1 Macc 2:50–60; 2 Macc 7:2; 8:21; 4 Macc 18; cf. 1 Macc 1:63; 2:32–41; Josephus *Ant.* 18.23–24.

53. 2 Macc 14:37–46; cf. Josephus *War* 7.320–401.

54. 1 Macc 2:50–64; *Jub.* 30.18–20; 2 *Bar.* 66.6; 4 Macc 18.

55. 1 Macc 3:19; cf. Josephus *Ant.* 18.51.

56. Cf. 4 Macc 17:20–22; *Num. Rab.* 21.3; John 16:2.

57. While interpretations vary, the significance of zeal for understanding Paul is recognized by a number of scholars: J. Dupont, "The Conversion of Paul and Its Influence on His Understanding of Salvation by Faith," in W. W. Gasque and R. P. Martin, eds., *Apostolic History and the Gospel* (Grand Rapids: Eerdmans, 1970) 183–85; James D. G. Dunn, *The Partings of the Ways* (London: SCM/Philadelphia: TPI, 1991) 120–22; Ulrich Wilckens, "Zur Entwicklung des paulinischen Gesetzverständnis," *NTS* 28 (1982) 154; K. Haacker, "Die Berufung des Verfolgers und die Rechtfertigung des Gottlosen," *ThBei* 6 (1975) 1–19; Hengel, *The Pre-Christian Paul*, 70.

58. For a stimulating recent treatment, see Craig C. Hill, *Hellenists and Hebrews: Reappraising Division with the Earliest Church* (Minneapolis: Fortress, 1992).

59. For treatments of the topic, see Hare, *Jewish Persecution*, 1–79; Richardson, *Israel in the Apostolic Church*, 43–47; Hultgren, "Paul's Pre-Christian Persecutions"; Steven T. Katz, "Issues in the Separation of Judaism and Christianity after 70 C.E.: A Reconsideration," *JBL* 103 (1984) 43–76.

60. Martin Hengel, *The Atonement* (Philadelphia: Fortress, 1981) 44; Stuhlmacher, *Paul: Rabbi and Apostle*, 14–15; Kim, *Origin*, 45; Bornkamm, *Paul*, 14; Dunn, *Partings*, 118–19.

61. In addition to Stuhlmacher and Bornkamm (see previous note), see: Bultmann, "Paul," 113; Lucien Cerfaux, *The Christian in the Theology of St. Paul* (New York: Herder & Herder, 1967) 17–18; J. Klausner, *From Jesus to Paul* (New York: Macmillan, 1943) 317; John Knox, *Chapters in a Life of Paul* (London:

A. & C. Black, 1954) 76; J. Christiaan Beker, *Paul the Apostle* (Philadelphia: Fortress, 1980) 143–44; Becker, *Paul: Apostle to the Gentiles,* 65–66.

62. In addition to Bultmann, Knox, Beker, and Becker (see previous note), see: Heikki Räisänen, "Paul's Conversion and the Development of His View of the Law," *NTS* 33 (1987) 406; Dunn, *Partings,* 122.

63. So Sanders (though with respect to a different suggestion): "The general freedom of the Jerusalem apostles from punishment seems decisive against the view . . . that the cause of persecution was the confession of a condemned man as messiah"; *Paul, the Law, and the Jewish People,* 204–5, n. 77. Cf. Walther Schmithals, *Paul and James* (London: SCM, 1965) 21–28.

64. For a sociological approach to persecution, see Adela Yarbro Collins, *Crisis and Catharsis: The Power of the Apocalypse* (Philadelphia: Westminster, 1984).

65. If Stephen's speech in Acts 7 can be taken as an indication of the viewpoint and attitudes of the persecuted group, it is to be noted that criticism of the temple is much clearer and more explicit than any criticism of the law.

66. Fredricksen has suggested a sociopolitical reason for Paul's persecution, viz., that the proclamation of a Messiah, especially one executed by the Romans, would have brought the Jewish community under Roman suspicion; Paula Fredriksen, "Judaism, the Circumcision of Gentiles, and Apocalyptic Hope: Another Look at Galatians 1 and 2," *JTS* 42 (1991) 548–58. But the selective nature of the persecution would serve to rule this out. Also to be rejected is Pfleierer's proposal that the veneration of one whom the Pharisees had opposed and helped to put to death was an affront to Pharisaism; O. Pfleiderer, *Paulinism* (2 vols.; London: Williams & Norgate, 1891) 1:8.

67. In which case Paul's "distinctive" views would have been just those of the community into which he converted; so, e.g., Bultmann, "Paul," 113–14.

68. See above, chap. 6, n. 16.

69. Those who see it as at least part of his motivation include: Kim, *Origin,* 44–48; Beker, *Paul the Apostle,* 143–44, 185–86; Ben Meyer, *The Early Christians* (Wilmington, Del.: Glazier, 1986) 162–63; W. D. Davies, *Invitation to the New Testament* (Garden City, N.Y.: Doubleday, 1969) 260–61; idem, "The Apostolic Age and the Life of Paul," in Matthew Black and H. H. Rowley, eds., *Peake's Commentary on the Bible* (London: Nelson, 1962) 873; Hultgren, "Paul's Pre-Christian Persecutions," 103; Hengel, *The Atonement,* 43–44; H. G. Wood, "The Conversion of St. Paul: Its Nature, Antecedents and Consequences," *NTS* 1 (1954–55) 278; F. J. Leenhardt, "Abraham et la conversion de Saul de Tarse," *RHPhR* 53 (1973) 334; P. H. Menoud, "Revelation and Tradition: The Influence of Paul's Conversion on His Theology," *Int* 7 (1953) 133; F. F. Bruce, *Paul* (Grand Rapids: Eerdmans, 1977) 70–71.

70. See the discussion below, pp. 289–92.

71. Pp. 269–72.

72. See, e.g., F. C. Baur, *The Church History of the First Three Centuries* (2 vols.; London: Williams & Norgate, 1878) 1:46; and the discussion in Beverly Roberts Gaventa, "Paul's Conversion: A Critical Sifting of the Epistolary Evidence" (Ph.D. diss., Duke University, 1978) 10–13.

73. F. C. Baur, *Paul: Apostle of Jesus Christ* (2 vols.; London: Williams & Norgate, 1876) 1:57.

74. Baur, *Church History*, 1:46.

75. See the survey by Gaventa; "Paul's Conversion," 10–24.

76. Rudolf Bultmann, *Theology of the New Testament* (2 vols.; London: SCM, 1952) 1:187–88; see also "Paul," 111–46. For Bultmann, this was not Paul's unique perception; it was already present in the Hellenistic church that he persecuted.

77. See Menoud, "Revelation and Tradition," 133; Hengel, *The Atonement*, 40.

78. See the scholars listed above, chap. 6, n. 11.

79. In addition to those discussed already, several other reasons have been suggested. Some have proposed that the proclamation of a new era opened up by Christ was itself offensive, though this is always linked with other reasons; see Kim, *Origin*, 44–45; Hultgren, "Paul's Pre-Christian Persecutions," 103; Leenhardt, "Abraham et la conversion de Saul de Tarse," 334. Schonfield has made the startling and wildly fanciful suggestion that Paul persecuted the followers of Jesus because he believed himself to be the Messiah; Hugh J. Schonfield, *The Jew of Tarsus* (London: Macdonald, 1946) 78–90.

80. See pp. 170–73.

81. Martin Dibelius, *Paul* (Philadelphia: Westminster, 1953) 50–52; Davies, *Invitation*, 260–61, and "The Apostolic Age," 873; Gaventa, *From Darkness to Light*, 39; idem, "Paul's Conversion," 347.

82. Ulrich Wilckens, "Die Bekehrung des Paulus als religionsgeschichtliches Problem," in *Rechtfertigung als Freiheit* (Neukirchen-Vluyn: Neukirchener, 1974) 11–32. See also Dupont, "The Conversion of Paul."

83. On this, see above, pp. 243–45.

# Chapter 12

1. See J. Christiaan Beker, *Paul the Apostle* (Philadelphia: Fortress, 1980) 3–6.

2. A sympathetic, nonreductionistic treatment of Paul's religious experience is one of the strengths of Segal's important work; Alan F. Segal, *Paul the Convert* (New Haven/London: Yale University Press, 1990).

3. For a full survey and discussion, see Beverly Roberts Gaventa, "Paul's Conversion: A Critical Sifting of the Epistolary Evidence" (Ph.D. dissertation, Duke University, 1978).

4. See F. C. Baur, *The Church History of the First Three Centuries* (2 vols.; London: Williams & Norgate, 1878) 1:46; see also the discussion in Gaventa, "Paul's Conversion," 10–13.

5. See above, esp. pp. 170, 289–92; see also the literature referred to in my article, "Zealot and Persecutor: The Origin of Paul's Christ-Torah Antithesis," *CBQ* 51 (1989) 656–68.

6. On conversion as a *Gestalt* shift, cf. Thomas S. Kuhn, *The Structure of Scientific Revolutions* (2nd ed.; Chicago: University of Chicago Press, 1970) 122.

7. See above, pp. 242–47.

8. Kuhn, *Scientific Revolutions*.

9. See the section "Call rather than Conversion" in his *Paul among Jews and Gentiles* (Philadelphia: Fortress, 1976) 7–23.

10. Early psychological approaches to religious conversion tended to concentrate on sudden and dramatic religious experiences such as were found in nine-

teenth-century revivalism, treating them as phenomena associated with what William James called "the divided self" (*The Varieties of Religious Experience* [New York: Longmans, Green and Co., 1902] 166–258); see also E. D. Starbuck, *The Psychology of Religion* (New York: Scribner's, 1899) 281–362; G. S. Hall, *Adolescence* (2 vols.; New York: Appleton, 1904) 281–362. In such studies, Paul's case was often viewed as typical. For more direct studies of Paul's conversion from a psychological perspective, see, e.g., O. Pfleiderer, *Paulinism* (2 vols.; London: Williams & Norgate, 1891) 1:3–13; idem, *Primitive Christianity* (4 vols.; London: Williams & Norgate, 1906) 1:84–95; J. Klausner, *From Jesus to Paul* (New York: Macmillan, 1943) 312–30; Hugh J. Schonfield, *The Jew of Tarsus* (London: MacDonald, 1946) 75–91.

11. Lewis R. Rambo, *Understanding Religious Conversion* (New Haven/London: Yale University Press, 1993) 12–14. For a similar, though less extensive typology, see Beverly Roberts Gaventa, *From Darkness to Light* (Philadelphia: Fortress, 1986) 8–14.

12. See esp. Gaventa, "Paul's Conversion"; idem, *From Darkness to Light*; Segal, *Paul the Convert*; John G. Gager, "Some Notes on Paul's Conversion," *NTS* 27 (1980–81) 697–704; Paula Fredriksen, "Paul and Augustine: Conversion Narratives, Orthodox Tradition, and the Retrospective Self," *JTS* 37 (1986) 3–34.

13. See the discussion in Rambo, *Understanding Religious Conversion,* 5–19.

14. A point well made by Carl Raschke, "Revelation and Conversion: A Semantic Appraisal," *ATR* 60 (1978) 420–36.

15. Cf. Fredriksen, "Paul and Augustine." This is not to deny either the appropriateness of the comparison she makes or the validity of her observations; still, the difference in situation needs to be recognized.

16. A point perceptively made by Larry W. Hurtado, "Convert, Apostate or Apostle to the Nations: The 'Conversion' of Paul in Recent Scholarship," *SR* 22 (1993–94) 280.

17. On the role of individuals in the shift from one paradigm to another, see Kuhn, *Scientific Revolutions*, esp. 62–64, 144.

18. For the application of Kuhn's model to conversions generally, see Raschke, "Revelation and Conversion"; for Paul in particular, see Gaventa, *From Darkness to Light*, 11.

19. Kuhn, *Scientific Revolutions*, 150; see above, pp. 43–46.

20. Ibid., 6.

21. "Since new paradigms are born from old ones, they ordinarily incorporate much of the vocabulary and apparatus, both conceptual and manipulative, that the traditional paradigm had previously employed. But they seldom employ these borrowed elements in quite the traditional way. Within the new paradigm, old terms, concepts and experiments fall into new relationship one with the other"; ibid., 149.

22. Helmut Koester, "Historic Mistakes Haunt the Relationship of Christianity and Judaism," *BARev* 21 (March-April 1995) 26–27.

23. On Christianity as a *genus tertium*, see, e.g., Aristides, *Apol.* 2; Tertullian, *Scorp.* 10; also Marcel Simon, *Verus Israel* (Oxford: Oxford University Press, 1986 [1948]) 107–11. Sanders sees Paul as essentially treating Christians as a third race, though "against his own conscious intention"; see E. P. Sanders, *Paul, the Law and the Jewish People* (Philadelphia: Fortress, 1983) 171–79.

# Bibliography

Achtemeier, Paul. *Romans.* Interpretation. Atlanta: John Knox, 1985.

Allison, Dale C. "Romans 11:11-15: A Suggestion." *Perspectives in Religious Studies* 12 (1985): 23–30.

Aus, Roger D. "Paul's Travel Plans to Spain and the 'Full Number of the Gentiles' of Rom. XI 25." *NovT* 21 (1979): 232–62.

Badenas, Robert. *Christ the End of the Law: Romans 10:4 in Pauline Perspective.* JSNTSup 10. Sheffield: JSOT Press, 1987.

Bamberger, B. J. *Proselytism in the Talmudic Period.* New York: Ktav, 1968.

Bandstra, Andrew J. *The Law and the Elements of the World.* Grand Rapids: Eerdmans, 1964.

Barnikol, E. *Die vorchristliche und frühchristliche Zeit des Paulus.* Kiel: Walter G. Mühlau Verlag, 1929.

Barrett, C. K. *A Commentary on the Epistle to the Romans.* London: A. & C. Black, 1962.

———. *Essays on Paul.* Philadelphia: Westminster Press, 1982.

Bassler, Jouette M. *Divine Impartiality: Paul and a Theological Axiom.* SBLDS 59. Chico, Calif.: Scholars Press, 1982.

———, ed. *Pauline Theology. Volume I.* Minneapolis: Fortress Press, 1991.

Baur, F. C. *The Church History of the First Three Centuries.* 2 vols. London: Williams & Norgate, 1878.

———. *Paul: The Apostle of Jesus Christ.* 2 vols. London: Williams & Norgate, 1876.

Beare, F. W. *St. Paul and His Letters.* Nashville: Abingdon Press, 1962.

Becker, Jürgen. *Paul: Apostle to the Gentiles.* Louisville: Westminster/John Knox, 1993.

Beker, J. Christiaan. "The Faithfulness of God and the Priority of Israel in Paul's Letter to the Romans." In *Christians among Jews and Gentiles*, ed. G. W. E. Nickelsburg and G. W. MacRae, 10–16. Philadelphia: Fortress Press, 1986.

———. *Paul the Apostle: The Triumph of God in Life and Thought*. Philadelphia: Fortress Press, 1980.

Best, Ernest. "The Revelation to Evangelize the Gentiles." *JTS* 35 (1984): 1–30.

Betz, Hans Dieter. *Galatians*. Hermeneia. Philadelphia: Fortress Press, 1979.

Bickerman, Elias J. "The Altars of the Gentiles." In *Studies in Jewish and Christian History. Part Two*, 324–46. Leiden: Brill, 1980.

Blair, Edward P. "Paul's Call to the Gentile Mission." *BR* 10 (1965): 19–33.

Boers, Hendrikus. *Theology Out of the Ghetto*. Leiden: Brill, 1971.

Borgen, Peder. "Paul Preaches Circumcision and Pleases Men." In *Paul and Paulism*, ed. M. D. Hooker and S. G. Wilson, 37–46. London: SPCK, 1982.

Boring, M. Eugene. "The Language of Universal Salvation in Paul." *JBL* 105 (1986): 269–92.

Bornkamm, Günther. *Paul*. London: Hodder & Stoughton, 1971.

Bousset, Wilhelm. *Kyrios Christos*. Nashville and New York: Abingdon, 1970.

Boyarin, Daniel. *A Radical Jew: Paul and the Politics of Identity*. Berkeley, Los Angeles, and London: University of California Press, 1994.

———. "Was Paul an 'Anti-Semite'? A Reading of Galatians 3–4." *USQR* 47 (1993): 47–80.

Bring, Ragnar. "The Message to the Gentiles: A Study to [*sic*] the Theology of Paul the Apostle." *StTh* 19 (1965): 30–46.

Brown, Raymond E. "Not Jewish Christianity and Gentile Christianity, but Types of Jewish/Gentile Christianity." *CBQ* 45 (1983): 74–79.

Bruce, F. F. *Commentary on Galatians*. NIGTC. Grand Rapids: Eerdmans, 1982.

———. *Paul: Apostle of the Heart Set Free*. Grand Rapids: Eerdmans, 1977.

Bultmann, Rudolf. "Paul." In *Existence and Faith*, 111–46. Cleveland and New York: Meridian, 1960.

———. *Theology of the New Testament*. 2 vols. London: SCM, 1952.

Burton, Ernest de Witt. *A Critical and Exegetical Commentary on the Epistle to the Galatians*. ICC. Edinburgh: T. & T. Clark, 1921.

Calvin, John. *The Epistles of Paul to the Romans and to the Thessalonians.* London: Oliver & Boyd, 1961.

Campbell, William S. *Paul's Gospel in an Intercultural Context.* Frankfurt: Peter Lang, 1992.

Cerfaux, Lucien. *The Christian in the Theology of St. Paul.* New York: Herder & Herder, 1967.

Cohen, Shaye J. D. "Crossing the Boundary and Becoming a Jew." *HTR* 82 (1989): 11–33.

———. *From the Maccabees to the Mishnah.* Philadelphia: Westminster Press, 1987.

Collins, John J. *Between Athens and Jerusalem.* New York: Crossroad, 1983.

———. "A Symbol of Otherness: Circumcision and Salvation in the First Century." In *"To See Ourselves as Others See Us": Christians, Jews and "Others" in Late Antiquity,* ed. J. Neusner and E. S. Frerichs, 163–86. Chico, Calif.: Scholars Press, 1985.

Cranfield, C. E. B. *A Critical and Exegetical Commentary on the Epistle to the Romans.* ICC. 2 vols. Edinburgh: T. & T. Clark, 1975, 1979.

———. "Some Notes on Romans 9:30-33." In *Jesus und Paulus: Festschrift für Werner Georg Kümmel,* ed. E. E. Ellis and E. Grässer, 35–43. Göttingen: Vandenhoeck & Ruprecht, 1975.

Cremer, H. *Die paulinische Rechtfertigungslehre im Zusammenhänge ihrer geschichtlichen Voraussetzung.* 2d ed. Gütersloh: Bertelsmann, 1900.

Cullmann, Oscar. "Le caractère eschatologique du devoir missionaire et de la conscience apostolique de S. Paul: Étude sur le κατέχον (-ων) de 2 Thess. 2:6-7." *RHPhR* 16 (1936): 210–45.

Cunningham, Philip A. *Jewish Apostle to the Gentiles: Paul as He Saw Himself.* Mystic, Conn.: Twenty-Third Publications, 1986.

Dahl, Nils A. "The Messiahship of Jesus in Paul." In *Jesus the Christ: The Historical Origins of Christological Doctrine,* ed. D. H. Juel, 15–25. Minneapolis: Fortress Press, 1991.

———. *Studies in Paul: Theology for the Early Christian Mission.* Minneapolis: Augsburg Press, 1977.

Davies, Glenn N. *Faith and Obedience: A Study in Romans 1–4.* JSNTSup 39. Sheffield: JSOT Press, 1990.

Davies, W. D. "The Apostolic Age and the Life of Paul." In *Peake's Commentary on the Bible,* ed. Matthew Black and H. H. Rowley, 870–82. London: Nelson, 1962.

———. *Invitation to the New Testament.* Garden City, N.Y.: Doubleday, 1969.

———. *Paul and Rabbinic Judaism.* London: SPCK, 1948.

———. "Paul and the Gentiles: A Suggestion concerning Romans 11:13-24." In *Jewish and Pauline Studies,* 356–60. Philadelphia: Fortress Press, 1984.

———. "Paul and the People of Israel." *NTS* 24 (1977): 4–39.

———. *Torah in the Messianic Age and/or Age to Come.* Philadelphia: SBL, 1952.

Deissmann, Adolf. *St. Paul: A Study in Social and Religious History.* London: Hodder & Stoughton, 1912.

Denis, A. M. "L'Apôtre Paul, prophète 'messianique' des Gentils." *EThL* 33 (1957): 245–318.

Dibelius, Martin. *Paul.* Philadelphia: Westminster Press, 1953.

Dietzfelbinger, Christian. *Die Berufung des Paulus als Ursprung seiner Theologie.* WMANT 58. Neukirchen-Vluyn: Neukirchener, 1985.

Dodd, C. H. *The Epistle of Paul to the Romans.* London: Hodder & Stoughton, 1932.

———. "The Mind of Paul." *BJRL* 17 (1933): 91–105.

Donaldson, Terence L. "The 'Curse of the Law' and the Inclusion of the Gentiles: Galatians 3.13-14." *NTS* 32 (1986): 94–112.

———. "'The Gospel That I Proclaim among the Gentiles' (Gal 2.2): Universalistic or Israel-Centred?" In *Gospel in Paul: Studies on Corinthians, Galatians and Romans for Richard N. Longenecker,* ed. L. A. Jervis and P. Richardson, 166–93. JSNTSup 108. Sheffield: Sheffield Academic Press, 1994.

———. "Proselytes or 'Righteous Gentiles'? The Status of Gentiles in Eschatological Pilgrimage Patterns of Thought." *JSP* 7 (1990): 3–27.

———. "'Riches for the Gentiles' (Rom 11:12): Israel's Rejection and Paul's Gentile Mission." *JBL* 112 (1993): 81–98.

———. "Zealot and Convert: The Origin of Paul's Christ-Torah Antithesis." *CBQ* 51 (1989): 655–82.

Dunn, James D. G. "'A Light to the Gentiles': The Significance of the Damascus Road Christophany for Paul." In *The Glory of Christ in the New Testament,* ed. L. D. Hurst and N. T. Wright, 251–66. Oxford: Clarendon Press, 1987.

———. "The New Perspective on Paul." *BJRL* 65 (1983): 95–122.

———. *The Partings of the Ways.* Philadelphia: Trinity Press International, 1991.

———. *Romans.* WBC. 2 vols. Waco, Tex.: Word, 1990.

Dupont, J. "The Conversion of Paul and Its Influence on His Understanding of Salvation by Faith." In *Apostolic History and the Gospel,* ed.

W. W. Gasque and R. P. Martin, 176–94. Grand Rapids: Eerdmans, 1970.

Ellis, E. Earle. *Paul and His Recent Interpreters.* Grand Rapids: Eerdmans, 1961.

———. *Paul's Use of the Old Testament.* Grand Rapids: Baker, 1981 [1957].

Enslin, Morton Scott. *Reapproaching Paul.* Philadelphia: Westminster, 1972.

Feldman, Louis F. "The Omnipresence of the God-Fearers." *BARev* 12, no. 5 (1986): 58–63.

Figueras, Pau. "Epigraphic Evidence for Proselytism in Ancient Judaism." *Immanuel* 24/25 (1990): 194–206.

Finkelstein, Louis. "Some Examples of Rabbinic Halaka." *JBL* 49 (1930): 20–42.

Fredriksen, Paula. *From Jesus to Christ.* New Haven: Yale University Press, 1988.

———. "Judaism, the Circumcision of Gentiles, and Apocalyptic Hope: Another Look at Galatians 1 and 2." *JTS* 42 (1991): 532–64.

———. "Paul and Augustine: Conversion Narratives, Orthodox Traditions and the Retrospective Self." *JTS* 37 (1986): 3–34.

Fuller, Daniel P. *Gospel and Law: Contrast or Continuum?* Grand Rapids: Eerdmans, 1980.

Gager, John G. *The Origins of Anti-Semitism.* New York and Oxford: Oxford University Press, 1983.

———. "Some Notes on Paul's Conversion." *NTS* 27 (1980–1): 697–704.

Gaston, Lloyd. "Abraham and the Righteousness of God." *Horizons in Biblical Theology* 2 (1980): 39–68.

———. *Paul and the Torah.* Vancouver: University of British Columbia Press, 1987.

———. "Paul and the Torah." In *Antisemitism and the Foundations of Christianity,* ed. by Alan T. Davies, 48–71. New York and Toronto: Paulist Press, 1979.

Gaventa, Beverly Roberts. *From Darkness to Light: Aspects of Conversion in the New Testament.* Philadelphia: Fortress Press, 1986.

———. "Paul's Conversion: A Critical Sifting of the Epistolary Evidence." Ph.D. diss., Duke University. 1978.

Georgi, Dieter. *Theocracy in Paul's Praxis and Theology.* Minneapolis: Fortress Press, 1991.

Getty, Mary Ann. "Paul and the Salvation of Israel: A Perspective on Romans 9–11." *CBQ* 50 (1988): 456–69.

Gilbert, Gary. "The Making of a Jew: 'God-Fearer' or Convert in the Story of Izates." *USQR* 44 (1991): 299–313.

Goodman, Martin. *Mission and Conversion: Proselytizing in the Religious History of the Roman Empire.* Oxford: Clarendon Press, 1994.

Goodspeed, Edgar J. *Paul.* Nashville and New York: Abingdon Press, 1947.

Grundmann, W. "Paulus, aus dem Volke Israel, Apostel der Völker." *NovT* 4 (1960): 267–91.

Haacker, Klaus. "Die Berufung des Verfolgers und die Rechtfertigung des Gottlosen." *ThBei* 6 (1975): 1–19.

———. "War Paulus Hillelit?" *Das Institutum Judaicum der Universität Tübingen* (1971–72): 106–20.

Hahn F. *Mission in the New Testament.* Naperville, Ill.: Allenson, 1965.

Hamerton-Kelly, R. G. "Sacred Violence and the Curse of the Law (Galatians 3:13): The Death of Christ as a Sacrificial Travesty." *NTS* 36 (1990): 98–118.

Hansen, G. Walter. *Abraham in Galatians: Epistolary and Rhetorical Contexts.* JSNTSup 29. Sheffield: Sheffield Academic Press, 1989.

Hare, Douglas R. A. *The Theme of Jewish Persecution of Christians in the Gospel According to St. Matthew.* SNTSMS 6. Cambridge: Cambridge University Press, 1967.

Harnack, A. von. *The Date of Acts and of the Synoptic Gospels.* London: Williams & Norgate, 1911.

Hay, David M., ed. *Pauline Theology.* Volume 2. Minneapolis: Fortress Press, 1993.

Hays, Richard B. *Echoes of Scripture in the Letters of Paul.* New Haven and London: Yale University Press, 1989.

———. *The Faith of Jesus Christ.* SBLDS 56. Chico, Calif.: Scholars Press, 1983.

———. "'Have We Found Abraham to Be Our Forefather according to the Flesh?' A Reconsideration of Rom 4:1." *NovT* 27 (1985): 76–98.

Hengel, Martin. *The Atonement: The Origins of the Doctrine in the New Testament.* Philadelphia: Fortress Press, 1981.

———. *The Pre-Christian Paul.* Philadelphia: Trinity Press International, 1991.

Hill, Craig C. *Hellenists and Hebrews: Reappraising Division within the Earliest Church.* Minneapolis: Fortress Press, 1992.

Holtzmann, H. J. *Lehrbuch der neutestamentlichen Theologie.* Freiburg: Mohr, 1897.

Hooker, Morna. "Paul and Covenantal Nomism." In *Paul and Paulinism,* ed. Morna Hooker and Stephen G. Wilson, 47–56. London: SPCK, 1982.

Howard, George. *Paul: Crisis in Galatia.* SNTSMS 35. Cambridge: Cambridge University Press, 1979.

———. "Romans 3:21-31 and the Inclusion of the Gentiles." *HTR* 63 (1970): 223–33.

Hultgren, Arland J. *Paul's Gospel and Mission: The Outlook from His Letter to the Romans.* Philadelphia: Fortress Press, 1985.

———. "Paul's Pre-Christian Persecutions of the Church: Their Purpose, Locale, and Nature." *JBL* 95 (1976): 97–111.

Hurd, John C. *The Origin of 1 Corinthians.* London: SPCK, 1965.

Hurtado, Larry W. "Convert, Apostate or Apostle to the Nations: The 'Conversion' of Paul in Recent Scholarship." *SR* 22 (1992–93): 273–84.

Hübner, Hans. *Law in Paul's Thought.* Edinburgh: T. &. T. Clark, 1984.

Jeremias, Joachim. "Paulus als Hillelit." In *Neotestamentica et Semitica,* ed. E. E. Ellis and M. Wilcox, 88–94. Edinburgh: T. & T. Clark, 1969.

Jervell, J. *Luke and the People of God.* Minneapolis: Augsburg Press, 1972.

Jewett, Robert. "The Agitators and the Galatian Congregation." *NTS* 17 (1970–71): 198–212.

———. "The Law and Coexistence of Jews and Gentiles in Romans." *Int* 39 (1985): 341–56.

Johnson, D. G. "The Structure and Meaning of Romans 11." *CBQ* 46 (1984): 91–103.

Johnson, E. Elizabeth. *The Function of Apocalyptic and Wisdom Traditions in Romans 9–11.* SBLDS 109. Atlanta: Scholars Press, 1989.

Käsemann, Ernst. *Commentary on Romans.* Grand Rapids: Eerdmans, 1980.

———. "Paul and Israel." In *New Testament Questions of Today,* 183–87. London: SCM, 1969.

———. *Perspectives on Paul.* Philadelphia: Fortress Press, 1971.

———. "'The Righteousness of God' in Paul." In *New Testament Questions of Today,* 168–82. London: SCM, 1969.

Katz, Steven T. "Issues in the Separation of Judaism and Christianity after 70 C.E.: A Reconsideration." *JBL* 103 (1984): 43–76.

Kaylor, R. David. *Paul's Covenant Community: Jew and Gentile in Romans.* Atlanta: John Knox, 1988.

Kim, Seyoon. *The Origin of Paul's Gospel.* Grand Rapids: Eerdmans, 1982.

Klausner, J. *From Jesus to Paul.* New York: Macmillan, 1943.

Klein, Günter. "Heil und Geschichte nach Römer IV." *NTS* 13 (1966): 43–47.

Knox, John. *Chapters in a Life of Paul.* London: A. & C. Black, 1954.

———. "Romans 15:14-33 and Paul's Conception of His Apostolic Mission." *JBL* 83 (1964): 1–11.

Kraabel, A. Thomas. "The Disappearance of the 'God-Fearers,'" *Numen* 28 (1981): 113–26.

Kuhn, K. G. "προσήλυτος." In *TDNT,* 6.727–44.

Kuhn, Thomas S. *The Structure of Scientific Revolutions.* 2d ed. Chicago: University of Chicago Press, 1970.

Kümmel, W. G. *Römer 7 und die Bekehrung Des Paulus.* Leipzig: Hinrichs, 1929.

Lapide, Pinchas, and Peter Stuhlmacher. *Paul: Rabbi and Apostle.* Minneapolis: Augsburg Press, 1984.

Leenhardt, F. J. "Abraham et la conversion de Saul de Tarse." *RHPhR* 53 (1973): 331–51.

Lieu, Judith, et al., eds. *The Jews among Pagans and Christians in the Roman Empire.* London and New York: Routledge, 1992.

Lindars, Barnabas. *New Testament Apologetic.* London: SCM, 1961.

———. "The Old Testament and Universalism in Paul." *BJRL* 69 (1986-7): 511–27.

Longenecker, Bruce W. "Different Answers to Different Questions: Israel, the Gentiles and Salvation History in Romans 9–11." *JSNT* 36 (1989): 95–123.

———. *Eschatology and the Covenant: A Comparison of 4 Ezra and Romans 1–11.* JSNTSup 57; Sheffield: Sheffield Academic Press, 1991.

Longenecker, Richard N. *Galatians.* WBC 41. Waco, Tex.: Word, 1990.

———. *Paul, Apostle of Liberty.* New York: Harper & Row, 1964.

Luther, Martin. *A Commentary on St. Paul's Epistle to the Galatians.* Grand Rapids: Zondervan, n.d.

McEleney, Neil J. "Conversion, Circumcision and the Law." *NTS* 20 (1973–74): 319–41.

McKnight, Scot. *A Light among the Gentiles: Jewish Missionary Activity in the Second Temple Period.* Minneapolis: Fortress Press, 1991.

Marquardt, Friedrich-Wilhelm. *Die Juden Im Römerbrief.* Zurich: Theologischer Verlag, 1971.

Menoud, P. H. "Revelation and Tradition: The Influence of Paul's Conversion on His Theology." *Int* 7 (1953): 131–41.

Meyer, Ben. *The Early Christians: Their World Mission and Self-discovery.* Wilmington, Del.: Michael Glazier, 1986.

Meyer, Paul. "Romans 10:4 and the End of the Law." In *The Divine Helmsman,* ed. J. L. Crenshaw and S. Sandmel, 59–78. New York: Ktav, 1980.

Montefiore, C. G. *Judaism and St. Paul: Two Essays.* London: Max Goschen, 1914.

Moore, George Foot. *Judaism in the First Centuries of the Christian Era.* Cambridge, Mass.: Harvard University Press, 1927–30.

Moxnes, Halvor. *Theology in Conflict: Studies in Paul's Understanding of God in Romans.* NovTSup 53. Leiden: Brill, 1980.

Munck, Johannes. *Christ and Israel: An Interpretation of Romans 9–11.* Philadelphia: Fortress Press, 1967.

———. *Paul and the Salvation of Mankind.* London: SCM, 1959.

Murphy-O'Connor, Jerome. "Paul in Arabia." *CBQ* 55 (1993): 732–37.

Mussner, F. *Tractate on the Jews.* Philadelphia: Fortress Press, 1984.

Nanos, Mark D. *The Mystery of Romans: The Jewish Context of Paul's Letter.* Minneapolis: Fortress Press, 1996.

Neyrey, Jerome H. *Paul, in Other Words.* Louisville: Westminster/John Knox, 1990.

Nickelsburg, George W. E. "An Ἔκτρωμα, Though Appointed from the Womb: Paul's Apostolic Self-description in 1 Corinthians 15 and Galatians 1." In *Christians among Jews and Gentiles,* ed. G. W. E. Nickelsburg and G. W. MacRae, 198–205. Philadelphia: Fortress Press, 1986.

Nickle, Keith F. *The Collection: A Study in Paul's Strategy.* SBT 48. Naperville, Ill.: Allenson, 1966.

Niebuhr, Karl-Wilhelm. *Heidenapostel aus Israel: Die jüdische Identität des Paulus nach ihrer Darstellung in seinen Briefen.* WUNT 62. Tübingen: Mohr [Siebeck], 1992.

Nolland, John. "Uncircumcised Proselytes?" *JSJ* 12 (1981): 173–94.

Novak, David. *The Image of the Non-Jew in Judaism: An Historical and Constructive Study of the Noahide Laws.* New York and Toronto: Edwin Mellen Press, 1983.

Ohana, M. "Prosélytisme et Targum palestinienne: Données nouvelles pour la datation de Néofiti I." *Bib* 55 (1974): 317–32.

Pannenberg, Wolfhart. *Jesus—God and Man.* Philadelphia: Westminster Press, 1968.

Parkes, James. *The Conflict of the Church and the Synagogue.* New York: Atheneum, 1985 [1936].

———. *Jesus, Paul and the Jews.* London: SCM, 1936.

Patte, Daniel. *Paul's Faith and the Power of the Gospel.* Philadelphia: Fortress Press, 1983.

Pfleiderer, O. *Paulinism*. 2d ed. 2 vols. London: Williams & Norgate, 1891.

———. *Primitive Christianity*. 4 vols. London: Williams & Norgate, 1906.

Porton, Gary. *Goyim: Gentiles and Israelites in Mishnah-Tosefta*. Atlanta: Scholars Press, 1988.

Räisänen, Heikki. "Galatians 2:16 and Paul's Break with Judaism." *NTS* 31 (1985): 543–53.

———. *Paul and the Law*. Philadelphia: Fortress Press, 1986.

———. "Paul, God and Israel: Romans 9–11 in Recent Research." In *The Social World of Formative Christianity*, ed. J. Neusner et al., 178–206. Philadelphia: Fortress Press, 1988.

———. "Paul's Conversion and the Development of His View of the Law." *NTS* 33 (1987): 404–19.

Rambo, Lewis R. *Understanding Religious Conversion*. New Haven and London: Yale University Press, 1993.

Raschke, Carl. "Revelation and Conversion: A Semantic Appraisal." *ATR* 60 (1978): 420–36.

Reicke, B. "The Law and This World according to Paul: Some Thoughts on Gal 4:1-11." *JBL* 70 (1951): 259–76.

Rhyne, C. Thomas. *Faith Establishes the Law*. SBLDS 55. Chico, Calif.: Scholars Press, 1981.

Richardson, Peter. *Israel in the Apostolic Church*. SNTSMS 10. Cambridge: Cambridge University Press, 1969.

Riesner, Rainer. *Die Frühzeit des Apostels Paulus*. WUNT 71. Tübingen: Mohr [Siebeck], 1994.

Rigaux, B. *The Letters of St. Paul: Modern Studies*. Chicago: Franciscan Herald Press, 1968.

Robinson, John A. T. *Wrestling with Romans*. Philadelphia: Westminster Press, 1979.

Ruether, Rosemary R. *Faith and Fratricide: The Theological Roots of Anti-Semitism*. Minneapolis: Seabury, 1974.

Sanders, E. P. "The Covenant as a Soteriological Category and the Nature of Salvation in Palestinian and Hellenistic Judaism." In *Jews, Greeks and Christians: Religious Cultures in Late Antiquity*, ed. R. Hamerton-Kelly and R. Scroggs, 11–44. Leiden: Brill, 1976.

———. "Defending the Indefensible." *JBL* 110 (1991): 463–77.

———. *Jesus and Judaism*. Philadelphia: Fortress Press, 1985.

———. *Paul*. Past Masters. Oxford and New York: Oxford University Press, 1991.

———. *Paul and Palestinian Judaism*. Philadelphia: Fortress Press, 1977.

———. *Paul, the Law, and the Jewish People.* Philadelphia: Fortress Press, 1983.

Sandnes, Karl Olav. *Paul — One of the Prophets?* Tübingen: Mohr [Siebeck], 1991.

Schechter, S. *Aspects of Rabbinic Theology.* New York: Schocken, 1961 [1909].

Schiffman, Lawrence H. "The Conversion of the Royal House of Adiabene in Josephus and Rabbinic Sources." In *Josephus, Judaism and Christianity,* ed. L. H. Feldman and G. Hata, 293–312. Detroit: Wayne State University Press, 1987.

———. *Who Was a Jew?* Hoboken, N.J.: Ktab, 1985.

Schlier, Heinrich. *Der Brief an die Galater.* Göttingen: Vandenhoeck & Ruprecht, 1965.

Schlueter, Carol J. *Filling Up the Measure: Polemical Hyperbole in 1 Thessalonians 2.14-16.* JSNTSup 98. Sheffield: JSOT Press, 1994.

Schoeps, Hans-Joachim. *Paul: The Theology of the Apostle in the Light of Jewish Religious History.* Philadelphia: Westminster, 1961.

Schulz, J. P. "Two Views of the Patriarchs: Noachides and Pre-Sinai Israelites." In *Texts and Responses,* ed. M. A. Fishbane and P. R. Flohr, 43–59. Leiden: Brill, 1975.

Schürer, Emil. *The History of the Jewish People in the Age of Jesus Christ.* Revised edition. 3 vols. Edinburgh: T. & T. Clark, 1973–87.

Schweitzer, Albert. *The Mysticism of Paul the Apostle.* New York: Seabury, 1968 [1931].

———. *Paul and His Interpreters.* London: A. & C. Black, 1950 [1912].

Scobie, Charles H. H. "Jesus or Paul? The Origin of the Universal Mission of the Christian Church." In *From Jesus to Paul,* ed. P. Richardson and J. C. Hurd. Waterloo, Ont.: Wilfrid Laurier University Press, 1984.

Scott, James M. "Paul's Use of Deuteronomic Tradition." *JBL* 112 (1993): 645–65.

Segal, Alan F. "Conversion and Universalism: Opposites That Attract." In *Origins and Method: Towards a New Understanding of Judaism and Christianity,* ed. by Bradley H. McLean, 162–89. JSNTSup 86. Sheffield: Sheffield Academic Press, 1993.

———. *Paul the Convert.* New Haven and London: Yale University Press, 1990.

———. "Universalism in Judaism and Christianity." *Bulletin of the Canadian Society of Biblical Studies* 51 (1991–92): 20–35.

Siker, Jeffrey S. *Disinheriting the Jews: Abraham in Early Christian Controversy.* Louisville: Westminster/John Knox, 1991.

Simon, Marcel. *Verus Israel: A Study of the Relations between Christians and Jews in the Roman Empire (135–425)*. Oxford: Oxford University Press, 1986 [1948].

Snodgrass, Klyne R. "Justification by Grace—to the Doers: An Analysis of the Place of Romans 2 in the Theology of Paul." *NTS* 32 (1986): 72–93.

Stacey, W. David. *The Pauline View of Man*. London: Macmillan, 1956.

Stanley, Christopher D. "The Redeemer Will Come ἐκ Σιων: Romans 11:26-27 Revisited." In *Paul and the Scriptures of Israel*, ed. C. A. Evans and J. A. Sanders, 118–42. Sheffield: Sheffield Academic Press, 1993.

Stendahl, Krister. *Paul among Jews and Gentiles*. Philadelphia: Fortress Press, 1976.

Stewart, James S. *A Man in Christ*. London: Hodder & Stoughton, 1935.

Strecker, Georg. "Befreiung und Rechtfertigung; Zur Stellung der Rechtfertigungslehre in der Theologie des Paulus." In *Rechtfertigung*, ed. J. Friedrich et al., 479–508. Tübingen: Mohr [Siebeck], and Göttingen: Vandenhoeck & Ruprecht, 1976.

Stuhlmacher, Peter. *Paul's Letter to the Romans*. Louisville: Westminster/John Knox, 1994.

———. "Zur Interpretation von Römer 11:25-32." In *Probleme biblischer Theologie*, ed. H. W. Wolff, 555–70. Munich: Kaiser, 1971.

Sukenik, E. L. *Jüdische Gräber Jerusalems um Christi Geburt*. Jerusalem: N.p., 1931.

Swetnam, J. "The Curious Crux at Romans 4,12." *Bib* 61 (1980): 110–15.

Tannenbaum, Robert F. "Jews and God-Fearers in the Holy City of Aphrodite." *BARev* 12, no. 5 (1986): 54–57.

Tannenbaum, Robert F., and Joyce M. Reynolds. *Jews and Godfearers at Aphrodisias*. Cambridge: Cambridge Philological Society, 1987.

Theissen, Gerd. "Judaism and Christianity in Paul: The Beginnings of a Schism and Its Social History." In *Social Reality and the Early Christians*, 202–27. Minneapolis: Fortress Press, 1992.

Thielman, Frank. *From Plight to Solution*. NovTSup 61. Leiden: Brill, 1989.

Tomson, Peter J. *Paul and the Jewish Law: Halakha in the Letters of the Apostle to the Gentiles*. CRINT 3/1. Assen: Van Gorcum, and Minneapolis: Fortress Press, 1990.

Tuckett, Christopher M. "Deuteronomy 21,23 and Paul's Conversion." In *L'apôtre Paul: Personnalité, style et conception du ministère,* 345–50. Leuven: Leuven University/Peeters, 1986.

van der Horst, P. W. "A New Altar of a Godfearer?" In *Hellenism — Judaism — Christianity: Essays on Their Interaction,* 65–72. Kampen: Kok, 1994.

van Minnen, Peter. "Paul the Roman Citizen." *JSNT* 56 (1994): 43–52.

Watson, Francis. *Paul, Judaism and the Gentiles.* SNTSMS 56. Cambridge: Cambridge University Press, 1986.

Weiss, K. "Paulus—Priester der christlichen Kultgemeinde." *ThLZ* 79 (1954): 355–64.

Westerholm, Stephen. *Israel's Law and the Church's Faith: Paul and His Recent Interpreters.* Grand Rapids: Eerdmans, 1988.

Wilckens, Ulrich. "Die Bekehrung des Paulus als religionsgeschichtliches Problem." In *Rechtfertigung als Freiheit,* 11–32. Neukirchen-Vluyn: Neukirchener Verlag, 1974.

———. "Zur Entwicklung des Paulinischen Gesetzverständnis." *NTS* 28 (1982): 154–90.

Williams, Sam K. "The 'Righteousness of God' in Romans." *JBL* 99 (1980): 241–90.

Wolfson, Harry A. *Philo.* Cambridge, Mass.: Harvard University Press, 1948.

Wrede, William. *Paul.* London: Green, 1907.

Wright, N. T. *The Climax of the Covenant: Christ and the Law in Pauline Theology.* Minneapolis: Fortress Press, 1991.

Zeller, Dieter. *Juden und Heiden in der Mission des Paulus: Studien zum Römerbrief.* 2d ed. Stuttgart: Verlag Katholisches Bibelwerk, 1976.

Ziesler, John A. *The Meaning of Righteousness in Paul.* SNTSMS 20. Cambridge: Cambridge University Press, 1972.

———. *Pauline Christianity.* Revised edition. Oxford and New York: Oxford University Press, 1990.

———. *Paul's Letter to the Romans.* London and Philadelphia: SCM; TPI, 1989.

# Index of Ancient Sources

## *Pseudepigrapha*

| | | | |
|---|---|---|---|
| 82.3–9 | 72, 224 | 8.5–7 | 83 |
| 82.6 | 54 | 8.9 | 63 |
| | | 10.12–13 | 63 |
| *4 Baruch* | | 11.3–18 | 63 |
| 8.1–12 | 319 | 11.4–6 | 63 |
| | | 11.4–5 | 58 |
| *1 Enoch* | | 11.7–11 | 57 |
| 14.8–23 | 203 | 11.10 | 63 |
| 50.1–5 | 324 | 11.17 | 63 |
| 63.1–12 | 90, 92 | 12.1 | 83 |
| 63.8 | 327 | 12.1–13.14 | 63 |
| 85–90 | 71 | 12.3–4 | 63 |
| 89.36 | 325 | 12.5–15 | 58 |
| 89.50 | 325 | 14.7 | 57 |
| 90.27–33 | 71 | 15.4 | 63 |
| 90.28–29 | 324 | 15.7 | 63 |
| 90.32–38 | 324 | 16.1–16 | 63 |
| 105.1 | 283, 350 | | |
| 108.11–12 | 324 | *Jubilees* | |
| | | 1.15–17 | 324 |
| *Epistle of Aristeas* | | 1.28 | 324 |
| 16 | 342 | 5.16 | 90, 327 |
| 37 | 322 | 7.20 | 67 |
| 40 | 322 | 15.25–32 | 83 |
| 185–97 | 342 | 15.26 | 53, 68, 69, 324 |
| | | 16.17–18 | 324 |
| *4 Ezra* | | 18.15 | 334 |
| 3.28–36 | 54 | 21.4 | 327 |
| 4.38–43 | 355 | 22.22 | 319 |
| 6.26 | 325 | 23.23–24 | 339 |
| 7.19–24 | 54 | 24.11 | 334 |
| 7.21 | 342 | 27.23 | 319 |
| 7.37–38 | 54, 224 | 30.12 | 53 |
| 7.72 | 53, 59, 207, 224 | 30.16 | 327 |
| 7.79–82 | 54 | 30.18–20 | 368 |
| 8.55–58 | 54, 224 | 30.18 | 368 |
| 9.10–12 | 54 | 31.20 | 319, 324 |
| 12.31–33 | 324 | 32.19 | 324 |
| 13.13 | 325 | 33.18 | 327 |
| 13.37–38 | 324 | 40.10 | 319 |
| 13.39–47 | 324 | | |
| | | *Psalms of Solomon* | |
| *Joseph and Asenath* | | 2.18 | 90, 327 |
| 7.1 | 63 | 2.22–35 | 90 |
| 8.4–5 | 63 | 11.1–3 | 324 |

## Greco-Roman Literature

## New Testament

## Other Early Christian Literature

# Index of Modern Authors